A History of Film

FIFTH EDITION

Jack C. Ellis

Northwestern University

Virginia Wright Wexman

University of Illinois at Chicago

Allyn and Bacon

Boston • London • Toronto • Sydney • Tokyo • Singapore

Series Editor: Molly Taylor
Editor-in-Chief, Social Sciences: Karen Hanson
Series Editorial Assistant: Michael Kish
Marketing Manager: Mandee Eckersley
Composition Buyer: Linda Cox
Manufacturing Buyer: Julie McNeill
Editorial-Production Administrator: Karen Mason
Editorial-Production Services: Susan Freese, Communicáto, Ltd.
Cover Designer: Kristina Mose-Libon
Electronic Composition: Omegatype Typography, Inc.

Library of Congress Cataloging-in-Publication Data

Ellis, Jack C.
    A history of film.—5th ed. / Jack C. Ellis, Virginia Wright Wexman.
        p.   cm.
    Includes filmographies, bibliographical references, and index.
    ISBN 0-205-31856-8
    1. Motion pictures—History.   I. Wexman, Virginia Wright.   II. Title.
PN1993.5.A1 E4 2001
791.43'09—dc21

                                                        2001022736

Printed in the United States of America

10 9 8 7 6 5 4 3 2 1   RRD-VA   05 04 03 02 01

Contents

Preface   vii

1 *Birth and Childhood
of a New Art* ★ *1895–1914*   1

*Brief Motion-Picture Records of
Actuality and of Performances*   1

*Telling Stories through Staged and
Filmed Pantomime*   6

*Telling Stories through
Filmic Means*   10

The Language of Film   16

*Increasing Films
to Feature Length*   20

Films of the Period   24

Books on the Period   25

2 *Rise of the American Film* ★
1914–1919   26

The First American Epics   27

*A Tradition of Screen Comedy
Is Established*   38

Emerging Patterns of Industry   45

Films of the Period   49

Books on the Period   49

3 *Great German Silents* ★
1919–1928   51

Predominant Types and Themes   52

*Principal Technical and Stylistic
Advances*   60

Mirror of the Culture   66

Influence on Hollywood   66

Films of the Period   68

Books on the Period   69

4 *Art and Dialectic in the
Soviet Film* ★ *1925–1929*   70

Historical Setting   71

Beginnings   72

Three Silent Masters   75

Montage: Theory and Practice   83

Films of the Period   87

Books on the Period   87

5 *Hollywood in the Twenties* ★
1919–1929   88

Movies Become Big Business   88

Ascendancy of the Director   91

Popular Genres   97

Sound Arrives   104

Films of the Period   110

Books on the Period   111

6 *France in the Twenties and Thirties* ★ *1919–1939*   **112**

The First Avant-Garde: Impressionism   113

The Second Avant-Garde: Pure Cinema   115

The Golden Age of the 1930s   117

Films of the Period   125

Books on the Period   126

7 *Hollywood in the Thirties and Early Forties* ★ *1929–1945*   **127**

The Industry   128

Censorship, Self-Regulation, and Pressure Groups   131

Notable Directors of the 1930s   132

Emergent Genres in the 1930s   137

Wartime   150

A 1940s Genre: Film Noir   152

Orson Welles: Boy Genius   155

Films of the Period   157

Books on the Period   159

8 *Postwar Italy: Neorealism and Beyond* ★ *1945–*   **161**

Theory and Practice of Neorealism   163

Two Major Directors of the Neorealist Era   166

Period of Transition: 1952–1960   168

Emergence of a New Style: Three Directors of the 1960s   170

Neo-Neorealism: Three Directors of the 1960s and 1970s   180

The 1970s and Beyond: A New Generation of Film Makers   182

Films of the Period   189

Books on the Period   192

9 *British Film after the War: Humor, Horror, and Social Criticism* ★ *1945–*   **193**

The Griersonian Documentary Tradition   194

Postwar Comedies   196

Free Cinema and Social-Realist Features   199

The Gothic Strain   204

Americans Abroad   210

State of the Industry   214

Films of the Period   216

Books on the Period   219

10 *Films of the Auteurs: The French New Wave and After* ★ *1954–*   **220**

Auteurism   220

Precursors to the New Wave   222

The New Wave Arrives   225

New Wave Directors   231

Left Bank Directors and Others   236

New Politics and New Theories of Authorship   241

After the New Wave   **243**

Films of the Period   **249**

Books on the Period   **252**

11 *Other Western European
Cinemas: National Cinemas
or Eurofilms?* ✭ *1945–*   **253**

Scandinavia   **254**

Germany   **261**

Spain   **269**

Films of the Period   **276**

Books on the Period   **279**

12 *Eastern European Cinema:
Film Making for the State* ✭
1954–   **280**

Poland   **282**

Hungary   **290**

Czechoslovakia   **293**

Yugoslavia   **298**

The Soviet Union and After   **301**

Films of the Period   **307**

Books on the Period   **311**

13 *Japanese Film: A Pictorial
Tradition and a Modernist
Edge* ✭ *1951–*   **312**

The Japanese Style   **313**

Three Japanese Masters   **315**

*Other Japanese Film Makers
of the Classic Era*   **322**

The Japanese New Wave   **324**

Recent Developments   **327**

Films of the Period   **329**

Books on the Period   **331**

14 *Other Asian Film-Making
Traditions* ✭ *1956–*   **332**

*India: Film and National
Identity*   **332**

China: Three Cinemas   **340**

Films of the Period   **351**

Books on the Period   **353**

15 *Hollywood in Transition* ✭
1945–1962   **354**

Television   **355**

New Screen Processes   **357**

*Fall of the Studios, Rise of the
Independents*   **361**

Internationalization   **362**

Loosened Controls on Content   **363**

*Liberalism, Communism, and
Anti-Communism: The House
Un-American Activities Committee
and Blacklisting*   **367**

Major Genres   **370**

American Directors of the 1950s   **375**

Films of the Period   **380**

Books on the Period   **381**

16 *American Reemergence* ✭
1963–1974   **382**

Popular Genres   **383**

The American New Wave   **385**

Independent Voices   **395**

Films of the Period   402

Books on the Period   403

17 *Recent National Movements* ★
1959–   404

Latin America   404

Africa   415

Australia   417

Canada   422

Iran   426

Films of the Period   429

Books on the Period   434

18 *Here and Now: United States* ★
1975–   435

The Economy and Technology   435

Emerging Genres   440

Studio Stalwarts   448

Independent Voices   453

Multicultural Agendas   459

Multinationalism   469

Films of the Period   471

Books on the Period   474

Index   475

Preface

Preparing the fifth edition of *A History of Film* with Jack Ellis has been a rewarding experience. Previous editions have treated the subject in an exemplary fashion, covering a broad array of material in a coherent, comprehensible, and accessible manner, while managing to be engaging, as well. In the fifth edition, we have tried to build on these strengths while carrying out major revisions that have both updated the coverage and expanded topics of special interest.

A new chapter on Japanese cinema broadens the book's global reach, as does expanded coverage of Indian and Chinese film and additional sections on new national cinema movements in countries such as Mexico, Iran, and Canada. Attention to women film makers and the genre of the woman's film has also been added along with coverage of minority film makers and genres that have targeted minority audiences, such as so-called race cinema and the blaxplotiation cycle. The more artisanal and politically oriented modes of avant-garde and documentary film making are also dealt with in greater detail. Mainstream cinema has been treated in greater depth, as well, especially in relation to its social and industrial context. Added attention has also been given to production personnel, such as actors, producers, screenwriters, and cinematographers, all of whom collaborate with the director to shape a film's final form.

We have further strengthened the book's emphasis on understanding a film within its cultural context, adding more background on the institutions and infrastructures out of which cinema is created. Despite the increasing complexity of the relations between films and nationhood, we feel it is important to continue to explore these ties rather than to elude them by resorting to terms such as *art cinema,* which situate movies outside time and place. In many of today's productions, touristic motifs coexist with nationalist agendas, creating a so-called "glocal" cinema of pastiche and hybridity. Often denigrated with labels such as *Europuddings* and *National Geographic Cinema,* these films nonetheless may embody multivocal discourses that allow their authors to speak to both a global arthouse market and a local constituency. We believe these connections between film and culture continue to be worthy of examination.

We have continued to emphasize full discussions of the films themselves. This approach implies selectivity; we have not tried to cover everything (which, in any event, is impossible). Some film history teachers may not agree with all our choices, but we hope that they and their students will appreciate the clarity and focus that our approach provides.

The fifth edition of *A History of Film* also includes an entirely new feature: a companion website. With the help of webmaster Kevin Smith, we have researched a multitude of valuable film history resources on the web and have installed relevant links to materials covered in the book on a chapter-by-chapter basis. We hope this feature will help both students working on papers or class reports and teachers looking for materials to include in lectures and class discussions. The website is <http://www.ablongman.com/ellis5e>.

Readers of earlier editions of *A History of Film* may notice a greater variety in the book's illustrations. We have added some frame enlargements to the publicity stills that have appeared in earlier editions. Although not as sharply focused as production stills, which are shot with a still camera on a film's set, frame enlargements represent shots taken from the films themselves. A mix of these two types of illustrations thus strikes a balance between clarity and accuracy. For the large role they played in preparing the illustrations, we owe a large debt of gratitude to Al DiFranco, Angelo Restivo, and Kevin Smith.

We also want to extend profuse thanks for work on the manuscript as a whole to the always patient, helpful, and professional editors at Allyn and Bacon—Karon Bowers, Molly Taylor, and Sarah McGaughey—and to Sue Freese of Communicáto, who oversaw production of this edition.

Thanks are also owed to Professor John Rohsensaw, who painstakingly reviewed the section on China and corrected many errors. And finally, we would like to thank those individuals who reviewed the fourth edition for Allyn and Bacon and provided useful comments and suggestions: Michael Ryan, Northeastern University; William C. Siska, University of Utah; and Donald E. Staples, University of North Texas. And once again, our thanks go to the reviewers of the third edition: Joseph A. Daccurso, Los Angeles Valley College, and William C. Siska, University of Utah.

Virginia Wright Wexman

1

Birth and Childhood of a New Art

★ ★ ★ ★

1895–1914

The most important reason motion pictures came into being had nothing to do with their artistic potential. The theory underlying the motion picture was demonstrated in a succession of optical toys. Its tools and materials were invented out of a desire to make visual records of life and to study the movements of animals, including humans. Its capacity to provide peep-show entertainment attracted impresarios and paying customers to what scientists and inventors had made available. Later, as the novelty of lifelike movement began to pale, the technicians and entrepreneurs who had discovered how to project moving images onto screens stumbled onto an old interest latent in audiences—the story. They began to offer simple narratives in a new form.

At first no one considered the storytelling potential of moving pictures, let alone their potential as an art form; but when still pictures began to move, they acquired duration, and the photographer was challenged to deal with that fourth dimension. Temporal organization was demanded in addition to spatial composition. As in the novel, the play, music, or dance, an ordering of events into a beginning, middle, and end was required in even the simplest motion picture.

Brief Motion-Picture Records of Actuality and of Performances

Initially the moving picture was scarcely more than still photographs extended into motion. The brief duration of the short strips of film demanded little beyond the still photographer's concern that there be an interesting subject appropriately lit and composed. The early motion picture camera operator sought something that moved, but otherwise the concept

1

was the same. The first films, made in the United States in the 1890s by the motion picture company founded by Thomas Alva Edison, the great inventor, were of vaudeville and circus acts. In France the Lumière brothers, Louis and Auguste, took their lighter-weight camera, developed from the Kinetoscope peep-show viewing machine manufactured by Edison from 1894 on, out into the everyday world. In one of their early films, *Feeding the Baby* (France, 1895, Louis Lumière), rather than a fixed instant of Mama and Papa Lumière at breakfast with baby, we see the infant being fed successive spoonfuls of cereal. In a short from the Edison Company (United States, c. 1894) we see two trained cats with tiny boxing gloves patting away at each other in a miniature ring, rather than standing in static pose. The novelty of captured motion was intriguing enough at first.

It was not self-evident from the outset that the motion picture image would be projected onto a large screen. Peep-show machines for individual viewing were a viable possibility, not unlike present-day video monitors. It was the Lumière brothers who thought to project the image (onto a sheet) and began paid public performances of their films in a basement café in Paris in December 1895. In April 1896 the first commercial projection in a theater took place at Koster and Bial's Music Hall in New York City. The films shown were those made by the Edison Company.

As they chose the actions they would record, film makers soon discovered what painters and still photographers had already known: that some subjects have more intrinsic (or in another sense extrinsic) interest than others do. Although the motions of knocking down a wall or of a woman feeding chickens satisfied the earliest audiences, such

"Black Maria"   ★   The Edison Studio in West Orange, New Jersey, c. 1893.

Kinetoscopes in the Peter
Bacigalupi Parlour ✳ San
Francisco, c. 1894.

everyday scenes were shortly supplemented by scenes of ships being launched and heads of state addressing large crowds. A strong man flexing his muscles (Edward Sandow) or a sharpshooter rapidly breaking targets thrown into the air ("Little Sure Shot," Annie Oakley) were soon followed by a somewhat more eventful vaudeville skit, *Fun in a Chinese Laundry* (1894), and then by a piece of a popular stage success, *Rip van Winkle* (1896) with its star, Joseph Jefferson,

Even with more interesting subjects, however, the film makers' further choices were limited to two: where they placed the camera and when they started cranking. They usually chose the ideal position of a human observer—straight in front, at eye level, and far enough back to take in all the significant action. The amount of time was fixed at half a minute or less by the length of the short film strips.

In offering perfect reproductions of unmanipulated reality, Edison and Lumière succeeded (given the limitations of silence, black and white, and two dimensions) as well as anyone has since. The rowboat rounding the pier in early Lumière, or Fatima dancing for the Edison camera, are appealingly fresh, revealing the delight the first film makers and audiences must have felt when looking at natural movement in a new way. "It is life itself," one Frenchman is supposed to have exclaimed at a premiere screening; Lumière's train pulling into the station definitively established the way to record such an event—the camera low, stationary, and at an oblique angle.

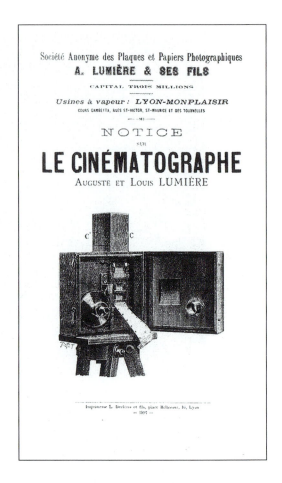

The Cinématographe, motion picture camera-projector-printer ★ Invented by Louis Lumière, France, 1895.

As stripped to essentials as these primitive films seem, there were seminal differences between the programs of the Grand Café in Paris and those at Koster and Bial's in New York City. These differences suggest, in fact, the two main and divergent aesthetic impulses that have continued to today, impulses that began in still photography—as Siegfried Kracauer emphasized in his *Theory of Film: The Redemption of Physical Reality.* One tendency, what Kracauer called the *formative,* was to strive for the "artistic," to use materials and models from the older arts. Even before the motion picture, certain photographers had begun to pose their subjects, arrange their decor and lights, and manipulate the photographic emulsion in various ways intended to make their photos look more like paintings and less like mere mechanical recordings. The other tendency, the *realistic,* was to take pride in the verisimilitude of photographic reproduction and in its ability to capture and preserve unadulterated actuality of events and views.

Perhaps largely because of the cumbersomeness of his camera, Edison started along the "artistic" way, in that he recorded performances that had originated on stage or in the circus ring. The pleasure afforded by a film of this sort depended almost entirely on the quality of the performance. Film merely preserved and made widely available what had been created and offered to the camera. In essence, this is the theatrical tradition, characteristic of fiction films in which actors perform roles with scripts that follow the time-honored rules of the earlier forms of storytelling.

Poster advertising early Lumière showings ★ *L'Arroseur arrosé* is the film being shown.

The "realistic" tradition, the documentary impulse, was the more vigorous at first. Louis Lumière, with a portable camera, had no need for a studio or prepared material. He could wander the streets and set up his camera in front of any aspect of observed reality that took his fancy. The large projected image supported the illusion that the viewer was looking out a window (rather than into a room with one wall missing, as on the stage). Another key factor sustaining the illusion was that in Lumière's work the people, animals, and vehicles frequently moved toward and away from the camera, not just laterally in relation to it—as in many Edison films that duplicated stage-bound movement. As a result of his subjects and method, Lumière and his followers left us a fascinating surface view of what the people and the world they lived in were like at the turn of the twentieth century.

Although film as record may not be film as art, these early topical and scenic views pointed to the capacity of film to find or to set its drama within real life. Lumière himself made a kind of fusion of the conceived and the actual, which seems to look way beyond Edison to the nonstudio fiction films of today. In the 1895 *L'Arroseur arrosé* (which means something like "the squirter is squirted") he set a concocted, vaudevillelike gag outdoors in an actual garden. A gardener is watering the lawn. When a boy steps on the hose, the water stops. The gardener peers into the nozzle to see what the trouble is. The boy takes his foot off the hose and the gardener is doused. In *A Game of Cards* (1896) Lumière made a somewhat similar attempt at a visual gag.

What *L'Arroseur* and *A Game of Cards* suggest, however, regarding an acted story in real settings would not be returned to for almost a decade. Instead, screens were filled

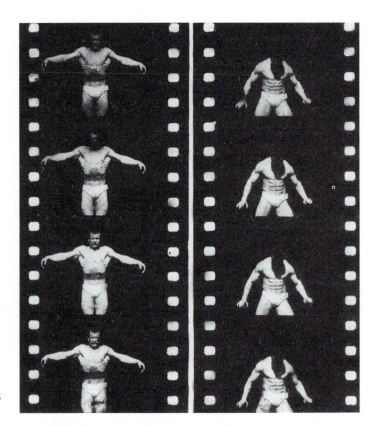

Early film taken at the Edison laboratory ✳ United States, 1890–1891, W. K. Laurie Dickson; Edward Sandow.

alternately with Lumière-type *actualités* and Edison-like stage attractions, and before the end of the decade both firms were producing both types of films. The films continued to be brief, with single shots from one camera position, and were shown characteristically as part of vaudeville programs. At first they were featured attractions; then, as the novelty began to wear off, they were reduced to the function of "chasers"—shown while one audience was leaving and another was entering the theater.

It is entirely possible that the art of the motion picture might have been stillborn, along with its capacity for entertainment, if the story ingredient hadn't been added. It is not possible, however, to establish when the first film to incorporate a story was made or who was responsible for it. Many of the early films have disappeared, so the "firsts" in film technique are subject to endless argument. National pride and individual partisanship further affect the writing of film history in this regard. But no one would deny the importance of Georges Méliès's contribution to the development of narrative full-length film.

Telling Stories through Staged and Filmed Pantomime

Unlike other of the earliest film makers, Méliès had a background in the arts, which led him to think of the motion picture in a different way. At the time of the first Lumière show-

Workers Leaving the Factory ★ France, 1895, Louis Lumière.

ings he operated the Théâtre Robert-Houdin (named in honor of a renowned French magician, who also received homage from an American who called himself Houdini). In Méliès's tiny theater, fantastic sketches and magical acts were performed with the aid of trap doors, mirrors, invisible wires, and other trappings of stage illusion. As a magician it was only natural that Méliès would be fascinated by the unprecedented apparitions offered with such seeming ease by the motion picture. Immediately after seeing the first Lumière program in the small café near his theater, he asked the brothers Lumière to sell him one of their cameras. They refused, adding that Méliès would eventually thank them for saving him from a folly certain to be ruinous once the public lost interest in the novelty. Undeterred, Méliès obtained apparatus from the English pioneer Robert Paul, assembled a machine, and soon was, like the Lumières, out on the streets photographing.

In April 1896 (the month the Edison Vitascope opened in New York) Méliès began showing movies at the Théâtre Robert-Houdin. His brief skits and slices of life on the street were evidently quite indistinguishable from those of others. But according to Méliès's later account, it was during that first year as a film maker that he discovered quite by accident what would make his contribution most distinctive: the capacity of the motion picture to move beyond the real into the fantastic. One day, while photographing in the Place de l'Opéra, the film jammed. When he succeeded in getting the camera functioning again, he indifferently cranked the film on through. Fortunately, he developed it to see if any of the footage would be usable. When projected, the film offered a succession of images that brought instant joy to the heart of the conjurer: a horse-drawn tram on the street suddenly metamorphosed into a hearse. What had happened, of course, was that the tram was passing in front of the camera when Méliès had first started cranking; by the time the film had gotten stuck and unstuck the tram had passed on and been followed by a funeral cortege.

Méliès took deliberate advantage of this accidental discovery in *The Vanishing Lady* and *The Haunted Castle* (both 1896), starting an early genre of "trick films." Within the next few years he mastered most of the technical means for what today are called "special effects." Using fades and dissolves, superimpositions and mattes, fast and slow motion, animation and miniatures, and even hand coloring of each frame, he created a delightful phantasmagoric world. Although he had many imitators, it was years later before film makers were able to figure out how some of his remarkable results had been achieved.

In addition to introducing trickery, Méliès also made the most important beginning steps in screen narrative techniques and helped increase the standard running time from less than a minute to ten to fifteen minutes—one reel. In 1897 he built France's first permanent film studio and founded Star Film Company, the first French firm devoted exclusively to making movies. By 1912 he had produced more than five hundred films of various types, but is best remembered for his fairy tales (beginning with *Cinderella* in 1900) and for a kind of fantastical science fiction (such as *An Impossible Voyage,* 1904; *The Conquest of the Pole,* 1912). Of the latter genre *A Trip to the Moon* (1902) is generally regarded as the master work; its enduring charm of conception and ingenuity of execution are easily appreciated today. It is one of the few early fiction films that modern audiences laugh with rather than at. This man of the theater brought to film an innate taste for eccentric humor and a developed sophistication of visual embellishment.

A *Trip to the Moon* is vaguely based on, but also parodies, a Jules Verne story; it lampoons scientific presumptions of the day as well. In making the film, an unprecedented thirty separate scenes were acted out by a sizable professional cast (including Méliès himself as the chief scientist) on the stage of his specially constructed glass-enclosed studio. Each scene is taken with an unbroken run of a stationary camera placed in an ideal position for viewing the whole—twelfth row center, as it were. The performers fully, not to say exaggeratedly, pantomime the action (intertitles were not yet in use), move laterally across the stage, make entrances and exits (for who was to know they didn't have to in this new medium?), and occasionally bow and gesticulate directly toward the audience (that is, the camera). The decor consists of painted canvas backdrops and highly stylized constructions and props; the robes and conical hats of the scientists, the shorts of the chorus-line guard of honor, and the devil suits of the moon men are all out of theater rather than life. Some of the trick effects are created by cinematic means; for example, scenes are joined by dissolves in place of opening and closing curtains. Other effects are achieved by such stage devices as scenery flats that are raised and lowered, trap doors, pulleys, and the like. What appears to be a dolly shot as the rocket ship approaches the moon (and lands right in the eye of its papier-mâché face) was achieved by moving the moon toward the camera rather than the camera toward the moon. In another shot, a matted drawing of the rocket enters an incongruously real ocean, proceeds down into an animated rendering of undersea life, then surfaces.

Méilès's marvelous contributions and ultimate limitations, in terms of film, are all clearly evident in *A Trip to the Moon.* He did manage to tell a complete story of many incidents in a coherent fashion; script, staging, and performances are carefully controlled to achieve a satisfying whole. The advance of what Méliès himself proudly called "artificially arranged scenes" over the single, undirected, and casually planned fragments that preceded

A Trip to the Moon ⋆ France, 1902, Georges Méliès.

him can only be admired. Where he stopped short, however, was in confining his camera to an uninterrupted view, making the photographic frame equivalent to the proscenium arch. Granting his intention "to push the cinema toward the theatrical way," we can say he succeeded too well. Although he achieved a theatrical sophistication of content and style, he failed to discover the capabilities of the unique tools of the motion picture—the camera and cutting shears. No one would want to be without those creations of his that remain (hundreds of them no longer exist). But once Méliès had established larger ambitions for storytelling in film, it remained for others to make further contributions by using methods unique to the new medium.

One other aspect of Méliès's importance should be acknowledged before we move on. With his trick films he established the basis for what would become the avant-garde tradition, which began in France in the 1920s and has continued to today in the experimental/underground/independent film.

It is possible to say, then, that the three main artistic modes of film were present in embryo form almost from the outset: narrative fiction, documentary, and experimental. The first represented a desire to tell stories with the new and increasingly rich effectiveness of moving pictures. The second had as its intention capturing the real world in a way that would help us to know and understand it more fully. The third creative impulse would lead beyond physical reality to humorous imaginings or frightful hallucinations, to the terrain of dream and the unconscious. The documentary and experimental possibilities were scarcely explored in the first decades of screen history; they did not evolve into mature forms until the early 1920s, when they did so with curious simultaneity. Though given their proper value by the cognoscenti, the documentary and experimental modes have never been as widely popular as the fiction film. It was storytelling that first attracted a loyal audience and built an economic base, and the art continued to move along fictional lines.

Telling Stories through Filmic Means

Edwin S. Porter, an American who began film work in 1896, was much less well equipped in artistic background or sensibility than Méliès. In the history of the motion picture, a lack of experience with the traditional arts has frequently proved an advantage, artistically as well as commercially. In a medium seeking its own way, vigor and vulgarity have often stimulated rather than inhibited valuable innovation. A film maker without preconceptions about the nature of artistic function and form is free to try anything. By his own admission Porter was more mechanic than artist. In choosing a career he had considered both the horseless carriage and the "flickers," coincidental new engineering fields carrying unknown potential—of industrial expansion and cultural influence. (Henry Ford built his first car in Detroit in 1896; the last Model-T was manufactured in 1927, the year the silent film ended.)

At the time Porter was hired by Edison, in 1900, film makers were first of all camera operators, valued more for their technical ingenuity in keeping the camera operating properly than for their creative imagination. Unconscious genius though he may have been, Porter made the next and crucial step—through primitive and tentative editing—that set film on its main road of advance.

One of the favorite subjects for the early actuality film makers was a horse-drawn fire engine rushing to a fire. It may have been commercial expediency that led Porter to use this available and conventional material in a new way, to "re-tread" what we would now call stock footage by adding some specially staged bits of action. At any rate, in late 1902 and early 1903 Porter made *Life of an American Fireman,* which raised the possibility of connecting different parts of a total action, all seeming to be happening at the same time but in various places.

The opening scene of *Life of an American Fireman* is of a fire chief who has fallen asleep in his office and is dreaming (in superimposition) of a mother and baby trapped by fire in a bedroom. The next scene, very brief, is a closeup (perhaps the first, and what would later be called an insert) of a fire alarm box. A hand (and part of a body) enters the frame to send an alarm. The third scene (which begins the stock footage) is of the firemen asleep in their fire station. They leap from their beds, presumably as the alarm is sounded. Note the narrative linkage that Porter has managed to imply with these three separate shots. The fire chief dreaming of a woman and child in danger foreshadows what we will see, economically evoking the tension and responsibility of his job. The hand pulling the alarm tells us that at that very moment someone has observed such a fire. The alarm, turned on, goes to the firehouse and awakens the firemen.

This apparently interconnected and simultaneous action is followed by more stock footage: interiors of the firemen sliding down the pole, hitching up their apparatus, and starting off; the exterior of an engine house as fire wagons rush out; and finally, a splendid shot (from a moving vehicle) of horses, pulling firemen and equipment, galloping down a wide

Life of an American Fireman ★
United States, 1903, Edwin S. Porter.

street. Now there appears what must have been a specially taken shot: A fire engine enters the frame, and the camera pans with it to reveal the house that is on fire. This is followed by a studio interior of the bedroom with mother and child amidst (rather unconvincing) wisps of smoke. At this point, Porter presents all the interior action—with mother and child and firemen entering the room to rescue them—and then presents the simultaneous exterior scene of the firemen, covering the same action and the same time *without cross-cutting.*

Porter followed *Life of an American Fireman* with a radically abridged adaptation of a popular stage melodrama of the day, *Uncle Tom's Cabin.* Although this production consists of little more than a series of tableaus played out against patently artificial backdrops, the intertitles that introduce each scene are the first known in an American film.

Representing a considerable advance over *Life of an American Fireman* and everything else that had gone before was Porter's next film, *The Great Train Robbery* (1903). It is a remarkable achievement, containing virtually all of the elements that might be needed for a super-western released tomorrow, and it warrants repeated study. Unlike *Life of an American Fireman,* all of *The Great Train Robbery* was specially shot for the film, exteriors "on location," interiors in the studio. Although using "artificially arranged scenes," Porter dealt with a topical subject much in the headlines and built from realistic materials. In this respect his work was very different from Méliès's stylized theatricality; Méliès offered the first filmed fantasies, but realism became the main artistic style of the fiction film.

The plot of *The Great Train Robbery* progresses along three lines with three principal sets of characters. The first scene is in a railway telegraph office. Bandits enter and force the telegrapher to order the approaching train to stop for water. After binding and gagging him, the bandits leave. In scene two the desperadoes hide behind the water tank, then sneak aboard the train as it departs. Scene three takes place in the interior of the express car, which the bandits enter and rob. Scene four shows them commandeering the locomotive and forcing the engineer to stop the train. In scene five the engineer is made to uncouple the locomotive, pull ahead, and stop again. Scene six furthers the course of the robbery as the passengers empty out of the train, line up while the bandits collect all their valuables, and then depart. The robbers board the locomotive in scene seven, and it moves off. In scene eight the locomotive comes to a halt and the bandits run off into the countryside. Scene nine shows them moving down a hill and across a stream to mount their waiting horses. Back in the telegraph office, scene ten, the telegrapher's daughter enters and frees her father, who then rushes out. In a dance hall, scene eleven, we see a number of couples square dancing; the telegraph operator staggers in; the men grab their rifles and leave. In scene twelve the robbers, and then the posse in pursuit, gallop by the camera. In the thirteenth and final scene the bandits, thinking they have escaped their pursuers, are inspecting their loot; the posse surrounds them, and shoots them all down. The famous epilogue, a medium closeup of one of the bandits firing directly at the camera, had no narrative function (as did the alarm box closeup in *Life of an American Fireman*); it was added simply to startle. In fact, the Edison catalogue of 1904 suggests that this scene "can be used to begin or end the picture."

Notice how neatly the thirteen scenes dovetail. The bandits enter the telegrapher's life, and then we follow them for the robbery and escape, which constitute the bulk of the picture. The dance hall is introduced without explanation, Porter evidently counting on our being patient for a moment until the telegrapher arrives—thus bringing the dance hall men into the story and leading to the final dramatic action, the gunning down of the bandits.

The film's structure and characterization are so basically sound that one can easily imagine how its twelve minutes might be further expanded to ninety. The telegrapher would be a widower, let's say, whose daughter badly wants him to marry the local school-teacher so she can have a new mother and so her father won't be so lonely. The Eastern dude who has his heels shot at in the dance hall is really a fearless secret service agent whose job is to track down train robbers. There is also the possibility of adding preceding events that explain how the gang's leader entered into a life of crime. The sturdy bones are all there; only flesh would be needed to give that first western large and full life today.

Note also how time and space are dealt with. Between most scenes brief or longer ellipses are suggested, and the order is straight succession, as in *A Trip to the Moon*. When the film cuts from the mounted bandits back to the telegraph office, however, a reversal in time seems implied—since the bandits are still in the vicinity for the posse to catch them. There are instances of implicit simultaneity as well: In the beginning of scene three, in the express car, the bandits are evidently approaching as we watch the expressman's actions; or, at the start of scene eleven, in the dance hall, the telegraph operator is presumably on the way from his office as we see the dancing.

Each scene is still one continuous take—scene equals shot. Porter does not cut to varying distances or angles within scenes: The camera remains resolutely at eye level in

The Great Train Robbery ✷ United States, 1903, Edwin S. Porter.

long shot. But there are some interesting beginnings of camera variety, most likely forced on Porter by the exigencies of location shooting. First of all, in photographing the action of the robbers on the topside of a train in motion, a sort of moving camera results: The camera itself is stationary but the scenery passes by. Second, given the substantial number of "extras" lined up alongside the train, Porter probably couldn't get straight back far enough to include them all in the frame; and the side of the roadbed no doubt sloped down to a ditch. So he may have been required to move up the track for that effective oblique angle emphasized by the man who runs toward the camera to do a little dance of death at closer range. Finally, if horsemen are going to ride down a bluff and then turn left in front of the camera, the choice is either to pan and tilt with them or let them leave the frame. Though Porter's camera moves most hesitantly, the hesitation would be caused partly by a tripod head not constructed to accommodate such movement properly. It is possible also that he thought the odd angle and movement regrettable deviations from prevailing propriety rather than positive assets.

To us, if not to Porter, the conventionally painted canvas interiors mix poorly with the fine outdoor settings; they seem part of another and less innovative film. Looking back over the history of cinema we can find many valuable additions to technique forced on film makers by the requirements of nonstudio shooting. In the studio everything can be constructed and adjusted for the convenience of the camera; outside, the film maker must adapt to the world as is. With *The Great Train Robbery* it is the exteriors that are inventive in composition, depth, and movement; the interiors are conventionally horizontal and unimaginative. Learning comes from the kind of improvisation demanded by the unanticipated.

This simplified account of the evolution of narrative film technique of necessity excludes other Porter films as well as hundreds of film makers and thousands of films that contained some of the same accidents and discoveries. These early films seem to evince a conscious pursuit of what would become standard narrative technique, but the motivation of the film makers at the time and what audiences were responding to may have been something quite different. Film historians are going back to the evidence of the films that still exist to try to understand better those original purposes. It seems evident, however, that Porter did not carry his remarkable discoveries much further than in the two seminal films previously discussed; in fact, he seems not to have been altogether clear about what it was he had achieved. In the time between them he made a most uninspired bit of recorded theater in *Uncle Tom's Cabin.* After *The Great Train Robbery* he frequently lapsed into earlier and less interesting modes, and never surpassed that 1903 achievement. Even the seductively entitled and brilliantly ingenious *The Dream of a Rarebit Fiend* (1906) appears to be a frank imitation of Méliès.

Porter's innovations were anticipated and developed by film makers in other countries whose work is now beginning to receive more scholarly attention. In the mid-1890s the British inventor R. W. Paul developed a camera and projection system that was widely used to create and show films all over the world. Subsequently a group based around the English resort town of Brighton, including George Albert Smith and James Williamson, produced films such as *Fire!* (1901) and *The Robbery of the Mail Coach* (1903), which bear striking similarities to Porter's later successes, *Life of an American Fireman* and *The Great Train Robbery.* The productions of another English entrepreneur, Cecil Hepworth, also met with great acclaim during these early years. Hepworth's best-known work, *Rescued by Rover,* which tells the tale of a baby kidnapped by gypsies and retrieved by the family pet,

Rescued by Rover ★ United Kingdom, 1905, Cecil Hepworth.

is distinguished by such innovations as smooth panning and a low angle shot. In France, Alice Guy made what was perhaps the first fiction film, *The Cabbage Fairy,* in 1896.

The man who most effectively took over leadership from Porter, and whom Porter himself regarded with deference, was another American, David Wark Griffith. Griffith's introduction to film was in Porter's *Rescued from an Eagle's Nest* (1907); he played the father hero, calling himself Lawrence Griffith to keep his real name unsullied for anticipated fame as a playwright. Lack of success in the theater (as a dramatist he had only one play produced, and that unsuccessfully) kept Griffith tied to the movies. While acting in them for five dollars a day he learned that he could earn an additional ten to fifteen dollars apiece for story ideas. In 1908 he directed his first film, *The Adventures of Dollie.*

In a remarkably short time Griffith mastered what there was to know about the new medium and progressed beyond his contemporaries. Working with characteristically prodigious energy, his output of short films, the prevailing form, advanced virtually all aspects of technique. The one- and two-reelers contained experiments or refinements that carried forward the rudiments established by Porter; and by the time of Griffith's monumental feature *The Birth of a Nation* in 1915, the whole syntax of silent film had been laid out for use. The essential nature of Griffith's contributions can best be appreciated by comparing his work with the film making that preceded him. The extent to which Porter, the Brighton School, and others were able to develop the narrative aspects of cinematic expression was severely limited. According to that most modern of film makers, Jean-Luc Godard, every development since Griffith had its origins in him. Whether Godard's statement is hyperbolic or not, it is unquestionable that Griffith contributed more to the evolution of film as an art form than any other individual in its history to date.

The Language of Film

Perhaps Griffith's single-most important insight was that the shot rather than the scene should be the basic unit of film language. With this discovery came the possibility of varying the standard, stationary, head-on long shot. Gradually Griffith moved his camera to setups closer to the action or farther away, altered its angle for the most effective view, let it follow a moving subject when appropriate or traverse a stationary scene for certain kinds of kinetic emphasis. These varied shots were then edited together to create the appearance of a continuous scene selectively viewed. Once understood, these options gave the film maker immeasurably greater control over the audience's emotional response, adding powerful connotations to the action itself. Méliès's framing, in unvaried long shots, had been emotionally neutral. Although Porter had begun to break away from fixed convention, the exceptions did not upset established rules even in his own films (and the deliberateness of his intentions is less than certain).

It was Griffith more than anyone who came to understand the separate psychological-aesthetic functions of the long shot, the medium shot, and the closeup, and who used this awareness consistently. In Griffith's work, and in that of his successors, the *long shot* usually begins a scene, establishing the action and its setting. It might be used to "reestablish," after closer and partial views, so that the parts could be kept related to the whole. Full of information—one could go on and on describing all the things seen in it—it is emotionally cool: We are literally distanced from the action. As the camera is placed closer, or a longer lens is used to achieve much the same effect, there are fewer things included within the frame, but we tend to be more interested in them, feeling closer to them emotionally as well as perceptually. The *medium shot* rather than the long shot became the standard framing from which the director departs for special purposes, just as we usually deal with life around us from middle distance. In it we are close enough to see and comprehend what is happening and what it means. Generally the stress of the medium shot is on relationships, on interaction: a person in conversation with another, or petting an animal, or cooking at a stove. When the camera is moved closer still, to a *closeup*, the visual information becomes quite limited—perhaps to one face, a hand stroking fur, a pot boiling over—but the emotional weight becomes very heavy. Our attention is directed to what we might not have noticed otherwise or might not have been able to discern at a distance. The closeup can also be used to draw us into strong identification with a character, and to suggest through facial expression what is being thought and felt. It is a freed visual statement that permits directors to show us exactly—and only—what they want us to see in the way they want us to perceive it.

Griffith called closeups "inserts," and he shot them after the scene had been filmed in long and medium shots. This frequently shifting point of view, especially to the closeup, offered a means of expression comparable to the use of spoken words in the theater. Although the stage director can block and light action in a way designed to lead our eye, we

David Wark Griffith directing.

are still free to regard the whole proscenium—no more, no less—from one fixed position. Broad gestures and conspicuous props and symbolic settings may be employed, but most of what we learn comes from what the characters say to each other. Lacking the power of spoken words, Griffith substituted a kind of visual language with its own conventions and limitations. Though never as intellectually precise as words, the affective use of images can cause us to feel directly and deeply in a manner both unique and compelling.

Alternation of tempo through the editing of detached shots is something that Griffith came to understand from intuition and experiment, and that Porter understood not at all. Although Porter shifted from one scene to another, he did not break up the run of the camera within scenes. The pursuit of the bandits by the posse in *The Great Train Robbery* remains one of the slowest chases in memory as the first party of horsemen, and then the second, enters and passes through the frame. Griffith might extend screen time beyond actual time, as he would cut back and forth from shots of bandits to shots of a posse, building to a rhythmic climax, but his chases (honored as "the Griffith last-minute rescue") seem incredibly more tense—and even faster. What he discovered, other film makers have learned and used since: Rapid cutting, or a succession of short shots, can create excitement; slow cutting, or shots held longer on the screen, will aid calm contemplation. Both the shifting spatial framing and the temporal alternation of shots give the film maker artistic resources extending well beyond the bare meaning of the action being recorded.

For transitions between shots Griffith used a larger range of optical effects than is generally employed today. The *cut* is basic within scenes; virtually unnoticed in itself, it is necessary for the variable ordering and pacing of the action. The *dissolve* is a more noticeable transition in which one image is gradually superimposed over, and then replaces, the other. As in early Méliès, it is usually used between scenes rather than within them, and signals a change of place and/or time. When one image *fades out* to darkness and a new image *fades in* to full exposure, a different place and lapse in time are usually being signaled also. (Griffith tended to favor fades over dissolves.) As the heaviest screen "punctuation," the only one in which we are given nothing to look at for a few seconds, fade-outs frequently indicate a larger break in the dramatic action as well, marking off groups of scenes that are called *sequences* by some critics. (Other writers and many film makers use *shot* and *scene* synonymously and *sequence* for what is here being called *scene,* leaving no term for a larger dramatic/narrative unit [comparable to an act or a chapter] short of the entire film.)

Griffith also liked *irises* as connective devices. An iris begins with a black screen containing only a small circle (or square or other shaped portion) of the total image: a girl's bowed head, for example. Then as the iris opens up it reveals the whole action and setting: a family standing over the girl at the dinner table in a farm kitchen. When the scene has run its course, with the girl explaining (in intertitles) how she has been orphaned and has come in desperation to these old friends of her parents, the final shot might iris out; within the contracting circle of black we see the girl's smiling, upturned face as she learns that the family will let her stay.

Griffith employed *masking* in several ways: the sides of the frame darkened to emphasize the height of a tower in the center; tops and bottoms darkened to form a CinemaScope-proportioned strip across the middle, stressing the horizontal movement and length of a column of galloping cavalry; or a cameo masking of the corners, to enhance the oval loveliness of Lillian Gish's face. He also experimented with *superimposition* and *split screen* for special effects—for the longing daydream in *Enoch Arden* (1911), or to make the awareness of burning Atlanta hang over the foreground of people fleeing in *The Birth of a Nation* (1915).

Griffith did not by any means limit his attention to the "grammatical" elements of screen language. Although of the theater, as Porter was not, Griffith soon began to sense that performance in film required a style quite different from that in fashion on the stage. If spoken words were lacking, the eloquence of body movement and gesture was magnified; in the new medium the camera registered and the projector projected. Actors on the screen appeared large, their every movement easily discernible from the back rows; as the camera came closer to them, its photographic authenticity rendered as false the prevailing theatrical histrionics. Griffith began to confine movement, dress, and makeup to an approximation of life; any exaggeration was kept small in scale and justified by character. Pantomime became more and more expressly tailored for the camera—the sad smile with only the face visible, the upper part of a body with hands plucking and fluttering in nervous excitement, the eyes revealing remorse or anger or frustrated passion. Richer and subtler characterizations began to replace the broad and simple performances of the first dramatic films. Faces and bodies, cut up and reassembled in edited sequence, were made to achieve a new precision of expression. Griffith commanded a thoughtfulness and invention from the actors in his developing stock company; with camera and cutting shears he shaped their performances into a dramatic entity that had existed initially only in his mind.

As for physical background to the action, Griffith's exterior locales were always carefully selected for their appropriateness to the events depicted and for their capacity to reinforce the mood of the story. Constructed sets in his films strike us as the real thing even when they're not; the style is invariably naturalistic in solidity and detail. What he couldn't find on location he had carefully and fully re-created on the back lot or in the studio. Griffith was able to achieve a scale that had no theatrical precedents: real trains rushing across a wide prairie, enemy hordes encircling a besieged city. His lighting initially advanced along existing stage lines and then, as brighter lights and more sensitive emulsions became available, finally surpassed theatrical possibility. At first he and cameraman G. W. "Billy" Bitzer were content to light scenes with sharp, even clarity, using controlled sunlight for interiors (with no ceiling or roof) as well as exteriors—standard practice at the time; but photographically the earliest Griffith/Bitzer films stand out from those of most of their peers, as they somehow manage to look fresh and sharp even today. In addition to exact exposure and focus, this quality must have something to do with choice of emulsion and care in processing. In later work Griffith began to experiment with the effective possibilities of modulated and directional artificial light, breaking some taboos in the process. An interior night scene might be lit as if suffused by the flickering softness of the firelight, underexposed by standards then current, or what is called "low-key lighting" today. In another scene the heroine's head might be lit from behind by simulated morning light streaming in through a window so that it bounced off her blonde hair to form a halo of overexposure, "halation" in photographic terms. Some of these experiments would be expanded and refined by the Germans in the 1920s, just as the Russians would further develop Griffith's editing.

The New York Hat ✶
United States, 1912,
D. W. Griffith; Mary Pickford.

Finally, Griffith was one of the leaders in the movement against the short length of films imposed by the American industry of the day. With few exceptions, the dominant companies were conservative in their adherence to established practice and their unwillingness to risk the capital that longer films would have required. At first Griffith was confined to the one-reel (ten to fifteen minutes) standard that Méliès and Porter had achieved. As film makers became more aware of the potential of the medium, they became increasingly ambitious in terms of subject matter. Larger subjects demanded more running time. In 1910 Griffith made a two-reeler entitled *His Trust,* which the studio released as two separate one-reel films. The same thing happened to his next two-reeler, *Enoch Arden,* but Griffith and others persisted until two reels became accepted as standard length. He continued to strive for more time and larger scale, and by the end of this first period of film history, he had reached a length of four reels, with *Judith of Bethulia* (1914). It was his last important film before *The Birth of a Nation,* and in narrative structure and historical spectacle it foreshadowed his even larger feature, *Intolerance.*

Increasing Films to Feature Length

In the early days movie makers experimented with a wide array of film forms, including *serial* films, which featured continuing story lines played out over many individual episodes, and *series* films, which featured a continuing set of characters engaged in various adventures, much like the *Star Wars* series of today. The best-known practitioner of these forms was the French director Louis Feuillade, whose masterful compositions created a striking visual style that has come to be known as *fantastic realism.* Utilizing elaborate, implausible plot lines built around the exploits of sinister criminal gangs who adopted multiple disguises, Feuillade crafted popular series such as *Fantômas* (1913); *Les Vampires* (1915–1916), featuring the master criminal Irma Vep; and *Judex* (1917), which was later remade by Georges Franju as a tribute to Feuillade. Series and serials were screened everywhere, including Argentina, which produced the widely shown *Gaucho Nobility,* directed by Humberto Cairo and Ernesto Gunche, in 1915, and Mexico, where the twelve-part *The Grey Car,* directed by Joaquin Coss and Juan de Homs, was released in 1919. Serials were also popular in the United States. The most famous, *The Perils of Pauline* (Louis Gassner and Donald MacKenzie, 1914), starring Pearl White, featured individual episodes finished off with so-called cliffhanger endings designed so that audiences would feel compelled to return for the next episode.

Another popular form during these years was the short *animated* film, in which still images are drawn or photographed on single frames and then joined in such a way as to suggest movement. Emile Cohl developed this technique, creating nonnarrative films such as *Brains Repaired* (1911) by combining drawings, photographs, and live action. Other animators active in this period created popular cartoon characters such as Gertie the Dinosaur (Windsor McCay), Felix the Cat (Otto Messmer), and Koko the Clown (Max and Dave Fleischer).

In reaching feature length, Griffith had been passed by the French and the Italians. Free from the stringent limitation on running time imposed by the U.S. industry, the Europeans had begun to exploit subjects that led naturally to films of an hour and more. Available to French film makers was a long and uniquely distinguished theatrical tradition.

Les Vampires serial ★ France, 1915–1916, Louis Feuillade.

From as early as 1908, with *The Assassination of the Duc de Guise,* directed by Charles de Bargy, they began to turn out film versions of successful plays starring well-known players. A company called Film d'Art was the first in the field, bestowing its name on the entire shortlived subgenre. In most respects the idea was retrogressive, extending back to Méliès, who had wanted to "push the cinema toward the theatrical way," and even to Edison, who had earlier recorded bits of popular theater. The principal difference of the *films d'art* was that the extreme deference paid to the older medium, however perverse, meant that whole plays rather than fragments were recorded exactly as performed. Intertitles were abridged substitutions for the unheard dialogue the actors mouthed. Except for the new length required, it was back to the camera in twelfth row center, the scene recorded in one shot, and using theatrical sets and gestures. These films did attract a certain following, however, especially among the middle class who knew or thought they ought to know the theater; and the somewhat snobbish appeal and contemporary prestige helped to drag films as a whole toward greater length.

The most consequential of the series was *Queen Elizabeth* (1912), directed by Louis Mercanton and Henri Desfontaines, and starring Sarah Bernhardt and Lou Tellegen (her leading man offstage as well as on). The divine Sarah, although sixty-eight years old at the time, still commanded an international audience. Unlike many theatrical artists, she seemed to have been extremely interested in film. "I rely on these films to make me immortal," she is supposed to have said. Alas, for Bernhardt and for us, much of her divinity must have resided in her reputedly remarkable voice and oral interpretation. What remains in *Queen Elizabeth* now seems more nearly a cruel travesty of a great talent and an exhumation of dead theatrical convention. Such problems only vaguely troubled contemporary observers, however. The film was acquired for distribution in the United States by the young Adolph Zukor and played with substantial and prophetic success in converted "legitimate" theaters at the unheard of price of one dollar a ticket. It provided the first capital as well as the precedent for Famous Players Film Company, which eventually became Paramount Pictures.

Although *Queen Elizabeth* opened up the possibility for successful American distribution and exhibition of feature-length films, it was the Italians who contributed more importantly to the form that features would take—along lines close to those Griffith had begun to explore in miniature. The inclination of the Italians was toward historical and religious spectacle set in their own glorious past. The first of these, *The Last Days of Pompeii,* was produced in 1908, the same year as the first of the films d'art. *The Fall of Troy* (1910) and *Dante's Inferno* (1911), at five reels in length, continued the trend. A static and dully literal illustration of the epic poem, the *Inferno* was followed by *Quo Vadis?* (1912), at nine reels. Both were road-shown in the United States, the latter even more successfully than *Queen Elizabeth.* Noteworthy among similar films were another *Last Days of Pompeii* (1913) and *Cabiria* (1914). Of the early Italian spectacles perhaps only *Cabiria* (twelve reels), a worldwide success at the time, is of more than historical interest today.

Queen Elizabeth ★ France, 1912, Louis Mercanton and Henri Desfontaines; Sarah Bernhardt.

Cabiria ⋆ Italy, 1914,
Giovanni Pastrone.

From a script credited to Gabriele D'Annunzio and directed by Giovanni Pastrone, it is placed in the Punic Wars. The plot centers on Hannibal's crossing of the Alps and the siege of Syracuse. Vast sets were employed as well as plaster models. The action is directed and shot with an unusual amount of energy and movement, and an appropriate symphonic score was specially composed. Like its predecessor *Quo Vadis?, Cabiria* had a definite influence on American production.

Massive in all respects, these extravaganzas not only established feature length but they also demonstrated film's superior claim over the theater to this kind of spectacle. Patterns laid down in them would be followed by Griffith, Cecil B. DeMille, and all those who have subsequently worked in the genre. They also moved the movies out of the nickelodeons and converted stores into large theaters and auditoriums, where they were often accompanied by full orchestra. The Italian lead was lost only with the outbreak of World War I.

During its first two decades the motion picture advanced from vaudeville turns and brief cinematographic records of life on the street to short film narratives using the rudimentary grammar of the medium. By the end of this period the length of films had increased until precedent had been established for the feature running over an hour, which would become the staple form around which the art and the industry further developed. The subsequent consolidation of these early advances and the move toward an expanded future initially occurred mainly in the United States.

Films of the Period

1894
Fun in a Chinese Laundry (U.S., Edison Company)

1895
The Arrival of a Train at the Station (L'Arrivée d'un train à la Ciotat) (France, Louis Lumière)
L'Arroseur arrosé (France, Louis Lumière)
The Execution of Mary, Queen of Scots (U.S., Edison Company)
Feeding the Baby (Repas de bébé) (France, Louis Lumière)
Workers Leaving the Factory (La Sortie des usines Lumière) (France, Louis Lumière)

1896
The Cabbage Fairy (La Fée aux choux) (France, Alice Guy)
The Kiss (U.S., Edison Company, starring May Irwin and John C. Rice)
The Vanishing Lady (Escamotage d'une dame au théâtre Robert Houdin) (France, Georges Méliès)

1899
The Dreyfus Affair (L'Affaire Dreyfus) (France, Georges Méliès)

1900
Attack on a China Mission (U.K., James A. Williamson)
Cinderella (Cendrillons) (France, Georges Méliès)
Grandma's Reading Glass (U.K., George Albert Smith)

1901
Story of a Crime (Histoire d'un crime) (France, Ferdinand Zecca)

1902
A Trip to the Moon (Le Voyage dans la lune) (France, Georges Méliès)

1903
The Great Train Robbery (U.S., Edwin S. Porter)

Life of an American Fireman (U.S., Edwin S. Porter)

1904
An Impossible Voyage (Le Voyage à travers l'impossible) (France, Georges Méliès)

1905
Rescued by Rover (U. K., Cecil Hepworth)

1906
The Dream of a Rarebit Fiend (U.S., Edwin S. Porter)

1907
Ben-Hur (U.S., Sidney Olcott)
Rescued from an Eagle's Nest (U.S., Edwin S. Porter)

1908
The Adventures of Dollie (U.S., David Wark Griffith)
The Assassination of the Duc de Guise (L'Assassinat du duc de Guise) (France, Charles de Bargy)
The Last Days of Pompeii (Gli Ultime giorni di Pompeii) (Italy, Luigi Maggi)

1909
The Lonely Villa (U.S., David Wark Griffith)

1911
Brains Repaired (La Retapeur de cervelles) (France, Émile Cohl)
The Lonedale Operator (U.S., David Wark Griffith)

1912
The Conquest of the Pole (La Conquête du pôle) (France, Georges Méliès)
The Musketeers of Pig Alley (U.S., David Wark Griffith)
The New York Hat (U.S., David Wark Griffith)

Queen Elizabeth (Les Amours de la reine Élisabeth) (France, Louis Mercanton and Henri Desfontaines)
Quo Vadis? (Italy, Enrico Guazzoni)

1913
The Battle at Elderbush Gulch (U.S., David Wark Griffith)
A House Divided (U.S., Alice Guy)

Fantômas (France, Louis Feuillade)

1914
Anthony and Cleopatra (Marcantonio e Cleopatra) (Italy, Enrico Guazzoni)
Cabiria (Italy, Giovanni Pastrone)
The Perils of Pauline (U.S., Louis Gassner and Donald MacKenzie)
Les Vampires (France, Louis Feuillade)

Books on the Period

Abel, Richard. *The Ciné Goes to Town: French Cinema 1896–1914.* Berkeley: University of California Press, 1994.

Abel, Richard. *The Red Rooster Scare: Making Cinema American 1900–1910.* Berkeley: University of California Press, 1999.

Bernstein, Matthew, ed. *Controlling Hollywood: Censorship and Regulation in the Studio Era.* New Brunswick, NJ: Rutgers University Press, 2000.

Brown, Gene. *Movie Time: A Chronology of Hollywood and the Movie Industry from Its Beginnings to the Present.* New York: Macmillan, 1995.

Cripps, Thomas. *Slow Fade to Black: The Negro in American Film, 1900–1942.* New York: Oxford University Press, 1993.

Dixon, Wheeler Winston, ed. *Re-Viewing British Cinema, 1900–1992: Essays and Interviews.* Albany: State University of New York Press, 1994.

Fuller, Kathryn H. *At the Picture Show: Small-Town Audiences and the Creation of Movie Fan Culture.* Washington, DC: Smithsonian Institution Press, 1996.

Harding, Colin, and Simon Popple, eds. *In the Kingdom of the Shadows: A Companion to Early Cinema.* Canbury, NJ: Fairleigh Dickinson University Press, 1996.

Hayward, Susan. *French National Cinema* ("National Cinemas Series"). New York: Routledge, 1993.

MacCann, Richard Dyer. *The Silent Screen* ("American Movies Series"). Lanham, MD: Scarecrow Press, 1997.

Maltby, Richard, and Ian Craven. *Hollywood Cinema: An Introduction.* Malden, MA: Blackwell Publications, 1995.

Phillips, Ray. *Edison's Kinetoscope and Its Films: A History of 1896.* Westport, CT: Greenwood Press, 1997.

Robinson, David. *From Peep Show to Palace: The Birth of the American Film.* New York: Columbia University Press, 1996.

Rossell, Deac. *Living Pictures: The Origins of the Movies.* Albany: State University of New York Press, 1998.

Slide, Anthony. *The New Historical Dictionary of the American Film Industry.* Lanham, MD: Scarecrow Press, 1998.

Sorlin, Pierre. *Italian National Cinema, 1896–1996.* New York: Routledge, 1996.

Stokes, Melvyn, and Richard Maltby. *American Movie Audiences: From the Turn of the Century to the Early Sound Era.* London: British Film Institute, 1999.

Toulet, Emmanuelle. *Birth of the Motion Picture* (tr. Susan Emanuel). New York: Harry N. Abrams, 1995.

Waller, Gregory A. *Main Street Amusement: Movies and Commercial Entertainment in a Southern City, 1896–1930.* Washington, DC: Smithsonian Institution Press, 1995.

2

Rise of the
American Film

★ ★ ★ ★

1914–1919

Except for the United States, the major film-producing countries—France, Germany, Great Britain, and Italy—were involved in World War I from its outbreak. The United States did not enter the war until 1917, and then our participation was far less than total. Since some of the materials required for the manufacture of high explosives are the same as those for photographic film (cotton, and nitric and sulfuric acids), film stock was in short supply abroad. A much more serious effect of war on European film producers was the curtailment of international distribution of completed films. Nations were separated from each other by battle lines; transportation was unavailable for many nonmilitary purposes; and the large American audience lay three thousand miles across a submarine-infested ocean.

Although the French and the Italians had been first to arrive at feature-length films, and although the French motion picture industry had achieved unquestioned world dominance by 1910, the United States was now in a position to pursue that development as no other country could. With its sizable moviegoing public, an economy stimulated rather than drained by war, a tradition of business expertise, and film makers of considerable inventiveness and occasional genius, the United States had a crucial advantage at this important stage. The Americans made full use of their resources, and that is to their credit. If there had not been that four-year lead at exactly that historical moment, however, the subsequent domination of the world's screens by the United States might never have occurred, at least not to the extent that it has.

As it happened, during the second half of the 1910s, the Americans were the ones who expanded the art to a fuller expression, discovered the sorts of ingredients that would make the entertainment universally popular, and devised systems of manufacture, wholesaling, and retailing that could support the new expense of feature production. In the United

States during those years, three parallel developments occurred that deserve particular attention. First was the culmination of Griffith's earlier experimentation in film form, his first features. Second, a very special tradition of American screen comedy began in the output of Mack Sennett and his co-workers, most notably Charles Chaplin. Finally, the new and prototypical systems of mass production, distribution, and exhibition evolved—with Thomas H. Ince among the leaders in organizing production—laying the groundwork for subsequent economic expansion.

The First American Epics

Griffith worked in both large and small scale. Many of his films that have aged well, or his scenes remembered with great pleasure, are close, intimate studies of character and feeling (for example, *Broken Blossoms* [1919]) or selective and heightened observations of everyday life in small-town America (*True Heart Susie* [1919]). Still, what was needed to shake film completely free from the stage, in a way so conspicuous that no one could fail to understand, was probably the kind of spectacular grandeur represented by Griffith's *The Birth of a Nation* (1915) and *Intolerance* (1916). Except for their length and expense, any other single element of these two films could no doubt be found in one or more of the over four hundred shorter Griffith films preceding them, especially in those produced from 1912 on. To bring together all these contributions, however, under complete control and on such a gigantic scale, was a truly staggering accomplishment. Nothing like these two films—in their size and intricacy of conception and in their mingling of history with passionate argument—had appeared before them.

The Birth of a Nation is the paradigm for the successful "big" Hollywood movie, through *Gone With the Wind* (1939) to *Titanic* (1997) and beyond. It also established the technique and style of film making that has come to be called classic Hollywood cinema. Today if *The Birth of a Nation* is not quite the fresh revelation of the breathtaking power of the screen that it was for its first audiences, it can still be an overwhelming experience, particularly when properly presented at silent rather than sound speed with a good print and the original music. It can come alive for those who free themselves from unjustified feelings of superiority to any film not in a current idiom, those who can accept Griffith's artistic postulates and understand that his racial attitudes are embedded in the myths and memories that formed such a dominant part of his life.

After completing *Judith of Bethulia* in 1913 (four reels, twice as long as any film he had previously made), Griffith left his first employer, the Biograph Company. Apparently he was restive under commercial restraints that had prevented him from proceeding to even larger projects. It is not clear to what extent Griffith was influenced by the Italian features; internal evidence suggests that *Intolerance* may owe more to them than does *Birth*. Griffith claimed not to have been influenced, and associates such as Lillian Gish have testified that he was so busy making films he rarely took time to see any. He was working along lines similar to the Italians, however, and their successes must have acted as competitive stimuli, if not models, demonstrating that the kind of thing he was trying to do could be done. In any case, after joining the small independent firm called Mutual, where he directed some routine productions to meet the payroll, he began to plan the huge film on the Civil War and Reconstruction that became *The Birth of a Nation*. Most of the latter part of the film was based on Thomas Dixon's novel *The Clansman* and the successful play made from it; there are lesser borrowings from Dixon's *The Leopard's Spots* and other sources.

The Birth of a Nation broke all sorts of precedents. Even in production, its cost, approximately $110,000, was said to be five times greater than the next largest sum spent on an American film up to that time. (*Judith of Bethulia* had cost $23,000—the most spent on a film prior to *Birth*, according to Seymour Stern, one of Griffith's biographers.) Having run through his backers' money, Griffith invested what he could raise and borrow on his own to finish it. There were six weeks of rehearsal; shooting extended from July into October of 1914; editing took another three months. This overall production time contrasted with the average in those days of six weeks or less. When completed, *Birth*'s length was an unprecedented three hours. It was accompanied throughout by a symphonic score specially composed by Joseph Carl Briel, and was the first American film to be so treated.

In 1915 the film opened as *The Clansman* in Los Angeles, and then as *The Birth of a Nation* in New York. This title change was suggested by Dixon, the author of the novel, who felt something was needed to suggest the epic scope of Griffith's achievement. The new title referred to the end of the sovereignty of the states, achieved by the victory over secession. Although it played in "legitimate" theaters for as much as two dollars per ticket, it has been estimated that the first six months of its national run drew more people than had attended all the performances of all the stage plays in the United States during any given five-year period. More than merely a motion picture, it was a cultural phenomenon that everyone felt obliged to witness. Because of its evident racial biases, it created enormous controversy, even riots, and the notoriety attracted still more customers.

Since it was distributed on a "states' rights" basis, with flat fees paid for regional distribution franchises, there are no accurate figures of what *Birth* earned at the box office. *Variety* estimated that it had grossed as much as $50 million, and until recent years it was acknowledged as the top money-maker of all time. It continues in active circulation among film societies and in nontheatrical series and academic courses, and receives occasional theatrical revivals. No doubt it is playing somewhere on the globe at this moment, and it is still capable of provoking picketing and threats of worse by civil rights groups who want to protect audiences from its depiction of African Americans.

Aside from the racial content (to be dealt with later), what may strike one most strongly about the film is the sheer massiveness of its subject. Part I deals with the North and South in the days before the War Between the States (as Griffith would have called it) and with the war itself; Part II covers the Reconstruction period in the South. The whole is much more than an "epic" in the vulgarized entertainment sense of a film loaded with extras; instead, it is a genuine effort to treat a national epoch in the fullest possible way.

Griffith's strategy included the portrayal of imaginary persons who touch on salient aspects of national events. Partly through the social positions and vocations of the characters—who help shape the historical forces at work as well as representing those persons affected by the forces—a structural pattern was created that allowed the large canvas to be colored and infused with personal drama. Historical tableaux frame and punctuate the fictional plot: the first slaves landing in Virginia, Lincoln brooding at night in the White House, Grant and Lee at Appomattox. (Griffith would use this sort of organization again in *Intolerance, Orphans of the Storm* [1921], and other historical works.) The fusing of fiction with history dates at least from Homer and was standard practice with Sir Walter Scott

The Birth of a Nation ★ United States, 1915, D. W. Griffith.

and other historical novelists; Griffith drew more or less consciously on nineteenth-century literary precedents for the shaping of his stories.

The dramatic parallels Griffith employed among his characters do not seem excessively schematic, given the full and lifelike detail of the incidents surrounding them. There are the two families, one northern and one southern, whose children become acquainted at a northern school—as they might well have done, given the southern aristocracy's practice of educating their sons in the North. The northern father, the Honorable Austin Stoneman, Leader of the House, is a powerful abolitionist politician (clearly modeled on Thaddeus Stevens, a prime factor in the passing of Reconstruction legislation). He is a widower whose dead wife has been succeeded by a scheming mulatto housekeeper. The southern father, Dr. Cameron, is an aging, wealthy planter with a gentle wife, thoroughly part of a chivalric tradition. Each family thus represents one of the strong causative elements in the impending conflict.

Because of their acquaintanceship, the invented characters can cross back and forth into each other's lives and surroundings: a friendly visit before the war, a fatal meeting on the battlefield, an encounter in a prisoner-of-war hospital, and the final merging through the postwar northern "occupation" of the South. They come in contact with actual personages at historical moments: when the Confederate mother approaches the Union president to plead for clemency for her captured son, when a brother and sister attend the play at the Ford Theatre on the night the president is assassinated, and so on. The fictional characters'

The Birth of a Nation ★ United States, 1915, D. W. Griffith.

lives are lived within the re-created events and conditions of those times. Griffith's structuring is also strangely persuasive, drawing us into an understanding and sympathy, if we allow it. President Woodrow Wilson, historian and southerner, is said to have exclaimed after seeing the film that it was "like writing history in lightning." After controversy arose over the film the White House disavowed any approval on the part of the president.

It is its passionate certainty that made *The Birth of a Nation* not only a *succès d'estime* but a *succès de scandale.* Although based in part on Dixon's novel, Griffith re-created the narrative world according to his own viewpoint. Born in Kentucky in 1875, he absorbed an understanding of the war and Reconstruction from his father—Colonel "Roaring Jake" Griffith of the Confederate Cavalry. The attitudes about black people in *Birth* are so much part of the total view of life the film encompasses that Griffith was evidently shocked when he was accused of racism.

Thoroughly embodied in the film, however, is an assumption of innate inferiority of black people. The bad, usually those of mixed blood, are led by evil or misguided white men, are vicious and greedy for power, and line up with the northerners. The good are dependent and childlike, and support the white South. Bad or good, these African Americans are given few individual attributes apart from caste role and function, and are mostly played by white actors in black face. Viewers today feel more uneasy with Griffith's approving patronization of "the faithful souls" than with his treatment of the villains.

Whatever documentation and evidence he might offer, it is the very unconsciousness of his assumption of black inferiority, that "that was how it was," that is most disturbing. The way in which this strand becomes an integral part of a credible whole makes it particularly effective "propaganda." The conviction of the film carries viewers along, and it is impossible to put aside one aspect of it as an aberration. Because the biases are so uncalculated and rawly emotional in their appeal, they may even get past our intellectual defenses. Given the film's enormous popularity, Griffith's assumptions must have been shared by a substantial number of his white contemporaries.

The nastiest aspect of Griffith's representation of black-white relationships is also the one closest to the national nerve—his preoccupation with possible sexual intermingling of the races. Would you want your sister to be molested by or married to a Negro? Griffith asks. For him the two possible fates exert an equally morbid fascination: Marriage to a black man is presented as unthinkable except as equivalent to rape. The much more prevalent forced submission of black women to white men is dealt with only through the congressman's weakness for his housekeeper. This is presented as close to a pathological failing on his part, with the woman exercising what is clearly a sexually based power over him. Stoneman's horrified reaction to his black political protégé's asking for his daughter's hand is of a piece with the rest. Perhaps more than any other white character in the film, the congressman seems to exist solely for rhetorical purposes.

There are many who cannot accept the content of Griffith's films—not just the racial bias in *Birth,* but the sentimentality and melodramatics that color so much of his presentation and possibly his view of life. Even in his own time, his conception—rooted in nineteenth-century Victorianism—apparently came to seem increasingly old-fashioned and irrelevant to his audiences. Some critics—unwilling to allow for what others see as a style, a set of conventions, a way of thinking about people and events—have tended to deplore the content while praising the form. But all agree that in *Birth of a Nation* Griffith's formal control over the medium achieved an unprecedented power.

Take, for instance, the extraordinarily moving scene of Ben Cameron's return from the war. (Ben, the Little Colonel, is played by Henry B. Walthall.) After an intertitle, "The homecoming" (less than 1 second), there is a long shot of the street and the Cameron front yard: Everything is in need of repair; the columns are scorched, the fence is falling apart, the street and sidewalks are littered. Ben enters left background, shattered and weary; he pauses, leans against the fence, and looks about at the marks of war. Limping, he walks slowly and weakly forward along the fence (34.5 seconds). In medium closeup in the living room, his younger sister, Flora, is by a mirror admiring the effect of "southern ermine" (strips of raw cotton daubed with soot) decorating her dress. Ben's older sister, Margaret, and his mother hurry in, indicating that they have seen Ben coming; Margaret runs to the door and back; all run out of the room (18 seconds). Medium shot of the hall: The three rush forward, excited, joined by the father (6 seconds). Medium long shot of Ben pausing by the gate, opening it, supporting himself against it a moment and then going in (11 seconds). Medium long shot of the family, waiting in the hall breathlessly, smiling at Flora's excitement (3.5 seconds). Medium long shot of the front yard as Ben comes to the porch (7.5 seconds). Medium long shot of the family in the hall; Flora rushes forward (4.5 seconds). Medium shot of the porch as Ben climbs the steps; Flora comes out the door and meets him, smiling. They gaze at each other; she points to his worn and dirty uniform; he pulls off a piece of her "ermine." She explains, giggles, and points to a hole in his hat. They

The Birth of a Nation, Ben's Homecoming ★ United States, 1915, D. W. Griffith; Henry B. Walthall (Ben), Mae Marsh (Flora), Miriam Cooper (Margaret), Josephine Crowell (Mrs. Cameron), and Spottiswoode Aiken (Dr. Cameron).

both pause and gaze off into space, thinking of all that has happened. Suddenly they stop pretending. Flora starts to cry, and embraces Ben; he looks into the distance, kisses her hair, and pats her. They start into the house, arm in arm (57 seconds). Medium shot from side angle of the front door: Ben and Flora start in; a woman's arm comes from inside and encircles Ben's shoulders, gently drawing him and Flora in (17.5 seconds). Fade-out.[1]

The shots in this example have a much longer average duration than those in most other scenes in the film. Here much more emotional content is conveyed by each shot, especially by the first two and last two. Only against Griffith's usual practice of presenting a scene from varying points of view in a rapid succession of shots did the tension of the Little Colonel's slow movement within that static frame (and the arm of the unseen mother appearing to encircle him) achieve the kind of eloquence it possesses. In the pre-Griffith years such a shot was the invariable standard in which an action took place, and thus it was not useful for special emphasis. An analogy might be made to silence, which had no dramatic meaning until the coming of sound: There had to be sound, and the cessation of it, before silence had significance. Not until the camera was freed to interrupt the action, which would then be synthesized through editing, could a long-running wide-angle shot be used for contrasting emphasis.

Performances in *The Birth of a Nation* are advanced well beyond the larger-than-life conventions of stage pantomime, growing out of a more subtle sense of persons moving through the surroundings and incidents of everyday life. Actors register emotions by means of small changes in their facial expressions (captured in closeups) or meaningul interactions with objects. Although simplified and heightened for dramatic communication without spoken words, the gestures and expressions are generally toned down in comparison with other contemporary films and Griffith's own earlier work. For example, the contrast with *The Battle* (1911—a sort of sketch for *Birth*) is quite marked. There is some exaggeration in the young people's high jinks, which Griffith associates with youthful good spirits; Mae Marsh is fluttery—painfully so if projected at twenty-four frames per second; and the villainies or buffooneries of the blacks appear caricatured to modern eyes. But by and large the acting style seems quite consciously created for the silent camera, rather than being a theatrical performance recorded by it. Henry B. Walthall and Lillian Gish rise considerably above minimum expectations to create characterizations unrivaled on the screen up to that point, comparable to the best the mature silent film would offer. Their intense, nuanced performances do much to imbue the whole with its sense of loss and sadness, of feelings warped and impoverished by the cruel demands of the historic time.

The care in selection and design of interiors and exteriors surpasses historical recreation to achieve a semblance of documentary veracity that makes the past seem present. So vividly particularized are the interior settings that the rooms look lived in. The huge, period tableaux come alive: the ball on the eve of battle, the gigantic battlefield scenes, the gathering and ride of the Klan, the rioting and fighting in the streets.

Before *The Birth of a Nation* was released Griffith had completed a feature to be called *The Mother and the Law,* its opening sequences based on an actual incident of conflict and violence in a contemporary labor dispute. After the grandeur of *Birth,* however, particularly after its enormous success on the one hand and the angry criticism it provoked on the

---

[1] This shot list is taken from Theodore Huff, *A Shot Analysis of D. W. Griffith's* The Birth of a Nation (New York: The Museum of Modern Art, 1961).

other, *The Mother and the Law* must have seemed an inadequate successor. As part of the *Birth* controversy, Griffith had published a pamphlet entitled *The Rise and Fall of Free Speech in America.* Then, apparently wanting to align himself clearly on the side of un-questionable social and moral rectitude to show his detractors how they had misunderstood him, and perhaps to castigate those he felt had been intolerant toward him, he conceived an even more elaborate narrative structure than that of *Birth.* Added to *The Mother and the Law* were three other stories, set in widely disparate historical periods and cultures. These four stories, according to a title prefacing the multilayered whole, would show "how ha-tred and intolerance, through the ages, have battled against love and charity." This under-taking, which perhaps remains the most ambitious in conception and largest in size of any film ever produced in the United States, became *Intolerance,* released in 1916.

The three stories added to the modern story were a re-creation of the fall of Babylon to the Persians (539 B.C.); vignettes from the life of Christ (27 A.D.), culminating in the cru-cifixion; and an account of the massacre of Protestant Huguenots in France on St. Bartholomew's Eve (1572). If the stories had been told consecutively, the task would have been difficult enough. But Griffith's design went even further, using intercutting so that narratives and characters became subservient to the overriding theme. He began with the modern story up to a certain point of development; then he moved to Jerusalem and an episode from the life of Christ; then to the introduction of the plotting at court in sixteenth-

Intolerance ★ United States, 1916, D. W. Griffith; Robert Harron and Mae Marsh, seated.

Intolerance ★ United States, 1916, D. W. Griffith.

century France; back to the modern story; on to the beginning of the Babylonian sequences; then to the modern story again; and so on.

These parts are announced, separated, and connected with an image of "The Woman Who Rocks the Cradle" (Lillian Gish) accompanied by Whitmanesque intertitles: "Endlessly rocks the cradle—Uniter of Here and Hereafter—Chanter of Sorrows," or "Out of the cradle endlessly rocking . . . " Later, as the tension in each of the stories increases, Griffith cuts ever more rapidly from one to another without interruption.

In order to finance this colossal spectacle, Griffith used all his profits from *The Birth of a Nation,* finally buying out the other backers when they lost their nerve. The total cost of the picture is said to have been $1.9 million; it has been estimated that it would cost much, much more to achieve the same results today. The sets of French streets, houses, and castles are all full scale, solid, and practicable. Babylon, constructed on a 254-acre site along Sunset Boulevard, is the most overwhelming: Its towers rise 200 feet; its walls are wide enough at their tops to allow two chariots to pass; and it took hundreds of extras to fill the courtyard and balconies in the film's victory celebration. *Intolerance* originally ran close to four hours, longer than *Birth,* and again a special score was composed by Joseph Carl Briel according to Griffith's specifications.

Although some critics praised the film lavishly, the public seemed to find the disjunctive organization and unprecedented length confusing and exhausting. The final climactic passages become almost an assault on the optical nerves as well as on the emotions, as the cutting tempo increases to many shots no longer than five frames. Also, the thematic material was out of keeping with the national mood by the time the film was released. Brotherly love was going out of fashion. President Wilson, who had been reelected on an isolationist peace platform, asserting that the United States was too proud to fight, was soon moving with the country itself toward entry into World War I. The sentimental idealism of *Intolerance* carries nothing of the direct conviction of *The Birth of a Nation* and was as dismal a financial failure as the preceding film had been an unrivaled success.

Griffith's career was deflected and probably permanently damaged by the necessity of paying the debts incurred with *Intolerance.* In a desperate effort to recoup some of the losses, he cut into the original negative—without printing a copy—to make versions of *The Mother and the Law* and *The Fall of Babylon,* which were subsequently released separately. As a result of these mutilations, the copies of *Intolerance* that exist today are reduced approximations of the original. Even so, the overall effect is undeniably impressive. In many ways, it is an advance on *The Birth of a Nation.* What it lacks in coherence and genuine passion it makes up in its sweeping imaginativeness of conception and increased perfection of technique.

Intolerance was to have an influence on film history quite disproportionate to its lack of popular appeal. After the war, Lenin arranged for it to tour the new Soviet Union, where it ran continuously for ten years. Very likely Lenin was most interested in the portrayal of exploitative and repressive managerial classes in the modern story—Griffith's viewpoint

Intolerance ★ United States, 1916, D. W. Griffith; Lillian Gish.

Intolerance ★ United States, 1916, D. W. Griffith.

being strongly anticapital and prolabor. But two future giants of Soviet cinema, Sergei Eisenstein and V. I. Pudovkin, saw much more in it than that. Griffith had shown them how argument (education and propaganda) could be conveyed through dramatic incident, and how its effectiveness could be heightened by the dynamics of editing. (Indeed, the strike in Pudovkin's *Mother* [1926] has some direct borrowings from *Intolerance.*) Most of what the Soviet masters formalized and articulated in theories of montage Griffith had understood intuitively. In *Intolerance* the evolving unity rests on generalized idea and emotion—rather than solely on characters' decisions that forward a plot—and depends on the unique resources of the film medium. Through skillful juxtaposition of images, disjunctive in physical place-time but related by each phase of the developing theme, the effect of the whole becomes greater than the sum of its parts.

In other respects *Intolerance* represents Griffith's growing mastery over the medium. The alternation between large vista and small human detail (the page boy sleeping in the throne room of Charles V, or the fat woman throttling her dance partner when he steps on her toes) is even more assured. Performances are completely nonstagelike and are carefully broken into shots, with especially forceful use of closeups (for example, the often cited shot of Mae Marsh's twisting hands in the courtroom, or Little Brown Eyes' face, enormous and haunting in the St. Bartholomew's Eve massacre). Griffith and Bitzer carried their experimentation with framing and lighting further than ever. Considerable camera movement was introduced: the long, cranelike dolly into Belshazzar's palace courtyard; the pan across the seated women in the marriage market, not to follow action but to compel our close attention to the women. There is some exterior night shooting in the Babylonian battle scenes, which seems almost impossible at that time. The full range of irises, fades, superimpositions, and masking (a CinemaScope shape to present the sun court of Cyrus) are employed throughout—all done in the camera. In total, *Intolerance* is felt by many to represent Griffith's fullest achievement; for all it must stand as one of the great landmarks in the history of film.

A Tradition of Screen Comedy Is Established

At about the time Griffith was contributing a new flexibility and power to screen language, a distinctive line of American film comedy began that would produce its own geniuses and masterworks. Although contrasting strongly with Griffith's high seriousness and Victorian sentimentality (in fact, sometimes subjecting those qualities to parody), the early film comics nonetheless contributed importantly to solving some basic problems of the art form that concerned Griffith. Given funny-looking people behaving oddly in situations filled with humor, the amount of laughter obtained could still vary considerably depending on how it was presented. The requirements of pictorial narrative, the selection and arrangement of shots, were as important to the effectiveness of the comedians as they were to Griffith. One of Griffith's former co-workers and informal students, Mack Sennett, came to understand this newly evolved technique and put it into practice for comic purposes. Like Griffith, Sennett didn't invent so much as he applied insights gained from his own and others' experiments. His essential contribution was to fashion a kind of systematic, though unarticulated, comic aesthetic that would become a standard basis from which others would continue to develop.

As with most film genres, screen comedy was present in embryonic form from the very beginning—in fact, before the screen (for instance, *Fred Ott's Sneeze,* 1893, one of Edison's peep-show Kinetoscope fragments). Other early Edisons included visual records of comic vaudeville skits: *Fun in a Chinese Laundry* (1894) involved a chase, a policeman, and a thrown prop (not yet a pie), foreshadowing the later Sennett Keystone comedies—as did, even more clearly, the brief but fully developed *A Wringing Good Joke* (1896). Then there were the French "trick films" begun by Méliès and added to, most notably, by Ferdinand Zecca and Emile Cohl. In these the "trickery" was usually designed for humorous as well as fantastic effect; for example, pumpkins roll off a wagon and bounce around town creating all sorts of havoc (*The Pumpkin Race,* Cohl, 1907). Méliès's *An Adventurous Automobile Trip* (1905) in many ways foreshadows Sennett's later fun with Model Ts.

It was another Frenchman, Max Linder, who from 1905 on established most clearly a pattern for the kinds of visual incongruities and surprises that were to screen comedy what verbal gags were to stage burlesque and vaudeville. The comic figure he created was a dapper, upper-class man-about-town involved with a hard-hearted lady love. Sennett admitted to having studied Linder closely, and Sennett's most brilliant discovery, Charles Chaplin, was even more obviously in Linder's debt. In Chaplin's first films for Sennett, before he developed his tramp persona, his costume and mannerisms not only suggest his own English music-hall background but also bear a resemblance to the smoothly maladroit and somewhat effete dandy that Linder had created. Sennett's work, however, which started a main line of film comedy lasting from 1912 (the year the Keystone Company was founded) through the 1920s and into the first years of sound, was vigorously and indigenously American. It was he who earned the broad popularity for the style known as *slapstick,* upon which Chaplin was to ring his own, subtler changes.

Whatever other influences there were, the precedents offered by Porter and Griffith would serve Sennett as a way of structuring his films. The chase, characteristic of the filmed action-melodramas, could be used for comedy as well as for pure suspense. With exciting action situations as backbone, comic muscle and flesh were added. Perhaps the essentials of the method can best be demonstrated by suggesting a composite Keystone comedy made up of remembered scenes from several of the actual comedies. It opens in a bungalow bedroom, with two seedy-looking robbers climbing through the window. They waken the rotund homeowner at gun point, gag him, and tie him to a conveniently available hot water heater, which they set at HOT (insert of gauge). They then rifle his bureau, scoop up valuables, and leave. A freckle-faced, gap-toothed urchin peers in the window, sees the trouble, and sets off, presumably to summon help. (Note the similarity so far to Porter and Griffith.)

Cut to the interior of a police station, where an outsized sergeant sporting a large brush of mustache (Mack Swain) is snoozing at the desk. He bounces awake, answers the phone, then shouts off screen. A gaggle of policemen stumble over each other through a

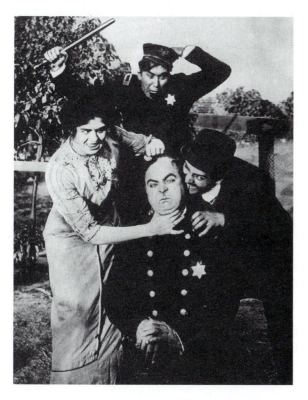

Keystone Kops in an unidentified comedy
☆ United States, 1913, Mack Sennett;
Sennett, with raised club, and Fred Mace, seated.

door and line up in front of the desk. An odder collection of physical types would be hard to imagine. There's a tall skinny one (Slim Summerville), a fat one (Roscoe "Fatty" Arbuckle), a wildly cross-eyed one (Chester Conklin), and so on. A number of them are decorated with bizarre mustaches, beards, and sideburns. Uniforms are too large or too small, and parts are as apt to be on backwards as not. They twitch and weave in an irregular line as the sergeant shouts at them, then rush toward a door leading outside. Emerging onto the sidewalk, they jump into a couple of open jalopies at the curb. The floor on the rear car gives way under the impact. Its occupants then leap in with the others in the front car, though one can scarcely believe it is holding them all. Starting up rapidly in reverse, they crash into the rear car, which then totally collapses. Roaring out into the street, they barely slip in front of an oncoming truck; zigzagging from one side to the other, they obliviously scatter pedestrians and opposing traffic in their wake. An undercranked camera speeds up the movement to a surreal tempo.

Back in the bedroom, the nightgowned captive is still spread-eagled on a now swelling boiler. The needle of the gauge moves from HOT to BOILING and toward DANGER and EXPLOSION. Return to the police car, now careening along a highway at an improbable speed; the cops are all standing, overflowing the sides, peering ahead, gesticulating frenetically with their elbows in each other's faces.

Cut to a single file of laborers walking along a country road; the shovel on the shoulder of the last man catches a detour sign and turns it to point to a road other than the one it had been indicating. The police arrive in the patrol car, pause, zip backward and forward, then drive off on the route we know is not the detour. Coming down a hill at breakneck speed, they fail to stop as the road dead-ends into a lake; instead, they go straight off the end of a pier, and submerge. On the other side of the lake, they emerge unfazed, still going full tilt toward their destination; and so on, with other impediments, other cross-cuts to the bulging boiler distending the fat man's stomach, until the final rescue.

Several things are noteworthy about this kind of comic invention. For instance, it is clear that the same Porter/Griffith excitement and suspense of crime, chase, and rescue or capture are here turned into comedy by visual and emotional exaggeration. Also, a recognizably real world (unlike that of Méliès) is madly distorted as if certain physical laws (of gravity, acceleration, solidity of objects, and the like) operated eccentrically or not at all. The incongruity between what is expected in the real world and what happens in Sennett's universe extends throughout the films. The pleasure we get from this sportive tampering with the expected is the same as would later be offered in animated cartoons. We know that floorboards usually remain in cars, that boilers have no rubbery elasticity, that humans and machines move at predictable speeds, and that no one can drive along the bottom of a lake and come up on the other side; still, it's fun to have the unlikely made manifest. As for the people in Sennett's films, they are incredibly incompetent; also, it is highly improbable that a random sample of beings would include the widely variant physical types and appearances of his cast. Further, they are always inhumanly unflappable: They cope with the irregularities of nature with a maniacal seriousness, only dimly aware that anything is amiss.

These funny-looking, oddball characters could be expected to send a less sophisticated, or perhaps only less inhibited, audience into gales of laughter merely by their cross-eyedness or fatness. This suggests that a certain sadistic pleasure in others' misfortunes underlies the jokes of physical discomfort that are such an integral part of silent screen

Keystone Kops in an unidentified comedy ⋆ United States, c. 1914–1919, Mack Sennett.

comedy, including pratfalls and pies in the face. We enjoy the robbery victim being grilled and splayed on the water heater; the car going off the end of the pier looks like a multiple drowning, and we howl with glee. An emotional catharsis of some sort is provided by this controlled display of aggression and violence. The magical power of the characters to survive annihilation is probably also an important cathartic element. There is no death; Sennett's people are invulnerable, and we are free to indulge in comic-hysterical relief and reaction to normally destructive actions. Our laughter no doubt arises from a feeling of comfortable superiority—we are not the ones afflicted.

In Sennett's films the powerful and socially exalted characters are comic butts, helpless in the face of an onslaught by nature or one of its minions. The choice of policemen is significant in this respect. Although he would turn in his grave at any suggestion of Freudian notions about authority figures as resented parental surrogates, Sennett evidently did realize that the incongruous and the uncomfortable were a lot more humorous when inflicted on types of people who were taken seriously by society and themselves. The indignities to which the grotesque and ineffectual policemen are subjected are funnier because they *are* policemen. And if soup spilled down a back is amusing, it is at least twice as comical if the back belongs to a plump dowager in an evening gown at a formal function.

By puncturing pomposity and pretension, by making the leaders and guardians his victims, Sennett heightened our enjoyment. To this extent there is a social edge to his comedy. It is usually on the side of the little guy in the audience and directed against institutions and conventions outside his sympathies. This general satirical intention was even more pointed in the Sennett parodies of certain popular films he felt suffered from pretentiousness. *Barney Oldfield's Race for Life* (1913), for example, was an early kidding of the Griffith last-minute rescue. In the 1920s the first of the epic westerns, *The Covered Wagon,* became Sennett's *The Uncovered Wagon;* Erich von Stroheim's *Foolish Wives* was lampooned in *Three Foolish Weeks;* and there was nothing quite like Ben Turpin playing a Rudolph Valentino in *The Shriek of Araby* to put passion and heroics in proper perspective.

Slapstick was as natural to the silent screen as were the action-melodramas and spectacles, and for the same reasons: It utilized those aspects of the world best communicated through the moving image, those not requiring the supplement of language. Most of us who didn't grow up in the tradition of silent comedy have trouble getting back to its essence except through the works of the later, greater clowns—Buster Keaton, Harold Lloyd, Harry Langdon, Stan Laurel and Oliver Hardy, and post-Keystone Charlie Chaplin. One difficulty in our appreciation of early silent comedies is that we too frequently see them in excerpted and anthologized snippets, projected at a speed faster than intended (which undercuts Sennett's use of fast motion for precise effect). Exaggerated music and sound effects, and perhaps a commentator's condescending asides, act as further distractions.

The essential point to be understood is that the best of Sennett had a disciplined lunacy. His work is not merely a succession of unrelated inanities; although not intellectual, it is not mindless either. When properly constructed and executed, the rules of silent comic geometry are consistent, and a coherence is built from gag to gag to entire film. Sennett's special genius lay in understanding the construction and timing of sight gags. Careful manipulation of the standard ingredients, plus a sure feeling for what each shot includes, at what point it appears, and how long it is held on the screen, make all the difference. Start with the basic comic situation of a man falling down; make that man a ridiculously pompous, rotund, middle-aged suitor on the way to his lady love's, carrying a dainty corsage, dressed in top hat, cutaway, and striped trousers; then select, quite properly, a small boy to deflate this dignity by placing a banana peel in the man's path. The comic effectiveness of character and incident may still be profoundly altered by whether we first see the man walking and falling in long shot, then the banana peel in closeup, then the boy peering around the fence in medium shot, or whether the order of these shots is reversed so we can share the boy's anticipation and sense of achievement. Of course, the film maker must judge when the audience will have gotten the full impact of a shot, and thus cut on the rising laugh—not before, not after.

In silent comedy the gag construction could advance unimpeded: No pause was needed for lines to be heard and laughs registered. The silent film maker could build steadily, milking the visual joke for all of the variations it offered. Roars of laughter crescendoed until the comic climax was reached; only then was there a slowing of pace, a transition, and a hooking into the beginning of the next gag—which started building all over again. Ideally, the audience was left weak and helpless, weeping with laughter. It was this kind of robust creation, one uniquely suited to silent film, that Sennett mastered. His work is directly related to the cinematic technique that engaged Griffith's attention.

The early generation of American film makers who did not get their training from Griffith got it from Sennett. His transcendently brilliant protégé was, of course, Charles Chaplin, whom George Bernard Shaw called the only genius at work in motion pictures (as he thought himself the only genius at work in theater). Sennett and his partner Adam

Kessel had seen Chaplin in the Fred Karno English music hall company, which had been touring the United States extensively between 1910 and 1913. Though Kessel didn't get the name quite right, he wired off for "Charlie Chapman" at a time when Keystone's then reigning star, Ford Sterling, was being difficult about salary. Charlie's first film—entitled *Making a Living* (1914), with prophetic understatement—was pure Sennett. *Tillie's Punctured Romance,* directed by Sennett in the same year, and featuring Chaplin, Marie Dressler, Mabel Normand, Mack Swain, and Charles Bennett, is generally considered the first feature-length comedy (six reels). It too represents Sennett's slapstick humor rather than the tragicomic elaboration of Chaplin's finest work.

From later accounts by Chaplin, and from the evidence of his early films compared to his subsequent successes, it is clear that he was not altogether comfortable in Sennett's broad, knockabout style. Gradually, especially after leaving Keystone, Chaplin would develop a comedy character rich and subtle beyond anything Sennett had conceived. Chaplin made that character into one of the great comic figures (along with Falstaff, Til Eulenspiegel, Don Quixote and Sancho Panza, and the creatures of the *commedia dell'arte*). The personality and costume of the little tramp, assembled through dozens of one- and two-reelers, evolved full-blown by the end of the 1910s. The little fellow, ingenuously and ingeniously triumphant while maintaining his cheerfulness and dignity in an adverse world, was quickly taken to the hearts of audiences everywhere.

In addition to the creation of this persona, rounded and complex enough to encompass strains of pathos, from *The Tramp* (1915) on, Chaplin developed his unique pantomimic grace, evident early in *The Rink* (1916) and *The Cure* (1917). He handled his body as a dancer would, and there is an exuberant joy in merely watching him skip through the world, pirouetting to offer himself to the blondly beautiful Edna Purviance, bounding into and out of an open utility hole without apparent hurt, or running and gliding around a table, just out of reach of the giant Eric Campbell. From large movements to small (the dissection of a clock in *The Pawnshop,* 1916), there was a constant flow of invention. Chaplin turned what could be done with arms, hands, legs, feet, and stiff backbones into unexpected and sometimes unimaginable physical potential, a playful and precise bodily commentary on the human condition. And this is not to mention his uses of a Murphy bed (*One A.M.,* 1916), a lamp shade (*The Adventurer,* 1917), and other props.

The social dimension implicit in Sennett was expanded by Chaplin, and tended to preoccupy him increasingly as his career progressed. Even in this early period his films generally included some pointed observations about people in relation to society. *Easy Street* (1917) is a veritable catalogue: The main theme of law and order includes a delightful reversal of police brutality; revivalist religion, slums, poverty, welfare, anarchists, and drug addiction are all touched upon along the way. *The Immigrant* (1917) is frequently quite sardonic as well as broadly amusing in its depiction of the experiences of new arrivals in the "Land of the Free." For example, as the ship passes the Statue of Liberty, the passengers are shoved and roped in like cattle; Chaplin takes a quizzical second look at the statue. In *Shoulder Arms* the satirical treatment of military life and basic antiwar stance are all the more remarkable when you realize it was released before the armistice of 1918.

Chaplin's enormous popular success and shrewd handling of the income he earned from it allowed him, throughout his career, freedom for social-political comment and a

The Rink ★ United States, 1916, Charles
Chaplin; Chaplin.

degree of artistic autonomy (which Griffith lost after the failure of *Intolerance*). Chaplin's
control over his films would become unique within the art industry. From the early 1920s
he was his own producer; his artistic virtuosity permitted him to write the scripts for, direct,
star in, compose the music for, and supervise all the other creative functions of his films.
To make fully certain his works would reach the screen exactly as he intended, in 1919 he
joined Griffith, Mary Pickford, and Douglas Fairbanks to form a distribution company
called United Artists. Thus not only did Chaplin succeed in preserving his independence,
but he was also able to proceed in a way quite opposite to the centrifugal, collective forces
generally at work in the industry.

The feature length of *Tillie's Punctured Romance* proved something of an exception
as far as comedies were concerned. Chaplin continued at two reels until 1918, when he left
Mutual and joined First National. He then began a Griffith-like extension of running time
(to three reels in 1918–1919) that would lead him to intermingle features and shorts in the
early twenties. Although the short comedies held their own against features in popularity,
the standard program by the late 1910s was organized around the feature attraction, with
the preceding shorts adding variety.

The Cure ★ United States, 1917, Charles Chaplin; Edna Purviance, Chaplin, and Eric Campbell, in front row.

Emerging Patterns of Industry

It was the independent producers who introduced and rose with the features. The Motion Picture Patents Company, the fixedly conservative combine that had included all of the principal early producers—most notably Edison, Biograph, and Vitagraph—finally failed in its efforts to exert a monopoly through its patent claims and its attempts to control the manufacture of equipment and film stock. Founded in 1908, the Trust, as it came to be known, consistently resisted longer films and stuck to the outright sale of prints—through its distribution arm, General Film Company, established in 1910. With the increasing acceptance of the more expensive features, a rental system evolved whereby after they had made the rounds of the theaters, the prints would return to the producers. By 1914–1915 the Trust was clearly being beaten by the amount and quality of its competition: The independents were too numerous, aggressive, and ingenious; there simply was no way to keep them from producing and distributing films. By 1917, through court decisions in a series of antitrust suits, the Motion Picture Patents Company was declared legally dead.

During those same years, partly as a result of the attempt by the independents to escape the legal harassment and goon squads of the Trust, the center of production shifted from New York to southern California. (From about 1907 to 1917 Chicago was also a production center, with three large Trust firms—Essanay, Selig, and Kalem—located there.) With the feature film as the staple commodity, with the former independents becoming the newly dominant powers as the old Trust companies faded away or were absorbed, with

Hollywood the production center, and with distribution controlled out of New York, the model was established for industrial expansion for the next decade and beyond.

The general lines followed were already standard in the manufacturing, wholesaling, and retailing of other products. The movie industry had the same requirements as any industry in which the annual costs of production were enormous—as its close contemporary, the automobile industry, for example. As far as manufacture was concerned, the motion picture and automobile industries were both geographically centered near raw materials and sources of power, with specialized labor pools developed around them (the workers often being imported from abroad). Detroit was within reach of coal, oil, iron ore, and the steel mills. Hollywood's distance from New York and proximity to asylum across the Mexican border were initially among its chief attractions to the independents who settled there. Later Hollywood proved to have attributes similar to the raw materials and sources of power sought in other industries. The extraordinary variety of California's scenery meant that virtually any sort of locale—mountain, desert, ocean, forest, rolling fields—could be duplicated within a few hundred miles of Los Angeles. In those days when sunshine was still the principal source of illumination for movie making—even for interior scenes—southern California had more of it than did the eastern centers.

Gigantic Hollywood studios became the equivalents of Detroit's River Rouge plant; enormously expensive facilities and equipment were constructed and assembled in both. Motion picture projection was standardized throughout the world. Any change that required retooling involved vast sums, and only economic crisis would induce it. The assembly-line method devised by Henry Ford eventually would have its analogue in the Hollywood production process; tendencies in that direction were already manifest in the late 1910s.

It was Thomas H. Ince who first functioned as a studio head/production supervisor, planning and overseeing an entire production program. He supervised the making of hundreds of films, developing especially the western genre (and its early star, William S. Hart) into a popularity that rivaled the melodramas of Griffith and the comedies of Sennett. In 1915 Ince joined Griffith and Sennett in the newly formed Triangle Film Corporation, named in honor of the three of them. When Ince left Triangle to form his own company, he built a big new studio at Culver City, which later became the M-G-M Studios.

The production methods that began with Ince would become standard Hollywood practice in the 1920s. This piecemeal assembly—especially the practice of shooting out of sequence—however efficient and economical, tended to make the creative process disjointed and strained. The notion of separate specialists in charge of each of the many aspects of production seemed a bitter paradox to those who thought a work of art demanded, by definition, the absolute domination of a single personality. But there just wasn't enough individual genius around to supply the theaters with a steady and frequent change of bill. What generally resulted from this "art by committee"—as with American automobile manufacture—was a high level of standardized technical excellence.

The mass-produced films inevitably came to look pretty much alike, especially to the critical eye. A crucial problem for the motion picture industry thus became how to create the illusion of variety without fundamental differences involving wasteful experimentation and expense. One of the solutions was not unlike the development of automobile types—the sport roadster, the family sedan—and the offering of (slightly) different models each year. There evolved types of formula pictures (the "woman's picture," the comedy, the action-adventure) and cycles within each type (the vamp, the rural comedy, the war drama).

The Edison Company film studio in Menlo Park, New Jersey, 1915.

Technicians could become expert at a particular kind of film making; one western, for example, could effortlessly follow the pattern of another. Audiences always had the choice of going to one of the popular genres one week and to another the next, keeping their entertainment sufficiently varied to obscure the similarities within the limited spectrum. Then, too, the familiar had its own attractions. Repetition with variation is pleasurable: Nobody wanted a western so different as to seem unlike a western.

Another device that kept audiences coming back for more was the cultivation of the star personality. People would go again and again to see Mary Pickford or Mabel Normand, Charlie Chaplin or Doug Fairbanks, just to be in their screen presence for an hour and a half on a Friday night. In this case, too, the fans didn't want radical innovation any more than did the producers; they enjoyed their favorites in vehicles carefully tailored to exploit their appeal. The stars commanded an automatic audience. As long as the range extended from femme fatale Theda Bara to melodramatic heroine Pauline Frederick, from robust comic John Bunny to matinee idol Francis X. Bushman, what more could be asked? Aspiring performers patterned themselves, or were patterned, along the lines of the already established, so that even the individuality of personality could be fitted into existing grooves.

Finally, the whole enterprise was enveloped in an unprecedented amount of promotion and advertising designed to whip up audience expectations. Each film, even if essentially indistinguishable from others preceding it, was presented as the most spectacular, the

Thomas H. Ince, center with cigar, probably producing and perhaps directing.

most action-packed, the funniest, the most heartwarming—in short, as something not to be missed. Press agentry soon encompassed the stars' lives off screen as well as on, and made them into demigods whose mythological existence commanded constant attendance and unswerving devotion. That was how the system came to work.

By the end of the first quarter-century, film production—which had begun in a tar-paper shack or out on the street—had moved into large, permanent studios, clustered for the most part around Los Angeles. Distribution initially was a simple and direct affair: The producers sold prints of films outright to those showing them—at so much per foot, like cordwood; ten cents per foot, or one hundred dollars per reel, was common, regardless of the quality of the entertainment. As audiences tired of seeing the same films over again, it occurred to someone to set up an "exchange" whereby exhibitors could trade in their prints and—for a small fee for the service—obtain used prints of different films from other exhibitors. With increased competition among producers and discrimination on the part of the public, the practice of rental instead of sale gradually evolved; producers then received a share of the actual box-office drawing power of their films, greater for the more attractive and expensive, less for the others. This practice made for one of the singularities of the industry: The product is not bought or sold; customers merely pay to spend some time looking at it. The retailers (exhibitors) return a share of that income to the wholesalers (distributors), who in turn subtract their expenses and profits and pass the remainder on to the manufacturers (producers).

Exhibition, which had started as part of vaudeville programs, began to take place in nickelodeons in 1905, when films became longer and more of them narrative. Named for the price of admission, these first movie houses characteristically were converted store fronts, perhaps with chairs rented from a local funeral parlor. The nickelodeons showed continuous programs of assorted short films; the enormously successful *The Great Train Robbery* opened many of them. With the arrival of features and the increasing popularity of film, former stage theaters were converted for motion picture exhibition. The big era of showing movies in the town's "opera house" and competing with stage road shows dates from 1913 to 1916. At that time, there were perhaps as many as 28,000 movie theaters of all types in the United States. A new and more pretentious type of screen theater was initiated in 1914 with the opening of the Strand on Broadway, soon to be followed by others with equal ambitions. Widespread construction of theaters designed especially for movies did not occur, however, until the 1920s.

By the time World War I ended, in late 1918, the American film had achieved all the essentials necessary to ensure its success as an art industry: a steady flow of features accompanied by shorts, especially by popular comedies; a national distribution in which prints circulated out of regional exchanges within a rental system that permitted the income to flow back through exhibitors and distributors to producers; and theaters gradually being formed into chains by enterprising exhibitors, accommodating larger and more demanding audiences paying higher prices. These fundamentals extended to an international scale gave the United States its lead in the conquest of the world's screens. Once the war was over, growth of the medium could resume unimpeded by national boundaries.

Films of the Period

1914
A Fool There Was (Frank Powell)
Judith of Bethulia (David Wark Griffith)
Making a Living (Charlie Chaplin)
The Squaw Man (Cecil B. DeMille)
Tillie's Punctured Romance (Mack Sennett)

1915
The Birth of a Nation (David Wark Griffith)
Carmen (Cecil B. DeMille)
The Cheat (Cecil B. DeMille)
The Tramp (Charlie Chaplin)

1916
Civilization (Thomas H. Ince)
Intolerance (David Wark Griffith)

The Pawnshop (Charlie Chaplin)
The Rink (Charlie Chaplin)

1917
Easy Street (Charlie Chaplin)
The Immigrant (Charlie Chaplin)
Teddy at the Throttle (Mack Sennett)

1919
Back to God's Country (Nell Shipman)
Blind Husbands (Erich von Stroheim)
Broken Blossoms (David Wark Griffith)
Male and Female (Cecil B. DeMille)

Books on the Period

Bernstein, Matthew, ed. *Controlling Hollywood: Censorship and Regulation in the Studio Era.* New Brunswick, NJ: Rutgers University Press, 2000.

Brewster, Ben, and Lea Jacobs. *Theatre to Cinema: Stage Pictorialism and the Early Feature Film.* New York: Oxford University Press, 1998.

Brown, Gene. *Movie Time: A Chronology of Hollywood and the Movie Industry from Its Beginnings to the Present.* New York: Macmillan, 1995.

Browne, Nick, ed. *Refiguring American Film Genres: History and Theory.* Berkeley: University of California Press, 1997.

Couvares, Francis G., ed. *Movie Censorship and American Culture* ("Studies in the History of Film and Television"). Washington, DC: Smithsonian Institution Press, 1996.

Cripps, Thomas. *Hollywood's High Noon: Moviemaking and Society Before Television* ("The American Moment Series"). Baltimore, MD: Johns Hopkins University Press, 1996.

Cripps, Thomas. *Slow Fade to Black: The Negro in American Film, 1900–1942.* New York: Oxford University Press, 1993.

Davis, Ronald L. *The Glamour Factory: Inside Hollywood's Big Studio System.* Dallas, TX: Southern Methodist University Press, 1993.

De Bauche, Leslie Midkiff. *Reel Patriotism: The Movies and World War I.* Madison: University of Wisconsin Press, 1997.

Eyman, Scott. *The Speed of Sound: Hollywood and the Talkie Revolution, 1926–1930.* New York: Simon & Schuster, 1997.

Fuller, Kathryn H. *At the Picture Show: Small-Town Audiences and the Creation of Movie Fan Culture.* Washington, DC: Smithsonian Institution Press, 1996.

MacCann, Richard Dyer. *The Comedians* (Vol. 4, "American Movies: The First Thirty Years"). Metuchen, NJ: Scarecrow Press, 1993.

MacCann, Richard Dyer. *The Silent Screen* ("American Movies Series"). Lanham, MD: Scarecrow Press, 1997.

Maltby, Richard, and Ian Craven. *Hollywood Cinema: An Introduction.* Malden, MA: Blackwell Publications, 1995.

Robinson, David. *From Peep Show to Palace: The Birth of the American Film.* New York: Columbia University Press, 1996.

Slide, Anthony. *The New Historical Dictionary of the American Film Industry.* Lanham, MD: Scarecrow Press, 1998.

Staiger, Janet. *The Studio System.* New Brunswick, NJ: Rutgers University Press, 1994.

Stokes, Melvyn, and Richard Maltby. *American Movie Audiences: From the Turn of the Century to the Early Sound Era.* London: British Film Institute, 1999.

Waller, Gregory A. *Main Street Amusement: Movies and Commercial Entertainment in a Southern City, 1896–1930.* Washington, DC: Smithsonian Institution Press, 1995.

3

Great German Silents

★ ★ ★ ★

1919–1928

Following the end of World War I, while the United States moved toward domination of the world motion picture industry, Germany led the art into newly urbane subject matter and refinement of technique. This brief period of cinematic ascendancy occurred at a time when the country itself was desperately unstable in its political, economic, and social life. Loss of the war and the humiliation of the Versailles Treaty peace terms were damaging to national pride. The shaky and directionless Weimar Republic faced rioting and anarchy. Inflation, unemployment, and food shortages crippled the economy and inflicted great hardship on the German people. Morale was lower than it had ever been during the war. The highest point of German silent film (1922–1924) was precisely the lowest point for the nation. French troops occupied the Ruhr industrial heartland; the Deutschmark was utterly worthless; revolt was incipient in Bavaria.

With the stabilization of the mark in 1924 and the election of war hero Field Marshal Paul von Hindenburg to the presidency in 1925, a kind of order was restored. Within German society, however, the amorality and decadence portrayed in the American musical *Cabaret,* in Rainer Werner Fassbinder's *Berlin Alexanderplatz* (1980) television series, and in Bertolt Brecht's and Kurt Weill's *The Threepenny Opera* (first produced in Germany in the late 1920s) succeeded the immediate postwar years and formed the setting for the triumph of Naziism. At the same time, the German film began to lose its particular excellence, a loss caused in considerable measure by American infiltration and dominance within the German film industry.

During the first half of the 1920s, however, there was a vitality in all the German arts, as if the nation's ill health had caused a feverish counteractivity. Literature and, especially, drama and the visual arts were released from the rigidities of a Hohenzollern monarchy and Prussian militarism. Prompted by the disillusionment of the war and the radically changed values that followed its end, newly expressive forms and styles were sought. At this time the plays of Bertolt Brecht, Ernst Toller, and Georg Kaiser were first produced; Max Reinhardt, in his more conventional historical-romantic stagings, added elements of lighting and handling of crowds that would be translated directly into film. Lyonel Feininger, Vasily Kandinsky, and Paul Klee were among the many active painters. Others affiliated with the Berlin *Sturm* group became stage and then film designers. The general aesthetic impulses would feed into film and in some ways find their ultimate expression in that collective and composite art.

In the United States, the West Coast center of film production was separated geographically (some would say culturally and spiritually as well) from the East Coast center of the other arts and communications media. In Germany, Berlin was not only the national capital but also the center for all the arts, including film. Those working in the traditional arts were free from feelings of condescension toward the movies like those of many Americans; on the contrary, German artists expressed a lively curiosity about the new art form and demonstrated their interest by trying their hands at it. It was possible for them to do so without changing their place of residence or lifestyle, and German films owed much of their sophistication to those trained in the older arts.

Whereas American films had been populated by good guys, bad guys, funny guys, and pretty women, the Germans started probing complex and frequently disturbed characters along loosely Freudian lines, which stimulated the additions to technique noteworthy in their work. While the Americans had concentrated on action and melodrama, the Germans explored the psychological and pictorial. In their quest for means to objectify inner consciousness, they created a world on film that represented not so much a physical reality, as most of us perceive it, as a state of mind: the universe distorted and stylized to express what we might feel about it. Expressionism, as opposed to American realism and naturalism, was the prevalent style. First appearing in extreme and sustained form in *The Cabinet of Dr. Caligari* (1920), it is also manifest in subtle ways in much of the German production of the 1920s, as will be noted.

Predominant Types and Themes

Looking at the German films of 1919–1925 as a body, film historians have identified three prominent types with concomitant themes that make evident most of the major German contributions. First were the historical/mythological films in which architectural settings, careful costuming, and romantic lighting, as well as the handling of massed crowds, reflect Max Reinhardt's theories and experiments in stage production. In these films, history is treated psychologically and spectacularly, rather than realistically; they might be called historical fantasies. Ernst Lubitsch, who had acted in Reinhardt's stage company, was one master of this genre. His accounts of the Bourbons (*Passion/Madame du Barry,* 1919) and the Tudors (*Deception/Anna Boleyn,* 1920) center on a bedroom-keyhole view of the past, which suggests that great historical events can be seen as extensions of sexual intrigue. Someone once observed that Cecil B. DeMille, much indebted to Lubitsch, presented the Crusades as if they were fought for the sole benefit of Loretta Young; the same might be said about Lubitsch, the French Revolution, and Pola Negri. Onto gossipy biographies Lubitsch overlaid massive spectacles of the Bastille and the Tower of London, using hundreds of extras.

Madame du Barry/Passion ★ Germany, 1919, Ernst Lubitsch; Pola Negri, kneeling.

Allied to the Lubitsch pageants were Fritz Lang's less popular but more innovative and significant mythological/historical evocations. *Destiny* (1921), part legend, part fairy tale, includes three episodes placed in earlier times: one in a Moslem city, another in Venice during the Renaissance, and the final one in a charmingly fantastic China. Much of the pleasure in Lang's film is derived from the stylized settings. The dominant image is the enormous blank wall—in the connecting story—that fills the whole screen and dwarfs the humans. Trained as an architect, Lang went on to even fuller expression of his themes in gigantic re-creations of the German saga *Die Nibelungen* (1924)—a film that became so vast it had to be released in two parts: *Siegfried* and *Kriemhild's Revenge.* (His *Metropolis,* 1926, though set in the future, is like the films about the past in that it re-creates another time and place through predominantly architectural means.) Much more serious in intent than Lubitsch's, Lang's spectacles are nonetheless offered as feasts for the eyes. The careful visual patterns and breathtaking scale are designed to be enjoyed in their own right as well as to be the expression of what seems an especially Germanic imagination about a prehistoric or fantasied past. Static they may be, but monumental too.

Also set in the past, though frequently even less specific as to time, were the second group of themes: the sinister, fantastic, macabre films in which expressionistic decor plays an important part and the subjects are often derived from old legends and ballads.

Siegfried ★ Germany, 1924, Fritz Lang.

The Cabinet of Dr. Caligari is the most famous of these. It could also be considered a precedent for the avant-garde film, predating the movement that would start in Berlin with Hans Richter's *Rhythmus 21* (1921) and Viking Eggeling's *Diagonal Symphony* (1925) and would then headquarter in Paris, while continuing to flourish in Germany with productions such as Walther Ruttmann's poetic documentary *Berlin: Symphony of a Great City*.

Originally Fritz Lang was to direct *Caligari*. When he withdrew to complete another film, Robert Wiene was appointed in his place. It was not the direction, however, so much as the eerily frightening story (by Carl Mayer and Hans Janowitz) and, particularly, the expressionistic settings, that made this film both seminal and enduring in its fascination. The names of the three painters who designed its sets—Hermann Warm, Walter Röhrig, and Walter Reimann—appear in various collaborations on the credits of many of the finest of the German films of this period. *Caligari* remains the purest and fullest use of the expressionist credo in film: "Films must be drawings brought to life," said Warm. The "exteriors" as well as the interiors were all constructed from wood, plaster, and canvas. The world created is that of a madman, a paranoid whose fears derive not only from the people and events around him but also from the shapes of nature, the town, a fairground, and an insane asylum. Jagged irregularity dominates: trees like barbed spears;

Berlin: Symphony of a Great City ★
Germany, 1927, Walther Ruttmann.

pools of black shadow cast by no discernible light (shadows and light were in fact painted in order to better control them); a maze of crooked streets; ramps and stairways foreshortened; and houses like clusters of strange geometrical blocks balanced precariously.

Scarcely the sort of film to inspire popular imitation (it was moderately successful), there was nonetheless a small group of films that reflected its influence. Perhaps best remembered are Paul Wegener's *The Golem* (1920) and F. W. Murnau's *Nosferatu* (1922). *The Golem* is based on a Jewish legend about a practitioner of black magic—a rabbi of great erudition—who brings to life a clay monster to aid the Jews against their governing Christian oppressors in Prague in the sixteenth century. As Doctor Frankenstein also discovered, such monsters often attack those who create them, punishing us for our presumption. The abstractly fashioned medieval town, with its skyline of sharply angled roofs and tilted chimney pots, looks like twisted gingerbread; not a straight line is visible. A gigantic gate into the walled ghetto dwarfs the human beings. Irregular arches and inverted Vs predominate. The camera frequently shoots through the archways, imposing their strange shapes on the frame itself. The citizens—the males in tall conical hats and pointed beards—are again part of a nightmarish world like that of *Caligari*.

The Cabinet of Dr. Caligari ★
Germany, 1920, Robert Wiene;
Conrad Veidt and Lil Dagover.

The Golem ★ Germany, 1920,
Paul Wegener; Wegener.

56

In Murnau's *Nosferatu,* the themes of somnambulism, a man under another's diabolical power, mass murder, and madness all recur, and the agent of death is destroyed while attacking the young female loved one in her bedroom. Count Orlock, who is Nosferatu-the-Vampire by night, strongly suggests Cesare of *Caligari* in appearance, bodily movement, and facial contortions. Tall, thin, grotesquely made up and costumed, he moves in a trance (not unlike Cesare) when under the curse of his vampirism. From real exteriors Murnau selected the sorts of buildings (the deserted castle, the town with its steep pointed roofs, the narrow twisting streets) and landscapes (rocky roads with abrupt inclines and turns, a deformed tree) that look as if they could have served as models for the abstractions created in the studio for *Caligari.* Going beyond the prototype, the expressionistic influence appears in specifically cinematic devices: fast motion, negative images, superimposition, and stop motion—which permits a tarpaulin to remove itself and a ship hatch to open of its own accord. The huge black shadow of Nosferatu, now created by light, moves horrifyingly toward and over his victims, unlike the painted theatrical shadows in *Caligari.* Unreal, irrational, and hauntingly disturbing, these expressionist works offered a totally new kind of film.

The third group of German films from this period, marked least obviously by expressionistic tendencies, and most important in advancing film technique, began with the *Kammerspielfilm* (literally "chamber play film"), which derived from Reinhardt theater. This style was marked by unity of time, place, and action, with virtually no intertitles; few characters, usually lower middle class; sparse decor, with objects given extraordinary

Nosferatu ✳ Germany, 1922, F. W. Murnau; Max Schreck.

importance; and intimate psychological content. Its characteristics are further described, lovingly and sensitively, by Lotte Eisner in *The Haunted Screen: Expressionism in the German Cinema and the Influence of Max Reinhardt.* Key films were Paul Leni's *Backstairs* (1921), Lupu Pick's *Shattered* (1921), and Murnau's *The Last Laugh* (1924). Scripts for all three were written by Carl Mayer.

Finest of the Kammerspielfilms, and arguably of all German silent cinema, is *The Last Laugh.* It chronicles the pathos of a proud and majestic doorman at an elegant hotel, who, having become too old to handle heavy baggage and perform his other functions adequately, is demoted to washroom attendant. Seemingly loved and respected by his family and neighbors in his earlier status, he is reviled and ridiculed when they learn of his demotion. In the epilogue an eccentric American millionaire dies in the men's room, with a will in his wallet leaving his fortune to whomever is with him at his death. This whimsical conclusion, while lifting us out of the despair of the poor old man (played by Emil Jannings), by its very improbability reinforces the sense that real life is unhappy and that only stories have happy endings.

A genre related to the Kammerspielfilm is the "street film," a term used by Siegfried Kracauer in his *From Caligari to Hitler: A Psychological History of the German Film.* Beginning with Karl Grune's prototypal *The Street* (1923), street films include G. W. Pabst's *The Joyless Street* (1925) and Bruno Rahn's *Tragedy of a Street* (1927). In these films, most typically, the male protagonists are drawn away from home, family, and bourgeois life

The Last Laugh ★ Germany, 1924, F. W. Murnau; Emil Jannings.

The Joyless Street ⋆
Germany, 1925, G. W. Pabst;
Werner Krauss, with hand
on dog.

by the lure of the city, the seductive promise of excitement and sensual pleasures. These were individualized studies of lower-middle-class life, often set within or alongside entertainment, and sometimes vaguely underworld, milieus. If extracted from the frequently superb skill of their realizations, the plot themes might appear melodramatic or morbidly sentimental. Though rooted in contemporary reality, these films were concerned primarily with character study—frequently with the personality disintegration of an individual or group of individuals.

The Joyless Street, featuring Scandinavians Asta Nielsen, Greta Garbo, and Einar Hanson, deals more directly with economic and political problems in postwar Vienna (inflation, black market, stock manipulation, ineffectuality of government) than do other street films. Its realistic visual style is also quite different from the other street films; it was said at the time to be an example of the *Neue Sachlichkeit* (new objectivity). Showing how these national problems lead to general corruption and dislocation of moral and spiritual values, Pabst concentrated on the pressures exerted on a bourgeois father: The man faces old age and poverty, and his beautiful daughter is about to be forced into prostitution; they are saved by a *deus ex machina* in the form of a U.S. aid commission.

Variety (1925), directed by E. A. Dupont, though not exactly a Kammerspielfilm or a street film, embodies some of the characteristics of both. It concerns trapeze artists involved in a romantic triangle; the husband (played by Emil Jannings) murders the partner who has cuckolded him. The film proper is presented as a long flashback within the framework of Jannings in prison, telling his story to the warden. It was a great international success, especially popular in the United States.

Variety ☆ Germany, 1925,
E. A. Dupont; Warwick
Ward, Lya de Putti, and
Emil Jannings.

Principal Technical and Stylistic Advances

An underlying psychological function of all three major types of the German silent film is posited by Siegfried Kracauer in *From Caligari to Hitler.* According to him, they offered escape from contemporary social reality—into the past (historical or mythological), into fantasy (expressionist), or into the recesses of individual psyches (Kammerspiel and street films). Certainly it is true that German film makers were preoccupied with the psychological rather than the sociological, and that their new intentions brought innovations of technique to camera, lighting, set design, acting, and script construction.

To some extent the Germans, like the Soviets who would follow in the international spotlight, organized their industry as a vehicle of state. In 1917, when Germany's last great offensive in the West had failed, the giant firm Universum Film A. G. (Ufa) was founded by General Erich Ludendorff; over a third of its initial capital was supplied by the Reich. Mergers and affiliations with other large production firms and control of the biggest chain of first-run theaters led to its dominance. Unlike the Soviets, who used film directly for purposes of education and propaganda, the postwar German cinema was designed primarily to add to Germany's prestige through artistic accomplishment and to project Germany's image before the eyes of the world.

For these purposes the huge Ufa studios at Neubabelsberg were erected. Its facilities were unrivaled, and the craftspeople working there were the finest known. Many of their names later appeared on screen credits outside Germany, especially in the United States, decades after this original brilliant period of experiment and training.

Probably the single most striking contribution by the Germans was their fuller use of the **moving camera.** The Kammerspiel and street films in particular developed this possibility in order to probe character, to follow and bore into protagonists, and to let the world be seen from subjective points of view. In this latter respect the moving camera became part of the general expressionist tendency.

As far back as Porter's *The Great Train Robbery,* the camera had panned and tilted; Griffith had used trucking and dollying as well; but moving the camera while shooting was relatively rare, and usually (not always) confined to the simple function of keeping a moving subject within frame. The standard Griffith method was to rehearse performances with actors, shoot them from the most effective angles and distances on a stationary tripod, then select and arrange the images, adjust the tempo of the action, and heighten the conflict through editing. Griffith thus transcended the spatial and temporal limitations of the stage, offering the varied filmic view rather than the fixed and continuous one available to the playgoer; but the viewpoint remained essentially objective, a recording of *dramatic* action.

The Germans made their camera part of the story in a more profound way. It became a *narrative* tool in addition to being a means of recording dramatic action. This potential was employed in two ways, both appearing together in many of the German silent films. First, the camera could become a narrator, like Joseph Conrad's Marlow, leading viewers into and through the story. *The Last Laugh,* for example, opens with the camera descending on an elevator, peering out through its wrought-iron grillwork at the passing floors of the hotel. In one continuous take it moves down to the lobby and across to the revolving door, where it offers a view of the street and of the doorman whistling up cabs, greeting guests, and unloading luggage. It is for all the world like a novelist writing, "Evening was approaching at the fashionable Hotel Atlantic. On the upper floors maids scurried back and forth with fresh linen while guests moved toward the elevator and down into the lobby. There a string ensemble played to seated guests sipping aperitifs. If one crossed the lobby to the tall revolving door awhirl . . . ," and so on. Later, the camera follows at the shoulder of the little night watchman as he makes his rounds, permitting us to see what the light from his electric torch reveals as it bounces along the walls and floors of the corridors.

In the earlier sequences the doorman is viewed from a low camera angle, which exaggerates his size and importance in his splendid uniform and flowing mustache. When he is reduced to washroom attendant he not only moves lower in social status (and physically below the street level), but the camera is frequently placed at a high angle, further emphasizing the crushed spirit that makes the now stooped body seem small and pitifully vulnerable. Again, this kind of film making seems more analogous to a novelist's descriptive capabilities than to anything that can be achieved on a stage.

Another special use of the moving camera fully exploited by the Germans was the possibility of its taking on a character's point of view and even state of mind—what is called "subjective camera." In *The Last Laugh,* after a wedding party at his flat, the doorman is sitting alone amidst postparty debris, amiably bemused by drink. First he is seen to spin in the room as the camera moves around him (the "narrator's" viewpoint); then the room itself revolves as the camera takes on his own tipsy vision. In *Variety,* the camera is mounted on a swinging trapeze to let us experience the vertigo of the disturbed catcher as the audience below seems to approach and then recede. In the same Wintergarten scenes, specially constructed lenses fragment and distort images to suggest psychological states, those of the excited members of the audience as well as those of the principals.

Karl Freund was cinematographer for both *The Last Laugh* and *Variety,* and it was the German camera work that most strongly impressed Hollywood. Freed entirely from a fixed base on a tripod and from a strictly objective view, the camera now ran or stumbled, got dizzy or suffered from hallucinations, and "saw" the sounds of a reveler's horn blown at midnight or of a woman's footsteps going down a corridor. In the less important films this use of narrative/subjective camera placement and movement was a mere trapping, a "special effect." In the best work this subtly profound innovation opened a whole new range of screen technique, not only affecting the way subjects could be dealt with but also making accessible themes and kinds of characters never before treated.

The other vital component of the cinematographer's craft, **lighting,** was important to all three major types of German silent film. In the historical-costume films it followed rather closely the stage lighting developed earlier by Reinhardt. The tableaux were bathed in pools of light and shadow, which enhanced the mood and fitted into the total composition of set design, massed extras, and featured players. In the expressionist films the lighting was one of the most evocative means of conveying the bizarre and the threatening as seen and felt by the characters. In the Kammerspiel and street films, often expressionistic in their subtler ways, lighting augmented camera movement to direct the viewer's eye where the film maker wanted it. Frequently the lighting was what most strongly evoked the feelings desired. Modeled lighting exposed a character's face (and soul) for examination. The essential significance of places and objects was rendered through the way they were lit. In these silent films things often seem to take on a life of their own, surrounding and commenting on the lives being led by the protagonists.

In all three types of German films the lighting was conceived and arranged specially to set the overall mood, and in the latter two types, to reflect the emotional states of the characters as well. Often eerie or sombre, at the same time romantic (softening) and decorative, it was vastly different from the consistent brightness and clarity of most American films. At its basic level, of course, film, the medium, is simply film, the material: the response to illumination by a coating of light-sensitive emulsion on a cellulose base. The title of cameraman John Alton's book, *Painting with Light,* suggests the way the Germans learned to conceive of and use this primary factor.

Two specific lighting contributions can be noted as well. First was the new prevalence of *low-key* lighting. Suddenly the screen went dark, with candlelit rooms, gloomy stairways, streets at night, cabarets, and all the other environments that would be habitual to the many "night people" of the German films. Sufficiently sensitive emulsions and expertness in laboratory processing had not been available before; nor, more important, had an understanding of the precise control that might be exercised over the cinematographic process. Second was the Germans' use of *key light* (not to be confused with low key, but often occurring in conjunction with it). The key light is the brightest light on the set, usually appearing to come from a source within the scene—a light fixture, a window, a street lamp. Griffith experimented with this possibility (notably in *Broken Blossoms*), but usually he led the eye and created emotional overtones by limiting the amount of area within the frame—cutting from long shot, to medium, to closeup—with the scene generally well and evenly lit.

The Germans came to realize that within a shot, if there is one brighter area amidst less brightly lit surroundings, it becomes the center of attention. They also sensed that it is much more satisfying aesthetically to have a variety of lighting intensities balanced around the frame—a monochromatic equivalent to the painter's placement of pigments. In short, they learned to lead the eye over the screen and to gratify it with the illumination, part of a total, ordered composition in which the main elements stand out and are reinforced by the lesser.

The importance of **set design** to the special effectiveness and unique qualities of the German silent film has already been noted, but can scarcely be exaggerated. Virtually all of the films were shot completely inside the studio, the "exteriors" frequently constructed painstakingly on a mammoth scale. In *The Last Laugh,* for example, the huge Hotel Atlantic and the busy intersection in front of it, with autos, buses, and pedestrians passing by, are studio creations. Even an exception like Arthur von Gerlach's *The Chronicle of the Gray House* (1923), shot in part out-of-doors, uses the East Prussian moors as Thomas Hardy used those of Dorsetshire. Nature is bent to human purposes and given an anthropomorphic coding to reinforce human conflicts. Most of the crucial action, however, takes place within large, ornate, and calculatedly oppressive sets of baroque rooms and castle courtyards.

Two prevalent impulses in German set design were rarely separate from each other. The pictorial beauty and grandeur of the historical films had psychological dimensions as well, especially in the work of Fritz Lang. The expressionist tendency offered visual design that was striking in its own right (*The Cabinet of Dr. Caligari*) and large in scale (*The Golem*) as well as being expressive of overall moods and subjective states. Even in the Kammerspiel and street films, which embodied a modified expressionism, the pictorial and psychological functions of the sets were commingled. The Wintergarten scenes in *Variety* dazzle us by their size and opulence, besides serving as the public setting for the private tensions of star performers.

The Chronicle of the Gray House ✷ Germany, 1923, Arthur von Gerlach.

In Lang's *Nibelungen* the huge re-creation of a forest is breathtaking, with its Klieg-light sunshine streaming through the branches of trees as big as sequoias. The blond Siegfried riding slowly into frame on a white horse approaches a sizable, and palpably real, waterfall. Even the smoke-breathing dragon carries a rare conviction. In a wide-angle long shot of a huge castle courtyard, human figures are placed on the checkerboard tiles to form part of a total visual pattern; Lang evidently intended that we study its vastness and ingenuity as the shot holds on the screen. The costumes, too, are geometrically patterned. This sense of persons being segments of a decorative whole is confirmed by a scene in a treasure cave: A large round table piled with ornaments and jewelry is supported by carved dwarfs in chains; when one of them moves slightly, we have an ultimate statement about person being interchangeable with object in a screen world remarkable for its nonhuman use of human beings. Lang seemed to like the idea of humans as statuary; he used it again in *Metropolis,* even more pointedly and ingeniously. The futuristic city of the latter film may have been Ufa's *magnum opus* as far as set construction was concerned. It also marks the last great burst of expressionism.

Obviously there was no **performance style** except the theatrical when film came into being, and the evolution of screen acting included breaking away from stage tradition—a progress to which Griffith and contemporary Scandinavian film makers had contributed substantially. Griffith's intentions were to make his actors perform with greater subtlety, and the Scandinavians continued and advanced that approach. The more intimate style of film acting would in turn influence the theater.

Metropolis ★ Germany, 1927, Fritz Lang.

In trying to delineate internal states without the help of dialogue, the Germans went beyond realism to a deliberate expressiveness. Actors began working out their characterizations by "becoming" as completely as possible the persons they were playing. Immersing themselves sufficiently in the roles, they would inevitably reveal the characters' feelings through small gestures, the slope of a back, the movement of a head, the eyes—especially the eyes. But to these intuitive physical responses was added an intellectual refinement to make fullest use of silent film limitations (in this sense its strengths). Through closely observed facial expression and bodily movement the camera can capture what is eloquent and seems true in the actors' understanding of the characters. This understanding is then "projected" effortlessly, to every seat in the house, by the projector shining a large likeness onto the screen. Gestures and expressions formed and shaped for the screen can reveal more than can actors on a relatively distant stage, or even people across a room.

The great actors in German silent film—Emil Jannings, Werner Krauss, Conrad Veidt, Lil Dagover, Asta Nielsen, Pola Negri, Greta Garbo—learned to retard and simplify their gestures to make precise psychological points. In *The Joyless Street* the neurotic energy of Asta Nielsen and the radiant inward beauty of Greta Garbo are conveyed without any of the stagelike busyness of Mae Marsh or Lillian Gish (fine as she was) in the earlier Griffith films. Nielsen, who appeared in Danish films (beginning with *The Abyss,* 1910) before moving to Germany after the war, remains one of the great artists of the silent screen. Perhaps she was the first to suggest a dimension and complexity of feeling beneath the surface of the screen presence. Her style of passionate intensity would be developed to even greater expressiveness by Garbo, who began in Sweden and worked in Germany before coming to the United States. Jannings created remarkable portrayals through a kind of stylization that called for an absolute comprehension of the psychological makeup of his characters and an abstraction and heightening of the physical expression of feeling—an artfulness that did not so much conceal art as transcend life. Jannings lived a great number of screen lives in the studio world, all of them consistent with the stylistic level of the carefully designed sets and lighting.

Given the complex interaction of the various elements of technique, the Germans needed more-detailed **scripts** than did the simpler, more open-air and improvised American films. (Neither Sennett nor Griffith used scripts at all.) If the camera was going to move in a sustained take down a studio street, lights had to be arranged along a predetermined path, sets built to accommodate the full range of its shifting angle and distance, and actors directed and rehearsed to move in relationship to it. Thus script writing, and the production planning growing out of it, achieved new importance. The German script writers could blueprint a film on paper, and the best of them, like Carl Mayer, could go beyond the mechanics to communicate a complete sense of a film. Through written descriptions of images, Mayer defined the kinds of emotional values required and suggested how to achieve them. He also understood clearly what sorts of themes, characters, and emotions lent themselves best to visual expression. The action in his scripts was invariably sparse and simple; the plots, tight in construction, required few intertitles—and ultimately almost none at all (for example, *Shattered,* 1921; *New Year's Eve,* 1923; and *The Last Laugh*). It seems paradoxical that Griffith, without scripts, tended toward the literary, and required screen words to connect and explain his action. Mayer, working with words, used them to evoke self-explanatory images that were given physical form by directors, set designers, cinematographers, and performers—the extraordinary collective of German talent in the 1920s.

Mirror of the Culture

E. W. and M. M. Robson, in their book *The Film Answers Back,* were possibly the first to note the ways in which German silent film reflected certain aspects of a nation suffering from social-political sickness that would ultimately lead to a cure worse than the disease. Siegfried Kracauer, in *From Caligari to Hitler,* systematized, elaborated, and extended their insights. His book is a film history with both a thesis and a provocative demonstration of the kinds of things that can be learned about a society by analyzing the content and style of a popular art form. Because of their collective creation and appeal to an anonymous multitude, Kracauer argues, the films of a nation reflect its "mentality," the "inner dispositions" of a culture, more directly than do other arts. In examining German films from the end of World War I to Adolph Hitler's accession to power, Kracauer finds revealed a steady succession of attitudes conducive to authoritarianism.

First, he observes that no alternative between tyranny and anarchic chaos is offered: Freedom is not depicted as a possibility. In *The Cabinet of Dr. Caligari* the options are the asylum (tyranny) or the fair (chaos). This is by no means the only film example assessed by Kracauer. According to him none of the major German films of this period suggests possible human control over destiny through rational, democratic action. He notes as well the studio construction of unreal worlds and the penchant for organization, which requires submission. Instinct and fate are shown to rule. This is as true of the strangely driven burgher of the street film, led into corruption by his own vague lusts and longings, as it is of the haunted worlds of the expressionist films, in which an unknowable and malevolent destiny shapes the lives of the characters. The extent to which this particular worldview was held by the German people and could be invoked in a propaganda program was well understood by Hitler. Finally, Kracauer asserts that fantasy and retrogression were ubiquitous: the escaping of real problems in an unreal world, as in the expressionist films; the recurring image of a repentant man's head on a maternal woman's breast, as in the street films. He reads these symbolic signs as indicating political paralysis and pointing ahead to the passive acceptance of Naziism.[1]

Influence on Hollywood

As the old Hollywood saw advises, "If you can't beat 'em, join 'em." In Hollywood terms this has often meant, "If you can't beat 'em, buy 'em up." There began in the 1920s an emigration of German film makers to the United States that would impoverish their native industry and further enrich the dominant American one. The entire principal cast and crew of *Variety* were imported—Erich Pommer (producer), E. A. Dupont (director), Karl Freund (cinematographer), Leo Birinski (scenarist), and Emil Jannings and Lya de Putti (stars). Pommer, the production head of Ufa and arguably the man most directly responsible for the German "Golden Era" just surveyed, was lured by Paramount in 1927. Among other directors who emigrated were Ernst Lubitsch, Paul Leni, F. W. Murnau, and Fritz Lang. Cameramen Kurt Courant and Theodore Sparkuhl, along with Freund, brought

---

[1] See *From Caligari to Hitler: A Psychological History of the German Film* (Princeton, NJ: Princeton University Press, 1947), Chapters 5–10, pp. 61–130, for Kracauer's development of his thesis.

German cinematography to American films. Actor emigrès also included Pola Negri and Conrad Veidt.

Murnau, who had achieved worldwide prominence with German expressionist productions such as *Nosferatu* (1921) and *The Last Laugh* (1923), enjoyed a successful American career until his untimely death in 1931. *Sunrise,* a domestic melodrama he directed for Fox Studios in 1927, is sometimes cited as the greatest film ever made. The tale of a young husband's seduction by a *femme fatale* from the city, it boasts a mise-en-scène filled with stunning expressionistic effects. The city becomes a place of dazzling beauty and daunting complexity in scenes featuring reflective glass surfaces and deep space compositions, including a sequence in a restaurant that used a slanted floor, out-of-scale furniture, and midgets in the background to achieve a feeling of endless space and activity. William Fox gave Murnau complete control and an unlimited budget to make *Sunrise* in the belief that the film would enhance the studio's prestige. However, despite the critical acclaim that greeted its release, *Sunrise* lost money, and Murnau was never granted similar freedom again.

Germanic influence on American films was persistent, lasting decades after the first invasion. The imitation of German successes and the presence of German creative personnel combined to alter prevailing American style in regard to moving camera, lighting, and the use of visual narrative transitions rather than titles. Often this "Germanization" was somewhat arbitrary, being applied to native plots and themes without the aesthetic logic that had made form and content so interdependent in the best of the German silent films. Certain film types that developed later in the United States had their roots in the earlier Ufa and became sturdy hybrids. The horror series of Universal Studios, which began with *Dracula* and *Frankenstein* (both 1931), is one example, relying on sinister and fantastic subjects; expressionistic lighting, makeup, and costuming; and special-effects cinematography. A later instance is the cluster of *film noir,* as the French called them. Reminiscent of the street films, these dark crime melodramas of the mid-1940s also involve the probing of disordered psyches in a predominantly nighttime studio world.

In addition to the loss of talented creators, technicians, and performers, a kind of "internationalization" of German films, which began after the middle of the 1920s, vitiated the very distinctiveness that had made them popular as well as significant. This marked the appearance of a recurring problem of commerce affecting art. Once a country earns an international prominence through a special national contribution, it attempts to compete with Hollywood on its terms; that is to say, ingredients that are thought to make American films so successful are employed in an effort to obtain an even larger piece of the global box office (which includes the huge American audience). At the same time, American studios set about to coproduce within countries that demonstrated a successful competitiveness, contributing further to a blurring of national distinctions. In 1925 both Paramount and Metro-Goldwyn-Mayer negotiated with Ufa regarding joint production on the continent, using American-German casts and technicians. What Kracauer calls a "synthesis of Hollywood and Neubabelsberg" resulted in a further dilution of German themes and styles.

This is not to say that the German industry suddenly ceased to produce films of enduring value: With the arrival of sound there was a flurry of innovative and valuable work. American Josef von Sternberg made what many regard his masterpiece—*The Blue Angel* (1930)—and Fritz Lang, a German about to become an American, made what could be argued to be his—*M* (1931). G. W. Pabst, another of the great German film makers about

Triumph of the Will ★ Germany, 1935, Leni Riefenstahl.

to emigrate, did some of his best work during the early 1930s: *Westfront* (1930), *The Three-penny Opera* (1931), and *Kameradschaft* (1931). Among other German film makers of the early sound era, it may be Leni Riefenstahl who remains the most discussed—and the most controversial. After making a successful example of the mountain film genre, *The Blue Light*, in 1932, she worked with Hilter's government to craft a spectacular documentary celebrating Nazi power—*Triumph of the Will* (1935)—which chronicles the mass political rally at Nuremberg. She followed this with another masterful documentary, *Olympia,* made in 1938, which showcased the German-hosted Olympic Games.

But the exceptions to a general decline have to be weighed against the dozens of uniquely fascinating films of the first half of the 1920s. From about 1925 onward the eyes of the film world shifted from Germany to a star rising in the east, a red star. Made for the new government in Russia, another remarkable body of work began to appear that could scarcely be more different from the German films in form, content, and purpose.

Films of the Period

1919
Passion/Madame du Barry (Ernst Lubitsch)

Deception/Anna Boleyn (Ernst Lubitsch)
The Golem (*Der Golem*) (Paul Wegener)

1920
The Cabinet of Dr. Caligari (*Das Kabinett des Doktor Caligari*) (Robert Wiene)

1921
Destiny (*Der müde Tod*) (Fritz Lang)

1922
Dr. Mabuse, the Gambler (*Dr. Mabuse, der Spieler*) (Fritz Lang)
Nosferatu (F. W. Murnau)

1923
The Street (*Die Strasse*) (Karl Grune)

1924
The Last Laugh (*Der letzte Mann*) (F. W. Murnau)
Die Nibelungen (Fritz Lang)

1925
The Joyless Street (*Die freudlose Gasse*) (G. W. Pabst)
Variety (*Varieté*) (E. A. Dupont)

1927
Berlin: Symphony of a Great City (*Berlin: die Symphonie einer Grosstadt*) (Walther Ruttmann)
Metropolis (Fritz Lang)

1928
Pandora's Box (*Büchse der Pandora*) (G. W. Pabst)

Books on the Period

Elsaesser, Thomas, with Martin Wedel, eds. *The BFI Companion to German Cinema.* London: British Film Institute, 1999.

Kreimeier, Klaus. *The UFA Story: A History of Germany's Greatest Film Company, 1918–1945.* (trans. Robert and Rita Kimber). Berkeley: University of California press, 1999.

Silberman, Marc. *German Cinema: Texts in Context.* Detroit, MI: Wayne State University Press, 1995.

4

Art and Dialectic in the Soviet Film

★ ★ ★ ★

1925–1929

The Russians were even more profoundly affected by World War I than were the Germans. While there had been no fighting within the borders of Germany, Russia had been a vast battlefield. It had suffered defeat at the hands of the Central Powers and the peace treaty signed at Brest-Litovsk was even more vindictive than that of Versailles. While in Germany an abortive rebellion in 1919 was quickly suppressed, the Bolshevik Revolution of 1917 succeeded. At least five years elapsed, however, before it was clear that the new government of Russia, a communist government, could survive, and that a beginning stability would be achieved.

Not until 1925 did the Soviets fully launch into the final, and some would say most brilliant, phase of the silent film before the introduction of sound. The contrast between Soviet and German silent film, in both subject matter and technique, was even greater than that between the German film of the early 1920s and American film preceding it. Though the German effort had been state supported in part, it was directed toward the prestige of art. It can be valued precisely because of its extreme artificiality, but a prevailing aestheticism cannot be denied. There was an anarchic indifference to the social-political implications of content, which Kracauer interpreted as reflecting a kind of national neurosis. The introspection and morbidity of the major themes led to a slowness of tempo. As the veteran British director Anthony Asquith observed of German contributions, "While the film was gaining in its ability to convey mood, emotion and character, it was gradually losing touch with its life-source—movement."

Soviet film, completely state supported, was socially purposeful above all else: intended primarily to educate and indoctrinate the Soviet people in the events and causes of the Revolution. Vigorous and optimistic, the films came out of the East like a blast of cold Siberian air, blowing away the hothouse atmosphere of the German studios. Objective in approach (as opposed to German subjectivism) and epic in form (as opposed to the personal dramas of the Germans), they brought rapid pace and physical action back to the moving picture and resumed the line that emphasized editing inaugurated by Porter and advanced by Griffith.

The German film makers' intellectual sources included Sigmund Freud. Their concern with the psychological led to expressionism and the subjective camera as means of portraying internal states. As used by the Germans the moving camera became a kind of visual equivalent to the psychoanalyst's probing of the patient's psyche; the expressionistic design conveyed dreams, nightmares, and hallucinations.

In the Soviet Union the ideological basis was provided by Karl Marx and V. I. Lenin, and the film makers' concerns were social, political, and economic. The predominant aesthetic mode was futurism, which attempted to depict vividly the energetic and dynamic quality of contemporary life influenced by the motion and force of modern machinery. In film, pictorial realism rather than expressionism was the visual style required to portray the actual, external world. Cutting—paralleling the conflict and resolution of opposites in Hegelian/Marxian dialectic—was the principal formative method. A neat symbolic point is made by G. W. Pabst having directed *Secrets of a Soul,* a popularization of Freudian psychology, in the same year, 1926, that V. I. Pudovkin made *Mechanics of the Brain,* explaining the Pavlovian scientific dialectic of stimulus-response. Even a comparison of the titles of the German and Soviet films is revealing: *secrets* versus *mechanics, a* versus *the, soul* versus *brain.*

Historical Setting

In czarist Russia movies were not a popular art as they were elsewhere. There were few theaters, tickets were expensive, and the working classes couldn't afford to attend regularly. The high illiteracy rate made printed intertitles a general burden, and the literary-theatrical bent of the Russian silent films further helped confine their patronage to the educated middle classes. Somewhat equivalent to *films d'art* and Adolph Zukor's famous players in famous plays, the highly theatrical tradition of the Russian film (as opposed to the later Soviet film) is generally agreed upon and is borne out by the few examples existing in archives in the United States. After the Bolshevik Revolution most of the film producers and actors emigrated, taking with them whatever equipment and film they could carry.

Those producers who chose to remain were at first allowed to continue along lines of private enterprise. Though they lacked revolutionary understanding, let alone zeal, not much attention was given to their output by a government preoccupied with more pressing matters. A Cinema Committee was set up, however, under playwright A. V. Lunacharsky, Minister of Education. With truly remarkable foresight, given the uses of film generally up to that time and the negligible Russian production, Lenin had said, "Of all the arts, the cinema is the most important for us." His statement contrasts as strongly as could be expected with one from the deposed Nicholas II, who had written: "I consider cinematography an empty, useless, and even pernicious diversion. Only an abnormal person could place this sideshow business on a level with art. It is all nonsense and no importance should be lent to such trash." At the same time it is known that this last of the czars was an ardent moviegoer who spent many evenings at private screenings in the palace basement.

The national conditions that prevented Lenin and the other communist leaders from promptly turning film into the voice for the Revolution that it eventually became were not unlike those of postwar Germany, and considerably more severe. In the first year of the new government famine was widespread. During one of the cruelest Russian winters on record there was no fuel. Typhus raged in epidemic proportions. After participation in the war dragged to a halt, the Soviets faced Allied armies within their borders and continuing civil warfare with the counterrevolutionaries. One curious instance of the general instability was an episode in which some 50,000 escaped Czech prisoners of war ravaged the countryside unresisted along the route of the Trans-Siberian railway.

It took five years (1918–1922) to fully establish the new political regime and two more years before the film industry was functioning with anything approaching productivity. (Even by the end of 1923 only 13 percent of the films shown in the country were Soviet.) In 1919 the industry had been completely nationalized when it became clear that the old capitalist economics and mentality would not serve the needs of a socialist state. In the same year the State Institute of Cinematography (VGIK) was established in Moscow to train new Soviet film makers; it was thus the oldest, as well as one of the largest and best, film schools in the world. In 1925 the Sovkino Trust was formed to try to bring some order into all aspects of the domestic industry and to reestablish distribution abroad.

Beginnings

The new Soviet cinema, which began its formative period about 1919, was thought of at the time as being divided into two creative camps. Although called the right and left wings, the labels weren't essentially political. At first the right wing carried on in the old theatrical tradition, using conventional methods and styles but substituting commissars, peasants, and Red Army soldiers for the upper-class characters of traditional theater. Romance, humor, and heroics persisted. The concerns of the new state motivated the action initially and appeared as background, but scarcely replaced standard dramaturgical elements: boy-girl, comic sidekicks, obstacles to be overcome, obstructive villains, and so on. *Kombrig Ivanov* (1923) is an example of this creative tendency; it was retitled *The Beauty and the Bolshevik* in the United States. Subsequently the work of the right wing achieved greater sophistication and addressed sociological problems. Abram Room's *Bed and Sofa* (1927), for example, deals with a romantic triangle, but the shifting allegiance of the woman toward the two men involves the housing shortage and her attitude and theirs toward the role of women in the new society. The general methods of the right wing became the only officially sanctioned approach after "socialist realism" was imposed in the 1930s, and continued to dominate Soviet cinema. *The Cranes Are Flying* (1957) and *Ballad of a Soldier* (1959) are later popular examples.

The left wing was much more radical in its innovation, which involved form as well as subject. When we think of the Soviet silent cinema, it is usually of the films growing out of the theories and experiments of two left-wing pioneers. One of these was Dziga Vertov, who followed Lenin's advice that the first work of Soviet film makers should be with newsreels and documentaries. This seemed advisable partly because of the drain on resources feature film production would have represented, but especially because of the urgency of communicating the history and spirit of the Revolution to the still largely apathetic and un-

Kino-Pravda series ★ Soviet Union, 1922–1925, Dziga Vertov.

informed Russian public. In 1919 Vertov founded his Kino-Eye Group and began publishing manifestos.[1] "Life caught unawares" was Vertov's credo. What he meant by this was not exactly candid camera (since the subjects usually knew they were being filmed) but that nothing be staged or directed. Life in front of the camera was permitted to run its natural course; the only creative control the film maker exerted was through choosing what and how to shoot, and the placement of one shot in relation to another during the editing. In 1922 Vertov began to produce "Kino-Pravda," a series of monthly newsfilms that lasted for twenty-three issues. The title, incidentally, is synonymous with *cinéma vérité* (film truth), a term French anthropologist-film maker Jean Rouch coined in 1961 to apply to a new kind of documentary. What *cinéma vérité* added to *kino pravda* was essentially the lightweight, synchronous sound equipment that permitted the film maker to shoot and record virtually anything without interrupting or altering it for the benefit of camera or microphone.

Since Vertov had no control over the action he was filming, unlike a director of fiction films, editing took on a peculiarly central role in his work. Moreover, the shortage of raw stock in the Soviet Union in the early 1920s (before the Soviets began to manufacture their own) meant that Vertov had to use pieces of film as he found them, frequently short

[1] Vertov's theories of film are available in *Kino-Eye: The Writings of Dziga Vertov,* edited and with an introduction by Annette Michelson, translated by Kevin O'Brien (Berkeley: University of California Press, 1984).

ends left over from other projects. In an impulse not unlike Porter's in *Life of an American Fireman,* Vertov learned that by juxtaposing shots from old czarist newsreels with newly shot materials he could create new meanings. Russian tanks crossing a no-man's-land in the war could be followed by Soviet tractors breaking ground for cultivation. Juxtaposing a shot of the formal and elegant Nicholas stiffly reviewing his palace guard with a shot of a shirt-sleeved Lenin energetically addressing the workers added significance not inherent in either shot alone. In embryonic form this was precisely the kind of editing Sergei Eisenstein would develop into montage; the title of his film *Old and New* (1929) concisely sums up a principal propaganda device of Vertov's. Beyond that, one can say of "Kino-Pravda" that all the subjects were socially purposeful: There are no beauty parades, no animals in the zoo. Inspirational in tone, the films seem to be urging that there's a job to be done. In general they show one region or aspect of national life to the rest of the country (a major mission of the documentary film later to be picked up in Britain, with proper credit always given to the Soviets). Vertov's reports are not all sweetness and light by any means; hard-hitting exposés are included. "Save the starving children" one title proclaims, as we see pitiful young victims of famine. The directness of communication with the people is further revealed in end titles that encourage the audience to mail its "inquiries regarding traveling film shows" and "all film and photo work" to Kino-Pravda.

Another left-wing pioneer was Lev Kuleshov, film director, theorist, lecturer (from 1920 on) and later head of the State Institute of Cinematography.[2] As Sergei Eisenstein came out of the Vertov line, another great Soviet film maker, V. I. Pudovkin, was Kuleshov's star pupil. Eisenstein's impressively talented cameraman, Eduard Tisse, had worked for Vertov, as Pudovkin's cameraman, Anatoli Golovnya, had for Kuleshov. Kuleshov coped with the shortage of raw stock by conducting acting experiments performed for an empty camera. Also, he and his students spent much time analyzing and recutting existing motion pictures to learn filmic construction. When Kuleshov gained access to film stock he came to emphasize editing as heavily as did Vertov, but for different purposes. He discovered how, through cutting, to make nonactors appear to give skillful performances and how to give the acting of professionals meanings of which they were unaware at time of performance. Following Vertov and Kuleshov, Eisenstein and Pudovkin made editing for the Soviet silent film makers virtually synonymous with the creative process itself.

A third early creative and theoretical group contributed to the scope of Soviet cinema. In 1922 a youthful Grigori Kozintsev (age 17) joined Leonid Trauberg (17), and Sergei Yutkevitch (18) to form the Factory of the Eccentric Actor: FEX. The virtually unlimited freedom for experimentation in the arts during the hectic years of revolution and civil war unleashed the progressive spirit among the young. (In 1922 Vertov was age 26, Kuleshov 23, Eisenstein 24, and Pudovkin 29.) This generation of Soviet artists, seeking new methods of expression, turned toward minor genres, "the kind of popular art which the aristocracy and bourgeoisie had scorned. To be precise: the music hall, the circus and the cinema." Eisenstein's first film, *Strike* (1925), is very closely related to these aesthetic impulses. After seeing it, Kozintsev told the FEX group, "All that we're doing is childish nonsense, we must all see *Strike* again and again, until we can understand it and adopt its power for our own."

---

[2] His theories are available in *Kuleshov on Film: Writings by Lev Kuleshov,* selected, translated, and edited by Ronald Levaco (Berkeley: University of California Press, 1974).

By the Law ★ Soviet Union, 1926,
Lev Kuleshov.

Three Silent Masters

Ranked alongside Eisenstein and Pudovkin among the great Soviet silent film makers
would be **Alexander Dovzhenko.** Because he stands somewhat apart from the principal
thrust of Soviet film making, his work will be discussed first. A Ukrainian from a family
of uneducated farmers, Dovzhenko includes in his films strange ethnic and mystical elements that color his Marxism and make his silent work quite distinct from that of the other
Soviet film makers. He was a painter before he became a film maker, and montage was not
as important for him as it was for the others; at least his use of it is quite different.

In Dovzhenko's three major silent films—*Zvenigora* (1928), *Arsenal* (1929), *Earth*
(1930)—the larger sequences seem separate from each other, circular in construction, and
strangely complete in themselves. He emphasizes the relationships of scenes to scenes, within
the sequences, rather than of shots to each other within the scenes. The numerous and varied
scenes tend to be brief, but the shots (or even a single shot) that they comprise are often sustained. Contrasting and elliptical combinations involve quite extraordinary shifts of mood and
statement. The connections of the parts to each other are often unclear or ambiguous on first
viewing. In *Earth,* in a scene of the kulaks weeping and wailing, which follows the scene of
the peasant grandfather dying, we assume initially that they are mourning his death. When we
learn that it is a threatened loss of possessions that has provoked their grief, the comment
about them becomes a negative one. Ambiguity of this sort is rarely allowed to occur in the

more didactic main body of Soviet work. It is as if Dovzhenko were serenely indifferent to conventional continuity in his pursuit of evocative, many-layered imagery.

Marking Dovzhenko's visual style are extremely wide-angled long shots in which a complexity of action and composition builds up within a single frame like an evolving painting. Also, there are the painterly "still" shots—the striking silhouettes of *Arsenal,* the trees heavy-laden with fruit in *Earth*—which convey a sense of timelessness, of fixity. In thinking of Dovzhenko's work we remember its many images of the Ukrainian country-side composed of low horizons and small human figures moving under an enormous open sky. The shocking and beautiful balletic death of Vasily in *Earth,* as he moves down a curving moonlit road toward the camera, to be cut down almost casually by a murderer's bullet, is not likely to be forgotten. Throughout his early films Dovzhenko's intentions are clearly more poetic than narrative (as with Pudovkin) or dramatic (as with Eisenstein).

His symbols and metaphors are not forced or belletristic, however; they grow out of a conception of the closeness of the people to the soil. They also contain dialectical contradictions that advance the revolutionary argument; but because Dovzhenko sees life whole, there is nothing of the agitprop about his work. In *Earth* he is saying it is right for an old man to die (at peace) but wrong (against nature) for a young man to die (by violence). Yet death is followed by life in both instances. As the old man munches one apple, a child munches another, completing the cycle of generations. A woman gives birth during Vasily's funeral, and his comrades are clearly fulfilling the potential of his abbreviated life in building for the future. The autumn rain in the epilogue appears at first to be like tears, but it is also life-giving as it falls on the fullness of harvest. The tractor is regarded by the elderly as a replacement of themselves and their animals, and by the young as an extension of the people's productivity.

Though working in the service of the state, Dovzhenko's humanism causes him to extend sympathy to the old as well as the new. One can imagine that a Joseph Stalin might have regarded the ambivalence uneasily, and ultimately as subversive. To a modern American viewer *Earth*'s unmistakably optimistic tone presents a remarkable argument for revolutionary change. But when it premiered in Moscow, it was attacked at length in *Izvestia* for being "defeatist" and "counterrevolutionary." Given its slowness of pace, ambiguities, obscurities, and dependence on the pictorial, it seems unlikely that it could have had the requisite popularity in the Soviet Union to do the indoctrinational job required of it by the sponsoring government. At any rate, after the brilliant experimental period of the 1920s, the hard line of "socialist realism" appeared; Dovzhenko never again achieved anything equal to the unique visual lyricism of his silent films. Even in the earlier time he seemed out of step with his colleagues. What attracted him most strongly was clearly the human and natural beauty that could be captured by the camera, rather than the arguments that could be fashioned by an editor's shears.

V. I. Pudovkin was educated as a physicist and chemist. (Dovzhenko's education, too, had been scientific and technological.) He became interested in acting for films, he said, as a result of seeing *Intolerance,* which had finally arrived in the Soviet Union in 1919. Although Pudovkin would appear as an actor in many of his own films as well as those of others, while studying under Kuleshov he came to see that the real creative fulfillment in motion pictures was for the director rather than the actor. Kuleshov, for his part, fully understood that Griffith had been working out of some of the same concepts that had begun to preoccupy him. A prominent concern of Kuleshov's was the difference between the actor's contributions to stage and to screen.

Earth ★ Soviet Union, 1930, Alexander Dovzhenko.

On stage, once the curtain rises the performer is in complete control of his or her performance. Direction and rehearsal are merely preparation to be used, or ignored for that matter, in interpreting a character in the presence of an audience. In film, the director is the principal "audience" of the live performance. The screen performance is constructed after the actor has finished his or her work, out of the selection made available by the camera: a long shot of the actor in a room full of people, a closeup of just the actor's profile, a reaction shot of someone else's face, and so on. It is no longer the actor's total performance that finally appears, no longer her or his rhythm or even whole body, but bits and pieces integrated into a synthetic whole. With systematic thoroughness Kuleshov began to test the possibilities of this basic cinematic technique.

His influence on Pudovkin was profound, and the latter claimed to have participated in a series of Kuleshov's experiments that explored the potential of editing to create a time and space existing (or seeming to exist) only on film. For one of these experiments Kuleshov assembled five shots. In the first a young man walks from left to right. In the second a young woman walks from right to left. In a third they meet and shake hands, and the young man points to something off screen. The fourth shot shows a large white building with a broad flight of steps. In the fifth the couple ascends steps. A viewer would accept this scene as one uninterrupted action, but in actuality the five pieces had been shot in completely different times and places—the man and woman (shots one and two) in separate parts of Moscow, and the handshake (shot three) in yet another. The white building (four) was in fact the White House, snipped from an American film, and the steps (five) were those of a cathedral.[3] Rudimentary and obvious as such experiments may seem, they

[3] V. I. Pudovkin, *Film Technique,* translated by Ivor Montagu (New York: Lear Publishers, 1949), pp. 60–61.

Mother ⋆ Soviet Union, 1920, V. I. Pudovkin; Nikolai Batalov, left, and Vera Baranovskaya, right.

nonetheless isolated and held up for examination the most basic aesthetic underpinning of the medium.

Returning from their practical experiments to a further study of *Intolerance,* Kuleshov and Pudovkin began to see how to apply their discoveries to the requirements of a new Soviet cinema. Although as far from being a Marxist as is conceivable, Griffith, in *Intolerance,* had carried on a moral and ethical argument through his separate historical episodes, and in the modern story economic and social ones as well. (Not only the strike in Pudovkin's *Mother,* 1926, but Eisenstein's *Strike,* 1925, contain unmistakable borrowings from the Griffith film.) In a succession of masterworks paralleling those of Eisenstein—warmer and more moving, if not as breathtakingly experimental and brilliant—Pudovkin gave full form to his learning. Unlike the highly intellectual appeal of Eisenstein's work, Pudovkin's films reach the emotions directly. They received instant acclaim and their power seems undiminished by the years. As with Dovzhenko, Pudovkin's major silent films—*Mother, The End of St. Petersburg* (1927), and *Storm over Asia* (1928)—stand as his finest and most personal achievements, but he too continued to work for several decades in the sound film. Although he became a greater director than Kuleshov, Pudovkin also wrote theoretical essays—*Film Technique* and *Film Acting*—which explain and show the applications of his former teacher's insights. They remain among the best texts for beginning directors, especially for those interested in documentary film and work with nonactors.

Sergei Eisenstein, like Dovzhenko and Pudovkin, had a technical education (as a civil engineer) prior to defecting to the arts—first to theater in his case. Before beginning stage work, however, Eisenstein had developed an intense interest in Japanese language and culture, which would feed into his later profound and erudite theorizing about film. He was fascinated by the Japanese hieroglyphic writing, in which the word *weeping* is formed by combining the pictograph for *eye* with that for *water; singing* by combining that for *mouth* and *bird; listening,* for *ear* plus *door;* and so on. He came to believe that the two drawn symbols combined like film shots to provide a third meaning. Also, he noted a Japanese technique for teaching drawing, which limited the student to the composition of segments of a cherry tree branch within a frame. This attention to frame area and composition within it became useful preparation for Eisenstein's own painstaking composing of images. Finally, Kabuki theater seemed to him to bring various artistic elements together in a balance not unlike that of film. In Kabuki, and in the Nō plays, spoken language is not the almost exclusive carrier of content that it is in Western drama. Japanese theater is visual as much as verbal. Words are part of an ensemble in which formalized gesture, choreographed body movement, music, and even costumes carry equal weight and add nuances and qualifications to a complex whole.

Eisenstein's theatrical beginning was as a scene designer for the Proletkult Theatre. From childhood he had been a prodigious sketcher and painter; the Proletkult, dedicated to the development of proletarian artists and the education of the working class, accommodated his sympathies for the revolution. From the Proletkult he learned to distrust the character-centered theater of the nineteenth century and to seek ways to make the masses the hero and to present social problems in place of bourgeois romantic triangles. Moving on to work with Vsevolod Meyerhold, a radically innovative theatrical producer and director, Eisenstein completed the theoretical education and practical experience that would propel him into film.

Meyerhold's theories of acting were in polar opposition to those of Konstantin Stanislavsky, the other great contemporary force in Soviet theater. Whereas Stanislavsky started from within, in a psychological approach, instructing his actors to search out the emotions of their characters, Meyerhold began from without, in a theory he called biomechanics. Related to Pavlov's experiments in conditioned reflexes and consistent with the scientific spirit of the new Russia, Meyerhold's method was based on the idea that emotions could be stimulated in the actor (and conveyed to the spectator) through analysis of the emotive connotations of movement and by developing the actor's body into a precise machine capable of producing the exact effects desired. This approach pulled the Meyerhold theater closer to the *commedia dell'arte* tradition and even to the technique of circus performers. It may have helped lay the groundwork for German revolutionary Bertolt Brecht's aesthetic stance; certainly it had a profound effect on Eisenstein.

Returning to the Proletkult, Eisenstein arrived at his own eclectic fusion of all he had come to understand up to that point. What he sought was a "montage of attractions"—a series of sensory experiences that would involve the spectators and carry them along a predetermined path of emotional response. His most successful realization of these theories on the stage seems to have been a parody production of Alexander Ostrovsky's *The Wise Man.* In it he combined acrobats, a tightrope walker, and satirical asides directed at foreign political figures with a caricatured religious procession bearing candles, chanting litany, and carrying placards inscribed "Religion is the opium of the people." A short comic film was specially produced for incorporation into the performance.

Eisenstein's final attempt to transform theatrical art and get closer to the emotional needs of contemporary audiences led him in a direction opposite from the circus and music hall toward the reality outside the theater. His production of *Gas Masks,* a play by Sergei Tretyakov, was performed by workers and staged in the actual Moscow Gas Factory. Eisenstein regarded this experiment as a failure. Rather than eliminating "art" and replacing it with "life," as he had intended by using real setting and nonactors, he had succeeded only in exposing the artificiality of conventions that would have seemed perfectly at home in the theater. Seeking a means of capturing the reality of factory and workers that so fascinated him, he arrived at film as the medium that could make art out of materials much closer to life than could theatrical drama. As he put it, "The cart fell to pieces and the driver dropped into the cinema."

Strike (1925), his first film, also used a factory setting, with the workers as the collective protagonists. The "montage of attractions" now became the rapid and rhythmic cutting together of shots, startling in their visual contrasts, physical in their impact. Although all of the elements of Eisenstein's mature silent work are present, traces of the kind of theater in which he had been working account for some excesses and discordances. The "circus" elements—caricatures, gross symbolism, and exaggerated action—although

Strike ★ Soviet Union, 1925, Sergei Eisenstein.

striking in themselves, fit rather strangely into the prevailing naturalism. On the other hand, there is a documentary-like looseness of structure that makes the film more successful within its sequences than it is as a whole. *Battleship Potemkin* (1925) advanced on the first work by stripping away some of the flamboyance and disciplining the fertility of imagination. Built on a tight and firm dramatic line, its five sequences proceed with the cumulative power of the acts of classical tragedy.

Both films make essentially the same ideological points. Although *Potemkin* deals with the mutiny of the crew of an armored cruiser in the abortive 1905 Revolution, its officers are equivalent to the capitalists of *Strike;* its White Guards and Cossacks, who cut down the populace on the Odessa Steps, are like the army and police of the preceding film. In both films, the actions of the ruling class are arrogant and deceitful and lead to slaughter. The sailors and workers are simple and loyal to each other; except for their proletarian leaders, they are naive in the ways of the world. Incapable of evil unless duped into it by the authorities, they resort to violence only to counter unendurable oppression. The working classes are portrayed as the most productive resource of the nation and its only democratic force. A version of the desired dictatorship of the proletariat is offered in these two films. A recurrent image shows the revolutionary leaders haranguing the sailors or

Battleship Potemkin ★ Soviet Union, 1925, Sergei Eisenstein.

workers who then move together in a single group decision: "All for one, one for all!" the *Potemkin* titles shout.

The "hero" of both films is the masses—played by people who would have lived through situations much like those portrayed. In both cases, an epic scale of action is based on real or composite events. The viewpoint is broadly social-political and there is little delineation of characters except as types. Both films were shot on location rather than in studios; in the case of *Potemkin,* Odessa was the actual place of some of the incidents portrayed. Eisenstein seized on and made full use of the accidents of setting—in *Strike,* the stairway tier of the workers' tenements; in *Potemkin,* the architectural characteristics of Odessa, a morning mist on the water, the stone lions, and the like. His play with mass, line, and movement is that of a dynamic painter; his handling of crowds is quite without peer. Always Eisenstein works through the kinetic. But, given the amount of movement within the frame and the rapidity of cutting, there is little moving camera. Instead there are an extraordinary number and variety of camera setups, as would be required by his kind of editing. At moments of climactic action some of the shots are as short as two frames, and their content is frequently horrifying: a Cossack's saber slashing downward, a woman's spectacles broken and her face bloodied. Through an intended physiological response, Eisenstein aimed to bring his viewers to a political attitude. Closeups abound and there is a prominent use of what in literature would be called synecdoche, the parts representing a larger whole. In *Potemkin,* the maggoty meat, the doctor's pince-nez which eventually dangle in the ropes, the pounding pistons of the ship's engines, and the final magnificent shot from below of its hull slicing through the water, all serve this function.

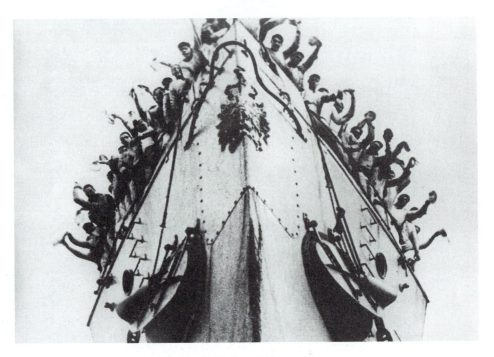

Battleship Potemkin ★ Soviet Union, 1925, Sergei Eisenstein.

October (or *Ten Days That Shook the World,* 1928) marks the height of Eisenstein's "intellectual montage," but it lacks the passion and coherence of *Battleship Potemkin*—at least the versions of it that appear in the West. Like Griffith's *Intolerance,* in comparison to *The Birth of a Nation, October,* although in some respects Eisenstein's ultimate achievement, is on a canvas so large that the monumental conception remains only partially realized. *Old and New* (also known as *The General Line,* 1929) was his final silent film. In it, though his aesthetic sensibility and intelligence are as evident as ever, they seem essentially of the wrong kind for this account of Soviet farm life and collectivization.

Dovzhenko and Pudovkin adjusted to the conventions of socialist realism and continued a steady if scarcely distinguished output into the first decades of sound. Eisenstein could not adjust, and was frequently the target of criticism from bureaucrats, critics, and other film makers. The problem was not that he was unwilling to serve the state in ways deemed socially useful, but that he was innately and supremely what he was accused of being—a formalist. His released sound films—*Alexander Nevsky* (1938), and *Ivan the Terrible,* Part I (1944), Part II (1958)—great though they are, are few. He spent much of the last fifteen years of his life teaching and writing. It may be that his theoretical writings, like George Bernard Shaw's prefaces to his plays, will retain a value beyond some of the creative work that grew out of them. In any event, Eisenstein's films and theories marked an enormous advance in a conscious and articulated understanding of how the cinema works as a means of communication—as a kind of language and as a form of art. Montage was the key concept.

Montage: Theory and Practice

The word *montage* was borrowed from the French; *monter* simply means to mount or assemble. For the Soviet film makers, however, this assembling and mounting through editing became the ultimate creative act. Although they had learned from Griffith and were nudged into the most economic use of the shot by the shortage of raw stock, their practical experiments, published theories, and finally the great works of Soviet silent film led them to a kind and level of accomplishment that has served to instruct film creators and critics ever since. Eisenstein and Pudovkin, friendly rivals as film makers, were also principal spokesmen in a running debate about the proper uses of montage. They agreed on the fundamental importance of editing, but for Pudovkin the cut was linkage, a joining of shots for the gradual accumulation of narrative meaning—the unfolding of a story. For Eisenstein its function was to achieve shock, the banging together of contrasting shots in a way that would force the audience into an understanding greater than the sum and different from any one of its parts. Eisenstein took particular satisfaction in what he regarded as the similarity of this process to the thesis-antithesis-synthesis of Hegelian dialectic. The argument is important as well as interesting, and worth pursuing through the words of the adversaries.

In *Film Technique,* Pudovkin, after acknowledging his indebtedness to Kuleshov and the importance of the concept of montage to Soviet film makers, writes:

> Kuleshov maintained that the material in film-work consists of pieces of film, and that the composition method is their joining together in a particular, creatively discovered order. He maintained that film-art does not begin when the artists act and the various scenes are shot—this is only the preparation of the material. Film-art begins from the moment when the

director begins to combine and join together the various pieces of film. By joining them in various combinations, in different orders, he obtains differing results.[4]

Pudovkin continues by describing two more of the practical experiments (like the one with the couple, the steps, and the White House) that Kuleshov and his students supposedly carried out to test their theories.

The first involves three short strips of film. On one is the image of a smiling face, on another a hand pointing a revolver, on the third a frightened face. Pudovkin observes that if the shots are assembled in that order the impression we get is that the second man is facing the revolver and that he is a coward. If the order is reversed—frightened face, revolver, smiling face—the impression we get is that the man facing the revolver is very brave. Thus the meaning of precisely the same images is altered, even reversed, by changing their order.

In the second experiment recalled by Pudovkin he and Kuleshov selected some close-ups of the Russian actor Ivan Mozhukhin. They were static, neutral shots of Mozhukhin's face expressing no particular emotion. Those shots were then intercut with closeups of other material. First was a bowl of soup on a table; it seemed quite obvious that Mozhukhin was looking at the soup. Then the actor's face was followed by shots showing a coffin in which lay a dead woman. In the third instance the face was followed by a shot of a little girl playing with a funny toy bear. When the three combinations were shown without explanation to an audience, they raved about Mozhukhin's acting! They pointed out the heavy pensiveness of the mood created as he regarded the forgotten bowl of soup, the deep grief expressed as he looked at the dead woman, and the light, happy smile that played across his features as he gazed at the little girl. In all three cases, according to Pudovkin, Mozhukhin's facial expression had been virtually the same, and expressing very little at that.

Pudovkin concludes his recounting of these experiments with an additional observation:

> The combination of various pieces in one or another order is not sufficient. It is necessary to be able to control and manipulate the length of these pieces, because the combination of pieces of varying length is effective in the same way as the combination of sounds of various length in music, by creating the rhythm of the film and by means of their varying effect on the audience. Quick, short pieces rouse excitement, while long pieces have a soothing effect.[5]

In other words Pudovkin offers a sort of formula: Film creation equals (1) what is in the shots, (2) the order in which they appear, and (3) how long each is held on the screen. "To be able to find the requisite order of shots or pieces and the rhythm necessary for their combination," he summarizes, "that is the chief task of the director's art. This art we call *montage*—or constructive editing. It is only with the help of *montage* that I am able to solve problems of such complexity as the work on the artists' acting."[6]

Note the final emphasis given to performance. Unlike Eisenstein's silent films Pudovkin's make heavy use of professional actors and contain some superb characterizations. He portrays the awakening of revolutionary consciousness through the microcosm of individual experience more than through the action of the masses—for example, Vera Baranovskaya as the title character in *Mother* and Ivan Chuvelyov as the peasant lad in *The End of St. Petersburg*. Still, Pudovkin regards actors as "plastic material" not unlike any objects that

---

[4] Pudovkin, *Film Technique*, pp. 138–139.

[5] Pudovkin, *Film Technique*, pp. 139–141.

[6] Pudovkin, *Film Technique*, p. 141.

might be photographed. They move and gesture, stare and weep, but for Pudovkin the film "performance" is created by the director cutting together strips of celluloid registering these actions. As might be expected, this is a position that horrifies and infuriates actors.

Pudovkin began the "Introduction to the German Edition" of *Film Technique* with: "The foundation of film art is *editing*." Eisenstein, in an essay in *Film Form,* echoes Pudovkin: "To determine the nature of montage is to solve the specific problem of cinema." He goes on to explain:

> The earliest conscious film makers, and our first film theoreticians, regarded montage as a means of description by placing single shots one after the other like building-blocks. The movement within these building-block shots, and the consequent length of the component pieces, was then considered as rhythm.[7]

That was precisely what Pudovkin had written, as Eisenstein acknowledges with what is perhaps a feigned superiority of disbelief and an implied distinction between the theorist and the artist: "According to this definition, shared even by Pudovkin as a theoretician, montage is the means of *unrolling* an idea with the help of single shots: the 'epic' principle." (*Epic* is here used in the classical sense—narrative as opposed to dramatic.) In Eisenstein's opinion, however, "montage is an idea that arises from the collision of independent shots—shots even opposite to one another: the 'dramatic' principle."[8]

Elsewhere, in an essay in the companion volume, *The Film Sense,* Eisenstein continues the argument and expands on his own position. As he sees the Soviet films, they are "faced with the task of presenting not only a narrative that is *logically connected,* but one that contains a *maximum of emotion and stimulating power.* Montage is a mighty aid to the resolution of this task," he asserts. Eisenstein goes on to ask rhetorically, "Why do we use montage at all?"

> Even the most fanatical opponent of montage will agree that it is not merely because the film strip at our disposal is not of infinite length, and consequently, being condemned to working with pieces of restricted lengths, we have to stick one piece of it on to another occasionally.
>
> The 'leftists' of montage saw it from the opposite extreme. While playing with pieces of film, they discovered a certain property in the toy which kept them astonished for a number of years. This property consisted in the fact *that two film pieces of any kind, placed together, inevitably combine into a new concept, a new quality, arising out of that juxtaposition.*
>
> This is not in the least a circumstance peculiar to the cinema, but is a phenomenon invariably met with in all cases where we have to deal with juxtaposition of two facts, two phenomena, two objects. We are accustomed to make, almost automatically, a definite and obvious deductive generalization when any separate objects are placed before us side by side. For example, take a grave, juxtaposed with a woman in mourning weeping beside it, and scarcely anybody will fail to jump to the conclusion: a widow. It is precisely on this feature of our perception that the following miniature story by Ambrose Bierce bases its effect. It is from his Fantastic Fables and is entitled "The Inconsolable Widow":
>
> > "A Woman in widow's weeds was weeping upon a grave.
> >
> > 'Console yourself, madame,' said a Sympathetic Stranger. 'Heaven's mercies are infinite. There is another man somewhere, besides your husband, with whom you can still be happy.'
> >
> > 'There was,' she sobbed—'there was, but this is his grave.'"[9]

---

[7] Sergei M. Eisenstein, *Film Form,* edited and translated by Jay Leyda (New York: Harcourt Brace, 1949), p. 48.

[8] Eisenstein, *Film Form,* p. 49.

[9] Sergei M. Eisenstein, *The Film Sense,* edited and translated by Jay Leyda (New York: Harcourt Brace, 1942), pp. 4–5.

It is neatly coincidental that Pudovkin referred to a coffin in the experiment with the actor Mozhukhin. Both Eisenstein and Pudovkin are suggesting how the meaning of an action can be changed into something other than the actual or original through associative montage. But Pudovkin's addition of a coffin merely makes the actor's face seem sad when it was not necessarily. The attraction of Bierce's anecdote for Eisenstein is clearly that the normal additive principle is replaced by a combination of the unexpected, opposites in a sense, and the "widow" becomes an adulteress.

Eisenstein's reference to an obscure piece of American literature to illustrate his conception, rather than a practical experiment with several pieces of film, represents fairly the difference between his critical method and that of Pudovkin. Eisenstein explored the arts of other cultures to show that montage as he understood it existed quite separately from film and had existed long before film appeared. His analyses of the shooting-script-like ordering of images found in passages from the poems of Pushkin and the novels of Dickens offer a contribution to literary criticism as well as provocative analogues for those studying film. For Eisenstein the form and sense of film aesthetic extended into a total philosophical view of the world. For Pudovkin the insights montage provided were carefully restricted to film technique and film acting.

In practice the argument between the two is happily muddled by some of the best examples of Eisensteinian shock montage appearing in films of Pudovkin and by Eisenstein necessarily having to resort to Pudovkinian narrative to hold together the brief pyrotechnical bursts of collision. Whether as linkage or juxtaposition, one result of this extreme fragmentation of the scene was that both film makers could use nonactors to a degree that more sustained takes would not allow. Any embarrassed self-consciousness could be stripped away and the usable moments selected and combined with other visual materials—like the actor Mozhukhin with soup, coffin, and child—to give the illusion of a performance that in fact never occurred. This new possibility led to theories of *typage,* of choosing people who looked the part regardless of their thespian skills.

Another characteristic of Soviet film technique was that the naturalistic materials of "real people" (as opposed to actors) and "actual locations" (in contrast to studio interiors or back lots) were subjected to an extreme degree of highly conscious manipulation through editing. Although the style is radically different from that of the Germans, in their own ways the Soviet films are just as stylized. Finally, in order to construct their intricate mosaics from small pieces of the total action, the Soviets—like the Germans and unlike Griffith—relied on highly detailed scripts and preplanning. Eisenstein sketched virtually all of his shots in advance; a substantial portion of Pudovkin's *Film Technique* is devoted to a method of precise script construction.

Unlike the films of any nation that had preceded them, however, all the Soviet films had social-political purposes and government sponsorship. Most of them interpreted the revolution in ways designed to improve the understanding and win the loyalty of the Soviet people. When *Battleship Potemkin* first went out into the world as a revolutionary emissary—feared and hated by reactionaries and philistines, elaborately praised by liberals and aesthetes—its success was as much a surprise to the Soviets as to anyone. That many of the Soviet silent films are universal and enduring works of art as well as being indoctrinational is a tribute to the sincere enthusiasm the film makers felt for the gigantic social experiment of which they were part.

Although the significance of this body of work in the history of film is enormous, specific applications of its themes and techniques, unlike those of the Germans, were limited in the capitalist countries. Soon the formal concerns and innovations of the left wing would become unacceptable in the Soviet Union itself. Perhaps the one clear and direct link between Soviet silent films and films elsewhere is with the British social documentaries of the 1930s, which were state supported for purposes of broad citizenship education and which indulged in their own experimentation with form—especially the joining of sound and image.

In the fictional film the arrival of sound largely reduced the use of montage to brief transitional sequences—of spinning locomotive wheels superimposed over a succession of billboards as the young opera star progresses toward fame and heartbreak, or of crowded beaches, golfers, and children eating watermelon to signal summer. To be sure, and for better or worse, every television commercial builds on the kinds of persuasiveness the Soviets discovered lay in the combination of short strips of film. But the body of Soviet silent cinema stands as a statement of the loftier purposes a theory of montage may serve.

Films of the Period

1925
Battleship Potemkin (*Bronenosets Potyomkin*) (Sergei Eisenstein)
Strike (*Stachka*) (Sergei Eisenstein)

1926
The Cloak (*Shinel*) (Grigori Kozintsev and Leonid Trauberg)
Mother (*Mat*) (V. I. Pudovkin)

1927
Bed and Sofa (*Tretya meshchanskaya*) (Abram Room)
The End of St. Petersburg (*Konets Sankt-Peterburga*) (V. I. Pudovkin)
The Fall of the Romanov Dynasty (*Padeniye dinastij Romanovykh*) (Esfir Shub)

1928
The Man with a Movie Camera (*Chelovek s kinoapparatom*) (Dziga Vertov)

October/Ten Days That Shook the World (*Oktyabr*) (Sergei Eisenstein)
Storm over Asia (*Potomok Chingis-Khana*) (V. I. Pudovkin)
Zvenigora (Alexander Dovzhenko)

1929
Arsenal (Alexander Dovzhenko)
Fragment of an Empire (*Oblomok imperij*) (Friedrich Ermler)
The New Babylon (*Novyj Vavilon*) (Grigori Kozintsev and Leonid Trauberg)
Old and New/The General Line (*Staroye inovoye*) (Sergei Eisenstein)
Turksib (Victor Turin)

1930
Earth (*Zemlya*) (Alexandra Dovzhenko)

Books on the Period

Attwood, Lynne, ed. *Red Women on the Silver Screen: Soviet Women and Cinema from the Beginning to the End of the Communist Era.* San Francisco: Pandora Press, 1993.

Shlapentokh, Dmitri, and Vladimir Shlapentokh. *Soviet Cinematography, 1918–1991: Ideological Conflict and Social Reality.* New York: Aldine de Gruyter, 1993.

5

Hollywood
in the Twenties

★ ★ ★ ★

1919–1929

Movies Become Big Business

The 1920s were characterized by intense competition among former independent companies that had become the new major studios. Old firms merged and disappeared; not one member of the Motion Picture Patents Company, with which the independents had competed between 1908 and 1915, survived.

In 1924 Metro-Goldwyn-Mayer was put together by Marcus Loew—president of Loew's, Inc., which had large theater holdings. Added to Metro Pictures Corporation (Loew's small production company) were the Goldwyn Picture Corporation and the Louis B. Mayer Pictures Corporation. Samuel Goldwyn had already left the Goldwyn Picture Corporation to become an independent producer; Mayer joined the newly created firm as studio head, beginning a reign that would last nearly thirty years. Also prominent were Universal (Carl Laemmle's outfit), Warner Brothers (Harry, Jack, Sam, and Albert), Paramount (which Adolph Zukor had brought along out of Famous Players-[Jesse] Lasky), Columbia (Jack and Harry Cohn), United Artists (Chaplin, Fairbanks, Pickford, Griffith), and the (William) Fox Film Corporation. The competition among these firms led to the need for increased capital, which was used to sign up stars, expand distribution and exhibition outlets, and buy out rivals. Public stock was issued, giving Wall Street a voice that would grow louder over the years.

The earlier economic battles had been fought largely in the field of production as the Motion Picture Patents Company trust attempted to stem the competition of the independents. During the first years after World War I, control of distribution was the major goal. National distribution became increasingly centralized and dominated by the major producing companies. The old "states' rights" franchise system, under which *The Birth of a Nation* and many of the first features had been distributed, faded away. For ultimate dom-

30,222 in Two Days!

Into this Paradise of luxury, color and enchantment they came, more than 30,000 in two days, Saturday and Sunday, thrilling with new excitement at every step! The spaciousness of the place! The superb height and dignity of the Grand Hall as they entered! The decoration and equipment throughout, so beautiful that work detail made people halt to admire it aloud! And then, a show worthy of the setting! These thousands are telling more thousands and they are all coming back, week after week, for there is nothing like the Paramount in all New York for sheer luxury and unprecedented entertainment values!

Continuous 10:45 A. M. to Closing. Popular Prices!

The Home of Paramount Pictures

Paramount THEATRE

Located in the Paramount Building, Times Square.

Advertisement for the opening of the Paramount Theatre, New York City, in 1926.

ination of the screen and long-term revenues, the struggle extended inevitably to ownership of the theaters themselves. There finally developed a pattern known as "vertical control," which lasted until it was outlawed by the federal courts in 1948. Under vertical control a few huge firms (eventually the roster became fixed at eight) produced, distributed, and exhibited their own films.

By the mid-1920s the fight for control of exhibition was being waged by three giants, which looked as if they might divide the whole pie, either forcing the other companies out or making them sit at table according to strict rules of etiquette. In 1919 Paramount had floated a $10 million issue of preferred stock, marking the beginning of the new phase. By 1921 that company was in virtual control of five hundred key theaters in the United States and first-run theaters in major cities around the world. By the end of the 1920s Adolph Zukor had built up the most formidable combination in the industry: Paramount had the stars, the production outfit, the distribution channels, and control of two thousand theaters.

First National, the next largest production-distribution firm, had been formed by a group of theater chains to get access to the product on their own terms. The third contestant was Loew's, Inc., the vast firm of which Metro-Goldwyn-Mayer, the production-distribution arm, was only one part. Within a few years nearly all the major and first-run houses in the United States and Canada had been acquired by Paramount, Loew's, or the large circuits affiliated with the First National group. Fox and Universal also had theater outlets, but on a lesser scale.

By 1927 some four hundred to five hundred feature films a year were being produced. Ideally, each of the large companies would release no fewer than fifty-two a year, permitting a weekly change of program for its own theaters. Distribution involved close to six hundred exchanges (that is, regional offices handling prints of the films) in forty-six key American cities. Approximately twenty thousand theaters in the country were attended by some eighty million customers a week. The center of return on investment and of ultimate control was where distribution and exhibition were headquartered: New York City, not Hollywood. Any would-be new independents were effectively kept out of this closed system. If they wanted to produce, the screens weren't available to them; if they wanted to exhibit, they couldn't get access to films.

The emphasis on exhibition made the 1920s the great decade of motion picture theater construction. The "movie palaces"—most of which have been torn down, divided into smaller theaters, or converted to other uses—stem from that era. The Capitol Theatre in New York

Rialto Theatre,
Joliet, Illinois.

City, for example, was built in 1919 and seated 5,300. *Photoplay* magazine wrote of it: "The mezzanine floor looks as if it had been designed for eight-day bicycle races." Grauman's Egyptian and Chinese Theatres in Hollywood along with large and ornate New York City theaters, including the fabled Roxy, were all part of this extraordinary architectural tradition.

If the appeal of the films didn't always measure up to their surroundings, at least the increasing expensiveness of production kept pace with the new lavishness of presentation. Extravagance reigned, and the notion of spending money to make money was unquestioningly accepted. Salaries soared for directors, writers, and especially stars. The epic *Birth of a Nation* had cost around $100,000 in 1915; *Ben-Hur* cost $6 million a decade later. By the end of the 1920s the average production expenditure on features was up to $200,000. The studios' steady incomes, however, came from the "program" or "B" pictures—unlike today, when television has taken over that kind of production, and theatrical features must offer something that seems special in order to attract an audience.

Ascendancy of the Director

With such expenditures, and attendant financial concern, by the mid-1920s the director had been replaced by the production supervisor as the person in charge of film making. The production supervisor made many of the artistic decisions as well as all of the business ones. Developing out of the pattern first established by Thomas Ince, this function was most brilliantly exercised by the legendary boy wonder at M-G-M: Irving Thalberg, model for the hero of F. Scott Fitzgerald's uncompleted novel *The Last Tycoon*. Sometimes called production chief, head of studio, or vice-president in charge of production, this executive oversaw a whole program of pictures, deciding which ideas or literary and dramatic "properties" were to be developed into scripts, then casting players and assigning directors. With the cost and complexity of sound, added at the end of the 1920s, the power of this position would become even more complete than in silent days. Film makers such as D. W. Griffith and Erich von Stroheim were temperamentally incapable of working within this system and eventually were discarded by it. Griffith directed two sound films; von Stroheim directed one. Directors mostly became "glorified foremen" and, with assembly-line specialization, were as much typecast as were the players. There were directors of westerns, comedies, romances, and so on, with second-rank directors hired to imitate the work of first-rank ones. Nonetheless, certain directors stand out as having battled for control over their work and their image. Griffith played a pivotal role in this struggle. Through a variety of strategies—from placing his initials on all of the intertitles of his films, to taking advertisements in newspapers that trumpeted his achievements, to creating his own studio—Griffith devoted himself to the tasks of imposing his vision on his movies and his name on the lips of the moviegoing public.

Another dominating figure, **Cecil B. DeMille,** has often been disregarded or disapproved of by critics and historians on grounds that his films are generally superficial and frequently meretricious, that they add nothing to film art. In recent years, a reevaluation has occurred in some quarters, based on the visual (as opposed to intellectual) merits of his films. In either case, no one can deny their enormous success. Unparalleled as a showman, publicist, and businessman, DeMille also had a unique ability to move with the times. Although the artist in him may have been uncertain, the social psychologist was uncannily accurate in his intuitions. By examining DeMille's invariably successful pictures, today's social historians can infer much about the cultural climate of the American 1920s. To some extent those films may have affected that climate.

DeMille's father and mother were of the theater; his brother was the playwright William C. DeMille. Cecil himself had been associated with David Belasco, the "Dean of the American Stage." DeMille's initial film effort, *The Squaw Man* (1914), was one of the earliest features and among the first films to be made in Hollywood; it established at the outset his ability to anticipate trends in the industry. From 1915 to 1924 he turned out a rapid succession of widely popular films aimed at middle-class audiences and reflecting postwar changes in manners and morals, the best of which is probably *The Cheat*. Released in 1915, *The Cheat* tells the story of society matron Edith Hardy and her relationship with an Asian man named Tori (a role subtly performed by the acclaimed Japanese actor Sessue Hayakawa). Despite Hayakawa's nuanced and underplayed performance, however, the movie's unsympathetic portrayal of his character led to protests by the Japanese American community; as a result, Tori's nationality was changed to Burmese.

In addition to its controversial treatment of ethnicity, *The Cheat* is notable for its influential technical innovations in editing and lighting. DeMille pioneered a subjective editing style in a scene between Edith and her husband, Richard, by crosscutting between Edith and Tori, who, although miles away, dominates her thoughts as she converses with

The Cheat ★ United States, 1915, Cecil B. DeMille; Sessue Hayakawa and Fannie Ward.

her husband. In addition, working with his talented art director, Wilfred Buckland, DeMille employed a distinctive lighting style in *The Cheat,* which is also featured in other films he directed in these early years. Widely known at the time as *Rembrandt lighting* or *Lasky lighting* (after the name of DeMille's studio), this technique, like Rembrandt's paintings, features large areas of shadow punctuated by brightly illuminated points of dramatic interest. In scenes that feature this style, most of the frame remains dark while intense spotlights highlight the main actors and their immediate surroundings. A striking example of this lighting technique occurs in the scene in *The Cheat* in which Edith shoots her lover. As Tori collapses against a vividly lit Japanese screen, we watch from the other side as his blood smears the screen; meanwhile the rest of the frame is shrouded in darkness.

As the titles of some of DeMille's other productions suggest, this was indeed the roaring twenties: *Old Wives for New* (1918); *Don't Change Your Husband, For Better or Worse, Male and Female* (all 1919); *Why Change Your Wife? Something to Think About* (both 1920); *Forbidden Fruit, The Affairs of Anatol, Fool's Paradise* (all 1921); *Saturday Night, Manslaughter* (both 1922); and *Adam's Rib* (1923). These were promoted as "typical DeMille productions—audacious, glittering, intriguing, superlatively elegant and quite without heart." Following these essays on contemporary mores (they were called the "divorce comedies"), a shift began to occur in DeMille's preoccupations. *The Ten Commandments* (1923) had a long Biblical prologue to a modern story, and *The King of Kings* (1927)

The King of Kings ★ United States, 1927, Cecil B. DeMille; H. B. Warner, as Christ.

was the first full work of the kind with which his name would subsequently become associated: religiosity along with sex and spectacle.

If DeMille's films of the 1920s were largely trivial in content, they had considerable influence on the craft of motion picture making and on the popular culture of the United States at large. Although he made movies that were "production-conscious" (he was painstaking with details—clothes, makeup, lighting, properties, and sets), he also offered styles of interior decoration and clothing fashions for imitation. He is often given credit for inaugurating the tendency of American bathrooms to aspire to the sumptuousness of throne rooms. Theatrical in his direction, he rarely used camera or cutting obtrusively, except for "special effects." His historical spectacles are like a series of separate illustrations brought to life. The performances tend to be stiff, broad, and simple.

It must be conceded, however, that DeMille is one of a very few directors who have gotten their names onto marquees. People went to see a "DeMille picture." He achieved this star status partly from the size and dazzle of his productions, but also from a vigorous publicizing of his own personality. It is to DeMille that we owe the assumption that you could tell a motion picture director by his open-neck shirt, jodphurs, boots, and megaphone. Also, people went partly out of curiosity to see what all the other people were seeing. The consistency of DeMille's box-office record remains remarkable: Not one of his films lost money. When DeMille died, the prop Ten Commandments tablet used in his second film of that title was placed on a kind of altar under his lighted portrait in the Paramount commissary. The color of the tablet was gold.

Erich von Stroheim resembled DeMille in flamboyance, meticulousness with details, and extravagance. But von Stroheim could not put those qualities to consistent commercial use. The iron will, artistic integrity, and rebelliousness for which he is respected by those who admire his films kept him from seeking out what the public wanted. Instead, he gave audiences the world as he saw it—in a style notable for scathing naturalism laced with irony—in place of the usual coating of reality covering a sentimental center.

Of the eight films von Stroheim made between 1918 and the end of his directorial career in 1928, *Greed* (1925) is unquestionably the masterpiece. It remains one of the most impressive films in the total history of the screen. The legend surrounding it contains omens pointing toward the end of his career as a director and his subsequent canonization: its staggering cost; its length of forty-five reels (over seven hours) cut to a conventional ten; von Stroheim's disavowal of the released version; and the power that remains in spite of the mutilation. Controversy about the film can still be heard, and there are still unshakable hopes and occasional rumors that a copy of the complete version may somehow have survived.

Today most would agree that a handful of his films (*Foolish Wives,* 1922; *The Merry Widow,* 1925; *The Wedding March,* 1928; and *Greed*) are original and extraordinary, powerful in a way and to a degree unlike anyone else's work. His camera-editing style rested on the long take/long shot not much in vogue during the ascendancy of montage, with its stress on fast cutting and closeups. The sort of spatial-temporal coherence and realism represented by von Stroheim's style would later become a dominant aesthetic tendency.

The mirror von Stroheim held up to nature not only reflected warts and all, it emphasized the warts—the venality, selfishness, and perversity present in most of us. Sexuality is usually interwoven with money, station, or power in an uncompromisingly un-

Greed ★ United States, 1925, Erich von Stroheim; Zasu Pitts and Gibson Gowland, center.

palatable view of life. Decadence and depravity are ubiquitous. In *Foolish Wives,* "Count" Wladislas Karamzin, played by Stroheim—"the man you love to hate"—evidently makes his way in the world through sexual enterprises based on seduction, blackmail, and the like. Although he seems to be involved with five women, there is no suggestion of love in any of these relationships. This character, whom von Stroheim had created in his first film, *Blind Husbands* (1919), appears in intermittent variation throughout his work—including his last released film, *Queen Kelly* (1928). Although he doesn't appear in *Greed,* the consistent point is made most explicit as a romantic attachment gradually deteriorates into a single-minded pursuit of gold.

For the audacity of his themes, as well as for his arrogance and financial disinterest, von Stroheim was denied access to the tools of his art. His directorial career ended about the same time as that of D. W. Griffith, for whom he had first worked in film. The last decades of von Stroheim's life, like Griffith's, were spent in semiretirement outside the film industry.

Unlilke Griffith and von Stroheim, **Ernst Lubitsch** adapted well to the changing realities of the Hollywood industry, becoming at one point head of production at the mammoth Paramount Studio. Lubitsch succeeded, in part, by attaching himself to tried-

The Marriage Circle ★
United States, 1924, Ernst
Lubitsch; Adolphe Menjou
and Marie Prevost.

and-true genres. His German films made within the romantic-historical tradition (*Passion/Madame du Barry* and *Deception/Anna Boleyn*) were discussed in Chapter 3. They were very popular in the United States and Lubitsch followed them here in 1922. But neither those films nor his earlier training as an actor in Max Reinhardt's company foreshadowed the kind of film Lubitsch would turn to and make peculiarly his own. After studying contemporary American production, Lubitsch moved into comedy and light drama of the sort DeMille was making so successfully. Before the end of the decade he had outstripped DeMille, in quality at least, while DeMille had moved to spectacles not unlike those Lubitsch had made earlier. But he is most amazing for his command of the medium: the subtlety and flexibility with which he was able to use silent film to communicate nuances of a situation, and later his experimental leadership in sound.

Though differences of style and outlook mask the similarities, the films of Lubitsch are like those of von Stroheim in one important respect: They are about sex and money. To increase his freedom for comment, and to add a bit of glamor and suavity, Lubitsch, like von Stroheim, tended to set his plots against European backgrounds. But in Lubitsch's films, sexual intrigue is merely frivolity engaged in by the wealthy to occupy their leisure time. With few exceptions his American pictures are comedies of manners, peopled entirely with the well-bred, urbane upper classes. He delineates their fads and foibles with a Viennese charm and worldliness that made them seem novel, fascinating, and a bit naughty to American audiences. His sophisticated humor came to be well known as "the Lubitsch touch." Of his American silent films, *The Marriage Circle*, *Forbidden Paradise* (both 1924), and *Lady Windermere's Fan* (1925) have best retained their charm.

Popular Genres

Perhaps more than the business acumen of the moguls or the technical resources of the big studios, more than the attractiveness of the stars and the skills of the directors, it is the popular genres that have most typified American film and given it its greatest strength and vitality. Until fairly recently, critics tended to discount or ignore the importance of genres. A case could be made, however, that the conventions of genre—fixed yet capable of infinite variation—have supported and given strength to the work of many of the finest American scriptwriters and directors (as Shakespeare, in Elizabethan England, had built on the conventional revenge tragedy introduced by Thomas Kyd). At the same time it must be acknowledged that genres bear a complex relation to the society that produces them, expressing the dreams, anxieties, and ambivalences of a given era.

During the 1920s all the major types of American film were present except, of course, the musical, which required sound. The **western** embodied some of the United States's most resonant national myths: the conception of land as private property and the rationalization of the conquest of indigenous peoples by the European settlers. The genre started at least with *The Great Train Robbery* (1903) and matured most notably in the films produced by Thomas Ince and starring William S. Hart (for example, *The Gun Fighter* and *The Aryan,* both 1916). In the 1920s the epic western was added to the line: *The Last of the Mohicans* (1921), directed by Maurice Tourneur; *The Covered Wagon* (1923), directed by James Cruze; and *The Iron Horse* (1924), directed by John Ford. Hart continued to work until 1925 (*Tumbleweeds* was his last and probably finest film) and was succeeded in popularity by Tom Mix, Buck Jones, Tim McCoy, Hoot Gibson, Ken Maynard, and some lesser stars.

When the **comedy** genre moved from one- and two-reelers to include features, the 1920s became "Comedy's Greatest Era," as James Agee called it in a famous essay on the subject. The wonderful clowns—Charles Chaplin, Buster Keaton, Harold Lloyd, and Harry Langdon—created their masterworks during that decade. They confirmed and advanced the early discoveries and pioneering insights of Mack Sennett, making silent film comedy an art form offering timeless and universal pleasure.

The Covered Wagon ★ United States, 1923, James Cruze.

The General ★ United States, 1927, Buster Keaton; Keaton.

The features included Chaplin's *The Kid* (1921) and *The Gold Rush* (1925), Keaton's *The Navigator* (1924) and *The General* (1927), Lloyd's *Safety Last* (1923) and *The Freshman* (1925), and Langdon's *The Strong Man* and *Tramp, Tramp, Tramp* (both 1926). Along with the continuing shorts of Stan Laurel and Oliver Hardy, and others, these films gave American screen comedy an impetus that carried it through the 1940s and perhaps beyond.

If we include the work of Danny Kaye, Red Skelton, Jerry Lewis, Woody Allen, and Mel Brooks within that tradition, and maybe of Dan Ackroyd and Bill Murray as well, the influence of the comedies of the 1920s has extended to the present. Although the introduction of sound required extreme modifications of style and introduced a new group of comics, the comedy, along with the western, the gangster film, and the musical, remains among the most distinctive, indigenous, and important American contributions to film forms.

The **"problem picture,"** dealing with social and moral concerns, had appeared among the first story films shortly after the turn of the twentieth century (for example, *The Ex-Convict,* 1905, and *The Eviction,* 1907). This has always been a significant genre and includes some of this nation's most substantial work. Often the problem pictures look at society from the vantage point of a new generation and deal with the alarms and discomforts caused by social change. A number of films attacked Bolshevism at home and abroad, revealing American uneasiness over the successful Soviet revolution. Other films dealt with strikes, usually portraying them as resulting from misunderstanding between management and labor, rarely acknowledging real economic causes. Director Lois Weber, working in collaboration with her scriptwriter husband, Phillips Smalley, created a number of noteworthy problem pictures during the 1910s and early 1920s, including *Where Are My Children* (1916), which deals with birth control; *The People vs. John Doe* (1916), on capital punishment; *The Blot* (1921), about the genteel poverty of college professors; and *A Chapter in Her Life* (1923), on Christian Scientism.

The overwhelming preponderance of "problems" considered in films of this genre had to do with morals and mores: the changing conception of marriage (*Wine of Youth,* 1924; *Trial Marriage,* 1929); women's increased independence (*Daring Youth, For Ladies Only,* both 1927); youthful rebellion (*Flaming Youth,* 1923; *Our Dancing Daughters,* 1928); promiscuity (*Husbands for Rent,* 1927; *Breakfast at Sunrise,* 1927); bootleg debauchery (*The House of Youth,* 1924; *The Mad Whirl,* 1925), and similar subjects. From the attempts of DeMille and others to treat the "jazz age," postwar morality, and the "modern generation" of the 1920s, there runs a more or less straight line to the Depression films of the 1930s.

In spite of a remark attributed to Samuel Goldwyn—"If you got a message, send it by Western Union"—the problem picture has been remarkably persistent in an industry presumably devoted to "escapist entertainment." This means, of course, that the problem

The Blot ★ United States, 1921, Lois Weber; Claire Windsor.

The Crowd ★ United States, 1928, King Vidor; Eleanor Boardman and James Murray.

picture has been good box office. Self-criticism and exposé form a strong thread that extends through American history beginning before Tom Paine and continuing past the "yellow journalism" of the 1920s to Sunday night's *60 Minutes* on CBS. Films in this tradition—even if frequently exploiting as well as examining problems—have remained significant in reflecting and changing an awareness of our culture.

War dramas were common before the 1920s but had only the old-fashioned wars for subjects and treated those from a historical perspective. Moviegoers of the 1920s had recently been through a world war, and the experience was influential to most of them. Although films about the war had been made during it, the "war is hell" prototypes were first offered in King Vidor's *The Big Parade* (1925) and Raoul Walsh's *What Price Glory?* (1926). A subspecies of the war dramas of the 1920s was the air-war cycle, including *The Lone Eagle* and *Wings* (both 1927); *The Legion of the Condemned* (1928); and *Lilac Time* (1928). The latter group suggest the impossibility of making an *anti*-war film—at least along standard lines. The ultimate drama of war cannot be denied: life and death, bravery and fear, selflessness and leadership, comradeship and love; they are present even within the impersonal slaughter of modern warfare. War may be hell; but on film, war has always been highly dramatic.

Action and adventure—a category, if not exactly a genre—takes various forms, most of which appeared in the 1920s. Often the action-adventure films deal with a chase and pursuit, or with survival in some distant and colorful locale. There are adventures on the sea, under water, in the jungle (*Tarzan of the Apes* began the Tarzan series in 1918), in

The Big Parade ☆ United
States, 1925, King Vidor;
Renée Adorée, with her arm
about John Gilbert.

the mountains, in the desert, and in polar regions. Documentaries and semidocumentaries of the period appealed more factually to the same sort of interest—*Nanook of the North* (1922), *Grass* (1925), *Moana* (1926), and *Chang* (1927). Another kind of action-adventure of the 1920s (and 1930s) was the animal picture, with animal stars; Rin-Tin-Tin and Rex, "King of the Wild Horses," were successful enough to have their imitators. The actress Nell Shipman also produced, directed, and starred in a number of animal pictures during this era, including *Baree, Son of Kazan* (1917) and *Back to God's Country* (1919).

If you think of action-adventure films of the 1920s, you might think first of the kind in which Douglas Fairbanks excelled. A star of considerable magnitude, his obvious attractions were a marvelous body, dazzling smile, acrobatic grace, and an ingeniously intricate way of moving about the world by scaling walls, sliding down draperies, leaping from roof to balcony and balcony to roof, and swinging on chandeliers. Those qualities and abilities, together with his enormous good cheer and easy superiority to the normal nagging concerns of the modern world, guaranteed the popular success of his films—*The Mark of Zorro* (1920), *The Three Musketeers* (1921), *Robin Hood* (1922), *The Thief of Bagdad* (1924), *The Black Pirate* (1926), and others. As the titles of the Fairbanks films suggest, their action and adventure were usually set in a past time as well as a distant place; the improbable could be given freest reign in exotic settings.

Another kind of historical film featured more **spectacle** than derring-do. *The Execution of Mary Queen of Scots* (1895) was the first of these, and it was Griffith who reached a level of spectacle—in *Intolerance* (1916)—that in some respects has never been equalled. DeMille, admitting his indebtedness to Griffith, took over the historical/Biblical extrava-

Robin Hood ★ United States, 1922, Alan Dwan; Douglas Fairbanks, second from left.

Ben-Hur ★ United States, 1926, Fred Niblo.

ganza with *The Ten Commandments* (1923) and *The King of Kings* (1927), and intermittently pursued his own special form of it until his last film, the second *Ten Commandments* (1956). Other especially noteworthy historical/religious spectacles of the 1920s were Griffith's *Orphans of the Storm* (1921), about the French Revolution, and Fred Niblo's *Ben-Hur* (1926). *Variety*'s annual listing of all-time box-office champions has a preponderance of the spectacular in its upper echelons.

Finally, the period saw the flourishing of what have come to be known as **race movies.** Galvanized by their outrage at the depiction of black characters in *The Birth of a Nation*, African American entrepreneurs and film makers set out to create an alternative cinematic tradition, producing *Birth of a Race* in 1919 in response to Griffith's controversial epic. At the same time companies such as the Colored Players in Philadelphia and the Lincoln Motion Picture Company in Los Angeles released a series of films for African American audiences, including *The Trouper of Troup K* (1916) and *Scar of Shame* (1926). The most notable creator of these movies was Oscar Micheaux, who often worked as his own distributor and exhibitor as well as functioning as a writer, producer, and director, driving prints of his films from town to town to show them in local venues. Two of his most widely admired productions are *Within Our Gates* (1920), a shocking story of incest, miscegenation, and attempted rape, featuring a climactic lynching sequence, and *Body and Soul* (1925), in which the distinguished actor Paul Robeson stars as an ex-convict posing as a clergyman.

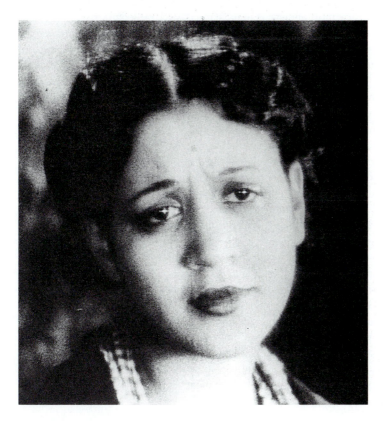

Scar of Shame ★ United States, 1927, Frank Peregini; Lucia Lynn Moses.

Within Our Gates ★ United States, 1920, Oscar Micheaux; William Stark and Ralph Johnson.

Sound Arrives

The phrase *silent cinema* implies an absence of sound, but this was not the way in which movies were experienced by most audiences in the early days. Live lecturers often spoke to those who attended showings of actuality films and travelogues as the visuals unrolled. In Japan, commentators called *benshi,* who narrated the action and spoke the dialogue, were an integral part of the pleasure of moviegoing; and in Brazil, a popular form known as *fitas can-tatas* involved filmed stage musicals lip-synched in theaters. In other cases, sound effects were created during projection. In addition, most early films were screened as music played. Such music took many forms, from pianola rolls to elaborate symphonic scores performed by full orchestras and choirs. In certain cases well-known composers created movie scores—for example, Saint-Saëns for *L'Assassinat du Duc de Guise* in 1908 and Shostakovich for *New Babylon* in 1929. The most common practice, however, was to have a pianist or organist draw on stock melodies and leitmotifs from standard cue sheets to improvise moods in keeping with the movie being screened. However, musicians using this method could not always be relied on to create an appropriate background for a given film, either because they lacked the requisite skill or because they were unacquainted with the movie until after the first showing. In some instances musicians simply chose to disregard the film entirely in favor of their own conception of what would make a suitable evening's entertainment. For example, an early reviewer writing in *The Chicago Defender* complained that a jazz band accompanying a movie presentation on the city's near south side played "Here Comes Charlie!" an up-tempo blues number, as a funeral scene was unfolding on the screen.

Sound accompaniments like these added a vital dimension to the moviegoing experience, but sound created in the theater rather than in the studio remained fundamentally separate from the film itself. From 1910 onward studios exercised increasing control over the sound accompaniments theater owners could add to their productions. However, the challenge of marrying sound and image in a permanent, predictable way remained unfulfilled for many years.

As with most technological innovations in film, synchronized sound was experimented with from the beginning. In fact, Edison seems initially to have conceived of the motion picture as illustration to go with his highly successful cylindrical phonograph—so that those purchasing the sound machines would have something to look at while they listened. W. K. L. Dickson, Edison's talented assistant (and the man most responsible for the development of motion picture equipment at the West Orange, New Jersey, laboratory), had joined sound to image prior to the first Lumière showings. A film made by Dickson shows a pair of Edison technicians dancing in eerie slow motion to a violinist, supposedly Dickson himself, playing into a huge phonograph horn. The further problem of amplifying sound sufficiently to fill a theater had been solved by 1914, primarily by Lee de Forest's invention of the silenium, or vacuum, tube which allowed for a "loud speaker" (audio amplifier).

Like the later additions of color, wide screen, and 3-D, it took strong economic motivation to bring on sound. In 1924 and 1925 the comparatively small production firm of Warner Bros., which owned no theater chains, was competing against the large companies that controlled distribution and exhibition. According to the Warners' account, accepted by earlier film historians, they decided in desperation to try the novelty of sound to see if it would help them out of their financial difficulties. Another, more credible and thoroughly documented explanation is offered in Robert C. Allen and Douglas Gomery, *Film History: Theory and Practice* (New York: Alfred A. Knopf, 1985, pp. 115–124). According to this version, Wall Street interests looking for a favorable opportunity for investment in the motion picture industry chose Warner Bros. Although a small firm, it was tightly managed and well run financially. The infusion of new capital permitted competitive expansion along a number of lines, one of them being experimentation with sound.

For whatever reason, Warner Bros. added a sound track to a silent feature entitled *Don Juan,* starring John Barrymore, and released it in August 1926. Their Vitaphone system, as they called it, having acquired the Vitagraph company in 1925, used disc recordings mechanically synchronized with the projector. In the case of *Don Juan* the track consisted of a symphonic score plus some sound effects—especially the clanging of swords in the dueling scenes. To the feature they attached a few shorts of distinguished musicians in performance, including violinist Mischa Elman and Metropolitan Opera stars Giovanni Martinelli and Marion Talley.

Leading off this program was a short in which Will Hays appeared. Former Postmaster General and national chairman of the Republican Party, Hays had become president of the Motion Picture Producers and Distributors of America. This trade organization of the major studios (today called the Motion Picture Association of America) had come into being mainly as an attempt by the industry to protect itself—through public relations—from threats of censorship being provoked by the new frankness of the postwar films. Mr. Hays welcomed the public to the epochal event presented by the Warner brothers and predicted a glorious future for the motion picture accompanied by recorded sound.

Although the opening night audience was enthusiastic enough, the success of Vitaphone was limited because of the few theaters equipped for it. It was not altogether clear that *Don Juan* with Vitaphone was making more money than it would have without recorded sound. Two other programs of shorts and features with synchronized musical scores released in the following year met with only moderate success. The Warners had gambled so much on the innovation, however, that they couldn't consider abandoning it.

With the exception of William Fox, who had begun experimenting with his own sound system, the rest of the producers were annoyed with the Warners for rocking the industrial boat. Box office was down slightly and competition from the new sound entertainment of radio seemed one possible cause, but it was by no means certain that the addition of recorded sound to movies would bring larger audiences into the theaters.

The other studios held back because of general uncertainty and for several specific reasons. First, the expense of changing equipment and facilities for production and, especially, for exhibition (in the eighty thousand theaters throughout the world) loomed as ominous as the national debt. Second, the studios didn't relish paying royalties to Warner Bros. or Fox for use of their patented sound systems, and losing face to a competitor. Third, it was possible that sound might change production technique radically, and no one was yet trained to make sound features. Fourth, there was the backlog of silent films and others in production that might have to be written off as complete losses if they didn't conform to the new technology. Fifth, if the movies ever began to talk (a prospect only vaguely foreseen), the long-term contracts with silent stars, foreign stars, and directors might prove frozen assets if those individuals couldn't adapt themselves to the altered medium or to the English language. Finally, if the marvelous esperanto of the silent film were sacrificed, audiences abroad would be curtailed: Whereas titles could easily and inexpensively be translated and reshot, what could the Hungarians, for example, make out of conversations in English? The industry continued to watch and wait.

For their fourth Vitaphone feature the Warners chose a popular musical play, *The Jazz Singer*, which had starred George Jessel on the Broadway stage. When they approached Jessel to repeat his performance for the film, negotiations broke down over the amount of money he asked. As it turned out, the enormously popular Al Jolson was hired for twice as much and insisted that his salary be in cash. Although the film's sound was thought of principally in terms of Jolson's six numbers (concluding with his theme song, "Mammy"), two of his four sound scenes contain a little dialogue that seems scarcely to have been planned. In one scene, after finishing a song in a nightclub, Jolson utters the words that had become his trademark on Broadway: "Wait a minute! Wait a minute! You ain't heard nothin' yet." In this context the expression became unexpectedly prophetic. In the second scene, a bit of dialogue leading up to and intervening between two renditions of "Blue Skies" is certainly unscripted. It consists of Jolson joshing his little old screen mother, who is obviously embarrassed and can't think of a thing to say. It's almost as if the conversation had been recorded accidentally, or as a kind of test, and only afterwards did the Warners decide to include it. Whatever the intent, the response of the moviegoing public was emphatic.

There are something like 354 words of dialogue in *The Jazz Singer*, but it was clearly those spoken words more than the songs that had audiences queuing up four-deep around the block of the Warner Theatre. The comparative indifference to the sound in *Don Juan* had apparently occurred because it consisted solely of recorded music plus a few sound effects in place of the usual live orchestra, organ, or piano to which audiences were accustomed. With the ensuing success of *The Jazz Singer*, the "talkie" was born, and a new dramatic dimension in the spoken word was suggested. Except for songs and fragments of dialogue, however, *The Jazz Singer* looks and sounds like the standard silent film of the time, with a recorded orchestral score (making heavy use of Tschaikowsky's *Romeo and Juliet* overture) and with printed intertitles carrying the bulk of the verbal communication.

The Jazz Singer ★ United States, 1927, Alan Crosland; Al Jolson and Eugenie Besserer.

On the basis of *The Jazz Singer*'s success, the Warners extended what looks as if it had been intended as a two-reel short into a seven-reel feature. Entitled *The Lights of New York* and released in July 1928, it became the first "100 percent talkie." It begins with a prologue, which transports the young hero from "Main Street" to "Broadway." There he and his sidekick get mixed up with a couple of con men, and with a gang of bootleggers who use their barbershop as a front. The film contains what is surely the longest exposition in history; in fact, it is all exposition. The characters talk about what has happened, will happen, should happen, and might happen; very little except conversation does happen on the screen.

We can feel a kind of morbid fascination in watching the limitations sound imposed at first on the brilliance of the best silent films. Everything is static, all is talk. The flexible fluency of the mature silent film is reduced to a jabbering infancy. (The M-G-M musical *Singin' in the Rain,* 1952, provides a marvelously enjoyable account of the pains of this transition; it is funny because it is so true.) Although we can relish *The Lights of New York*'s authentic "roaring twenties" flavor, it is impossible not to notice how much more dated it seems than many of its silent contemporaries (such as *The Crowd, The Wind,* or *The Last Command,* also released in 1928). Speech is more firmly rooted in the particularities of time and place than is image.

The Lights of New York ⋆
United States, 1928, Brian
Foy; Cullen Landis and
Helene Costello.

At first, some observers thought sound merely a fad, one that would pass away once audiences got over their fascination with lips moving and voices seeming to come from them. Others felt that the talkies might coexist with the silents, the one appealing to the rubes who liked the yackety novelty, the other for the more sensitive and intelligent. Whatever view was taken, the lines at the box office dictated that the rest of the industry could no longer afford to ignore the Warners' unsettling contribution.

By the close of the 1920s there was no doubt that the synchronous sound film would be the universal form of the future. At the end of 1928 Hollywood had only 16 recording machines in use; by the end of 1929 there were 116, and almost half the more than twenty thousand theaters in the United States were equipped for sound reproduction. The consensus was that a sound system using optical patterns along the edge of the film (Fox Movietone), rather than discs (Warner Vitaphone), would provide more reliable synchronization. In 1931, in order to achieve standardization, the patents on the various sound systems held by most of the major studios and others were pooled and divided between Western Electric and Radio Corporation of America (RCA). The sound systems of those two firms became the only ones in use.

As the industry borrowed money to retool, the financial center of gravity, which had gradually moved eastward with the expansion of exhibition and the mergers, now rested firmly in the big banks of New York City and Boston. Among the major studios, there were shifts in power (Warner up, having absorbed First National; Paramount down) and new alignments (RKO and Twentieth Century-Fox). Incidentally the *R* in RKO stands for Radio Corporation of America, which had become involved in motion pictures because of sound;

the *K* and *O,* for the Keith-Orpheum theater circuit, which stemmed from the days when vaudeville was still competing with film for popular audiences. As for the Fox (William) in Twentieth Century-Fox, he was forced out of his firm by the new large financial interests. He then commissioned a socialist author to expose the evils of capitalism, as he had experienced them, in the book *Upton Sinclair Presents William Fox.*

In general, Hollywood turned to Broadway for people who had had experience with spoken words. For awhile, the Twentieth-Century Limited pulling out of New York City headed west with a load of actors, writers, and voice coaches. The silent directors were joined by a new crop who would carve their careers out of the possibilities opened up by sound; George Cukor, Leo McCarey, Rouben Mamoulian, Busby Berkeley, John Cromwell, and Tay Garnett all began to direct films in the first years of sound.

Three technical problems were solved during the early 1930s, allowing the sound film to return to the movement of the silent film, reducing the dependence on dialogue, and regaining the visual richness. The first of these problems was to find a means of removing the camera from its soundproof booth. For that purpose a "blimp" was constructed: a metal cover filled with acoustic insulation that encased the camera. As heavy and large as the blimped cameras were, they still could be moved about quite freely on dolly and crane.

The second problem was to free the actors so they could move about without regard to the stationary microphones. Lionel Barrymore, who directed as well as acted in those days, claimed credit for solving this difficulty. As an actor he no doubt felt the performer's frustration in being rooted to one spot; he insisted, against technicians' protests, that a mike be swung overhead from a fishpole and moved around to follow the actors. The directional

Hallelujah! ★ United States, 1929, King Vidor; Harry Gray and Fannie B. DeKnight, as Parson and Mammy.

boom microphone, able to capture sounds from overhead while remaining out of frame, completely replaced the nondirectional fixed microphones that had been hidden about the set.

The blimped camera and boom microphone permitted more dynamic studio shooting, but they did not help the camera get outside the sound stages into the world of unwanted noises, bad acoustic conditions, and wind roaring in the microphone. *In Old Arizona* (1929), codirected by Raoul Walsh and Irving Cummings, was the first sound feature known to be recorded principally out-of-doors. "Location shooting" was made fully possible when sound technology advanced sufficiently so that sight and sound did not have to be recorded at the same time: Footage could be shot silent; sound could be recorded separately, then added to the images. Noteworthy early experiments included King Vidor's *Hallelujah!* (1929). In a frightening chase scene at night in a swamp, snapping twigs, splashing water, and the heavy breathing of the actors are the principal sounds. The battle scenes of Lewis Milestone's *All Quiet on the Western Front* (1930) were shot with the sort of tracking camera movement and rapid cutting that marked the best silent work. The addition of rattling machine gun fire, the detonation of high explosives, and the screams of dying men made the images even more horrifying.

Since it was to the United States that sound first came, the Americans were the first and the most prolific (given their output of four to five hundred feature films per year) in their successes and mistakes. Their work will be surveyed in a subsequent chapter on Hollywood in the 1930s and early 1940s. By the mid-1930s the "100 percent all talking," "canned theater" had been largely transcended and the mature sound film achieved.

Films of the Period

1920
The Last of the Mohicans (Maurice Toumeur and
    Clarence Brown)
The Mark of Zorro (Fred Niblo)
Way Down East (David Wark Griffith)
Within Our Gates (Oscar Micheaux)

1921
The Blot (Lois Weber)
The Four Horsemen of the Apocalypse (Rex
    Ingram)
The Kid (Charles Chaplin)
Orphans of the Storm (David Wark Griffith)
Tol'able David (Henry King)

1922
Foolish Wives (Erich von Stroheim)
Nanook of the North (Robert Flaherty)
Robin Hood (Allan Dwan)

1923
The Covered Wagon (James Cruze)
Safety Last (Harold Lloyd)
The Ten Commandments (Cecil B. DeMille)
A Woman of Paris (Charles Chaplin)

1924
The Iron Horse (John Ford)
The Marriage Circle (Ernst Lubitsch)
The Navigator (Buster Keaton)
Sherlock Junior (Buster Keaton)
The Thief of Bagdad (Raoul Walsh)

1925
The Big Parade (King Vidor)
Body and Soul (Oscar Micheaux)
The Freshman (Harold Lloyd)
The Gold Rush (Charles Chaplin)
Greed (Erich von Stroheim)

Lady Windermere's Fan (Ernst Lubitsch)
The Phantom of the Opera (Rupert Julian)

1926
Ben-Hur (Fred Niblo)
Moana (Robert Flaherty)
The Scarlet Letter (Victor Sjöström/Seastrom)
What Price Glory? (Raoul Walsh)

1927
The General (Buster Keaton)
Hotel Imperial (Mauritz Stiller)
The Jazz Singer (Alan Crosland)
The King of Kings (Cecil B. DeMille)
Seventh Heaven (Frank Borzage)
Sunrise (F. W. Murnau)

Underworld (Josef von Sternberg)
Wings (William Wellman)

1928
The Crowd (King Vidor)
The Docks of New York (Josef von Sternberg)
The Last Command (Josef von Sternberg)
The Lights of New York (Bryan Foy)
Steamboat Willie (Walt Disney)
The Wind (Victor Sjöström/Seastrom)

1929
Applause (Rouben Mamoulian)
Hallelujah! (King Vidor)
The Love Parade (Ernst Lubitsch)

Books on the Period

Brewster, Ben, and Lea Jacobs. *Theatre to Cinema: Stage Pictorialism and the Early Feature Film.* New York: Oxford University Press, 1998.

Brown, Gene. *Movie Time: A Chronology of Hollywood and the Movie Industry from Its Beginnings to the Present.* New York: Macmillan, 1995.

Browne, Nick, ed. *Refiguring American Film Genres: History and Theory.* Berkeley: University of California Press, 1997.

Couvares, Francis G., ed. *Movie Censorship and American Culture* ("Studies in the History of Film and Television"). Washington, DC: Smithsonian Institution Press, 1996.

Cripps, Thomas. *Hollywood's High Noon: Moviemaking and Society Before Television* ("The American Moment Series"). Baltimore, MD: Johns Hopkins University Press, 1996.

Cripps, Thomas. *Slow Fade to Black: The Negro in American Film, 1900–1942.* New York: Oxford University Press, 1993.

Davis, Ronald L. *The Glamour Factory: Inside Hollywood's Big Studio System.* Dallas, TX: Southern Methodist University Press, 1993.

De Bauche, Leslie Midkiff. *Reel Patriotism: The Movies and World War I.* Madison: University of Wisconsin Press, 1997.

Eyman, Scott. *The Speed of Sound: Hollywood and the Talkie Revolution, 1926–1930.* New York: Simon & Schuster, 1997.

Fuller, Kathryn H. *At the Picture Show: Small-Town Audiences and the Creation of Movie Fan Culture.* Washington, DC: Smithsonian Institution Press, 1996.

MacCann, Richard Dyer. *The Comedians* (Vol. 4, "American Movies: The First Thirty Years"). Metuchen, NJ: Scarecrow Press, 1993.

MacCann, Richard Dyer. *The Silent Screen* ("American Movies Series"). Lanham, MD: Scarecrow Press, 1997.

Maltby, Richard, and Ian Craven. *Hollywood Cinema: An Introduction.* Malden, MA: Blackwell Publications, 1995.

Robinson, David. *From Peep Show to Palace: The Birth of the American Film.* New York: Columbia University Press, 1996.

Slide, Anthony. *The New Historical Dictionary of the American Film Industry.* Lanham, MD: Scarecrow Press, 1998.

Staiger, Janet. *The Studio System.* New Brunswick, NJ: Rutgers University Press, 1994.

Waller, Gregory A. *Main Street Amusement: Movies and Commercial Entertainment in a Southern City, 1896–1930.* Washington, DC: Smithsonian Institution Press, 1995.

6

France in the Twenties and Thirties

★ ★ ★ ★

1919–1939

The economy of the French film has so persistently tended toward anarchy and chaos that it is easy to imagine its trade press keeping headline type standing to prophesize and then report "TOTAL COLLAPSE OF INDUSTRY." Made up of numerous small firms and individual impresarios, rather than a few huge studios, production companies have been born and laid to rest with single films. Individual successes and fitful bursts of popularity have been supplemented by various forms of government protection and subsidy in efforts to achieve sustained good health. The French have released only between one hundred and one hundred thirty films each year; as is the case in most countries, American movies have consistently dominated as popular entertainment. Nonetheless, the French film industry has produced a high proportion of carefully crafted works that are the equal of any in terms of artistic quality.

The contribution of France to the maturing art of the silent cinema was much more limited in appeal than that of either Germany or the Soviet Union, yet it followed some of the same lines and in particular instances even antedated achievements in the other two countries. Its strengths, like its limitations, came from the fact that it was rooted firmly in the aesthetic ferment that marked Paris in the 1920s and made it the artistic capital of the world. The outpouring of creation in many arts was accompanied by ongoing argument and polemic about the nature of art itself. Theory fed into practice, and practice back into theory—from the ateliers and garrets to the cafés and salons. A premium was placed on the new and the experimental, the daring and the shocking, in the search for artistic styles—for forms and functions—that would speak for and to the modern age.

The First Avant-Garde:
Impressionism

Louis Delluc—theorist, practitioner, crusader—set out not only to link film with the other arts and aesthetic movements of the time but also to find in what ways it was special and how it could be superior to the traditional modes of music, literature, and theater. He and other French intellectuals and artists had a particular appreciation for the popular American film genres. As they had earlier done with the mystery stories of Edgar Allan Poe, the French pointed out the formal and aesthetic beauties encased in the Hollywood western, for example, and insisted that those responsible for them were genuine artistic talents.

While editing a succession of film journals, Delluc wrote prolific criticism applauding the work of the Americans—especially Ince, Griffith, and Chaplin—as well as the Swedes. He also attacked the French tendency to revert to the theatrical tradition of *films d'art* or to blandly imitate the commercial successes of other nations. Around Delluc there gathered a group of film makers who have been labeled the *impressionists:* Marcel L'Herbier, Jean Epstein, Abel Gance, and Germaine Dulac, for whom Delluc wrote his first scenario, *La Fête espanole* (1919).

What Delluc and his followers wanted was a cinema that was distinctively filmic, with emphasis on the rhythmical and lyrical possibilities of the medium, and one that was distinctively French, with indigenous themes and images. In his early theoretical writings and in his films, Delluc championed what he termed *photogenie,* which could be defined as the camera's transformation of the actual world through lighting, framing, and the like. Movement was the most prized quality. Delluc's emphasis on the natural world as a precondition for cinematic art meant that he disapproved of films such as those produced by the German expressionists, which featured artificial sets and performances. Of the movies directed by Dullac, *Fièvre* (1921) and *La Femme de Nulle Part* (1922) are most often cited as those that best exemplify his theories. But he made his greatest impact through his intellectual leadership, his influence on other film makers, and his organization of the *ciné club* movement to build support for the kinds of films he valued.

The films of the impressionists contained elements of stylization and experimentation that set them apart from the bulk of French commercial production of the time. Eventually they embraced the term *cinématographie* to signal their growing interest in using film to render interior states rather than the external world. Germaine Dulac's *The Smiling Madame Beudet* (1923) exemplifies this new principle perfectly. Focusing on the fantasy life of a Madame Bovary–like young matron living in the French provinces, *Madame Beudet* makes little distinction between what happens without and within the young protagonist's mind. When quotidian reality takes over after the woman's scheme to murder her husband fails, the world appears bleak and meaningless.

Of those associated with the impressionists, Abel Gance is the most special case—too large and long-lasting a creator to be contained within a single school. As the one gigantic figure of the French silent film, he not only rivaled Griffith during the silent years but continued to be ahead of his time up to the 1970s. Although his work was enormously influential, the vastness of Gance's conceptions and the originality of his technique were what made him unique in the history of film. The subjectivity and distortion in his *La Folie du Docteur*

The Smiling Madame Beudet ★ France, 1923, Germaine Dulac.

Tube (1915), achieved through the camera, preceded the later experiments of the impressionists, but its innovations so alarmed the producer that the film wasn't released at the time. The impressionistic technique and complex rapid cutting of his *La Roue* (1922) antedated the Soviet films and strongly influenced the French avant-garde just then developing.

In his enormous *Napoléon* (1927), Gance first employed a triptych screen process called *Polyvision,* which preceded *Cinerama* (the U.S. version of a wrap-around film experience) by a quarter century. Unlike the film makers of Cinerama, Gance used his separate panels to carry contrasting and complementary images as well as to extend one image to panoramic proportions. The film's force, however, did not depend solely on the novelty of those scenes projected in multiscreen (only four out of the whole). The eighty-minute single-screen version released originally in the United States by M-G-M is, as a historical-dramatic work, as powerful as the best of Griffith or Eisenstein. Numerous subsequent efforts have been made to reconstruct the film as close to the six-hour definitive version as possible. The most popular of these was sponsored by Francis Ford Coppola. Shown initially at New York's Radio City Music Hall in 1981 (the year Gance died), this four-hour version, with original live orchestral score composed by Coppola's father Carmine, then toured the United States. Many people who had never seen silent films, or even thought about them, were overwhelmed by this one. Its amazing power remains intact.

Napoléon ⋆ France, 1927, Abel Gance.

The Second Avant-Garde:
Pure Cinema

Working alongside the impressionists in the 1920s, carrying their technical and stylistic experimentation even further, were another group of French avant-garde film makers. The production of impressionist films was virtually ended by 1924; the second avant-garde waxed most strongly from about 1925 to the end of the decade. It emerged, however, quite directly from a nonfilmic historic line—one that began with the impressionist painters of the late nineteenth century and departed from the film impressionists' reliance on literary material. These avant-garde films, usually short, are like visual poems, jokes, or dreams—more akin to abstract or surrealist painting than to novels, plays, or feature films. The film makers who produced these kinds of films advocated a concept called *pure cinema (cinéma pur),* a cinema without plots.

Avant-garde film making was practiced in France more than elsewhere primarily because the right kind of personnel were there. French intellectuals and artists were among the most enthusiastic admirers of "the seventh art," as critic Ricciotto Canudo called film at the time. Even more than the Germans, many French artists were demonstrating an eagerness to try their hands at more than one medium. Jack-of-all-arts Jean Cocteau—poet, novelist, playwright, painter, film maker—was one extreme case. Cocteau, along with other notable figures from the world of painting who made forays into film, gravitated toward animation. In 1930 he produced *Blood of a Poet,* which mixed animation with live action. Similar experiments with animation were carried out by the cubist painter Fernand Léger (*Ballet mécanique,* 1924), the dadaist painter and photographer Man Ray (*The Starfish,* 1927), and the futurist artist Marcel Duchamp (*Anemic Cinema,* 1928).

The avant-garde movement in France was bolstered by the comparatively easy access to the tools and materials of the medium and by an audience receptive to experiment. In this period the French film industry was so loosely organized and lightly financed as to be almost amateurish by standards prevailing elsewhere. Rather than an oligopoly of a few large studios, there were many small companies and individual entrepreneurs. Given the relative inexpensiveness of the silent film, it was quite possible for a painter to raise a little money from the owner of an art gallery (to pay for raw stock and processing), borrow a camera from the studio where a friend worked, arrange for the use of an aristocratic art lover's château, invite friends (other artists) there, and then shoot a short, improvised experimental film in which they appeared. When completed it could be shown in one of the small cinemas on the left bank and among the *ciné clubs* founded by Delluc and Canudo that were beginning to show specialized programs. If the painter's reputation was sufficient, general public interest in the arts, including film, could assure enough of an audience to pay back the modest costs. Man Ray's *Les Mystères du Château de Dés (The Mysteries of the Chateau de Dés)* (1929), for instance, was produced and exhibited that way. With their new creative impulses, young poets and especially painters simply wrote themselves off their pages and painted beyond their canvases onto the cinema.

Another strand of the second avant-garde, *surrealism,* came out of the new psychological sciences pioneered by Sigmund Freud, whose equivalence in literature can be found in Proust (in his obsession with early memories) and Joyce (in his stream of consciousness and dream episodes). In painting, the surrealists informed their canvases with Freudian symbols and insights. Some thought the motion picture might be the art best able to capture and reveal the dream state so significant for Freud. Cinema's capacity for representing the fantasy world of dreams was as great as its ability to record the objective reality of the physical world; and so a number of surrealist artists turned to the film medium. A number of significant films were produced during this period under the surrealist banner. In 1924 René Clair made *Entr'acte,* a short movie consisting of logically unrelated images intended to be shown as a prologue and intermission entertainment at a ballet composed by fellow avant-garde artist Eric Satie. In 1928 Germaine Dulac made a surrealist-influenced short entitled *The Seashell and the Clergyman* with the participation of the theatrical innovator Antonin Artaud.

The best known of the surrealist films is *Un Chien andalou,* made in 1927 by the surrealist painter Salvador Dali working with his fellow Spaniard Luis Buñuel. *Un Chien andalou* might best be called an antinarrative film rather than a nonnarrative film insofar as it repeatedly violates one's expectations about spatial, temporal, and logical continuities. Characters open doors and find themselves on a beach. Intertitles contain phrases, such as "eight days later," that have no discernible relation to the action being shown. Characters behave erratically, with no rational motivations for their actions. Insofar as *Un Chien andalou* can be said to be "about" something, it deals with three people, a woman and two men, who participate in fantastical episodes, many of which focus on elemental sexual drives and hostility toward everyday civilized values. An especially shocking sequence near the beginning of the film shows a man (played by Buñuel) slitting a woman's eyeball. Buñuel and Dali went on to make another surrealist short film, *L'Age d'or,* in 1930, which continued to exploit surrealist shock tactics. Its most famous image features a woman sucking on the toe of a statue.

The expense of sound production and the inaccessibility and complexity of sound equipment and technique effectively ended the avant-garde film movements at the end of the 1920s. In the new technology, there was no place for the inspired amateur. However, several of the avant-garde film artists—including Clair, Buñuel, and Cocteau—later managed to establish careers for themselves in feature film making.

A second cause for the demise of the avant-garde spirit was the changing attitudes of the 1930s. Art for the sake of art seemed worthy of artists' full attention in the 1920s, but the 1930s became the years of art for society's sake. The Depression and rising fascism prompted new artistic intentions. The avant-garde film was replaced by the documentary as the artistic form most attractive to the artists and intellectuals of the 1930s. It is no

Un Chien andalou ★ France, 1927, Luis Buñuel and Salvador Dali.

coincidence that several of the avant-garde film makers of the 1920s became socially committed documentary film makers in the decade following their avant-garde successes.

The Golden Age of the 1930s

During certain periods of rapid change the lack of economic ballast, which has otherwise been a liability, has given the French a peculiar advantage. This was the case at the time sound was introduced at the end of the 1920s. At first the greatly increased expense meant that only the two largest firms, Gaumont and Pathé, were capable of exploiting the new medium. When both collapsed from overextension of their resources, the situation changed. In part because they didn't have the heavy investments the American industry did, the French moved more readily into the experimental stage with sound, and hence exerted considerable leadership in the development of the altered art. In France the individual film maker frequently enjoyed a freedom of and control over expression seldom granted in Hollywood's major studios, or, for that matter, in the Ufa of Germany or the state-financed cinema of the Soviet Union. A French film maker who could find a backer—wealthy lover, moribund aunt, reckless stock broker—could hope to make a film. With sound, French production returned to an international prominence it had relinquished with the outbreak of World War I.

First there was a series of René Clair successes—*Sous les toits de Paris* (1930), *À nous la liberté* (1931), *Le Million* (1931). Clair used music and noises fantastically (a flower in the field bursting into song, a crowd scrambling for a lottery ticket as an off-screen announcer delivers a play-by-play description of a soccer game) or satirically (assembly-line work performed to the same music and monotonous sounds in the factory as in the prison). Although dialogue had little place in his first sound works, Clair vastly expanded the range of cinematic effects sound could create.

In those same early sound years Marcel Pagnol began his memorable trilogy of *Marius* (1931), *Fanny* (1932), and *César* (1936). In these a warmly human story about simple people is enacted in definitive performances against a Marseilles setting. For Pagnol dialogue was perhaps too important and the overall style remained "theatrical."

Only a little later, Jean Vigo, the supreme poet of French cinema, made his two enduring and influential features before his tragically premature death. *Zero for Conduct* (1933), also concerning children, deals with life in a strangely surreal boys' school—a film to which Lindsay Anderson paid obvious and respectful homage in his own film *If . . .* (1968). *L'Atalante* (1934) is the tender and somewhat haunted, as well as haunting, love story of young newlyweds and a bizarre, elderly Caliban—set in a barge on the Seine. Both films are models for sparse and assured use of sound in support of images. The poetry is primarily visual rather than verbal, and the words, noises, and music coming from the loudspeakers add reverberations to what is already clear and rich on the screen.

Le Million ★ France, 1931,
René Clair; René Lefèvre
and Annabella, as the lovers.

Zero for Conduct ★
France, 1933, Jean Vigo.

In 1934, however, the year of *L'Atalante,* it looked to many observers as if the French industry finally had reached that state of total collapse frequently predicted. Major cause of the catastrophe was the worldwide Depression that had by then hit France. Now no investment money was available for production, no films were being made, and film artists and technicians joined the millions of unemployed. Not unlike 1919 in Germany, 1934 was a year of grave political unrest in France. Demonstrations and riots preceded the formation of the Popular Front, a short-lived effort by the parties of the left to keep France from succumbing to fascism, as had Italy and Germany, and as Spain soon would. Perhaps this is yet another instance of periods of great national film expression growing out of troubled times. In any case, out of the ashes of 1934—and for reasons that aren't altogether clear in the general quirkiness of French film economics—a phoenix arose, becoming what is still referred to as the Golden Age of French Cinema.

One of the causes of revival seems more evident to the historian of today than it would have been to investors at the time. France was specially blessed with a cultural tradition that, though not fully accessible to the silent film, offered the stuff of which the best sound films are made. Whereas action-melodrama, spectacle, and slapstick comedy were ideal forms for the strictly visual requirements of the silent medium, the addition of dialogue demanded a new thoughtfulness, subtlety, and refinement of dramatic values. From 1935 until the end of the decade French film makers utilized the resources of the new technology to emphasize intellectual content, to explore philosophical and psychological themes. Intelligent screenplays and superior screen acting were France's chief additions to the maturation of the sound film, contributed by some of its distinguished literary and theatrical talents. Those qualities, all of prime importance in the new medium, were often achieved without loss of visual brilliance—owing in no small measure to the well-known French affinity for the graphic arts. As tangible evidence of their excellence, it can be noted that French films of the late 1930s became the first substantial body of foreign-language pictures to interest American audiences. In major U.S. cities a few little "art theaters" sprang up to show them, somewhat as *The Great Train Robbery* had opened the nickelodeons in the earlier days. The first five annual New York Film Critics' Awards for the Best Foreign Film, which began in 1936, went to France.

In general, because of the avant-garde inheritance, the best of French cinema of the 1930s was saved from the "staginess" that often marred Hollywood studio output. The avant-garde's attention to *cinéma pur,* and the fact that some of France's major directors came out of that informal school, kept the French aware that *motion* and *picture* was still the best two-word aesthetic of the motion picture, even when accompanied by sound.

But the French sound feature film, although showing the influence of a painterly tradition and of silent avant-garde film making, drew even more heavily on literary and theatrical sources available to it. Historically, the French novel has been noteworthy for a kind of realism closely akin to the dominant style of the sound film. The works of Stendhal, Balzac, Flaubert, Zola, and de Maupassant comprise a main line in French literature; much of French cinema of the latter half of the 1930s can be seen as an extension of that inheritance. Often the films are set firmly within the provinces (*Carnet de Bal,* 1937; *The Baker's Wife,* 1938) or amongst the urban working classes (*La Belle Équipe,* 1936; *Le Jour se Lève,* 1939). Violence and crime frequently occur but, in French fashion, more out of passion than hatred or greed. Robust, sexually based humor alternates with worldly *tristesse.* The earthiness and honesty strike the viewer at once. Small important details of a scene are searched out; nearly tangible contact between characters and audience is established. Principal script writers were Jacques Prévert, Charles Spaak, and Henri Jeanson—all of whom had literary as well as filmic reputations—and they can claim a substantial share of the creative credit for films bearing their names. Most of the finest work of the period had scripts by one or another of them.

Excelling in psychological depth and intimate characterization, these films also depended to considerable extent on the skill of French acting. Sound film was obviously more attractive than silent film to actors trained in the theater. France had its great heritage of private and state-supported theatrical companies which for decades, even centuries, had provided one of the finest cadres of performers in the world. French cinema owes much of its luster and subtlety to the contributions of such actors as Arletty, Jean Gabin, Louis Jouvet, Michèle Morgan, Raimu, and Michel Simon. They approached the new medium with enthusiasm and quickly learned to adapt their talents and techniques to its special requirements.

One of the most distinctive trends to emerge during this period was **poetic realism.** Concerned primarily with working-class protagonists trapped in a dark universe, these films featured low-key lighting and fatalistic themes. Jean Gabin became the personification of the tragic proletarian hero in many of these films. In this guise Gabin came to stand for the French proletarian leader, called by the critic André Bazin "Oedipus in a cloth cap." Among Gabin's many poetic-realist films were *Pépé le Moko* (Julien Duvivier, 1936), *Port of Shadows* (Marcel Carné, 1938), and *Daybreak* (Carné, 1939). In each of these productions he plays a doomed criminal ennobled by love.

Marcel Carné, director of some of the most accomplished poetic realist films, was a superb craftsman who did his best work in collaboration with the poet/screenwriter

Jacques Prévert; in fact, it seems quite possible that Prévert was the *auteur* (author) in the filmic as well as the literary sense. Their attention to tight dramatic structures, themes of doomed love, and evocative, studio reconstructions of the real world give their work a distinctive aura of serene melancholy. Their two greatest films of the period, *Port of Shadows* (1938) and *Daybreak* (1939), are also remarkably consistent in the dark and despairing view they present of society. In them Carné and Prévert follow the ubiquitous Jean Gabin through urban lowlife on the fringes of the criminal world. Forced and led into a crime of passion that causes his own destruction, Gabin meets his end with the special sort of stoicism that he carried with him from film to film. Even individual scenes seem almost interchangeable: The lighting and wallpaper in the forlorn hotel rooms look alike; a woman (Michèle Morgan or Arletty), with a kind of tired sensuousness, peels off a silk stocking; the same little bistro reappears, as do the same unadorned and cheerless flights of stairs. It's as if a bleak vision of the society had been frozen on the screen and Carné-Prévert insist that we see it over and over again with them.

The best-loved collaboration between Carné and Prévert took place under the German occupation in the 1940s. *Children of Paradise,* which was released immediately after World War II ended in 1945, creates a tapestry of plot lines set in the world of the nineteenth-century French theater. Prévert's witty script focuses on Debureau, the greatest pantomimist France had ever known, masterfully played by Jean-Louis Barrault. The film's most prominent female character is Garance, a free-spirited actress, played by the charismatic Arletty. With its spectacular sets and large crowd scenes, *Children of Paradise* is epic in scope, but it also offers intimate and nuanced views of individual characters.

Daybreak ★ France, 1939, Marcel Carné; Jean Gabin.

Out of the eclectic mix of film makers active in France during this time, one figure emerged whose work transcended all conventions and formulas: **Jean Renoir.** Renoir's total corpus places him among the foremost film makers in the history of cinema to date; he is protean, experimenting in many forms and styles, yet usually saying essentially the same things. For Renoir, life is fundamentally good—the life of the heart and of the senses. Sexual love and natural countrysides are to be celebrated along with food and wine. In Renoir's world there are no bores and few villains. (In *The Rules of the Game* one of his characters, played by Renoir himself, remarks, "Everyone has his own good reasons.") His people may cause themselves and others difficulties, but they are never less than human.

Renoir's worldview had already been formed in his sound films preceding the high years of French cinema. *La Chienne* (1931), *Boudu Saved from Drowning* (1932), *Madame Bovary* (1934), and *Toni* (1934) can stand alongside his later work without apology. This is particularly true of *Boudu.* In it Renoir developed the notion of the social group, with the "outsider" (in one sense or another) serving as catalyst. This protagonist stirs up the group, unhinges it a bit; when he or she leaves, the group re-forms, changed by the experience. But the cohesiveness of the social unit, the need of people for each other, is one of the *idées fixes* in Renoir's universe of discourse.

In *The Crime of Monsieur Lange,* made in the landmark year 1935, Renoir restates these thematic materials in even fuller detail and more controlled form. He depicts the cooperative workplace established by the employees of a publishing firm, contrasting this utopian world with the oppression and exploitation they had suffered in the past under their corrupt capitalist boss Batala. One of Renoir's few unredeemed villains (played by Jules Berry in a tour-de-force performance), Batala asserts explicitly fascist sentiments near the end of the film. *The Crime of Monsieur Lange* was widely viewed at the time of its release as an endorsement of France's antifascist Popular Front movement. Yet with Renoir, these social themes never seem schematic: They are made manifest through close observation of particular, idiosyncratic human beings rather than through reliance on types.

Renoir's use of the camera is designed to capture what is happening to his characters without intruding on them. He favors wide-angle moving shots of considerable duration, composed in depth. At the climactic moment in *The Crime of Monsieur Lange,* for example, as the eponymous protagonist resolves to commit his "crime," the camera executes an elaborate panning movement around the courtyard as if to honor the wholeness of the idealized world the workers have created within this space, a world that Lange has come to feel he must protect at any cost.

Renoir's framing typically has a casual air. By allowing characters to enter and leave the cinematic stage freely, he creates an impression of a series of snapshots rather than posed portraits. He has referred to this style as one that fosters "the feeling of a frame too narrow for the content." The performances he elicits from his actors are so fresh and spontaneous they surpass an impression of improvisation to convey a sense of authenticity, of real persons at their core. At the same time, Renoir often alludes to the artificial quality of his creations by including amateur theatricals in many of his films. These performances within the films suggest the pleasure people take in make-believe and, by extension, refer to the activities of the film maker himself.

The Grand Illusion is unquestionably one of Renoir's masterworks. The script, which he wrote with Charles Spaak, is based on his own experiences during World War I and those recounted to him by others. He has said that the film is about "how to belong, how to meet."

The Grand Illusion ★ France, 1937, Jean Renoir; Jean Gabin, Pierre Fresnay, and Marcel Dalio, front row.

The tale is that of French prisoners of war in German prison camps, of two of the prisoners who have escaped, and of a German woman and her child with whom they stay for a while. According to the film, it is an illusion that war can solve national problems; instead, it merely frustrates human needs. For the two aristocratic professional soldiers, one French the other German, modern warfare doesn't even grant the traditional satisfactions of chivalry and male comradeship. (The latter character is played by Eric von Stroheim, popularly known as "the man you love to hate," in one of his few sympathetic roles.) For the remaining soldier-prisoners, war represents other kinds of deprivation—of freedom, primarily, but also of women's love. In one memorable scene the French prisoners try on costumes as they re-hearse for an amateur show. When one emerges in a woman's dress and wig, the others stand transfixed. The camera lingers on their awestruck stares as it slowly tracks among them. At this moment, the soundtrack lapses into silence, and the audience is invited to share the force of the emotional starvation these men feel as a result of the absence of women in their lives.

Renoir said that he was a pacifist, but *The Grand Illusion* is not a conventionally pacifist film. It contains no bloodshed, no atrocities, not even unbearable cruelties. (Punishment by solitary confinement comes closest; how like Renoir to regard being deprived of human companionship the cruelist of tortures.) If this is an antiwar film, it is even more profoundly a prohuman film, against all those restrictions placed on the human potential—nationality, class, military rank, religious prejudice—that keep us from solidarity.

After *La Marseillaise* and *The Human Beast* (both 1938) there came the final master-piece of the 1930s: *The Rules of the Game* (1939). It was completed just before French liberty was extinguished by the nation's collapse in the face of German onslaught. The "game" refers to the behavior of the upper-class hosts and guests during a house party. We see much of the servants of the estate as well. Their jobs are to serve the masters; the masters' jobs are to entertain themselves. The chief entertainment (game) is sexual intrigue, in which all the principal players indulge. In addition there are the host's collection of mechanical toys, a costume party, a rabbit hunt, and a variety show (another of Renior's characteristic set-pieces built around a performance within the film).

The "rules" in general require that things be done properly, style taking precedence over feeling. (The feelings of the characters seem atrophied, or, at most, light and variable.) Passion is not permitted, sexual infidelity is accepted; embarrassment is avoided; decorum is preserved; and the appearance of friendship, frankness, and generosity is maintained. It is not just that the rules don't relate to human wishes and desires, they are in opposition to them (similar to the illusions of *The Grand Illusion*). Although essentially a comedy, the diagnosis of social illness is disturbing enough that the film was banned by the French during the Occupation. One of Renoir's few dark films, *The Rules of the Game* became a requiem marking the end of an era.

If Renoir stands apart from all others in this period of diverse activities and movements, he is also emblematic of the high quality that has consistently marked French film culture. The era of the 1920s and 1930s in France ended as it had begun, with renewed efforts to under-

The Rules of the Game ★
France, 1939, Jean Renoir;
Roland Toutain, Renoir,
Nora Grégor, Pierre
Magnier, and Marcel Dalio,
front row.

stand and document the development of motion picture artistry. A new generation of what the French call *cinéphiles,* or lovers of film, took up the work begun by Louis Delluc but in a more disciplined way. Henri Langlois, Georges Franju, and Jean Mitry began the Cinémathèque Française, an institution dedicated to archiving and screening the films of the past. At the same time Jean Mitry, Georges Sadoul, and others began projects to create authoritative film histories and to theorize this new aesthetic phenomenon. Through such projects the French consolidated their position as leaders not only in the creation of film art but also in the production of film scholarship—a position they have maintained to the present day.

Films of the Period

1919
J'accuse (Abel Gance)

1922
La Roue (Abel Gance)

1923
L'Inhumaine (Marcel L'Herbier)
The Smiling Madame Beudet (*Le Souriante Madame Beudet*) (Germaine Dulac)

1924
Ballet Mécanique (Fenand Léger)
Entr'acte (René Clair)

1927
Napoléon (Abel Gance)
The Starfish (*L'Etoile de mer*) (Man Ray)
Un Chien andalou (Salvador Dali and Luis Buñuel)

1928
The Fall of the House of Usher (*La Chute de la maison Usher*) (Jean Epstein)
The Little Match Girl (*La Petite Marchande d'allumettes*) (Jean Renoir)
The Seashell and the Clergyman (*La Coquille et le clergyman*) (Germaine Dulac)

1930
L'Age d'or (Luis Buñuel and Salvador Dali)
The Blood of a Poet (*Le Sang d'un poet*) (Jean Cocteau)
Sous le toits de Paris (René Clair)

1931
À nous la liberté (René Clair)
La Chienne (Jean Renoir)

Marius (Marcel Pagnol)
Le Million (René Clair)

1932
Boudu Saved from Drowning (*Boudu sauvé des eaux*) (Jean Renoir)
Fanny (Marcel Pagnol)

1933
Zero for Conduct (*Zéro de conduite*) (Jean Vigo)

1934
L'Atalante (Jean Vigo)
Madame Bovary (Jean Renoir)
Toni (Jean Renoir)

1935
Carnival in Flanders (*La Kermesse héroïque*) (Jacques Feyder)
The Crime of Monsieur Lange (*La Crime de Monsieur Lange*) (Jean Renoir)

1936
César (Marcel Pagnol)
A Day in the Country (*Un Jour du campagne*) (Jean Renoir) (released 1946)
Pepé le Moko (Julien Duvivier)

1937
Carnet de bal (Julien Duvivier)
The Grand Illusion (*La Grande Illusion*) (Jean Renoir)

1938
The Baker's Wife (*La Femme du boulanger*) (Marcel Pagnol)

The Human Beast (Le Bête humaine) (Jean Renoir)
La Marseillaise (Jean Renoir)
Port of Shadows (Quai des brumes) (Marcel Carné)

1939
Daybreak (Le Jour se lève) (Marcel Carné)
The Rules of the Game (La Règle de jeu) (Renoir)

Books on the Period

Andrew, Dudley. *Mists of Regret: Culture and Sensibility in Classic French Film.* Princeton, NJ: Princeton University Press, 1995.

Crisp, Colin. *The Classic French Cinema, 1930–1960.* Bloomington: Indiana University Press, 1997.

Hayward, Susan. *French National Cinema* ("National Cinemas Series"). New York: Routledge, 1993.

Hayward, Susan, and Ginette Vincendeau. *French Film: Texts and Contexts.* New York: Routledge, 1999.

Rees, A. L. *A History of Experimental Film and Video.* London: British Film Institute, 1999.

Vincendeau, Ginette, ed. *Cassell Film Guides: France.* Herndon, VA: Cassell Academic, 1997.

7

Hollywood in the Thirties and Early Forties

★ ★ ★ ★

1929–1945

The 1930s in the United States were the years of the Depression and of the New Deal—of business collapse and bank failure, of unemployment and poverty, and of the WPA, the CCC, and the NRA (Works Progress Administration, Civilian Conservation Corps, and National Recovery Administration). They were years of economic stagnancy, industrial strife, and individual frustration. At the same time, they were years of rediscovery of American tradition, of affirmation of an American character, of unearthing and preserving folklore and folk music, and of attempts at restoring and conserving our land and water through federal government efforts after decades of neglect and despoilation.

During these years the movies continued as a vital form of popular culture. Usually they seemed to avoid direct confrontation with the problems of the time, but inevitably they carried along its themes and concerns—even into seemingly escapist entertainment. Sometimes social stance was implicit in what was omitted or disguised. In other instances the movies spoke more or less directly to national fears and aspirations. The populist rhetoric and symbols of the first government documentaries, Pare Lorentz's *The Plow That Broke the Plains* (1936)and *The River* (1937), had their analogues in the fiction films of Frank Capra, *Mr. Deeds Goes to Town* (1936) and *Mr. Smith Goes to Washington* (1939).

American entertainment films of the 1930s were designed to function in a way quite different from theatrical feature films of today, at which attendance becomes something of a special occasion. Those earlier movies were more like current television series, and with similar audience expectations. Admission prices were much lower then; theaters were more easily accessible; and they were attended with greater casualness, more frequently—by 80 million customers a week. The men and women who created films for that mass audience conceived of themselves as making entertainment. They didn't think of their work as art.

A standard technique for screen narrative became fixed—what is now sometimes called classic Hollywood cinema. It involves a master long shot covering the whole scene, which introduces it and is returned to from time to time to reestablish spatial orientation. Within it are inserted medium shots and closeups in shot/reverse shot order, back and forth between action and reaction to speaker and listener(s). Screen direction and screen action are matched perfectly from shot to shot, and sight lines are carefully observed: When an actor looks, we see what she or he is looking at from approximately the same angle and distance. American film makers working within that style aspired to the well-made film, and the best of them had very high standards for their craft. But to regard the motion picture as a means for personal expression would generally have been considered a somewhat peculiar idea. Art existed in the movies of course, but in comparison to other more self-conscious artistic endeavors it was arrived at surreptitiously, sometimes unconsciously. We can tell this from the evidence of the five thousand or so features produced during the decade, and from an understanding of the industrial system within which they were made and marketed.

The 1930s were the years of the giant studios having nearly complete control over the careers of their employees, more absolute than that of today's professional football teams over their players. The studios assembled their rosters of creators, performers, and technicians who, as they worked together over the years, became expert indeed. Because of this continuity of personnel, which extended from top management to lowliest grip, each studio had its own "look." In some ways we can deal with the American films of the 1930s more adequately by identifying them with their studios rather than with individual film makers.

As much as we have come in recent years to think of the director as principal creator of a film, we must remember that in Hollywood in the 1930s producers and stars would generally have been considered the major factors in each production. Producers, with a stable of scriptwriters at their disposal, put together vehicles for stars. Producers such as Irving Thalberg, Hal Wallis, and Darryl F. Zanuck left strong imprints on films they produced. Actors such as Katharine Hepburn, Clark Gable, Marlene Dietrich, and James Stewart had their wishes carefully attended to. The director was sometimes merely a supervisor who oversaw the recording of images and sounds. It makes sense, then, to look first at the industrial system before considering its product and the work of a few powerful creative figures who emerged.

The Industry

After seismic upheavals and shifts during the transition from silence to sound, the Hollywood economic terrain hardened into a pattern that would remain virtually unchanged for two decades. In fact, vestiges of the modus operandi of the 1930s still characterize what is left of the once mighty feature film industry.

The system was built around eight major companies—five more major than the other three—and around the *vertical control* exerted by those firms over distribution and exhibition as well as production. Chains of theaters were owned by the five largest studios: Metro-Goldwyn-Mayer (M-G-M, the production arm of Loew's, Inc.), Twentieth Century-Fox, Paramount Pictures, Warner Bros., Radio-Keith-Orpheum (RKO). Each studio produced upward of fifty features a year for its theaters and for those of the others. "Program" or "B" pictures might play only within their producing company's chain as weekly or semi-weekly filler between hits. The more popular films were sought by all the exhibitors regardless of which studios produced them. Whatever part of the country you are from, chances are that names of local theaters still pay tribute to their former owners: the RKO Grand, the Paramount, Loew's, and so on. The three smaller studios—Universal, Columbia Pictures, United Artists—produced and distributed, but to survive had to have their films shown in the theaters owned and controlled by the big five. Besides the eight major studios there were also those producers called independents. Some of them were reasonably large and well established (Samuel Goldwyn Productions, Walt Disney Studio, Republic, Monogram); others were individual entrepreneurs working out of one of the major studios (David Selznick at M-G-M, Walter Wanger at Paramount).

In 1939 the eight majors were responsible for 76 percent of feature films released, and took in 86 percent of total rental income. These studios were the members of the Motion Picture Producers and Distributors of America—the trade organization that self-censored the content of the films produced, bargained with foreign governments regarding export abroad, and performed other functions on behalf of the industry as a whole. Through the MPPDA (now the MPAA—Motion Picture Association of America) the majors dominated the industry. If control of exhibition was crucial to their power, they also controlled distribution.

The distribution branches of the majors undertook to "sell" the films to exhibitors and to physically handle and circulate prints to theaters. Selling involved advertising and promotion, which took two forms. First, each film was presented through advertisements and reviews in the trade press, and by sales representatives and advance screenings at regional offices. Second, the distributor developed a promotional campaign to attract general public attention to the new release—through the national press, radio, billboards, sky writing, and any other means available or thinkable. The budget allocated for promotion of each film was a key factor in determining the rental the exhibitor would pay for it. The more important the studio thought the picture, the more money it spent on the campaign, and the more the exhibitor might expect to take in at the box office.

The distributor worked out the kinds of appeals thought to be best suited and most effective for selling each picture. Its staff designed the graphics, wrote advertising copy, even prepared canned "reviews" for those newspapers that didn't choose to hire their own reviewers. Often the approaches to the public and to the trade were strikingly different. We are all aware that sex and violence are not only staples of popular entertainment but of the advertising for it. It may be less obvious that novelty is stressed almost as often: "For the first time on the screen . . . ," "At last it can be told . . . ," "Never before in the history of the motion picture . . ." Usually pains were taken to disguise the probability that the film would be rather like the ones shown last week and a month ago, and to promise a unique experience no one could conceivably miss. To the exhibitor, however, the exact opposite (and a bit more honest) appeal was more often used: "The studio, the director, and the star who gave you *Dark Victory*," "Judy and Mickey together again in the kind of story that made *Babes in Arms* a smash." The exhibitor sought known quantities in relation to audience tastes as demonstrated by their purchase of tickets in the past.

Some two hundred to four hundred prints of each film, costing around $250 apiece, were shipped from the laboratories to the regional film "exchanges." There were roughly thirty distribution centers in the country—Chicago, Dallas, Seattle, Atlanta, and so on—the same cities used as wholesale outlets by the garment manufacturers, meat packers, and other industries. Each distributor had an exchange along "film row." Prints were delivered from the exchanges to the theaters in time to open; prints of the closing program were returned for inspection and repair, then made available to other theaters in the region. In the eighteen to twenty thousand theaters across the country (estimates vary), nine thousand bookings were considered a good average for individual pictures. The first thirty-five hundred to four thousand bookings were scrutinized carefully to determine likelihood of success. If the projected income looked hopeful, more money might be spent on promotion. If not, the film was allowed to die quietly; prints would be kept in the exchanges, but no more money would be spent on promotion. Many fine films, particularly some small ones with quiet tone and subtle appeal, met this fate without being given a chance to reach the audience that might have existed for them.

The flow of money that started at the box office moved from the exhibitor to the distributor and finally back to the producer. Each took a cut to cover costs and make a profit, if any. With a looseness of accounting that flabbergasted people in other businesses, the distributor had to trust the exhibitor's report, and the producer the distributor's. Everyone cheated, it was said, and yet there was usually enough income to go around.

Helping to ensure the profits of distribution and production were certain characteristic trade practices. *Block booking,* for example, meant the exhibitor had to rent films in packages that included the "dogs" along with the "hits." This assured some return on even the weakest items in a studio's annual program. *Blind buying* occurred when an exhibitor was forced to book films unseen—sometimes even before they were made—to guarantee an advance market that would cover at least some of the considerable production and distribution costs. Block booking and blind buying led to *overbuying.* In those days of surplus product, the exhibitor might have to book more films than could be shown in order to get those that would attract the largest audiences. In return for what might be regarded as economic harassment (in 1940 the federal courts ruled the practices illegal), the exhibitor got *clearance* and *zoning.* If the theater was a downtown first-run "house" in a city, the exhibitor was assured that the film booked would not be shown in any other theater downtown or in the neighborhoods or suburbs until a certain time had elapsed—six months, say; or, if the theater was in a small town, the exhibitor knew that the film would not be shown in a town closer than perhaps twenty miles away.

In the days of vertical control this set of ungentlemanly agreements successfully kept out independents in any of the three phases—production, distribution, exhibition—except by tolerance of the major studios. Since profits could be made at any of the three levels, competition was largely internal within a single company: among its production, distribution, and exhibition branches. As for competition among the eight firms, since the members of the MPPDA parceled out their spheres of influence (kinds of production, regions in which theaters were owned), they competed with one another only in somewhat the manner of the several divisions of General Motors Corporation—Buick with Oldsmobile with Pontiac. Vertical control also meant that the industry could thoroughly police itself in terms of kinds of screen content it felt would be acceptable to the public. By self-censoring it was able to forestall outcries of moral indignation that might hurt the box office and invite government intervention.

Censorship, Self-Regulation, and Pressure Groups

To some creators, the system of self-regulation that developed was an even more onerous feature of the industrial organization than was the single-minded pursuit of profits by front office and stockholders. Certainly it had substantial effect on what would appear on the screen or, more accurately, what would not. This "production code" remained in operation with only minor revisions until 1968, when the industry adopted the practice, common abroad, of regulating attendance (the G/PG/R/X ratings) rather than content. The United States is almost unique among nations in never having had federal censorship of motion pictures.

As noted earlier, the move toward self-regulation began in the years immediately following World War I. It came in response to public criticism and the industry's fear of increased state and municipal censorship, and perhaps even federal government involvement. Eight states and a number of cities had passed film censorship laws by the early 1920s. Public indignation had been provoked by films reflecting (exacerbating, some argued) a new, freer morality that featured hip flasks, knee-length skirts, and petting in the rumble seats of roadsters. Rocked by scandals surrounding the death of a starlet after an orgy (comedian Roscoe "Fatty" Arbuckle was accused of having caused her death), and by the unsolved murder of director William Desmond Taylor, Hollywood became the subject of particularly strident criticism.

In 1922 the Motion Picture Producers and Distributors of America hired Will H. Hays, Postmaster General and former national chairman of the Republican Party, to become its head. The response of the "Hays Office" to new threats of economic boycott and government intervention was the Motion Picture Production Code. Like the Ten Commandments, the Code's language was largely negative. Restrictions on what could be dealt with and how appeared under twelve main headings: crimes against the law, sex, vulgarity, obscenity, profanity, costume, dances, religion, locations (that is, bedrooms), national feelings, titles ("salacious, indecent, or obscene"), and repellent subjects (actual hangings or electrocutions, third degree, brutality, branding of people or animals, apparent cruelty to children or animals, the sale of women, surgical operations). Totally forbidden were presentations of drug traffic or the use of drugs, sexual perversion, "white slavery," sexual relationships between the white and black races, and nudity.

In 1934 Catholic forces, particularly unhappy about Hollywood flouting the Code drafted by two of their own, formed the Legion of Decency. Since the Legion's program rested on boycotting films that violated the Code (their titles to be announced from pulpits across the country), the industry finally became sufficiently alarmed to institute a mechanism to enforce adherence: the Code seal, to be applied by the Production Code Administration. Joseph I. Breen, a young Catholic newspaperman, was appointed director. The members of the MPPDA agreed not to release or distribute films unless they carried the seal. A $25,000 penalty was instituted for producing, distributing, or exhibiting any picture that had not received it. Given vertical and nearly complete control of the industry by the major studio members of the association, not a single important feature was released without the seal in the next two decades.

This enforced, official morality imposed on the creative personnel by the business leaders resulted in a screen world that many found more than a little removed from life. Though it was argued to be "self-regulation," the Code was embraced much more warmly by studio heads than by those who actually made the pictures. Writers, directors, and actors—who often came out of theater and the other less financially encumbered traditional arts whose audiences were smaller and more select—felt particularly inhibited by it. One principal problem was that the Code sapped creative energy at its source. Staying within the Code's standards of conventional, conservative middle-class mores became at least as important as creating a fine work. Another problem was the patent hypocrisy involved. The real reasons for the Code and the seal were financial rather than moral. If organized pressure groups succeeded in keeping audiences away from theaters, a substantial loss of income would result. If local and state censorship bodies increased in number and were joined by a threatened federal agency, the considerable expense of providing several versions of a film to meet the varying standards might be entailed.

Naturally film makers working within the Code tried to suggest what they could not show; the leer replaced a frank look at many of life's realities. Since restrictions were greatest on sexual matters, sexuality was replaced by violence (regarded with more equanimity by the society as well as by the Production Code Administration). Hollywood's adherence to the Code ensured that reality was not so much excluded (as was argued by the social critics of the 1930s) as dealt with obliquely and within the fixed rubrics of the popular forms. In *Trouble in Paradise* (1932), for example, after Gaston and Lily embrace passionately on a couch, the culmination of that embrace is expressed by a dissolve to the same couch, now empty, followed by a cut to Gaston's hand hanging a "Do Not Disturb" sign on the bedroom door. The indirection of content, like the stylization of technique, frequently adds to rather than detracts from the charm and resonant effectiveness of the best films of the 1930s.

Notable Directors of the 1930s

In part as a result of the efforts of the Directors Guild of America, which was formed in 1935 to advance the power and image of its members, directors as a group gained more control over the film-making process during the late 1930s than they had enjoyed in the early part of the decade. A few of the directors who did important work in the 1930s and early 1940s stand as emblems of how respect and recognition accorded to directors were beginning to grow. Josef von Sternberg, Howard Hawks, Frank Capra, and John Ford would appear on the lists of many historians as preeminent. Often with the help of valuable collaborators, each of these film makers managed to cultivate an identifiable personal style by ingeniously navigating a path through the headwinds, storms, and shoals that were part and parcel of the studios that employed them. Although all started in silent film in the 1920s and some continued to work fruitfully for decades after the 1930s, they all reached creative maturity during this time.

Joseph von Sternberg is the supreme visual stylist. With him the shadow is the substance. In a series of films starring Marlene Dietrich—*Morocco,* 1930; *Dishonored,* 1931; *Shanghai Express,* 1932; *The Scarlet Empress,* 1934; and *The Devil is a Woman,* 1935— he fashioned and perfected his own unique, exotic screen world. Von Sternberg believed that a film should be capable of offering an aesthetic experience when projected upside down and backward. He had a thorough background as an editor and cameraman, and there is evidence suggesting he did much of the cinematography on the films he directed.

The Scarlet Empress ☆ United States, 1934, Josef von Sternberg; Sam Jaffe and Marlene Dietrich.

Certainly he understood lighting and used it for extraordinarily intricate and consistent effect. It may be a mixed compliment to observe that a still from a von Sternberg film gives a fuller sense of its essence than would a still from any other director's work.

Howard Hawks is a quite different sort of artist. His is the art that conceals art. Working within genre conventions he nonetheless manages to state and restate what evidently were for him persistent preoccupations having to do with professionalism, individual courage (and cowardice, its complement), loyalty to the group, friendship among men, and the battle between the sexes. He began and ended the 1930s with films dealing with flying (*The Dawn Patrol,* 1930; *Only Angels Have Wings,* 1939), and he himself had been a flyer in World War I. In both films Hawks is obviously admiring in his treatment of the aviators. Dangerous flying can be senseless and frightening, but the camaraderie, pride, and bravery it allows for are to be honored. In *Dawn Patrol* there are no women (not even a mention of them except for the mothers of dead aviators), and their absence is filled by a "female" tenderness among the flyers toward each other. *Only Angels Have Wings* sets Jean Arthur off in pursuit of Cary Grant; but, since she is a woman, she can't really understand why the men behave as they do, and she represents a tacit threat to the group. These are some of the consistent thematic materials of Hawks the action director, the director of men's pictures

Peter Wollen, in *Signs and Meaning in the Cinema,* acknowledges the dynamism and stress prevalent in all of Hawks's work. Wollen also sees what he calls the crazy comedies

Only Angels Have Wings ★
United States, 1939, Howard
Hawks; Cary Grant (seated at
table in dark jacket), Thomas
Mitchell, and Jean Arthur
(standing close to table).

(including *Twentieth Century,* 1934, and *Bringing Up Baby,* 1938) as the inverse of the adventure dramas. "They are the agonized exposure of the underlying tensions of the heroic dramas," he writes. "Whereas the dramas show the mastery of man over nature, over woman, over the animal and childish; the comedies show his humiliation, his regression. The heroes become victims; society instead of being excluded and despised, breaks in with irruptions of monstrous farce."[1] The two strata must be taken together, Wollen argues, if we are to get a full sense of the meanings Hawks offers in the recurrent motifs of his films.

Frank Capra's comedies are essentially social. They present an explicit view of American society, its economy and its politics—a view traditionally seen as uniquely Capraesque—though Joseph McBride's 1992 biography of the director called attention to the important contributions of Capra's longtime screenwriter Robert Riskin in establishing Capra's distinctive themes. *Mr. Deeds Goes to Town* (1936) and *Mr. Smith Goes to Washington* (1939) celebrate the "little guy" (played by Gary Cooper or James Stewart)—not as dumb as he seems and, once aroused, able to defeat the city slickers and the power figures. His victories are achieved through pluck, persistence, Jean Arthur, and his overwhelming decency, which is matched by the decency of the American people when they see the true situation. Frequently even the villains are redeemed in Capra's films, since at heart they too are usually well intentioned. This rosy portrait of America was typically depicted in crisp, glowing images contributed by Joseph Walker, who photographed many of Capra's best films.

Capra country is essentially an idealized small-town America (no matter that *Mr. Deeds* ostensibly takes place in New York City and *Mr. Smith* is set in Washington, DC). His films celebrate lovable eccentricities and homely virtues. Even in the 1930s this view

---

[1] Peter Wollen, *Signs and Meaning in the Cinema* (London: Secker & Warburg, 1972), p. 91.

Mr. Smith Goes to Washington ★ United States, 1939, Frank Capra; James Stewart.

was clearly nostalgic. Richard Griffith, in *The Film Till Now,* labels Capra's conception the "fantasy of goodwill." The huge popular success of his pictures attests to the appeal his vision had in those troubled times. If Capra's sensibility was uniquely tuned to the prevailing mood of the 1930s, his post-1930s films suggest a man who has lost his popular touch. In 1941 Capra and Riskin fashioned a darker variation on the theme of the little guy making good in *Meet John Doe.* In this tale, a cynical newspaper columnist played by Barbara Stanwyck invents a character (John Doe) who is threatening to commit suicide because of the corruption rampant in American society. A good-looking hobo (Gary Cooper) is subsequently hired to play the character Stanwyck has created. The logical conclusion of this story would have Cooper's character kill himself. But Capra could not live with such a tragic finish. "In desperation—setting some kind of pointless record," he recalled in his autobiography, "I was to photograph five different endings, and then try them out on theater audiences; all collapsed like punctured balloons." Retreating from the confusion that *John Doe* created, Capra returned to the ingredients that had fueled his early successes with *It's a Wonderful Life* (1946). Although it is as finely crafted as any of his films (it's Capra's favorite and has become a television tradition at Christmastime), it flopped at the box office. Its failure suggests that the country in the mid-1940s was a radically different place after the experience of World War II. In spite of his own contribution to the war effort in the *Why We Fight* series of documentaries made for the armed forces, Capra's own thinking and feeling seem to have remained in the earlier time.

John Ford, who, like Hawks and unlike Sternberg and Capra, continued to do some of his finest work after the 1930s, nevertheless established his reputation during those years. The cycle that began with *Steamboat 'Round the Bend* (1935) and continued with *The Prisoner of Shark Island* (1936), *Stagecoach* (1939), and *Young Mr. Lincoln* (1939) showed Ford as the chronicler of American history and the reworker of American folklore, especially of its frontier West.

Stagecoach set a standard for westerns that were to follow, with a script by Ford's frequent collaborator Dudley Nichols and a career-making performance by another Ford stalwart, John Wayne (who is introduced in a striking short tracking shot). The film is an ensemble piece, chronicling the adventures of a group of people thrown together in the confined interior of a moving vehicle. The plot follows a classic journey structure as the stagecoach traverses the arid landscape of Utah's Monument Valley. The spectacular setting was ever afterward identified as an archetype of the western genre, as were many of the film's characters: Wayne's good badman on the run from the law, Claire Trevor's warm-hearted dance-hall girl, Thomas Mitchell's alcoholic doctor, and Berton Churchill's corrupt banker. Even gravel-voiced western icon Andy Devine was on board as the stagecoach driver.

Stagecoach ★ United States, 1939, John Ford.

In his westerns that followed *Stagecoach*, including *My Darling Clementine* (1946) and *The Searchers* (1956), Ford continued to explore the forces set in motion by the European expansion in the New World. The savagery of the wilderness was frequently symbolized in these films by the figure of the Native American, bands of whom are often shown rampaging over the plains in wild disorder in contrast to the neat columns of cavalry troops led by widely admired stars such as John Wayne, Henry Fonda, and James Stewart. For Ford, as for other directors of westerns, the indigenous peoples of America represented what stood in the way of the advance of a civilizing order. In later years, Ford rethought his attitude toward the Native Americans; his elegiac 1962 western *Cheyenne Autumn* focuses on their plight of being displaced from their ancestral homelands by the policies instituted by an Anglo government.

Almost all of Ford's films of whatever genre reveal a profound reverence for nature. Ford favors outdoor scenes, often featuring expansive skyscapes that contrast with cramped, overcrowded interior spaces. To achieve an effect of oppressive closeness in his interiors, he frequently took the unusual step of putting ceilings on his sets; in many scenes these ceilings can be seen looming just above the characters' heads. Ford's traditional outlook also embraced the values of the family and the past: Graveside scenes, old-fashioned folk music, and the need to avenge wrongs done to relatives are recurring motifs in his films.

Emergent Genres in the 1930s

Although genres came about because of the requirements of mass production and popular appeal, they have nonetheless been consistently developed by American film makers. Of the popular genres that had formed into recognizable patterns during the 1920s, silent comedy was affected most radically by the introduction of sound. While lamenting the loss of comic pantomime and the great clowns who made it the universal and timeless form it is, we would still want to welcome the new kinds of comedies and the creators who entered with sound. Westerns, of course, could only be hampered by the sound stages; during the the first half of the 1930s they were relegated largely to "B" and "C" production budgets and comparable prestige. They became the "oaters" beloved by rural adult populations and small boys everywhere on Saturday afternoons, but had little to do with the advance of the motion picture generally. Of the narrative forms emerging with the new sound medium, most vigorous and characteristic of the 1930s were the musical, the gangster film, the horror film, the sound comedy, and the animated cartoon.

The **musical** was dependent on sound for its existence. In such harbingers as *The Merry Widow* of 1925, von Stroheim's most popular film, audiences had to be content with a live pit orchestra or organist providing a potpourri of Franz Lehar melodies to accompany the pantomimed action and printed titles. Fittingly, the film that caused the revolution, *The Jazz Singer* (1927), foreshadowed the backstage musical, an important early subgenre. What it lacked most essentially was dancing, for the appeal of the musical often came to depend as much on choreography as on music. From *The Hollywood Revue of 1929* through *Saturday Night Fever* (1977), *All That Jazz* (1979), *Flashdance* (1982), and *Dirty Dancing* (1987), the creators of musicals frequently have been men and women of dance as well as song.

The Hollywood Revue of 1929 was a prototype for one line of musical, the revue, which flourished in the 1930s and first half of the 1940s. It disappeared after World War II, with only a few exceptions (*Ziegfeld Follies,* 1946; *New Faces,* 1952). Consisting of separate "acts" unconnected by narrative linkage, like its stage counterpart, the screen revue let audiences throughout the world see the great entertainers whose performances had formerly been confined to Broadway and infrequent tours. Generally presented very much as they might have been on a superstage (by impresario Florenz Ziegfeld, for example), the film revues substituted the possibility of perfection—ideal performers in their best performances—for the special excitements of live theater.

Another early film musical form deriving from theater was the filmed operetta. It began with the romantic musical comedies of Ernst Lubitsch (starting with *The Love Parade,* 1929) and Rouben Mamoulian (*Love Me Tonight,* 1932). These operetta-like screen originals were made at Paramount and starred Maurice Chevalier and/or Jeanette MacDonald. Moving to M-G-M, in 1934 Lubitsch directed the same stars in his version of *The Merry Widow.* It was at M-G-M that the operetta continued, in a series of standard stage favorites beginning with *Naughty Marietta* in 1935. In them Chevalier was replaced by Nelson Eddy; he and MacDonald helped make a great deal of money for everyone concerned.

The first backstage musical may have been *Broadway Melody* (M-G-M, 1929), which was also the first Academy Award winner, but it was at Warner Bros. that the cycle was launched. In 1930 Warners imported Broadway veteran Busby Berkeley, who became master of the production number. His ranks and clusters of chorines moving with military

42nd Street ★ United States, 1933, Lloyd Bacon/Busby Berkeley; Ruby Keeler.

precision through elaborate patterns are understandably the subject of "camp" appreciation today. Those extravagant creations nonetheless contain an exotic charm. Early in the period Berkeley's spectacular staging and bravura use of camera, cutting, and special effects were brought together in the narrative musical.

In *42nd Street* Berkeley started full scale on that special kind of creation we associate with his name. The massed chorines are viewed by the camera from almost any position except a stationary one in front of a theater stage. They are seen from overhead as they form floral patterns or strange concentric rings suggesting interconnecting gears. Or the camera gets down on the floor and moves through their spread legs in a slyly elegant bit of erotica. Costumes and settings are designed to support and underscore the extravagant fantasy of the total choreographic conception; or, to put it the other way around, the dances grow out of and take full advantage of every suggestion provided by the visual decor. The chorus line performs a jerky, syncopated march up stairs, they turn toward the camera and raise cardboard profiles of skyscrapers, covering themselves and becoming a miniature Manhattan. Berkeley would later sustain and elaborate on delights of this sort at their most breathtaking (and bizarre) in the *Gold Diggers* series (*of 1933, 1935, 1937*).

A series of films starring Fred Astaire and Ginger Rogers were the first to drop the theatrical setting as an excuse for music and dancing. Although they play professional dancers, thus making their terpsichorean skill plausible, they move from the theater out into the world, breaking into song and dance whenever the emotional charge is sufficient.

Swing Time ★ United States, 1936, George Stevens; Ginger Rogers and Fred Astaire.

Astaire and Rogers, whose films together extend from 1933 to 1949, served to link the backstage musical inaugurated by *42nd Street* (same year as *Flying Down to Rio,* the first Rogers/Astaire) and the vintage cluster of M-G-M musicals beginning with *On the Town* (same year as the last Astaire/Rogers, *The Barkleys of Broadway*), which offered song and dance as the normal response to life. The M-G-M cycle, overseen by producer Arthur Freed, included some of the films many historians feel mark the high point of the genre: *Meet Me in St. Louis* (Vincente Minnelli, 1944), *Singin' in the Rain* (Gene Kelly and Stanley Donen, 1952), and *The Band Wagon* (Minnelli, 1952). In more recent times the traditional musical has been eclipsed by mutant forms: "rock docs" such as *Woodstock* (Michael Wadleigh, 1970), dance contest pictures such as *Saturday Night Fever* (John Badham, 1977), and music videos.

Although there were many films about gangsters in the 1920s (von Sternberg's *Underworld,* 1927, is one example), the **gangster film** is indissolubly linked with the 1930s. It thrived on the growling of limousines in low gear, the squealing of tires and screeching of brakes, the ratchet noise of tommy guns, and the explosions and tinkling of glass. It was born and brought up within that decade. *Little Caesar* (1930) began the cycle; *Public Enemy* (1931) and *Scarface* (1932) confirmed its power. Later decades would retool the genre's "success at any price" theme to speak to social dilemmas different from the economic desperation that characterized the United States in the 1930s: the psychic dislocation occasioned by World War II (*White Heat,* 1940); post-Watergate cynicism about political corruption (*The Godfather* cycle, 1972, 1974, and 1990); and the amoral accumulation of wealth (*Goodfellas,* 1990).

Little Caesar ★ United States, 1931, Mervyn LeRoy; Edward G. Robinson, center right.

As the prototype, *Little Caesar*, directed by Mervyn LeRoy, contains the essential thesis of the classic gangster film in its simplest and clearest form. Rico (Edward G. Robinson), the hero, or perhaps the antihero, begins as a gun-toting thug with ambition—the toughest, most ruthless of the lot. What motivates him is the exercise of power. The film makers don't feel obliged to justify their dramatic premise: It is presented as a given. Those on top are enviable because they are rich and powerful. But as one climbs upward there's a danger of becoming soft. Refinement and sentiment make people vulnerable and lead to destruction through "loss of nerve." The film begins with Rico murdering a robbery victim and ends with Rico being gunned down by the police after he fails to shoot his friend, Joe Massara (Douglas Fairbanks, Jr.), who becomes indirectly responsible for his death.

While the musical and gangster genres flourished at Warner's, **horror films** were the specialty of Universal. The appearance of these successors to *The Golem* and *Nosferatu* seems to have had less to do with the advent of sound technology than with American mastery of the lighting techniques originated earlier in Germany. Chiaroscuro lighting was crucial to the evocation of terror, and the names of German emigrés dot the technical credits of this series. Also, as in Germany, it may be that audiences respond especially to horror on the screen during times of national instability. At any rate, as with the gangster films, the two prototypical American horror films set forth fully the traits of their progeny. *Frankenstein* and *Dracula*, both released in 1931, are still in active circulation on video and in college series and courses.

The opening graveyard scene of *Frankenstein*—with its low-angled shots among the tombstones, an iconic cross, and a figure of death—establishes the mood. The desolate landscapes, the remote ancestral castle, the forbidding stone tower in which Dr. Frankenstein conducts his experiments, the laboratory interior with its flashing electrodes—all would

Frankenstein ☆ United States, 1931, James Whale; Boris Karloff.

become familiar images of the gothic horror movie. A sense of impending doom hangs over the film like a pall. Stylized Ruritanian settings and the bleak black-and-white cinematography create the visual atmosphere of shadowy gloom that dominates successive films of the genre.

As an outcast of society, the monster prompts an empathic response drawn from our own feelings of loneliness and alienation. Perhaps a Depression-ridden society, economically and culturally deprived, was particularly attuned to this appeal—and also to the suggestion that there is madness in high places, which can set loose a monstrous, impersonal, uncontrollable, destructive force.

The archetypical horror film, like the gangster film, waxed in the 1930s and waned after that decade, degenerating into more simplistic tales of horror, and finally even to self-parody (the series of *Abbott and Costello Meet* films; *Frankenstein,* 1948; the *Invisible Man,* 1951; and others). Though ailing, the genre didn't die with the 1930s. Instead, the horror films produced by Val Lewton in the 1940s—such as *Cat People* (1942), *I Walked with a Zombie* (1943), and *The Body Snatcher* (1945)—mark a sharp departure from the broad effects of the earlier cycle and are noteworthy for their subtlety. Later the horror film was restored to something like full health by Roger Corman in his series of Edgar Allan Poe adaptations (such as *The Fall of the House of Usher,* 1960; *The Masque of the Red Death,* 1964) made in England. Though not as distinctively American as the musical or gangster film, like the other genres, the horror film has been worked at consistently by American film makers including Corman, Brian De Palma, George Romero, John Carpenter, and Wes Craven. It is another lasting contribution of the American 1930s.

One line of **sound comedy** took advantage of the new possibilities for repartee and double entendre. Although like drawing room comedies of the theater, in the best film examples (Lubitsch's *Trouble in Paradise,* 1932) visual interest was retained and sight and sound were worked into counterpoint. A second line, out of vaudeville and stage, and replacing the silent clowns, featured talking comic stars in vehicles tailored to their special talents and the verbal styles associated with them. The Marx Brothers, for example, merely transferred to film their theatrical hits *The Cocoanuts* and *Animal Crackers,* in 1929 and 1930. W. C. Fields had been a popular vaudeville performer whose most memorable film bits (for instance, the crooked cue-stick routine) had frequently been worked out before on stage. Mae West, long before she appeared in movies, had played her particular version of herself on stage. The point is that the great comic movie stars of the 1930s were experienced with sound, especially with their own distinctive voices, as supplement to pantomime. In fact, they required sound for full comic effect.

A third kind of comedy developed in the 1930s was called the "screwball" comedy. This style combined intellectual sophistication with slapstick behavior. It depended on fast, witty dialogue and a battle of the sexes in which male and female roles were often reversed (in terms of traditional expectations of male strength and dominance). The performers most frequently inhabiting the screwball world were Claudette Colbert, Gary Cooper, Irene Dunne, Cary Grant, Jean Harlow, Katharine Hepburn, Carole Lombard, Rosalind Russell, Barbara Stanwyck, and James Stewart.

Frank Capra's enormously successful *It Happened One Night* (1934) may have been the first of the screwball comedies. Howard Hawks also directed effectively in this subgenre (*Twentieth Century,* 1934; *Bringing Up Baby,* 1938; *His Girl Friday,* 1940; *Ball of Fire,* 1941). Other directors who did memorable work in this style were Gregory La Cava

A Night at the Opera ★ United States, 1935, Sam Wood; Groucho Marx, Chico Marx, Sig Rumann, and Harpo Marx.

My Little Chickadee ★ United States, 1940, Edward Cline; W. C. Fields and Mae West.

Hail the Conquering Hero ☆ United States, 1944, Preston Sturges; Ella Raines, Eddie Bracken, and Franklin Pangborn.

(*My Man Godfrey,* 1936), William Wellman (*Nothing Sacred,* 1937), and Leo McCarey (*The Awful Truth,* 1937). The distinctive series of comedies written as well as directed by Preston Sturges are also of this type (*The Lady Eve,* 1941; *The Palm Beach Story,* 1942; *The Miracle of Morgan's Creek,* 1944; and others).

Scripts, even more than direction or performance, seem to provide the basis for the screwball cycle; the writers (especially Ben Hecht, Robert Riskin, Charles Brackett, Billy Wilder, and Preston Sturges) worked out the typical patterns of theme, plot, and dialogue. Ludicrously improbable situations were devised and then dealt with as if they were every-day occurrences. In *Bringing Up Baby,* screenplay by Dudley Nichols and Hagar Wilde, the plot is furthered as Katharine Hepburn, playing an heiress, has her dress torn off while in an elegant dining room—much to the embarrassment of Cary Grant, a paleontologist. Subsequently: (1) they collide with a truck full of chickens; (2) Grant chases her aunt's dog around a country estate, to find a brontosaurus bone; and (3) a wild leopard is mistaken for a tame one (Baby of the title). The dialogue is filled with unmistakably American exuberance. These films all evidence a close and sensitive attention to the native idiom—wisecracks, slang, and wrenched clichés are rapped out with uproarious effect.

What the trade called the **woman's picture,** aimed at the female customers who comprised most of the matinee audience, consisted mainly of love stories and domestic melodramas. The genre originated in the 1920s, when women attending entertainments on their own became socially acceptable; it came into full flower during the 1930s. As vehicles for glamorous stars, love stories fed the enormous fan appeal of actors such as Rudoph

Bringing Up Baby ★ United States, 1938, Howard Hawks; Cary Grant and Katharine Hepburn.

Valentino and Greta Garbo. The incandescent Garbo was set off to advantage in vehicles such as *Flesh and the Devil* (Clarence Brown, 1927), *Queen Christina* (Rouben Mamoulian, 1933), and *Camille* (George Cukor, 1937), whereas Valentino had earlier made millions swoon when he commanded Agnes Ayres, "Lie down, you little fool!" in *The Sheik* (1921). A series of memorable love stories directed by Josef von Sternberg during the 1930s showcased screen goddess Marlene Dietrich (*Morocco,* 1930, and *Blonde Venus,* 1932).

In *Queen Christina,* Garbo plays a sexually ambiguous Swedish monarch whose aborted love affair with a foreign envoy leads her to abdicate her throne. In the film's famous final shot, Christina stands at the prow of the ship that will take her away from Sweden and into the unknown. She gazes at the sea with an inscrutable expression. Mamoulian reportedly told Garbo to clear her mind of all thoughts for this shot so that viewers could read into it their own desires about what Christina's future might be like. Recent films, such as *The English Patient* (1997) and *Titanic* (1998), have attempted to revive the genre of the tragic love story, but in a certain sense *Queen Christina* and other films like it are irreproducible today. For whatever reasons, Hollywood is no longer able to manufacture the kind of love goddesses and matinee idols who could carry off such grandiose fantasies.

Domestic melodramas, which chronicle the travails and rewards of family life, came to the fore during this time as well, with stars Barbara Stanwyck, Bette Davis, and Joan

Stella Dallas ☆ United States, 1937, King Vidor; Barbara Stanwyck and Anne Shirley.

Crawford delivering tour-de-force performances in productions such as *Stella Dallas* (King Vidor, 1937), *Now, Voyager* (Irving Rapper, 1942), and *Mildred Pierce* (Michael Curtiz, 1945). In these films, all problems become family problems as issues such as illegitimacy, adultery, and parent-child relationships are explored.

Stella Dallas, a moving tribute to mother love, marks a high point in the cycle. Stanwyck won an Oscar for her role as a mother whose lower-class background drives a wedge between her and her upwardly mobile daughter Laurel. As Laurel becomes more refined, Stella becomes more frowzy and vulgar. She is ultimately reduced to watching Laurel's wedding through a picture window, where the spectacle created by her garish clothes and loud manner is placed at a safe distance from the elegant society marriage into which her daughter is entering.

Bette Davis undergoes another kind of transformation in *Now, Voyager,* this one from dowdy old maid to glamorous foster mother. Under the care of an avuncular psychiatrist played by Claude Rains, Davis's Charlotte Vale rebels against her dominating mother and meets her soul mate Jerry Durrance (Paul Henreid) on an ocean voyage. Although the two are prevented from marrying, Charlotte takes Jerry's troubled daughter Tina under her wing. The film's final scene, in which Jerry lights Charlotte's cigarette as the two stand together on a balcony gazing into the night sky, concludes with a famous statement of womanly renunciation. "Oh, Jerry, don't let's ask for the moon!" Charlotte exclaims, "We have the stars!"

Mother-daughter relationships again take center stage in *Mildred Pierce,* starring Joan Crawford as a self-made restaurateur who uses her hard-earned wealth to spoil her daughter Veda. The story was given a dark edge by a climax that featured murderous passions and romantic betrayals. The film's director Michael Curtiz used two styles for this domestic melodrama-whodunit: an evenly lit balanced look for the early scenes and a dramatic deeply shadowed style for the later ones.

Dorothy Arzner, the only major female director working in Hollywood during this era, made a specialty of women's pictures, turning out a series of films celebrating women's lives and women's relationships. Her work with actresses—especially Clara Bow in *The Wild Party* (1927), Katharine Hepburn in *Christopher Strong* (1933), and Rosalind Russell in *Craig's Wife* (1936)—showcased their talents to great effect and played a significant role in furthering their careers. Arzner's best-known film, the 1940 *Dance, Girl, Dance,* juxtaposes Judy, an aspiring ballerina (Maureen O'Hara) with Bubbles, a burlesque queen (Lucille Ball), in a story about female rivalry and female friendship. The film's climactic scene depicts Judy performing before a jeering audience at a burlesque house where her desperate financial situation has forced her to accept employment. Suddenly turning her gaze back on the crowd, she stops the show to challenge the audience's complacent assumption that the position they occupy as spectators makes them invulnerable to criticism. "Go ahead and stare!" she exclaims. "I'm not ashamed. Go on. Laugh! Get your money's

Dance, Girl, Dance   ★   United States, 1940, Dorothy Arzner; Maureen O'Hara and Lucille Ball.

worth. Nobody's going to hurt you. I know you want me to tear my clothes off so's you can look your fifty cents worth." At this point in the film, the spectators in the movie house who are watching O'Hara pirouette may begin to feel that the comfortable, passive role they enjoy is also being impugned.

In the 1930s and early 1940s, what weren't genres and originally conceived for the screen were **adaptations** from literature, drama, history, or a combination of those sources, and included the most expensive and prestigious productions of the decade. In 1935 alone there were the spectacular *Mutiny on the Bounty;* Max Reinhardt's production of Shakespeare's *A Midsummer Night's Dream; Becky Sharp,* the first feature in three-color Technicolor; *Captain Blood,* with some marvelously conceived and executed sea battles; *David Copperfield;* and *Lives of a Bengal Lancer.* All manifested the scale and skill associated with the big-studio Hollywood film of the 1930s. They cost a lot and made a lot. Created by experts at that special sort of opulent illusion, they were enjoyed by audiences who responded to it unselfconsciously and in large numbers.

Foremost among the Hollywood professionals who created these prestigious products was William Wyler, who won Academy Awards for *Mrs. Miniver* (1942) and *The Best Years of Our Lives* (1946), both based on well-known literary sources. Also nominated for Oscars were Wyler adaptations of Sinclair Lewis's *Dodsworth* (1936), Sidney Kingsley's *Dead End*

Mutiny on the Bounty ★ United States, 1935, Frank Lloyd; Clark Gable and Charles Laughton, white shirts center.

(1937), Emily Brontë's *Wuthering Heights* (1939), Somerset Maugham's *The Letter* (1940), and Lillian Hellman's *The Little Foxes* (1941). The complex character interactions that characterized these literary works found eloquent cinematic expression in Wyler's celebrated compositions in depth, which enabled audiences to focus on more than one dramatic center in a given scene. One memorable example occurs in *The Best Years of Our Lives,* when several characters gather at a bar. A group at the piano, including two of the protagonists, is in the right foreground; several persons at the bar are in left middle ground, reacting to the piano playing; the third protagonist is telephoning in center background.

The live-action comedies and other feature films of the 1930s were often preceded on the program by the enormously popular cartoon shorts. **Animated cartoons,** which had appeared intermittently from the early days, were given a boost by sound, color, and Walt Disney. Disney's first big hit, *Steamboat Willie* (1928), was also one of the first animated films with synchronized sound. Soon cartoon shorts, provided by Disney and his imitators, became almost obligatory in theater programs, and Disney's ambitions carried him on to animated features. Among twentieth-century comic figures only Charlie's Tramp could rival the universal affection in which Walt's Mickey Mouse was held.

What Disney started, others continued. Ub Iwerks seems to have become the principal creative force at the Disney Studio as Walt concerned himself more and more with

Steamboat Willie ★ United States, 1928, Walt Disney; Mickey Mouse.

administration. The Fleischer Studios followed up their Koko the Clown character with the sexy Betty Boop and later Popeye, and M-G-M produced a mischievous cat and mouse named Tom and Jerry. In 1938 Chuck Jones, who had worked with Iwerks and Disney, moved to Warner Bros. and created a rival menagerie in Bugs Bunny, Tweetie Pie, Daffy Duck, Speedy Gonzalez, Road Runner, and Wile E. Coyote. Others who left Disney about the same time later established United Productions of America (UPA). It was UPA that offered the first radical departure from Disney in the extreme simplification and stylization of its drawings, much in the manner of modern French painting, and in the use of the human characters Mr. Magoo and Gerald McBoing Boing.

Poorly paid animation workers staged a series of strikes at various studios during the early 1940s. The strikes, along with the labor shortages occasioned by World War II, contributed to the waning enthusiasm for the animation genre among the studios that were its main producers. The disappearance of short subjects from movie programs was also a factor in the commercial decline of the form. Creative leadership passed from the Disney Studio to UPA and to government film making like that of the National Film Board of Canada, with Norman McLaren, and especially to animation units in Poland, Czechoslovakia, Yugoslavia, and Japan.

Who Framed Roger Rabbit? produced by the Disney Studio in 1988, was a technically extraordinary fusion of live action (directed by Robert Zemeckis) with animation (by Richard Williams). Along the way cartoon characters created by animators at Disney, Warner Bros., M-G-M, and other studios in the 1940s were reintroduced. With new animated features such as *Beauty and the Beast* (1991), *The Prince of Egypt* (1998), and the Japanese animé film *The Princess Mononoke* (1999), as well as the new forms of computer animation on display in *Toy Story* (1997) and *Toy Story 2* (1999), the enthusiastic critical as well as popular response that had greeted earlier Disneys was repeated, perhaps even exceeded.

Wartime

Along with other social and economic abrasions, the 1930s contained the beginnings of World War II in military conquest and imperialist expansion. Japan gobbled up chunks of a China weakened by internal factionalism. Italy overran a defenseless Ethiopia. Germany joined Italy in testing weapons and tactics and helping to defeat the Republicans in Spain. The Germans continued to bluff their way through a series of territorial acquisitions culminating in the notorious Munich agreement concluded between Reichskanzler Adolph Hitler and Prime Minister Neville Chamberlain. On September 1, 1939, German dive bombers took to the skies, and tanks and trucks rolled across the Polish border, causing England and France to declare war on Germany. By some ten months later, not only Poland but France (along with Denmark, Norway, the Netherlands, and Belgium) had been ignominiously defeated. Germany's occupation of virtually all of Western Europe was complete and Britain was left to fight on alone against that massed power.

The preceding decade ended with the outbreak of World War II in Europe, but for the United States 1940 and 1941 were pretty much a continuation of the 1930s. The United States had been backing into the war, pushed by the commitment President Roosevelt and other opinion leaders felt to Great Britian and its struggle against Nazi Germany. But the majority of the American public remained isolationist, preoccupied with ongoing domestic dificulties. When the Depression finally ended, it didn't die of natural causes; it was merely replaced by the artificial boom of a wartime economy after the Japanese attack on Pearl Harbor pulled the nation into the conflict in December 1941.

The United States would continue to provide the Allied and neutral countries with the bulk of their screen entertainment. The Hollywood films of wartime, for the most part, were more an extension of those of the 1930s—appropriately trimmed with references to the war—than a prelude to those of the second half of the 1940s. The memorable *Casablanca* (1943) is one prominent example, its bittersweet romance tinged with antifascist idealism. Aljean Harmetz's book on the making of this consummate Hollywood product attributes the film's initial popularity to the timeliness of its release, just after Roosevelt and Churchill were finishing a crucial meeting in Casablanca. But the production was marketed on the basis of its human drama rather than its historical importance. A voice-over narrator for the trailer stated, "Against this fascinating background is woven the story of an imperishable love and the enthralling saga of six desperate people, each in Casablanca to keep an appointment with destiny." The story features a romance between Rick (Humphrey Bogart) and Ilsa (Ingrid Bergman) as Dooley Wilson plays and sings "As Time Goes By."

Casablanca ★ United States, 1943, Michael Curtiz; Claude Rains (in dark uniform), Paul Henreid, Humphrey Bogart, and Ingrid Bergman.

Some of the films dealing directly with the war, derived from popular genres and toughened by wartime realities, antedated a postwar tendency toward realism. Among the most popular were *Wake Island* (1942); *Air Force, Bataan, The Moon Is Down* (all 1943); *Lifeboat, Thirty Seconds Over Tokyo* (both 1944); and *The Story of G. I. Joe* (1945). But it has been estimated that fewer than a third of the wartime films dealt with the war. More characteristic was the continuation, with home-front themes or military ruffles and flourishes added, of the comedies, the light romantic or family dramas, and the musicals, now increased in number and vitality. Still, the bulk of American films of World War II undoubtedly contributed to the war effort. When not inspirational and hortatory, they were wholesomely entertaining and supportive of the culture the war was being fought to preserve.

A 1940s Genre: Film Noir

During the first half of the 1940s a body of films began that represented a sort of substratum amidst wartime patriotism and wholesomeness. This subgenre or style subsequently identified by French critics as ***film noir*** was referred to in the close of Chapter 3. These dark melodramas of crime and corruption, of psychological dislocation and aberration, reveal a Germanic influence in their intricate and artificial visual style and their preoccupation with disordered psyches. *Noir* is an attitude as well as a style, however, and is descended not only from German expressionism of the 1920s but also from French poetic realism of the 1930s, especially the films of Marcel Carné and Jacques Prévert.

Some would say that the success of *The Maltese Falcon* (1941), John Huston's first directorial effort, established not only a private-eye formula but also the beginning of *film noir* as well. *Noir,* however, was subsequently developed especially in the work of a few German and Austrian expatriates. Austrian-born Billy Wilder was one of the masters of the black film; his *Double Indemnity* (1944), coscripted by Raymond Chandler, is a prime example. Along with Wilder there were Robert Siodmak (*Phantom Lady,* 1944; *The Spiral Staircase,* 1945; *The Killers,* 1946), Otto Preminger (*Laura,* 1944; *Fallen Angel,* 1945), and Fritz Lang (*The Woman in the Window,* 1944; *Scarlet Street,* 1945). The style spread to include films of a number of other distinguished Hollywood professionals, among them Edward Dmytryk (*Murder, My Sweet,* 1944) and Howard Hawks (*The Big Sleep,* 1946). Prominent among later examples are *Gilda* (Charles Vidor, 1946), *Kiss of Death* (Henry Hathaway, 1947), *Out of the Past* (Jacques Tourneur, 1947), and *Kiss Me Deadly* (Robert Aldrich, 1955).

The fantasies the *noir* films offered were nightmare hallucinations full of indecipherable complications, a pervasive sense of fear and helplessness in the face of enigmatic human malevolence. The protagonists are typically trapped, seeking to find a way out of a tortuous labyrinth of violence and evil. The antagonists are frequently seductive women, career criminals, worldly foreigners, or members of a decadent and sexually permissive upper class. As opposed to the idealism of a society fighting together to combat the political evil of fascism, *film noir* dealt with individuals conspicuously antisocial in their greed and selfishness, driven to crime out of an incurable sickness. Their malaise was presented as endemic to the human species, and the world they inhabited was a dark one literally as well as morally. The films take place mostly at night, in seedy furnished apartments and

Murder, My Sweet ★
United States, 1944, Edward
Dmytryk; Dick Powell.

on rain-washed streets of big cities. Studio sets were fashioned into urban jungles with predators stalking prey and danger lurking in the shadows, intermittently revealed by flashing electric signs. Perhaps even more than most other cinematic styles, *film noir* depends for its impact on nonverbal, essentially visual effects, where form far outstrips content. The scene in *Phantom Lady* featuring a hopped-up jazz drummer (Elisha Cook, Jr.) surrounded by swirling cigarette smoke, glaring lights, and harsh shadows and photographed from low, oblique angles is characteristic of *noir.*

The most accomplished director of *noir* films was **Fritz Lang.** As the film maker responsible for such German masterpieces as *Metropolis* and *M,* Lang came to the United States with a distinguished pedigree that was ideally suited to the *noir* style. He continued his exploration of dark themes, typically expressed through hard lighting and occasional overhead shots that pinned characters to the ground like ants. His two *noir* films with Edward G. Robinson, Joan Bennett, and Dan Duryea, *The Woman in the Window* (1944) and *Scarlet Street* (1945), stand as classics of the cycle. In *The Woman in the Window,* Robinson, playing a timid professor called Richard Wanley, becomes enmeshed in a tangled web of intrigue with Alice Reed (Joan Bennett), an alluring stranger whose portrait he greatly admires. In Alice's apartment, Richard repeatedly confronts his image reflected in mirrors as he begins to confront new facets of his personality. In a coldly analytical style, the film examines the way in which illicit behavior and criminality emerge from hidden parts of people's personalities.

Another influential director whose career is closely identified with the *noir* style was **John Huston.** Following the *noir* tradition of dark passions, criminality, and

The Woman in the Window ★ United States, 1944, Fritz Lang; Joan Bennett and Edward G. Robinson.

pessimism, Huston's films often feature groups of people undertaking dangerous enterprises at great risk; most of these endeavors end in failure. In Huston's world of male adventurers, women are typically seen as weak, manipulative, and not to be trusted; his films rarely end with the traditional Hollywood romantic clinch. *The Maltese Falcon,* which Huston adapted from a novel by hard-boiled writer Dashiell Hammett, features Mary Astor as the worldly temptress Brigid O'Shaugnessey and *noir* icon Humphrey Bogart as detective Sam Spade. Like many *noir* films, *The Maltese Falcon* features a cast of villains obliquely identified as homosexuals and associated with the cosmopolitan cultures of Europe and Asia. Bogart stands in contrast as unambiguously heterosexual and American. The film's many tightly composed three-shots make palpable the threat represented by the villains' otherness. Later in the decade Huston followed *The Maltese Falcon* with other downbeat *noir*-inspired dramas, including *Key Largo* (1948) and *The Asphalt Jungle* (1950).

Because *noir* films typically told stories of weak men ensnared by manipulative *femme fatales,* critics have sometimes viewed them as a response to the anxiety caused by women taking jobs that men had vacated to go to war. Perhaps they also appealed to something in audiences that distrusted the official rhetoric and optimism espoused by the dominant political forces. If not among the big hits, for the most part, the noir films have continued as a steady stream to the present day, including such productions as *Chinatown* (1973), *Body Heat* (1982), and *L. A. Confidential* (1998).

The Maltese Falcon ★ United States, 1941, John Huston; Mary Astor.

Orson Welles: Boy Genius

Orson Welles came to Hollywood following a phenomenal burst of creative leadership and experimentation in theater and radio. He was twenty-six years old when his first film, *Citizen Kane,* was released in 1941. It became a landmark like *The Birth of a Nation* and *Battleship Potemkin* before it. Although influenced by the emerging *noir* style, it went far beyond genre conventions. *Citizen Kane* moved American film into the modernism present in the other arts. With its unconventional approach to theme, character, and narrative, as well as its range of cinematic technique, it became a sourcebook for future film makers. If modernist narrative is usually associated with the foregrounding of filmic language, multiple levels of narration, and estrangement of the spectator, *Citizen Kane* might be said to be fully if not overly qualified for modernity.

The fictional Charles Foster Kane, played by Welles, was modeled closely enough on the real William Randolph Hearst to make Hearst furious and vengeful. After trying unsuccessfully to suppress the film, he ordered the reviewers in his newspaper chain to trash it. As a result, *Citizen Kane* had little success at the box office and was largely passed over for Academy Award consideration.

Like Hearst, Kane is a newspaper tycoon, a lonely and egocentric man of vast wealth and failed political ambition. We learn the facts of his life as a reporter questions people close to him for a filmed obituary. Using investigative journalism as a device, scriptwriters Herman J. Mankiewicz and Orson Welles track back through Kane's life with

Citizen Kane ★ United States, 1941,
Orson Welles; Welles.

interview and flashback recollection from his banker-guardian, his business manager, his best friend, his second wife, and his butler. From their divergent points of view, we are presented with different Kanes. Although we learn about the complexity of his activities, neither we nor the reporter get at Kane's essence. We do find out what *rosebud,* his final word, referred to, as the reporter does not; rather, we are left standing at a distance from him—the sort of distancing or estrangement of the spectator employed by Bertold Brecht.

To complement its kaleidescopic narrative, *Citizen Kane* pushes filmic language into the foreground. Low angles and chiaroscuro lighting abound. The great depth of field of the images was provided by cinematographer Gregg Toland and made possible by improvements in film stock, light sources, and optics. It introduces a new intricacy in the relationship of characters to setting and to each other as well as demands a fuller "reading" than was necessary to interpret the selective emphasis that had become the standard technique for creating filmed narratives by this time. For example, in an early scene that focuses on Kane's childhood, his mother, having unexpectedly come into a fortune, relinquishes her son to be raised in privileged surroundings by Thatcher, a heartless banker. As the transaction is finalized, we see Mrs. Kane and Thatcher in the foreground, Kane's skeptical father in the middle background, and, through a window in the far background, the oblivious young boy playing outside in the snow. This single shot thus contains three distinct centers of dramatic interest.

The sound track takes on the acoustical character of the surroundings. Sound montage, growing out of Welles's radio work, includes sequences in which a character begins a sentence in one scene and completes it in another. For example, at one point, we see Thatcher wishing a nine-year-old Kane "Merry Christmas," but in the following shot, as the stuffy banker completes his thought by adding "and a Happy New Year," his young charge reappears as a twenty-one-year-old.

One of the most famous scenes in *Kane* combines sound and image montage by splicing together numerous shots of Kane and his first wife, Emily, as they breakfast together over a period of years. In less than a minute of screen time, the film signals the disintegration of the marriage by juxtaposing brief snippets from a series of increasingly acrimonious conversational exchanges between the two.

Welles's career continued until his death in 1987, but he was never again to enjoy the freedom and financial support that made *Citizen Kane* possible. Nonetheless, he made a number of other *noir*-influenced films such as *The Lady From Shanghai* (1948) and *Touch of Evil* (1959) as well as several adaptations of Shakespearan plays and other literary works, among them *The Magnificent Ambersons* (1942) and *Macbeth* (1948). In his later years he made several films in Europe, including *The Trial* (1962) and *Chimes at Midnight* (1966), a conflation of Shakespeare's *Henry IV, Part 2* and *The Merry Wives of Windsor* with Welles as Falstaff. As a film maker, Welles had some inspired flashes and some partially realized creations, but it is for *Citizen Kane* that he is most remembered.

In addition to the pleasures they may offer individually, the American films of the 1930s and early 1940s are studies in paradox. The studio system with its big bosses and front office, mass production and distribution, allowed and even encouraged the scattering of masterpieces among the thousands of films made within its purview. The system's prodigious resources and the opportunities for ongoing team activity enabled by the studio structure set the stage for a fuller panoply of creative opportunities than may ever have existed in human history. At the same time, the studio system fostered a repressive self-regulation that attempted to bleach art into the palest imitation of life. In the face of this kind of censorship, Hollywood craftspeople managed to abide only by the letter of the law, often playing with the prim conventions in inventive ways. The genres, cycles, and formula pictures with their fixed patterns, which the studios loved for their predictability and easy marketability, could also be manipulated in ingenious ways, enabling inventive directors to create some of their best work.

Films of the Period

1929
The Cocoanuts (Joseph Stanley and Robert Florey)

1930
Little Caesar (Mervyn LeRoy)
Morocco (Josef von Sternberg)

1931
City Lights (Charles Chaplin)
Dracula (Tod Browning)
Frankenstein (James Whale)
The Public Enemy (William Wellman)
Tabu (F. W. Murnau and Robert Flaherty)

1932

I Am a Fugitive from a Chain Gang (Mervyn LeRoy)

Scarface (Howard Hawks)

Shanghai Express (Josef von Sternberg)

Trouble in Paradise (Ernst Lubitsch)

1933

Christopher Strong (Dorothy Arzner)

Duck Soup (Leo McCarey)

42nd Street (Lloyd Bacon)

Gold Diggers of 1933 (Mervyn LeRoy)

King Kong (Merian C. Cooper and Ernest B. Schoedsack)

1934

It Happened One Night (Frank Capra)

Queen Christina (Rouben Mamoulian)

The Scarlet Empress (Josef von Sternberg)

Twentieth Century (Howard Hawks)

1935

A Night at the Opera (Sam Wood)

1936

Fury (Fritz Lang)

The Great Ziegfeld (Robert Z. Leonard)

Mr. Deeds Goes to Town (Frank Capra)

Modern Times (Charlie Chaplin)

The Story of Louis Pasteur (William Dieterle)

Swing Time (George Stevens)

1937

The Awful Truth (Leo McCarey)

Camille (George Cukor)

The Life of Emile Zola (William Dieterle)

Snow White and the Seven Dwarfs (Walt Disney)

A Star Is Born (William Wellman)

Stella Dallas (King Vidor)

You Only Live Once (Fritz Lang)

1938

Angels with Dirty Faces (Michael Curtiz)

Bringing Up Baby (Howard Hawks)

1939

Gone with the Wind (Victor Fleming)

Mr. Smith Goes to Washington (Frank Capra)

Ninotchka (Ernst Lubitsch)

Only Angels Have Wings (Howard Hawks)

Stagecoach (John Ford)

Young Mr. Lincoln (John Ford)

1940

Dance, Girl, Dance (Dorothy Arzner)

Fantasia (Walt Disney)

Foreign Correspondent (Alfred Hitchcock)

The Grapes of Wrath (John Ford)

The Great Dictator (Charlie Chaplin)

The Great McGinty (Preston Sturges)

His Girl Friday (Howard Hawks)

The Letter (William Wyler)

The Philadelphia Story (George Cukor)

Rebecca (Alfred Hitchcock)

1941

Citizen Kane (Orson Welles)

High Sierra (Raoul Walsh)

How Green Was My Valley (John Ford)

The Lady Eve (Preston Sturges)

The Little Foxes (William Wyler)

The Maltese Falcon (John Huston)

Sergeant York (Howard Hawks)

Sullivan's Travels (Preston Sturges)

Suspicion (Alfred Hitchcock)

1942

Casablanca (Michael Curtiz)

The Magnificent Ambersons (Orson Welles)

Mrs. Miniver (William Wyler)

Now, Voyager (Irving Rapper)

The Palm Beach Story (Preston Sturges)

To Be or Not to Be (Ernst Lubitsch)

Yankee Doodle Dandy (Michael Curtiz)

1943

Air Force (Howard Hawks)

Meshes of the Afternoon (Maya Deren)

Ox-Bow Incident (William Wellman)

Shadow of a Doubt (Alfred Hitchcock)

1944

Double Indemnity (Billy Wilder)

Gaslight (George Cukor)

Hail the Conquering Hero (Preston Sturges)

Laura (Otto Preminger)

Meet Me in St. Louis (Vincente Minnelli)
The Miracle of Morgan's Creek (Preston Sturges)
The Woman in the Window (Fritz Lang)

1945
The House on 92nd Street (Henry Hathaway)
The Lost Weekend (Billy Wilder)

Mildred Pierce (Michael Curtiz)
Scarlet Street (Fritz Lang)
The Southerner (Jean Renoir)
Spellbound (Alfred Hitchcock)

Books on the Period

Altman, Rick. *Film/Genre.* London: British Film Institute, 1999.

American Film Institute Staff and Carolyn B. Mitchell. *American Film Institute Catalog of Motion Pictures Produced in the United States: Feature Films 1931–1940.* 3 vols. Berkeley: University of California Press, 1993.

Balio, Tino T. *Grand Design: Hollywood as a Modern Business Enterprise, 1930–1939.* (Vol. 5, "History of the American Cinema"). New York: Charles Scribner's Sons, 1993.

Barrier, Michael. *Hollywood Cartoons. American Animation in Its Golden Age.* New York: Oxford University Press, 1999.

Barrios, Richard. *A Song in the Dark: The Birth of the Musical Film.* New York: Oxford University Press, 1995.

Bernstein, Matthew, ed. *Controlling Hollywood: Censorship and Regulation in the Studio Era.* New Brunswick, NJ: Rutgers University Press, 2000.

Black, Gregory D. *The Catholic Crusade Against the Movies, 1940–1975.* New York: Cambridge University Press, 1998.

Borowiec, Piotr. *Animated Short Films: A Critical Index to Theatrical Cartoons.* Lanham, MD: Scarecrow Press, 1998.

Brown, Gene. *Movie Time: A Chronology of Hollywood and the Movie Industry from Its Beginnings to the Present.* New York: Macmillan, 1995.

Browne, Nick, ed. *Refiguring American Film Genres: History and Theory.* Berkeley: University of California Press, 1997.

Cameron, Ian. *The Book of Film Noir.* New York: Continuum, 1993.

Christopher, Nicholas. *Somewhere in the Night: Film Noir and the American City.* New York: The Free Press, 1998.

Copjec, Joan, ed. *Shades of Noir.* New York: The Free Press, 1998.

Cormack, Mike. *Ideology and Cinematography in Hollywood, 1930–39.* New York: St. Martin's Press, 1993.

Couvares, Frances, G., ed. *Movie Censorship and American Culture* ("Studies in the History of Film and Television"). Washington, DC: Smithsonian Institution Press, 1996.

Crafton, Donald. *The Talkies: American Cinema's Transition to Sound, 1926–1931.* (Vol 4 "History of the American Cinema"). New York: Charles Scribner's Sons, 1997.

Cripps, Thomas. *Hollywood's High Noon: Moviemaking and Society Before Television* ("The American Moment Series"). Baltimore, MD: Johns Hopkins University Press, 1996.

Davis, Ronald L. *The Glamour Factory: Inside Hollywood's Big Studio System.* Dallas, TX: Southern Methodist Unviersity Press, 1993.

Doherty, Thomas. *Projections of War: Hollywood, American Culture, and World War II.* New York: Columbia University Press, 1994.

Doherty, Thomas. *Pre-Code Hollywood: Sex, Immorality, and Insurrection in American Cinema, 1930–1934.* New York: Columbia University Press, 1999.

Dyson, Jeremy. *Bright Darkness: The Lost Art of the Supernatural Horror Film.* Herndon, VA: Cassell Academic, 1997.

Fine, Richard. *West of Eden: Writers in Hollywood, 1928–1940.* Washington, DC: Smithsonian Institution Press, 1993.

Fyne, Robert. *The Hollywood Propaganda of World War II.* Lanham, MD: Scarecrow Press, 1994.

Henderson, Amy, and Dwight Blocker Bowers. *Red, Hot and Blue: A Smithsonian Salute to the American Musical.* Washington, DC: Smithsonian Institution Press, 1996.

Klein, Norman M. *Seven Minutes: The Life and Death of the American Cartoon.* New York: Verso, 1996.

Maltby, Richard, and Ian Craven. *Hollywood Cinema: An Introduction.* Malden, MA: Blackwell Publications, 1995.

Muller, Eddie. *Dark City: The Lost World of Film Noir.* New York: St. Martin's Press, 1998.

Muscio, Giuliana. *Hollywood's New Deal.* Philadelphia: Temple University Press, 1997.

Naremore, James. *More than Night: Film Noir in Its Contexts.* Berkeley: University of California Press, 1998.

Palmer, R. Barton. *Hollywood's Dark Cinema: The American Film Noir.* New York: Twayne, 1994.

Sarris, Andrew. *"You Ain't Heard Nothin' Yet": The American Talking Film: History and Memory 1927–1949.* New York: Oxford University Press, 1998.

Schatz, Thomas. *Boom and Bust: Hollywood in the 1940's* (Vol. 6, "History of the American Cinema," Charles Harpole, Gen. Ed.). New York: Charles Scribner's Sons, 1997.

Schindler, Colin. *Hollywood in Crisis: Cinema and American Society 1929–1939.* New York: Routledge, 1996.

Sevastakis, Michael. *Songs of Love and Death: The Classical American Horror Film of the 1930's.* Westport, CT: Greenwood Press, 1993.

Silver, Alain, and James Ursini, eds. *Film Noir Reader.* New York: Limelight Editions, 1996.

Silver, Alain, and James Ursini. *The Noir Style.* London: Aurum Press, 2000.

Slide, Anthony. *The New Historical Dictionary of the American Film Industry.* Lanham, MD: Scarecrow Press, 1998.

Smoodin, Eric. *Animating Culture: Hollywood Cartoons from the Sound Era.* New Brunswick, NJ: Rutgers University Press, 1993.

Staiger, Janet, ed. *The Studio System.* New Brunswick, NJ: Rutgers University Press, 1994.

Stokes, Melvyn, and Richard Maltby. *American Movie Audiences: From the Turn of the Century to the Early Sound Era.* London: British Film Institute, 1999.

Tapert, Annette. *The Power of Glamour: The Women Who Defined the Magic of Stardom.* New York: Random House, 1996.

Whissen, Thomas. *Guide to American Cinema, 1930–1965.* Westport, CT: Greenwood Press, 1998.

8

Postwar Italy: Neorealism and Beyond

★ ★ ★ ★

1945–

The eruption of a brilliant cluster of Italian films that began with Roberto Rossellini's *Open City* (1945) was stimulated by the removal of fascist power after nearly a quarter century and the release of bottled-up feelings of frustration and humiliation generated by Italy's ambiguous and shifting position in World War II. Beginning as a nominal equal to the other two Axis powers, Germany and Japan, Italy subsequently was reduced to a subservient role. When Mussolini was overthrown, a separate peace was signed with the Allies. The Germans in Italy then turned into an occupying force, retreating slowly as the Allies advanced up the peninsula to replace Germany as the new occupier. It is against this background that *Open City* is set, at the point when Allied forces were approaching Rome and had already begun bombing its outskirts. An agreement was then reached whereby the Germans did not attempt to hold the Eternal City, thus averting its destruction.

In *Open City* Rossellini chronicles in cross-sectional form the activities of the partisans, the raids and reprisals of the German military and the Italian police, the painful tensions among collaborators, resisters, and the great majority of people who simply wanted enough bread and wine, and an end to the killing and misery of war. The film begins with German soldiers arriving outside the building lived in by Manfredi (Marcello Pagliero), a partisan activist. After he flees, his former lover (Maria Michi), now dependent on the Gestapo to supply her with drugs, tries to reach him by phone. Manfredi goes to the apartment of a friend and fellow partisan, whose fiancée (Anna Magnani) takes him in and sends for a Catholic priest who is aiding the resistance. The friend returns from work and the action proceeds with the Gestapo net closing in on Manfredi and the priest. But equal attention is given to the daily lives of the Roman people under the stress of a foreign presence, from child resistance-fighters to an irritable old man who scarcely comprehends what is happening but attempts to supply his needs nonetheless.

Open City ★ Italy, 1945,
Roberto Rossellini; Aldo
Fabrizi and Marcello
Pagliero, foreground.

Scriptwriters Sergio Amidei and Federico Fellini, and director Rossellini, make as good a case as they can for the instances of courage, heroism, and martyrdom that occurred in a generally demoralized Italy. *Open City* seems in part an attempt to ease the national conscience in regard to the immediate past and, for the grim postwar problems yet to be solved, to provide models of behavior. The Catholic priest and the professional communist revolutionary unite in their efforts and sacrifice their lives in the fight to free their country from fascist rule. The film is a passionate requiem, like Verdi's for his novelist friend Alessandro Manzoni, and its rough beauty and emotional intensity carry all before it.

The Italian industry had become heavily controlled and subsidized by the fascist government, and dictator Benito Mussolini used it as a relatively harmless field in which to place some of his less able relatives. After a few unsuccessful attempts to use the fiction film for direct propaganda—invoking the glories of ancient Rome and associating them with the contemporary Italy of the black shirts, for example—the fascists had to accept the evidence that audiences would simply stay away. Instead, the authorities became content to keep films from making any significant statement about modern reality; the filmed opera, costume melodrama, and romance built around a box-office idol became ubiquitous. The latter type were known as the "white telephone films," since an ultimate in luxurious dalliance was frequently portrayed as a langorous heroine lounging in negligee on an elaborate bed cooing to her lover on the phone.

At the same time, the fascist regime managed to put into place an infrastructure that was to serve the industry well in the decades to come. A national film school, inaugurated in 1935, trained future star directors such Roberto Rossellini, Pietro Germi, and Michelangelo Antonioni, as well as other production personnel. In 1937, the mammoth Cinecettà

Studios, subsequently known as "Hollywood on the Tiber," was built. Cinecettà later housed the production of American blockbusters such as *Cleopatra* (Joseph Mankiewicz, 1963) along with distinguished home-grown features mounted by film makers Luchino Visconti, Federico Fellini, and others. Although the neorealist directors of the immediate postwar era turned away from the artificiality implied by the studio style, they benefitted from these initiatives insofar as they created a cadre of trained production workers, provided material resources, and gave momentum to the ideal of a national film culture.

That *Open City* was made at all is something of a marvel. Rossellini filmed secretly between 1943 and 1945, scraping together funds from various sources. The money kept running out and at one point Rossellini and Magnani, who plays her first great screen role in the film, sold all their clothes to obtain enough lire to carry on for a few more days. Production conditions were incredibly primitive. Shooting was done on odds and ends of raw stock of various manufacturers. Studios weren't available to them, and nearly all the scenes were enacted on the actual locations they represent in the film. Even the electrical power in wartime was so erratic that maintaining consistent exposure was a constant problem. In spite of the technical and financial difficulties (dead broke, Rossellini is said to have sold the rights for $28,000; *Open City* grossed $5 million in the United States alone), the film emerged as a towering achievement that would inspire other Italian film makers to emulate its concepts and its method of dealing with contemporary reality.

Theory and Practice of Neorealism

The working principles of the neorealist films that Rossellini had first improvised partly by necessity and accident, partly out of conviction, became loosely codified into a theory of cinema. The premises underpinning neorealism were most forcefully articulated by scriptwriter Cesare Zavattini, who became spokesman for, as well as one of the principal creators in, the movement. Perhaps the only other screenwriter to have achieved a comparable intellectual-aesthetic dominance in a period of national excellence is Carl Mayer, in relation to the German-expressionist films of the 1920s.

In a famous interview, Zavattini had the following things to say about the content and purposes of neorealism:

> The most important characteristic, and the most important innovation, of what is called neorealism, it seems to me, is to have realized that the necessity of the "story" was only an unconscious way of disguising a human defeat, and that the kind of imagination it involved was simply a technique of superimposing dead formulas over living social facts. Now it has been perceived that reality is hugely rich, that to be able to look directly at it is enough; and that the artist's task is not to make people moved or indignant at metaphorical situations, but to make them reflect (and, if you like, to be moved and indignant too) on what they and others are doing, on the real things, exactly as they are.

Asking himself what effects on narrative structure the neorealist style had, Zavattini answered:

> To begin with, while the cinema used to make one situation produce another situation, and another, and another, again and again, and each scene was thought out and immediately related to the next (the natural result of a mistrust of reality), today, when we have thought

Umberto D ★ Italy, 1952, Vittorio de Sica; Maria-Pia Casilio and Carlo Battisti.

out a scene, we feel the need to "remain" in it, because the single scene itself can contain so many echoes and reverberations, can even contain all the situations we may need. Today, in fact, we can quietly say: Give us whatever "fact" you like [a stolen bicycle, for example], and we will disembowel it, make it something worth watching.[1]

The newly realistic Italian films were based on a real incident or a composite of several events; they had factual rather than fictional bases. For example, a film might be based on an actual situation of a staircase collapsing under the weight of hundreds of unemployed young women applying for jobs as typists (*Rome, Eleven O'Clock,* 1952) or on a typical one like that of an old man finding it difficult to live on his pension (*Umberto D,* 1952). The problems treated by these films had some degree of immediacy and broad concern. Their themes were not necessarily universal and timeless, as those of the arts tend to be; they were more tied to the here and now, like documentary: sociological as much as psychological in their approach. Among the prevalent concerns were poverty (*Miracle in Milan,* 1951; *Two Cents Worth of Hope,* 1952), prostitution (*Without Pity,* 1948), collaboration with and resistance to occupying military forces (*Outcry* and *To Live in Peace,* both 1947), exploitative agricultural conditions (*The Tragic Hunt,* 1947, and *Bitter Rice,* 1949),

[1] Cesare Zavattini, "Some Ideas on the Cinema," *Sight and Sound,* 23 (October–December 1953): 64, 65.

and continuing tensions between the industrial north and the agrarian south that had simmered since the time of Italian unification in the late nineteenth century.

In these semidocumentary-like films there *is* a plot and there *are* characters, but they are less fully developed than in pure fiction, and are used quite directly to embody the theme and ideas. The conflict and resolution are apt to be drawn out of the larger situation rather than out of interpersonal relations. A poor fishing family is in contention with the boat owners; when the owners win, the fishermen are forced to work the boats on the owners' terms. The family that had been resisting is broken (*La Terra Trema,* 1948). In other words, in films of this sort the characters and their lives (plot incidents) are used deliberately to express an ideology.

Finally, in these films the film-making methods are drawn from both fiction and documentary. They tend to depend less on performance and dialogue than do conventional fiction films. Actors may appear in principal roles, but frequently nonactors are used in lesser roles and as extras (*Open City,* 1945; *The Tragic Hunt,* 1947) and even as leads (*Shoeshine,* 1946; *The Bicycle Thief,* 1948; *Umberto D,* 1952). In any event there is usually an avoidance of stars. Considerable location shooting (exteriors) is combined with studio (interiors). Sometimes candid or newsreel footage is interpolated. Frequently commentary, montage, and even maps suggest a broader scope and help bridge a less-tight plot. Lighting, costumes, makeup, and sets are actual, or naturalistic in style. The editing is less "smooth"

La Terra Trema ★ Italy, 1948, Luchino Visconti.

than in the usual story picture, being dictated by the subject-matter requirements. The cutting pace is frequently more rapid, too, as it tends to be when ideas more than emotions are being dealt with, and when film makers (as in documentary) are working with persons (nonactors) who cannot sustain performances. There tends to be emphasis on source sounds and avoidance of heavy musical scoring.

Two Major Directors of the Neorealist Era

Many of the basic strategies of neorealism had been put into practice during the early days of cinema by Neapolitan director Elvira Notari. Notari's widely distributed productions of the 1910s and 1920s featured location shooting, amateur actors, and a focus on the poor. Her films had, in turn, been influenced by the *sceneggiata,* a popular Italian theatrical form that mixed melodrama with songs and was performed by nonprofessionals. After World War II, these time-honored conventions gained new relevance by virtue of Italy's political and economic woes. At the same time, the theoretical writings of Zavattini and others provided such traditions with deeper meanings. In the cultural context thus created, the careers of two major directors peaked during this period: Roberto Rossellini and Vittorio de Sica. The films of both represent the characteristics of the neorealist movement as a whole.

Rossellini quickly followed *Open City* with his other major film fully within the general terms of neorealist style and intention, *Paisan* (1946). In six separate episodes it traces the Allied campaign up the long boot of Italy, exploring the contacts between the conquerors (principally American) and the conquered. Maps and newsreel footage connect the parts, suggesting that the dramatic vignettes are incidents happening within the larger historical context. Each episode sketches one aspect of the complex and changing American-Italian relationships, which move from an initial distrust to a growing closeness.

Rossellini worked the stories out as he went along, with the aid of a group of writers that included Federico Fellini. Each incident is particularly representative of that phase of the campaign. Taken together they treat, with extraordinary comprehensiveness as well as precision, the significance of the American presence in Italy. The camera and editing techniques are as sparse and unprettified as the stories. Of *Paisan's* large cast only four members had had previous acting experience (the GI and the prostitute in Rome, the nurse in Florence, the Catholic chaplain in Bologna); the others were picked up by Rossellini as he found them on location. The whole achieves a directness and power through its spontaneity. Rossellini's style is in perfect keeping with the material and his attitude toward it.

De Sica and his scriptwriter, Cesare Zavattini, continued this national saga with an examination of the immediate postwar years. Before directing, de Sica had been a well-known screen actor in the 1930s. His first important film as director, *The Children Are Watching Us* (1943), was also his first collaboration with Zavattini. Roughly contemporary with Visconti's *Ossessione,* it was somewhat comparable in its realistic tendencies. In the main line of postwar neorealism, de Sica's *Shoeshine* (1946) is concerned with the Roman *ragazzi* who eked out a living shining GIs' shoes, pimping, and dealing in black market American cigarettes, candy bars, and, in this instance, blankets. Two boys are apprehended, tried, convicted, and sent to a reformatory, where their affection for each other is turned

Paisan ★ Italy, 1946, Roberto Rossellini.

into hatred, resulting in the death of one of the boys. There are no villains, however, but simply a bad system. We are not sure why there aren't enough staff and money to run this institution properly, except that there never are in institutions of this sort. Nor are we told what steps might be taken to obtain adequate resources. Although the neorealist films dealt with social problems, they tended to hold them up for examination in terms of their effects on individual lives rather than explain causes or propose solutions.

Zavattini's and de Sica's most successful collaboration, and among those films closest to the neorealist ideal, was *The Bicycle Thief* (1948). It deals with the simplest possible situation. An unemployed laborer with his first chance to work for some time has the bicycle stolen that he must have in order to keep his job. The events leading up to the theft and the attempt to recover the bicycle provide sufficient "plot" for a complete and significant work of art, even including implied social and political criticism. In following the man's and his young son's search for the bicycle, various aspects of Italian society are sketched, with apparent casualness it may seem at first; on reflection the highest degree of economy and skill become evident. *The Bicycle Thief* was shot almost entirely outside the studio, in the streets and apartments and offices of Rome. The father in the film was in real life a machinist in the big Breda steelworks. The boy who plays his son was a Roman newsboy. The performances elicited from the pair can only be described as miraculous. De Sica's work with nonactors, especially children, is always sensitive and sure; here he surpassed himself. Although methods formerly found only in documentary are

Shoeshine ⋆ Italy, 1946, Vittorio de Sica; Rinaldo Smordoni and Franco Interlenghi, standing left rear.

basic to its conception, the emotional richness of *The Bicycle Thief* depends to considerable extent on the portrayals of its Everyman and his small son.

Period of Transition: 1952–1960

It must be admitted that cosmic meaning arising from the ordinary was not always, and seldom completely, attained in neorealist films. Melodrama superimposed on reality was still the rule. But films of the neorealist style attracted Italy's most talented directors, writers, and performers; received the widest foreign distribution; and exerted the strongest influence on the film production of other countries during the immediate postwar years. The neorealist films began in a defeated and occupied country, with a badly disorganized economy and political life, widespread poverty and unemployment, and uncontrolled inflation—another instance of a film movement growing out of troubled times, like the post–World War I German and Soviet cinemas.

Problems of national identity, political turmoil, economic misery, and social dislocation continued, but by 1949 neorealism had begun to wane as the predominant force in Italian film making. Pressure from the Roman Catholic Church and the Italian government

The Bicycle Thief ⋆ Italy, 1948,
Vittorio de Sica; Enzo Staiola and
Lamberto Maggiorani.

in the early 1950s resulted in a decline of the export of "social problem" films to the United States, the chief source of economic support for neorealism. A realization by the film makers themselves that the neorealist conception of reality, with its externalized nonpsychological approach, was limiting, led to an enlargement or alteration of their scope of concern. An often quoted comment by Michelangelo Antonioni about *The Bicycle Thief* is revealing. He said that if he had directed the film, he would have told more about the people and less about the bicycle.

If neorealism began with Rossellini's *Open City* in 1945, it ceased, or changed direction anyway, after the de Sica-Zavattini *Umberto D* of 1952. The latter is about an old man whose fixed income had become insufficient to support life with any dignity, let alone pleasure. After that last great neorealist film, Italian film makers began shifting their attention from the lower classes and poverty to the upper classes and the unsatisfying and corrosive values of much of modern life that are most evident among them. Some of Rossellini's films of the middle and late 1950s look ahead to a later kind of cinema, exerting great influence on the upcoming generation of French as well as Italian film makers. His *Voyage to Italy* (1953) is startlingly predictive; Antonioni's *L'Avventura* (1960) seems to grow directly out of it—though on its initial release, the Italian critics panned it as a betrayal of neorealist ideals. (One wrote, "*Viaggio in Italia* does nothing but confirm the absolute, progressive, and irredemable decadence of Rossellini.")

Fellini also can be considered a transitional figure who moved from the essentially materialistic concerns of the neorealist films to the (for want of a better word) spiritual concerns of the next generation of Italian film makers. "For me," he said, "neorealism means looking at reality with an honest eye—but at any kind of reality; not just social reality, but also spiritual reality, metaphysical reality, anything man has inside of him." His *La Strada* (1954) might in many ways be regarded as a pivotal film. Although set among the lower classes, it is not concerned with poverty but with inadequacies in human relationships. With a haunting musical score by Nino Rota and a delicately stylized performance by Fellini's wife, Giulietta Masina, which was modeled on the ancient *commedia dell'arte* tradition, *La Strada* came across more as a fable than as a study in quotidian reality. When the film was attacked by the Italian critics as a betrayal of neorealist traditions, Fellini replied, "Reality needs poetry."

De Sica attempted to return to neorealism with *The Roof* (1955), but this tale of a young couple trying to obtain their own place to live seemed strangely old-fashioned and inessential in the newly prosperous Italy. Rossellini's *General della Rover* (1959) and de Sica's *Two Women* (1960) are also efforts to recapture some of the themes of the immediate postwar films. In spite of the professional polish, in part because of it of course, and some excellent things in each, both seem anachronistic. It may be fitting that in the former film Rossellini is directing de Sica, playing the lead as the General's impersonator who dies a hero. Those two films were a kind of final reprise, not so much for the two directors—because by then even those stalwarts of neorealism were making other kinds of films—but for the original movement.

The practice and the theory of neorealism did not cease to exist, however, and its influence has been discernible ever since the initial period. In Italy the films of Ermanno Olmi (*Il Posto,* 1961; *The Fiancés,* 1962) embodied it most directly. Also the works of Vittorio de Seta (*The Bandits of Orgosolo,* 1961) and Pier Paolo Pasolini (*Accatone,* 1961), in their methods and explicitly Marxist ideologies, recalled the earlier films, as did the films of Francesco Rosi (*Salvatore Giuliano,* 1961; *Hands Over the City,* 1963). The French New Wave, Eastern European cinema, and the British social-realist features, all to be dealt with later, owed something to the kind of film making practiced in Italy between 1945 and 1952.

Emergence of a New Style: Three Directors of the 1960s

A new kind of Italian cinema emerged at the Venice International Film Festival in 1960. The films were by experienced directors whose landmark works of that year were set within careers that extended back into immediate postwar neorealism. The films also pointed ahead to the subsequent development of their directors and to a younger generation that would quickly grow up around them. The films were *Rocco and His Brothers, La Dolce Vita,* and *L'Avventura;* their directors were, respectively, Luchino Visconti, Federico Fellini, and Michelangelo Antonioni.

The Italian film makers were reacting against classical Hollywood narrative with a basic orientation that might be called modernist (Visconti being the exception). *Rocco and His Brothers* looked back to neorealism, although, like the bulk of Visconti's work, it departed from accepted neorealist tenets in its melodramatic emotionality and its heightening of character and incident. *La Dolce Vita* and *L'Avventura,* on the other hand, contained much identifiable as new in both subject and form.

The films had an existentialist base, derived from the novels of Cesare Pavese, whom Antonioni much admired, as well as the writings of Sartre and Camus: the sense that life was merely the sum of actions lived, the emphasis on alienation and the failure of communication. There was also a similarity with Ingmar Bergman, acknowledged by both Antonioni and Fellini, in picturing a world in which divine faith has been lost and human love seems unattainable.

The narrative structure of the new Italian films was loose. Both *L'Avventura* and *La Dolce Vita* are episodic, rather than tightly woven, and picaresque. The first is organized around a journey and search for a missing person; the second centers on a sort of spiritual quest for values amidst various physical settings and social groups in and near contemporary Rome. Much of Fellini's work gives us the sense of being on the road; *La Strada* (1954) is the extreme case, the emphasis acknowledged in the title. Antonioni's films, too, set people in motion through countrysides and across cities. He is resolutely narrative rather than dramatic, in a low key of slight action and sparse, inconclusive dialogue. Of all film makers perhaps he is closest to certain tendencies in the modern novel in his attempts to deal with the interior lives of his characters. Since little is accidental in an Antonioni film, significance can be attached to a copy of F. Scott Fitzgerald's *Tender Is the Night* lying open on a footstool in *La Notte* (1961). The characters and themes of his "trilogy" (*L'Avventura, La Notte, The Eclipse,* 1962) suggest Fitzgerald. Perhaps he is closer still to the French *nouveau roman* and a novel like Alain Robbe-Grillet's *Jalousie* in his efforts to convey feeling states through presentation of the particularities of physical surroundings. *The Eclipse* ends with a seven-minute montage of images devoid of people: Places and objects that had appeared earlier were stripped of anthropomorphic meaning.

Unlike the French film makers of the New Wave (to be dealt with later), new Italian film makers as a whole have shown little interest in manipulating time and space in extra-real, purely filmic ways. Fellini, of course, does make use of fantasy (in *8½,* 1963, and *Juliet of the Spirits,* 1965, for example), in which he plays with the physical laws of the universe as well as with subjective and hallucinatory emotional states, but he clearly sets the imagined and remembered apart from the ongoing present reality. In *La Dolce Vita* and elsewhere, in his approach to the "real world," time and space are dealt with in a perfectly straightforward manner—that is, within the conventions generally employed in realistic films. Antonioni, on the other hand, gets even closer than the conventional to the felt passage of time and experienced movement across space. After seeing Antonioni's long-held shots, with slow panning and trucking, in *L'Avventura,* the filmgoer could make out a complete itinerary, with a journal and a map. Fantasy scenes occur only rarely in Antonioni's work—for example, in *Zabriskie Point* (1969), in the ghostly desert love-in, and in the conclusion, in which the heroine imagines the destruction of her boss's modern mansion.

Fellini's films can be playful, but his fun and games are more likely to be drawn from the circus and music hall than from the characteristics of the film medium or the work of other film makers. Antonioni and Visconti, by contrast, are notably unplayful in every respect, though the former in later work undertaken abroad—*Blow-Up* (Britain, 1966), *Zabriskie Point* (United States), and *The Passenger* (Italy/United States, 1975, shot in Algeria, Spain, England, and Germany)—departed sharply from the austerity of his Italian films. *Blow-Up* offers a rich aesthetic, even ontological commentary on the very nature of the photographic image (upon which motion as well as still pictures depend) and its relationship to reality. *The Passenger* so emphasizes the shifting frame area and perspective of a moving camera that it too forces the viewer to consider the cinematic process that adds to the cryptic nature of the events observed.

What the new Italian cinema was moving away from and toward was consolidated at the Venice Festival of 1960. In an Italy that had recovered with astonishing rapidity from the social-political-economic upheaval and aftermath of World War II, the concerns were with the beliefs one might live by now that life itself and the living of it were more assured and comfortable. One indication of the change was that the new Italian film makers turned their attention from the lower to the upper classes. With their capacity to spend life more or less as they chose, the wealthy made most clearly evident the moral vacuum, the angst, the idle pursuit of meaningless pleasures that had accompanied the "economic miracle." In Italy of the 1960s, gone or seriously eroded were, on the one hand, the support of traditional Catholic morality and faith in God and His church, and on the other, the solidarity and militancy of the Left that had infused Italian society and political life in the immediate postwar years. Whatever the differences among their films, Visconti, Fellini, and Antonioni established a newly prominent moral, even spiritual, concern, and redirected attention to individual psyches, rather than collective conditions, in a contemporary Italy.

Luchino Visconti, along with Rossellini and de Sica, could lay claim to being one of the founders and principal practitioners of the neorealist movement. His *Ossessione* (1942) was clearly a precurser, with its harshly naturalistic approach to character, theme, and setting at a time when Italian films were either patriotic or escaping the realities of wartime Italy—optimistic or cheery in either case. *La Terra Trema* (1948) is among the great neorealist films, although its overlay of highly stylized studiolike cinematography and staged groupings onto actual fishermen and Sicilian village make us think of Eisenstein of *Old and New* rather than of the other neorealists.

In *Rocco and His Brothers* Visconti in a sense returned to his southern Italians of *La Terra Trema,* but now they are immigrants in Milan. Although social and economic forces are shown as contributing to the destruction of the family, the drama grows out of the personal conflicts and psychological flaws of the characters. Subsequently Visconti used various sorts of historical and literary materials—initiated in *Senso* (1954) and *White Nights* (1957) and continued in *The Leopard* (1963), *Sandra* (1965), *The Stranger* (1967), *The Damned* (1969), *Death in Venice* (1971), and *Ludwig* (1972). As a nobleman whose distinguished family had figured prominently for centuries in Italian history, Visconti had the deep concern for tradition (at odds with his Marxism) and the cultivated taste you would expect. His penultimate film before his death in 1976, *Conversation Piece,* offers an elegiac commentary on an aristocratic intellectual and art lover forced into uneasy but fascinated contact with the strident exigencies and vulgarities of modern political and social reality. We can imagine that the protagonist (played by Burt Lancaster, who also had played the prince in *The Leopard*) must have been seen by Visconti as some kind of equivalent to himself.

The Visconti who evolved out of neorealism traveled as far from it in style and subjects as could be imagined. If Marxism and the scenographic baroque combined in his earlier films, the creation of lush imagery and re-creation and examination of various forms of decadence, usually aristocratic, seem to carry the main weight in the total body of his work. An interest in homosexual motifs, overt or implied, also marks his *oeuvre.* His lyrical tracking and crane shots were most often orchestrated by his longtime collaborator, master cinematographer Giuseppe Rotunno. A film maker of international scope as well as

Rocco and His Brothers ★ Italy, 1960, Luchino Visconti; Alain Delon, center, white T-shirt.

stature, Visconti can be thought of as Italian primarily because of the "operatic" qualities of his films.

Federico Fellini had been the scriptwriter on *Open City, Paisan,* and *Europe 51* (for Rossellini), *Without Pity* and *Mill on the Po* (for Alberto Lattuada), and *In the Name of the Law* (for Pietro Germi), among other noteworthy neorealist films. The first works he directed as well as wrote—*Variety Lights* (1951, with Lattuada), *The White Sheik* (1952), and especially the autobiographical *I Vitelloni* (1953)—fell clearly within the neorealist tradition, even if they already began to reflect Fellini's predilection for the popular arts and his own personal experiences as source material. The enormously successful *La Strada* (1954) represented a turning point. Although set amidst the poverty and drabness of small-town rural Italy, its protagonists are vagabonds (a traveling strong man and his female assistant) rather than workers or peasants. Fellini was onto new themes quite outside the persistently materialistic view of the earlier neorealism. What we care about in *La Strada* is not that times are hard and social institutions culpable, but that Zampanò fails to learn to receive the warmth and comfort of Gelsomina's love.

Fellini's films, more obviously Italian in attitude and subject than Visconti's, departed more gradually from the accepted limitations of neorealism. What attracted him, instead of the historical and literary, was the subjective and fantastic. The only films of his that have literary-historical bases are *Fellini Satyricon* (1969) and *Fellini's Casanova* (1976). In these, as their titles imply, Petronius's ancient Rome and Casanova's eighteenth-

The Leopard ★ Italy, 1963, Luchino Visconti; Claudia Cardinale, Burt Lancaster, and Alain Delon.

century Europe are converted into the director's fantasies of debauchery and sexuality, and into extravaganza. Fellini has remarked of his *Satyricon* that it may be even more autobiographical than his much more obviously autobiographical *8½* (1963). Even the two filmed essays, *The Clowns* (1970) and *Fellini's Roma* (1972), keep the film maker's own interests, experiences, tastes, and, yes, fantasies at their center: It is *his* fascination with clowns from young boyhood on, *his* Rome. *Amarcord* (1973) is a sort of compendium of his recollections filtered through the exaggeration and imagination of adolescent perception. *City of Women* (1980) brought together and made quite explicit (as dreams) the sexual fears and desires that appear throughout his work.

From the beginning of Fellini's directorial career the autobiographical elements are present either in foreground or background, and usually both. *Variety Lights* deals with the music-hall milieu that he had experienced first hand. *The White Sheik* satirizes the comic book industry, and Fellini had been a cartoonist. *La Strada* is again about touring entertainers. *Il Bidone* (1955), although perhaps not drawn so directly from experience, contains many of the recurring themes and images, especially the religious ones. *The Nights of Cabiria* (1957) portrays the life of Roman prostitutes as Fellini had come to understand it. A special aspect of Fellini's "personalizing" of his work is that his wife, Giulietta Masina, played in all but one of those early films, as well as in many of the later ones.

Up through *Nights of Cabiria,* however, Fellini maintained that he was still working within the neorealist tradition, that he had simply shifted his concentration from external to internal reality. Certainly his films have much the look of the earlier neorealism. If shot more carefully and intimately, with emphasis on composition and the symbolic reverberations of the images, they are still objective in point of view. *I Vitelloni* is especially remarkable in the feeling it gives that the camera just happened to be there to capture bits of lives as they are being lived. Also, those early films make significant use of actual locations and nonactors and are set among the lower classes, the outcasts and dispossessed. But the poverty that concerned Fellini most was the impoverishment of the spirit. In his work, as in the original neorealist films, there are things to be sad about and no solutions are outlined; however, the hope that is offered for the human condition lies not in working-class solidarity but in the joy and love, in an almost religious sense, of which the individual soul is capable. The ending of *Nights of Cabiria,* with the little prostitute picking herself up after a near drowning and walking down a lane encircled by playing children, is very different in its implications from that of *The Bicycle Thief,* with father and son walking hand in hand off into the crowd, however similar the action. Both attest to human resiliency, but Antonio and his son, though comforted by their love for each other, merge into the masses to face another jobless day; Cabiria, through the children, recovers her own optimism and sense of self-worth.

With *La Dolce Vita,* Fellini took a long step farther away from neorealism. It is concerned with the effete idle rich of Rome and the sensational press that reports their doings to a voracious public. The journalist-protagonist (played by Marcello Mastroianni, who

La Dolce Vita ★ Italy, 1960, Federico Fellini.

would become "Fellini" in *8½*) is in search of meaning in life and values to live by. His passage through the sort of café society life well known to Fellini is like a descent into Dante's *Inferno*. The various pursuits to which he might devote himself—wife and family, business success, sexual excitement, religious fervour, philosophical contemplation—are successively shown to be corrupting or insufficient to support meaningful existence. By inference we learn that God is absent from this world. (The pointedly ironic opening scene of a gilded statue of Christ being hauled by helicopter over the rooftops of modern Rome, and the sequence of a highly publicized fake miracle flail at the hollow and superstitious religion subscribed to by the masses and tacitly approved by the Church.) Although it deals with the upper classes and matters of the spirit, *La Dolce Vita* is still in a completely realistic style. It is merely that the locations now include *palazzi* and the nonactors are actual members of Roman high society.

It wasn't until "The Temptation of Dr. Antonio" episode for *Boccacio 70* (1962) that Fellini turned to fantasy—one of his own, more than likely. Not until *8½* did he combine the autobiographical and the extravagant personal phantasmagoria that would depart from neorealism entirely and mark the remainder of his work. Certainly his most complex film, *8½* may also be his finest. It is a witty and revealing account of a director's harried life and the difficulties he has in conceiving his next film. (That was this film, hence the title. Fellini had

8½ ★ Italy, 1963, Federico Fellini; Marcello Mastroianni, center, arm outstretched.

directed eight films up to that point.) Just to make certain there would be no mistake, Mastroianni wore a wide-brimmed western hat like the one Fellini habitually wore on the set.

Fellini died in 1993. In his last films he moved away from the autobiographical, with indifferent results. *And the Ship Sails On* (1983), a slight tale unfolding during an Adriatic cruise in 1914, parodies the conventions of early cinema and the inflated emotions of the operatic world. In *Ginger & Fred* (1986) the object of satire is television. A 1930s dance team (played by Masina and Mastroianni, whose dancing is scarcely up to that of their namesakes, of course) are reunited for a superproduction variety show. *Frederico Fellini's Interview* (1987) returned more directly to his own past: to his early days at Cinecittà studios, in fact. It includes an homage to *La Dolce Vita*—Fellini coming full circle, you might say.

Michelangelo Antonioni served his apprenticeship as a critic and scriptwriter, including work on films in the neorealist tradition, such as Giuseppe de Santis's *Tragic Hunt* and Fellini's *White Sheik*. He also directed a number of documentary shorts. But his features, aside from *Il Grido* (1957), which is set amidst working-class surroundings in the Po Valley, treat personal values and interpersonal relationships of the middle and upper classes.

In extreme contrast to Fellini's ebullience is Antonioni's austerity. Although *La Dolce Vita* and *L'Avventura* deal with the same social strata (and both are organized around protagonists on the fringes rather than part of the aristocracy) and contain the same themes (loss of meaning and values replaced by promiscuity and debauchery), these two films and the subsequent work of their respective makers could scarcely be more different from each other. Whereas Fellini's films are informed with a Catholic humanist view of the world (evidently deep-rooted if informal and anticlerical), Antonioni's view is that of a postreligious Marxist and existentialist intellectual. While Fellini exposes the shoddiness of the moral values offered by "the sweet life," at the same time he is clucking moralistically he seems to be enjoying the naughtiness and the glamor.

Antonioni offers no such titillation or spectacle. In *L'Avventura* and his Italian films that follow it—*La Notte* (1961), *The Eclipse* (1962), *The Red Desert* (1964), *Identification of a Woman* (1982), and *Beyond the Clouds* (1995)—he dissected the values he saw operative in upper-class modern Italy with the disinterested precision and functional grace of a skilled surgeon, or perhaps of a weary but alert coroner conducting a postmortem. The "sweet life" in Antonioni's portrayal of it seems closer to death in that the souls have left the bodies. Not only is meaning lacking, but so is feeling, except for the instinctual sexual twitching as bodies refuse to acknowledge what minds know. Eroticism is prominent in the films of Antonioni, as it is in those of Fellini; Antonioni has described it as "a dominating factor in our civilization." The orgy at the end of *La Dolce Vita* has some prurient appeal (the striptease and the horsey-back ride on the bovine blonde actress), the sexual interludes in *L'Avventura* leave us cold and sad: the early scene with Anna in Sandro's apartment, Sandro with Claudia outside the deserted town and later in the hotel room after his encounter with the young architect, and Sandro with the high-class prostitute in the early morning. Never has "sin" looked less inviting. The sensuality, pleasure, guilt, and remorse felt by Fellini's characters are replaced by pervasive ennui and irritability, and a sense of the inability of any person to make contact with another even in the most intimate moments. Sex in Antonioni's world may stem from a desire to communicate, but it frequently takes the form of aggression or tired surrender to habit. Among his characters a life in which the sexual act has meaning or even offers enjoyment seems unavailable and perhaps unimaginable.

The extraordinary visual surface of *L'Avventura,* and of Antonioni's succeeding work, seems less radical now than it did when it first appeared precisely because it has been incorporated into the language of film as one of the prominent styles. Growing out of Antonioni's artistic intentions and statements, of course, it also took peculiar advantage of the attributes of the wide screen, seems almost to require it. The camera is placed at a medium distance more often than close in, frequently moving slowly; the shots are permitted to extend uninterrupted by cutting. Thus each image is more complex, containing more information than it would in a style in which a smaller area is framed, and the shots are briefer in duration. In this respect he harks back to Murnau or Dovzhenko rather than Eisenstein. In Antonioni's work we must regard his images at length; he forces our full attention by continuing the shot after others would cut away. This obsessive focus on the environment that forms the background for human interaction led Seymour Chatman to entitle his book on the director *Antonioni: Or, the Surface of the World.*

Antonioni offers us a view in certain respects closer to life than is usual. He is an artist of superb control, which extends into and balances every aspect of his films. His method does not include the spontaneity and improvisation of Fellini, nor does it permit the rough edges that Visconti allows to go uncorrected in his impatience to outline a grand plan. Consider, for example, the much-noted island sequence in *L'Avventura.* In it the characters are continually being commented upon, linked, and separated by their positions in relation to each other and within the frame: Their movements and the camera's are chore-

L'Avventura ✶ Italy, 1960, Michelangelo Antonioni; Monica Viti and Gabriele Ferzetti.

ographed with equal care. The growing awareness and desire of Sandro and Claudia for each other is initially signaled through such means. For instance, one shot begins with the camera looking down on Sandro. Then it tilts up and, on another plane above him, frames Claudia in the distance as she walks toward the camera (and Sandro's position). In another shot, there is a slight, slow pan from left to right with Claudia in the background. As the shot proceeds, Sandro enters frame left, mid-foreground. Then there is the *pas de deux* in successive shots when Claudia is trying to avoid Sandro and he, somewhat unconsciously and helplessly, tries to attach himself to her. Sometimes the camera even becomes like a member of the group as it moves ahead of the actors until they catch up with it and walk into frame again.

But with Antonioni, that kind of visual calculation—the framing and movement of actors and camera, the settings (barren rocky island, eerie deserted town), the way the light falls (the cold gray of early morning in the halls of the palatial hotel)—is everywhere designed to enrich narrative. A director like Eisenstein, who planned and executed his films with equal attention to detail, for all of his visual and kinetic brilliance, was saying simple things. The complexity in his films resides almost entirely in their visual artistry. Antonioni, on the other hand, has provided the sorts of ambiguity considered proper to modernist art. It is his kind of imagery and storytelling, rather than the more selective and directive method of Eisenstein, that has come to characterize the best of modern cinema and to represent a profound break with what had gone before.

The Passenger ★ Italy-France-Spain, 1975, Michelangelo Antonioni; Maria Schneider and Jack Nicholson.

Neo-Neorealism:
Three Directors of the 1960s and 1970s

Following Visconti, Fellini, and Antonioni were a cluster of other talented Italian film mak-ers whose careers came to fruition during the 1960s and 1970s and who, rather than par-alleling the concerns of their celebrated contemporaries, returned to some of the earlier neorealist impulses. One had accumulated extensive documentary experience before turn-ing to fiction; another began his film career as assistant director on a neorealist feature; and the third was committed to a Marxist philosophy that prompted him to follow a neo-realist path.

Ermanno Olmi's first features contain socially significant themes, were shot on location, and use nonactors as in the earlier tradition. But instead of unemployment and poverty, he deals with jobs that offer little satisfaction and the difficulties of achieving ful-filling lives and relationships within the conformist demands of an industrialized society. What Olmi provides is a subtle and absorbing attention to the individual among the work-ing classes. *Il Posto* (1961) is about a teen-age boy from a small village on his first job as messenger for a large firm in Milan. The tenderness and gentle humor with which the director regards the boy's tentative relationship with a girl, his loneliness at a dreary office party, and his feelings when he first sits at a clerk's desk are uniquely Olmi's own. *The Fiancés* (1963) concentrates on a worker who goes from the North to a new plant in Sicily. The slender story deals largely with his efforts to come to a better understanding of the

Il Posto ★ Italy, 1961, Ermanno Olmi; Sandro Panzeri, second from right.

fiancée he has had to leave behind and of their relationship. In later films, *One Fine Day* (1968) and *The Circumstance* (1974), for example, Olmi moved to the middle and upper classes, from workers to bosses, fragmented his narrative, and sometimes intermingled the present and recollected past. In *The Tree of Wooden Clogs* (1979), about the life of a peasant community in Lombardy at the close of the nineteenth century, Olmi returned to his earlier lyrical and unadorned style. But in *Long Live the Lady!* (1987) he mixes his special comedy of behavior, in this case that of ordinary kids, with a fantastic banquet hosted by the incredibly ancient lady of the title. And *The Legend of the Holy Drinker* (1988) is a fable about a tramp in Paris. The two hundred francs loaned him by a mysterious stranger helps him rehabilitate himself but he never manages to repay the loan as he had promised; finally, he dies in a drunken stupor. In 2001 Olmi returned to a historical theme with the medieval war drama *The Profession of Arms.*

Francesco Rosi, little known in the United States, is much admired in Italy and in Europe generally. His first considerable achievement was *Salvatore Giuliano* (1962), shot entirely on location in Sicily with an almost exclusively nonprofessional cast. It concerns a Mafia leader whose murder becomes the occasion for tracing political machinations in Sicily. *Hands Over the City* (1963), in many ways similar in method and ultimate intent, examines the exploitation of capitalist power and political corruption by an unscrupulous housing developer in Naples. *The Mattei Affair* (1972) retains its basis in actuality but

Hands Over the City ★ Italy, 1963, Francesco Rosi.

extends to a national, even international, scale. Enrico Mattei was an industrial manager who created a state-controlled oil company that loomed large in Italian political-economic affairs and competed against other national and multinational oil interests in the world market. *Christ Stopped at Eboli* (1979) is Rosi's version of the Carlo Levi book about the condition of rural southern Italy in the 1930s. *Three Brothers* (1981) traces the fortunes of three sons of a farmer in the Puglia region whose lives mirror the development of post–World War II Italy. It is a meditation on the conflicting values of the South and the North, the rural and the urban, and on the political violence and social fragmentation prevalent in modern Italy. The enigma of power, the pervasiveness of political influence, and the factual source remain characteristic of Rosi's finest work. Of the neo-neorealist directors, perhaps it is Rosi who has made most fully manifest the ideology implicit in the original movement.

Rosi's next two films departed from that main line, however. Both are adaptations of masterpieces, one an opera and the other a novel. His version of Bizet's *Carmen* (1984) was his first substantial success in the United States, partly due to the excellent interpretation and performance and most especially to the compelling sensuality of Julia Migenes Johnson in the title role. It was followed by his version of Gabriel García Márquez's *Chronicle of a Death Foretold* (1987). Although both films follow the neorealist tenet of shooting on location—*Carmen* in the Andalusian region of Spain and *Chronicle* in Colombia—in other respects they are closer to the later Visconti. (Rosi began in film as assistant director on *La Terra Trema.*)

Piero Paolo Pasolini—a novelist, poet, linguist, and film theorist before he directed his first feature, *Accattone!* in 1961—consistently dealt with the "subproletariat"—beggars and outcasts. Even *The Gospel According to St. Matthew* (1964), his best-known film, conforms to that generalization. In it Christ is portrayed as a revolutionary orator-leader from the masses, of a sort common in the history of the Middle-Eastern peoples. Shot as if it were reportage rather than re-creation, hand-held camera and nonactors give the Biblical story a feeling of contemporary actuality and urgency. *The Hawks and the Sparrows* (1966), an allegorical comedy, reveals and examines the interdependency between Christianity and Marxism, between religion, ideology, and existence. *Teorema* (1968) and *Pigpen* (1969) include strange mythic evocations of transcendental states, perverse sexuality, and cannibalism in their attacks on capitalist society. Pasolini's ability as a writer and translator led him to attempt new interpretations of classic literary works. Following *Oedipus Rex* (1967) were *Medea* (1970), *The Decameron* (1971), *The Canterbury Tales* (1972), and *The Arabian Nights* (1974). His last film, *Salò—The 120 Days of Sodom,* suggested by a work of the Marquis de Sade and full of violence, was completed just before his own violent death in 1975. Brilliant and multitalented, at the same time idiosyncratic and unpredictable, Pasolini occupied a position of leadership among the new Italians.

The 1970s and Beyond:
A New Generation of Film Makers

Following the extraordinary flowering of Italian film from 1945 through the 1960s, the end of the century brought hard times to the industry. As in all of the Western world, the late 1960s was a time of political turbulence. In Europe, especially, Marxist readings of class

The Gospel According to St. Matthew ★ Italy, 1964, Piero Paolo Pasolini; Enrique Irazoqui as Christ, center, hand to mouth.

warfare were taken up with renewed passion, especially by young people. Most movie industry workers and students then enrolled in Italian film schools were deeply affected by these developments. In 1968 there were widespread protests and turmoil in the institutions devoted to Italian cinema, including the Venice Film Festival, which was canceled for political reasons. With the 1970s, overt political activity largely ceased, although Italy saw a series of political assassinations mounted by terrorist groups beginning in 1972.

The film industry suffered during these years and has never managed to regain its vigor. Despite continued help from the government and additional sponsorship from television, production has fallen off: In 1965 Italy produced three hundred films; by 1999 the number had dropped to one hundred. Many of these films failed to find distributors; audiences for those that were released were typically siphoned off in short order by Hollywood blockbusters. Some industry analysts blamed the crisis on a lack of strong, hands-on producers, such as the late Franco Cristaldi, who could reign in the excesses of headstrong directors. Cristaldi helped shape many of the legendary productions of an earlier era, such as Germi's 1961 *Divorce, Italian Style,* Rosi's 1962 *Salvatore Giuliano,* Visconti's *Sandra,* and Fellini's *Amarcord.* He was credited with much of the international success enjoyed by Giuseppi Tornatore's 1988 *Cinema Paradiso,* cutting forty-seven minutes from the original version; the resulting version went on to win an Academy Award as best foreign film. Italy has no new generation of producers of this caliber. As the Italian critic Otello Angeli observed as early as 1979, "The rigidity of today's film market has resulted in the absorption of the figure of the producer and the transformation of his role into a managerial and bureaucratic function." In the late 1990s American independent distributor Miramax and its owners Bob and Harvey Weinstein stepped into the void. The Weinsteins ordered deep cuts in Roberto Benigni's 1998 *Life Is Beautiful,* enabling it, too, to garner an Oscar. Despite such rescue efforts by producers and distributors, however, Italian films were entirely shut out of the competition at Cannes in 2000, causing much consternation in the industry. A few film makers have continued to produce valuable work, however, most notably Bernardo Bertolucci, one of the preeminent directors now active anywhere in the world.

Again, Roberto Rossellini showed the way for a younger generation. In the 1960s and 1970s he had shifted his own attention to what he called "informational" films made for television, the most admired of which is his 1966 production *The Rise to Power of Louis XIV.* A manifesto signed by Rossellini and other Italian film makers, including Bertolucci, during this time states, "We wish, again, to present man with the guidelines of his own history, and depict drama, comedy and satire, the struggles, the experiences and the psychology of the people who have made the world what it is today, making it a criterion to fuse together entertainment, information and culture."

This statement articulated a renewed interest among Italian directors in taking up political subjects—this time from a perspective informed by the radical movements of the 1960s, often combined with a sophisticated Freudian worldview. Film historian Mira Liehm has called the resulting movement "metaphoric" cinema, because in it the realities of Italian life are rendered obliquely. This move to a more allegorical representational mode, arising from a distrust of the tenets of realism, can be inferred from a statement made by director Marco Bellocchio in 1980 about the political movements of the 1960s of which he was a part: "At the time of the union of Marxist-Leninist communists," he observed, "the conjecture was that in order to change, the bourgeois intellectuals should serve the people, live among the people, for the people have the correct ideas, etc. But actually the people in question did not exist, were nowhere to be found. It was a myth, an abstraction, and all that came to nothing." Some of the most significant works by Italian film makers made during the 1970s, 1980s, and 1990s grew out of this politically sophisticated world view, including Bertolucci's *The Conformist* (1970) and *1900* (1976), Gianni Amelio's *Lamerica* (1994), and Bellocchio's own *In the Name of the Father* (1971) and *The Nanny* (1999).

Bernardo Bertolucci, who served as assistant director on *Accatone!* achieved a prodigious international success with *Before the Revolution* (1964), which he completed at the age of twenty-four. (His first feature, *The Grim Reaper,* based on a rough draft by Pasolini, had been made two years earlier.) His films resemble those of the later Visconti, in their concern with intertwined personal relationships and political attitudes, and in their bold painterly style—*The Conformist* and *The Spider's Stratagem,* both 1970, for example. In these two films he put together a talented production team consisting of cinematographer Vittorio Storraro, production designer Ferdinando Scarfiotti, and editor Kim Arcelli, all of whom helped craft the sinuous camera work, striking art deco *mise-en-scène,* and seductive rhythms of *The Conformist,* perhaps Bertolucci's most influential film.

Last Tango in Paris (1972) bears some resemblance to Antonioni thematically and aroused something of the same excitement as *L'Avventura* in suggesting a new sort of film language, or personal idiom at least. It was followed by the vast panorama of *1900* (1976), covering some seventy years of life and social conflict in the Emilia region of Italy, which

Last Tango in Paris ✶ Italy, 1972,
Bernardo Bertolucci; Marlon Brando
and Maria Schneider.

the director later called "the nicest cinematic adventure of my life." The film treats class
conflict and the rise of fascism through the story of two young men, one a peasant (Gerard Depardieu) and one an aristocrat (Robert De Niro), both born on the same estate on the
same day at the turn of the century.

Bertolucci followed this sprawling chronicle with a more intimate film, *La Luna*
(1979), the intimate study of an incestuous relationship between mother and son. This sensitive topic occasioned controversy at least equal to that caused by *Last Tango*. *La Luna* was
followed by *Tragedy of a Ridiculous Man* (1981), involving a father-son relationship, kid-
naping, and terrorism in present-day Italy. Bertolucci's next film, *The Last Emperor* (1987),
was a triumph on all counts. A huge multinational production, it tells the story of Pu Yi, the
last emperor of China. The film can be seen in several ways. It is a sumptuous visual feast
of elegance and display on a colossal scale. As cultural and political history it is less satis-
factory; too much is crammed into too little time, with large events hinted at or dealt with
obliquely. Perhaps it can best be understood as the story of a person whose emotional life
becomes constricted and empty as a result of early traumas. He is torn from his mother and
then from his wet nurse; ritual obeisance is substituted for love and nurturing. He is told he
is the most powerful person in the world who can do anything he wants, when in fact he is
someone who experiences one loss after another. In a sense he is a prisoner throughout
his life. This aspect of the film is consistent with Bertolucci's persistent fascination with

psychological tensions that lead to loneliness and aberrant behavior. He has suggested that his films and his method of film making are part of his own psychoanalysis. In any event, the gamble at high stakes paid off handsomely. *The Last Emperor* attracted great critical attention, won eight Academy Awards, and became an international financial success.

The subjects of Bertolucci's films of the 1990s have moved away from overt politics and history to a more personalized concern with romantic obsession, often blended with a motif of cultural otherness rendered as an alluring exoticism. *The Sheltering Sky* (1990), *Stealing Beauty* (1996), and *Besieged* (1998) fall into this pattern. In these films the director's genius for rendering intense emotional states is given full play. *The Sheltering Sky* is perhaps the most effective of the three. Its long, complex traveling shots of North Africa, accompanied by Ryuikchi Sakamoto's haunting love theme, weave a spellbinding web of ineffable longing. Bertolucci's *Little Buddha* (1993) omitted the romance, treating the exotic myths of the Buddhist faith as a kind of fairy tale, sumptuously mounted, with Keanu Reeves playing the young god.

Similar to Bertolucci in his early commitment to Marxism and psychoanalysis, **Marco Bellocchio** began his career at about the same time as his more internationally celebrated colleague. With a style more coldly allegorical than Bertolucci's, he relies more heavily on the aberrant and grotesque. Bellocchio's first feature, *Fists in the Pocket,* released in 1965, drew a mordant portrait of a middle-class family in which epilepsy, matricide, fratricide, and incestuous longings form the basis of the plot. His follow-up film, *China Is Near,* in 1967, was less successful, failing to pull its myriad thematic and narrative strands together into a coherent whole. In 1971 Bellocchio was more successful with another black comedy, *In the Name of the Father,* this one set in a boys' boarding school. *The Conviction,* in 1994, explored the ambiguities surrounding the issue of rape and won a Silver Bear at the Berlin Festival.

By the late 1990s, Bellocchio had begun to couch his social criticism in more mellow, sympathetic terms. His 1999 film *The Nanny,* made for Italian television, is set in the early part of the century. Its story centers around a peasant girl who is hired by a psychiatrist to wet-nurse his new baby. With a style featuring Bellocchio's characteristic chiaroscuro photography and an elegantly designed *mise-en-scène,* the film, based on a story by Luigi Pirandello, showcases a broad range of issues, including parenthood, class difference, Italian nationalism, and literacy.

Among the films of the newer Italian film makers especially popular in the United States have been those by the ***Taviani brothers,*** Paolo and Vittorio. Though *St. Michael Had a Rooster,* made in 1971, is considered by some to be their most fully realized work, they first became known in the United States chiefly for *Padre Padrone* (1977), an adaptation of a best-selling account of the progress of an ignorant Sardinian from shepherd to university professor. *The Night of the Shooting Stars* (1982), shot in their native Tuscany, was based on their own experiences as young boys and on oral accounts of fellow Tuscans. It concerns a group of villagers who in 1944 left their town in defiance of the retreating Germans and resident Fascists to search for the advancing Americans. It was followed by *Chaos* (1984), adaptations of several Pirandello stories shot in Sicily with a cast that included many nonprofessional actors. The best of the Taviani films return to the emotional territory of neorealism, or at least have their roots in the history and traditional culture of the Italian people. *Night Sun* (1990), set in southern Italy in the eighteenth century, is a tale of a young nobleman who becomes something of a tortured saint. Although based on Leo Tolstoy's "Father

Night of the Shooting Stars ✦ Italy, 1982, Paolo and Vittorio Taviani.

Sergius," the film is richly reflective of the Italian heritage. Another Taviani brothers' film that draws on motifs from Italian history is *Fiorile* (1993), which tells a story about the corrupt past of a prosperous Italian family and its repercussions on the present.

Two controversial Italian women directors also rose to international prominence during the 1970s but have since dropped from view on the international festival circuit. **Liliana Cavani** caused an international sensation with *The Night Porter,* her 1974 chamber piece on sadomasochistic relationships between former inhabitants of a Nazi concentration camp. **Lina Wertmüller** achieved a comparable notoriety with a series of broad social satires focused on gender relations and political follies, including *The Seduction of Mimi* (1972), *Love and Anarchy* (1973), and *Seven Beauties* (1976).

Other directors of note also did significant work during this era. **Marco Ferreri,** a director highly regarded by the Italian critical community, enjoyed his greatest international success with *La Grande Bouffe* in 1973, a black comedy about four men who commit suicide by overindulging in gourmet food. **Sergio Leone** tempered the extreme stylistic quirks he had cultivated in earlier "spaghetti westerns"—such as *The Good, the Bad and the Ugly* (1966) and *Once Upon a Time in the West* (1967)—to produce his greatest work, the 1984 gangster saga *Once Upon a Time in America.* Anchored by Giusseppi Rotunno's bravura camera work, Ennio Morricone's distinctive musical score, and Robert De Niro's riveting performance in the story's central role, *Once Upon a Time in America* ranks with Coppola's 1972 *Godfather* as one of the most accomplished of gangster films produced during the last half of the twentieth century.

The most critically acclaimed Italian director to emerge in the 1990s was **Gianni Amelio.** Best known in the United States for his prize-winning 1994 production *Lamerica,* he also directed *Stolen Children* (1992) and *The Way We Laughed* (1998), both of which received major international awards. *Lamerica* tells the tale of a pair of Italian capitalists who attempt to exploit the newly opened market in Albania after the fall of communism there. One, who becomes the story's protagonist, finds himself drawn into an increasingly fantasmagorical world of ambiguous identities and economic ruin. The gaunt faces of the Albanians and the arid, rocky devastation of the landscape gradually grind down his cocky self-assurance until he is reduced to the status of a nameless refugee, like the thousands of Albanians he had formerly treated with insouciant contempt. *Lamerica* is replete with haunting images of droves of starving people, especially children, who descend like waves on anything that might present them with a means of escape from the intolerable world in which they are imprisoned. In the tradition of neorealism, the film tackles a social problem affecting the poor and socially downtrodden, but its allegorical style has more in common with the metaphoric cinema of early Bertolucci and Bellocchio.

One of the enduring pleasures of the Italian cinema has always been comedy, with a string of classic titles running from Pietro Germi's *Divorce, Italian Style* in 1961 to Franco Brusati's *Bread and Chocolate* in 1974. In the 1990s, this tradition took on a new significance internationally as Italian comedies, often given a bittersweet edge, captured world-

Il Postino ★ Italy, 1994, Michael Radford; Linda Moretti and Philippe Noiret.

wide interest. The trend began in 1988 with Giusseppe Tornatore's *Cinema Paradiso,* a touching tale of a young provincial boy's love affair with the movies. *Il Postino* followed in 1994. Although directed by British film maker Michael Radford, this story about the relationship between an idealistic mailman and a famous poet was spearheaded by its star, the venerable Italian comedy actor and director Massimo Troisi, who died shortly after production was completed. Also in 1994, another comic talent, Nanni Moretti, directed and starred in *Dear Diary,* a humorous jaunt through his life, told in three chapters; it, too, became an international prize winner. And in 1997, yet another well-known Italian comic, Roberto Benigni, directed *Life Is Beautiful,* a moving fable about a winsome little man and his family caught up in the nightmare of World War II.

Seen as a whole, Italian film from 1945 onward represents a tradition of artistic innovation tempered by a continuing awareness of the role of film in society. From the neorealism of the late 1940s to the modernism of the 1960s to the metaphoric cinema of the 1970s, 1980s, and 1990s, a common sense of national identity among the film makers has strengthened individual efforts. In spite of obvious personal and generational differences, contemporary Italian directors share many aesthetic and political as well as cultural assumptions. That cohesiveness permitted artists of the stature of Rossellini, de Sica, Visconti, Fellini, and Antonioni to have long productive careers. It has also provided a background from which newcomers such as Bertolucci, Bellocchio, and Amelio have emerged to command worldwide attention. The story of postwar Italian cinema is one of an evolving sense of national purpose and of the ongoing search for a filmic style best suited to represent that purpose. A similar pattern appears in the history of film in Great Britain, the subject of the next chapter.

Films of the Period

1942
Ossessione (Luchino Visconti)

1945
Open City (Roma, Città Apperta) (Roberto Rossellini)

1946
Paisan (Paisà) (Roberto Rossellini)
Shoeshine (Sciusià) (Vittorio de Sica)

1947
Germany, Year Zero (Germana anno zero) (Roberto Rossellini)

1948
The Bicycle Thief (Ladri di biciclette) (Vittorio de Sica)
La Terra Trema (Luchino Visconti)

1949
Bitter Rice (Riso amero) (Giuseppe de Santis)
Stromboli (Stromboli, terra de dio) (Roberto Rossellini)

1950
Chronicle of a Love Affair (Cronaca di un amore) (Michelangelo Antonioni)

1951
Miracle in Milan (Miracolo a Milano) (Vittorio de Sica)

1952
Umberto D (Vittorio de Sica)
The White Sheik (Lo sceicco bianco) (Federico Fellini)

1953
I Vitelloni (Federico Felllini)
Voyage to Italy (Viaggio in Italia) (Roberto Rossellini)

1954
Senso (Luchino Visconti)

1956
The Nights of Cabiria (La notti di Cabiria)
   (Federico Fellini)

1957
Il Grido (Michelangelo Antonioni)

1959
General Della Rover (Il Generale della Rover)
   (Roberto Rossellini)

1960
L'Avventura (Michelangelo Antonioni)
La Dolce Vita (Federico Fellini)
Rocco and His Brothers (Rocco e i suoi fratelli)
   (Luchino Visconti)
Two Women (La ciociara) (Vittorio de Sica)

1961
Accatone! (Piero Paolo Pasolini)
The Bandits of Orgosolo (Banditi a Orgosolo)
   (Vittorio de Seta)
Divorce, Italian Style (Divorzio all'Italia)
   (Pietro Germi)
La Notte (Michelangelo Antonioni)
Il Posto (Ermanno Olmi)

1962
The Eclipse (L'eclisse) (Michelangelo
   Antonioni)
Salvatore Giuliano (Francesco Rosi)

1963
8½ (Federico Fellini)
The Fiancés (I fidanzati) (Ermanno Olmi)
The Leopard (Il Gattopardo) (Luchino Visconti)

1964
Before the Revolution (Prima della revoluzione)
   (Bernardo Bertolucci)
*The Gospel According to St. Matthew (Il vangelo
   secondo Matteo)* (Piero Paolo Pasolini)
The Red Desert (Il Deserto Rosso) (Michelangelo
   Antonioni)

1965
Fists in the Pocket (I pugni in tasca) (Marco
   Bellocchio)
Juliet of the Spirits (Giulietta degli spiriti)
   (Federico Fellini)
Sandra (Vaghe Stelle dell'orsu) (Luchino
   Visconti)

1966
The Battle of Algiers (La battaglia di Algeri)
   (Gillo Pontecorvo)
*The Good, The Bad, and the Ugly (Il buono, il
   bruto, il cattivo)* (Sergio Leone)
*The Hawks and the Sparrows (Uccellacci e
   Uccelllini)* (Piero Paolo Pasolini)

1967
China Is Near (La Cina è vicina) (Marco
   Bellocchio)
*Once Upon a Time in the West (C'era una volta
   il West)* (Sergio Leone)

1968
Dillinger Is Dead (Dillinger è morte) (Marco
   Ferreri)

1969
Burn! (Queimada!) (Gillo Pontecorvo)
The Damned (La caduta degli dei) (Luchino
   Visconti)
Fellini Satyricon (Federico Fellini)
Zabriski Point (Michelangelo Antonioni)

1970
The Conformist (Il conformista) (Bernardo
   Bertolucci)
*The Garden of the Finzi-Continis (Il giarino dei
   Finzi-contini)* (Vittorio de Sica)
*Investigation of a Citizen above Suspicion
   (Indagene su un cittadino al di sopra di ogni
   sospetto)* (Elio Petri)
The Spider Stratagem (Strategia del ragno)
   (Bernardo Bertolucci)

1971
In the Name of the Father (Nel nome del padre)
   (Marco Bellocchio)

Death in Venice (Morte a Venezia) (Luchino Visconti)
St. Michael Had a Rooster (San Michele aveva un gallo) (Vittorio and Paolo Taviani)

1972
Last Tango in Paris (L'ultimo tango à Parigi) (Bernardo Bertolucci)
The Seduction of Mimi (Mimì metallugico ferito nell'onore) (Lina Wertmüller)
The Mattei Affair (Il caso Mattai) (Francesco Rosi)

1973
Amarcord (Federico Fellini)
Diary of a Schoolteacher (Diario di un maestro) (Vittorio de Seta)
La Grande Bouffe (La grande abbouffatta) (Marco Ferreri)
Love and Anarchy (Film d'amore e d'amore e d'anarchia) (Lina Wertmüller)

1974
Bread and Chocolate (Pane e cioccolata) (Franco Brusati)
The Night Porter (Il potiere de notte) (Liliana Cavani)

1975
The Passenger (Professione: reporter) (Michelangelo Antonioni)

1976
Fellini's Casanova (Federico Fellini)
1900 (Novocento) (Bernardo Bertolucci)
Seven Beauties (Pasqualino Settebellezze) (Lina Wertmüller)

1977
Padre Padrone (Vittorio and Paolo Taviani)

1978
The Tree of the Wooden Clogs (L'albero degli zoccoli) (Ermanno Olmi)

1982
The Eyes, the Mouth (Gli occi, la bocca) (Marco Bellocchio)

Identification of a Woman (Identicazione de una donna) (Michelangelo Antonioni)
The Night of the Shooting Stars (La Notte de San Lorenzo) (Vittorio and Paolo Taviani)

1984
Carmen (Francesco Rosi)
Chaos (Kaos) (Vittorio and Paolo Taviani)
Once Upon a Time in America (C'era una volta in America) (Sergio Leone)

1987
The Last Emperor (Il ultimo imperatore) (Bernardo Bertolucci)

1988
Cinema Paradiso (Nuovo cinema paradiso) (Giuseppe Tornatore)

1990
The Sheltering Sky (Il tè nel deserto) (Bernardo Bertolucci)

1991
Mediterraneo (Gabriele Salvatores)

1992
Stolen Children (Il ladro di bambini) (Gianni Amelio)

1994
Dear Diary (Caro Diaria) (Nanni Morretti)
Lamerica (Gianni Amelio)
Il Postino (Michael Radford)

1997
Life Is Beautiful (La vita è bella) (Roberto Bengini)

1998
Besieged (L'Assedio) (Bernardo Bertolucci)
The Way We Laughed (Così ridevano) (Gianni Amelio)

1999
The Nanny (La Balia) (Marco Bellocchio)

2001
The Son's Room (La Stanza del Figlio) (Nanni Moretti)
The Profession of Arms (Il Mestiere delle armi) (Ermanno Olmi)

Books on the Period

Nowell-Smith, Geoffrey, ed. with James Hay and Gianne Volpi. *Cassell Film Guides: Italy.* Herndon, VA: Cassell Academic, 1996.

Sitney, P. Adams. *Vital Crises in Italian Cinema: Iconography, Stylistics, Politics.* Austin: Unversity of Texas Press, 1995.

Sorlin, Pierre. *Italian National Cinema, 1896–1996.* New York: Routledge, 1996.

Vincendeau, Ginette, ed. *The Encyclopaedia of European Cinema.* New York: Facts on File, 1995.

9

British Film after the War: Humor, Horror, and Social Criticism

★ ★ ★ ★

1945–

American money and personnel are so inextricably interwoven with British production and distribution that it is difficult to determine where one industry leaves off and the other begins. If in the days of gunboat diplomacy commerce followed the flag, in modern economic imperialism culture follows the dollar. American films had so overwhelmed the British market during the 1920s that the British government passed the Quota Act in 1927, which restricted the distribution of Hollywood films in Britain and required U.S. distributors to finance a set number of British films every year. Through the years, a large number of British actors, directors, and production personnel have been quick to move across the Atlantic, and many of these are rewarded for their change of allegiance by being honored in Hollywood on Academy Awards night. The trend reached a crescendo of sorts at the end of the twentieth century when British productions *The English Patient* and *Shakespeare in Love* swept the Oscars in 1997 and 1999, respectively.

To be sure, Britain has a cache of subject matter all its own. British films about World War II, for example, dealt with British wartime experiences: *The Cruel Sea* (1953, Charles Frend), *The Dam Busters* (1953, Michael Anderson), and *The Battle of the River Plate* (1956, Michael Powell and Emeric Pressburger). Also, many individual British films followed a sort of "academic" tradition—significant subjects treated with self-effacing expertise—but prestigious ventures of this sort have become increasingly multinational in conception, financial backing, and creative personnel. John Huston's *The African Queen*

(1952), *Moulin Rouge* (1953), and *Moby Dick* (1956) as well as David Lean's *Summertime* (1955) and *The Bridge on the River Kwai* (1957) are prominent examples.

The problem that British films present, then, is one of national identity, not of artistic quality. However, the British have made certain kinds of films with a particular excellence, such as films drawn from their literary, dramatic, or historical heritage, or a type of sophisticated crime or espionage thriller. Prominent British heritage films include the David Lean versions of literary works by Noël Coward and Charles Dickens (*Blithe Spirit,* 1945; *Brief Encounter,* 1945; *Great Expectations,* 1946; and *Oliver Twist,* 1948), adaptations of William Shakespeare by Laurence Olivier (*Henry V,* 1944; *Hamlet,* 1948; and *Richard III,* 1955) and later Kenneth Branaugh (*Henry V,* 1989 and *Hamlet,* 1996), the Carol Reed collaborations with Graham Greene (*The Fallen Idol,* 1948 and *The Third Man,* 1949), Michael Powell and Emeric Pressburger's *The Red Shoes* (1949), and in the 1980s and 1990s, the productions of director James Ivory and producer Ismael Merchant (*A Room with a View,* 1986 and *The Remains of the Day,* 1993). In the realm of thrillers, Alfred Hitchcock's work is preeminent, although his British films were all produced before the war (most notably, *The Thirty-Nine Steps* in 1935 and *The Lady Vanishes* in 1938). After the war, Michael Powell's psychologically acute *Peeping Tom* (1960) became a critical favorite, although its interest in perverse sexuality made it atypical of the British thriller mode. More conventionally British were *The Ipcress File* (Sidney J. Furie, 1965), starring Cockney actor Michael Caine, and the wildly popular, over-the-top James Bond cycle initially featuring the urbane, ironic Edinburgh native Sean Connery.

Distinctive cultural strengths have nurtured British cinema over the years. At its most characteristic, British film making draws on indigenous traditions of comedy and progressive politics as well as a less pronounced vein of gothic fantasy and horror. From Chaucer to Hogarth to Dickens, British humor has long been an honored form. The British have a keen eye for identifying the foibles of a rich assortment of social types, and the large cohort of highly skilled British actors are adept at bringing such portraits to life. An equally fruitful tradition has been that of progressive politics. An impulse toward reformist agendas has historically distinguished the British social and political scene. A less prominent element in the British cultural character is a gothic mode of horror and fantasy, historically represented in literary works such as *Frankenstein* and *Dracula.* These three traditions, singly and in combination, have formed the basis of every significant British film-making movement since the war: the comedies of the 1950s and later those of Bill Forsyth and Mike Leigh; the socially progressive films of directors such as Tony Richardson and Ken Loach; and the gothic fantasy and horror tales of the Archers during the 1950s and the Hammer Studios during the 1960s. Even American directors who have worked in Britain—for instance, Joseph Losey, Richard Lester, Stanley Kubrick, and Terry Gilliam—have been decisively influenced by the fertile cultural traditions of their adopted country. Underlying all of these developments was a series of prewar documentaries that created a distinctive identity for British cinema on which later film makers could build.

The Griersonian Documentary Tradition

A politically progressive documentary movement that exerted a major influence on the evolution of many postwar British genres was initiated by John Grierson before the war.

More than any other person, Grierson is responsible for the documentary film as it has developed in English-speaking countries. The first person to apply the term *documentary* to a mode of film, he understood the value of nonfiction film making to reside in its ability to use the documents of modern life as materials to spread the faith of social democracy. He believed passionately in the capacity of film to educate audiences and to aid in creating a global culture of understanding and tolerance. The documentary films Grierson produced in the 1930s, including *Industrial Britain,* which he codirected with Robert Flaherty in 1931–1932, and *The Song of Ceylon,* directed by Basil Wright in 1936, were financed not by box-office revenues but by government and industry sponsorship, and they were shown in commercial cinemas as well as community gathering places such as churches, schools, and union halls. *Industrial Britain,* sponsored by the British government's Empire Marketing Board, contrasts images of traditional craftspeople such as glassblowers and potters with portraits of industrialized workers in the steel industry, arguing that the success of British industry rests on the skill of its artisans. A voice-over commentator states at the beginning, "The human fact remains, even in this machine age, the final fact." *Song of Ceylon* was sponsored by the Ceylon Tea Propaganda Board (although the film did little to sell the sponsor's product). A moving hymn to a native people, their work, their ways, and their values in conflict with the imposed requirements of modern commerce, it contains exquisite images of a golden time and a golden place. The Griersonian documentary tradition reached its height during the war in the semidocumentary features (for example, *Target for Tonight* [1941] and *Fires Were Started* [1943]) that combined fact and fiction.

Industrial Britain ☆ United Kingdom, 1933, John Grierson and Robert Flaherty.

It is for his multifacted, innovative leadership that Grierson is to be most valued. The three hundred or more British documentaries made during the 1930s and the system that spawned them became models for other countries, including New Zealand, Australia, South Africa, and most significantly Canada, where Grierson established the National Film Board in 1939. The documentary film culture Grierson nurtured among associates Basil Wright, Humphrey Jennings, and Paul Rotha cast a long shadow over subsequent feature film production in Great Britain, inspiring generations of film makers who came of age following the Second World War: documentarians such as Peter Watkins, whose 1965 production *The War Game* presented a searing portrait of life after a nuclear holocaust, and an array of fiction film makers both at home and abroad.

Postwar Comedies

If the British semidocumentary became as rare soon after the war as it had been prevalent during wartime, it might be argued that it didn't so much cease as go underground and come up looking and sounding like the **Ealing comedy.** Michael Balcon, head of Ealing Studios, had always been a friend of the documentary movement and favored fiction films that were distinctively British rather than imitatively American. When the documentarians began to cross over into feature film making via the wartime semidocumentary it was to Ealing they came. Alberto Cavalcanti, former production head of the government Crown Film Unit, as well as Harry Watt, one of its star directors, were among these. Three of the principal directors of the Ealing comedies—Charles Crichton, Charles Frend, and Alexander Mackendrick—had had considerable documentary experience. The result of these biases and this personnel, plus the fine writing talents Balcon acquired, especially T. E. B. Clarke, gave the string of comedies their distinctive flavor.

The first of the series was *Hue and Cry,* directed by Crichton in 1947. The lower- and middle-class milieu, location shooting, bumbling crooks and police, and fast pace all typify the Ealing manner. There followed, in fairly rapid succession, *Whiskey Galore* (1949, Mackendrick; *Tight Little Island* in the United States), *Passport to Pimlico* (1949, Henry Cornelius), *A Run for Your Money* (1949, Frend), *The Lavender Hill Mob* (1951, Crichton), *The Man in the White Suit* (1951, Mackendrick), *Genevieve* (1953, Cornelius), *The Titfield Thunderbolt* (1953, Crichton), *The Maggie* (1954, Mackendrick; *High and Dry* in the United States), and *The Ladykillers* (1955, Mackendrick). In 1952 financial problems caused Ealing to sell its studios to BBC-TV; in 1955 the company itself was dissolved. Between 1951 and 1955 similar kinds of comedies were being made at Group 3, a government-financed experiment in feature production headed by Grierson.

These British comedies turn documentary seriousness on its ear. The themes of the Ealing films are notably social, economic, political, or at least cultural (in the anthropologist's sense), designed to bring out a particular facet of national life. They deal with the Scots' fondness for a wee drop, strict Calvinism, dislike of the English (*Tight Little Island*), the bureaucratic entanglements in which the British found themselves after the war (*Passport to Pimlico*), the expected honesty and trustworthiness of the English middle class (*The Lavender Hill Mob*), the collusion among management and labor, and government and opposition within the English system (*The Man in the White Suit*). Laughter is provoked only through the incongruities and exaggerations with which these subjects are treated; even so, the comic style is noteworthy for its deadpan seriousness, underplaying, and throwaway delivery of lines.

Casting called on nonglamorous, quintessentially British actors (rather than stars)—Alistair Sim (*Hue and Cry*), Stanley Holloway (*Passport to Pimlico*), and Alec Guinness (*The Lavender Hill Mob, The Man in the White Suit, The Ladykillers*)—and used local citizens as extras. Their performances were built around mimickery of a wide array of social types rather than on subtle renditions of the interior lives of complex individuals, as is the custom among American method performers. In a performance *tour de force* Alec Guinness created a gallery of these broadly satiric portrayals in *Kind Hearts and Coronets,* where he played eight different characters, from a doddering old lady to an urbane country squire.

In *Tight Little Island* the documentary influence is especially pervasive. The novel on which it is based—by Compton Mackenzie, who appears in the film in a small part as Captain Bucher—was drawn from an actual disaster to a whiskey-laden ship during World War I. Mackenzie (assisted on the screenplay by Angus MacPhail) elaborated a hilarious plot about the reactions of the citizens of a small Scottish village to having such a ship wrecked off their coast with its cargo intact. The cast is a blend of well-trained actors, many of them Scottish by birth, and local inhabitants. Alexander Mackendrick, who directed, was trained in wartime documentary; this was his first feature. It was shot almost entirely on location, interiors as well as exteriors. A kind of mobile studio unit was established on the Hebridean island so that no time would be lost waiting for good weather. Mackendrick even set up processing equipment so he could look at the rushes without undue delay, just as Robert Flaherty had done for his famous documentary feature *Man of Aran,* shot on an island off the coast of Ireland some fifteen years earlier.

Whiskey Galore/Tight Little Island ★ United Kingdom, 1949, Alexander Mackendrick.

Bill Forsyth, a Scot, has worked within what can be described as a revival of the Ealing comedy tradition. Forsyth-directed films—such as *That Sinking Feeling* (1979), *Gregory's Girl* (1981), and *Comfort and Joy* (1984)—have offered Scottish looks and Scottish ways with a knowing and affectionate humor that marks them as emanating from the British Isles. Like many of the earlier Ealing directors, Forsyth began film making with documentaries. His most widely seen feature, *Local Hero,* released in 1983, was shot on location in Fort William. The plot concerns the oil strike in the North Sea and a visiting agent for a Houston oil company. It is reminiscent of the situation in *Tight Little Island* (1949), with an American intruder replacing the earlier English one. In this case, however, the foreigner succumbs to the charms of the villagers and longs to be one of them.

In the 1980s and 1990s a new group of directors revived the tradition of British comedy, the most innovative of whom was **Mike Leigh.** Leigh's films draw on the considerable resources represented by the large pool of talented British actors, making performers partners in the creative process by developing scripts from scenes they improvise together. In time-honored British fashion, Leigh's films, including *High Hopes* (1989) and *Life Is Sweet* (1991), focus on strongly defined social types, often from the lower classes. At times, however, his characters reveal depths of feeling not often seen in comedies. Leigh's most admired production, *Secrets and Lies,* which won the Palme d'Or at Cannes in 1996, features a scene in which a middle-aged matron is confronted by a young woman who unexpectedly reveals that she is the former's long-lost daughter. In the role of the mother, actor Brenda Blethyn improvised an in-character response to this news that is one of the greatest performances ever recorded on film. Leigh followed this triumph in 1993 with *Naked,* a dark story about an angry drifter played by David Thewis. Both Leigh and Thewis

Local Hero ★ United Kingdom, 1983, Bill Forsyth; Burt Lancaster and Peter Riegert.

Topsy Turvy ★ United Kingdom, 1999, Mike Leigh.

won prizes at Cannes for their work in this film. In 1999 Leigh made a more conventional costume drama, *Topsy Turvy,* about the collaboration of the popular nineteenth-century operetta composers, Gilbert and Sullivan. The emphasis on the collaborative nature of theater artistry in this production can be seen as a comment on Leigh's own philosophy of shared creative endeavor.

Free Cinema
and Social-Realist Features

The year 1956 was a crucial one in the political and cultural life of Britain. It was the year of a last gasp of imperial arrogance in the foolish and failed invasion of Suez. As a result of that debacle the whole governmental system was discredited. To many on the Left, the Labour Party, which worked within the system, seemed as culpable as the ruling Conservatives. It was also in 1956 that Khrushchev ordered the Soviet invasion of Hungary, which caused many Marxist intellectuals finally to become disillusioned with Stalinist communism. Partially in reaction to those events, a politically sophisticated younger generation of dissidents arose around the universities—particularly at Oxford, which most of the Free Cinema group had attended. The label "New Left" was attached to them, and their publication was entitled *New Left Review* (originally *Universities and Left Review*). The New Left wanted to go beyond the old-line socialists, with their basis in dialectical materialism, trade unionism, nationalization of industry, and social welfare. They were concerned more with theory and a fundamental reorganization of society that would affect the total quality of people's lives. As an intellectual movement that also encompassed the arts, the New Left in Britain was more like the continental Left.

The artists in various media who arose out of the spirit of the time, many of them from the working classes, were dubbed the Angry Young Men for their attacks on the establishment and the rigidities and inequities of the class system. In 1956 John Osborne's play *Look Back in Anger,* directed by Tony Richardson, opened at the Royal Court Theatre. At about the same time Joan Littlewood's Theatre Workshop was started. Playwrights such as Arnold Wesker and Shelagh Delaney soon joined Osborne to create an outpouring of plays set among the lower classes that were articulate and sometimes strident in their social criticism. A new crop of actors—Albert Finney, Rita Tushingham, Rachel Roberts, Tom Courtenay, Richard Harris, and Ronald Fraser—also came out of that sort of theater and later worked in film. Novels of a similar tone began to appear as well, with John Braine's *Room at the Top* in 1957 followed by Alan Sillitoe's *Saturday Night and Sunday Morning,* Stan Barstow's *A Kind of Loving,* and David Storey's *This Sporting Life,* among others.

In this dynamic atmosphere, the British documentary tradition was again revived in a movement called Free Cinema. Early in 1956 a program of three short films was shown at the National Film Theatre under the Free Cinema banner. *O Dreamland* (1954), by Lindsay Anderson, castigated the dull and synthetic pleasures being offered the bemused masses at a seaside amusement park. *Momma Don't Allow* (1955), by Karel Reisz and Tony Richardson, celebrated a lively London jazz club patronized by working-class teenagers. *Together* (1955), by Lorenza Mazetti and Denis Horne, described the emotionally impoverished lives led by two deaf-mute dock workers in the East End. The films' makers stated in their program notes for the occasion that Free Cinema was free from serving the sponsor's purpose (as in documentaries) and free from pandering to the demands of the box office (as in fiction features). It was to be an "entirely personal cinema," socially committed but also poetic. "Implicit in our attitude," they wrote, "is a belief in freedom, in the importance of people and in the significance of the everyday." The Free Cinema trio of Anderson, Reisz, and Richardson were later joined by John Schlesinger, an Oxford classmate of Richardson's. Together they constituted the main directorial talent of the social-realist features of the early 1960s. All of their films were based on the writings of the so-called Angry Young Men (or Women, as the case might be).

Although Free Cinema had in fact appeared slightly before the explosions in the other arts, it wasn't until it connected with the new drama and literature that its kind of expression moved over into the feature film and became economically viable. Following *Nice Time* (Claude Goretta and Alain Tanner) and *Every Day Except Christmas* (Anderson) in 1957, the Free Cinema movement as such virtually ceased with *We Are the Lambeth Boys* (Reisz) in 1959. Nonetheless, the attitudes and some of the rough-hewn style of Free Cinema were carried into the new social-realist features that began as the Free Cinema shorts ended. Although much more conventional than Free Cinema in both content and form, the 1959 production *Room at the Top,* directed by Jack Clayton, who had come up through the commercial industry, launched the new phase. Set in an industrial northern town, the plot deals with the compulsions and confusions of a cynical young arriviste determined to climb up out of his slum origins. Its romantic conflict is class based—to marry the daughter of a local industrialist in order to get ahead, or to stay with the mistress he loves but who would impede his chances for success.

Look Back in Anger, released in the same year and directed by Free Cinema stalwart Tony Richardson, put some of the same matters, and others, in a clearer and less ambiguous way. Through the Jimmy Porter character's brilliant and paranoiac monologues, we could begin to understand what the anger was all about. At least it was clear what he was trying to tear down (the Establishment, personified by his wife's parents) and what he was trying to preserve (the working-class virtues represented by his friend Ma Tanner). It was not so clear (if at all) what the replacement society would be like, and certainly not how it might come about.

In any case, these two films, double-billed in the United States, began the social-realist cycle that dealt with various aspects of working-class character and problems. The cycle continued with such notable titles as *Saturday Night and Sunday Morning* (Reisz, 1960) and *The Loneliness of the Long Distance Runner* (Richardson, 1962). As a body the films tended to be set in the industrial regions north of London. Thus they contrasted with British entertainment films up to that time which, according to the Free Cinema group at least, had reflected almost exclusively the outlook of metropolitan southern English culture and the middle and upper classes. Here were efforts to include "the rich diversity of tradition and personality which is the whole of Britain" called for in one of Free Cinema's manifestoes.

Lindsay Anderson, although acknowledged as leader and spokesman of the Free Cinema group, was the last to arrive at features. Curiously, his first, *This Sporting Life* (1963), if it marked a high point in the social-realist cycle, also indicated a turning away from the sources that had given that demimovement its character and strength. From a

Saturday Night and Sunday Morning ★ United Kingdom, 1960, Karel Reisz; Albert Finney, right rear.

The Loneliness of the Long Distance Runner ★ United Kingdom, 1962, Tony Richardson; Tom Courtenay.

novel and script adaptation by David Storey, it has the requisite general characteristics of a northern industrial town and working-class background. Where it departs from the other films is in its concentration on the tortured love affair between the miner-turned-football player and his widowed landlady, and in its flashback sequences of surrealist exaggeration. At the time of its release Anderson was complimented by British reviewers for having broken out of the confines of the social-realist films, with their air of objectivity and use of the representative to make their criticism stick, into richer areas of individual feeling, the traditional concerns of great art. Perhaps what was by then being referred to as the "kitchen sink" school of film making was limited in certain important ways and had run its course. Whatever the reasons, *This Sporting Life* along with *Billy Liar* (directed by John Schlesinger in 1963) proved to be the last films directly connected with the line that had begun with *Room at the Top.* Of the directors who worked in it, Anderson stuck closest to the earlier commitments (and made the fewest features). *If . . .* (1969), *O Lucky Man!* (1973), and *Britannia Hospital* (1982), although different in subjects and settings, grew out of the same impulses of social criticism as the earlier films—even though their fantastical style had little in common with the documentary mode that had initially given birth to the Free Cinema movement.

The advent of a conservative government led by Prime Minister Margaret Thatcher in 1979 gave renewed impetus to the British cinema of social criticism. In response to Thatcherism, artists in all media created works that protested the large-scale cutbacks in social programs and hawkish foreign policies that were adopted. Prominent among the film directors who reflected this attitude were Terrence Davies (*Distant Voices, Still Lives,* 1988), Danny Boyle (*Trainspotting,* 1996), Stephen Frears, and Ken Loach. All produced memorable portraits of British working-class life that updated the project of the so-called kitchen sink school.

Beginning with *Kes,* his first feature, in 1969, **Ken Loach**'s films all deal with the plight of the poor and those who have progressive political ideas. "I think it is very important to let people speak who are usually disqualified from speaking or who've become non-persons," he has said, "activists, militants, or people who really have any developed political ideas." Loach has made many incisive films about the English social scene, including *Family Life* in 1973, which deals with the efforts of a working-class family to deal with mental illness; *Raining Stones* in 1993, about the effects of chronic unemployment on a well-meaning husband and father; and *Ladybird, Ladybird* in 1994, about a lower-class woman whose children are taken away from her. He has also made films about international issues, including *Land and Freedom* in 1995, which deals with the British radicals who fought in the Spanish Civil War, and *Carla's Song* in 1996, which tells of an Edinburgh bus driver who follows his Nicaraguan girlfriend to her homeland and becomes involved in the conflict there. Loach's unprettified *mise-en-scènes* reflect the grungy lifestyles of his characters, and his loose narrative structures follow their adventures in a *laissez faire* manner. Many Loach films are highly comedic, but the humor is always carried off with a feeling of affection for the characters, who are seen as constrained more

Trainspotting ★ United Kingdom, 1996, Danny Boyle.

Carla's Song ★ United Kingdom, 1996, Ken Loach; Oyanka Cabezas.

by social circumstances than by innate limitations. Although he uses skilled actors, they typically speak in the thick dialects characteristic of their characters' class and region, making Loach's films generally unattractive to American distributors.

      Stephen Frears began his career as an assistant to Lindsay Anderson, but he has developed a much more eclectic body of work. His most memorable films, however, contain an undercurrent of social criticism that is identifiably British, often combined with an emphasis on ethnic and gender issues. The most radical of these, *My Beautiful Laundrette* (1985) and *Sammy and Rosie Get Laid* (1987), were the results of a collaboration with scriptwriter Hanif Kureishi, whose screenplays reveal facets of English ethnic and homosexual subcultures never before committed to film. "Hanif took me to a different country and brought me out alive," Frears later commented. Frears has gone on to direct a number of beautifully crafted productions made on both sides of the Atlantic that have had a less clearly discernible social agenda, most notable among which are *Dangerous Liaisons* (1988), *The Grifters* (1990), *The Snapper* (1993), and *High Fidelity* (2000).

The Gothic Strain

After World War II the British gothic tradition, with its emphasis on horror and magic, found its most viable outlet in film, an art form uniquely well suited to showcase the atmospheric effects that were the genre's stock-in-trade. British movies took the gothic form in new directions, adding unconventional sexuality to the mix of terror, suspense, and eerie locales for which such stories have long been known. Hammer Studios turned out a series of stylishly lurid horror movies of this type during the 1950s and 1960s, most of the best

My Beautiful Laundrette ★ United
Kingdom, 1985, Stephen Frears; Daniel
Day-Lewis and Gordon Warneke.

directed by Terrence Fisher. The Hammer films featured a new stable of British acting talent, including Peter Cushing and Christopher Lee, the latter of whom became a popular postwar reincarnation of Bela Lugosi's famous movie vampire. Notable among the Hammer productions are *The Curse of Frankenstein* (1957) and *Dracula* (1958), both directed by Fisher. Other British directors have also been drawn to the Gothic tradition, including Michael Powell, John Boorman, and Neil Jordan, as well as postmodernists such as Peter Greenaway and Sally Potter. These film makers typically rely heavily on expressive cinematography to set an appropriate mood; the striking effects they often achieve give the lie of François Truffaut's remark that the English are constitutionally incapable of handling a camera.

Michael Powell has produced some especially beautiful images, carefully photographed and lushly colored. The series of romantic fantasies he created in collaboration with Emeric Pressbuger after the war include *The Red Shoes* (1948) and *Tales of Hoffman* (1951). Powell and Pressburger called their production company The Archers and took joint credit for writing, directing, and producing all the films they made together. Despite its fairy-tale atmosphere, *The Red Shoes* provides a realistic inside look at the world of ballet and also functions as a meditation on the meaning of art. The Archers' 1947 release, *Black Narcissus,* is set in a convent deep in the Himalayas. The film's exotic locale (reproduced in a gloriously artificial manner in London's Pinewood Studios) becomes a backdrop for a study of repressed sexuality. These two themes, art and sexuality, come together in the 1960 release, *Peeping Tom,* which Powell made following his breakup with Press-burger. In this strikingly self-reflexive film, often regarded as Powell's masterpiece, an emotionally twisted photographer combines his penchant for voyeurism and sadism by tak-ing pictures of women as he murders them.

Another British director whose work fits into the gothic mold is **John Boorman.** Boorman's connection with film began as a movie reviewer. He then worked in British tele-vision, first as a film editor and eventually as a director of documentaries for BBC-TV (in-cluding one on D. W. Griffith). In his films, even in the more realistic ones, Boorman has been drawn to the mythic and fantastic motifs of the British tradition, including quests and magic. His romantic vision of nature also connects him to the gothic mode. *Deliverance* (1972), *Zardoz* (1974), and *Excalibur* (1981) are noteworthy examples of his work. With *Hope and Glory* (1987), perhaps his best film, he draws themes from his own remembered past as a nine-year-old during the Blitz in London and subsequently at his grandparents' home on the Thames at Shepperton. The special charm of the film is the way in which it deals with life going on in the midst of bombs and wartime separations. In fact the blitzed London, with its collapsed buildings and rubble, becomes a kind of playground. And when his vacant school receives a direct hit, permitting the boy to return to his grandparents and the river, he mutters, "Thank you, Adolf." It is as if the historical moment chronicled by the British wartime semidocumentaries is overlaid with the amused, gentle, and affection-ate spirit of the Ealing comedies. Boorman followed up this nostalgic memoir in the 1990s with *Where the Heart Is* (1990), *Beyond Rangoon* (1995), *The General* (1998), and *The Jailor of Panama* (2001).

Hope and Glory ☆ United Kingdom, 1987, John Boorman; Sebastian Rice-Edwards and Geraldine Muir.

Neil Jordan's films can also be characterized as gothic. The Irish Jordan was a writer before becoming a film maker. (He was age twenty-five when his collection of short stories, *A Night in Tunisia,* was published; he has scripted most of his films, and most of them are original stories.) Jordan's first two directorial efforts—*Angel* (*Danny Boy* in the United States, 1982) and *The Company of Wolves* (1984)—are squarely in the gothic tradition: the former a thriller, the latter a horror story. His third film, *Mona Lisa* (1986), was a resounding success. Set in London, it introduces the motifs of unorthodox sexuality and racial differences, which also characterize his 1992 hit *The Crying Game.* The latter film added the element of political conflict, as it begins in Ireland with an IRA kidnapping of a British soldier before moving on to London. Jordan followed up this success in 1994 with another gothic tale, *Interview with the Vampire.* Based on a novel by Anne Rice, it was made in the United States and starred Tom Cruise and Brad Pitt. In 1999 he returned to his British roots with *The End of the Affair,* a poignant love story tinged with metaphysical overtones based on a book by English writer Graham Greene.

In the latter part of the twentieth century, British gothicism took a postmodern turn. Foremost among the directors who gave expression to this new direction were Derek Jarman (*Carravagio,* 1986) and Isaac Julien (*Young Soul Rebels,* 1991), along with **Nicolas Roeg,** Peter Greenaway, and Sally Potter. Roeg, who had become a topflight cinematographer (for example in Truffaut's *Fahrenheit 451,* 1966; Schlesinger's *Far from the Madding Crowd,* 1967; and Lester's *Petulia,* 1968), turned to direction with the surrealistic *Performance* (1970, codirected by its scriptwriter, Donald Cammell). It features rock star Mick Jagger and a plot that intermingles music, drugs, sex, and identity confusions.

The Crying Game ★ United Kingdom, 1992, Neil Jordan; Stephen Rea and Jaye Davidson.

Walkabout (1971), filmed in Australia, is a more realistic narrative about a teenage girl and her younger brother who become lost in the bush and are saved by an aboriginal youth. Roeg's most widely seen film, *Don't Look Now* (1973), with Julie Christie and Donald Sutherland, combines murder, illusion, and perhaps the supernatural somewhat in the manner of Hitchcock's *Vertigo*. It offers what is surely one of the most ravishing portraits of Venice ever committed to film. Roeg followed this success with *The Man Who Fell to Earth* (1976), an eerie science-fiction story featuring rock star David Bowie as the alien being. In *Bad Timing* (1980), two Americans meet in a Viennese art gallery; the Gustav Klimt paintings on exhibit suggest the fragmented style adopted by Roeg in this tale of tortured erotic love. Some consider it the peak of his career to date.

In keeping with the spirit of postmodern gothicism, Roeg's films present increasingly complex and dazzling mosaics in which logic is transcended; the images, extraordinarily sensual, are cut together in pursuit of feeling, like the stories of Argentinian writer Jorge Luis Borges (who is in fact invoked in *Performance*). Roeg's output during the 1980s and 1990s—including *Eureka* (1983), *Track 29* (1987), *The Witches* (1990), and *Cold Heaven* (1992)—became increasingly recondite and hermetic, although always providing the pleasures of stylish photography. Many starred his wife, Theresa Russell. In the late 1990s Roeg turned his attention to productions made for television, with *Full Body Massage* (1995) and *Samson and Delilah* (1996).

Bad Timing ★ United Kingdom, 1980, Nicolas Roeg; Theresa Russell and Art Garfunkel.

Another director in the postmodern tradition, **Peter Greenaway,** began as a painter. Although not appealing to all tastes, Greenaway's work is stylish, inventive, and enigmatic, offered as a delightful game between film maker and audience. From 1966 he made experimental shorts; in 1980 he turned to features. The first of these to receive international attention was *The Draughtsman's Contract* (1982). An extremely clever, mannered evocation of the mores and morals of aristocratic seventeenth-century England, it revolves around seduction and murder in a stately country house. Eventually it becomes a metaphysical puzzle that proves insoluble, at least in terms of the evidence offered. *The Cook, the Thief, His Wife, and Her Lover* (1989), thought by some to be his best film, benefited at the box office from the notoriety earned by its scandalous content: adulterous copulation being carried on mostly in the washrooms of a posh London restaurant while the title characters are engaged in sumptuous dinners. Its form includes sets and lighting palettes of red, blue, or dazzling white, and references to famous painters' paintings. It was followed in 1991 by *Prospero's Books,* a stylish, erudite reworking of Shakespeare's *The Tempest* starring John Gielgud, and in 1995 by *The Pillow Book, which* combines an essayistic retelling of a book of maxims written by a medieval Japanese lady-in-waiting with the picaresque adventures of a Japanese model in contemporary London who is obsessed with the project of having men cover her body with calligraphy.

The Cook, the Thief, His Wife, and Her Lover ⋆ United Kingdom, Peter Greenaway, 1989; Alan Howard, Richard Bohringer, Helen Mirren, and Michael Gambon, in foreground.

Orlando ✭ United Kingdom-Russia-France-Italy-Netherlands, 1992, Sally Potter; Tilda Swinton and Charlotte Valandrey.

In the 1970s a British academic film journal, *Screen,* became the English language voice for a new, more politically and theoretically engaged way of looking at cinema. Represented most infuentially by critic–film maker Laura Mulvey's seminal 1975 essay "Visual Pleasure and Narrative Cinema," *Screen* led film scholars on both sides of the Atlantic to turn their attention to the ways in which mainstream cinema portrays the female body as an object displayed for the benefit of what became known as "the male gaze." A British director whose style evolved in sympathy with this feminist perspective on the nature of film narratives was **Sally Potter.** Potter's first production, the thirty-minute *Thriller,* released in 1979, was conceived as a deconstruction of the gender politics of the opera *La Boheme.* Her most widely seen feature, the 1993 *Orlando,* takes as its guiding principle the proposition that gender roles are social constructions. Based on a Virginia Woolf novella, *Orlando* traces the adventures of a Renaissance man who is reincarnated as a woman and lives many lives throughout the centuries that follow. The film's spectacular *mise-en-scène* features lavish costumes and sumptuous backgrounds of castles and estates in England and on the continent.

Americans Abroad

British cinema of the last half of the twentieth century was distinguished by a cluster of sometimes brilliant directors whose films, for the most part, had an international rather than a national identity. They worked on either side of the Atlantic and for American money in any case. Of the former social-realist directors, Reisz (*Who'll Stop the Rain?* 1978; *The*

French Lieutenant's Woman, 1981; and *Sweet Dreams,* 1986) has worked in the United States and on U.S. projects; Richardson (*The Charge of the Light Brigade,* 1968; *The Border,* 1982; and *Blue Sky,* 1991, released in 1994) and Schlesinger (*Midnight Cowboy,* 1969; *Sunday Bloody Sunday,* 1971; *Cold Comfort Farm,* 1995; and *The Next Best Thing,* 2000) have alternated between the United Kingdom and the United States. Another group of British directors who work in Hollywood are hardly distinguishable from their U.S. colleagues, including Adrian Lyne (*Flashdance,* 1973, and *Fatal Attraction,* 1987), Alan Parker (*Mississippi Burning,* 1988, and *Evita,* 1996), Mike Figgis (*Leaving Las Vegas,* 1995), and Ridley Scott (*Blade Runner,* 1982; *Thelma and Louise,* 1991; and *Gladiator,* 2000). On the other hand, four Americans, long-time residents in England, clearly became English to the extent that Henry James and T. S. Eliot became English: Joseph Losey, Richard Lester, Stanley Kubrick, and Terry Gilliam. Each drew on aspects of the British cultural heritage to create works that built on the traditions of which they subsequently became part.

After a modestly successful Hollywood career, **Joseph Losey** exiled himself in 1951 in order to escape the blacklisting of the McCarthy era. In Britain his reputation was first established with a succession of moderately budgeted pictures within conventional idioms that are packed with political meaning and psychological, even philosophical, complexities. With *The Servant* (1963) Losey began his association with playwright Harold Pinter and moved from the partially covert investigation of British society to a clear emphasis on social observation less restricted by rigid and complex plotting. To be more exact, beginning with *The Servant* and continuing with *King and Country* (1964), *Accident* (1967), *The*

The Servant ★ United Kingdom, 1963, Joseph Losey; Dirk Bogarde and James Fox.

Go-Between (1971), *The Romantic Englishwoman* (1979), and *Steaming,* completed just before he died in 1984, a group of Losey's films comment directly on a culture that he observed with the eye of an outsider who has experienced fresh what others had absorbed from birth. Implicit criticisms of British manners and the British class system abound in these films, which differ from earlier "kitchen sink" productions in their emphasis on middle- and upper-class characters and their stylish cinematography.

Richard Lester was attracted to a much different kind of England than was Losey—the rock, the mod, and the trendy. Lester drew lavishly on the tradition of British comedy, updating it with a hip 1960s spin. Moving to London in 1955 (at the age of twenty-three) Lester worked on television commercials during his first years there, developing the technical facility—including rapid cutting, freely moving camera, and improvisational performance style—that is associated with his earlier, and some of his later, work. *The Running, Jumping, and Standing-Still Film* (1959), a short for BBC-TV's *The Goon Show,* set forth his special talents in capsule form. It was followed by two features starring the Beatles: *A Hard Day's Night* (1964) and *Help!* (1965). *Petulia* (1968), his first feature shot in the United States, may also be his best. Following the British tradition of acute social analysis, it appraises the American scene through the revealing exaggerations that California manners and mores offer. Featuring American Method actors George C. Scott and Shirley Knight along with British star Julie Christie, it also attempts a much more intense and sustained probing of character than any of Lester's other films.

A Hard Day's Night ★
United Kingdom, 1964,
Richard Lester; Paul
McCartney, George
Harrison, Ringo Starr,
and John Lennon.

Stanley Kubrick, who arrived in Britain ten years after Losey and six years after Lester, had an even more substantial career before leaving the United States. In his American films Kubrick seemed to be setting off in several directions at once, however: antiwar statement (the youthful outcry of *Fear and Desire,* 1953, and the mature condemnation of *Paths of Glory,* 1957); gangster film (the experimentally expressionistic *Killer's Kiss,* 1955, and the expertly professional *The Killing,* 1956); and even historical spectacle (*Spartacus,* 1960). Beginning with his first film made in Britain, *Lolita* (1962), he began gradually to settle into a consistently cynical, increasingly misanthropic view of humankind, a mordant variant on the British legacy of social criticism, which he combined with corrosive satire, his own version of English humor. Kubrick came to depend on strong literary figures for sources and/or collaboration: Vladimir Nabokov for *Lolita,* Terry Southern for *Dr. Strangelove, or, How I Learned to Stop Worrying and Love the Bomb* (1964), Arthur Clarke for *2001: A Space Odyssey* (1968), Anthony Burgess for *A Clockwork Orange* (1971), William Thackery for *Barry Lyndon* (1975), Stephen King for *The Shining* (1980), and Arthur Schnitzler for *Eyes Wide Shut,* which he completed just before his death in 2000. Each of those films is laced with dark humor and enlivened by extraordinary set constructions. All feature the clean, hard-edged cinematography for which Kubrick has become known. Perhaps the most conspicuous aspect of his films is the consistency of the world they portray. Of the somberness of this spectacle Kubrick has said, "We're never going to get down to doing anything about the things that are really

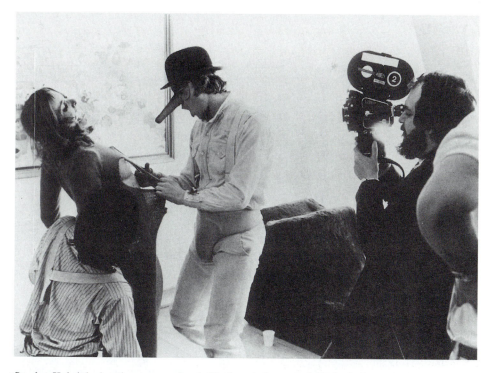

Stanley Kubrick shooting a scene for *A Clockwork Orange* ★ United Kingdom, 1971; Adrienne Corri and Malcolm McDowell.

bad in the world until there is recognition within us of the darker side of our natures, the shadow side."

Having made his home in England since 1963 and begun his career creating animations for the popular British TV comedy series *Monty Python,* **Terry Gilliam** has absorbed much of the British sensibility. Although he has worked on both sides of the Atlantic, his taste for distopic fantasy and mordant social satire are reminiscent of the work of Irish writer Jonathan Swift. *Brazil* (1985), *The Adventures of Baron Munchausen* (1988), and *Twelve Monkeys* (1995) are Gilliam's most highly regarded productions to date, the first two cartoonish portraits of fantasmagoric worlds, the last a more subdued reworking of French director Chris Marker's short science-fiction film about time travel.

State of the Industry

The ebb and flow of the British film industry is inextricably tied to the ebb and flow of American production dollars and American audiences. In the early 1980s there was talk of a British film renaissance. *Chariots of Fire* (1981), directed by Hugh Hudson, had become the most successful British film ever released in the United States and won the Oscar for best picture of 1981. In the exhilaration of the moment the cry "The British are coming!" was uttered (by a Brit, admittedly). *Gregory's Girl* (1980), *Gandhi* (1982), *Educating Rita* (1983), and other films were well received by critics as well as the public at home and abroad.

Chariots of Fire ★ United Kingdom, 1981, Hugh Hudson; Ian Charleson, waving.

In these promising circumstances, producer David Puttnam came to the fore. The driving force behind *Chariots of Fire,* Puttnam has produced first features of a number of directors who have made important films. Although drawn to talent, he does not regard the director, nor himself for that matter, as the film artist. He began his career in advertising, but in the early 1970s he started to produce theatrical features, including Ken Russell's *Mahler* (1973) and *Lisztomania* (1975). Then in 1976 Puttnam formed his own production company, Enigma; its first release was Ridley Scott's *The Duellists* (1977), widely praised in the United States. His first great international box-office hit was Alan Parker's *Midnight Express* (1978), followed by *Chariots of Fire* (1981), *The Killing Fields* (Roland Joffe, 1984), and *The Mission* (Joffe, 1986). On the basis of his success he was named head of Columbia Pictures. Hollywood has long attracted and imported foreign talent, but the appointment of a foreigner as head of a major studio was unprecedented. Given Puttnam's commitment to making films he cared about and his lack of experience with megacorporations (Columbia was a subsidiary of Coca-Cola), this turn of events was surprising. His acceptance was announced in September 1986; his resignation followed in September 1987.

Adding support to the British film renaissance was a television channel, Channel 4 of the quasi-governmental BBC, named in reference to the other two BBC channels plus the commercial channel, ITV. Set up in 1980, Channel 4 went on the air in 1982. In that year it began to finance feature films in the manner of Italian (RAI) and West German (ZDF) state television. *The Draughtsman's Contract* (1982) and *Dance with a Stranger* (Mike Newell, 1984) were made because Channel 4 was prepared to supplement funds obtained elsewhere as required. In 1984 ten out of twenty-eight British features had financial investment from Channel 4; several of the others were presold to the network (*Insignificance,* for example). In 1985 *My Beautiful Laundrette* was fully financed by Channel 4, as was most of *Wetherby* (1985). The British Film Institute, another partly governmental agency, has also contributed to the financing and cofinancing of a number of British successes, as has a related organization, British Screen. After these sources had run short of funds in the late 1980s, the government stepped in again, dedicating some of the proceeds from the national lottery to the support of film production. Supplementing these resources in the 1990s was a commercially oriented group of U.S. and multinationally financed British-based production companies, such as Polygram (*Four Weddings and a Funeral,* Mike Newell, 1994; *Elizabeth,* Shakhar Kapur, 1998), Pathé (*An Ideal Husband,* 2000), and the short-lived HAL, an offshoot of the American independent powerhouse Miramax (*Mansfield Park,* 1998). By the late 1990s, as a result of these varied initiatives, the industry was again on a roll, though its scale remained modest in relation to the American behemoth. As one British producer commented, to compare the English movie industry to that of Hollywood is "like comparing the space program with people in the Hebrides knitting scarves."

What seems remarkable about the resurgence of British cinema in the 1980s is not only that it managed to retain a national identity but also that its success was due to its national flavor. Many of these films comment critically—directly or metaphorically—on the political, economic, and social stresses that have preoccupied Britain since the mid-1950s, and this later success seems even more substantial than that of the earlier social-realist features. As American distributors have increasingly shied away from films with subtitles, the English-language British art film has become the dominant entry in the American market, including such notable hits as *A Fish Called Wanda* (Charles Crichton, 1988), *Four*

The Full Monty ★ United Kingdom, 1997, Peter Cattaneo.

Weddings and a Funeral (Mike Newell, 1994), *The English Patient* (Anthony Minghella, 1996), *Trainspotting* (Danny Boyle, 1996), *The Full Monty* (Peter Cattaneo, 1997), *Lock, Stock, and Two Smoking Barrels* (Guy Ritchie, 1999), and *Shakespeare in Love* (John Madden, 1999). Ealing's influence seems to have come full circle with the biggest British hit of 1988, *A Fish Called Wanda,* directed by former Ealing director Charles Crichton.

But the question What is a British film? isn't altogether answered by *Wanda,* as redolent as it is with reminders of *The Lavender Hill Mob* and *Fawlty Towers.* Creatively it may be British, but it was an M-G-M movie, financed in Hollywood. Whatever Britain looks like in the atlas, it is no island entire of itself but part of the main. Even its specifically national film types and most distinctive creators fit into an international economic context. It is to other successful examples of distinctive national film expression developed in the face of American hegemony that the next chapters are devoted.

Films of the Period

1946
Black Narcissus (The Archers [Michael Powell and Emeric Pressburger])
Great Expectations (David Lean)

1947
Hue and Cry (Charles Crichton)
Odd Man Out (Carol Reed)

1948
Hamlet (Laurence Olivier)
Oliver Twist (David Lean)
The Red Shoes (The Archers)

1949
Kind Hearts and Coronets (Robert Hamer)
Passport to Pimlico (Henry Cornelius)

Whiskey Galore (Tight Little Island) (Alexander
  Mackendrick)
The Third Man (Carol Reed)

1951
The Lavender Hill Mob (Charles Crichton)
The Man in the White Suit (Alexander Mackendrick)

1954
The Maggie (High and Dry) (Alexander
  Mackendrick)

1955
The Lady Killers (Alexander Mackendrick)

1957
The Curse of Frankenstein (Terence Fisher)

1958
Dracula (Terence Fisher)

1959
Look Back in Anger (Tony Richardson)
Room at the Top (Jack Clayton)

1960
The Entertainer (Tony Richardson)
Saturday Night and Sunday Morning (Karel Reisz)

1961
A Taste of Honey (Tony Richardson)

1962
A Kind of Loving (John Schlesinger)
Lawrence of Arabia (David Lean)
The Loneliness of the Long Distance Runner
  (Tony Richardson)

1963
Billy Liar (John Schlesinger)
This Sporting Life (Lindsay Anderson)

1964
Dr. Strangelove (Stanley Kubrick)
A Hard Day's Night (Richard Lester)
King and Country (Joseph Losey)

1965
Darling (John Schlesinger)
Help! (Richard Lester)

The Knack (Richard Lester)
The War Game (Peter Watkins)

1967
Accident (Joseph Losey)
Blow-Up (Michelangelo Antonioni)
How I Won the War (Richard Lester)

1968
Petulia (Richard Lester)
2001: A Space Odyssey (Stanley Kubrick)

1969
If . . . (Lindsay Anderson)
Kes (Ken Loach)
Women in Love (Ken Russell)

1970
The Music Lovers (Ken Russell)
Performance (Nicolas Roeg)

1971
A Clockwork Orange (Stanley Kubrick)
The Devils (Ken Russell)
The Go-Between (Joseph Losey)
Sunday Bloody Sunday (John Schlesinger)
Walkabout (Nicolas Roeg)

1972
Family Life (Ken Loach)

1973
Don't Look Now (Nicolas Roeg)
O Lucky Man! (Lindsay Anderson)

1975
Barry Lyndon (Stanley Kubrick)

1976
The Man Who Fell to Earth (Nicolas Roeg)

1977
Providence (Alain Resnais)

1979
That Sinking Feeling (Bill Forsyth)
Thriller (Sally Potter)

1980
Bad Timing (Nicolas Roeg)
The Shining (Stanley Kubrick)

1981
Chariots of Fire (Hugh Hudson)
Gregory's Girl (Bill Forsyth)

1982
The Draughtsman's Contract (Peter Greenaway)
Gandhi (Richard Attenborough)

1983
Eureka (Nicolas Roeg)
Local Hero (Bill Forsyth)

1984
Comfort and Joy (Bill Forsyth)
The Killing Fields (Roland Joffe)

1985
My Beautiful Laundrette (Stephen Frears)
Brazil (Terry Gilliam)
Insignificance (Nicolas Roeg)
A Passage to India (David Lean)

1986
Carravagio (Derek Jarman)
Mona Lisa (Neil Jordan)
A Room with a View (James Ivory)

1987
Full Metal Jacket (Stanley Kubrick)
Hope and Glory (John Boorman)
Maurice (James Ivory)
Sammy and Rosie Get Laid (Stephen Frears)

1988
Dangerous Liaisons (Stephen Frears)
Distant Voices, Still Lives (Terence Davies)
A Fish Called Wanda (Charles Crichton)
High Hopes (Mike Leigh)

1989
The Cook, the Thief, His Wife, and Her Lover (Peter
   Greenaway)
Henry V (Kenneth Branaugh)

1991
Edward II (Derek Jarman)
Howard's End (James Ivory)

Life Is Sweet (Mike Leigh)
Prospero's Books (Peter Greenaway)
Young Soul Rebels (Isaac Julien)

1992
The Crying Game (Neil Jordan)
Orlando (Sally Potter)

1993
Naked (Mike Leigh)
The Remains of the Day (James Ivory)

1994
Four Weddings and a Funeral (Mike Newell)
Ladybird, Ladybird (Ken Loach)

1995
Land and Freedom (Ken Loach)
The Pillow Book (Peter Greenaway)

1996
Carla's Song (Ken Loach)
The English Patient (Anthony Minghella)
Frantz Fanon: Black Skin, White Mask
   (Isaac Julien)
Hamlet (Kenneth Branaugh)
Secrets and Lies (Mike Leigh)
Trainspotting (Danny Boyle)

1997
The Tango Lesson (Sally Potter)

1998
Elizabeth (Shakhar Kapur)

1999
The End of the Affair (Neil Jordan)
Lock, Stock and Two Smoking Barrels
   (Guy Ritchie)
Shakespeare in Love (John Madden)
Topsy Turvy (Mike Leigh)

2000
Bread and Roses (Ken Loach)

Books on the Period

Caughie, John, and Kevin Rockett. *The Companion to British and Irish Cinema.* London: Cassell/British Film Institute, 1996.

Dixon, Wheeler Winston, ed. *Re-Viewing British Cinema, 1900–1992: Essays and Interviews.* Albany: State University of New York Press, 1993.

Friedman, Lester, ed. *Fires Were Started: British Cinema and Thatcherism.* Minneapolis: University of Minnesota Press, 1993.

Hill, John. *British Cinema in the 1980s: Issues and Themes.* New York: Oxford University Press, 1999.

Johnson, Lucy, ed.; interviews by Graham Jones. *The Talking Pictures: Interviews with Contemporary British Film-Makers.* London: British Film Institute, 1996.

Meikle, Denis. *A History of Horrors: The Rise and Fall of the House of Hammer.* Lanham, MD: Scarecrow Press, 1996.

Murphy, Robert, ed. *British Cinema of the 90s.* London: British Film Institute, 2000.

Pym, John. *Film on Four:* London: British Film Institute, 1993. (*Four* is Channel 4 of BBC-TV.)

Street, Sarah. *British National Cinema.* New York: Routledge, 1997.

10

Films of the Auteurs: The French New Wave and After

★ ★ ★ ★

1954–

Auteurism

In January 1954 an article by a young critic named François Truffaut, published in *Cahiers du Cinéma,* established the designation and first premise for a critical position that would gain increasing strength both in France and elsewhere in the years to come. Quietly entitled "A Certain Tendency in the French Cinema," Truffaut's piece was against the writer's film—the well-wrought "literary" scenario executed by expert craftsmen. In place of the creations of script writers, Truffaut called for films that would reflect as totally as possible the creative personalities of their directors. He argued that only in this way could French cinema overcome literary stasis and utilize the dynamic filmic potential available. A handful of French directors were capable of this sort of creation, he wrote, and they were the "authors" of their films—that is, in control of, or at least fully involved in, conception as well as execution. He cited Jean Renoir, Robert Bresson, Jean Cocteau, Jacques Becker, Abel Gance, Max Ophüls, Jacques Tati, and Roger Leenhardt as *auteurs* who often wrote their dialogue and some of whom invented the stories they directed. In asking for the elimination of the old psychological realism and dominance by scriptwriters, to be replaced by strongly original directors in creative control, Truffaut declared that he could not believe in the peaceful coexistence of the *tradition of quality* and a *cinema of auteurs*. What his criticism pointed toward was the French New Wave, which would break a few years later and carry him along with it.

The background for Truffaut's manifesto extends at least to Alexandre Astruc's call, as early as 1948, for *la caméra-stylo* (camera as pen)—that is, creating the film in its making rather than merely supplying images and sounds for a fully realized and prefixed conception. Also, by those early postwar years, the French national film archive and screening center, the

Cinémathèque Française, had been thoroughly reestablished, making available a systematic viewing of great amounts of the international history of the motion picture. It became possible to see that the moments of aesthetic excitement among the hours upon hours of films were provided by directoral vision, like that of Griffith or Eisenstein, Murnau or Gance.

Perhaps of even greater consequence was the arrival of the backlog of American films that had been kept from France by the German Occupation. Seeing in rapid succession films produced over a period of years permitted comparisons that provoked new insights. Even among the popular generic entertainments turned out by the big Hollywood studios there were differences, not only of artistic quality but, more important, of artistic personality attributable to certain directors. Both Howard Hawks and John Ford made excellent westerns, and yet a Ford western was subtly but nonetheless surely and consistently advancing different themes and offering a different visual style than one by Hawks. The same was true of the musicals of Vincente Minnelli compared to those of Stanley Donen and Gene Kelly. Further, directors who had been thought of only as having been involved with a few good pictures along with some less good ones could be seen to carry with them a certain special vision; among these were Orson Welles, Fritz Lang, and Alfred Hitchcock. For the young French critics, films by the latter kind of director were much more interesting and rewarding than those of others, however prestigious and expert, whose direction was impersonal. Especially was this so when they regarded all of a director's films together—that is, the director in relation to the total body of work. Even—sometimes especially—the humble action directors working on "B" budgets were able to maintain and articulate their own particular visions: Raoul Walsh in gangster films, Anthony Mann in westerns, Samuel Fuller in war pictures, and Edgar G. Ulmer in horror stories, for example.

It was the application of *la politique des auteurs* to the popular American movie that created the most excitement and controversy. Reevaluations of the total corpus of the American sound film were prompted by the young writers of *Cahiers,* who announced and defended newly discovered masters and masterpieces with enthusiastic rhetoric. The criterion was the consistency with which a uniquely personal point of view was expressed through recurring themes, characters, situations, imagery. Pushed to its extreme, the position was that any film directed by Otto Preminger, Nicholas Ray, or Douglas Sirk (among the auteurists' favorites) was of more value than any film directed by William Wellman, William Wyler, or Robert Wise. The former were auteurs, the latter merely interpreters, realizers of someone else's conception. What's more, auteurists seemed often to value most those auteur films in which the script was weakest or the content slightest precisely because they allowed the director's creative personality to be disclosed most nakedly, without the cloak of satisfying literary content.

Whatever the merits of the arguments, the French word *politique* translated badly as *theory;* what it means more nearly is *position* or *policy.* As with Truffaut initially, the auteur critics' positions were partisan and polemical. What they were insisting was simply that, after looking at hundreds of films in relation to who directed them, certain directors they valued and others they did not.

As the "auteur theory," it moved westward to the United States in 1961, as evidenced by Andrew Sarris's writing in *Film Culture* and by the appearance of the *New York Film Bulletin.* The auteur theory appeared in Great Britain in 1962, upon the publication of *Movie* magazine. Auteurism was attacked by the more conventional critics for ignoring the collective nature of film making, especially Hollywood's, and for turning critical standards upside down by insisting that bad films were good merely because they were made by favored directors. Eventually, however, even the founts of English-language criticism that had been under attack by the auteurists—*The New York Times, The New Yorker,* and *Sight and Sound,* for example—gradually came to reflect their tastes. In 1968 Sarris consolidated the auteur position in his book *The American Cinema: Directors and Directions 1929–1968.*

Precursors to the New Wave

Among the directors Truffaut cited as important French auteurs of the past were Jacques Tati, Max Ophüls, and Robert Bresson. Although very different from one another, each cultivated a readily distinguishable style that set his films apart from those of others and allowed him to create distinctive *oeuvres.*

Jacques Tati preceded the New Wave with *Jour de fête* (1949), *Mr. Hulot's Holiday* (1953), and *Mon Oncle* (1958). During its height he produced nothing, but in his last two films before his death in 1982, *Playtime* (1968) and *Traffic* (1971), he created intricate, oblique, amusing commentaries on contemporary life that have served as texts for postmodernist theorists. The character he conceived and performed, Hulot, remains one of the enduring comic figures of the screen.

Max Ophüls, father of the documentary film maker Marcel Ophüls, began his career as a director in Germany but produced most of his most memorable films in France. An incurable romantic, he celebrated passionate commitments and the sensitivity of women in

Mr. Hulot's Holiday ★ France, 1953, Jacques Tati; Tati.

films such as *La Signora di tutti* (*Everybody's Woman*) (Italy, 1934), *Letter from an Unknown Woman* (USA, 1948), *La Ronde* (France, 1950), *The Earrings of Madame de . . .* (France/Italy, 1953), and *Lola Montèz* (France/Germany, 1955). The stories of these films are frequently presented in flashback, accompanied by voice-over narrators. Ophüls favored period settings that could give free reign to his taste for opulent decorative effects. He also had a predilection for complicated crane and dolly shots. During one such shot in *Letter from an Unknown Woman* the narrator offered a self-reflexive commentary on the meticulous planning that went into the creation of such effects. "I know that nothing happens by chance," she states. "Every moment is measured; every step is counted."

Lola Montèz is often regarded as Ophüls's masterpiece, though it was clumsily re-edited by its American distributor and only partially restored in 1968. A chronicle of the life of the most famous courtesan of the nineteenth century, the film begins in a circus where Lola (Martine Carol), at the end of her career as an *amoureuse*, has been hired to sell kisses. Part of the show is built around the scandalous events of her former life; the ringmaster (Peter Ustinov) recounts her past exploits, which appear on the screen as flashbacks.

Ophüls once commented that *Lola Montèz* was about "the annihilation of the personality through the cruelty and indecency of spectacles based on scandal." The film's style supports this theme via a thoroughgoing critique of its own status as spectacle. Each episode of Lola's life is preceded by a clownish dumb-show created as part of the circus performance. She is displayed to the audience in a cage, like an animal; as the cage revolves to provide each member of the audience under the big top an unrestricted view, the camera tracks around it in the opposite direction, assertively calling attention to its presence even as it collaborates with the ringmaster's titillating narration by creating a sensation of dizzying romanticism. The film's sumptuous decor, lavishly displayed in wide-screen color

Lola Montez ★ France-Germany, 1955, Max Ophüls; Martine Carol.

images, also implicitly announces the constructed nature of what is depicted. Ophüls's overall strategy thus puts the film audience into a position not far removed from that of the gawking, sensation-seeking spectators at the circus—but his technique presents this voyeuristic position in terms that are self-conscious rather than crudely exploitative.

A wholly antithetical approach to Ophüls's self-reflexive romanticism is represented in the restrained, straightforward style of **Robert Bresson.** Bresson's important films began shortly after those of the great French film makers of the 1930s and extend to the early 1990s. Throughout his career he remained an isolated figure, among the most personal of film makers. The austerity of his subject matter, concerned more with moral and theological questions than with psychological analysis, and his insistence on rigorous control over every aspect of production, have kept him removed from critical and creative fashion and have limited his output to thirteen films, which stand as monuments to his intellectual and aesthetic integrity. Although Bresson is part of the Catholic humanist tradition, his views take on a particular severity, which led to his being called the Jansenist of French cinema.

With *Diary of a Country Priest* (1950), adapted from a novel by Georges Bernanos, Bresson moved into the main themes and mature style of his subsequent work. Set firmly in the midst of French provincial Catholicism, it is concerned not so much with religion as with faith, with the preservation and sharing of belief in God. Shot on location in the Artois region in bleak fall and early winter weather, it is about the misunderstanding and mis-

Diary of a Country Priest ★ France, 1951, Robert Bresson; Claude Laydu, right.

interpretation of motives to which the truly saintly are subjected in a world of petty self-ishness, rivalry, ambition, and smallness of spirit.

Bresson followed *Diary of a Country Priest* with a series of somber studies of the connection between human and divine love, including *A Man Escaped* (1956), *Pickpocket* (1959), *The Trial of Joan of Arc* (1962), *Un Femme Douce* (1969), *Four Nights of a Dreamer* (1971), *Lancelot of the Lake* (1974), *The Devil, Probably* (1977), and *L'Argent* (1983). In all of these the low-key quality of his visual style is complemented by his use of nonprofessional actors who were instructed to remain expressionless.

Although his films have never been widely popular with audiences, Bresson has emerged as one of the rare examples of a consummate individual stylist. Like Tati and Ophüls, his films offer an inimitable aesthetic experience that provided a model from which a new generation of French film makers could build.

The New Wave Arrives

Having constructed a critical system exalting the director, it is little wonder the young *Cahiers* critics soon left criticism to become directors themselves. Most of them had from the outset considered criticism only a stepping stone to creation. Still, the ensuing development of a creative movement out of a critical movement is unique in the history of film and seems, to Anglo-Saxons at least, particularly Gallic. In the United States to date only Peter Bogdanovich and Paul Schrader have come to film directing from writing about film. In France, however, many of the leading film makers of the New Wave, which began at the end of the 1950s, were *Cahiers* alumni and auteurists. Aside from Alexandre Astruc and Roger Leenhardt, already established directors at the time they were writing for *Cahiers,* there were among the younger generation of critics-turned-film-makers François Truffaut, Jean-Luc Godard, Claude Chabrol, Jacques Rivette, and Eric Rohmer.

While the critical context of auteurism was being constructed, conditions in the French film industry also came to favor a new kind of film maker. The glut of Hollywood film released during the late 1940's—a backlog from the Occupation years plus current releases—not only gave rise to its reevaluation by the *Cahiers* critics but also provoked an important series of responses from French producers and government attempting to meet the competition.

Immediately after the war, in 1946, a rather half-hearted quota system was established. Known as the Blum-Byrnes agreement (Léon Blum, President of France, and James F. Byrnes, U.S. Secretary of State), it required French cinemas to show French films at least sixteen weeks of the year. All this did was to establish modest limits on importation. It did not encourage French production, which dwindled in the years immediately following the agreement. In short, it scarcely checked the Americans and further contributed to the stagnation of French film about which Truffaut would complain.

In 1948 a new agreement was reached that stretched the period for exclusive showing of French films to twenty weeks and offered what was intended as temporary government subsidy to the French industry. The aid was financed through a tax on admissions. Money was refunded to the producers in proportion to the amount taken in at the box office. It was a system that favored the established and already successful: The rich got richer while the poor remained poor. Because producers were afraid to risk a share of future admissions, the norm became the repetition of tested ingredients. Kinds of films that had made money in the past were repeated; scriptwriters who had solid success to their credit were hired again; stars who were in public favor had vehicles created for them. But audiences became restive with the standard programming, and the industry soon had yet another crisis on its hands as it became more and more difficult to anticipate public reaction on the basis of the old formulas.

In 1953 André Malraux, Minister of Culture, put forth a new variation on the "temporary" assistance offered to producers. Feature films were given an *avance sur recettes,* a method of funding before the film was finished if the project looked worthwhile to the government advisers. Bresson's *A Man Escaped* (1956) was financed in that manner when he had difficulty finding private backing. Shorts as well as features were covered under the new system, being awarded money in relation to their artistic quality. These *primes de qualité* for the production of short films encouraged directors such as Georges Franju, Alain Resnais, and Chris Marker.

Taken together, the developments in France by the mid-1950s—an industry that began to support talented individual film makers, the critical climate created by the *Cahiers* group, the beginning rise of European auteurs such as Ingmar Bergman plus new works by Max Ophüls, Jacques Becker, Jean-Pierre Melville, and Robert Bresson—prepared an audience to accept innovation and a more personal kind of film making. The dominating scriptwriter's cinema of standard dramaturgy based on psychological realism began to give way to the director's cinema of eccentric artistic vision and varied style.

At the same time what would prove to be the precursors of the New Wave began to appear: Alexandre Astruc's *Les Mauvaises rencontres* (1955), Jean-Pierre Melville's *Bob le flambeur* (1955), Agnès Varda's *La Pointe courte* (1955), and Roger Vadim's *And God Created Woman* (1956). The last, enormously successful and creating a new sex goddess in Brigitte Bardot, also bore—superficially at least—many of the thematic and stylistic marks of the supsequent body of New Wave work. Louis Malle's *The Lovers* and Claude Chabrol's *Le Beau Serge* were so close to the main upswing, both in their year of release (1958) and in their artistic character, as to be part of the larger whole. But 1959 was the decisive year and the Cannes Film Festival the appropriate occasion on which three French features signaled to the world the beginning of the first new period of heightened national creativity since Italian neorealism of the late 1940's and early 1950's.

Of the three the most popular was *Black Orpheus,* the second feature of Marcel Camus, who had worked for many years as an assistant director. Based on the Greek legend of Orpheus and Eurydice, shot on location in Rio de Janeiro among Brazilian blacks at carnival time, it became an international success, winning an Academy Award as best foreign picture of the year. However, with its exoticism on the one hand and derivative narrative technique on the other, it belongs to the New Wave only by virtue of its year of release. Camus, in his mid-forties at the time, was part of an earlier generation; he made no other important film after *Black Orpheus.*

Hiroshima, mon amour, directed by Alain Resnais, whose background was in editing and documentary film making, was a far less conventional work. The script for *Hiroshima,* by the eminent *nouveau roman* novelist Marguerite Duras, concerns a transient and strained love affair between a French actress and a Japanese architect. The personal relationship is embedded in painful memories of the German occupation of France and the atomic holocaust in Japan. Its innovative transcendence of temporal-spatial unities,

Hiroshima, mon amour ⋆ France, 1959, Alain Resnais; Eiji Okada and Emmanuelle Riva.

Proustian emphasis on memory, and linkage of sexual love and global war were strange and absorbing—and typically Resnais, as it would turn out.

The 400 Blows, by former critic François Truffaut, also heralded major changes in French film making. An account of a young boy estranged from his parents, who is caught up in the juvenile judicial and penal system, *The 400 Blows* began Truffaut's semiautobiographical Antoine Doinel series, with the twelve-year-old Jean-Pierre Léaud playing his first role. If the film's warmth and humanity owe something to Renoir, one of Truffaut's heroes, it bears resemblances to Italian neorealism as well, specifically to de Sica-Zavattini's *Shoeshine*. It was, however, a very personal project. In addition, bravura flourishes—tracking shots in wide screen and the famous final freeze-frame closeup of the young Léaud—announce the presence of an individualistic stylist and look ahead to Truffaut's later work and to the work of other young French directors.

The year 1960 saw the release of Jean-Luc Godard's first feature, *Breathless*, an idio-syncratic tribute to the American gangster film. Filled with verve and originality in its fragmented storytelling and iconoclastic camera and editing style, Godard's debut film showcased the radical experimentation that would characterize the director's subsequent output. Deeply indebted to Jean-Pierre Melville's *noir*-ish existential crime film *Bob le flambeur*, it told the story of the last days of a self-destructive small-time criminal, played by Jean-Paul Belmondo as a self-conscious tribute to Humphrey Bogart. Like many of Godard's early films, *Breathless* conveyed a certain misogyny. Nonetheless, more than any other film, it epitomized the salient aspects of the New Wave style with its episodic plot,

The 400 Blows ★ France, 1959, François Truffaut; Jean-Pierre Léaud.

improvised dialogue, hand-held camera work, jumpy editing, grainy images shot on location with available light, and ubiquitous references to American culture—especially Hollywood movies.

These first films marked the beginning of what was not so much a movement as an explosion. Approximately one hundred directors made their film debuts in France between 1959 and 1962. Naturally the majority of these young and new film makers were less than geniuses and the bulk of their films scarcely masterpieces. When the novelty and excitement began to wear off, self-indulgence and ineptitude became a kind of commercial undertow. Audiences grew increasingly resistant and producers wary. But before the New Wave receded an extraordinary number of valuable and/or interesting films were produced that left a permanent mark on the international history of film and established a whole new generation of French film makers.

The term *nouvelle vague* was said to have been coined by a journalist. Used for promotional purposes, it covered a diversity of film makers many of whom had little in common with each other. If the New Wave was not as cohesive a movement as, say, German expressionism in the 1920s or post–World War II Italian neorealism, still there are certain characteristics that were either shared or that received a new and strong emphasis beginning about 1959 in France.

First was a base in the existentialist philosophy of Jean-Paul Sartre and Albert Camus, especially the latter. Camus's short novel *The Stranger* seems in many ways prototypical of

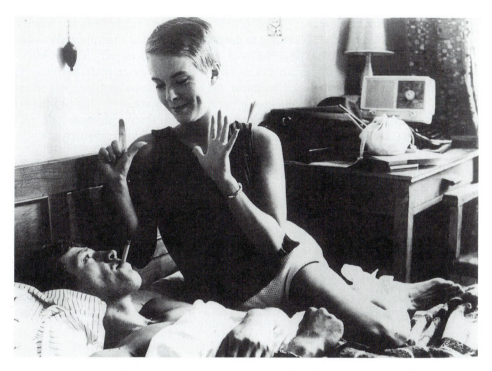

Breathless ★ France, 1960, Jean-Luc Godard; Jean-Paul Belmondo and Jean Seberg.

the attitudes and approaches of the New Wave. There is, arguably, a direct line between it and *Breathless.* A distanced, antisentimental stance on the part of their creators typifies both works and much of the New Wave (Truffaut being generally a notable exception). Within those films it is as if no preexisting, external moral codes operate, even to be rebelled against. Events happen that are not prepared for or explained in the usual manner, like the seemingly gratuitous death of the heroine at the end of Godard's *My Life to Live* (1962), and the sui-cide-murder of two of the three principals climaxing Truffaut's *Jules and Jim* (1961). Char-acters make decisions that appear arbitrary or lacking in motivation, of a conventional sort at least (Resnais's *Last Year at Marienbad,* 1961, is an encyclopedia of such behavior). They conceive of themselves as responsible only to themselves (Charles Aznavour in Truffaut's *Shoot the Piano Player* is one instance) in a world devoid of logic, justice, or even order.

Then there is the looseness and openness of narrative construction—the picaresque quality that dominates so many of the films (Godard's *Pierrot le fou,* 1965, a prime ex-ample of the general tendency). At the least they are narrative rather than dramatic, more allied to the New Novel than the well-made play. The ascending climaxes of traditional dramaturgy were abandoned, even the ends of narrative threads were no longer neatly tucked in. Randomness replaced the mechanisms of omnipresent fate at work in the French films of the 1930s noted earlier. Audiences were left to put together the disjointed experi-ence as they exited the theater. When asked by an exasperated interviewer if a film shouldn't have a beginning, middle, and end, Godard thought a moment and replied, "Yes, but not necessarily in that order."

Accompanying the freedom from strict narrative confines was a tendency to organize time and space according to the dictates of feeling (the film maker's and the characters') rather than the requirements of chronology or contiguity. The intricacies of memory are so dealt with in Resnais's work. *Last Year at Marienbad* seems to contain three tenses—past, present, and future conditional; the real and the imagined are jumbled as the protagonist tries to persuade the heroine and perhaps himself of what had happened between them during the previous summer. The jump cuts, abrupt transitions, and asides of Godard and Truffaut in *Breathless* and *Shoot the Piano Player* similarly defy orderly linear perception.

Finally, many of the New Wave films are about films and film making. Because these young film makers, many of them former critics, felt so at home in their medium, they played with it in uninhibited ways. These included encouraging improvisation by actors (Jeanne Moreau, Jean-Paul Belmondo, and Charles Aznavour rose to stardom in their films), taking advantage of the accidents of location shooting, and using new lightweight equipment to attach onto the unfolding action without making it conform to the restraints imposed by the studio method. (*Breathless* was shot in four weeks in indoor and outdoor locations, night as well as day, using "fast" still-photographic stock, a hand-held camera, and postrecorded sound.) There are allusions to other film makers and films, a use of the full range of cinematic conventions, some of them stemming from the silent years (irises,

Last Year at Marienbad ★
France, 1961, Alain Resnais;
Giorgio Albertazzi and
Delphine Seyrig.

intertitles, masking to change the size and shape of the images), and in-jokes (film friends appearing in apt and amusing bit parts, such as director Jean-Pierre Melville as a novelist in *Breathless* as well as two critics from *Cahiers* as blind men in *A Woman Is a Woman*, 1961). Truffaut's *Day for Night* (1973) is, of course, a summation of this tendency: Its subject *is* film making. Often the films were created as objects for contemplation in their own right rather than as commentaries on the world outside the darkened confines of the theater. These were "movie movies," dedicated to the proposition that if not more real than life, film is a good deal more interesting. In general the New Wave seems not so much art imitating life as life, at least as it is portrayed in those films, imitating art.

One way of thinking about these aesthetic and stylistic innovations is that the modernism percolating in the other arts since the turn of the century had at last seeped into narrative fiction film. The modernism of the French avant-garde films of the 1920s was allied to and mostly came out of painting and painters. The New Wave modernism was literary in origins, sometimes bearing striking resemblances to what James Joyce had explored in *Ulysses,* published in Paris in 1922. What we now generally think of, in relation to the feature film, as contemporary cinema or modern film can be said to have begun in France at the end of the 1950s.

New Wave Directors

As the New Wave began to roll in the 1960s it was Godard and Truffaut who first emerged as the major figures. Like Eisenstein, Pudovkin, and Dovzhenko in the Soviet 1920s, the French duo maintained their preeminence. Along with additional New Wave directors such as Chabrol, Rivette, Rohmer, and others, they created a filmic tradition that commanded critical attention worldwide throughout the 1960s.

Perhaps it is **Jean-Luc Godard** who represents better than any other single film maker the sort of experimental stretching of the medium the New Wave provided. In fact, it may be only Griffith and Eisenstein who have contributed as much formal innovation— additions to the "language" of the medium—as Godard. His early work included variations on the melodrama and chase conventions of popular American movies. It is not surprising that his first feature, *Breathless*, was dedicated to Monogram Pictures, a defunct Hollywood studio of "B" production. *Band of Outsiders* (1964), another "gangster film," has musical numbers as well, with Anna Karina singing on the Metro and dancing with two of the petty crooks; in *A Woman Is a Woman* (1961), Karina says she wants to be in a musical choreographed by Bob Fosse.

On the other hand, Godard employed the sort of "distancing" associated with avant-garde theater, or with Bertolt Brecht, whom Godard frequently invoked in interviews. To this end, he repeatedly disrupted the films' narratives with printed intertitles and interludes in which actors addressed the camera directly, often offering commentary that had little or nothing to do with the story being told. His visual rhetoric was similarly designed to disrupt the audience's suspension of disbelief through patently artificial devices that included the use of bold, primary colors that mimicked the style of advertising posters and ostentatious camera movements, such as the long tracking shot of a series of supermarket checkout counters in the 1972 *Tout va bien*. In the opening scene of *My Life to Live* (1962) the camera remains mostly on the backs of Nana and Paul, preventing, us from seeing their facial expressions as they converse. Its twelve episodes are punctuated by titles, pulling us further out of the narrative, which is already deliberately disjunctive, and suggesting a series of moral lessons (Montaigne furnishes the text for one of the tableaux).

But a new kind of realism was also present in Godard's cinematic collages. In *Sympathy for the Devil* (1968) and elsewhere, cinéma vérité actuality mingles with fictive elements. Godard has said that there are two kinds of cinema, Flaherty and Eisenstein: There is documentary and there is theater; but that ultimately, at the highest level, they are one and the same. Through documentary realism we arrive at the structure of theater, and through theatrical imagination and fiction we arrive at the reality of life. Even when working with actors, as he generally did, Godard observed aspects of their actual personalities as much as the created roles they played. In *Breathless*, Belmondo's energy and toughness, coiled-spring tension and handsome-ugliness were first revealed. Jean Seberg, who had failed badly as Joan of Arc in Preminger's film, succeeded completely in playing a young American in Paris whom we suspect might be rather like herself. The series of films with Anna Karina, Godard's wife for a time, were, among other things, essays on the difficulties of understanding and communicating with her (*Le Petit Soldat*, 1960; *A Woman Is a Woman, My Life to Live, Band of Outsiders, Pierrot le fou,* and *Alphaville,* 1965). In *Contempt* (1963) Fritz Lang played himself as a renowned film director.

My Life to Live ★ France, 1962, Jean-Luc Godard; Anna Karina and Bruce Parain.

As Godard's work progressed his philosophical observations came increasingly to obtrude. Concomitant with this move toward philosophical abstraction, the dialogue became denser and was assigned a more significant share of the total communication. In *My Life to Live*, Brice Parain, a philosopher in real life, carried on a long dialectical near-monologue that was only tangentially related to the slight plot. Later in the same film Godard's voice on the sound track reads an Edgar Allan Poe story to the heroine. In *See You at Mao* (also called *British Sounds*, 1969) there is so much speech over the images that the words become incomprehensible. Despite this alienating tendency, however, Godard's films of the 1960s stand as models of how far film language can be stretched and what forms it can take.

After *The 400 Blows,* **François Truffaut** made *Shoot the Piano Player* (1960), *Jules and Jim* (1961), and the other films (see Films of the Period) that earned for him the appellation of auteur that he first coined to apply to others. He has written or cowritten all of his films. Generally they are imbued with the sort of romantic realism we would expect from a spiritual godson of Bazin and Renoir. But they also, especially the earlier ones, contain amusing and astute references to the conventions of the medium within which he was working. Throughout there are signs of the well-informed former *cinéphile* and critic, and *hommages* to particular films and favorite film makers, most pointedly to Hitchcock in *The Bride Wore Black* (1967).

Jules and Jim ★ France, 1961, François Truffaut; Henri Serre, Jeanne Moreau, and Oscar Werner.

Among his later films the most effective and commercially successful was *The Last Metro* (1981). It deals with the theater in affectionate and knowledgeable detail (as *Day for Night* does with film making) and as a means of getting at the strange, muted, complicated, unnerving human tensions in German-occupied Paris of 1942. A wife (Catherine Deneuve) continues to run the Théâtre Montmartre in place of her Jewish husband. But the husband did not flee the country, as was assumed; he hides in the cellar of the theater and observes its continuation, including the addition of a young actor (Gérard Depardieu) with whom his wife has an affair.

Aside from the undervalued *Shoot the Piano Player* and *Jules and Jim,* which many regard as his masterwork, the Antoine Doinel series (*The 400 Blows;* an episode in *Love at Twenty,* 1962; *Stolen Kisses,* 1968; *Bed and Board,* 1970) may be Truffaut's most distinctive contribution to the history of film. In addition to their worth as separate art works, they represent the closest fictional feature films have come to sustained use of autobiographical material, except perhaps those of Fellini. In *Day for Night* (1973) Truffaut added his own performance to Léaud's to infuse his art with his life. This sort of creation is recognized as the basis for much of the world's great literature, from Cervantes to Faulkner. The idea of a director's life, at least his personal vision, being reflected in his films was inherent in *la politique des auteurs.* Truffaut brought his own experiences more directly to the screen through the evolving Doinel character than any other director has so far done. *L'Amour en fuite* (*Love on the Run,* 1979) was his farewell to Antoine Doinel. He died in 1984 at the age of 52.

Claude Chabrol has continued—with increasing strength and control in later years— a succession of cohesive works. Narrow in vision (usually they involve an ill-fated triangle and often end in death), they nonetheless gain power from their concentration. Overtaking Godard as the most prolific of the New Wave directors, Chabrol has consistently pictured a dark underside of bourgeois morality. Among the most carefully wrought, intense, and disturbing of his films are *Les Biches* (1968), *La Femme infidèle* (1969), *Le Boucher* (1970), and *Just Before Nightfall* (1971). His work would seem to be the most conventional of the New Wave directors—frequently following lines laid out by Lang and Hitchcock, whose films Chabrol admires—steadily produced and commercially successful.

While Truffaut, Godard, and Chabrol were being prolific, **Jacques Rivette** made only two films in the 1960s following *Paris nous appartient,* released at the beginning of the decade: *La Religieuse* (1965) and *L'Amour fou* (1968). In 1971 he completed *Out One* (running twelve hours and forty minutes and never released), which became *Out One: Spectre* (1974), reedited from the same footage. The most eccentric and obscure of the New Wave directors, he has nonetheless been influential. *Celine and Julie Go Boating* (1974) is his most "accessible" film, whimsical and amusing. All of his films maintain the enigmatic qualities of his first feature, either attacking or toying with the whole notion of illusionistic storytelling. In most of them the characters are in some ways involved in the production of plays from classical drama that are intricately interwoven with the modern stories. Rivette has said that his films "are about theater, about truth and lies."

Rivette's *La Belle Noiseuse* (1991, which means something like "The Beautiful Trouble Maker"), transfers the central setting from theater to a famous painter's studio, but it explores the process of creation even more intently and the development of characters and their shifting interactions remain linked to drama as in his earlier works. (It is credited as being "Based on the story *Le Chef d'oeuvre inconnu*" by Honoré de Balzac [that is, "The

Les Biches ★ France, 1968, Claude Chabrol; Jacqueline Sassard, Jean-Louis Trintignant, and Stephane Audran.

Unknown Masterpiece."]) Also its length, at four hours, is characteristic. But, while being something of a personal statement, it became the first commercial hit of Rivette's career.

Eric Rohmer's passage has been much smoother, his films much more within the main lines of French production. Although a late bloomer, *My Night at Maud's* (1969), the first feature of his *Six Moral Tales* to be released, achieved commercial success and established his international reputation. In Rohmer's work the "literary" is even more conspicuous than in Rivette's (whose films abound in references to books) and even in Resnais's. Whereas Resnais has collaborated with authors, Rohmer is one. His *Six Moral Tales* (published in translation under that title by Viking in 1979) were written as stories before he made them into films between 1962 and 1972. *The Marquise of O . . .* (1976) and *Perceval* (1978) are films of world literary classics. Consistent with this literary quality, the settings within which his characters are placed are observed with a particularity that suggests the term *described,* and his characters talk a lot. The way Rohmer thinks of his films is that they deal "less with what people do than with what is going on in their minds while they are doing it." (They have been referred to as "talking cure" films.) His intricate explorations of what are essentially conservative moral positions—supported by a perfection of performance, intelligent and witty dialogue, and subtle and exact psychological observation—continue to intrigue. *The Aviator's Wife* (1980) began a new series that Rohmer entitled "Comedies and Proverbs," and continued with *A Good Marriage* (1982), *Pauline at the*

Celine and Julie Go Boating ★ France, 1974, Jacques Rivette; Bulle Ogier, Marie-France Pisier, and Barbet Schroeder.

Beach (1982), *Full Moon in Paris* (1984), and *Summer* (1986). Truffaut, interviewed twenty years after the New Wave began, when asked about "the new directors in France," said, "The one I like best is Eric Rohmer, but of course he is of my generation." Rohmer was sixty-eight years old at the time the last film of his *Comedies and Proverbs* series, *Boyfriends and Girlfriends* (1988), was released. *A Tale of Springtime* (1990) launched a new series, *Tales of the Four Seasons,* completed with *An Autumn Tale* in 1999.

Left Bank Directors and Others

Not all veteran French film makers currently at work were part of the New Wave. Another group of intellectuals, known as the Left Bank directors, included Alain Resnais, Agnès Varda, Chris Marker, Alain Robbe-Grillet, and Marguerite Duras. Chantal Akerman and Louis Malle were other directorial talents that emerged during this period. Together with New Wave films, the output of these movie makers created a critical mass of cinematic art that made France the unquestioned leader of international film culture and created a legacy that continues to reverberate around the world.

A skilled film maker, **Alain Resnais** makes movies that display a dazzling technical virtuosity and formal elegance, separating them from the films of the New Wave proper. Also, his concern with older characters and the past contrasts with the youthful protagonists and current attitudes dominant in the films of Truffaut and Godard. With noteworthy

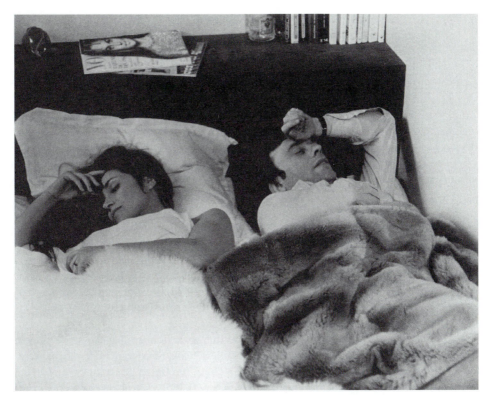

My Night at Maud's ★ France, 1969, Eric Rohmer; Françoise Fabian and Jean-Louis Trintignant.

consistency Resnais has pursued his absorption with the processes of memory, his features—*Hiroshima, mon amour; Last Year at Marienbad;* and *Muriel* (1963); *La Guerre est finie* (1966); *Je t'aime, je t'aime* (1968); *Stavisky* (1974); *Providence* (1977); *Mon Oncle d'Amerique* (1981); *La Vie est un roman* (1983); *L'Amour à mort* (1984); and *Mélo,* 1987—all reveal and insist on the presence of times past in every present moment. This was true even of the earlier shorts, especially the greatest of them, *Night and Fog* (1955). In *Mon Oncle d'Amérique* the real-life biologist Dr. Henri Laborit, on whose theories the film is based, says, "A living creature is a memory that acts." This might be a description of the protagonists of Resnais's films.

The problem Resnais presents in his candidacy for authorship is that on his features he has usually collaborated with strong literary figures such as Marguerite Duras and Alain Robbe-Grillet (who subsequently directed their own scripts) or Jean Cayrol. He has always been generous (perhaps more than) in acknowledging his indebtedness to others, and self-effacing in regard to his own contributions to the conceptions. According to published statements from some of those collaborators, Resnais is almost insistent that the scripts be conceived quite apart from his personal style as a film maker and without special deference to the medium of film. "Give me an original 'literary' work," he seemed to be saying, "and I will make it into cinema."

Resnais's English-language film *Providence* (1977) is about literary creation. The script was by playwright David Mercer. Its protagonist, a famous novelist, draws from his relationships with his children and dead wife to shape and reshape scenes intended for his final novel. His characters are at variance with what we are permitted to see of the "real" persons who exist outside his imagination, and the whole, of course, is presented to us in a filmic illusion that is, ultimately, Resnais's interpretation and creation.

His next three films, *Mon Oncle d'Amérique, La Vie est un roman,* and *L'Amour à mort* were scripted by Jean Gruault. The first two are complex three-part narratives: the former telling the stories of three quite different modern characters whose lives interact; the latter consisting of three stories set in different times and filmed in different styles, but yet connect thematically. Both are based on philosophical propositions: The first relates to the aggression innate in humans and human responses to it; the second relates to utopias, education and imagination, and adulthood and childhood. *L'Amour à mort* is also experimental in its narrative structure and stylized imagery—in this case the philosophical argument concerns the dictates of love.

Although the level of achievement may vary, it nonetheless seems clear that as a body of work Resnais's films remain notably coherent regardless of who is credited with the script. We can assume that, whatever the creative relationship between writer and director during production, Resnais is not altogether part of the tradition of writer's cinema about which Truffaut complained.

From the 1960s on **Agnès Varda** has had scattered successes. Following *Cleo from 5 to 7* (1961)—close enough to the New Wave to be part of it—there were *Le Bonheur* (1965), *Lion's Love* (1969), and *One Sings, the Other Doesn't* (1977). Generally regarded as a more solid achievement is *Vagabonde* (1985), a bleak and existential story of a lonely vagrant, Mona, wandering through the wintry landscapes of the South of France. It won the Golden Lion at Venice.

Another member of the Left Bank group, **Chris Marker**, developed a form of personal essay film within the documentary mode in films such as *Letter from Siberia* in 1958 and *Le Joli Mai* in 1963. Not only are his movies set in specific places, but they are about those places. He is especially interested in transitional societies, in "life in the process of becoming history," as he put it. His tone is frequently ironical and implicitly judgmental. In 1962 he directed a much admired short fiction film about time travel, *La Jetée,* composed almost wholly of still images. His 1982 production, *Sans Soleil,* which many critics consider his best work, grafts a similar time-travel story onto a documentary-like series of scenes shot in Tokyo and Guinea Bissou.

Marguerite Duras also belonged to the Left Bank group. After collaborating with Resnais on *Hiroshima, Mon Amour* she went on to direct a series of films on her own, including *Drive, She Said* in 1969 and *India Song* in 1975. As one of the French New Novelists, Duras had a strong interest in formal experimentation; her films feature elliptical narratives in which image and sound are only tangentially related. Their unorthodox style represents, in part, the search for a distinctively female film language. Many of Duras's later films, including *India Song* (perhaps her best), also took up colonial themes through their use of stories set in 1930s Vietnam.

Duras's search for a cinematic discourse that would foreground a woman's sensibility was a project also taken up by **Chantal Akerman,** a Belgian film maker who did most of her work in France. Influenced by French New Wave directors, Akerman was also

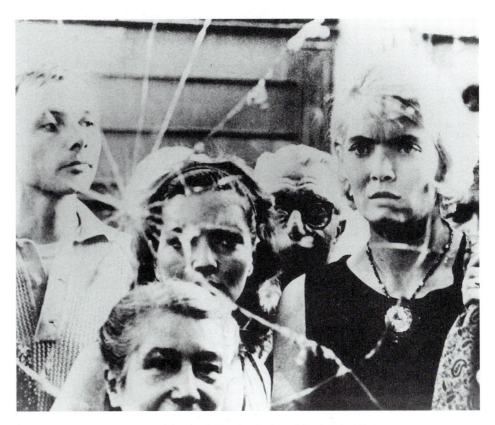

Cleo from 5 to 7 ★ France, 1961, Agnès Varda; Corinne Marchand, right.

deeply impressed by the work of North American avant-garde film makers such as Stan Brakhage and Michael Snow. Her most widely admired film, the four-hour *Jeanne Dielman, 23 Quai de Commerce, 1080 Bruxelles,* released in 1974, focuses on a Belgian house-wife and part-time prostitute (Delphine Seyrig) who unexpectedly murders one of her clients. But rather than building up suspense surrounding this shocking act, the film directs most of its attention to Jeanne's daily routine, which includes activities such as doing the dishes, making a meatloaf, taking a bath, and searching the local shops for a button. These tasks are typically observed impassively, by a motionless camera that watches her head-on, but from a distance. Although Akerman's approach has been labeled minimalist because so little of seeming consequence occurs, films such as *Jeanne Dielman* can none-theless prove more absorbing than many more conventional productions.

A director more traditional in formal terms if not in his choice of content was **Louis Malle**, who died in 1999. Malle's output was varied and innovative, alternating documen-tary and fiction and later French and American. His most memorable documentary work was the series "Phantom India," shown on French television in 1970. Malle won a Golden Lion at Venice with *Au revoir, les enfants* (1987), an autobiographical account of a boarding school for upper-class boys in German-occupied France that gave sanctuary to three Jewish youngsters in 1944. Of his French work beginning in the 1960s, *Zazie dans le Metro* (1960)

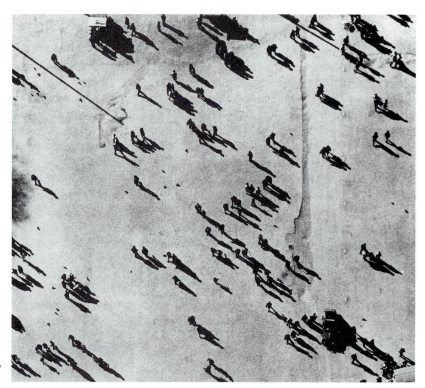

Le Joli Mai ★ France, 1963, Chris Marker.

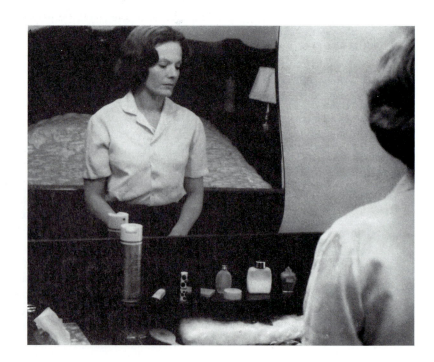

Jeanne Dielman, 23 Qaui de Commerce, 1080 Bruxelles ★ France, 1974, Chantal Akerman; Delphine Seyrig.

240

Au revoir, les enfants ⋆ France, 1987, Louis Malle; Gaspard Manesse, second from left.

and *A Very Private Affair* (1962) are contemporary with the New Wave and somewhat related in spirit. The first explores the conventions of film making in a comedy centered on a young girl; the second caricatures the harried movie star (played by Brigitte Bardot).

New Politics and
New Theories of Authorship

May 1968 was a watershed moment in French history. Galvanized by the escalation of the war in Vietnam and other political events, student radicals joined striking workers to stage violent protests in Paris and around the country, hoping to bring down the government. Although the movement failed to meet its immediate goals, these disturbances and the sentiments leading up to them had a lasting effect on the outlook of many young people. The cinema world was additionally galvanized by the attempted removal of Henri Langlois, long-time champion of film preservation, from his post as director of the French Cinémathèque. Reacting to these occurrences, a new generation of *Cahiers* critics turned away from a romantic, idealist conception of film *auteurs* to a more political approach to cinema informed by the theories of the Marxist German playwright Bertolt Brecht and others. Brecht had espoused a political art that actively engaged audiences by foregrounding its formal structures. In the words of one *Cahiers* critic, "What is needed is an attempt to understand the work not at the level of the 'humanistic' intentions of its *auteur* but at the level of its meanings—the work understood as a *mediation*." The idea was that auteurs—and, indeed, all artists who created works with the goal of expressing their inner feelings—were furthering the goals of a corrupt capitalist system that fostered competition and the hero worship of individuals divorced from culture in place of cooperation and group activity. The critic's job as now defined was to understand the way in which films related to the larger society that produced and consumed them, not to the transcendent vision of an isolated individual.

The most immediate consequence of this more politicized understanding of art was a renunciation of the concept of individual authorship altogether, not only by the *Cahiers* critics but also by some radical film makers as well, most notably Godard and Marker. Godard, as has been noted, had been interested in a politicized, Brechtian cinema from the beginning of his career. Following Brechtian precepts to their logical, antiauteurist conclusion, his work in the late 1960s and early 1970s was carried out either in partnership with Anne-Marie Miéville or with a collective that called itself "the Dziga Vertov Group" in honor of the visionary Soviet film maker of the 1920s. (The Dziga Vertov group was actually composed of Godard and Marxist intellectual Jean-Pierre Gorin.) The move to a model of anonymous group authorship by Godard and other French film makers was echoed in the policies of *Cahiers* itself, as the editors began to sign their articles as a collective rather than as individual writers. However, these attempts to deny individuality were destined to be short-lived. By the mid-1970s both Godard and the *Cahiers* writers were again signing their works as individual authors.

Godard's films made just before and after the May 1968 uprising were extraordinarily daring in their push to dismantle realist illusionism and narrative, which Godard denounced as bourgeois. Intended as spurs to discussion for committed Marxist groups, they presented too daunting a viewing experience for most general audiences. Films such as *Made in USA* (1966), *La Chinoise* (1967), and *Weekend* (1967) were defiantly expository and didactic. In *Le Gai Savoir* (1969), Godard's first film after the uprising, he abolished narrative altogether in an effort to find a revolutionary form suitable to revolutionary content.

Produced immediately before the events of May and released immediately afterward, *Weekend* begins with a caption that identifies it as "a film found on a scrap heap" and ends with another that reads "The end of cinema." Its minimal plot concerns a young bourgeois couple who set out on an automobile trip to borrow money from the woman's parents. En route they are waylaid first by a traffic jam, then by an encounter with a group of cannibalistic revolutionaries. Filled with digressions, the action meanders from incident to incident. A series of unconnected set pieces includes three 360-degree tracking shots around a farmyard to the accompaniment of a lecture on a Mozart sonata and a long closeup of an Algerian garbage collector, who glares silently into the camera as the voice of another garbage collector delivers an offscreen monologue. The film abounds in shock tactics, from the four-minute tracking shot of the devastation wreaked by the monumental traffic tie-up to the on-screen slaughter of a pig. In part, *Weekend* is constructed as an assault on its audience. Watching it is a frustrating but unforgettable experience.

Godard's absorption with politics and formal rarefactions meant that with the exception of *Tout va bien* (1972) and *Numéro deux* (1975)—both of which received limited commercial distribution—his work disappeared from public view after 1968. Later, however, *Sauve qui peut (la vie)* (*Every Man for Himself,* 1980) seemed to connect back to *Weekend* (1967) and the films that preceded it. The narrative structure and character psychology offer difficulty to be sure—like Resnais's *Mon Oncle d'Amérique* it is built around three characters whose lives become intertwined—but there is a story and there are characters. Formal experimentation is present—video techniques and stop motion, for example—along with Godard's abiding concern for "the politics of the image," and there is much visual beauty.

If *Sauve qui peut* might be thought of as being about the nature of cinema, as was said at the time, *Passion* (1982) most certainly can be. At its center are two East European film makers making a film called *Passion*. However, their film-within-the-film, and therefore Godard's film, is full of famous paintings (by Rembrandt, Goya, Delacroix, El Greco) brought to life in *tableaux vivant* accompanied by famous music (extracts from Mozart, Fauré, Ravel). Although art and politics are linked in *Passion*, as they are in Godard's thinking, the political problems don't receive as much attention as the aesthetic ones. It is then a familiar Godardian jumble of elements treated with philosophical engagement and emotional detachment—a truly "modern" film, we might say.

Passion was followed by *First Name: Carmen* (1983), which won the Golden Lion at the Venice Film Festival. It connects only vaguely with the story by Prosper Merimée on which Bizet's opera is based. Set in modern France, Carmen is a member of a gang of bank robbers; Don José is a bank guard. (Godard plays Carmen's dotty Uncle Jean, a washed-up film maker.)

Hail, Mary (1985) is a modern retelling of the immaculate conception, with Mary a sullen basketball-playing teenager pumping gas in her father's station, Joseph a sexually frustrated cab driver, and the archangel Gabriel an unshaven tough. Of course it aroused religious groups and scared distributors (as had Rossellini's 1948 *The Miracle* and as would Martin Scorsese's 1988 *The Last Temptation of Christ*). To many it was "shocking and profoundly blasphemous"; to others it was a continuation of Godard's recurrent meditations on the alluring mystery of woman and her ultimate strangeness, which he began with *Breathless* and *A Woman Is a Woman* twenty-five years earlier.

Following a series of marginally more conventional productions, such as *Détective* in 1984, a star-studded *King Lear* in 1987, and *Nouvelle Vague* in 1990, Godard turned to investigating the past of his chosen art form in a video series entitled *Histoire(s) du cinéma,* completed in 1994. Regarded by some critics as one of the cinematic highlights of the 1990s, *Histoire(s) du cinéma* is made up of film clips and commentary rendered in Godard's customary ellipitical style.

The inventiveness and freedom with which Godard employs all of the technical and stylistic resources available to the film maker has not been equalled. It could be argued that no matter what his subject matter, Godard continues to be preoccupied with formal explorations of the possible combinations of moving images and accompanying sounds. He makes one think of the painter Marcel Duchamp, who outlined so many of the forms of modern art. Godard is like Duchamp, too, in his intellectualism and coolness. If, ultimately, he withholds, or is unable to provide, kinds of aesthetic experience that may be valued most, within the humanist tradition at any rate, the importance of his contributions to an evolving art form and his influence on the work of others is unquestionable.

After the New Wave

Despite the political upheaval that characterized the late 1960s and the subsequent move by the *Cahiers* group as well as film makers such as Godard and Marker to a more politicized and heavily theorized critical approach to cinema that was less preoccupied with its

Romance ★ France, 1999, Catherine Breillat; Caroline Ducey and Rocco Siffredi.

creators than with its effects, the French film public continued to value its auteurs. As the twentieth century drew to a close, new directors continued to appear, supported by the system of state subsidies that continues to be the highest in Europe. The *avance sur recettes* system was further refined by the socialist government that came into power in the early 1980s. Its minister of culture, Jack Lang, added film industry representatives to the group of government bureaucrats who served on judging panels and made awards available directly to directors as well as to production companies. These policies encouraged more adventuresome films as well as more films directed by women, such as Diane Kurys (*Entre Nous*, 1983), Euzhan Palcy (*Sugar Cane Alley*, 1983), and Catherine Breillat (*36 Fillette*, 1988; *Romance*, 1998).

Throughout the high-pressure negotiations carried on with the United States during the 1980s and 1990s, the strong-willed Lang managed to exclude film from the new free trade agreements. Singling it out in treaties by using the phrase "cultural exception," he thereby kept in place quotas on the importation of Hollywood films and protected the market for home-grown productions. Lang's proactive strategy has met with limited success. Film production has risen, reaching 183 features by 1998. The mammouth French pay-television company Canal-Plus has steadily increased its support of ambitious film-making projects. As is true everywhere, it has been difficult for the French to keep Hollywood at bay; nonetheless, the film industry in France has remained far healthier than those of other European nations. After a miserable 2000, which saw domestic films account for less than 30 percent of French box office revenues while Hollywood fare overwhelmed locally produced offerings, the French industry came roaring back in the first quarter of 2001, taking almost half of the domestic box office gross with hits such as Thomas Gilou's *You*

Shouldn't Worry, Francis Veber's *The Closet,* and Christophe Gans's *Brotherhood of the Wolf.* Theater attendance also rose 24 percent over the year before. To further foster the efforts of French film makers, additional government subsidies were earmarked in 2001 to support distribution. At the same time, to prove that it didn't believe in honoring directors to the exclusion of all others involved in the movie-making process, the government also created a subsidy for script development, which is earmarked for writers.

In this supportive environment, new auteurs appeared, but, as if exhausted from the radical experimentation of the previous decades, the first of the new generation tended to make more conventional films, appealing to audiences around the world through their sensitivity and intelligence. Among these newer figures were Bertrand Tavernier (*A Sunday in the Country*, 1974), Maurice Pialat (*Under the Sun of Satan*, 1987), Claude Sautet (*Un Coeur en Hivre*, 1991), André Téchiné (*My Favorite Season*, 1993, and *Wild Reeds*, 1994), and Jacques Doillon (*Ponette*, 1996).

In the more politicized post-1968 environment, a group of documentary film makers also appeared, producing a series of magisterial works that often took a critical look at the past. Foremost among these documentarians is Marcel Ophüls, whose 1971 *The Sorrow and the Pity* delves into the history of French collaboration with the Nazis during World War II. In 1981 Ophüls produced another meditation on the events of World War II, *The Memory of Justice,* which focuses on the trials of German war criminals. Claude Lanzman's nine-and-a-half-hour *Shoah* (1985) carries on the project of revisioning the past. Consisting solely of interviews, it examines the impact of the Holocaust on the psyches of some of its victims. The work of French anthropologist Jean Rouch, another documentarian, took a more ethnographic

A Sunday in the Country ★ France, 1984, Bertrand Tavernier; Sabine Azema and Louis Ducreux.

Café au lait ★ France, 1994, Matthew Kassovitz; Hubert Koundé and Julie Maude Uech.

direction, including a number of films shot in West Africa. Rouch coined the phrase *cinéma vérité,* an updating of Dziga Vertov's notion of *kinó-pravda* (described in Chapter 4) to designate a documentary mode in which the film makers openly acknowledge their presence within the film itself. His most influential documentary, *Chronicle of a Summer* (1961), made in collaboration with the sociologist Edgar Morin, brings ethnographic investigation home; it is made up of the responses of average French people to the question Are you happy?

Popular genres also continued to flourish during this period, especially thrillers, comedies, and heritage films, typically directed by film makers who functioned more like highly professional craftspeople than like idiosyncratic auteurs. The French tradition of ingenious, finely crafted thrillers (*polars*) was kept alive by such international hits as *La Balance* (Bob Swaim, 1982) and *Monsieur Hire* (Patrice Leconte, 1989). Comedy also flourished—notably *Café au lait* (Matthew Kassovitz, 1994) and *Ma Vie en rose* (Alain Berliner, 1997). A number of these French comedies, such as *La Cage aux folles* (Edouard Molinero, 1979) and *Three Men and a Cradle* (Coline Serreau, 1985), were subsequently remade in Hollywood (as *The Birdcage* [Mike Nichols, 1998] and *Three Men and a Baby* [Leonard Nimoy, 1987], respectively). The heritage film, which dealt with events in French history and with significant individuals and works from the cultural past, was perhaps the most successful of all French genres during these years, benefitting from the high regard in which such productions were held by culture minister Jack Lang, and the large subsidies they received as a result. Sumptuous productions such as *The Return of Martin Guerre* (Daniel Vigne, 1982), *Cyrano de Bergerac* (Jean-Paul Rappeneau, 1990), and *Indochine* (Régis Warnier, 1992) recuperated France's cultural and political past with taste and style, finding large audiences both at home and abroad.

The tradition of auteurism, however, was not forgotten. The 1980s saw the advent of a new group of directors with highly distinctive styles whose films were labeled *cinèma du look*. Featuring glossy, high-tech surfaces that announced their high production values combined with jazzy rhythms inspired by advertising and music videos, films of this sort became cult favorites around the world, but did not always find favor with critics. Most prominent among the films of the *cinèma du look* was Jean-Jacques Beinex's 1981 *Diva*, Luc Besson's 1990 *La Femme Nikita*, and, in a more subdued vein, Leos Carax's 1991 *Lovers on the Bridge*.

In the 1990s a more introspective and ironic group of directors came to the fore. Called "Young French Cinema," their films frequently concern the problems of youthful relationships, especially sexual ones, treated in a style reminiscent of Jean Eustache's post–New Wave production *The Mother and the Whore* (1974). The travails of youth depicted in these films are wittily yet sensitively portrayed by skilled ensemble casts. The actors are encouraged to improvise subtle interactions, supported by the long takes and deep-focus photography favored by the Young French Cinema directors. The paradigmatic examples of the style are Arnaud Despechin's *My Sex Life (Or, How to Get into an Argument)* and Olivier Assayas's *Irma Vep*, both released in 1996. The former is a gentle satire about an immature young philosophy professor; the latter is a more unforgiving lampoon of French film making, featuring a burned-out director, played by New Wave stalwart Jean-Pierre Léaud, who is attempting to mount a remake of Louis Feuillade's classic 1915 French production *Les Vampires* starring the Hong Kong action star Maggie Cheung.

A more politically minded group of film makers also emerged in the 1990s. Concerned with the struggles of working-class and ethnic peoples, these directors produced a

Ma Vie en rose ★ France, 1997, Alain Berliner; Georges du Fresne.

series of films that reveal the underside of the economic prosperity of the *fin de siècle*. Foremost among the searing portraits of deprivation and alienation these film makers have produced are Matthew Kasssovitz's 1995 *La Haine*, a raw portrait of a violent gang of lower-class youths from the Paris suburbs; Claire Denis's 1995 *I Can't Sleep*, a loosely intertwined series of narratives centering on immigrants existing uneasily on the margins of Parisian society; Eric Zonka's 1998 *The Dreamlife of Angels*, about the class barriers faced by two young working-class women who share a flat; and Bruno Dumont's 1999 *L'Humanité*, a controversial Cannes Film Festival winner about a *lumpen* provincial policeman investigating the rape and murder of a young girl. Except for *La Haine*, which is filmed in grainy, high-contrast black and white, these films use muted colors and a drab *mise-en-scène* to create an ambience of bleak hopelessness.

Perhaps the most honored of this last group of directors are the Dardenne brothers (Jean-Pierre and Luc), a pair of Belgians working within the French industry. In 1996 they produced *La Promesse*, which told the story about the moral dilemmas faced by the young son of a brutal man who smuggles illegal workers into Belgium from North Africa. The Dardennes followed this success in 1999 with the remarkable *Rosetta*, which won top honors at the Cannes Film Festival. Its plot concerns a young girl living in a trailer park whose main ambition is to get a job as a street vendor. For the duration of the action the camera follows Rosetta in relentless, hand-held closeups as she battles with the world and especially with her alcoholic mother, trying vainly to achieve a measure of dignity and self-worth. In the brutal hard-scrabble environment she inhabits, it is doubly surprising to witness the young girl's encounter with a person who offers her a kind of spiritual salvation, even though she is unable to respond to the lifeline he represents. The hyperkinetic style of *Rosetta* is the polar opposite of the contemplative serenity that characterizes the films of Robert Bresson, yet the Dardenne brothers' thematic preoccupations are not far removed from those of the earlier film maker. Although *Rosetta* was made by two directors rather than a single auteur, it conveys a unique and highly personal vision in which the sacred and profane world inextricably echoes the concerns depicted in Bresson's films of forty years before.

Although the New Wave movement lasted only a few years, roughly from 1959 to 1962, its effects have extended down to the present. It completely revitalized French cinema and spawned most of the major directors subsequently at work. Together with the critical reevaluation of *la politique des auteurs* that preceded it, it gave more emphasis than had previously been the rule to a personal cinema under individual artistic control. Thinking of film as an art, and of the director as the controlling artist, became a predominant view in France and extended widely abroad.

Further, the influence of the New Wave extended not only to other countries but also into popular cinema. New Wave elements can be seen in Tony Richardson's *Tom Jones* (1963), Arthur Penn's *Mickey One* (1964, shot by one of the New Wave cameramen, Ghislain Cloquet), the Beatles films of Richard Lester (*A Hard Day's Night* [1964] and *Help!* [1965]) and his *American Petulia* (1968), John Schlesinger's *Darling* (1965), Stanley Donen's *Two for the Road* (1967, set appropriately in France), Nagisa Oshima's *Death by Hanging* (1968), and Wong Kar-Wei's *Chungking Express* (1994). These are only a few among the many films made subsequently elsewhere using styles and themes that first came to the fore during the New Wave.

Films of the Period

1955
Lola Montèz (Max Ophüls)
Night and Fog (Nuit et brouillard) (Alain Resnais)
La Pointe courte (Agnès Varda)

1956
And God Created Woman (Roger Vadim)
Bob le flambeur (Jean-Pierre Melville)
*A Man Escaped (Un Condamé à mort s'est
   échappé)* (Robert Bresson)

1958
Le Beau Serge (Claude Chabrol)
Black Orpheus (Marcel Camus)
Mon Oncle (Jacques Tati)

1959
The Cousins (Les Cousins) (Claude Chabrol)
The 400 Blows (Les Quatre cents coups)
   (François Truffaut)
Hiroshima, mon amour (Alain Resnais)
Pickpocket (Robert Bresson)

1960
Breathless (À Bout de souffle) (Jean-Luc Godard)
Les Bonnes Femmes (Claude Chabrol)
Paris nous appartient (Jacques Rivette)
Shoot the Piano Player (Tirez sur le pianiste)
   (François Truffaut)
Zazie dans le Metro (Louis Malle)

1961
Chronicle of a Summer (Chronique d'un étè)
   (Jean Rouch)
Cleo from 5 to 7 (Agnès Varda)
Jules and Jim (François Truffaut)
Last Year at Marienbad (Alain Resnais)

1962
My Life to Live (Vivre sa vie) (Jean-Luc Godard)
The Trial of Joan of Arc (Robert Bresson)

1963
Contempt (Le Mépris) (Jean-Luc Godard)
Le Joli Mai (Chris Marker)

1964
Band of Outsiders (Bande à part) (Jean-Luc
   Godard)
La Jetée (Chris Marker)
A Married Woman (Une Femme mariée)
   (Jean-Luc Godard)
*The Umbrellas of Cherbourg (Les Parpluies
   de Cherbourg)* (Jacques Demy)

1965
Alphaville (Jean-Luc Godard)
Le Bonheur (Agnès Varda)
Pierrot le fou (Jean-Luc Godard)

1966
Au hasard, Balthasar (Robert Bresson)
Belle de jour (Luis Buñuel)
La Guerre est finie (Alain Resnais)
Masculine-Feminine (Jean-Luc Godard)
*The Rise to Power of Louis XIV (La Prise de
   pouvior par Louis XIII* (Roberto
   Rossellini)

1967
Mouchette (Robert Bresson)
Playtime (Jacques Tati)
Le Samourai (Jean-Pierre Melville)
Weekend (Jean-Luc Godard)

1968
Les Biches (Claude Chabrol)
One Plus One (Sympathy for the Devil)
   (Jean-Luc Godard)

1969
La Femme infidèle (Claude Chabrol)
My Night at Maud's (Ma Nuit chez Maud)
   (Eric Rohmer)
A Very Curious Girl (La Fiancée du pirate)
   (Nelly Kaplan)
Wind from the East (Le Vent d'est) (Dziga Vertov
   Group [Jean-Luc Godard and Jean-Pierre
   Gorin])
Z (Constantin Costa-Gavras)

1970
Le Boucher (Claude Chabrol)
Claire's Knee (La Genou de Claire) (Rohmer)
The Wild Child (L'Enfant sauvage) (François Truffaut)

1971
Coup pour coup (Martin Karmitz)
The Sorrow and the Pity (Le Chagrin et la pitié) (Marcel Ophüls)
Two English Girls (Le Deux Anglasises et le continent) (François Truffaut)

1972
Chloe in the Afternoon (L'Amour l'après-midi) (Rohmer)
The Discreet Charm of the Bourgeoisie (Le Charme discret de les bourgeoisie) (Luis Buñuel)
Letter to Jane (Dziga Vertov Group [Godard and Gorin])
Tout va bien (Dziga Vertov Group [Godard and Gorin])

1973
Day for Night (La Nuit Americaine) (François Truffaut)
Lacombe, Lucien (Louis Malle)
The Mother and the Whore (La Maman et la putain) (Jean Eustache)

1974
Celine and Julie Go Boating (Celine et Julie vont en batteau) (Jacques Rivette)
The Clockmaker (L'Horloger de St. Paul) (Bertrand Tavernier)
Get Out Your Handkerchiefs (Préparer vos mouchons) (Bernard Blier)
Jeanne Dielman, 23 Quai de Commerce, 1080 Bruxelles (Chantal Akerman)
Lancelot of the Lake (Lancelot du lac) (Robert Bresson)
Stavisky (Alain Resnais)

1975
India Song (Marguerite Duras)
Numéro deux (Jean-Luc Godard and Anne-Marie Miéville)

1975
The Story of Adele H. (L'Histoire de Adele H.) (François Truffaut)

1976
The Marquise of O . . . (Die Marquise von O . . .) (Rohmer)

1977
The Devil, Probably (Le Diable, problement) (Robert Bresson)
The Man Who Loved Women (François Truffaut)

1979
La Cage aux folles (Edouard Molinero)
Loulou (Maurice Pialat)
Percival (Percival le Gallois) (Rohmer)
Sauve qui peut (la vie) (Every Man for Himself) (Jean-Luc Godard and Anne-Marie Miéville)

1980
Coup de Torchon (Bertrand Tavernier)
The Last Metro (Le Dernière métro) (François Truffaut)
Mon Oncle d'Amerique (Alain Resnais)

1981
Diva (Jean-Jacques Beineix)

1982
Passion (Jean-Luc Godard)
The Return of Martin Guerre (Le Retour de Martin Guerre) (Daniel Vigne)
Sans Soleil (Chris Marker)

1983
L'Argent (Robert Bresson)
City of Pirates (LaVille des pirates) (Raúl Ruiz)
Entre nous (Diane Kurys)
First Name: Carmen (Prenom Carmen) (Jean-Luc Godard)
Sugar Cane Alley (Rue Casse Nègres) (Euzhan Palcy)

1984
Rendezvous d'Anna (Chantal Akerman)
Subway (Luc Besson)
A Sunday in the Country (Un Dimance à la campagne) (Bertrand Tavernier)

1985
Hail, Mary (Je vous salue Marie) (Jean-Luc Godard)
'Round Midnight (Bertrand Tavernier)
Shoah (Claude Lanzmann)
*Three Men and a Cradle (Trois Hommes
    et un couffin)* (Coline Serreau)
Vagabonde (Sans toît ni loi) (Agnès Varda)

1987
Au revoir, les enfants (Louis Malle)
King Lear (Jean-Luc Godard)
Under the Sun of Satan (Sous le soleil de satan)
    (Maurice Pialat)

1988
Chocolat (Claire Denis)
Story of Women (Un Affaire de femmes)
    (Claude Chabrol)
36 Fillette (Catherine Breillat)

1989
Monsieur Hire (Patrice Leconte)

1990
Delicatessen (Jean-Pierre Jeunot and Marco Caro)
La Femme Nikita (Luc Besson)

1991
La Belle Noiseuse (Jacques Rivette)
Un Coeur en Hivre (Claude Sautet)
Lovers on the Bridge (Les Amants du Pont-Neuf)
    (Leos Carax)
Treasure Island (L'Isle au tresor) (Raúl Ruiz)
Van Gogh (Maurice Pialat)

1992
Indochine (Régis Warnier)

1993
My Favorite Season (Ma Saison preferée)
    (André Téchiné)

1994
L'Eau froide (Oliver Assayas)
Histoire(s) du cinéma (Jean-Luc Godard)
Queen Margot (La Reine Margot) (Patrice Chéreau)

Wild Reeds (Les Roseaux sauvages)
    (André Téchiné)

1995
City of Lost Children (La Cité des enfants perdus)
    (Jean-Pierre Jeunot and Marco Caro)
Hate (La Haine) (Mathew Kassovitz)
I Can't Sleep (Claire Denis)
The Ceremony (La Cérémonie) (Claude
    Chabrol)

1996
Irma Vep (Oliver Assayas)
Ponette (Jacques Doillon)
La Promesse (Jean-Pierre Dardenne and Luc
    Dardenne)
*My Sex Life (Or, How to Get into an Argument)
    (Comment je me suis disputé ["ma vie
    sexuelle"])* (Arnaud Desplechin)

1997
Ma Vie en rose (Alain Berliner)

1998
The Dinner Game (Le Diner de cons)
    (Francis Veber)
*The Dreamlife of Angels (La Vie rêvée
    des anges)* (Eric Zonca)
I Stand Alone (Seul contre tous)
    (Gaspar Noé)

1999
L'Humanité (Bruno Dumont)
Rosetta (The Dardenne Brothers)

2000
Beau Travail (Claire Denis)
L'Anglaise et le duc (Eric Rohmer)

2001
*Amelie from Montmartre (Le Fabuleux destin
    d'Amelie poulain)* (Jean-Pierre Jeunet)
Éloge de l'amour (In Praise of Love)
    (Jean-Luc Godard)
Laisser passer (Bertrand Travernier)
Savage Souls (Les Âmes fortes) (Raúl Ruiz)
Va Savior! (Who Knows) (Jacques Rivette)

Books on the Period

Austin, Guy. *Contemporary French Cinema: An Intro-duction.* New York: St. Martin's Press, 1996.

Biggs, Melissa E. *French Films, 1945–93: A Critical Filmography of the 400 Most Important Releases.* Jefferson, NC: McFarland, 1996.

Crisp, Colin. *The Classic French Cinema, 1930–1960.* Bloomington: Indiana University Press, 1994.

Forbes, Jill. *The Cinema in France: After the New Wave.* Bloomington: Indiana University Press, 1994.

Hayward, Susan. *French National Cinema ("National Cinema Series").* New York: Routledge, 1993.

Hayward, Susan, and Ginette Vincendeau. *French Film: Texts and Contexts.* New York: Routledge, 1999.

Powrie, Phil, ed. *French Cinema of the 1990s: Nostalgia and the Crisis of Masculinity.* New York: Oxford University Press, 1997.

Vincendeau, Ginette, ed. *Cassel Film Guides: France.* Herndon, VA: Cassel Academic, 1997.

Vincendeau, Ginette, ed. *The Encyclopedia of European Cinema.* New York: Facts on File, 1995.

11

Other Western European Cinemas: National Cinemas or Eurofilms?

★ ★ ★ ★

1945–

Like Italy, Britain, and France, other western European nations struggled after the Second World War to rebuild their film industries. All viewed their cinematic traditions as a source of pride at home and good will around the world. Unlike the United States, where narrative film making has mostly been privately financed and hugely profitable, European countries have felt the need to subsidize their motion-picture industries to ensure the viability of home-grown movies. Ironically this process has increasingly taken the form of international rather than national initiatives, sponsored in part by the European Community. MEDIA, set up by the European Community in 1987, provides production loans through a variation of the French *avance sur recettes* system, and the European Film Distribution Office has provided financial incentives to nationally based distributors for handling films from other European nations. Some commentators have seen this trend as the source of a new breed of culturally bland Eurofilms (sometimes disparagingly referred to as *Europuddings*), including an ever-larger group of so-called heritage productions that celebrate the histories and cultures of individual countries in an impersonal style that adds nothing new or distinctive to film language. The increasing role of television, both public and privately owned, in European movie financing has also fostered a large number of stylistically conservative productions. Many of the films produced under these new forms of financing, however, have also managed to incorporate the traditions of individual national film cultures and have at times carried those traditions in new directions. At the same time, although such productions may come to the fore at international festivals, they are rarely box-office hits in their countries of origin. Nonetheless, the patriotically motivated policies of support for local movie making that have increasingly held sway all over Europe since World War II have produced many undeniably significant films that could not otherwise have been made, and have given birth to a number of influential nationally based cinema movements as well. Three film industries that have developed under these conditions are Scandinavia, Germany, and Spain.

Scandinavia

The story of Scandinavian cinema begins during the early days of the medium. Like the Americans, whose initial noninvolvement and later brief participation in World War I had given them such an advantage at a crucial time in film history, the neutral Swedes and Danes were free to pursue movie-making activities during the war years. Denmark was in the best position to take advantage of the opportunity, having a well-established industry that had competed successfully throughout the world in the years before 1914. In certain ways, Denmark provided a transition from the forms and styles of the American film being developed by Griffith, Sennett, Ince, and others, to the distinctive Swedish cinema arising during the War, which in turn was succeeded by the high period of German silent film. As had the Americans, the Danes made important use of the outdoors; and Scandinavian films have continued to be marked by the beauty and moodiness of their landscapes.

The stories, however, began to take advantage of the darker and more mystical tradition of Scandinavian folklore and literature. Predominantly psychological rather than sociological in their concerns, the narratives are frequently subjective, seen from a character's point of view—more often than not from the perspective of a woman. The stories the Danes told tend to dwell on spiritual or, alternatively, sexual conflicts. In these latter respects they foreshadowed the Swedes as well as the Germans. Given their themes, the acting style was required to be more subtle and introspective than the broad, emphatic performances generally employed in the American historical spectacles, action-melodramas, and comedies. Asta Nielsen, who appeared in Danish films (beginning with *The Abyss* in 1910) before moving on to Germany after the War, remains one of the great artists of the silent screen. Perhaps she was the first to suggest a dimension and complexity of feeling beneath the surface of the screen presence. Her style of passionate intensity would be developed to even greater expressiveness by her successor, Greta Garbo, who began in Sweden and worked in Germany before coming to the United States.

Giant directorial figure **Carl-Theodor Dreyer** links the early contributions of the Danish cinema most directly to the near present. Dreyer began in film as a writer of titles for the Danish studio Nordisk in 1912. He then took on various jobs, including editing and script writing, until directing his first film, *The President,* in 1920. His second film, *Leaves from Satan's Book,* in 1921, although based on a novel (by Marie Corelli), was clearly influenced by Griffith's *Intolerance.* It also had much in common with *Witchcraft through the Ages* (1922), the most well known film of his pioneering countryman Benjamin Christiansen. Dreyer's career continued in Berlin, Copenhagen, and France with a steady succession of features during the first half of the 1920s. Beyond that period stand his scattered

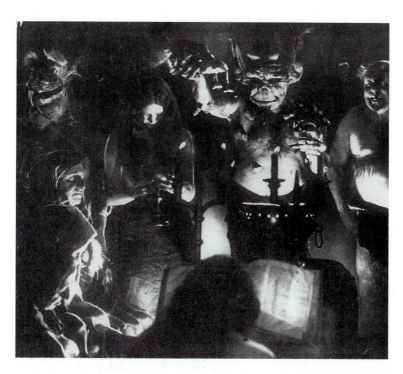

Witchcraft through the Ages
☆ Sweden, 1922, Benjamin
Christensen.

masterpieces: *The Passion of Joan of Arc* (1928), *Vampyr* (1932), *Day of Wrath* (1943), and *Gertrud* (1964).

It is this latter body of work—sparse because of Dreyer's rigid integrity, the difficulty of his themes, and the absolute control he demanded over every phase of production—that has assured Dreyer of his place in film history. He moved increasingly away from dependence on editing as a primary means of creative control and toward lengthy wide-angle shots with almost imperceptible camera movement, framing a succession of painterly compositions. His obsessive concern for the effects of organized religion in relation to individual belief—effects that he sees as usually repressive but capable of being transcended by the human spirit—characterizes *Joan of Arc, Day of Wrath,* and *Ordet.* The ambiguous malignity of what would have been a much more mechanical horror story in other hands gives *Vampyr* metaphysical dimensions; in *Gertrud* human love is expressed in terms of a creed. Only the Swedish Ingmar Bergman (who owes much to Dreyer), Robert Bresson in France, and the Spaniard Luis Buñuel have devoted themselves in such a consistent manner to themes that are religious in a broad sense and sometimes theological in their bases.

In the same year that Dreyer began work for Nordisk, 1912, **Victor Sjöström** entered the Swedish film industry. As early as 1913 he had commanded attention with *Ingeborg Holm,* an analysis of madness in a workhouse setting, with powerful performances under his direction. In *Terje Vigen* (1917), from an Ibsen poem, Sjöström directed himself as the bitter old sailor who lives alone on an island. The natural setting of ocean, cliffs, and sea birds strongly reinforces the mood. *The Outlaw and His Wife* (1917), marking the beginning of the best years of Swedish silent cinema, again has Sjöström in the role of an outsider—

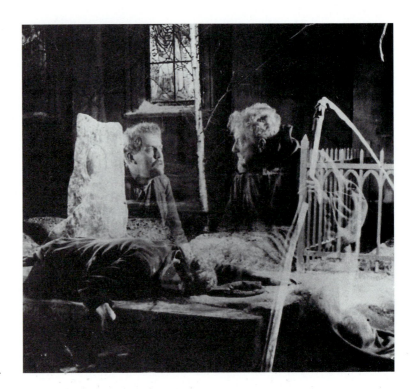

The Phantom Chariot ★
Sweden, 1921, Victor
Sjöström; Sjöström, on left.

a thief hiding in isolation, attempting to escape his fate, who finally meets death in the snow and cold of a northern winter. Of the several films that he directed based on the works of Swedish novelist Selma Lagerlöf, *The Phantom Chariot* is the most exceptional. Contemporary in setting, the subject matter suggests a deadly serious variant on George Bernard Shaw's play *Major Barbara*—replete with Salvation Army, dedicated heroine, and the chap who doesn't want to be saved—but with the theme reversed. Shaw maintains that economics is the underlying cause of drunkenness and brutality, and that faith is of no use in helping to eradicate them. Lagerlöf and Sjöström say that drink is the cause that creates brutality and that the problem can be solved only through religious salvation.

In 1923 Sjöström went to the United States. His best Hollywood work (in which he is officially credited as Victor Seastrom) retains some of the characteristics prominent in Scandinavian films. The moral and religious conflict featured in his adaptation of Nathaniel Hawthorne's *The Scarlet Letter* (1928) is very much like the kinds of thematic materials that attracted Dreyer. The lonely countryside and hostile elements of *The Wind* (1928) have their counterparts in many Swedish films. Both movies starred Griffith's favorite actor, Lillian Gish, who had never appeared to greater advantage than she did in Sjöström's productions. Sjöström's own film acting career later extended to his affecting performance as the old doctor in Ingmar Bergman's *Wild Strawberries* (1958), but he died in 1960, after a lengthy illness, without having seen his final contribution to Swedish film.

In the late 1910s and early 1920s Swedish film had achieved artistic heights and a unique national expression, primarily in the work of Victor Sjöström (*The Outlaw and his Wife*, 1917, and *The Phantom Carriage*, 1920) and Mauritz Stiller (*The Treasure of Arne*,

1919, and *The Story of Gösta Berling,* 1924). Following this period it descended to a kind of accomplishment appreciated mainly by Scandinavian audiences. The one major director at work in the years between Sjöström and Stiller and the rise of Ingmar Bergman was Alf Sjöberg. It was with Sjöberg that Bergman began his film career, as scriptwriter of *Torment,* the first postwar Swedish international success (produced in 1944). Coming out of theater, as playwright and director, Bergman continued his theatrical work alongside the cinematic, directing plays in winter and making films in summer. He has said that the theater is his wife, the cinema his mistress.

To date **Ingmar Bergman** stands unchallenged as Sweden's preeminent film maker. To a remarkable extent, his productions were responsible for inspiring the widespread serious intellectual consideration of film in the United States during the late 1950s. His great appeal to this new kind of audience was that his films dealt with matters of transcendent importance, and the manner in which he addressed those issues resonated powerfully in modern consciousness.

Stylistically Bergman is conservative and somewhat theatrical in manner. He emphasizes script and performance and makes heavy use of closeups. In addition to providing script and direction, he commanded a devoted stock company of some of the finest performers in film, including Ingrid Thulin, Bibi Andersson, Liv Ullmann, and Max von Sydow. He also oversaw a crew of technicians who, after years of working together, had grown accustomed to making tangible his every inclination; most notable among these was the master cinematographer Sven Nykvist. "There's a sensual satisfaction in working in close union with independent and creative people," Bergman wrote in his autobiography.

Bergman's debut film as director was *Crisis* (1945), from his own script, interesting now chiefly as a harbinger of things to come. The first works of stature were *Three Strange Loves* (1949), *Summer Interlude* (1951), and *Secrets of Women* and *Monika* (both 1952). All were shown abroad. *The Naked Night* (1953, also called *Sawdust and Tinsel*) marked a turning point; it is a small masterpiece. But it was *Smiles of a Summer Night* (1955), *The Seventh Seal* (1957), and *Wild Strawberries* (1957) that confirmed the earlier promise and set forth fully the thematic preoccupations we associate with the mature Bergman.

The familiar image of the game of chess between the Knight and Death in *The Seventh Seal* suggests a visual metaphor for the fifty some films of Bergman. Taken collectively, his work is like a huge chessboard on which a single game is being played. Parts of the game—the characters and themes—may receive his concentration in a particular film, with the rest of the board receding into the background, but most or all are present in each film. This was true at least up through his trilogy—*Through a Glass Darkly* (1961), *Winter Light* (1962), and *The Silence* (1963)—in which he claimed to have exorcised his religious preoccupations.

In *The Seventh Seal* we could see clearly what Bergman felt to be the essential problems confronting humanity, or at least himself. First of all was the human need for God, and His apparent absence, or was it merely silence? Then there was death, the inevitable, unknown, and unknowable end. What lay beyond life, if anything? If something, how could we find our way to it? Salvation, for Bergman, had to come through faith rather than knowledge or good works—the young couple Jof and Mia, and their baby, apparently have it and are saved; the Knight and his companions do not have it and are not saved (although the Knight, in his one meaningful deed, does distract Death so that Jof's family can escape). If in Bergman's world you can't learn or earn your way to faith, it is occasionally granted to the elect, who are saved. Invariably the faith is simple and unquestioning. On the other hand, we might see human love, although largely unattainable, as the key to salvation: the love of the young couple for each other and their child in *The Seventh Seal,* and the beginning love of the old doctor for his daughter-in-law in *Wild Strawberries,* which brings him an almost paradisiacal dream. Through love between human beings, faith may come, and from faith, salvation.

Sex in Bergman's films is frequently presented as a compulsive and destructive itch (*The Silence*), the scratching of which can sometimes quite literally draw blood (*Cries and Whispers,* 1972). Sex is the field of conflict rather than the source of fulfillment between the sexes (*Smiles of a Summer Night,* 1955, and *The Passion of Anna,* 1970, each in its own different way). Marriages evidently contain their own heavens and hells, but we see much more of the latter (*Scenes from a Marriage,* 1973).

Finally, Bergman is consistently absorbed with the role and function of the artist in society, and even in the cosmos. Bergman sees the artist as a charlatan, a kind of fake who may *almost* achieve understanding of the inscrutable mysteries of the universe and the mysterious ways of humankind. Artists may come closer to this understanding than other people, but thereby suffer more for their ultimate failure and the exposure of their pretensions and pretenses. The artist is invariably subjected to humiliation. *The Magician* (1958) is one of the serious films in which this concern is the center of attention; *Now About These Women* (1964) is one of the comedies. It is hard to say whether Bergman is sincere in this view or whether it is merely an engaging conceit. But in *Persona* (1966), which many regard as the most profound statement of all of his recurrent philosophical/psychological probings, he takes pains to remind us that we are seeing a movie. A projector shines its beam directly at us, a break in the film is simulated, and so on. He has expressed his delight with the basic technology and perceptual illusion on which his medium is based: that about half the time while one is watching a film the screen is in darkness as successive frames are moved into place. In a figurative sense, it's "all done with mirrors," as is said scornfully about certain kinds of magic performances.

In some quarters Bergman is faulted for the narrow range and frequent morbidity of his themes. Increasingly he became vulnerable to this sort of criticism after he abandoned God altogether and concentrated on the ways in which human beings can torture each other out of impulses that may have started as (and may still contain something recognizable as) love. It is true that in his pictures there isn't room for the pleasures and positive aspects of human existence celebrated by, say, Jean Renoir. Although Bergman's people are mostly physically attractive, intelligent, successful in their vocations, well-to-do, and living in pleasant surroundings, they are generally miserable. Part of their suffering is caused by their inability to understand why they are miserable. In Bergman's films misery seems to come from a lack (an absence of meaning, significance, or fullness) rather than from an active cause.

Fanny and Alexander (1983), regarded by many critics as Bergman's most fully realized achievement, is like a huge old-fashioned novel. Or, to return to a simile suggested earlier, Bergman here attempts to include most of the chessboard in his view. The well-worked themes are present, but this time Bergman's regard is mellow and valedictory. Beginning on Christmas Eve in 1907 in a Swedish town that might be Uppsala, where Bergman was born, it is about a large, influential family, almost a dynasty. There are many sharply differentiated characters and varied relationships among those living and visiting in the seemingly vast apartment presided over by the grandmother of twelve-year-old

Alexander and his younger sister, Fanny. It has elements traceable to what we know of Bergman's own growing up, and Alexander serves as the observer. Although a lot of curious and awful things may happen in this world, life is colorful and full, rich in its stimulations, and tender and tranquil in old age—well worth living. A very similar constellation is on view in Bille August's award-winning 1992 production, *Best Intentions,* based on a Bergman script about his parents' courtship.

Bergman's work is unique and highly personal, but it is also part of a tradition. The stylistic line from Sjöström's work, especially *The Phantom Chariot,* seems clear and direct. Bergman must have been thinking of this film especially while making *Wild Strawberries.* Not only does Sjöström play the principal role in both films, nearly forty years apart, but Bergman opens with a scene involving a horse-drawn hearse, the central symbol of the Sjöström film. Intricate flashback construction underpins both films as each shifts from a crucial moment in the protagonist's life (New Year's Eve and a university convocation) to let us discover how life has gone wrong for him. The character in each film faces his past as he nears death. In Bergman's *The Seventh Seal,* Death is remarkably close to the servant of death in *The Phantom Chariot;* close in function—as he moves about the earth collecting the dead—and close in visual treatment (the cowl).

Bergman's towering achievement has tended to dwarf the contributions of his peers and successors, but other Scandinavian directors emerged during the last decades of the

Wild Strawberries ★ Sweden, 1957, Ingmar Bergman; Victor Sjöström and Ingrid Thulin.

twentieth century to make distinctive contributions to world cinema. A number of these have participated in the growing European trend toward heritage productions that drew on the rich history of that part of the world and attracted international audiences. Bo Widerberg's lyrical *Elvira Madigan* (1967) was the first of these, followed by Jan Troell's eloquent portraits of Swedes struggling to make new homes in America, in *The Emigrants* (1970) and its sequel *The New Land* (1971), both starring two of Bergman's favorite actors: Max von Sydow and Liv Ullmann. Ullmann herself went on to a career in directing, most notably with another heritage film, *Kristin Lavanstdatter* (1995), this one set in the medieval era. Bille August also produced a notable heritage film with his 1987 Cannes prize-winner *Pelle the Conqueror,* again starring von Sydow, this time as a down-and-out nineteenth-century Swedish peasant who emigrates to Denmark with his young son in search of a better life. Like most heritage films, these productions were all distinguished by elegant, straightforward visuals designed to bring out the drama of the events chronicled. In a different vein, a Scandinavian comedy, Lasse Hallström's *My Life as a Dog* (1985), propelled its director into a hit-and-miss Hollywood career, the high point of which to date has been the 1993 *What's Eating Gilbert Grape?,* which offered a young Leonardo di Caprio the chance to shine in a plum role, and the 1999 Oscar-nominated production, *The Cider House Rules.*

In the 1990s Danish cinema regained center stage through the iconoclastic work of the audacious **Lars von Trier.** Although von Trier's irreverence and brash style place him at a distance from the austere, conservative Bergman, he too is interested in spiritual questions. His 1996 *Breaking the Waves,* made in England and winner of the Grand Jury Prize at Cannes, tells of a young married woman who achieves a kind of spiritual transcendence through sexual martyrdom. It was distinguished by a career-making role for British actor Emily Watson, who played the part with breath-takingly raw emotional bravado. An equally provocative von Trier production, *The Kingdom,* was originally a Danish television series he wrote and directed in 1994 and 1997. Its story examines a hospital that is haunted by the ghost of a dead child; in the process it satirizes the scientific pretensions of a medical profession that denies the power of spirituality. In 2000 von Trier's work took a new direction with the melodramatic musical, *Dancer in the Dark,* starring the Icelandic pop star Björk. Winner of the grand prize at Cannes, it features a story set in the United States during the 1960s. "Every time he makes a film, it's a great shock to everyone," his protégé Thomas Vinterberg has said of von Trier, "and therefore a great amusement to himself."

Von Trier banded together with Thomas Vinterberg, Soren Kragh-Jacobsen, and Kristian Levring to form the Dogma 95 group. The "vow of chastity" the group presented at the 1998 Cannes film Festival championed non-genre films shot in 35mm on location with hand-held cameras, available light, diegetic sound, and no special effects. Von Trier's 1998 *The Idiots* followed this formula to a certain degree (though it was shot on video), as did Vinterberg's 1998 *The Celebration.* Then came Kragh-Jacobsen's *Mifune* (2000). "I was losing spontaneity over the years," Kragh-Jacobsen commented on the release of this film. "Dogma taught me to play the game again." Although all of these productions attempted to simplify the filmmaking process and to make it more actor-friendly, none conformed in spirit to the most radical statement in the Dogma document, which forbade any directorial credit. The manifesto concluded with the pledge, "I swear as a director to refrain from personal taste! I am no longer an artist. . . . My supreme goal is to force the truth out of my characters and settings."

Meanwhile, the Scandinavian heritage film continues to thrive. A noteworthy addition to the genre was offered in 1997 by director Bille August. Originally produced as a

The Celebration
☆ Denmark, 1998,
Thomas Vinterberg.

television miniseries, *Jerusalem* tells the tale of a Swedish agrarian community torn apart by religious strife. The last part of the story is largely set in Palestine, where some of the group has resettled, joining an American colony that had established itself there. This plot turn provides an opportunity for exotic locations, English dialogue, and the addition of U.S. actor Olympia Dukakis, who plays the group's American leader—all features designed to appeal to the international market. However, the film is, at the same time, deeply Scandinavian. The story is adapted from a novel by Selma Lagerlöf, who had provided material for many of the earliest Swedish productions by Victor Sjöström and others. In keeping with its feeling for Scandinavian artistic traditions, its Swedish scenes are shot in subdued colors against the background of a harsh, unforgiving landscape, and its cast of characters are driven by moral and religious obsessions. As the work of a Swedish film maker who had, only a few years before, directed a production based on a Bergman script, could it be entirely coincidental that the patriarchal figure in *Jerusalem* is named Ingmar and that his young son—also named Ingmar—must struggle to make his own place in this world?

Germany

For Germany, the issue of the heritage film presents special problems, for modern German history is itself a problem for those who live there. After World War II Germany declared 1945 "Year Zero," the year of a new beginning. Until early 1989, when the wall dividing

East and West Berlin came down, it was a divided country: East Germany, part of the Soviet Bloc, and West Germany, allied with Western powers. Much of West German postwar culture, including cinema, involved attempts to escape or, alternatively, to come to terms with the events of the recent past, a process seen by some historians as a form of cultural mourning. West German film making took a leading role in this political self-examination, achieving international stature in a movement known as New German Cinema.

Before the process of enlisting cinema to exorcize the demons of the past could be undertaken, however, West Germany had to patch together the remnants of its film industry, which had been dismantled by the occupying forces after the war. Unlike other European nations, Germany had no quota on the number of American films that could be shown in its theaters. The low cultural prestige of cinema among the German people and the advent of television made the situation worse; by the early 1960s the film audience had dwindled to one-quarter of its former size. Despite these unpropitious conditions, however, an internationally recognized cinema movement emerged in Germany during the late 1960s and early 1970s. Film historian Thomas Elsaesser singles out four factors that enabled this movement to thrive: (1) a system of public funding for feature film production (begun in 1966); (2) a legal framework for television coproductions; (3) the establishment of international reputations for a group of "star" directors; and (4) the appearance of a new audience culled from the group of media-oriented student radicals of the era.[1] Despite the support of this new domestic audience, however, New German Cinema remained more of an international than a national phenomenon, winning prizes at festivals and attracting fine arts audiences around the world while never achieving significant popularity at home.

At the Oberhausen Film Festival of 1962, a group of young film makers presented a manifesto denouncing "Papa's cinema" and offered to make better films at half the cost. The group soon came to be regarded by the world at large and eventually in Germany itself as the new *Wunderkinder.* Under the leadership of Alexander Kluge, the movement became known as the Young German Film during the 1960s and the New German Cinema during the 1970s. The energy and influence of the New German Cinema were at their height during the 1970s; after the death of Fassbinder, its most innovative figure, in 1982, the movement offered little further in the way of significant innovations; its moment had passed.

The Oberhausen Manifesto represented an attempt to reject the past completely, espousing what it called "free cinema." "The old film is dead," the document declared. "We believe in the new film." The group's politics was Leftist: critical of Germany's Nazi heritage and the fascist movies it had produced. The films that emerged from this new vision were marked by unconventional narratives, new kinds of heroes, and novel ways of involving spectators. The directors were drawn to the politically potent images of documentary as well as to the portraits of society's victims found in melodrama. The conventions of Hollywood film making served as a model for some members of the group, as did images and motifs from American popular culture. A few of the new German directors, especially Werner Herzog and Wim Wenders, were inspired by these techniques and materials to create works designed to escape politics altogether in what was called a cinema of "pure being as pure seeing"; others, such as Rainer Werner Fassbinder, Volker Schlöndorff, Margarethe von Trotta, and Alexander Kluge, attempted a more engaged form of film making that could offer a revisionist view of modern German history.

---

[1] Thomas Elsaesser, *New German Cinema: A History* (New Brunswick, NJ: Rutgers University Press, 1989), p. 8.

Alexander Kluge's own film-making style combines fictional and documentary footage in collage structures in which fragmented story lines often center on female protagonists. His features include *Yesterday Girl* (1966), *Artists at the Top of the Big Top: Disoriented* (1968), and *The Part-Time Work of a Domestic Slave* (1974). The last deals with a twenty-nine-year-old woman trying to achieve some order, meaning, and effectiveness in a life that includes roles as wife and mother, abortionist, and political militant. Kluge has also championed the production of collectively made films, the most famous of which is the 1978 *Germany in Autumn,* which lists no less than ten directorial credits, including some of the most illustrious names of the New German cinema. A prolific writer as well as a film maker, Kluge has been profoundly influenced by the ideas of the Frankfurt school, a group of German Marxist intellectuals that had come together before the Nazi era. Since the late 1980s, he has devoted his attention to television, in which realm he has been active in producing noncommercial programming. "You only need one percent of alternative television, of calmness within the television set," he has said. "If you have it, people will accept that this television world isn't the only one."

Volker Schlöndorff, the most commercially successful member of the New German Cinema, also made his first feature (*Young Törless*) in 1966 and has remained active since, both as a director and as a movie executive. He is probably the most internationally oriented of the group, having been trained at the Institut des Haute Études Cinématographique in Paris and apprenticed under Louis Malle, Jean-Pierre Melville, and Alain Resnais. He subsequently worked all over Europe and America. In 1973 Schlöndorff founded his own production company with two partners; in 1992 he was named Chief of Production at Studio Babelsberg Grots, a company that represented a merger between the old Ufa studios and the East German studio DEFA.

Schlöndorff's *The Lost Honor of Katharina Blum* (1975) was written and directed in collaboration with his wife, Margarethe von Trotta. It concerns a young woman who spends the night with a fugitive political activist and is, as a result, hounded and exposed to humiliation by the authorities and the tabloid press. *The Tin Drum* (1978), Schlöndorff's adaptation of Günter Grass's novel, is his most substantial international success to date, winning top honors at the prestigious Cannes Film Festival. Subsequently, he has become something of a specialist in literary adaptation and a leading creator of Eurofilms. His *Swann in Love* (1984) presents part of the first novel of Marcel Proust's multivolume *Remembrance of Things Past.* A French film, its cast and crew were multinational. In the United States he directed the film-for-television *Death of a Salesman* (1985), starring Dustin Hoffman. His features during the 1990s have been financed under the banners of many nations: *The Handmaid's Tale* (1990) by Germany and the United States; *The Voyager* (1992) by France, Germany, Greece, and the United Kingdom; *The Ogre* (1996) by France, Germany, and the United Kingdom; and *Palmetto* (1998) by Germany and the United States. In 1999 he returned to a more nationally oriented model with *Legends of Rita,* a film based on the life of a well-known German radical.

Following her initial collaboration with her husband, **Margarethe von Trotta** became active on her own, producing a body of work focused on issues concerning women that has won her a large international following. Throughout the 1970s and 1980s her productions were financed by Schlöndorff's production company; during the 1990s she had a more difficult time finding support and her production slowed. Many of her films explore aspects of modern women's lives: the symbiotic relationship between sisters

Marianne and Juliane ★ Germany, 1981, Margarethe von Trotta; Jutta Lampe and Barbara Sukora.

(*Sisters, or the Balance of Happiness,* 1979, and *Three Sisters,* 1988) and the effect of politics on romantic attachments (*The Promise,* 1994). In another group of her films women are viewed in the context of historically significant radical movements, offering moving accounts of the lives of people on the far left, such as a female member of the terrorist Baader-Meinhoff group (*Marianne and Juliane,* 1981) and a legendary Marxist political leader (*Rosa Luxemburg,* 1986). Throughout her career, von Trotta has favored conventional narrative forms, although her interest in psychological interiority leads her to include many dream and fantasy sequences. "The unconscious and subconscious behavior of the character is more important to me than what they do," she has said. To emphasize the complexity of her characters' inner lives she uses a large number of closeups, typically set off by dark, pared-down settings. Her films are elegant yet intense studies of women whose deepest fears and desires are shaped by large social forces.

A more radical group of German women film makers have clustered around the journal *Frauen und Film,* launched in 1974. This group has experimented with unconventional techniques to present their vision of female angst and anger, turning to such techniques as fragmented narratives, direct address to the camera, and mosaic-like forms that mix documentary and fictional footage. Foremost among these German feminist directors are Helke Sander (*Redupers, or the All-Around Reduced Personality,* 1977), Helma Sanders-Brahms (*Germany, Pale Mother,* 1979), Ulrike Ottinger (*Ticket of No Return,* 1979), and Jutta Brückner (*One Glance, and Love Breaks Out,* 1986).

Another experimentalist, **Jean-Marie Straub,** an Alsatian, was in exile from France for political reasons from 1958 on. A committed Marxist, he is associated with the development of what he has called a minimalist cinema. His later films have been made in collaboration with his wife, **Danièle Huillet.** *Not Reconciled* (1965) probed the ways in which the dominant Junkerism and Nazism of past generations carried over into contemporary German life, accompanied by lingering guilt and continuing need for explanations. *Chronicle of Anna Magdalena Bach* (1967) presents performances of Bach's music with reverence but also attempts to imply the feelings and social ambience that surrounded the life of the composer. *History Lessons* (1973), a freely adapted version of a novel by Bertolt Brecht, combines a Marxist interpretation of the economic motives underlying the usual rendering of the history of ancient Rome with a slow automobile drive through the crowded streets of the present-day city. *Moses and Aaron* (1975) is a faithful rendition of Arnold Schönberg's twelve-tone opera with added ideological emphasis and characteristic straining of the formal conventions of narrative cinema. *Class Relations* (1985), an adaptation of Franz Kafka's *Amerika,* is literary and minimalist, in black and white. Its thesis is that the nature of human relationships is determined by class and capital rather than by individual psychologies. Of the modern German film makers the Straubs are the most "difficult," the least "accessible" to general audiences. At the same time their work is valued by the few as the most innovative in their attempts to analyze and expose the medium itself, and to make it serve the purposes of truly radical, politically committed film making.

Three German film makers who speak to the pit as well as the gallery and who emerged as the major names of the New German Cinema movement were Rainer Werner Fassbinder, Werner Herzog, and Wim Wenders. **Rainer Werner Fassbinder**'s style is characterized by cold colors and harsh lighting. He usually worked with a loyal stock company of actors, including Hanna Schygulla, Briggitta Mira, and Irm Hermann. Often, too, he himself acted in his productions. Committed to an avant-garde approach, especially as articulated in the theories of Bertolt Brecht and Antonin Artaud, he frequently drew attention to the film-making process by framing his characters in doorways, windows, and mirrors, and by hyperbolically foregrounding their gazes at one another. His early films, including *Katzelmacher* (1969) and *Beware of a Holy Whore* (1970), are squarely in the avant-garde mode.

As his career progressed, Fassbinder was increasingly influenced by the audience-pleasing model represented by Hollywood melodrama. He was especially drawn to the films of Douglas Sirk, a German expatriot who made a number of popular women's pictures in Hollywood during the 1950s that subtly critiqued the social system that victimized his characters. Carrying Sirk's approach one step further, Fassbinder's melodramas infused the dilemmas of his characters (who were frequently women or homosexuals) with broad political meanings. *The Merchant of the Four Seasons* (1971), for example, about a *lumpen* fruit peddler hounded by the women in his life (mother, girlfriend, and wife) into drinking himself to death, is essentially a critique of bourgeois manners. In it wildly incongruous behavior becomes part of everyday reality. *The Bitter Tears of Petra von Kant* (1972), dealing with female homosexuality, explores various permutations of freedom and slavery evident in the women's relationship with each other in an extraordinarily bizarre and artificial visual style. *Ali: Fear Eats the Soul* (1974), a remake of Sirk's 1955 *All That Heaven Allows,* is about a sixty-year-old German cleaning woman who falls in love with and marries a much younger immigrant Moroccan laborer and is ostracized by her family and the community because of racial prejudice and ageism. A subtitle suggests that "happiness is not always fun."

At the end of his career, Fassbinder began to produce more politically pointed studies of the German past. The first and best known of these is the *The Marriage of Maria Braun*

The Marriage of Maria Braun ★ West Germany, 1979, Rainer Werner Fassbinder; Ivan Desny, Gisela Uhlen, Gottfried John, Anton Schirsner, Hanna Schygulla, and Elizabeth Trissenaar.

(1979). It stars Hanna Schygulla as a woman buffeted by and adapting to the changing social conditions in Germany, from the stressful end of World War II to later affluence. The material success she achieves does not free her, however, from the constraints of the patriarchal capitalist system of which she is a part. The devastated urban landscape that forms the backdrop to her struggles reflects and shapes her own psychic economy. History is presented here as a never-ending cycle: The film begins and ends with explosions, and the last words we hear are "Germany is master of the world!"(uttered in the 1970s by the announcer of a soccer game). *Maria Braun* is the first of a trilogy that includes *Lili Marleen* (1980) and *Veronica Voss* (1981). All three films mount harsh criticisms of German history as revealed in microcosm through the lives of the heroines of each story, creating a devastating triptych of capitalism in crisis. The picture of a lost society was rounded out with Fassbinder's masterful 1980 television miniseries, *Berlin Alexanderplatz,* which some consider his greatest achievement. Based on a classic novel, it chronicles the misadventures of a down-and-out petty criminal in 1930s Berlin. "I try to illustrate that we have been led astray by our upbringing and the society we live in," the director once commented. "When I show people on the screen the ways things can go wrong, my aim is to warn them that that is the way things *will* go if they don't change their lives."

A film maker who resists making films about his homeland as strenuously as Fassbinder embraced this project is **Werner Herzog.** Herzog's style is characterized by slow pacing, frequent repetitions, and a focus on aberrant characters. The performances in his films often betray an eerily unreal quality—for example, the actors in *Even Dwarfs Started Small* (1970) are all dwarfs, and in *Hearts of Glass* (1976) all are hypnotized. The leading role in *The Mystery of Kaspar Hauser* (1976) is played by a derelict. Herzog's settings—the Amazon jungle (*Aguirre, the Wrath of God,* 1973, and *Fitzcarraldo,* 1981), the Sahara Desert (*Fata Morgana,* 1970), and an island with a volcano that is about to erupt (*La Soufrière,* 1978)—range from exotic to bizarre. "There is no harmony in the universe," he has said. "We have to get used to this idea."

Herzog's documentaries, including *Fata Morgana* and *La Soufrière,* make the real world appear more fantastical than fiction. In 1994 he made *The Transformation of the World into Music,* the title of which could stand as a symbol of his film-making project as a whole. Repeatedly drawn to the abstract, the mystical, and the sublime, he offers up a world of cosmic wonder and inchoate emotional resonance that is more closely related to musical themes than to ideological ones.

Like Herzog, **Wim Wenders** has been interested in creating a cinema of "pure being as pure seeing." Of his feelings about the German past, he has said, "Trying to remember how it was to grow up in post-war Germany seems so . . . there are so many other layers of experience over it that I can't even get back to the feeling of it." Wenders, too, is interested in the spiritual and the fantastic, a vision typically rendered in carefully composed images created by ace cinematographer Robby Müller. Slow rhythms add a dimension of other-worldliness to the stories he tells. Drawn to self-reflexive strategies and fragmented forms, he is the most clearly postmodern of the major New German directors.

Aguirre, The Wrath of God ★ West Germany, 1973, Werner Herzog; Klaus Kinski and Cecilia Rivera.

We first knew Wenders for *The Goalie's Anxiety at the Penalty Kick* (1972), *Alice in the Cities* (1974), *False Movement* (1975), *Kings of the Road* (1976), and *The American Friend* (1977). All of these involve, to one degree or another, individual alienation from society, aimless wandering, cities, and a fascination with the United States. One of the characters in *Kings of the Road* says, "The Americans have colonized our subconscious." Two of his other films, *The American Friend* (1977) and *Lightning Over Water* (1980), feature the American director Nicholas Ray.

Wenders's fascination with America quite naturally took him there. *Paris, Texas* (1984) is the best film to have come out of his stay. Although shot in the United States with a script by two Americans, Sam Shepard and L. M. "Kit" Carson growing out of the former's *Motel Chronicles,* it was said by many to be a German picture made in America (as had been said of Murnau's *Sunrise* before it). If *Paris, Texas* is a continuation of Wenders's road pictures and of his personal preoccupations, within that body of work, it surely would have to be recognized as one of the finest. It won the Grand Prix at Cannes.

At that festival in 1987, Wenders was awarded the prize for best direction for *Wings of Desire,* his first German-language film in a decade. It is a homecoming in a profound sense, an effort to capture the feeling of Berlin in the years since the end of World War II to the present, including the wounds left by that war. The fanciful elements that distinguish it from anything Wenders had done before are both daring and effective. These include angels (males and females in black overcoats) who fly the heavens and also patrol the streets of Berlin, listening to the unspoken thoughts of its inhabitants. The angel protagonist (played by Bruno Ganz) falls in love with a trapeze artist (Solveig Dommartin) and has to

Wings of Desire ★ West Germany, 1987, Wim Wenders; Solveig Dommartin and Bruno Ganz.

choose whether to continue his spiritual existence or opt for mortality with its attendant pains and uncertainties. It was remade in Hollywood in 1998 by director Brad Silberling as *City of Angels,* with Nicholas Cage and Meg Ryan in the leading roles. In 1994 Wenders made a sequel to *Wings of Desire;* entitled *Faraway, So Close,* it tells the tale of another angel who becomes mortal.

The escape from the German past represented in the work of the Romantic visionaries Wenders and Herzog has been countered by the thematic thrust of several films that explicitly attempt a revisionist history of modern Germany through the lives of individuals—a variant of the heritage genre that sees it as a means of purging a national sense of guilt and loss. One of the most admired of these is Edgar Reitz's television miniseries of the early 1980s, *Heimat (Home),* which chronicles the sweep of twentieth-century German history as it affects the members of a single family. "Heimat" raises the issue of German nationalism by questioning what it means to be "home." A similar project is represented in Helma Sanders-Brahms's *Germany, Pale Mother,* which also explores the interaction of the personal and political in Germany, in this case through the experiences of a young mother who must fend for herself during the Second World War. In one dramatic instance of the interrelation between the personal and the historical, a scene of the heroine giving birth is intercut with images of bombs being dropped on Berlin. *Germany, Pale Mother* begins with a 1933 Brecht poem which, in a foresightful mode, raises the question of how Germany can mourn for its past. "What have your sons done to you," the poem concludes. "That you sit among the peoples a mockery or a threat!" Many of the major film makers of the New German Cinema have attempted to answer this question, while others have rejected it to create an apolitical art. In both cases the result has been a distinctive national style that is recognizably German.

The close of the twentieth century saw Tom Tykwer's jazzy, ahistorical *Run, Lola, Run* become an international hit; at the same time, an increasing number of German films focused on the matter of the country's past, including Max Färberböck's *Aimée and Jaguar* and Roland Suso Richter's *After the Truth.* Other productions in a similar vein are planned. "The Second World War period still represents the most captivating and morally ambiguous challenge of the century," German producer Ortwin Freyermuth has said. "Ten years after reunification and with the government moving to Berlin again, Germany seems to have come around in a historical sense. German talent may feel even more encouraged to deal with this period in a historical way." Ironically, this project, as German film making in general, will likely prove more appealing to international audiences than to the Germans themselves.

Spain

The most prominent director to emerge from Spain is more an international figure than a national one, though his iconoclastic films have little in common with the bland Eurofilm formula.

Luis Buñuel was not only a truly independent and therefore isolated artist, like Bresson and Bergman, but his work stands outside a particular national culture. Perhaps one might better say that he carried his Spanish inheritance and later adoption of surrealism with him in films made in a number of countries, both in Europe and the New World, over a period of fifty-five years. His films can be divided into two types: the psychoanalytic, which explore the sexual proclivities of an individual, and the ethnographic, which examine the mores of an entire culture or social class.

Buñuel's first work in cinema was in France in the 1920s, as an assistant to Jean Epstein and other impressionist film makers, culminating in his turn to surrealism and collaboration with Salvador Dali on *Un Chien Andalou* (1928) and *L'Age d'or* (1930). After a long fallow period spent mostly in the United States—except for *Land Without Bread* (1932), a seering documentary about the impoverished Las Hurdes region of Spain—Buñuel settled in Mexico in 1946. There his production became steady and commercially successful, for the most part, within the popular Latin American genres of melodrama and comedy.

The most exceptional film in the Mexican period was *Los Olvidados* (1950), which won the international critics prize at Cannes. It extends out of the naturalism of *Land Without Bread,* examining the violence and squalor in a shantytown on the edge of Mexico City as experienced by a gang of juvenile delinquents. An introductory title asserts that the film is "entirely based on actual incidents and all characters are authentic." But, as with *Land Without Bread,* Buñuel's unsparing and unsentimental observation of the horrors created by poverty and the inadequacies or callousness of social institutions in the face of human need moves beyond the usual ways of presenting social problems. As in the earlier Spanish film, reality in *Los Olvidados* becomes *surreal* because we are not used to being forced to contemplate a situation as hopeless as this, or its implications about the structure of society and perhaps the nature of humankind. More conventionally surreal is the beautiful dream sequence in slow motion. Dreams and hallucinations appear throughout Buñuel's work as part of his efforts to capture the irrational drives and fears underlying human behavior.

In 1955 Buñuel returned to France and began a body of films, some of them cofinanced by Italian, Mexican, and Spanish sources and shot outside France, which constitute his latter-day career and confirm his position among the great auteurs of international cinema. Among these is *Viridiana* (1961) which, although made in Spain, was denounced and banned in that and other Catholic countries after its completion. *Viridiana* represents Buñuel's most unambiguous attack on what he views as the unhealthy sentimentality and restrictive and warped morality of institutionalized Christianity. The film climaxes as the filthy and deformed, cynical and misanthropic collection of beggars—whom Viridiana has assembled in order to save their souls through prayer—enter into a drunken orgy that includes an outrageous parody of da Vinci's *The Last Supper.* In his own way Buñuel was preoccupied with religion—"Thank God I am still an atheist," he would say.

Buñuel's last films satirized the social and sexual conceits of wealthy Europeans. Among the most admired of these is *The Exterminating Angel* (1962), which concerns a group of guests mysteriously (miraculously?) unable to leave a sumptuous dinner party for days, maybe even weeks, and the ways in which their enforced proximity to each other brings out the idiosyncracies and destructiveness lurking beneath their conventionally elegant exteriors. In *Diary of a Chambermaid* (1964), based on the novel about the French upper classes by Octave Mirbeau (from which Renoir also made a film, in Hollywood, almost twenty years earlier), Buñuel examines the pervasive evil and moral decadence of an updated, crypto-fascist society. The heroine/protagonist of *Belle de jour* (1967), frigid and sexually unfulfilled with her husband, whom she nonetheless loves, attempts to bring alive her masochistic fantasies of sexual debasement by volunteering her services to a chic brothel. *The Discreet Charm of the Bourgeoisie* (1972) is a loosely structured, amusing, and

Viridiana ★ Spain, 1961, Luis Buñuel; Silvia Pinal, fifth from left.

anecdotal attack on the values of polite society. It reverses the situation of *The Exterminating Angel,* with six persons attempting to hold a dinner party that is constantly interrupted. *The Phantom of Liberty* (1974) is a darker companion piece to *The Discreet Charm.* It turns on a series of chance encounters that expose the illogic at the core of modern society.

Throughout Buñuel's work his unflinching contemplation of human cruelty reminds us that he comes from the land of the Inquisition and the bullfight. Some of his films seem clearly to follow the tradition of Goya's horrifying documentation of the human capacity for inhumanity in his series of etchings entitled *The Disasters of War.* (A live reenactment of a Goya painting opens *The Phantom of Liberty.*) On the other hand, Buñuel's surrealism led him to explore the unconscious and powerful forces of sexuality, dangerous and destructive when suppressed, rendering any view of life incomplete and invalid when unacknowledged. His attacks on bourgeois institutions (religion and state, class distinctions, and conventional morality) carry the political charge of the surrealists' revolt. Closer to the anarchist's goal of individual freedom than to the Marxist's credo of cooperative endeavor, yet we can infer from *The Phantom of Liberty* that for Buñuel the concept of individual freedom remained a ghostly one.

An easing of censorship that began in the early 1970s has allowed a newly serious and critical examination of the national culture. Following the death of dictator Francisco Franco in 1975, a variety of topics that had long been off limits—church, army, sexual relations, and the Civil War, for example—have been treated with candor and humor. Spanish politics, from the turn of the twentieth century to the present, is the note that recurs most frequently. Three Spanish film makers who stand out clearly are Carlos Saura, Victor Erice, and more recently Pedro Almodóvar.

Carlos Saura's *The Hunt* (1966) was one of the first Spanish films to return to the painful experience of the Civil War with an honesty designed to lay bare and perhaps to cauterize the old wounds. It proceeds obliquely, however, from a kind of allegory of a hunting expedition undertaken by a group of friends who had earlier fought together in that dreadful conflict under Franco. In *Cousin Angelica* (1974) Saura also looked back to the 1930s from a modern perspective, with a protagonist who revisits a town for the first time in thirty years and relives episodes of his childhood, especially those centering on his relationship with his cousin Angelica. Saura's distinctive narrative style, combining allusion and association with chronological disruption, the past falling into place alongside the present, grew out of his need to deal with subjects that would otherwise have been taboo. *Hurry, Hurry* (1980) seems to be the first film in which he confronted a present reality, probing the lives of four young delinquents rushing headlong into tragedy. He also directed a stylish "flamenco trilogy" of ballets based on well-known literary works: *Blood Wedding* (1981), *Carmen* (1983), and *El amor brujo* (*Love, the Magician,* 1985). In the 1990s he continued to explore the political and cultural traditions of his country in internationally popular films such as *¿Ay! Carmela* (1990), an account of a performance troup sympathetic to the Republican cause caught behind enemy lines during the Spanish Civil War; and *Tango* (1997), a self-reflexive fantasy about a director engaged in making a film about the tango.

Victor Erice has directed only a few films. Best known is *The Spirit of the Beehive* (1973), which takes place in the period just after the Civil War. In it he evokes a strange

The Hunt ★ Spain, 1966, Carlos Saura.

The Spirit of the Beehive
★ Spain, 1973, Victor Erice;
Ana Torrent and Terésa
Gimpera.

dream world seen through the childhood games and fantasies of two sisters. There are allusions to surrounding events (for example, a fugitive soldier hides in their barn), but mostly it is the mood of unstated tension and fragile unreality which conveys Erice's sense of what it was like living in those first years of fascist rule. Following *The Spirit of the Beehive,* the next film, *The South* (1983), is also about a Spanish provincial family, as seen through the childhood memories of a young woman. It is a tale of mystery and romance in which her father is the dominant figure. *Dream of Light* (1991) chronicles the impossible attempt of the painter Antonio López to capture on canvas the moment of golden splendor when the fruit on a quince tree in his garden ripens. An oblique and strange document, it pursues the subtle mystery of an artist and his creation.

Contrasting as sharply as could be imagined with Erice's high seriousness is **Pedro Almodóvar**'s playful postmodernism. Also, against the sparsity of Erice's output is the fecundity of Almodóvar's: almost a film a year since his first feature in 1980. And then there is the audience: Erice's small, devoted following; Almodóvar's widespread popularity. Not only was *Women on the Verge of a Nervous Breakdown* the most successful Spanish film in Spain up to that point, but it was also the highest grossing foreign film in North America in 1989. At present, all the films he has made since 1982 are available on video in the United States, and all have made a profit here. Critical reaction to Almodóvar's work has varied from critic to critic and film to film, probably because of the paradoxical nature of the films themselves. They grow out of a gay sensibility and yet have women at their centers, played most notably by the actress Carmen Maura. Dark and deviant sexual fantasy and violence (including death) abound. Though situations and characters may seem

*Women on the Verge of a
Nervous Breakdown* ★
Spain, 1987, Pedro
Almodóvar; Julieta Serrano.

bizarre, they are treated with a seriousness and sensitivity that enable us to identify and empathize with them. Plot outlines more often than not are straight melodrama, which is then undercut with witty references to pop culture, citations of earlier films (*Duel in the Sun, Johnny Guitar*), and parodies of the styles of pantheon film makers (Buñuel and Bergman). Perhaps this eclectic mix is most satisfyingly achieved in Almodóvar's prize-winning 1999 release *All About My Mother,* thought by many to be his best effort. Almodóvar's style is so distinctive as to have become almost a cliché. "I became commonplace," the director has said. "They made me an adjective. 'This is Almodóvarian.'"

Almodóvar's films are sometimes thought of as representing a new Spain—democratic and permissive, sophisticated and irreverent—totally different from the Spain of the Franco years and reflecting the egalitarian ethos of the Socialist government of Felipe Gonzàlez, which came to power in 1982. Spanish film historian Marsha Kinder places Almodóvar at the forefront of a rethinking of Spanish national identity in terms of gender during the 1980s. "Almodóvar succeeded in establishing a mobile sexuality as the new cultural stereotype for a hyperliberated Socialist Spain," she writes.[2]

Thanks in part to Almodóvar's energy and popularity, a new generation of Spanish film makers emerged on the international scene during the 1990s, including Bigas Luna

---

[2] Marsha Kinder, "Refiguring Socialist Spain: An Introduction." In *Refiguring Spain: Cinema/Media/Representation* (Durham, NC: Duke University Press, 1997), p. 3.

(*Jamón Jamón,* 1992), Fernando Trueba (*La Belle Époque,* 1993), Julio Medem (*Lovers of the Arctic Circle,* 1998), and José Luis Cuerda (*Butterfly,* 2000), leading to talk of a New Spanish Cinema. Film attendance in Spain swelled; cutbacks on government subsidies in 1994 were compensated for by newly available funding from television. Production soared from forty-four features in 1994 to ninety-six in 1998. In 1995 the National Film School, which had been closed for twenty-five years, reopened.

The new directors have moved away from a reliance on heritage productions (over three hundred of which were released between 1976 and 1992); instead, in the 1990s, Hollywood formulas such as the thriller and the screwball comedy became the norm—a trend that gave Spanish cinema tremendous appeal not only at home but also around the world. María Lozano, director of the Instituto Cervantes in New York, has commented on this trend. "Whether for good or bad, we've become more Euopean," she says.

The vitality of Spanish film making in the 1990s, and of Almodóvar in particular, is deceptive; even at its healthiest, the scale of European cinema is miniscule compared to that of Hollywood. At their peak in the heyday of Ingmar Bergman in the 1950s, foreign films represented 7 percent of American box-office revenue; at the turn of the twenty-first century, however, they accounted for less than 1 percent of the pie. Although a few productions from abroad, such as *Life Is Beautiful, Shine,* and *Shakespeare in Love,* generated considerable interest during the 1990s, few foreign films find American distributors. Cable

Butterfly ★ Spain, 2000, José Luis Cuerda; Alexis de los Santos, Uxia Blanco, and Mañuel Lozano.

stations, such as the Independent Film Channel and the Sundance Channel, have compensated for this lack to some degree by showing foreign titles on a regular basis, as has the availability of videos, but there is no doubt that television and videos offer a diminished experience of most films—even those made with television money. In September of 2000, *Variety,* the show business Bible, reported the latest among many cooperative European financing ventures to produce English-language films for the international market, this one between England, Germany, and Spain. So the Eurofilm mentality continues to thrive. But as suggested in this chapter, the manifestations of this trend and the alternatives to it have provided an array of worthy cinematic offerings throughout the major western European nations. In eastern Europe, historically, the issue of the marketplace that has driven so much of the development of the cinemas of neighboring countries to the West has meant something quite different, as will be explored in the next chapter.

Films of the Period

SCANDINAVIA

1944
Torment (Alf Sjöberg)

1953
Summer with Monika (*Sommaren med Monika*) (Ingmar Bergman)
The Naked Night (*Gycklarnas afton*) (Ingmar Bergman)

1954
A Lesson in Love (*En Lektion i kärlek*) (Ingmar Bergman)

1955
Smiles of a Summer Night (*Sommarnattens leende*) (Ingmar Bergman)

1957
The Seventh Seal (*Det Sjunde inseglet*) (Ingmar Bergman)
Wild Strawberries (*Smultronstället*) (Ingmar Bergman)

1958
The Magician (*Ansiktet*) (Ingmar Bergman)

1960
The Virgin Spring (*Jungfrukällan*) (Ingmar Bergman)

1961
Through a Glass Darkly (*Säsom i en spegel*) (Ingmar Bergman)

1963
The Silence (*Tystnaden*) (Ingmar Bergman)

1966
Persona (Ingmar Bergman)

1968
The Girls (*Flickorna*) (Mai Zetterling)
Hour of the Wolf (*Vargtimmen*) (Ingmar Bergman)

1969
The Passion of Anna (*En Passion*) (Ingmar Bergman)

1971
The Emigrants (*Utvandrarna*) (Jan Troell)

1972
Cries and Whispers (*Viskningar och rop*) (Ingmar Bergman)
The New Land (*Nybyggarna*) (Jan Troell)

1973
Scenes from a Marriage (*Scener ur ett äktenskap*) (Ingmar Bergman)

1978
Autumn Sonata (*Höstonaten*) (Ingmar Bergman)

1982
Fanny and Alexander (*Fanny och Alexander*) (Ingmar Bergman)

1985

My Life as a Dog (Lasse Hallström)

1987

Pelle, the Conqueror (*Pelle erobreren*) (Bille August)

1991

Zentropa (Europa) (Lars von Trier)

1992

Best Intentions (*Den Goda viljan*) (Bille August)

1994

"The Kingdom" ("Riget") (TV miniseries) (Lars
   von Trier)

1995

Kristin Lavanstdatter (Liv Ullmann)

1996

Breaking the Waves (Lars von Trier)

1997

Jerusalem (Bille August)
"The Kingdom II" ("Riget II") (Lars von Trier)

1998

The Idiots (Ideoterne) (Lars von Trier)
The Celebration (*Festen*) (Thomas Vinterberg)

GERMANY

1966

Yesterday Girl (*Abschied von Gestern*) (Alexander
   Kluge)
Young Törless (*Der junge Törless*) (Volker Schlöndorff)

1967

Chronicle of Anna Magdelena Bach (*Chronik der
   Anna Magdalena Bach*) (Jean-Marie Straub and
   Danièle Huillet)

1971

The Merchant of the Four Seasons (*Der Händler der
   vier Jahreszeiten*) (Rainer Werner Fassbinder)

1972

The Bitter Tears of Petra von Kant (*Die bitteren
   Tränen der Petra von Kant*) (Rainer Werner
   Fassbinder)

1973

Aguirre, the Wrath of God (*Aguirre, der Zorn
   Göttes*) (Werner Herzog)

1974

Ali: Fear Eats the Soul (*Angst essen Seele auf*)
   (Rainer Werner Fassbinder)
The Mystery of Kaspar Hauser (*Every Man for
   Himself and God Against All*) (*Jeder für sich
   und Gott gegan alle*) (Werner Herzog)
The Part-Time Work of a Domestic Slave (*Gelegen-
   heitsarbeit einer Sklavin*) (Alexander Kluge)

1975

The Lost Honor of Katherina Blum (*Die verlorene
   Ehre der Katharina Blum*) (Volker Schlöndorff
   and Margarethe von Trotta)
Moses and Aaron (*Moses und Aaron*) (Jean-Marie
   Straub and Danièle Huillet)

1976

Kings of the Road (*Im Lauf der Zeit*) (Wim Wenders)

1977

The American Friend (*Der amerikanische Freund*)
   (Wim Wenders)
Our Hitler (*Hitler—Ein Film aus Deutschland*)
   (Hans-Jürgen Syberberg)

1978

Germany in Autumn (*Deutschland im Herbst*) (Alf
   Brustellin, Hans Peter Cloos, Rainer Werner
   Fassbinder, Alexander Kluge, Maximiliane
   Maintan, Edgar Reitz, Katja Ruppé, Volker
   Schlöndorff, Bernard Sinkel)
The Tin Drum (*Die Blechtrommel*) (Volker
   Schlöndorff)

1979

Ticket of No Return (*Bildnis einer Trinkerin*)
   (Ulricke Ottinger)
Germany, Pale Mother (*Deutschland, bleiche
   Mutter*) (Helma Sanders-Brahms)
The Marriage of Maria Braun (*Die Ehe der Maria
   Braun*) (Rainer Werner Fassbinder)
Nosferatu (Werner Herzog)
Sisters, or the Balance of Happiness (*Schwestern
   oder die Balance des Glücks*) (Margarethe
   von Trotta)

1980
"Berlin Alexanderplatz" (TV miniseries) (Rainer
    Werner Fassbinder)
Lili Marleen (Rainer Werner Fassbinder)

1981
Das Boot (The Boat) (Wolfgang Peterson)
*Marianne and Juliane, or The German Sisters
    (Die Bleierne Zeit)* (Margarethe von Trotta)
Veronika Voss (Rainer Werner Fassbinder)

1982
Fitzcarraldo (Werner Herzog)
Parsifal (Hans-Jürgen Syberberg)

1984
"Heimat" (Home) (television series) (Edgar Reitz)
    (begun in 1981)

1986
*One Glance—and Love Breaks Out (Ein Blick—und
    die Liebe bricht aus)* (Jutta Brückner)
Rosa Luxemburg (Margarethe von Trotta)
Sugarbaby (Zuckerbaby) (Percy Adlon)

1987
Cobra Verde (Werner Herzog)
Wings of Desire (Himmel über Berlin) (Wim Wenders)

1994
Faraway, So Close (In weiter Feine, so nah!) (Wim
    Wenders)
The Promise (Das versprechen) (Margarethe von
    Trotta)
*The Transformation of the World into Music (Die
    Verwandlung der Welt in Musik)* (Werner Herzog)

1999
Legends of Rita (Die Stille nach dem Schub)
    (Volker Schlöndorff)
Run, Lola, Run (Lola Rennt) (Tom Tykwer)

2001
Invincible (Werner Herzog)

SPAIN
1952
*Welcome, Mr. Marshall! (Bienvenido, Mr.
    Marshall!)* (Luis García Berlanga)

1955
Death of a Cyclist (Muerte de un ciclista) (Juan
    Antonio Bardem)

1961
Viridiana (Luis Buñuel)

1966
The Hunt (La caza) (Carlos Saura)

1967
Peppermint Frappé (Carlos Saura)

1970
Tristana (Luis Buñuel)

1973
*The Spirit of the Beehive (El Espiritu de la
    colmena)* (Victor Erice)

1974
Cousin Angelica (La Prima Angelica)
    (Carlos Saura)

1975
Poachers (Furtivos) (José Luis Boreau)

1976
Cria (Cria Cuervos) (Raise Ravens) (Carlos Saura)

1977
*That Obscure Object of Desire (Cet Obscur
    objet du desir)* (Luis Buñuel)

1980
La Sabina (José Luis Boreau)

1981
Blood Wedding (Bodas de sangre)
    (Carlos Saura)

1983
Carmen (Carlos Saura)
The South (El Sur) (Victor Erice)

1984
*What Have I Done to Deserve This? (Qué me
    hecho yo para merecer esto?)* (Pedro
    Almodóvar)

1987
Women on the Verge of a Nervous Breakdown
 (*Mujeres al borde de un ataque de nervios*)
 (Pedro Almodóvar)

1990
¿Ay! Carmela (Carlos Saura)

1991
Dream of Light (*The Quince Tree Sun*) (*El Sol del*
 Membrillo) (Victor Erice)
High Heels (*Tacones leganos*) (Pedro Almodóvar)

1992
Jámon, Jámon (Bigas Luna)

1993
La Belle Époque (Fernando Trueba)

1995
The Flower of My Secret (*Le Flor de mi secreto*)
 (Pedro Almodóvar)

1996
Tierra (Julio Medem)

1997
Open Your Eyes (*Abre los ojos*) (Alexandro
 Aménabar)

1998
All about My Mother (Pedro Almodóvar)
Lovers of the Arctic Circle (*Les Amantes del*
 Circulo Polar) (Julio Medem)
Tango (Carlos Saura)

2000
Butterfly (*La Lengua de las Mariposas*) (Jorgé Luis
 Cuerda)
Goya in Bordeaux (*Goya en Burdeos*) (Carlos
 Saura)

2001
The Devil's Backbone (*El Espinazo del diablo*)
 (Guillermo del Joro)

Books on the Period

SCANDINAVIA

Bono, Francisco, and Maaret Koskinen, eds. *Film in Sweden.* Stockholm: Svenska Institutet, c. 1997.
Soila, Tytti, and Astrid Widding Soderbergh. *Nordic National Cinemas.* New York: Routledge, 1998.
Vincendeau, Ginette, ed. *The Encyclopaedia of European Cinema.* New York: Facts on File, 1995.

GERMANY

Davidson, John, E. *Deterritorializing the New German Cinema.* Minneapolis: University of Minnesota Press, 1999.
Fehenbach, Heide. *Cinema in Democratizing Germany: The Reconstruction of National Identity in the West, 1945–1962.* Chapel Hill: University of North Carolina Press, 1995.
Silberman, Marc. *German Cinema: Texts in Context.* Detroit: Wayne State University Press, 1995.
Vincendeau, Ginette, ed. *The Encyclopaedia of European Cinema.* New York: Facts on File, 1995.

SPAIN

De España, Rafael, ed. *Directory of Spanish and Portuguese Film-Makers and Films.* Westport, CT: Greenwood Press, 1994.
Deveny, Tomas G. *Cain on Screen: Contemporary Spanish Cinema.* Metuchen, NJ: Scarecrow Press, 1999.
Jordan, Barry, and Rikki Morgan-Tamosunas. *Contemporary Spanish Cinema.* New York: St. Martin's Press, 1998.
Kinder, Marsha. *Blood Cinema: The Reconstruction of National Identity in Spain.* Berkeley: University of California Press, 1993.
Kinder, Marsha, ed. *Refiguring Spain: Cinema/Media/Representation.* Durham, NC: Duke University Press, 1997.
Vincendeau, Ginette, ed. *The Encyclopedia of European Cinema.* New York: Facts on File, 1995.

12

Eastern European Cinema: Film Making for the State

★ ★ ★ ★

1954–

Throughout the first years of the new revolutionary government in the Soviet Union, in the 1920s, considerable freedom and experimentation existed in the arts as well as in other aspects of life. With Stalin's consolidation of power, permissiveness and variety gave way to enormous monolithic control. By the early 1930s "socialist realism" was the official and only state aesthetic. Prescribed content was locked into straightforward unambiguous narrative form. The seductive artistry of the Soviet silent films was replaced by the positive, wholesome, uplifting, and bland portrayal of communist heroes whose lives might have some implication for the revolution, or by the presentation of ideologically "correct" modern peasants, workers, and professional people. Socialist realist films were expected to feature groups rather than individuals. Their plots focused on collective endeavors that always ended triumphantly. *Chapayev* (1934) was the prototype.

With rare exceptions contemporary Soviet films aroused little interest in the West. Conversely, when Fellini's *8½* was shown at the first Moscow Film Festival, in 1963, it was subjected to violent criticism as a decadent bourgeois work full of "vagueness and morbidity." Only after considerable argument and insistence on the part of the invited Western judges was it awarded first prize. Neither it nor other of the new French and Italian films were shown generally in the Soviet Union.

In the communist countries the effect of a film on the audience's social and political attitudes was regarded as more important than the money it brought in. Given this concern, film content was carefully scrutinized and regulated to one degree or another by the state. Consequently film production in the Soviet bloc could be analyzed as a kind of barometer measuring political pressure operating within a society at any given time. A few months before the 1963 Moscow Festival, Communist Party Chairman Nikita Khrushchev delivered an important speech regarding his attitude toward the arts in the Soviet Union. He said, in part:

> We adhere to class positions in art and resolutely oppose peaceful coexistence between socialist and capitalist ideologies. Art belongs to the sphere of ideology. . . . Abstractionism and formalism, whose right to a place in socialist art is advocated by some of their champions, are forms of capitalist ideology.

Only near the end of the century did this position change. The breakup of the Soviet Union in 1989 occasioned a new challenge to film-industry practices to adapt to a market-driven economy.

In the eastern European countries within the Soviet sphere, the situation was not as consistently restrictive as within the Soviet Union itself. On the contrary, the idealistic aspects of communism melded with an apparently unquenchable nationalism, and exposure to new films from the West accounted for fertile periods of creativity in the cinema of Poland, Hungary, Czechoslovakia, and the former Yugoslavia.

Prior to World War II the film production of eastern European countries was negligible in quantity and quality. Few of their films found audiences beyond their own borders, and the small national populations could not be counted on to return the profits necessary to private enterprise. With the establishment of communist governments in those countries immediately after the war, there were new incentives for production, like those in the Soviet Union earlier, and a new base for economic support in the form of state funding. It took a few years for the ground to be prepared, but once the state film schools had begun turning out graduates, and film production, distribution, and exhibition had been stimulated and coordinated, the Eastern People's Republics were ready to take their places in the international spotlight.

These governments wanted films that would inform and indoctrinate, that would interpret events of the immediate past to give a sense of solidarity, and that would instill attitudes contributing to future progress. Replacing the subject of the Bolshevik Revolution, dealt with by the first Soviet film makers, was the resistance to Nazi Germany during World War II. The national traumas of the war were returned to again and again. Often the social and psychological insights they contained were clearly if indirectly applicable to the postwar societies. Communism was represented as the only force with the people's interest at heart capable of opposing fascism effectively and offering an alternative, more democratic way of life. At the same time, many of the young film-school graduates were critical of prevailing conditions. To avoid censorship, they often cloaked their views by adopting strategies of indirection and allegory. Some disaffected film makers went so far as to emigrate to the West; others drew on international financing to reach out to foreign audiences and gain leverage that would allow them to tackle unorthodox themes in their home countries.

As in Russia itself, the political situation under which eastern European directors worked changed radically after the fall of the communist regime. The 1990s saw a good deal of turmoil in the former eastern bloc countries, both politically and within the film industries themselves.

Poland

A Pole once remarked that his homeland was "a fine country, but badly located." Historically, Poland has been overrun by almost every nation in Europe; and during World War I, Poles were drafted into the Austrian, German, and Russian armies. Given their historical affinity with the West, Poles felt trapped and betrayed when, after the debacle of Naziism and World War II, the Western allies decided to barter Poland off to its traditional enemy, Russia.

In the realm of art, Poland has been deeply affected by western European traditions, especially those of France, a country with which the Poles feel a special bond. The nineteenth-century romantic movement in music found one of its foremost exponents in Polish composer Frédéric Chopin. Polish writers such as Adam Mickiewicz and Stanisław Wyspiański created mystical, dreamlike works that have been seen as forerunners to the surrealist art of the twentieth century. In more recent times this tradition has merged with that of absurdism, most importantly in the work of Stanisław Ignacy Witkiewicz (known as Witkacy) and Witold Gombrowicz. The most powerful force in the Polish contemporary theater is the director Jerzy Grotowsi, whose approach closely follows surealist and absurdist principles. Grotowski's minimalist or "poor" theater (as he calls it) draws on theories of myth and the unconscious, which were first sketched out by Witkacy but bear a close affinity with ideas espoused by the French surrealist Antonin Artaud.

Immediately following World War II the communist regime in Poland rigidly followed the Stalinist line, including tight controls on the arts. During those years only a few Polish films achieved distinction: Wanda Jakubowska's *The Last Stage* (1948), a tragic account of suffering and endurance in the notorious concentration camp at Auschwitz, and the films of veteran Aleksander Ford (*Border Street,* 1948, and *Five Boys from Barska Street,* 1953), about wartime and immediate postwar problems. These and other Polish productions of the time had in common as major or minor themes the inability of individuals to discover places for themselves in the national community. At the end of the 1940s the most famous and influential of the new national film schools of the eastern European republics was established at Łódź. As a result of its training and leadership a whole generation of young film makers emerged who would change the nature of Polish film and bring it to worldwide attention.

After Stalin died in 1953 a lessening of Soviet domination, a relaxation of internal controls, and a growing expression of national sentiment gradually began at the rate of two steps toward liberalization followed by one step back to repression. In September 1954, Jerzy Toeplitz, director of the Łódź Film Academy, publicly condemned the simplistic approach of socialist realism. Together with Jerzy Bossak, head of the school's documentary production unit, as well as others, Toeplitz produced a series of films that dealt with social and political problems in sober, naturalistic terms. Their efforts were enabled by a reorganization of the national film industry into independent production groups, which took place in the same year.

From the early days of cinema Poland has nurtured a tradition of documentary film making. The 1920s saw the formation of the Society of Devotees of the Artistic Film (START), which had much in common with the Italian neorealist movement. Carrying this tradition forward, Jerzy Bossak originated a "black series" of documentaries that were released from 1954 to 1956, presenting harsh political and social realities that undermined the sanguine optimism of socialist realism.

Another distinguished Polish film maker of this era, **Andrzej Munk,** began his career by making documentaries. His later fiction films played documentary-like methods against black humor and grotesquery. Munk's first feature, *Man on the Track* (1956), departed from the broad historical settings of other Polish films of the time for a close observation of an old locomotive engineer at odds with the new order. With *Eroica* (1958) Munk turned to the war. The first of its two complementary but separate parts, "A Scherzo in the Polish Manner," is set in the Warsaw uprising of September 1944. What is amazing about this episode of Munk's film is that it completely deprives the rebellion of sentimentality in a macabre and at times hilarious tale of a con man who becomes a hero in spite of himself. The second episode, "Lugubrious Obstinacy," takes place in a German prisoner-of-war camp for resistance fighters. The sham values of the Polish officers frequently compel them to join their captors in a bizarre partnership to maintain a false myth so as not to destroy their own morale. The "heroism" of the title is clearly intended ironically since Munk took a skeptical view of the efficacy of Polish valor.

In 1961 Munk was killed in an auto accident while working on his last film, *Passenger.* The material he had shot was pieced together and released posthumously in 1963. From the evidence it might well have been Munk's masterpiece. With a base in the present, *Passenger* reflects on the past of Auschwitz through recollections of a German woman who had been a guard there. Like the second part of *Eroica,* it explores the complex power relationships among the prisoners and their captors with considerable irony.

Eroica ★ Poland, 1958, Andrzej Munk.

After the Poznan uprising of 1956, during which Poles protested Soviet control over their country, censorship loosened. Polish directors began to express their predilections more openly, although by so doing they largely cut themselves off from their colleagues in the eastern European bloc. In 1957, at a conference of eastern European film makers held in Prague, the main spokesman condemned the new Polish films as "hostile to the socialist system." Thereafter, the productions of the Polish school were rarely shown in other communist countries.

Andrzej Wajda led a sudden upsurge of Polish production that reached a peak between 1955 and 1958. Wajda's *A Generation* (1954) began an unplanned trilogy completed with *Kanal* (1956) and *Ashes and Diamonds* (1958). Together the three films explored the conflicting loyalties, confused politics, bravery, and sacrifice that had characterized Poland's sad history during the years following German invasion and occupation to the first days of peace.

With their romantic attachment to the past, Poles have always encouraged historical films. Although Wajda's romanticism tends to soften and mythologize, his intellectual stance is often antiheroic, probing, and implicitly critical of the leadership and causes for which so many young men his age died. In *Ashes and Diamonds,* and in his and others' subsequent films, the actor Zbigniew Cybulski frequently portrayed a young man trying to sort out values and create a life amidst the shifting and unclear postwar conditions. He resembled an existentialist antihero more than a working-class hero of orthodox socialist

Ashes and Diamonds ★ Poland, 1958, Andrzej Wajda; Zbigniew Cybulski and Adam Pawlikowski.

realism. (He and his roles occasioned comparison with his contemporary, American actor James Dean.) Wajda's *Everything for Sale* (1968) was in part a tribute to Cybulski, who was killed accidentally in 1967 as he jumped from a train. It is also Wajda's reflection on his own relationship to life and art. With a film director protagonist and a film within a film, as in works of Fellini and Godard earlier and Truffaut later, it is one of the major examples of this reflexive tendency of modern cinema. In *Landscape After Battle* (1970) Wajda returned to the war, but now the underlying philosophy seemed truly existential and some of the action and imagery almost surreal.

Wajda's visual style is romantic, dramatic, and symbolic all at the same time. *Ashes and Diamonds,* for instance, contains a scene in which Cybulski lights glasses of vodka lined up along the bar in salute to dead comrades. In another scene, a discordant but still stately polonaise is danced in the early morning hours, a dreamlike souvenir of former patriotic sentiments now tired and faded. The film ends as the mortally wounded Cybulski staggers through sheets hanging on a clothesline to fall to his death on a garbage heap.

In 1980 the shipyard workers in Gdansk struck and wrested from the authorities concessions that created Solidarity, eastern Europe's first independent labor union. The national euphoria that followed was shortlived, but before and during it two of Wajda's films were released that expressed to Poland and the rest of the world the spirit of the times (and also the deeply embedded official distrust that might cause it to end). *Man of Marble* (1977) encompassed the events of 1970, when workers rebelling against food prices were shot down in Gdansk and elsewhere along the Baltic coast. Although it was temporarily suppressed and kept from export for several years, the film had such an impact it is said to have precipitated a government shake-up. *Man of Iron* (1981), its sequel, carried the story into the 1980 events. Its frankness about government control and manipulation of the media

Man of Iron ⋆ Poland, 1981, Andrzej Wajda; Krystyna Janda and Jerzy Radziwilowicz.

and its obvious commitment to Solidarity are breathtaking, particularly in light of subsequent developments. It was considered by many to be the most important and courageous film to have been made in eastern Europe up to that time. Both *Man of Marble* and *Man of Iron* were produced by the so-called X unit, which Wajda had formed in the early 1970s and subsequently used to nurture a new generation of Polish film makers, including Agnieszka Holland and Ryszard Bugajski.

In 1981 martial law was imposed, in part to counter the threat of Soviet invasion, and Solidarity was outlawed. Wajda left for France, where he made a number of films during the 1980s. Late in the decade, after Solidarity had been reinstated in 1986, he became a senator in the Polish parliament while continuing to pursue his film-making activies. Although the films he produced during the 1990s were often international coproductions, he continued to feature Polish themes. His examination of the effects of World War II on his homeland continued in such films as *Dr. Korczak* (1990), *The Ring with a Crowned Eagle* (1993) and *Holy Week* (1995). *Miss Nobody,* released in 1996, focuses on life in Poland after communism, and *Pan Tadusz,* in 1999, is based on a poem by Polish writer Adam Mickiewicz.

The abstract, oracular nature of absurdist and surrealist art makes it ideally suited to represent the humiliation and trauma the Poles have suffered in allegorical terms. Such a style can speak to the Polish experience in an acceptably apolitical manner while at the same time appealing to an international audience. Out of this aesthetic came introspective, expressionistic Polish films, the best known of which include Jerzy Kawalerowicz's *Mother Joan of the Angels* (1961), Walerian Borowszyk's *Story of Sin* (1974), Wojcieck Has's *Saragossa Manuscript* (1965), and Jerzy Skolomowski's trilogy *Identification Marks: None* (1964), *Walkover* (1965), and *Barrier* (1966). Typical of this approach was the work of **Roman Polanski,** whose films show the influence of both absurdist theater and surrealist painting. After his first feature, *Knife in the Water* (1962), a tight triangle of latent sexuality and violence with an absurdist sense of psychological inertia, Polanski moved on to England and the United States, where he directed a number of surrealist-influenced horror films, including *Repulsion* in 1965 and *Rosemary's Baby* in 1968. *Chinatown* (1974), a Hollywood production featuring Jack Nicholson and Faye Dunaway, has a warmer, more romantic edge than his other work and is generally regarded as his masterpiece. Following a scandal in his personal life in 1977, Polanski moved to Paris, where he continues to turn out the surrealist-tinged horror tales and thrillers for which he has become famous, including *Bitter Moon* (1992), *Death and the Maiden* (1995), and *The Ninth Gate* (1999). His frequent collaborator is French scriptwriter Gerard Brach.

In 1968 a violent repression of students and intelligentsia took place in Poland. The film-production groups were once again reorganized and controls on film content became tighter. Among the directors working in Poland in the 1970s it was **Krzysztof Zanussi** whose films, along with the continuing work of Wajda (*Promised Land,* 1974, *Without Anesthetic,* 1979), received the most attention abroad. Zanussi stuck to contemporary themes, often dealing with moral and existential issues of corruption, careerism, and exploitation. *Family Life* (1970), *Illumination* (1973), *Camouflage* (1976), and *The Contract* (1981) are particularly noteworthy. In *The Contract* the gathering of diverse people at a wedding party becomes a microcosm of Polish intellectual life. The narrative wanders through this well-heeled throng of bizarre characters and relationships, bouncing one person off another. Its scathing indictment of Poland's privileged classes is presented through

The Contract ★ Poland, 1981, Krzysztof Zanussi.

wild and anarchic humor. In the 1980s and 1990s Zanussi, like others, turned to international coproductions in films such as *Year of the Quiet Sun* (1985) and *The Silent Touch* (1990), the latter starring the Swedish actor Max von Sydow. However, his base remained in Poland, and he actively participated in the restructuring of the Polish motion-picture industry that took place after 1989, heading up the Tor film unit during the 1990s.

Joining Wajda and Zanussi was a younger generation whose films were labeled the "cinema of moral concern." **Agnieska Holland** is among these. In addition to scripting for others she has directed her own scripts, including films made outside Poland. *Europa, Europa* (1991), a French-German coproduction based on a true story of a German Jew who takes on the identity of a Nazi during World War II, was a considerable international success. *Olivier Olivier* (France, 1991), also said to be based on an actual person and events, deals with the disappearance of a son and his subsequent replacement by an impostor who causes incestual sexual tensions and confusions within the family. Holland followed this with another intimate family drama, *The Secret Garden* (U.S., 1993), from the 1911 children's classic by Frances Hodgson Burnett. An $18 million production of Francis Ford Coppola's Zoetrope Studio for Warner Bros., it differs from her earlier films in the elegance of its *mise-en-scène*. In 1997, she directed another American-produced literary adaptation, *Washington Square* (1997), based on a novel by Henry James.

Europa, Europa ★ France-Germany, 1991, Agnieska Holland; Marco Hofschneider.

The most important, original, and highly respected member of the younger Polish generation identified with the cinema of moral concern is **Krzysztof Kieślowski,** who has been called "the most truly European director." His fiction features at first continued the realist, aggressive approach of his documentary shorts. *The Calm Before the Storm* (1976) was about then current Polish working conditions; *Camera Buff* (1979) revealed a reportedly quite accurate picture of the way the film-making system functioned in Poland. Following the 1981 crackdown Kieślowski's *No End* (1984) was much admired. It deals with the private tragedies and public conflicts under martial law as seen through the eyes of a widow whose husband had been a defense lawyer for the accused. Eventually she decides to commit suicide, not able to bear her personal loss.

No End was Kieślowski's first film coscripted with Kryzysztof Piesiewicz. Subsequently the two created a series of ten films for Polish television based on the Ten Commandments (*Decalogue*). All are set in a bleak post-war Warsaw high-rise apartment complex. Featuring coldly lit, starkly simple compositions, the films ponder complicated ethical and spiritual dilemmas as we witness characters becoming entangled in unfamiliar, stressful situations. Two of these productions, *A Short Film about Killing* (Thou shalt not kill) and *A Short Film about Love* (Thou shalt not commit adultery) were released as theatrical features in 1988. The former won a Special Jury Prize at Cannes and an Oscar for best foreign feature. Its story focuses on a young boy who murders someone for no apparent reason and the moral quandary this situation creates for the lawyer who must defend him.

After completing this magisterial work, Kieślowski moved his base of operations to France, as so many other Polish film makers have done. There he produced a series of stylish, metaphysically tinged character studies, including *The Double Life of Veronique* (1991) and a trilogy based on the colors of the French flag (*Three Colors: Blue,* 1993; *Three Colors: White,* 1993; and *Three Colors: Red,* 1994). In *The Double Life of Veronique,* he and cowriter Piesiewicz imagine two girls—one a Polish Veronika, the other a French Veronique—born on the same day, who are alike in all respects, including lovely singing voices and potentially fatal heart conditions. The film moves back and forth between them in their separate countries as one gives up her boyfriend to pursue her singing career and dies, while the other abandons singing, engages in a love affair, and lives.

Kieślowski died in 1996. The evolution of his preoccupations during the course of his relatively brief career evolved from a resolute social realism focused on political and societal issues to an increasing concern with moral choices being made by ordinary people well outside the public issues of their time and finally to the more supernaturally inflected preoccupations evidenced in his last French productions. (Someone remarked that Kieślowski's films of the past decade represent an "agnostic mysticism.") In 1998 his producer, Martin Karmitz, initiated the *Prix Kieślowski,* which is awarded annually to the winner of an international competition for young film makers.

In response to the forces of free enterprise prevailing in the 1990s, Polish cinema became more commercialized, with American movies dominating the marketplace. Native-

A Short Film about Killing ★ Poland, 1988, Krzysztof Kieślowski; Miroslaw Baka, on the left.

Schindler's List ★ United States, 1993, Steven Spielberg; Liam Neeson and Ben Kingsley.

born film makers scrambled to patch together financing packages from advertising, television, international funding entites, and a new Ministry of Film that granted monies on a matching basis. As the country's economy continued to struggle toward stability, the number of movie houses dropped, from twenty-five hundred in the 1970s to nine hundred in 1992. In the 1990s, however, Polish cinema received welcomed international recognition when Hollywood's Steven Spielberg chose to shoot his prestigious production *Schindler's List* in Poland in 1993, resulting in Academy Awards for the film's Polish cinematographer Janusz Kamiński and Polish art director Allan Starski.

Hungary

In 1956 there were uprisings in Poland and Hungary. Both occurred in populations who, having been given a small taste of increased liberty and independence, wanted more. In the case of Poland, concessions were made to "the Polish road to socialism." Soviet troops were withdrawn, a new era of greater freedom and nationalism began, and the Polish film flourished. As for Hungary, the Soviet army quashed the rebellion; hundreds were killed, nearly 200,000 fled the country, and the national film flowering just beginning was temporarily ended.

Most prominent among Hungarian directors at work at the time was Zoltán Fábri. His *Merry-Go-Round* (1955) and *Professor Hannibal* (1956), made just before the uprising, moved well outside the confines of prevailing socialist realism. The first dealt with contemporary youth trying to find their way to new attitudes in a changed society. Its humor and lyricism were especially original. The second went even further, taking as target for social satire the question of historical revisionism, a sensitive subject in communist countries.

It wasn't until about 1963 or 1964 that a new era began with the reorganization of the film industry and of the Academy of Film and Dramatic Art. The first works of a younger generation appeared during those same years, including films by András Kovács (it was the later *Cold Days,* 1966, that gained him international attention), István Gaál (*The Falcons,* 1970, his fourth and best-known feature), and István Szabó (whose *25 Fireman's Street,* 1974, presented a brilliant kaleidoscope of the Hungarian historical experience).

Two major factors were evident among the twenty to twenty-five Hungarian films produced each year. One was their emphasis on life in the villages rather than life in the big city. The other was their strong ties to Hungarian literature. For example, Károly Makk's *Love* (1970), which won a batch of international prizes, was an adaptation of a famous novel by Tibor Déry. A second successful example from this period, *Sinbad* (1971), directed by Zoltán Husárik, was based on novels by one of the greatest Hungarian writers of the twentieth century.

A conspicuous exception to this literary connection was **Miklós Jancsó.** It was Jancsó who—beginning with his third feature, *My Way Home* (1964)—carried Hungary's banner most prominently out into the world. Dominated by an obsessive subjective vision and intricate formal design that make it unique within eastern European cinema, his work is coherent and consistent almost to a fault. The strange world of his films has no exact counterpart anywhere, for that matter; reviewers habitually referred to it as "Jancsó country." Among his films are: *Cantata* (1963), *The Round-Up* (1965), *The Red and the White* (1967), *Silence and Cry* (1968), *The Confrontation* (1969), *Winter Wind* (1969), *Agnus Dei* (1971), *Red Psalm* (1972), and *Hungarian Rhapsody* (1978). All are part of a distinctively Hungarian subgenre that Jancsó initiated, the historical parable, which treats past events in symbolic form.

The Red and the White, seen most widely, is typical. Like so many of Jancsó's films, it takes place on a vast windswept plain. The historical setting is the civil war following the Russian Revolution. Armies battle, but the causes seem arbitrary and unavailing in relation to universal and casual inhumanity. Sides cannot be told apart once uniforms are removed; nationalities are not distinguishable except when characters speak. At one moment the Whites are winning, at the next the Reds. Everyone is subject to pursuit, capture, humiliation, and execution.

Applied to this disturbing narrative material, and informing and affecting its meaning profoundly, is an equally extraordinary visual style. Shot in wide-screen black-and-white, the takes are long in duration. Camera movement is almost continuous and exceptionally varied: pans, tilts, dollies, tracking, and helicopter shots all combined. In addition to the insistently moving camera, there is constantly shifting and complex movement within the frame—mainly of men and horses. The movement is unusually frantic, with much running and galloping, and its meaning tacitly ironic. These humans behave instinctively, like other animals; their capacity for reason and emotion merely causes unnatural self-destruction. All

The Red and the White ★ Hungary, 1967, Miklós Jancsó.

of the frenzied activity leads only to death in this land of the still. The highly stylized and decorative visual treatment applied to ugly human actions formalizes and distances them from us—they form part of a *danse macabre.* The choreographic quality plus the repetition of event, as each side achieves temporary victory or suffers more certain defeat, turns the action into arcane ritual.

In the 1980s and 1990s Jancsó worked mostly in theater and television (including a nine-hour TV series entitled *Faustus Faustus Faustus,* which covers Hungarian political history from its hero's birth in 1927 to his death in 1973). Meanwhile, the films of István Szabó and Márta Mészáros attracted considerable attention outside Hungary. **István Szabó**'s hugely successful *Mephisto* (1981) is concerned with an opportunistic actor in Hitler's Germany who shifts his personal allegiances (including wife and mistresses) and adjusts his principles to conform to the requirements placed on an artist in a totalitarian state. His *Colonel Redl* (1985), with the same star, Klaus-Maria Brandauer, covers similar thematic ground in the earlier Austro-Hungarian Empire.

Meeting Venus (1990) was a British production (David Puttnam producer) about a Hungarian orchestra leader invited to conduct a pan-European performance of *Tannhäuser* in Paris to be broadcast to twenty-seven countries via satellite. The romantic entanglements and bureaucratic travails that nearly scuttle the production seem accurately, and certainly acidly, observed. His most recent film at time of writing, *Sweet Emma, Dear Böbe* (1992), evidently resembles *Meeting Venus* in its portrayal of a dysfunctional social system mired in bureaucracy and petty feuds, and a clandestine love affair with no future. During the 1990s he continued to produce internationally financed, accessible films, including *Sunshine* (1999) with Ralph Fiennes and *Taking Sides* (2001) with Harvey Keitel.

Mephisto ✶ Hungary, 1981, István Szabó; Klaus Maria Brandauer.

The films of **Márta Mészáros** deal resolutely with the problems of women in contemporary Hungary. The life presented is bleak; the view of it unsparing. Her first film, *The Girl,* in 1968, was followed by *Riddance* in 1973. Her most well-known production, *Adoption,* was released in 1975 and won the Golden Bear at the Berlin Film Festival. In the 1980s Mészáros turned to a trilogy of autobiographical works, *Diary for My Children* (1984), *Diary for My Loves* (1987), and *Diary for My Mother and Father* (1990), in which she chronicles the effect Stalinist repression has had on her personal relationships.

Despite the economic confusion of the 1990s, Hungarian film making has remained relatively healthy. More than a dozen first films were made in the early 1990s, and directors such as Béla Tarr (*Satantango,* 1994) attracted a good deal of international attention. Among the socialist states, which generally demanded of their film makers positive and constructive service in the building of new societies, Hungary has consistently allowed surprisingly personal and critical examinations of the shared cultural experience. Under capitalism, it continues to do so.

Czechoslovakia

In Czechoslovakia the stirrings of 1956 were quietly quelled by the indigenous communist hierarchy so that the Czechs neither gained additional freedom and independence, as did the Poles, nor were subjected to Soviet invasion, as were the Hungarians. It wasn't really until the 1960s that the political and cultural climate warmed sufficiently for the Czechs to expand freely into their own equivalent to the New Wave. Unlike the melancholy Poles or

The Girl ★ Hungary, 1968, Márta Mészáros; Teri Horvath and Zsuzsa Pálos

the historically minded Hungarians, the Czechs created a cinema of sharply observed social comedy.

In 1963 a generation of graduates of the national film academy in Prague (FAMU), which included Miloš Forman and Věra Chytilová, made their feature debuts. Following these in the "Prague spring" were other features by new young film makers: Miloš Forman's *Black Peter* (1964) and *Loves of a Blonde* (1965), Jan Němec's *Diamonds of the Night* (1964), and Věra Chytilová's *Daisies* (1966). But the big international success was *The Shop on Main Street* (1965), by two veterans, Ján Kadár and Elmar Klos. The first Czech film to win an Academy Award, it is made up of known ingredients skillfully and movingly blended. Set in a small town under German occupation it exposed the evils of fascist mentality and its most heinous manifestation in anti-Semitism and genocide. *Shop on Main Street* treats these large themes on an intimate scale. The horrors inflicted on inconceivable millions are expressed through events occurring in the lives of a simple carpenter, his greedy wife and fascist brother-in-law, and an ancient Jewish shopkeeper. Their paradoxical situation, as the carpenter tries to save the old lady from extermination, becomes credible through the fully rounded performances. Warmly and delicately observed detail and humor mingled with pathos characterize script and direction. Satisfying within its own terms, *The Shop on Main Street* was more conventional than the Czech films that would follow.

One of the leaders of a truly new Czech cinema was Miloš Forman, whose widely seen *Loves of a Blonde* and *The Firemen's Ball* (1967) might be compared to Italian Ermanno Olmi's early work. Like *Il Posto, Loves of a Blonde* is about a young person experiencing the impersonality and loneliness of the industrial world in a first job away from home. Forman uses a style similar to *cinéma vérité* and draws the same remarkable

The Shop on Main Street ★ Czechoslovakia, 1965, Ján Kadár and Elmar Klos; Ida Kamińska and Jozef Króner.

performances from casts surely composed largely of nonprofessionals. In *The Firemen's Ball,* Forman's observation of average people and everyday situations is more humorous and satiric than Olmi's. The cross-purposes, confusions, and inarticulateness of the petit-bourgeois characters in their relationships with each other, the tensions and misunderstandings between generations, and the hopeless incompetence and self-inflated importance of bureaucracy are all wryly commented on in a totally disarming way. Despite its aura of unassuming charm, it was widely viewed in Czechoslovakia at the time of its release as a comment on the communist system and was banned there from 1973 to 1989.

Other Czech film makers with similarly comic sensibilities who came to promience during this era were Ivan Passer and Jiří Menzel. Passer, who coscripted *The Fireman's Ball,* conceived and directed *Intimate Lighting* (1966) in much the same warmly humorous manner. In it he observes the reunion in a provincial Czech town of two old musician friends, one with a wife and family, the other with a mistress. Of Jiří Menzel's films, the best known in the West is *Closely Watched Trains* (1966). (It, too, won an Academy Award.) Like Forman and Passer, Menzel observes with careful attention and detached amusement the actions of "the little people." Although set in World War II and including partisan sabotage of the German-controlled railway, instead of epic events, *Closely Watched Trains* concentrates on the coming of age of a shy and ineffectual young station attendant and the peculiar sexual goings-on around him in the isolated post.

The Firemen's Ball ☆
Czechoslovakia, 1967,
Miloš Forman.

A Czech New Wave director of a different stripe was **Jan Němec.** Němec makes one think of the Poles, especially of Jerzy Skolimowski. *Report on the Party and the Guests* (1966) carries the surrealist impulses of Skolimowski's *Barrier* even further. In fact, it is a sort of political allegory clothed in trappings of the avant garde; at times it looks like Resnais's *Last Year at Marienbad* with overtones of Kafka. The party takes place at formally set tables beside a lake in a lonely wood. The characters move and behave as if they are part of some sort of game with arcane rules, frenetic endeavor being followed by somnambulistic languor. The threat of violence and punishment hangs over the whole. Promptly banned after completion, it was defiantly awarded the Czech Critics Prize a year later. Němec was forcibly exiled in 1974.

The Czechs have long fostered a proud tradition of world-class animation, the leading figures of which are Jiří Trnka (*The Emperor's Nightingale,* 1948, and *Old Czech Legends,* 1953), Karel Zeman (*A Journey to Primeval Times,* 1955, and *An Invention for Destruction,* 1958), and Jan Švankmajer (*Dimensions of Dialogue,* 1982, and *Alice,* 1987). The skills of these and other Czech animators were honed in one of the state-supported animation studios set up throughout eastern Europe after World War II. Profoundly influenced by surrealism, they produced short and feature-length fantasies intended for both adults and children. Like their colleagues in the animation industries of other eastern bloc nations, many left the country during times of repression and found ready employment in Hollywood.

Even if unenthusiastic and vacillating, an official liberalization had clearly occurred within Czechoslovakia that permitted statements from film artists who were either openly or covertly critical of the society. The Czechs, like the Poles and Hungarians before them, responded by striving for still more freedom from Communist Party conformity and for

Closely Watched Trains ⋆ Czechoslovakia, 1966, Jiří Menzel; Václav Neckář and Jitka Bendová.

self-identification as Czechoslovaks. The years 1966 to 1968 saw the greatest ferment. Then, in the summer of 1968, an uprising was crushed by Soviet tanks, and Czechoslovakia once again became an occupied country for a time. As with the Hungarians earlier, many who weren't killed, imprisoned, or forced underground fled. Some came to the United States and continued to work here—for example, Ján Kadár (*Lies My Father Told Me*, 1975), Miloš Forman (*One Flew Over the Cuckoo's Nest*, 1975; *Hair*, 1979; *Ragtime*, 1981; *Amadeus*, 1984; *Valmont*, 1989; *The People Versus Larry Flynt*, 1996; and *The Man in the Moon*, 1999), and Ivan Passer (*Cutter's Way*, 1981).

In 1976–1977 there seems to have been a mild "thaw" and some of the leading figures returned to the studios after an absence of five or six years. Jiří Menzel made *Seclusion Near a Forest* and Věra Chytilová made *The Apple Game* (both in 1977). Following a reorganization of the studios in 1983, films of somewhat greater boldness began to appear.

In 1993, the country divided itself into its two ethnic components: Czech and Slovak. Despite the country's political and economic upheaval, however, Czech films again began attracting international acclaim during the latter part of the decade, with productions such as Jan Sverák's *Kolya* and Petr Zelenka's *Buttoners* in 1997, and Sasa Gedeon's *Return of the Idiot* in 1999. About twenty Czech and Slovak films were produced every year during the 1990s, and between 1993 and the turn of the century thirty first films by

Report on the Party and the Guests ★ Czechoslovakia, 1966, Jan Němec.

new Czech and Slovak directors were released, most of these produced by graduates of the famed FAMU film-making school. These productions build on the tradition of the Czech "Golden Age" cinema of the 1960s by focusing on intimate portraits of ordinary people, frequently leavened with gentle humor. Some critics have hailed these developments as heralding a new Czech New Wave, a claim that will be tested in the new century.

Yugoslavia

Among the eastern European countries Yugoslavia was special in that its communism was resolutely national and its economy was a compromise between socialist and capitalist. In 1948 it removed itself from the Soviet orbit and maintained its independence in spite of every effort short of invasion to make it return to the fold. Stalin took out his resentment on the other "satellite" nations in severe repressive measures designed to make certain they did not follow the Yugoslav example. After Stalin's death the new Soviet leaders journeyed to Belgrade to offer public apologies for past Soviet policies. From that time on, Yugoslavia's territorial integrity, as the phrase goes, was more assured.

Although the Yugoslavs, following earlier Czech example, developed an animation industry in Zagreb that remained among the most imaginative if not most prolific in the world, its live-action features plodded along the path of socialist realism as doggedly as if still being guided by the Soviets. It wasn't until the late 1960s that there appeared a new generation of feature film makers, including Dušan Makavejev, Aleksander Petrović, Živajin Pavlović, and a cluster of their innovative films (such as *Man Is Not a Bird,* 1965; *I Even Met Happy Gypsies,* 1967; and *When I Was Dead and White,* 1967). The group was labeled the Yugoslav Black Wave for the corrosive, iconoclastic satires they mounted against the Communist system. Their films had no heroes; instead they used kaleidoscopic techniques to unmask bureaucratic corruption and hypocrisy.

Dušan Makavejev burst on the scene like some sort of Slavic bombshell. His early works—*Love Affair or The Case of the Missing Switchboard Operator* (1967), *Innocence Unprotected* (1968), *WR: Mysteries of the Organism* (1971), and *Sweet Movie* (1974)— were seen widely abroad. His experimental bent went even beyond that of the Pole Skolimowski or the Czech Němec. Makavejev's work makes one think of the most stylistically mixed of Godard's features. Or perhaps a better comparison would be with the Swedish Vilgot Sjöman's *I Am Curious* (1967), with its similar combination of sex and politics, fantasy and fact, fiction and newsreel.

In subject matter *Innocence Unprotected* is quite different from Makavejev's other films; in technique it has aspects in common. An affectionate recall of the first Serbian talkie, made in 1942 during the German occupation, it is subtitled "A New Edition of a Good Old Film." Interspersed with the original are interviews with its surviving creators, who talk about its production, and newsreels of military and political events of that time. *Love Affair, WR,* and *Sweet Movie,* on the other hand, all elaborate on the relationship between sexuality and the social-political restraints and expectations faced by the individual. Wildly funny, bawdy (if not obscene), and irreverent, jumbled, and complex, they are finally impossible to describe, even thematically. Of the three, *Love Affair* is the most

WR: Mysteries of the Organism ★ Yugoslavia, 1971, Dušan Makavejev; Vica Vidovic, Jagoder Kaloper, and Milena Dravic.

coherent, with two central characters and a slender thread of plot spun out in flashes forward as well as back, preceded by a lecture on sex and interrupted by another on murder.
WR includes an informal television-style "profile" of psychologist Wilhelm Reich, replete
with interviews of people who knew him, a fragmented account of two zany sexually
preoccupied young women and their encounters with men, satirical political references,
phallic jokes about Stalin, and other odds and ends including a demonstration by a
markedly strange lady making a cast of a penis. Makavejev encapsulated the film's message in an interview published in *Film Quarterly:* "The main thing in sexual repression or
sexual freedom is actually the political content of human personal freedom," he stated.

After this extraordinarily creative period, Makavejev's work began to fall off as he
began to work abroad. *Sweet Movie,* made partly in the United States, is a dark mixture of
diverse elements, scatology added to sexuality and politics. It threw haymaker punches at
both the capitalist and communist mythologies, in about equal proportion, and provoked
enraged responses from all sides. *Montenegro* (1981), shot in Sweden, was much more
straightforward in narrative form but its content reiterated Makavejev's fascination (obsession?) with sexual homicidal mania. His *The Coca-Cola Kid* (1985) is about an American representative of the title company in Australia.

A successor Yugoslavian star director is **Emir Kusturica,** whose first film, *Do You
Remember Dolly Bell?* (1981), won a Golden Lion at Venice. His next project, *When Father
Was Away on Business* (1985), won the Palme d'Or at Cannes and has been seen widely

When Father Was Away on Business ★ Yugoslavia, 1985, Emir Kusturica.

abroad. It is a Bosnian comic drama set in Sarajevo in 1950. Father isn't really away on business but in a political prison camp during the period following the momentous break with the Soviet Union. He has been accused of "Stalinist tendencies." The film examines the family under the pressures that stem from the nation at a crossroads. The warmth and understated humor of its observation of individuals and society are in a manner reminiscent of the Czechs. And, in fact, Kusturica, and other Yugoslav directors and cinematographers of his generation, attended the FAMU school in Prague.

Kusterica is the formost exponent of what has come to be known as the gypsy genre of films. The gypsies (or Romanys) are found all over eastern Europe and are identified with a distinctive cultural style that is interpreted by these movies in terms of celebratory feasting, passionate love affairs, a streetwise mentality, and a colorful nomadic lifestyle. The protagonists of such stories are frequently worldly young people. Although the films sometimes exoticize and sentimentalize the Romany, they may also view the group's situation as a prototype of the region's political woes. As a universally oppressed ethnic minority, the gypsies provide a means of examining the phenomenon of ethnic hatred, which has inflamed such destructive passions throughout the eastern European world. Of all the European nations, Yugoslavia has taken up this genre most energetically, the foremost cinematic examples being Alexander Petrović's picaresque *I Even Met Happy Gypsies* (1967) and Slobodan Sijan's wildly popular *Who's Singing Over There?* (1980), which chronicles the adventures of two gypsy musicians during the Second World War. Kusterica's *A Time of the Gypsies* (1990) is crafted as a folktale about a homely and unlucky gypsy lad who sets out to steal enough money to marry the girl he desires. Kusturica returned to the topic of the Romany in 1998 with *Black Cat, White Cat,* a high-spirited fantasy about a family of gypsy gangsters, featuring Fellini-esque imagery and earthy humor.

The peaceful breakup of Czechoslovakia into two states was preceded by the dissolution of Yugoslavia into separate republics beginning in 1990, which devolved into a bloody civil war among the three main ethnic/religious factions: Serbs, Croats, and Muslims. In this politically charged atmosphere, Kusturica returned to the topic of Yugoslavian history in his 1995 film *Underground,* which spans the period from 1941 to the early 1990s. Despite being honored with the Palme d'Or at the Cannes Film Festival, this production proved controversial, and was seen by some as Serbian propaganda. As a result of the criticism he received, Kusterica withdrew from movie making in 1996. However, his retirement proved to be shortlived and he was soon back at work, joining others in the newly constituted nations of his homeland in crafting a cultural agenda that could help to define them afresh.

The Soviet Union and After

In the dominant power of the eastern bloc, trends of reform began in 1985 at the 27th Congress of the Communist Party that eventually would lead to the breaking up of the Soviet Union. At that time Mikhail Gorbachev became First Secretary, and *glasnost* (openness) and *perestroika* (restructuring) became key terms in his program. By 1986, when Gorbachev announced his commitment to "frank debate," films that had been "shelved," going back as far as 1966, were reexamined and many of them released. One of the most shelved of contemporary Soviet film makers, Elem Klimov, became one of the major figures involved in bringing revision, reassessment, and new latitude into the cinema. Klimov's films include *Rasputin* (1975, released in the United States in 1986), *Come and See* (1985, released in the United States in 1987), and *Farewell* (1983, released in the United States in 1987). Following a tense and significant election, Klimov became First Secretary of the Union of Soviet Filmmakers in 1986.

Klimov's wife, Larisa Sheptiko, who met an untimely death in an automobile accident in 1979, was also rediscovered after *glasnost. The Ascent* (1976), which won the Golden Bear at Berlin, chronicles the fate of a group of Soviets during the Second World War with strong spiritual overtones. Skeptiko's next project, *Farewell* (1983, released in the United States in 1987), deals with a Siberian village that is destroyed by a flood and is based on a story by Valentin Rasputin. It was completed by Klimov after her death.

Another exceptional find in the reexamination was *The Commissar* (completed in 1967, released in 1987), directed by Alexander Askoldov. Set in the Ukraine during the Civil War that followed the Revolution, *The Commissar* is about an iron-willed Russian woman who waits out her pregnancy amidst a Jewish family whose house has been requisitioned. Their loving gentleness contrasts with her fierce revolutionary zeal. The compassionate treatment of Jews, including a surrealist vision of the Holocaust to come, is most likely the reason it was suppressed. Askoldov's continuing efforts to have the film released earned him official disfavor. He was branded "professionally incompetent" and not allowed to make another film.

Two films made during the period of *glasnost* were especially popular at home and were exported abroad. Both are about young people and contemporary life in the Soviet Union. *Is It Easy to be Young?* (1987), a documentary, offers a broad survey showing the

The Commissar ★ Soviet Union, 1967/1987, Alexander Askoldov; Raisa Nedashkovskaya, Nonna Mordyukova, and Rolan Bykov.

complex and problematic nature of the choices being faced by the young generation. *Little Vera* (1988), although fiction, is both sociological and satiric in its depiction of a working-class family in the midst of a breakdown of moral norms under the pressures of consumerism and the influence of pop culture in the West.

One of the most uniquely talented of contemporary Soviet film makers resumed his career after fifteen years of enforced idleness. **Sergei Paradjanov** is known abroad for his *Shadows of Our Forgotten Ancestors* (1964) and *The Color of Pomegranates* (1969). *Shadows* is an extraordinary and unique epic blend of fact, fiction, and poetry in celebration of peasant life, lore, and mythology in a remote part of the Ukraine. Loose and elliptical in construction, "formalistic" and at the same time sensual, it is a film that would seem to stand quite outside the requirements of a modern socialist state, as did Dovzhenko's *Earth* before it. *The Color of Pomegranates* is about Sayat Nova, an eighteenth-century Armenian poet monk who suffers in an alien society. It was shelved after completion and reedited by others, over the film maker's protest, before release in 1973. Paradjanov's subsequent projects were either not accepted for production or not permitted to be completed. In 1974 he was convicted of homosexuality (a criminal offense in the Soviet Union), illegal currency dealings, and "incitement to suicide," and sentenced to six years of hard labor. Although tried as a citizen and not as an artist, considerable suspicion was expressed that his real crime may have been his ebullient and rebellious spirit and the individualistic and iconoclastic nature of his finest and most important films.

Shadows of Our Forgotten Ancestors ★ Soviet Union, 1964, Sergei Paradjanov; Ivan Nikolaichuk, in tub.

By 1983 Paradjanov was out of prison and working on *The Legend of the Suram Fortress* (1985). Based on Georgian sources, it apparently contains the sort of folk elements and pagan traditions mixed with Christianity and nationalism, heroism and sacrifice and breathtaking imagery, as did his earlier films. He died of cancer in 1990.

Another contemporary Soviet film maker, to whom Paradjanov's last film, *Ashik Kerib* (1988), was dedicated, managed to escape the dictates of socialist realism and express a strong personal vision through structures and styles more nearly resembling those of contemporary film makers in western Europe. **Andrei Tarkovsky**'s *Ivan's Childhood* (1962), *Andrei Rublev* (1966), and *Solaris* (1972) all won prizes at festivals abroad. *Ivan's Childhood,* with its strong and clear humanist message carrying along its unusual display of technical virtuosity, was extremely popular at home as well. *Andrei Rublev,* however, a more involuted and complex film about a monk icon painter who lived at the turn of the fifteenth century, was held up for several years and then released in a cut version. It seems to bear certain resemblances to Paradjanov's *The Color of Pomegranates,* and to have suffered a somewhat similar fate. Evidently it was suspect because of its religious themes, unorthodox view of history, and scenes of brutality. *Solaris,* a science-fiction film, evoked comparisons with Stanley Kubrick's *2001,* although Tarkovsky eschewed spectacular technology and psychedelic fantasy in favor of the philosophical implications of his vision of the future and its effects on human lives. *The Mirror,* released in a very limited way in the Soviet Union in 1974 and not until nearly a decade later in the United States, is autobiographical as well as experimental, mingling dream and reality, childhood memories with an ongoing marriage.

Tarkovsky's next two films were made in Italy. In *Stalker* (1979) he returned to science fiction. It is a grim odyssey of two Russian intellectuals led by the title character into "the Zone," a devastated postapocalyptic wasteland sealed off by the authorities. *Nostalgia* (1983), a brooding account of a journey through Italy by a Russian scholar, was made for European television. Its main theme seems to be the impossibility of transcultural understanding.

In 1984 Tarkovsky sought political asylum in the West. His last film, *The Sacrifice* (1986), was made in Sweden with a mostly Swedish crew, including Sven Nykvist, Bergman's cinematographer. Erland Josephson, from Bergman's repertory company, is the principal actor (as he is in *Nostalgia*). Like Bergman, Tarkovsky tends toward the poetic and the mystical, makes much use of philosophical dialogues, and creates his visual style by relying on prolonged takes with a slowly moving camera. There are similarities other than those just suggested, and the two film makers are known to have admired each other's films.

In *The Sacrifice* a woefully unhappy collection of humans on an isolated estate, most of them family members, torture themselves and each other psychologically. A nuclear war may break out or may be imagined; it may be countered by religious belief or by supernatural forces, if it ever happened. As the sacrifice promised to God for release from his fear of dying, the father burns down the house and is taken away by medical attendants. Although some aspects of the film parallel *Shame* and *The Seventh Seal,* it is slower than Bergman's films, more attuned to the visual—remarkably so. Tarkovsky seems to be trying to transcend the limitations of plot, character, and dialogue to arrive at pure feeling states; images that don't advance narrative meaning but intensify the desperate dark despair are held relentlessly and returned to repeatedly. It is a strange and troubling metaphysical inquiry.

Tarkovsky died in Paris in 1986. His slender body of work may well be the most important and lasting by a Russian film maker since that of the Soviet artists of the 1920s. It

The Sacrifice ★ Soviet Union, 1986, Andrei Tarkovsky; Allan Edwall and Erland Josephson, on right.

is markedly different from theirs and from the socialist realism that followed, in subject matter and themes particularly—intensely personal and private rather than public and social. The individual preoccupied Tarkovsky more than the society; the society is seen only through individuals. So it is not to Eisenstein, Pudovkin, or Dovzhenko that we would compare Tarkovsky; rather, the comparison is to Bergman and other western European auteurs, and in many respects his creation seems unique.

But the country from which Tarkovsky emigrated has itself changed more radically than could have been imagined at the time of his death. Following an attempted coup in 1991 aimed at unseating Gorbachev and reversing the changes he had begun, the Soviet Union itself has ceased to exist, being replaced by twelve autonomous republics, and the planned economy of communism has been succeeded by attempts toward achieving the market economy of capitalism.

Given the near anarchy that has characterized the political and economic life of the country during the 1990s, it is little short of miraculous that film making has continued in Russia. Although the number of motion pictures produced dropped from three hundred in 1990 to about one-tenth this number by the mid-1990s, that level of production has held steady since then. In the absence of the old state-controlled monolithic film industry, European coproduction arrangements have been sought, film festivals and prizes have been established, and television financing and exhibition have been welcomed. In 1996 a new state funding organization, Roskomkino, was founded. In 1997, Nikita Mikhalkov, the acclaimed director of films such as *Burnt by the Sun* (1994), was elected chair of the Union

Prisoner of the Mountains ★ Russia, 1996, Sergei Bodrov; Oleg Men'shikov, on left.

of Film Makers of the Russian Federation and initiated sweeping reforms in the movie industry, from the building and refurbishing of theaters to taxes on videos and sales to television to subsidize new production. Late in the 1990s, films such as Sergei Bodrov's *Prisoner of the Mountains* (1996) and Alexander Sokurov's *Mother and Son* (1997) garnered honors around the world.

Over the past four decades the films of Poland, Hungary, Czechoslovakia, Yugoslavia, and Russia have had intermittent periods in which critical self-examination, doubt, and even despair have appeared. Often the questioning, criticism, and satire seemed remarkably pointed and frank to Westerners whose biases and ignorances may have precluded an understanding of how these nations actually functioned socially and politically. Also, within the Soviet bloc there was an equally surprising amount of experimentation with form and the development of personal styles that include the ambiguous and the obscure. In these societies the French New Wave has affected film makers' creations and audiences' responsiveness.

    Beginning in the late fifties eastern European countries, joining France and Italy, achieved their own versions of a New Wave. Despite prominent differences, one thing common to all of these countries was a new emphasis on personal expression in film with the director as artist. Another was the use of new methods and techniques, defiance of former conventions, and the breaking up of traditional forms. In a general way the most interesting and important films from the countries on the continent, West and East, departed from the usual entertainment "package" as commercially conceived and from earnest Marxist exhortation. Instead they attempted to offer directly the kinds of moral, ethical, and aesthetic sustenance looked for in art works. It is these qualities in total that roughly characterize the New Wave, or Contemporary Cinema, or Modern Film, as the terms have come to be understood.

Two films made in eastern Europe during the 1990s encapsulate the challenges these countries have been facing and the aesthetic forms in which these challenges may be cast. Milcho Mikhalov's *Before the Rain* (1994) and Sergei Bodrov's *Prisoner of the Mountains* (1996) both deal with religious strife between Christians and Muslims, the former in Macedonia, the latter in the Caucasian Mountains of Russia. Both show families driven to the extreme of slaughtering their own relatives. Both set their brutal tales in barren mountain landscapes that isolate warring factions in a world that offers little in the way of natural sustenance. The vast scale of these majestic backdrops make the characters' acts seem insignificant and unavailing in comparison to the mighty forces that surround them. Despite the fatalistic message conveyed by this harshly drawn *mise-en-scène* and by the action as a whole, both films dwell on romantic attachments formed between a pair of young people on opposing sides of the conflict that seem to offer them a kind of spiritual if not physical salvation. Just as devastation follows from divisiveness and the delineation of differences, the films seem to argue, so does connectedness imply hope for a better world. Such a belief, perhaps, is what sustains the film-making activities of the eastern European nations; for films, too, are a way of forging connections, in this case initiating a larger connection between countries in turmoil and the larger world of which they see themselves as part.

Films of the Period

POLAND

1954
A Generation (Pokolenie) (Andrzej Wajda)

1956
Kanal (Andrzej Wajda)
Man on the Tracks (Człoiek na torze) (Andrzej Munk)

1958
Ashes and Diamonds (Popiół i diament) (Andrzej Wajda)

1960
Bad Luck (Zezowta szczéscie) (Andrzej Munk)

1961
Mother Joan of the Angels (Matka Joanna od aniołp) (Jerzy Kawalerowicz)

1962
Knife in the Water (Nóż w wodzie) (Roman Polanski)

1963
Passenger (Pasażerka) (Andrzej Munk)

1964
Identification Marks: None (Rysopis) (Jerzy Skolimowski)

1965
The Saragossa Manuscript (Rękopis znaleziong w Saragossie) (Wojcieck Has)
Walkover (Walkower) (Jerzy Skolimowski)

1968
Everything for Sale (Wszystko na sprzadaz) (Andrzej Wajda)

1969
The Structure of Crystal (Sturctura krysztalu)
   (Krzysztof Zanussi)

1970
Landscape After Battle (Krajobruz po bitwie)
   (Andrzej Wajda)

1973
Illumination (Illuminacja) (Krzysztof Zanussi)

1977
Man of Marble (Człowisk z marmura) (Andrzej
   Wajda)

1980
The Contract (Kontract) (Krzysztof Zanussi)

1981
Blind Chance (Przpadek) (Krzysztof Kieślowski)
Man of Iron (Człowisk z żelaza) (Andrzej Wajda)

1984
No End (Bez Końca) (Krzysztof Kieślowski)
The Year of the Quiet Sun (Rok spokojnego slonka)
   (Krzysztof Zanussi)

1988
*A Short Film about Killing (Krótki Film o zabi
   janiu)* (Krzysztof Kieślowski)
A Short Film about Love (Krótki Film o milósci)
   (Krzysztof Kieślowski)

1990
Korczak (Andrzej Wajda)
The Silent Touch (Dotknięci) (Krzysztof Zanussi)

1991
*The Double Life of Veronique (Podwójne życie
   Weroniki)* (Krzysztof Kieślowski)
30 Door Key (Ferdydurke) (Jerzy Skolimowski)

1993
Three Colors: Blue (Trzy Kolory: Niebieshy)
   (Krzysztof Kieślowski)

1994
Three Colors: Red (Trzy Kolory: Czerwory)
   (Krzysztof Kieślowski)

Three Colors: White (Trzy Kolory: Bialy)
   (Krzysztof Kieślowski)

1997
Love Stories (Historie milosne) (Jerzy Stuhr)

1999
Pan Tadusz (Andrzej Wajda)
With Fire and Sword (Ogniem i mieczem) (Jerzy
   Hoffman)

HUNGARY

1955
Merry-Go-Round (Körhinta) (Zoltán Fábri)

1956
Professor Hannibal (Hannibál tanár ur) (Zoltán
   Fábri)

1963
Cantata (Miklós Jancsó)

1965
The Round-Up (Szegénylegények) (Miklós Jancsó)

1967
The Red and the White (Csillagosok, katonák)
   (Miklós Jancsó)

1968
The Girl (Eltánozott nap) (Márta Mészáros)

1970
Love (Szerelem) (Károly Makk)

1971
Agnus Dei (Égi bárány) (Miklós Jancsó)

1972
Red Psalm (Még ker a nép) (Miklós Jancsó)

1975
Adoption (Örökbefogadás) (Márta Mészáros)

1976
The Fifth Seal (Ciz Ötödik pecsét) (Zoltán Fábri)

1981
Mephisto (István Szabó)

1982
Prefabricated People (Panelkapscolat) (Béla Tarr)

1984
Diary for My Children (Napló gyermekcimnek)
(Márta Mészáros)

1987
Diary for My Loves (Napló szerelmeimnek) (Márta
Mészáros)

1988
Damnation (Kárhozat) (Béla Tarr)

1990
*Diary for My Mother and Father (Napló apámnak,
anyámnek)* (Márta Mészáros)
My Twentieth Century (Az én xx. századom)
(Ildykó Enyedi)

1992
*Sweet Emma, Dear Böbe (Édes Emma, drága
Böbe)* (István Szabó)

1994
Satantango (Béla Tarr)

2000
Werkmeister Harmonies (Werckmeister harmóniák)
(Béla Tarr)

CZECHOSLOVAKIA

1964
Black Peter (Miloš Forman)
Diamonds of the Night (Jan Němec)

1965
Intimate Lighting (Intimitri osvĕteni) (Ivan Passer)
Loves of a Blonde (Lásky jedné plavovlásky)
(Miloš Forman)
The Shop on Main Street (Obchod na korze)
(Ján Kadár and Elmar Klos)

1966
Closely Watched Trains (Ostre sledované vlaky)
(Jiří Menzel)
Daisies (Sedmirkrásky) (Věra Chytilová)
*Report on the Party and the Guests (Oslavnosti a
hostech)* (Jan Němec)

1967
The Fireman's Ball (Horí má panenko)
(Miloš Forman)

1969
The Apple Game (Ovoce strp, i rakslucj jíme)
(Věra Chytilová)
Skylarks on a String (Skrivábcu na niti)
(Jiří Menzel)

1987
Alice (Nĕco z Alenky) (Jan Švankmajer)

1997
Buttoners (Knoflíkári) (Petr Zelenka)
Kolya (Kolja) (Jan Sverák)

1998
Traps (Pasti, pasti, pasticky) (Věra Chytilová)

1999
Return of the Idiot (Navrat idiota)
(Sasa Gedeon)

YUGOSLAVIA

1965
Man Is Not a Bird (Čovek nije tica) (Dušan
Makavejev)

1967
I Even Met Happy Gypsies (Sakupljaci perja)
(Alexandar Petrović)
*Love Affair, or the Case of the Missing Switchboard
Operator (Ljubavni slučaj ili tragedija
službenice P.T.T.)* (Dušan Makavejev)

1968
Innocence Unprotected (Nevinost bez zaštite)
(Dušan Makavejev)
*When I Was Dead and White (Kad budem mrtav
i beo)* (Živojin Pavlović)

1971
*WR: Mysteries of the Organism (W. R.—misterije
organizma)* (Dušan Makavejev)

1980
Who's Singing Over There? (Ko to tamo peva?)
(Slobodan Sijan)

1981
Do You Remember Dolly Bell (Sječaš li se Dolly Bell) (Emir Kusturica)

1985
When Father Was Away on Business (Otac na službenom putu) (Emir Kusturica)

1990
Time of the Gypsies (Dom za vešanje) (Emir Kusturica)

1994
Before the Rain (Pred dozhdot) (Milcho Manćhevski)
Underground (Bila jednom jedna zemlja) (Emir Kusturica)

1998
Black Cat, White Cat (Crna macka, beli macor) (Emir Kusturica)

RUSSIA

1957
The Cranes Are Flying (Letyat Zhuravli) (Mikhail Kalatozov)

1959
Ballad of a Soldier (Ballada o soldate) (Grigoy Chukrai)

1962
Ivan's Childhood (Ivanovo detstvo) (Andrei Tarkovsky)

1964
Shadows of Our Forgotten Ancestors (Teni zabytykh predkov) (Sergei Paradjanov)

1966
Andrei Rublev (Andrei Tarkovsky)

1969
The Color of Pomegranates (Tsvet granata) (Sergei Paradjanov)

1972
Solaris (Solyaris) (Andrei Tarkovsky)

1974
The Mirror (Zerkalo) (Andrei Tarkovsky)

1976
The Ascent (Voskhozhdenie) (Larisa Shepitko)
A Slave of Love (Raba lubvi) (Nikita Mikhalkov)

1979
Moscow Does Not Believe in Tears (Moskva slezam ne verit) (Vladimir Menshov)

1983
Farewell (Proschchanie) (Larisa Shepitko and Elem Klimov)

1984
The Legend of Suram Fortress (Legenda o Suramskoi kreposti) (Sergei Paradjanov)

1988
Little Vera (Malen'kaya) (Vasili Pichul)

1991
The Inner Circle (Blizhnii krug) (Andron Mikhalkov-Konchalovsky)
Urga, Territory of Love (Urga, Territoriya lyubvi) (Nikita Mikhalkov)

1994
Burnt by the Sun (Utomlennye solntsem) (Nikita Mikhalkov)

1996
Prisoner of the Mountains (Kavkazskii plennik) (Sergei Bodrov)

1997
Mother and Son (mat' i syn) (Alexander Sokurov)

1998
The Land of the Deaf (Strana glukhikh) (Valeri Todorovsky)

1999
The Barber of Siberia (Sibirski tsiriul'nik) (Nikita Mikhalkov)

2001
Taurus (Alexander Sokurov)

Books on the Period

Beumers, Birgit, ed. *Russia on Reels: The Russian Idea in Post-Soviet Cinema.* London and New York: Tauris, 1999.

Burns, B. *World Cinema: Hungary.* Cranbury, NJ: Farleigh Dickinson University Press, 1996.

Lawton, Anna. *Kinoglast: Soviet Cinema in Our Time.* New York: Cambridge University Press, 1993.

Taylor, Richard, Nancy Wood, Julian Graffy, and Dina Iordanova, eds. *The BFI Companion to Eastern European and Russian Cinema.* London: British Film Institute, 2000.

Woll, Josephine. *Reel Images: Soviet Cinema and the Thaw.* London and New York: Tauris, 2000.

13

Japanese Film: A Pictorial Tradition and a Modernist Edge

★ ★ ★ ★

1951–

The Japanese film industry has been strong from the earliest days, leading the world in the number of films it produces for most of the century. The first Japanese studios were established in 1904–1905; they continued to expand until the devastating Tokyo earthquake in 1923 forced them to regroup. Because of the popularity of the *benshi,* live performers whose spoken narration accompanied silent films, sound was slow in coming to Japanese cinema, arriving finally in the mid-1930s. The Second World War brought about another hiatus, and the subsequent American occupation, from 1945 to 1952, carried with it a policy of censorship that cramped the style of many major Japanese film makers. Nonetheless, Japanese cinema has remained notable not only for the quantity of films produced but also for the high quality many attained. Despite its rich tradition, however, Japanese movies remained largely unknown abroad until after World War II. Even now, few Japanese films made before 1940 are available to Western audiences because over 95 percent of them have been lost or destroyed.

The structure of the Japanese industry was curiously like the "classic" American one of the 1930s and 1940s (which was breaking up in the 1950s): Six major production companies controlled distribution and the theater circuits as well. Japanese film also had popular genres, some with close American counterparts. In a general way Japanese films were divided into two main categories: *jidai-geki,* or historical films, and *gendai-geki,* or contemporary films. The division between "historical" and "contemporary" times was marked by the year 1868, when the Emperor Meiji acceded to the throne and first opened Japan to commercial and cultural exchange with the West. It was during his reign that the country passed from feudalism to a modern way of life. Because the change was both sudden and radical, Japanese society in the contemporary period offered a striking contrast to that of the historical period. The two categories of films were also in sharp contrast to each other because each faithfully depicted the mores, thought, and feeling of the two periods. Each category had its own conventions, not only in regard to sets and costumes, but also production style and even acting. Studios, directors, and actors tended to specialize in one or the other of the two modes. The *jidai-geki* (historical) accounted for only 40 percent of Japanese production, but it enjoyed constant popularity with the domestic audience and achieved the first successes abroad.

Japanese film became internationally celebrated in 1951 when *Rashomon,* directed by Akira Kurosawa, won the grand prize at the Venice Film Festival. After its victory at Venice, *Rashomon* was distributed worldwide. Daie Motion Picture Company, which had produced it, was Japan's most prestigious studio, like an earlier M-G-M. Daie followed *Rashomon* with other films sent out for (and possibly in part produced for) world distribution. Masaichi Nagata, the Irving Thalberg of Daiei, to pursue the analogy, was producer of many of these. *Ugetsu* (1953) came next, directed by the veteran Kenji Mizoguchi. *Gate of Hell* (1953), the first Japanese film in the new Eastman Color, was directed by Teinosuke Kinugasa. Kurosawa's *Seven Samurai* (1954) reached the United States in a truncated version: two-and-a-half rather than three-and-a-half hours long. His *Ikiru,* though produced earlier (1952), followed. The latter was the first of the *gendai-geki* (contemporary films) to be seen here. The lovely Machiko Kyo, who appeared in the first three Japanese films to be imported, was much appreciated abroad, and Toshiro Mifune, whose finest work has been done with Kurosawa, established an international reputation with *Rashomon* and *Seven Samurai.*

The Japanese Style

Although the world hadn't seen Japanese films until the early 1950s, the Japanese had been seeing the world's films since the late 1890s, and their use of the medium had developed along lines parallel to those of other countries. Whereas American film makers most frequently concerned themselves with action and Europeans with the psychology of character, the Japanese often seemed to be more interested in overall mood and atmosphere. Even when the themes are universal, they embody unfamiliar assumptions and artistic conventions. In treatment there often seems to American audiences a sentimentality different in kind from their own. A didactic quality is also common in Japanese cinema, as is slower pacing. Shots and scenes are allowed to extend beyond the requirements of the narrative point being made to let audiences savor the feelings just expressed.

Other, more precise formal characteristics were equally noteworthy, especially in contrast to the immediately preceding Italian neorealism. Many of the Japanese films are beautifully and visually elegant. If one of them were stopped at random during projection, any frame held on the screen would probably be perfect in terms of composition and lighting. Long passages without dialogue give emphasis to the image. Coming from a cultural tradition that places great importance on the visual arts, Japanese directors and cinematographers thought as painters. Their frame lines always serve as organizational matrices for graphic design as well as for enclosing chunks of content. Planes of action seem constantly to be considered and shots painstakingly composed in depth—foreground in relation to middle ground in relation to background.

These visual qualities are especially striking in *Ugetsu* (and in Mizoguchi's work generally, later discovered). In it images are designed not only to create feelings of unease or of calm security but also to offer aesthetic pleasure in the very arrangement and balance of the blacks, whites, and grays. The full-color palette of *Gate of Hell* allows for the most dynamic and dramatic use of color film anyone had seen up to that point—especially in its first glowing orange-red scenes of violent action in a civil war. Camera movements, too—for these films are full of kinetic energy along with their careful pictorial patterns—have a calculation and control in relation to subject movement that frequently results in a kind of cinematic dance. In *Rashomon* the shots of the woodsman moving through the forest, the camera tracking with him and tilting up into the sunlight glinting down through the tall trees, are a breathtaking example. *Rashomon* suggested what would be confirmed by *Seven Samurai:* Kurosawa was a special master of camera movement. Another even more extraordinary instance in *Rashomon* occurs when Machiko Kyo weaves about after yielding to the bandit, confronting her husband's accusing stare as the camera swoops, backs, and glides with her. Reviewers resorted to phrases like "painting in motion" to describe the visual riches the Japanese films offered.

Stylistically still, but in terms of performance, the Japanese films drew on another ancient artistic tradition—that of the theater. Classical Nō plays, which go back for centuries, and the popular Kabuki have both reflected and influenced Japanese culture generally. They express national sentiments and beliefs, at least of the older Japan, which gave way more slowly and less fundamentally than appeared on the surface. Donald Richie, American authority on Japanese cinema, has insisted that Kabuki hasn't really affected the Japanese film to any great extent. Kurosawa has said much the same in regard to his own work, with an obvious exception in *The Men Who Tread on the Tiger's Tail* (1952), which was based on a Kabuki play. Yet there is something very different from western performance styles in the Japanese historical (not the contemporary) films. A composite outline of the conventional samurai films (of which *Gate of Hell* is one example; another is *Samurai,* 1954, directed by Hiroshi Inagaki) may suggest some of the differences.

A young warrior is in love with his lord's wife. Out of loyalty to his master he does not show that love. The acting in the first two-thirds of the picture would be not only restrained but extremely formalized. We can infer that each gesture and every movement (as well as costumes, makeup, and hairdos) have some sort of fixed and known meaning. An enormous tension is built up through this constraint of powerful feeling expressed in behavior limited by rigid, social/aesthetic convention. Then, when the young warrior can bear it no longer and his passion overleaps those self- and society-imposed bounds, he pursues the lady, fights the lord, and gives vent to his charged-up store of emotion. These scenes feature full-blown representations of lust and anger, complete with lunging and sweating, crawling and panting. The cold, inscrutable Oriental indeed! *Rashomon* first showed us these two extremes of performance—theatrical stylization in the trial scene, earthy naturalism in the bandit's behavior—within a single film.

Assessing the implications of such exotic charm is part of the problem in evaluating these films, which come out of a culture and tradition so vastly different from the Greco-Judeo-Christian one. The historical films usually are based on ancient legends well known to the Japanese audience. The stories about the Forty-Seven Ronin (masterless samurai), for example, have been the source for a good many films, those of Inagaki among the most popular. These period films reveal that the Japanese historical experience has had certain similarities to that of western nations, feudalism for instance, as well as certain differences, such as religion. It is the differences that fascinate most.

Three Japanese Masters

That initial cluster of five films opening the world's screens to Japanese cinema introduced two of Japan's greatest film makers: Akira Kurosawa and Kenji Mizoguchi. Both carry their personal concerns from film to film, whether the setting is modern or feudal. The work of the third, Yasujiro Ozu, is even more resolutely fixed on certain themes and is always set in contemporary Japan. Of the three, in terms of content and style, **Akira Kurosawa** is the most easily appreciated by Westerners. A number of his films are adaptations of European literary classics: Dostoyevsky's *The Idiot* (1951) and Gogol's *The Lower Depths* (1957) as well as Shakespeare's *Macbeth* (*Throne of Blood,* 1957) and *King Lear* (*Ran,* 1985). He also filmed an adaptation of a novel by the popular American mystery writer Ed McBain (*High and Low,* 1963). In turn, some of Kurosawa's productions have inspired Hollywood remakes, notably *Rashomon* (*The Outrage,* Martin Ritt, 1964) and *The Seven Samurai* (*The Magnificent Seven,* John Sturges, 1960). *Rashomon* is based on two stories by the popular author Ryunosuke Akutagawa, who was much influenced by western culture. Although set in the Heian period (794 to 1184), its four-times-told tale of a rape (or seduction), murder (or suicide), and robbery (or disappearance) is indebted to Robert Browning's novel-length poem *The Ring and the Book,* while the musical score is a close imitation of Maurice Ravel's *Bolero;* thus it makes use of a cinematic *lingua franca* available to all. With its fragmented narrative and pointed ambiguities, *Rashomon* was received by many Occidental critics as a continuation of the tradition of European modernism.

Kurosawa's action-filled samurai films, such as *Yojimbo* (1961) and *Sanjuro* (1962), share many features with American westerns. Substitute swords for six-guns and samurai warriors for professional gunslingers and much else remains the same. An acknowledged admirer of the westerns of John Ford, Kurosawa has directed a number of samurai sagas. *Seven Samurai,* the best of these, is set in the sixteenth century at a transitional time when the ancient and honorable profession of the samurai was coming to an end as gun powder and new military tactics appeared. The samurai we see have fallen on hard times, and in their unemployment a group of them accept a proposal by a committee of peasants to protect their village from bandit raids. The film combines discerning psychological observation with stunningly choreographed action and violence. Each of the seven warriors is carefully delineated. The leader and eldest (played by Takashi Shimura, who also plays the woodcutter in *Rashomon* and the lead in *Ikiru*) is a compelling personality. He eschews wasteful bloodshed, advocates strategy over force, and is wise, calm, and compassionate, with a sad acceptance of his destiny for leadership. Of the others, one samurai is tired of fighting, another is cool and skillful, a third bloodthirsty, a fourth a frightened youth, and so on. Crammed with action, the larger scenes of the bandits attacking the village are shot and cut with immense dynamism. His *Throne of Blood* (1957), a Japanese version of *Macbeth,* offers more of the same.

In *Seven Samurai* the action of the smaller, more intimate scenes carries with it fuller emotional meaning. But even then Kurosawa works through physical movement, and camera and cutting in relation to it. For example, there is the scene in which the preeminent

Rashomon ★ Japan, 1950, Akira Kurosawa; Toshiro Mifune, Masayuki Mori, and Machiko Kyo.

swordsman is introduced. He is challenged by another samurai to a test of skill, using staffs in place of swords. The result is contested: The challenger says that their blows landed at the same time; the master says the other would be dead. The former foolishly insists they fight again, with swords. When the great swordsman cuts his adversary down, he shows little emotion, simply having proved what he already knew. His interest is solely in further perfecting his awesome skill. The two seduction scenes between the youngest samurai and a peasant girl—one on a sunny flower-covered hillside, the other in the dark interior of a hut dappled by light—are also played largely with their bodies. His intense shyness and uneasy attraction and her almost wild abandonment to awakened sensuality are portrayed wordlessly. A final instance of Kurosawa's exceptional ability to transmute the physical into the emotional occurs in the scene of the raid on the bandits' fort. In the eerie early-morning light amidst a surrealist, Dantesque inferno of fire, torn bodies, and steaming pool, there is a haunting exchange between a husband and wife. She has come out of the burning fort after having been kept there as a concubine since the last raid. As she stands at the door, he runs to her; they look at each other for a full minute; nothing is said; then she turns and runs back into the flames.

In Kurosawa's films set in contemporary times he tends to subdue this kind of direct sensory appeal. Instead he keeps us focused on the subtler, more complex characters and on the sorts of social problems that more clearly show his dimension as a humanist. *Ikiru,* made in the same year as de Sica's and Zavattini's *Umberto D,* bears some resemblance to

Seven Samurai ★ Japan, 1954, Akira Kurosawa.

the Italian film. It concerns an inconsequential petty official who, after learning he has terminal cancer, tries to instill some meaning into his life as he faces death. His final positive act of helping create a children's playground in a poor section allows him to die satisfied, but it sets off social and political reverberations that are reviewed and discussed in a crazy drunken Joycian wake. In its complicated and experimental structure *Ikiru* descends in personal tragedy during the first two-thirds and then ascends back over the same material throughout the last third, with wry social comment and a sort of bitter comedy reinterpreting on a broader scale what we have seen. *Red Beard* (1965) is regarded by Richie as Kurosawa's masterpiece. At the same time he concedes that we must be able to look through and beyond its sentimental surface to get at the greatness of the film. The title character (played by Toshiro Mifune) is a crotchety, selfless, driven physician who devotes his whole life to treating the poor. His qualities are revealed to us as they are discovered by a young intern who comes to study under him. The film follows the young man's maturation and final success in finding his true self—his vocation, almost in the religious as well as practical sense. The kind of spiritual journey and discovery at the core of these two contemporary films appear frequently in Kurosawa's work. Even in his historical pieces he is always commenting on contemporary life, and the concerns are profoundly social and moral.

Kurosawa died in 1998. In his later years he produced some notable *jidai-geki,* some set during the period of change in the last quarter of the sixteenth century, when Japan was beset by ceaseless internal wars. Featuring militaristic spectacle and themes of charismatic authority, these films were well received internationally. In *Kagemusha* (*The Shadow Warrior,* 1981) a poor thief is chosen for his resemblance to the dying leader of the Takeda clan to take the latter's place, to become a "shadow warrior." At first frightened, the thief gradually falls under the spell of the visionary leader he is impersonating. The most accomplished of Kurosawa's late films, *Ran,* balances the pageantry of its elaborately staged battle sequences with the mental agonies suffered by its protagonist, Hidetora. Unlike Shakespeare's *King Lear*, on which it was based, *Ran* (which means "chaos") shows a hero driven mad not simply by the ingratitude of his children but also as a consequence of the guilt he has incurred in the course of a long reign marked by conquest and aggression. Numerous virtuoso battle sequences punctuate the action of the film, including one in which the massacre of Hidetora's army is viewed in slow motion with no audible sound save for somber and foreboding music. In both *Ran* and *Kagemusha*, Kurosawa exploits color to create magnificent pictorial effects in battle sequences by outfitting the soldiers with brightly hued flags, which are strapped to their backs. The flags provide a dramatic means of distinguishing among the clashing forces. In *Ran* the flags correspond to the colors of the king's three sons: red, yellow, and blue. The army of a neighboring warlord, which enters the fray near the film's conclusion, is identified by white flags.

Kurosawa's final films were personal and nostalgic reveries. *Dreams,* made in 1990, was a collection of eight tales based on the director's actual dreams; it was difficult for many critics and viewers to follow at times but universally praised for its stunning cinematography. *Rhapsody in August* (1991) starred Richard Gere in a tale about a Japanese and Japanese American family sorrowfully confronting the tragedy of the bombing of Hiroshima and Nagasaki. His last film, *Madadayo* (1993), is a poignant treatment of old age and the creation of community, a gentle conclusion to a career that had often been characterized by energetic action fare.

If much of Kurosawa's best work consisted of variations on the historical *jidai-geki,* the second of Japan's triumverate of top-ranked directors, **Kenji Mizoguchi,** favored this genre to an even greater degree. Because Mizoguchi's attitudes, subjects, and style are more traditionally Japanese than those of Kurosawa, his films have been less widely appreciated in the United States and Europe. Mizoguchi had a long career, beginning in 1923, but only with the international success of *The Life of O'Haru,* which won the grand prize at Venice in 1952, was he able to achieve a meaningful stability and independence, working at the prestigious Daiei Motion Picture Company to create a series of masterpieces during the 1950s that ended with his death in 1957.

Following in the footsteps of earlier Japanese directors such as Mikio Naruse, Mizoguchi frequently focused on the plight of women. Scripted by his long-standing scenarist Yoshikata Yoda, many of his films make a case for women's rights. This concern, which built on Mizoguchi's early experience as a director of "tendency" films that dealt with social problems, is especially apparent in such productions as *Sisters of the Gion* (1936), *Women of the Night* (1957), and *Street of Shame* (1956), which treat prostitution; *The Life of O'Haru* and *Princess Yang Kwei Fei* (1955), which focus on society's obsession with women's appearance; and *Osaka Elegy* (1936), which highlights the powerlessness of women within the Japanese family structure.

The varied visual environments Mizoguchi creates as a background for his stories invariably contain thematic overtones. He often presents leisurely tracking shots that move across a scene before the characters enter the frame as a way of emphasizing that human behavior is inevitably conditioned by and reflected in the context (both physical and, by extension, social) in which it occurs. *Crucified Lovers* (1954), for example, contrasts the constrictions and obstructions of its interior spaces, where the lovers are constrained by a repressive social system, with later scenes in which the delicate play of light in a leafy forest and the gentle rocking of a small boat in the water suggest the fragility of their happiness together after they elope. *Princess Yang Kwei Fei* employs an exquisite palette of pastel hues to chronicle the fate of an innocent young woman who is no match for the palace intrigue that surrounds her. In this film deep space compositions give visual expression to the rigid formality of the emperor's court, a world based on a set of intricate rules that mask political power plays. *The Story of the Last Chrysanthemum* (1939) contains many images in which the top and/or bottom of the screen is shrouded in darkness, creating a wide-screen look. In one pivotal scene the protagonist, a young actor, receives some crucial advice from the woman who later gives her life to help him succeed. The scene is photographed with long tracking shots taken from a conspicuously low angle below the boardwalk on which the two characters are walking; the camera looks up at them in such a way as to emphasize the precariousness of their situation.

Ugetsu, Mizoguchi's best-known film, deals with war and peace in relation to work and love—or perhaps, even more simply and broadly, war as it affects the total human condition. Set in the sixteenth century, the story centers on two brothers, a potter and a farmer, and their wives. The profiteering that wartime makes possible goads both men into an inordinate desire for gain. The potter wants money to buy extravagant presents for his wife and child, the farmer to equip himself as a samurai in order to impress his wife. While in the city selling his pots, the potter is seduced (partly through flattery about the aesthetic qualities of his pottery) by a mysterious and finally sinister Lady Wakasa. She causes him to abandon his wife for the carnal pleasures and luxury she seems to offer. During the same time the farmer comes to be regarded as a military commander through a faked heroic exploit. But the potter is no more an artist (nor should be) than the farmer is a warrior, Mizoguchi seems to be saying. Work ought to be for its own sake, not for money (or false praise for creativity) or glory (based on feigned valor). Also, it should be part of the family, not done away from home with the results brought back. The end of the film marks a return to the original state: work in peace, and conjugal and parental love.

Stylistically *Ugetsu* is even more "painterly" than Kurosawa's films. Mizoguchi's shaping of the visual-dramatic content takes place within the shot more than through juxtaposition of shots. Composition is always conceived in depth, often with objects at the side of the frame in the foreground to accentuate the perspective. Also, he uses the long shot quite deliberately to frame action at a distance—for example, there are the repeated views across the courtyard of Lady Wakasa's house, the scenes of the soldiers pillaging the village, and the shot of the farmer shopping for armor seen at a distance and from behind the armorer. Mizoguchi's frequent pans, too, are used pointedly as a compositional device rather than merely to follow action. One particularly memorable usage of the sort is the high-angled pan across the refugees from the village as they are camping for the night. In constructing his scenes he typically allows the camera to pick up action and then follow it remorselessly to its conclusion. But unlike the films of the German silent film makers who worked this way, there is an enormous amount of action within Mizoguchi's shots, and sharp contrasts—calm to frenetic, lyrical to horrifying—from scene to scene. He likes to have action explode into frame. Looting soldiers move around a corner and emerge in the middle of the frame, the potter's wife rushes directly toward the camera (shot from low angle with short-focal-length lens) and scoops up her child right under our noses. Entrances are frequently from behind the camera— from right or left and sometimes from below—which creates a startling, disruptive effect.

In *Ugetsu* the music is extremely important. More of it is Oriental than Western, the opposite of Kurosawa's usual practice, and it is fully integrated with the visuals. It

Ugetsu ★ Japan, 1953,
Kenji Mizoguchi; Kinuyo
Tanaka and Masayuki Mori.

complements and frequently takes precedence over the dialogue. In part it is used in place of natural sounds; elsewhere it is used as *leit motif,* evocative and symbolic. The bright piercing bell of Lady Wakasa's theme is matched by a gently melodic ensemble of bells in the return of the potter's wife. On the other hand, cries in the background sometimes supply an almost musical accompaniment to the action. When the two men and the farmer's wife leave the potter's wife and child on the shore of the lake, the farewells become a melancholy round. The ghost of Lady Wakasa's father groans in eerie and wordless recitative accompanied by strange and discordant instrumentation.

In contrast not only to the work of Mizoguchi and Kurosawa but also to that of almost any other film maker of any country one might think of, the style of **Yasujiro Ozu** is marked by the most rigorous austerity. In later films he rarely moved the camera, and then slightly and slowly solely to accommodate the action. Interiors predominate in his films and the action consists almost entirely of conversation among a few people. He worked exclusively in the formerly standard three-by-four screen ratio; although he used color when it became available to him for his last pictures, it was always muted and unemphatic, as if he were trying to keep the full palette from distracting. Characteristically, his camera sits at seated eye level, as if taking part in a formal tea ceremony, unblinkingly observing two of his characters reacting to each other. Very often the pair is made up of one old person and one young adult—an old man and a young woman perhaps most frequently in the final films. Above all Ozu, who began his career in 1922 and died in 1963, was concerned with the relationships between the traditional ways and the newer ones in a changing Japan. Implicit in all his films is an awareness of the extraordinary cultural dislocations that began to occur when Japan was opened to the West in the late nineteenth century. Ozu observed these changes and tensions not on a broad social scale but within the intimacy of the family unit—parents and children, husband and wife—where they finally have their deepest effect. Of the three giants of Japanese cinema, Ozu is unquestionably the most "Japanese." His view is a calm and balanced one. Although sad to see the old go, he has to acknowledge its passing, with sympathy but without complaint.

A philosophical stance growing out of the Japanese historical experience appears in the modern as well as the period films. It is distinctively and characteristically Japanese and is identified by one of those terms for which translators offer a sensible-enough English explanation but add that the concept remains essentially untranslatable. The phrase in this case is *mono no aware.* According to Richie, in *Japanese Cinema,* it means something like "that awareness of the transience of all earthly things; the knowledge that it is, perhaps fortunately, impossible to do anything about it; and celebration of resignation in the face of things as they are." Ozu's films have this attitude in abundance. Many of them are names to reflect the changing seasons: *Late Spring* (1949), *Early Summer* (1951), *Late Autumn* (1960), and *An Autumn Afternoon* (1962). Such titles suggest the cyclical movement of nature in which change takes place within a larger pattern of order and stability. Frequently the films include tranquil montages of cityscapes that create a comforting, solid background

Late Autumn ★ Japan, 1960, Yasujiro Ozu; Setsuko Hara and Yoko Tsukasa.

within which human behavior and customs can find a meaningful context. In *Tokyo Story* (1953), often considered Ozu's masterpiece, an old woman dies. Immediately afterward we see a fishing boat slowly leaving the harbor and hear the gentle putt-putt of its engine. We subsequently witness the grief and loneliness of the woman's husband. In the final shot of the film we watch as a similar fishing boat again crosses the harbor. The image overlays the widower's sorrow with a feeling of serenity: Death is part of life; the world goes on. The lives and events we have just witnessed are part of a universal and timeless human condition.

Ozu's films are incalculably rich in the observation of human behavior in the most ordinary and universal of situations. In *Late Autumn* (1960), for example, he is concerned with a widow, her twenty-four-year-old daughter, and the deceased husband's three old college friends who involve themselves with trying to find suitable mates for both mother and daughter. At the emotional center of the film is the mother's reluctance to lose her daughter, which she tries to check, and the daughter's growing desire to marry, stubbornly denied even to herself out of loyalty and affection for her mother. The so subtly changing situation is observed most discreetly—we learn no more about the characters than they know about each other—but for all of the quietness and control of Ozu's people, they possess a wonderful amount of robustness. Practical and realistic, they are willing to restrain their desires when necessary; at the same time they know the pleasures to be found in this world are those of the senses and feelings—eating, drinking, sex, and, most of all, love and companionship.

Abundant humor is interlaced throughout with tenderness and sadness; bawdy talk can exist within the confines of good manners. Ozu's narratives are like those of a kindly and merry old grandfather who doesn't need the large and exceptional events and characters conventionally required by storytellers. With astounding clarity and economy—through a few words, a tentative gesture, a partial smile—he makes a viewer feel "Yes, I know that person" or "Yes, something like that has surely happened countless times in many cultures." Ozu's genius was very special: an ability to put life back together whole out of closely observed bits and pieces. His films, in total, form an extraordinary tapestry, depicting the everyday, the intimate, the habitual, the lived-in world of unglamorous work and a few enduring relationships that comprise life for most of us.

Other Japanese Film Makers of the Classic Era

Accompanying the work of Kurosawa, Mizoguchi, and Ozu are the films of a small host of other noteworthy directors. Among those whose films have elicited the most sympathetic and sustained appreciation abroad are Kon Ichikawa and Masaki Kobayashi. The major works of both contain elements of social criticism, one of the characteristics of modern Japanese cinema.

Kon Ichikawa is concerned with dramatizing the conflict within people under peculiar stress. His films combine visual refinement with philosophical, even political statement; they tend toward allegory, or at least metaphor. *The Burmese Harp* (1956), his first international success, takes place at the end of World War II. The protagonist, a Japanese soldier separated from his unit, becomes converted to Buddhism. The values that had sustained him during the war are now meaningless to him, and he remains alone in Burma to bury his fallen comrades. *Enjo* (1958) is about a young monk who, tortured by the hypocrisy and evil he sees around him, sets fire to and destroys a temple he loved more than anything else in the world. *Odd Obsession* (1959), a dark comedy, is an even more convoluted psychological study, centering on the hypereroticism, bizarre sexuality, and voyeurism of a kind of *ménage à quatre* made up of a middle-aged husband, younger wife, daughter, and her fiancé. *Fires on the Plain* (1959) returns to the Japanese army in defeat. Suffering the horrors of starvation while straggling across a hostile and alien landscape, some of the soldiers are finally driven to cannibalism. *Alone on the Pacific* (1963) deals with the obsession of a single man who attempts to cross the Pacific in a small sailboat. *An Actor's Revenge* (1963) is the story of a female impersonator in Kabuki theater. The subject of *Tokyo Olympiad* (1965), a gigantic documentary tribute to that athletic event, permitted Ichikawa to continue the themes of obsession and unusual stress. In it he humanizes the competition with emphasis on the athletes and individuals in the crowds rather than on the events; his splendid visual flare and superb imagery of human bodies being pushed to their utmost raise sports to the level of poetry.

Of **Masaki Kobayashi's** films, *Kwaidan* (1964), an elegantly beautiful anthology of several period ghost stories, has been most popular in the United States. It does not represent the main thrust of his work, however. He is especially noted for the consistent criticisms his films have leveled at aspects of Japanese social tradition, particularly as it extends into political and military systems. *Black River* (1957) exposed the crime and corruption surrounding American military bases in occupied Japan. Kobayashi's massive trilogy, *The Human Condition* (comprising *No Greater Love, Road to Eternity,* and *A Soldier's Prayer*), was made between 1958 and 1961. The action takes place in Japanese-occupied Manchuria from 1943 to 1945. It chronicles the fate of a young pacifist intellectual forced into military service. He survives combat and, after the Japanese collapse, is captured by the Russians. Escaping from prison, he dies on his way to rejoin his wife. Antimilitary as

The Burmese Harp ★
Japan, 1956, Kon Ichikawa;
Shoji Yasui.

Harakiri ★ Japan, 1962, Masaki Kobayashi;
Tatsuya Nakadai.

well as antiwar, the trilogy aroused enormous controversy in Japan. Although *Harakiri* (1962) is a *jidai-geki* samurai film, it presents the traditional code of honor as senseless and destructive, a system ruled by a corporate class that wreaks the cruelest of punishments on the individual (an impoverished young samurai is forced to disembowel himself with a bamboo sword blade) in their efforts to keep themselves in power and the feudal system intact. The message is clearly directed toward contemporary Japan.

The Japanese New Wave

In the postwar years, the Japanese cinema developed new formulas, including the youth film and the action film. Gradually individual studios began to specialize exclusively in specific popular genres: Toho made monster movies and science-fiction spectacles, including the international blockbuster *Godzilla* (Ishiro Honda, 1954), whereas Toei produced *yakuza* or gangster films. During the 1970s Daiei went bankrupt, and Nikkatsu Studios began to specialize in soft-core pornography, or *pink films* (also called *roman poruno*). Increasingly, quality film making suffered as a result of these developments. Nonetheless a group of innovative directors emerged during the 1960s and 1970s, supported in part by the Arts Theater Guild, which had begun to finance and exhibit more adventuresome fare than the big studios were willing to risk. These directors—including Shohei Imamura, Nagisa Oshima, and Masahiro Shinoda—produced films with an iconolastic modernist bent. They were soon labeled the New Wave in recognition of their kinship with the contemporaneous New Wave directors in France. Often the films they made reworked the popular genres of the day, such as the pink film (Oshima's *In the Realm of the Senses,* 1976) and the yakuza film (Imamura's *Vengeance Is Mine,* 1975).

Shohei Imamura's films might best be described as ethnographic, a quality announced in the title of his 1966 production, *The Pornographers: An Introduction to Anthropology.* Imamura's films describe groups and individuals whose habits and traditions are unfamiliar and frequently repellent. For example, his 1983 *Ballad of Narayama* tells a tale about the nineteenth-century inhabitants of a mountain village in Japan who practice infanticide, bestiality, and ritual suicide, and who bury wrongdoers alive. Dispite their monstrous practices, however, Imamura's characters typically inspire sympathy as well as repugnance. His stories are often punctuated with shots of insects or reptillian life; like the characters themselves, these creatures inspire disgust but are also possessed of compelling beauty and grace. Even the titles of some of Imamura's films (for example, *The Insect Woman,* 1963, and *The Eel,* 1997) make the connection between human beings and lower forms of life. *The Eel,* which, like *The Ballad of Narayama,* took the Palme d'Or at Cannes, contains numerous shots of a pet eel belonging to the film's protagonist, a murderer who is trying to begin his life anew as a barber. Similarly one of the main characters in *The Pornographers* feels a strong affinity to her pet carp, which she believes contains the soul of her dead husband. A closeup of this creature opens the film. "We all want to be animals," one of the other characters comments at one point. "We want to be free." Imamura takes a similarly ethnographic approach to a horrific event in modern world history in his 1988 production *Black Rain,* which depicts the bombing of Hiroshima and its aftereffects on the people who lived there.

Of the Japanese film makers discussed in this chapter, **Nagisa Oshima** is the most "modern." Using narrative structures and techniques comparable to those of the French Jean-Luc Godard, Oshima is yet profoundly Japanese in his sensibility. The gentle, humanist criticism implicit in Ichikawa and the direct social-realist confrontation apparent in Kobayashi, become radical and revolutionary statements in Oshima. He challenges the moral assumptions underpinning Japanese society as well as its institutions. The values of the older generation are seen as neither valid nor relevant to the problems faced by youth, with whom he identifies.

Death by Hanging (1968) not only attacks capital punishment but goes further to suggest that the very concept of crime (and punishment) is a conception of the police, at considerable variance with actual human conduct and the motives behind it. It is the police rather than the criminal who are obsessed with crime. *Diary of a Shinjuku Thief* was made in the same year. Within an extremely fragmented structure and a mixture of modes, from the actuality of student riots to the artificiality of a ghost play, it links themes of sex as performance with theft as a revolutionary act. The film is dense and difficult; the actions of its individuals are intended to be read as symbolic statements about Japan. *Boy* (1969), based on a real incident, as was *Death by Hanging,* is about a child trained by his parents to run in front of moving autos to be hit and injured slightly so they can collect damages. It is about that particular situation, but the indictment, as Oshima has said, is not of the parents, but of a society that makes it necessary for them to live in that manner. In *The Ceremony* (1971), often regarded as Oshima's masterpiece, the plot revolves around a family for a period of twenty-five years since the end of the war. As they come together for weddings and funerals their traditional attitudes become increasingly divorced from the realities of modern life, their behavior ever more ritualistic, abstract, and finally strange.

Black Rain ★ Japan, 1988, Shohei Imamura.

Disjunctive narrative, diverse styles within a given film, reality mingled with surrealist fantasy, formalized patterns achieving the effect of ritual—all are present in Oshima's work. As a Japanese film maker Oshima also offers images of exquisite beauty, especially unnerving when they are of events horrifying in their human meanings. He received his greatest international attention, not to say notoriety, with *In the Realm of the Senses* (1976). It centers exclusively on a couple obsessed with each other and with sensual experience; sexual activity is its content, death and madness its conclusion. *Empire of Passion* (1979), dealing with a pair of rural lovers, is a companion piece, though more restrained emotionally, less explicit sexually, and more social in its content.

At the end of the 1970s Oshima increasingly turned away from movie making and became active as a political commentator—a more direct form of social protest. Nonetheless, his films have remained influential. Like other modern political film makers, he has fashioned new forms to express new ideas. Disjunctive narrative, diverse styles within a given film, reality mingled with surrealist fantasy, and formalized patterns achieving the effect of ritual are present in his work.

Together with Oshima, **Masahiro Shinoda** began his career as an assistant director at the Ofuna branch of Shochiku studios, whose specialty in the highly stratified Japanese film industry was roughly equivalent to Hollywood's "women's pictures." Shinoda's *Pale*

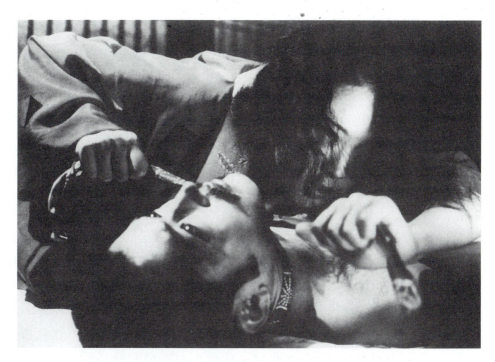

In the Realm of the Senses ★ Japan, 1976, Nagisa Oshima; Tatsuya Fuji and Eiko Matsuda.

Flower (1964) is his first important film, followed by *With Beauty and Sorrow* (1965), *Punishment Island* (1966), and *The Scandalous Adventures of Buraikan* (1970). It was *Double Suicide* (1969), however, that swept the festivals and earned him international notice. Based on a classical play about the conflict between love and duty, the film features stylistic devices of the traditional puppet theater from which the story was taken; these are fused with a fluid moving-camera style. The black-garbed puppeteers from the opening scenes in the theater remain hovering about the human characters throughout as a strange chorus, heightening the sense of destiny and impending doom.

Recent Developments

The golden age of Japanese cinema of the 1950s and 1960s came to an end by the mid-1970s. The situation in Japan paralleled developments in the United States, which will be dealt with in Chapter 15. Television broadcasting began in 1954; by the early 1980s, 99 percent of Japanese homes had color television sets. The old studio system broke down in the 1960s as the major companies faced declining audiences. Significant films from established directors were few in number and exceptions to the general scramble to match popular taste.

In the 1980s and 1990s, however, a new generation of Japanese film makers appeared, along with a new genre of Japanese film—irreverent satire focusing on contemporary society. The cycle began in 1983 with *Family Game,* directed by Yoshimitsu Morita. That film's

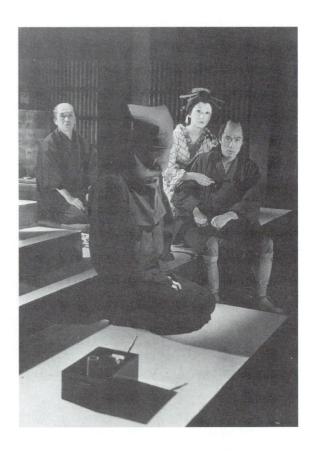

Double Suicide ☆ Japan, 1969, Masahiro
Shinoda; Kichiemon Kakamura and Shima
Inashita, right of black-garbed figure.

main targets were the shortcomings of a family in which false standards for achievement
and lack of communication prevail. Following its success, the actor who starred in it, Juzo
Itami, then wrote and directed a number of brilliant satires, including *The Funeral* (1984),
Tampopo (1985), *A Taxing Woman* (1986), *A Taxing Woman Returns* (1988), *Minbo; or, the
Gentle Art of Japanese Exploitation* (1994), and *Supermarket Woman* (1996).

The Funeral is said to have evolved out of Itami's own experience in handling his
father-in-law's funeral rites. It is a concentrated study of the three days of a Buddhist wake
seen from a comic perspective. The arcane intricacies of the ritual, scarcely remembered,
and the cross-purposes, misunderstandings, and hypocrisies among the mourners provide
the basis for a subdued sort of farce with an admixture of tenderness.

Tampopo does for food what *The Funeral* did for death. The story centers on the title
character (whose name means Dandelion) and her efforts, aided by others, to cook a perfect noodle. An assortment of characters and situations, all of them related to food, are
added to this main line, and film conventions, especially those of the American film, are
parodied throughout. (It was promoted in the United States as the first noodle western.)

Most of Itami's films star his wife, Nobuko Miyamoto. In *A Taxing Woman* she plays
the role of a resourceful government tax auditor obsessed with her job, who substitutes the
satisfaction of bringing tax evaders to justice for sexual relationships, including in particular an attractive, corrupt tax dodger she relentlessly pursues. The sequel also is a hilarious exposure of the corruption and inherent criminality of the patriarchal-capitalist power

The Funeral ★ Japan, 1984, Juzo Itami; Nobuko Miyamoto and Tustomu Yama, first row of black-clad mourners.

structure. The motif of Japanese criminality is further explored in *Minbo,* which focuses on Yakuza gangs. So telling was the film's satirical bite that Itami was attacked by members of these gangs after its release and was forced to go into hiding.

An increasing number of new Japanese movies are being released commercially in the United States. In addition, film festivals around the world, especially those in Pordenone, Italy, and Kyoto, Japan, have unearthed many older Japanese productions that had been believed lost, helping us fill in the huge gaps in our knowledge about Japanese film tradition. New English-language studies of Japanese cinema are also adding to our knowledge of Japanese film history. As America develops closer ties to its neighbor across the Pacific, Japanese cinema is becoming more familiar to us, prized not only for its aesthetic qualities but also for what it reveals about the values and sensibilities of an ancient and fascinating culture.

Films of the Period

1950
Rashomon (Akira Kurosawa)

1952
Ikiru (Akira Kurosawa)
The Life of O'Haru (*Saikaku ichidai onna*)
   (Kenji Mizoguchi)

1953
Gate of Hell (*Jigokumon*) (Teinosuke
   Kinugasa)
Tokyo Story (*Tokyo monogatari*) (Yasujiro
   Ozu)
Ugetsu (Kenji Mizoguchi)

1954
Chikamatsu Monogatari (Kenji Mizoguchi)
Sansho Dayu/The Bailiff (Kenji Mizoguchi)
Seven Samurai (Akira Kurosawa)

1955
Princess Yang Kwei Fei (*Yôkihi*) (Kenji Mizoguchi)

1956
The Burmese Harp (*Biruma no tategoto*) (Kon
    Ichikawa)

1957
The Lower Depths (*Donzoko*) (Akira Kurosawa)
The Throne of Blood (*Kumonosu jo*) (Akira
    Kurosawa)

1958
Enjo (Kon Ichikawa)

1959
Fires on the Plain (*Nobi*) (Kon Ichikawa)
Floating Weeds (*Ukigusa*) (Yasujiro Ozu)
Odd Obsession (*Kagi*) (Kon Ichikawa)

1961
An Autumn Afternoon (*Sanma no aji*) (Yasujiro Ozu)
The Human Condition (*Ningen no joken*)
    (1958–1961, Masaki Kobayashi)
The Island (*Hadaka no shima*) (Kaneto Shindô)

1962
An Actor's Revenge (*Yukinojo henge*) (Kon
    Ichikawa)
Harakiri (Masaki Kobayashi)

1964
Kwaidan (Masaki Kobayashi)
Onibaba (Kaneto Shindô)
Woman of the Dunes (*Suna no onna*) (Hiroshi
    Teshigahara)

1965
Red Beard (*Akahige*) (Akira Kurosawa)

1968
Death by Hanging (*Koshikei*) (Nagisa Oshima)
Diary of a Shinjuku Thief (*Shinjuku dorobo nikki*)
    (Nagisa Oshima)

1969
Boy (*Shonen*) (Nagisa Oshima)
Double Suicide (*Shinju ten no amijima*) (Masahiro
    Shinoda)

1970
Dodeska-den (Akira Kurosawa)

1971
The Ceremony (*Gishiki*) (Nagisa Oshima)

1975
Dersu uzala (Akira Kurosawa)
Kaseki (Masaki Kobayashi)

1976
In the Realm of the Senses (*Ai no corrida*) (Nagisa
    Oshima)

1979
Realm of Passion (*Ai no borei*) (Nagisa Oshima)

1981
Kagemusha/The Shadow Warrior (Akira Kurosawa)

1983
Family Game (*Kazoku geimu*) (Yoshimitsu
    Morita)

1984
The Funeral (*Ososhiki*) (Juzo Itami)

1985
Ran (Akira Kurosawa)
Tampopo (Juzo Itami)

1986
A Taxing Woman (*Marusa no onna*) (Juzo Itami)

1987
Gonza the Spearman (*Yari no gonza*) (Masashiro
    Shinoda)

1990
Dreams (*Yume*) (Akira Kurosawa)

1991
Rhapsody in August (*Hachigatsu no kyoshikyoku*)
    (Akira Kurosawa)

1992
Minbo; or, the Gentle Art of Japanese Exploitation
   (*Minbo no onna*) (Juzo Itami)

1993
Madadayo (Akira Kurosawa)

1996
Supermarket Woman (*Supa no onna*) (Juzo Itami)

1997
The Eel (*Unagi*) (Shohei Imamura)

1998
Afterlife (*Wandafuru raifu*) (Hirokazu Kore-eda)
Dr. Agaki (*Kanzo Sensei*) (Shohei Imamura)

2000
Taboo (*Gohatto*) (Nagisa Oshima)

2001
Distance (Hirokazu Kore-eda)
Lukewarm Water Under the Bridge (*Akai hashi
   noshitano nurui mizu*) (Shohei Imamura)

Books on the Period

Davis, Darryl William. *Picturing Japaneseness: Monumental Style, National Identity, Japanese Film.* New York: Columbia University Press, 1996.

Dissanayke, Winal, ed. *Cinema and Cultural Identity: Reflections on Film from Japan, India, and China.* New York: Cambridge University Press, 1993.

14

Other Asian Film-Making Traditions

1956–

At the time of *Rashomon's* appearance in 1951, scholars in the West knew little about film production in Asia except that reputedly large and heavily commercial industries seemed to be turning out entertainment aimed mainly at huge domestic audiences, at other countries in Asia, and at Asian populations living elsewhere in the world. Along with Japan, eventually India, China, Hong Kong, and Taiwan, in roughly that order, caught the attention of Western critics with world-class films that have received some distribution internationally. What has appeared at international festivals, however, does not always reflect the robust film cultures that have flourished in these countries, which, although often influenced by Western styles and Hollywood models of storytelling, have developed distinctive cinematic traditions of their own that speak to both domestic and diasporic communities around the world.

India: Film and National Identity

The Indian industry gained Western consideration through another single entry in an international film festival. In 1956 at Cannes, *Pather Panchali* was voted the "best human document." It was the first film of a young director named Satyajit Ray. Appropriately, its screening followed right after a Kurosawa film, *I Live in Fear.* Unlike Kurosawa's works, however, Ray's film was created completely apart from his national film industry and was not representative of it. Whereas *Pather Panchali* recalled the Italian neorealist films in its deep social concern as well as in its use of nonactors and location shooting, the big studios in India were producing a very different kind of product.

The Indian film audience is huge—roughly three-and-a-half million a day. To meet this demand, the number of films produced is the largest in the world, currently in the range of 800 features a year, more than that of any other nation. The main center of production for the popular Hindi cinema is Bombay, dubbed "Bollywood" because of its focus on big budget entertainments for the masses. In contrast to the "all-India" orientation of Bombay film making, smaller production centers in Calcutta, Madras, and other cities produce films to serve regional populations with movies in the sixteen officially recognized languages as well as in others. These regionally oriented productions sometimes turn into Bollywood-style blockbusters as well. Running times are long—typically three hours—to give as full an evening's entertainment as possible. Exhibition venues in rural areas are often primitive; Indian film producer Ismael Merchant writes, "Villagers gravitate to the makeshift cinemas, sometimes nothing more than wooden structures with a tin roof, to sit on the floor or on benches to be transported to another world."

India remains the only film industry to have developed under colonial rule: The British raj controlled the country until 1947. As a colonialist culture, many of the country's popular entertainments have traditionally been derived from Western models. But indigenous art forms also flourished, encouraged by the political philosophy of "swadeshi" espoused by the liberation forces led by Mohandas Gandhi and Jawaharlal Nehru, which called for support of locally made products over foreign imports. As a result, India is the only third-world country that has a larger audience for its own cinema than for foreign imports—this despite government policies in relation to the film industry that have historically included heavy taxation, burdensome censorship laws, and no subsidies.

In 1913 the nationalist impulse that was to define future Indian film making was made explicit. This was the year of *Raja Harishchandra,* directed by D. G. Phalke, often called "the father of Indian film." Phalke, whose writings declare his support of the swadeshi policy, was inspired to make a film about the Indian religious pantheon after viewing a Western religious epic. "Could we, the sons of India, ever be able to see Indian images on the screen?" he later recalled thinking at the time. A huge hit on its release, *Raja Harishchandra* became the first in a long line of Indian films that drew on Indian mythology for their subject matter.

Other distinctively Indian genres developed soon afterward, including the devotional (*Sant Tukaram,* V. Shantaram, 1936), the social (*Two Acres of Land,* Bimal Roy, 1953), the epic melodrama (*Mother India,* Mehboob Khan, 1957), and the historical (*Mughal-e-Azam,* K. Arif, 1960). All include musical numbers, a convention that undoubtedly plays a major role in their ability to reach a linguistically diverse audience across the country. Highly publicized stars, along with lavish sets and costumes, also add to the wide appeal of these productions. In their history, *Indian Film,* Erik Barnouw and S. Krishnaswamy observe that every film requires "a star, six songs, three dances." Favorite themes include the plight of the rural poor, the position of women, and the caste system.

A representative production is *Awara (The Tramp),* directed by its star, Raj Kapoor, in 1951 from a script by the left-wing writer Ahmad Abbas. The film's theme about the determining role played by the social environment rather than genetic inheritance in shaping human personality is implicitly critical of the Indian caste system. Kapoor plays Raj, son of Judge Raghunath, who is played by Kapoor's own father, Prithviraj Kapoor. Disowned by the Judge, Raj is cast into poverty and becomes a criminal. Later, on trial for murder in his father's courtroom, he is defended by the judge's adopted daughter, Rita, a lawyer, played by popular star Nargis. Raj and Rita fall in love. Ultimately, Judge Raghunath, who has advocated the belief that heredity is more important than environment in shaping character, recants his opinion and accepts his son. Although Raj is condemned to serve a three-year prison sentence for the crimes he has committed, Rita promises to wait for him. Symbolic overtones are created by the judge's name, which recalls the name of the Hindu god who is thought to watch over the Indian caste system.

This socially progressive fable is played out against a lavish background that counters its sombre message. The judge's house, where Rita resides, is like a palace, with vast, marble-floored rooms and sweeping staircases. Bathed in glowing, romantic lighting, the lovers sing many ballads of longing and fulfilment. An extravagant dream sequence uses expressionist techniques to render Raj's tortured state of mind, evoking visions of heaven and hell in the process. Using gestures and expressions reminiscent of a melodramatic Charlie Chaplin, Kapoor himself exudes a wholesome energy that belies the seriousness of his character's plight. Like many other Indian films, *Awara* resembles a sugar-coated pill, cloaking its message of social reform in a frothy package of engaging spectacle.

The Second World War and the move to independence that soon followed affected the Indian film industry in numerous ways. The economic turmoil of the war led to the breakup of the studios and the rise of independent production (a development that was also to occur in Hollywood). In addition, the new government headed by Nehru commissioned

Awara ★ India, 1951, Raj Kapoor; Nargis.

a report recommending more proactive policies to regulate India's film culture. Eventually, a film school was established at Poona and government financing was put in place to encourage what would become an alternative cinema. At the same time a radical grass-roots organization, the Indian People's Theater Association (IPTA), sprang up. The IPTA's philosophy of mixing folk art with international avant-garde techniques was applied to film as well as to the stage. Its political platform emphasized rural activism and took the devastating 1943 famine as a rallying point. A number of India's most influential directors were associated with this movement, including Mehboob Khan, Guru Dutt, Mrinal Sen, Ritwik Gatwik, and Shyam Benegal. The first production sponsored by the IPTA, *Children of the Earth* (1946), directed by the group's general secretary, K. A. Abbas, told a tale of a Bengali immigrant family in the city. It was advertised with the IPTA slogan "People's Theater Stars the People."

With these elements in place, the stage was set for a new Indian cinema. Ironically, however, the Indian filmmaker who first broke through to international prominence stood apart from all of these developments. From the outset **Satyajit Ray** was a maverick. A commercial artist by profession, he was one of the founders of the Calcutta Film Society and a passionate student of film. In his free time he saw as many movies as he could and paid particular attention to the work of such American directors as John Ford, William Wyler, Frank Capra, John Huston, and Billy Wilder. He was influenced strongly, he has said, by Flaherty's *Nanook of the North,* Jean Renoir's *The Southerner,* and "of course, all the Chaplins."

In 1950 Ray met Renoir, who was in Calcutta shooting *The River.* Renoir encouraged him and permitted him to observe production. Later that year Ray was sent by his advertising agency employers to their headquarters in London for six months. While there he talked with leading British film critics and theorists and attended movies daily. He was especially inspired, he said, by Vittorio de Sica–Cesare Zavattini's *The Bicycle Thief.*

On the boat going home he wrote the first draft of the script for *Pather Panchali,* adapted from a popular novel. The film was almost an amateur production—in personnel as well as scale. Only two of the cast and only one of the crew of eight—the art director— were professionals. The cinematographer was an amateur still photographer. To show him what he wanted, Ray, who had never directed a film before, drew pen-and-ink sketches from the camera's viewpoint. Shot on weekends over a period of almost four years, production was frequently halted for lack of funds. Eventually the money ran out. Ray was about to give up when the West Bengal government agreed to back him in return for ownership of the film.

First of a trilogy (followed by *Aparajito,* 1956, and *The World of Apu,* 1958), *Pather Panchali* (1955) begins the account of a Bengali family of five during the 1920s, which extends from the time the boy Apu is about age twelve, until he himself has a son about that age. In spite of its total three-feature length (each of the films can stand by itself, of course), the trilogy is not an epic in conception; it is epic only by implication. When social, religious, and economic themes and problems appear, it is within the detailed texture of the family's daily life.

Ray's trilogy is made up solely of diverse incidents; the films have no story in the usual sense. *Pather Panchali* ends when Apu's father, who has been away trying to earn enough money to support the family, returns home. In his absence the aged aunt has died, and more recently and cruelly, his older child, a lovely adolescent girl, died of pneumonia

Pather Panchali ★ India, 1955, Satyajit Ray; Karuna Manerji, Uma Das Gupta, and Subir Banerji.

caught while playing in the first of the rains. Father, mother, and Apu—their grim and intractable economic situation unresolved—load their few belongings onto an ox cart and depart for Benares. Early in *Aparajito* the father dies, and the remainder of the film, with its sustained note of moving sadness, concerns the gentle and loving tension created by Apu's ambition for an education (which also means westernization) and his mother's conflicting need for his affection and the traditional ways. *The World of Apu* deals with Apu's early manhood-his life in Calcutta and his marriage—and concludes with his relationship to his young son after his wife dies in childbirth.

Following the trilogy, Ray moved toward more strictly Indian and personal concerns. Yet, with dialogue in Bengali rather than the more widely spoken Hindi, his films were accessible only to a relatviely small audience in his homeland. Somewhat like the Italian film makers, he shifted from the poorer to the middle and upper-middle classes of which he was a member and away from material to spiritual and psychological themes. In *Devi* (*The Goddess,* 1960), a deeply religious feudal landlord becomes obsessed with the notion that his daughter-in-law is a goddess. *Kanchanjungha* (1962), his first film in color, *Charulata* (1964), *Days and Nights in the Forest* (1970), and *The Home and the World* (1984) are all concerned with complicated and shifting family, marital, and sexual relationships among the well-to-do and well educated. Frequently, like Ozu in Japan, Ray treated the old in a changing India, and the peculiar and fascinating mixture of East and West left as a legacy of the British raj. *The Music Room* (1958), for example, deals with a vanishing feudal culture, the protagonist being the last in a line of landed aristocrats in British India. It contains a fine selection of traditional Indian music. *The Chess Players* (1977) is set amidst nineteenth-century expansion of British colonial power. Ray has also been consistently concerned with the role of females. *Mahanagar* (*The Big City,* 1963), addressing attitudes about women and work and independence from male-dominated households and traditional roles, is one example.

Although Ray stands as a somewhat isolated figure against the panoply of forces that define Indian cinema, his more elite style of filmmaking found further expression in the work of other, more politically grounded, directors. Around 1969–1970 there developed what was called New Indian Cinema, or Parallel Cinema, financed in part by the government's National Film Development Corporation and more recently by the government-sponsored Doordarshan television network. Ritwik Ghatak and Mrinal Sen are considered the movement's founding fathers. Other notable directors associated with New Indian Cinema are Shyam Benegal, Mani Kaul (*Our Daily Bread,* 1969) and Kumar Shahini (*The Wave,* 1984).

Ritwik Ghatak, who died in 1976, directed only eight feature films, but he made a good many documentaries and wrote scripts for others' features. A Marxist activist, it is said of his films that practically all are about the social stress and turmoil in Bengal. Perhaps one of the most gentle and one of the few to arrive in the West, *Ajantrik* (*Pathetic Fallacy,* 1958) is about a taxi driver in a small provincial town and his ancient and decrepit Ford. The taxi is his only, and highly valued, companion, except for his brief encounters with the varied fares who join him in it. The film ends with the death and dismemberment of his faithful friend, the taxi; his sense of loss is shared by the audience, thanks to the special blend of enchantment and realism that Ghatak managed to create.

Mrinal Sen's features, some twenty-five or more in number, are quite different from those of either Ray or Ghatak, although all three men are Bengalis. Also a Marxist, Sen experimented for awhile with form as well as content, in the manner of Frenchman Jean-Luc Godard, in an effort to create a revolutionary cinema. *Bhuvan Shome* (*Mister Shome,* 1969), Sen's biggest success, was the first low-budget feature financed by the Indian government. Its title character is a stuffy senior executive of the Indian railways. During a holiday in rural India he is transformed by his experience of country people and country ways, especially those of the cheeky young wife of a lowly railway clerk. It is both funny and lyrical. *In Search of Famine* (1980) is about film makers visiting a rural settlement in order to get the villagers to reenact the terrible famine of 1943 (also the subject of *Ray's Distant Thunder,* 1973). The interaction between the urban film crew and their rural subjects generates friction and ultimately forces the crew to abandon the actual and retreat to the security of the make-believe world of the studio. Biting irony is the prevailing tone. *The Ruins* (1983), less didactic than Sen's work generally, also concerns urban in relation to rural. A city-bred photographer spends a country weekend with some friends at a ruined estate where a lonely girl, foresaken by her betrothed, tries to keep her ailing mother alive with the hope that he will return. *Genesis* (1986), too, is set amidst ruins, but those of a town long deserted, which two men and a woman try but fail to bring back to life.

Bhuvan Shome/Mister Shome ★ India, 1983, Mrinal Sen; Suhasini Mulay.

Among the directors of New Indian Cinema proper, **Shyam Benegal,** who lives and works in Bombay, is perhaps the best known. *Ankur* (*The Seedling,* 1974), his first feature, was a considerable success. It is a strong, tragic protest against the feudal society that has persisted in rural India. *Manthan* (*The Churning,* 1976) was financed by individual contributions from the farmers of Gujarat State and deals with the attempts of an Indian government administrator to set up a milk cooperative in a little village. The official becomes ensnared in caste and hierarchical entanglements that arise to thwart his efforts. The film portrays the difficulties, misunderstandings, and cross-purposes that surely would face an outsider attempting to bring about change in a tradition-bound society. *Bhumika* (*The Role,* 1977), another considerable success, is based on the biography of a female star of theater and film in the 1940s, dubbed the "Joan Crawford of India." It reveals much about the world of popular entertainment and the constrictions placed on the life of even a successful woman in Indian culture. Benegal's concerns seem to embody feminism and Marxism; his style is more extravagant and sensuous than that of other directors of the New Indian Cinema. In fact one of his films, *Trikal* (1986), fit into a Middle Cinema category, somewhere between the commercial mainstream and the small-budget, small-audience Parallel Cinema.

While the New Indian Cinema was developing, popular film continued to thrive. In recent years Tamil productions have seized the Indian public's imagination. The Tamil star and political figure M. G. Ramachandran had produced a series of wildly popular quasi-historical films in the 1950s and 1960s, some of which were supported by the progressive

DMK party and posed new interpretations of Tamil history. In the 1990s Tamil film maker **Mani Rathnam** came to the fore, especially with the controversial *Roja* (1992), which plays provocatively on Hindu-Muslim tensions within the country.

Another recent trend is the film-making activity of Indians living abroad. Notable among this group are two women directors: Mira Nair and Deepa Mehta. **Mira Nair** enjoyed great international success with the 1988 *Salaam Bombay!,* which used actual slum children to portray the grim lives of many of India's orphans and castoffs. Her 1996 *Kama Sutra,* a lushly erotic mythological tale, was less well received, and its explicit sexuality led to its being banned in India. During most of the 1990s Nair worked in the United States on productions with ethnic themes, such as *Mississippi Masala* (1991), starring Denzel Washington and Sarita Choudbury, and *The Perez Family* (1995), with Marisa Tomei and Chazz Palminteri. **Deepa Mehta,** based in Toronto, Canada, has also made controversial productions about India. Her 1996 *Fire,* about a love affair between two women, mounted a scathing critique of the treatment of women in traditional Indian households. The film created a stir in India because of its implicit comparison of the lesbian couple with revered goddesses. Mehta followed up this *success de scandale* in 1998 with *Earth,* a compelling tale of a young girl in Lahore caught up in the religious and cultural strife that accompanied the India-Pakistan partition. A third contemporary Indian director who has found success abroad is **Shakhar Kapur.** His searing epic drama *The Bandit Queen,* made in India in 1994, is putatively based on the actual life of a low-caste woman who, after undergoing unthinkable degradations and hardships, rose to become a national political figure. By 1999, Kapur had moved his base of operations to Great Britain to direct another tale about a powerful woman, *Elizabeth,* an austere and formal study of Queen Elizabeth the First of England, focusing on her ascension to the throne and her consolidation of power. In 2001,

Fire ★ India, 1996, Deepa Mehta; Nandita Das.

Kapur completed a U.S.-financed blockbuster, a remake of the British colonialist melodrama *The Four Feathers.*

The arc of Indian film history as a whole suggests a growing tendency toward Balkanization. Ray and the New Indian Cinema movement have split popular and elite audiences, and regional and diasporic film-making traditions have appealed to disparate linguistic, religious, and cultural traditions. But India is a country of unity as well as diversity. The Indian public's fascination with the songs, dances, stars, stories, and spectacle of its cinema transcends regional boundaries, creating bonds among Indian communities both at home and abroad as well as reaching out to audiences in other nations with a message of progress and good feeling in the face of adversity.

China: Three Cinemas

Unlike India, where a unifying film culture holds sway, China has three cinemas, each associated with a different location: the People's Republic of China, Hong Kong, and Taiwan. Separated geographically and politically, they share a common heritage but little else. Until the 1980s mainland China had largely been closed off to the rest of the world and its films unavailable. The world's largest and most widely known producer of Chinese entertainment films is Hong Kong, a tiny area perched on China's southern coast and until 1997 a British crown colony. In Taiwan, an island off the country's southeast coast, many of the most artistically distinguished films reflect a nativist value system not readily accessible to Western audiences. Although quite a number of Hong Kong films have been shot in China, and coproduction deals among the three film centers have increased, their diverse aesthetic approaches continue to set them apart from one another.

Until 1949, China's film industry, based in Shanghai, was overwhelmed by American and British imports. The People's Republic of China (PRC), established in that year, first produced so-called worker-peasant-soldier films mainly for revolutionary indoctrination and education, much as had its Communist mentor, the Soviet Union. In 1956, however, Communist leader Mao Zedong announced a new policy: "Let a hundred flowers bloom and a hundred schools of thoughts contend." As a result, censorship temporarily loosened. An exceptional fiction feature made during this period was *Two Stage Sisters* (1964), directed by Xie Jin, China's most highly regarded veteran director. It chronicles the parallel lives of two actresses during the political turmoil of 1935 to 1950, intermingling melodramatic and dialectic treatment, bravura camera style, and fine performances. Following the precepts of the revolutionary realist style dominant during this era, the plot turns on the desirability of valuing one's loyalty to the group over aspiring to an individualized form of stardom—a message encapsulated in a striking mirror shot in which the heroine recognizes that all Chinese women are her sisters.

During the so-called cultural revolution (1966–1976), very few films were made and those were mostly confined to the themes of the "revolutionary operas" approved by Communist authorities. Studios were closed; writers, directors, actors, producers, technicians (and millions of others) were sent off to the countryside to be "reeducated." In 1978, however, a second "hundred flowers" policy was announced, and constraints on the studios were again loosened. Since then, Chinese film production has resumed on a larger scale with a more sophisticated approach to the needs of the nation and its vast population. Now

Two Stage Sisters ★ China, 1964, Xie Jin; Cao Tindi and Xie Fang, left rear.

fully financially accountable, the studios began to create movies for entertainment rather than indoctrination. By the end of the 1990s, between 130 and 140 films a year were being produced. In 1982 the People's Republic was represented for the first time in the official competition at Cannes with *The True Story of Ah Q*. Though the Tiananmen Square massacre of student protesters by the government in 1989 led to yet another temporary censorship crackdown, the momentum that had been established has continued to drive film production in new creative directions.

Outside the major cities, exhibition practices are primitive. Until recently, exhibitors traveling on foot carried films and equipment to remote villages where viewers screened educational and entertainment productions on crudely improvised screens set up outdoors. In the past, these screenings were supported by the government; now the villagers must pay. Often special screenings are arranged for weddings and other community celebrations.

For the past twenty years some of the films attracting most attention at the Hong Kong International Film Festival—and more recently in Cannes, Venice, and Berlin—have come from the People's Republic of China. These have been directed by graduates of the Beijing Film Academy—especially by members of the class of 1982, the so-called Fifth Generation. Although these films vary widely from director to director, they have in common stories set in the past and a brilliant pictorial sense (greatly enhanced by the Technicolor laboratory still extant in China, which can produce images of incomparably rich hues). Often critical of Chinese society and history, Fifth Generation films have been subjected to harsh treatment at home, often looked on with disfavor by a government with a limited tolerance for dissent; in fact, some of the films have been banned in China. The *oeuvres* of the Fifth Generation directors fall into two periods: first, a cluster of exploratory films featuring elliptical narratives and extended poetic passages, and second, a more widely appealing series of productions with more conventional plot lines and fully developed characters. The first group includes *One and Eight* (1984) and *The Horse Thief* (1987). In the second group are most of the Chinese films that received international distribution during the 1990s, especially those directed by the best-known practitioners of the Fifth Generation style: Chen Kaige and Zhang Yimou.

Chen Kaige's *Yellow Earth* (1984), the first of the Fifth Generation films sent out to international festivals, is widely known abroad and was also influential at home. It tells the story of an encounter in the late 1930s between a soldier of the Communist Eighth Route Army and peasants in Shaanxi Province in northwestern China. Anthropological notations on the feudal culture and the superstitions of the tradition-bound peasant community are contrasted with observations on the ways in which some of the characters become "liberated" and react positively toward revolution. The film is distinguished by the inclusion of traditional Chinese folk songs and by Zhang Yimou's ravishing cinematography, which features extreme long shots of the stark, mountainous countryside in pictorial compositions with high horizon lines reminiscent of traditional Chinese landscape painting

Yellow Earth ☆ China, 1984, Chen Kaige; Xue Bai and Wang Xueqi.

Chen's second feature, *The Big Parade* (1986), is about a group of military cadets who train and rehearse for the huge celebration in 1984 of the Chinese Revolution's thirty-fifth anniversary. *Life on a String* (1991), Chen's first film made with foreign backing, is a folkloristic tale of the lifelong quests of a master musician and his pupil. Its narrative is abstract, even metaphysical. Again, cinematographer Zhang Yimou's choreographed views of breathtaking scenery are stunning. *Farewell My Concubine* (1992), starring the exquisite Gong Li, was made with Taiwanese money by a producer based in Hong Kong. It concerns a Beijing Opera star's fifty-year unrequited passion for his costar. Both characters are male. A reformed prostitute is the wife of the lover, romantic rival of the loved one. In 1999 Chen made his most conventional film to date, *The Emperor and the Assassin,* again starring Gong Li. Featuring lavish costumes and sets, it tells the story of palace intrigue during China's struggle for unification in ancient times.

Chen's relationship to his homeland is equivocal. While dealing resolutely with Chinese subjects and themes, his films veer from political correctness. Alhough his background includes passionate commitment to Maoist policies in the 1960s (he was, in fact, a Red Guard), he has subsequently spent much time in New York, living there for more than three years. Chinese film scholar Rey Chow has argued that Chen's 1988 *King of the Children* constitutes a patriarchal affirmation of traditional Chinese national identity, which positions him as a conservative presence among the Fifth Generation directors.

Zhang Yimou, the cinematographer for two of Chen's early films, directed his own first feature, *Red Sorghum,* in 1988. Injecting a powerful erotic element into the Fifth Generation style, it won the Golden Bear at the Berlin Film Festival, thus becoming the first PRC film to achieve the highest honor at one of the leading international festivals. The film was also selected as the closing-night film of the New York festival and was subsequently released in the United States. Its look was characteristic of Zhang's early cinematographic technique, with low lighting, radiant Technicolor images, and studied, asymmetrical compositions. It typified Zhang's outlook in its ardent championing of individualism over group values.

Throughout his career Zhang has been concerned with the oppression of women. The story of *Red Sorghum,* which is set in the 1930s, is based on a northern Chinese legend of a young woman sold into wifehood by her unfeeling father. His second feature, *Ju Dou* (1990), wholly Japanese financed, is an earthy sexual melodrama of an old and vicious owner of a textile factory who buys a lovely bride and mistreats her. His nephew and she become lovers, and violence and revenge ensue. Studded with shimmering images of freshly dyed swathes of silk drying on the rafters of the factory, the film met with considerable success abroad. *Raise the Red Lantern* (1991), set in northern China in the 1920s, concerns a beautiful young woman from an impoverished family who becomes the fourth wife of an elderly potentate. *The Story of Qiu Ju* (1992) features a contemporary setting; the central figure is again a young woman of fierce will. In 1994 the epic-scale *To Live* was about a Chinese family—especially its women—living through the seismic upheavals of twentieth-century China. Zhang's rendition of a gangster tale, *Shanghai Triad* (1996), tells its saga of corruption and social upheaval through the eyes of a young boy; here again, however, the focus is on a woman, the doomed mistress of an underworld chieftain.

Gong Li, featured in Chen's *Farewell My Concubine* and *The Emperor and the Assassin,* starred in all of Yimou's films in the late 1980s and early to mid-1990s; as a result, she became China's best-known performer internationally and was labeled the most

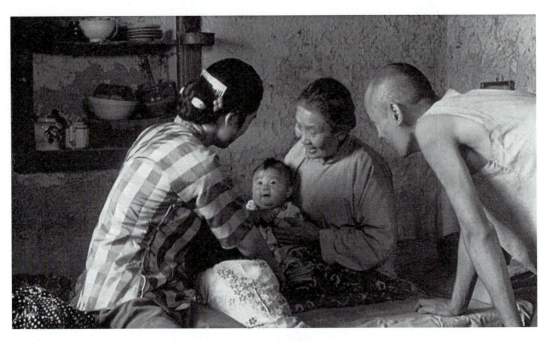

To Live ★ China, 1994, Zhang Yimou; Gong Li and Ge You.

beautiful woman in the world by one Western critic. "Almost all her parts were bigger-than-life women," the director later recalled, "symbols living under the oppression of feudalism and patriarchy." When the professional and personal relationship between director and star broke up in the late 1990s, he turned to other performers and cultivated a more subdued style of cinematography and *mise-en-scène.* His 1999 production, *Not One Less,* about a young girl who teaches school in a small Chinese village, uses nonprofessional actors and is shot in the documentary style he had experimented with in *The Story of Qiu Ju,* sometimes using a hidden camera. The film won him a Golden Lion at the Venice Film Festival.

The antithesis of the tightly controlled film making of mainland China is the free-wheeling capitalist film industry of Hong Kong. Productions there typically proceed at breakneck speed on tight schedules, often with fragmentary scripts. At its peak in the early 1990s the industry released two hundred thirty films a year. Movie making suffered a temporary setback in the mid-1990s due to uncertainty about the Chinese takeover of the former British colony in 1997, but fears were quickly allayed when it became clear that the mainland government would maintain a hands-off policy. Thus, by 2000 the industry had rebounded; one hundred thirty new films were released that year. The staples of Hong Kong production are the popular genres of martial arts, crazy comedies, gangster films, and soft-core pornography. To serve a population divided between Mandarin- and Cantonese-speaking audiences, virtually all Hong Kong movies are subtitled in Chinese.

Hong Kong films are distributed mostly within Asia, but in the 1970s and 1980s the style achieved international renown through the global appeal of two of its major stars: Bruce Lee and Jackie Chan. Both were masters of martial arts technique, engaging in sequences of violence and mayhem that made liberal use of filmic techniques such as fast-motion photography and flash editing to create visually flamboyant set pieces of surpassing grace and energy. The sinewy Lee starred in a series of riveting action pictures, culminating in the 1973 Hollywood-sponsored blockbuster *Enter the Dragon,* made just before he died. Chan combines martial arts with comedy; extended reaction shots allow him to showcase his rubber-faced expressivity and to create mischievous yet sympathetic comic characters with whom the audience can identify in productions such as the 1978 *Drunken Master* (Woo-ping Yuen).

At Cannes in 1975 Hong Kong's *A Touch of Zen* won the Grand Prix. Directed by King Hu, it was large in scale, three hours in length, and added Buddhism to martial arts. Hu's *Legend of the Mountain* and *Raining in the Mountains,* shown at Edinburgh in 1979, also evoke the legends of ancient China and contain much visual elegance and a philosophical dimension along with their balletic fight scenes. More recently, Tsui Hark, a major player in the Hong Kong industry, has made a name for himself through a series of fast-paced "chop-socky" productions with incomprehensible plots, such as the 1986 *Peking Opera Blues.* Hong Kong film scholar Steven Jao has labeled Tsui's style "nationalism on speed."

The virtuoso of Hong Kong action movies is **John Woo,** who deploys formulaic martial arts elements and gunplay in hyperstylized action sequences of overpowering visual energy, replete with special effects-aided acrobatics and shock cutting. In films such as *A Better Tomorrow* (1986), *The Killer* (1989), *Hard-Boiled* (1992), and the 1997 American production *Face-Off,* Woo embellishes formulaic Hollywood crime story elements with flashy visual flourishes, frequently relying on the kaleidoscopic patterns of light and reflections created by shattering glass. *The Killer,* for example, begins with a scene in which Woo's frequent leading man Chow Yun-Fat, playing a reluctant mob hit-man, enters a church illuminated by thousands of candles. The next scene finds him engaged in a

A Touch of Zen ★ Hong Kong, 1975, King Hu.

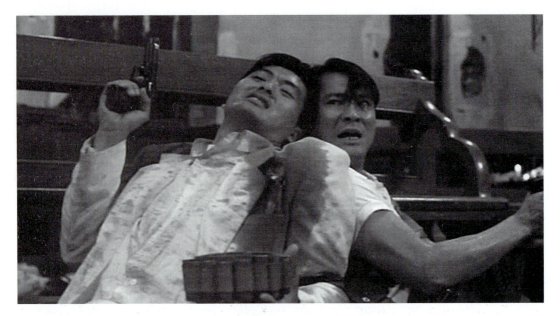

The Killer ★ Hong Kong, 1989, John Woo; Chow Yun-Fat and Danny Lee.

ferocious gun battle in which a seemingly endless barrage of windows and mirrors are smashed, creating meteoric showers of light over the proceedings. At one point the weary hit-man confides in a friend that he seeks the solace of a church to find peace and quiet, a quality conspicuously lacking in the world Woo creates.

Unlike Woo, who specializes in action movies, **Ann Hui** has worked in a variety of genres. Her first film, *The Secret* (1979), was a thriller; her next, *The Spooky Bunch* (1980), was a comedy. She followed these commercially successful productions in 1982 with *Boat People,* a searing portrait of South Vietnamese refugees, which was shot on location in China and premiered at Cannes. In 1990 Hui made *Song of the Exile,* a semiautobiographical exploration of the emotional and cultural gap between a British-educated Hong Kong girl and her Japanese mother. *My American Grandson* (1991), a Taiwanese production, focuses on a Chinese American child visiting his grandfather in Shanghai for the summer. In 1996 Hui made another award-winning drama, *Summer Snow,* about a middle-aged woman who must care for a father-in-law with Alzheimer's disease.

The career of Hui's protegé, **Stanley Kwan,** has also been characterized by versatility. He first drew international attention with his 1987 *Rouge,* a ghost story. Then, in 1991 he made *Center Stage,* a biopic about the legendary Chinese film star Ryan Ling-yu. *Center Stage,* his most acclaimed film, is crafted as a Brechtian collage of old movie clips, interviews, and fictional footage. Maggie Cheung, who won the best actress award at the Berlin Festival for her portrayal, plays the lead.

Center Stage marked the advent of a more postmodern mode of Hong Kong film making that came to the fore in the 1990s, most prominently in the work of **Wong Kar-Wei.** Thanks to the efforts of the American film maker Quentin Tarantino, who arranged for Wong's 1994 comedy *Chungking Express* to be commercially distributed in the United

States, this unconventional Hong Kong director has achieved considerable international renown, with a number of commentators labeling him as one of the most significant presences on the contemporary movie-making scene. *Chungking Express* tells two stories about a pair of young police detectives getting over failed romances. One falls for a mysterious female drug smuggler, played by Brigitte Lin (known as "the Asian Garbo"), a character putatively inspired by the Gena Rowlands character in the American independent film *Gloria,* directed by John Cassavetes. The other police detective is pursued by a pixie-ish fast-food worker, played by Hong Kong pop singer Faye Wong. Like other Wong productions *Chungking Express* focuses on characters reminiscent of those in American "B" pictures. Adding to their sleazy Hollywood feel, Wong's movies are littered with American pop culture references. His edgy style comes across as a kind of updated *film noir* look, featuring grainy, darkly lit images of a nighttime urban world sometimes accompanied by *noir*-ish voice-over narration. Jumpy, hand-held camerawork, slow motion and stop motion photography, shock cutting, strobe-effect lighting, frequently shifting points of view, sudden time shifts, and a dearth of establishing shots complete the look, keeping the viewer off balance but wide awake. Wong followed *Chungking Express* with *Fallen Angels* in 1995 and, in 1997, *Happy Together,* which won the best director prize at Cannes. A tale of two gay Chinese men caught in a destructive sadomasochistic relationship, *Happy Together* is set against the backdrop of modern Buenos Aires, reflecting the director's affection for Latin American novelists, such as Manuel Puig and Julio Cortázar. In 2000 Wong turned to a more traditional love story with *In the Mood for Love,* a nostalgic vision of romantic longing for which he toned down his style to achieve an aura of elegance and restraint.

In Taiwan, martial law was lifted in 1987 and it became possible to show previously taboo aspects of the island's history and to undertake coproductions with mainland China

Happy Together ★ Hong Kong, 1997, Wong Kar-Wei; Tony Lung and Leslie Cheung.

(though officially forbidden). Taiwanese films have been honored at international film festivals but not shown widely in the United States. Influenced by the reigning aesthetic philosophy of nativism, they often emphasize Taiwanese history and traditional Chinese formal techniques, making many of them somewhat daunting for Western audiences.

City of Sadness (1988), directed by **Hou Hsiao-hsien,** was Taiwan's first international artistic success (awarded the Golden Lion at the Venice Film Festival), while also doing very well commercially at home. Hou went on to make a series of nativist-oriented cinematic meditations on Taiwanese and Chinese history, including *The Puppetmaster* (1993), *Good Men, Good Women* (1995), *Goodbye, South, Goodbye* (1996), and *Flowers of Shanghai* (1998). Hou favors contemplative long shots in which the camera remains at a distance from his actors; thus his films lack the dramatic intensity American filmgoers are accustomed to. "I always tell my cameraman, 'Pull back! More detached!' " Hou says. Often there is more than one center of dramatic interest—or perhaps none at all. Nonetheless, the results can be deeply affecting. The three-hour *City of Sadness* tells the traumatic tale of the massacre of thousands of native Taiwanese by the incoming Chinese Nationalist government in 1947. Although Hou claims to have been influenced by *The Godfather* in his conception of this film, it takes a far more stoic and externalized perspective on the action than its American predecessor. *Flowers of Shanghai,* which a number of critics have labeled Hou's most accomplished work, is set in a Shanghai brothel at the end of the nine-

Good Men, Good Women ★ Taiwan, 1995, Hou Hsiao-hsien

teenth century. Softly lit rooms photographed with long, flowing camera movements reveal the intrigues that seal the fate of the female inhabitants of the house, who are at the mercy of their powerful male patrons. The film's first shot, lasting ten minutes, introduces us to a number of the major characters, then surveys the room, lingering on objects and views that, although void of immediate dramatic interest, create a richly textured vision of a surrounding world against which the action unfolds.

Besides directing, Hou has also acted. Among other roles, he starred in the 1985 *Taipei Story,* the breakthrough production of fellow Taiwanese film maker **Edward Yang.** Yang was born and raised in Taiwan but received his graduate education in America (Florida State University and University of Southern California). Like Hou, Yang has followed the nativist line, turning out a series of emotionally detached studies of Taiwanese culture. "The future of Western civilization lies right here," one of the characters in *Taipei Story* remarks. Unlike Hou, however, Yang usually sets his films in the present rather than in the past. Although he has been compared to Antonioni, his films lack the psychologically complex central characters that mark the work of the Italian director. Instead, he favors multiple plot lines made up of intricately woven narrative strands involving many characters, who may act in seemingly unmotivated ways. Among his most notable films, *The Terrorizor* (1986) follows the activities of three modern Taiwanese couples and their interactions with a police detective. The four-hour *A Brighter Summer Day* (1991), set in Taiwan in the early 1960s, concerns teenagers who have no memory of life on the Chinese mainland and who gravitate toward gangs as they reject the ideals of their parents. With a cast made up of mostly nonprofessionals, the film was inspired by a true incident in which a fourteen-

A Brighter Summer Day ★ Taiwan, 1991, Edward Yang.

year-old girl was murdered by a male high school student. In 2000 Yang made *Yi yi (A One and a Two),* a tangled family drama that won him a best director award at Cannes.

A more Westernized and accessible Taiwanese sensibility is represented by **Ang Lee,** whose interests have shifted from Chinese to Western subjects and back again. Lee is particularly adept at depicting self-deluded characters with gentle humor, revealing their quirks and foibles without causing the audience to lose sympathy for them. His first film, *The Wedding Banquet* (1993), portrays the travails of a gay Taiwanese man living in New York City who must conceal his relationship with his lover from his traditional parents. In a plot device that recalls the popular French farce *The Birdcage,* the Taiwanese parents arrange a marriage for their son, and the three young people must engage in an elaborate charade to prevent the truth from coming out. Lee followed up this success in 1994 with an equally engaging comedy, this time set in Taiwan rather than New York. Entitled *Eat, Drink, Man, Woman,* it concerns an eminent Taiwanese chef and his relationship with his three marriageable daughters. More recently, Lee has worked on large-scale Hollywood productions such as the 1995 *Sense and Sensibility* with Emma Thompson and Kate Winslet, and the 1997 *Ice Storm* with Sigourney Weaver and Kevin Kline. In 2000 he returned to mainland China to make *Crouching Tiger, Hidden Dragon,* a light-hearted martial arts film with a feminist slant. It went on to win a number of Academy of Awards and became the most widely seen foreign film in the United States.

If the experience of Ang Lee is any guide, globalization will operate to bring the three Chinese cinemas closer together in future years. As a Taiwanese film maker who has worked in his home country, in America, and in mainland China, he is a truly international figure. Yet, if we are to judge from developments thus far, increased globalization need not operate to create a homogeneous film culture that will obliterate the venerable traditions of Asian art. Rather, what we observe in Chinese film is an aesthetic of hybridization: allusions to American-style pop culture, Hollywood storytelling techniques, and a Latin American-inspired postmodernism combined with traditional Chinese subjects and tech-

Crouching Tiger, Hidden Dragon ☆ Taiwan, 2000, Ang Lee; Zhang Ziyi.

niques. Similarly in the development of Indian cinema, one finds Italian neorealism and Brechtian modernism enriching the indigenous materials of Indian culture. Even Hollywood is not immune to the effects of hybridization; international influences infiltrate the most powerful film industry in the world, as we will see in the next chapter.

Films of the Period

INDIA

1951
Awaara (Raj Kapoor)

1952
Nagarit (Ritwik Ghatak)

1955
Panther Panchali (Satyajit Ray)

1956
Aparajito (Satyajit Ray)

1957
Mother India (Mehboob Khan)

1958
Pathetic Fallacy (*Ajantrik*) (Ritwik Ghatak)
The World of Apu (*Apur Sansar*) (Satyajit Ray)
The Music Room (*Jalsaghar*) (Satyajit Ray)

1960
The Goddess (*Devi*) (Satyajit Ray)

1964
The Lonely Wife (*Charulata*) (Satyajit Ray)

1969
Mister Shome (*Bhuvan Shome*) (Mrinal Sen)
Our Daily Bread (*Uski Roti*) (Mani Kaul)

1970
Days and Nights in the Forest (*Aranyer Din Ratri*) (Satyajit Ray)
Daily Bread (*Uski Roti*) (Mani Kaul)

1973
Distant Thunder (*Ashani Sanket*) (Satyajit Ray)

1976
The Churning (*Manthan*) (Shyam Benegal)

1977
The Role (*Bhumika*) (Shyam Benegal)
The Chess Players (*Shatranj Ke Khiladi*) (Satyajit Ray)

1979
And Quiet Rolls the Dawn (*Ekdin pratidin*) (Mrinal Sen)

1980
In Search of Famine (*Aakaler Sandhaney*) (Mrinal Sen)

1983
The Ruins (*Khandahar*) (Mrinal Sen)

1984
Home and the World (*Ghare-Baire*) (Satyajit Ray)
The Wave (*Tarang*) (Kumar Shahani)

1986
Genesis (Mrinal Sen)
Trikal (Shyam Benegal)

1988
Salaam Bombay! (Mira Nair)

1991
Agantuk (Satyajit Ray)

1992
Roja (Mani Rathnam)

1994
The Bandit Queen (Shakhar Kapur)

1996
Fire (Deepa Mehta)

1998
Earth (Deepa Mehta)

THE PEOPLE'S REPUBLIC OF CHINA

1964
Two Stage Sisters (*Wutai jiemei*) (Xie Jin)

1984
One and the Eight (*Yi ge he ba ge*) (Zhang
     Junzhao)
Yellow Earth (*Huang tudi*) (Chen Kaige)

1986
The Big Parade (*Da yue bing*) (Chen Kaige)
The Black Cannon Incident (*Hei pao shijian*)
     (Huang Jianxin)

1987
The Horse Thief (*Dao ma zei*) (Tian
     Zhuangzhuang)

1988
King of the Children (*Haizi wang*) (Chen Kaige)
Red Sorghum (*Hong gaoliang*) (Zhang Yimou)

1990
Ju Dou (Zhang Yimou)

1991
Life on a String (*Bian zou bian chang*) (Chen
     Kaige)
Raise the Red Lantern (*Da hong denglong gao gao
     gua*) (Zhang Yimou)

1992
Farewell My Concubine (*Ba wang bie ji*) (Chen
     Kaige)
The Story of Qiu Ju (*Qiu Ju da guansi*) (Zhang
     Yimou)

1995
Shanghai Triad (Zhang Yimou)

1999
Not One Less (*Yi ge dou bu neng shao*) (Zhang
     Yimou)
The Road Home (*Wo de fugin muqin*) (Zhang Yimou)

HONG KONG

1975
A Touch of Zen (*Hsia nu*) (King Hu)

1982
Boat People (*Tou bun no hoi*) (Ann Hui)

1986
A Better Tomorrow (*Ying huang boon sik*) (John Woo)

1987
The Horse Thief (*Daoma zei*) (Tian Zhuangzhuang)

1989
The Killer (*Die xue shuang xiong*) (John Woo)

1990
Song of Exile (*Ketu qiuhen*) (Ann Hui)

1992
Hard-Boiled (*Lashou shentan*) (John Woo)

1994
Chungking Express (*Chonging Samlam*) (Wong
     Kar-Wei)

1995
The Blade (*Dao*) (Tsui Hark)

1997
Happy Together (*Cheun guong tsa sit*) (Wong Kar-Wei)

2000
In the Mood for Love (Wong Kar-Wei)

2001
Time and Tide (*Seunlau ngaklau*) (Tsui Hark)

TAIWAN

1985
Taipei Story (*Qingmei Zhuma*) (Edward Yang)
A Time to Live and a Time to Die (*Tong nien
     wang shi*) (Hou Hsiao-hsien)

1986
The Terrorizer (*Kongbu fenzi*) (Edward Yang)

1988
A City of Sadness (*Beiqing chengshi*) (Hou Hsiao-
     hsien)

1991
A Brighter Summer Day (*Guling jie shaonian sha
     ren shijian*) (Edward Yang)

1993
The Wedding Banquet (*Hsi yen*) (Ang Lee)
The Puppet Master (*Hsimeng jensheng*) (Hou
  Hsiao-hsien)

1994
Eat, Drink, Man, Woman (*Yin shi nan nu*) (Ang Lee)

1996
Goodbye, South, Goodbye (*Nanguo zaijan, nanguo*)
  (Hou Hsiao-hsien)

1998
Flowers of Shanghei (*Hai shang hua*) (Hou
  Hsiao-hsien)

2000
Crouching Tiger, Hidden Dragon (Ang Lee)
Yi yi (Edward Yang)

2001
Millenium Mumbo (Hou Hsiao-hsien)

Books on the Period

INDIA

Chakavarty, Sumitra S. *National Identity in Indian Popular Cinema, 1947–1987*. Austin: University of Texas Press, 1993.

Dissanayke, Wimal, ed. *Cinema and Cultural Identity: Reflections on Film from Japan, India, and China*. New York: Cambridge University Press, 1993.

Garga, B. D. *So Many Cinemas: The Motion Picture in India*. London: Eminence Designs, c. 1998.

Gazdar, Mushtaq. *Pakistan Cinema 1947–1997*. New York: Oxford University Press, 1998.

Narwekar, Sanjit, comp. *Directory of Indian Film-Makers and Films*. Westport, CT: Greenwood Press, 1994.

Rajadhyaksha, Ashish, and Paul Willemen, eds. *Encyclopedia of Indian Cinema* (2nd ed.). Bloomington: Indiana Unversity Press, 1999.

CHINA (PEOPLE'S REPUBLIC OF CHINA, HONG KONG, TAIWAN)

Bordwell, David. *Planet Hong Kong: Popular Cinema and the Art of Entertainment*. Cambridge, MA: Harvard University Press, 2000.

Browne, Nick, Paul Pickowicz, Vivian Sobchack, and Esther Yau, eds. *New Chinese Cinema: Forms, Identities, Politics*. New York: Cambridge University Press, 1994.

Chow, Rey. *Primitive Passions: Visuality, Sexuality, Ethnography, and Contemporary Chinese Cinema*. New York: Columbia University Press, 1995.

Dannen, Fredric, and Barry Long. *Hong Kong Babylon: An Insider's Guide to the Hollywood of the East*. Boston: Faber and Faber, 1997.

Dissanayke, Wimal, ed. *Cinema and Cultural Identity: Reflections on Film from Japan, India, and China*. New York: Cambridge University Press, 1993.

Fonoroff, Paul. *At the Hong Kong Movies: 600 Reviews from 1988 till the Handover*. London: Odyssey Publications, 1999.

Hammond, Stefan, and Mike Wilkins. *Sex and Zen and a Bullet in the Head: The Essential Guide to Hong Kong's Mind-Bending Films*. New York: Simon and Schuster, 1996.

Hoover, Michael, and Lisa Stokes. *City on Fire: Hong Kong Cinema*. New York: Verso, 1999.

Logan, Bey. *Hong Kong Action Cinema*. New York: Overlook Press, 1996.

Semsel, George S., Chen Xihe, and Xia Hong, eds. *Film in Contemporary China: Critical Debates, 1979–1989*. Westport, CT: Greenwood Press, 1993.

Stokes, Lisa Oldham, and Michael Hoover. *City on Fire: Hong Kong Cinema*. London: Verso, 1999.

Tam, Kwok-kan, and Wimal Dissanayake. *New Chinese Cinema*. New York: Oxford University Press, 1998.

Teo, Stephen. *Hong Kong Cinema: The Extra Dimensions*. London: British Film Institute Publishing, 1998.

Weisser, Thomas. *Asian Trash Cinema*. Kingwood, TX: ATC/ETC Publications, 1994.

Widmer, Ellen, and David Den-Wei Wang. *From May Fourth to June Fourth: Fiction and Film in Twentieth Century China*. Cambridge, MA: Harvard University Press, 1993.

Zhang, Xudong. *Chinese Modernism in the Era of Reforms: Cultural Fever, Avant-Garde Fiction, and the New Chinese Cinema*. Durham, NC: Duke University Press, 1996.

Zhang, Yingjin, ed. *Cinema and Urban Culture in Shanghai, 1922–1943*. Stanford: Stanford University Press, 1999.

Zhang, Yingjin, and Zhiwei Xiao. *Encyclopedia of Chinese Film*. New York: Routledge, 1999.

Hollywood
in Transition

★ ★ ★ ★

1945–1962

After World War II ended in 1945, the United States lost no time in returning to a settled state. The early postwar years were given over to readjustment. Then, in 1952, General Dwight Eisenhower, hero of World War II, was elected President of the United States; he was reelected in 1956. These were the Cold War years, in which the United States defined itself largely through its ideological differences with the Soviet Union. The struggle between these two superpowers for global dominance led to a war in Korea, which ended in 1953. Apart from this conflict, the Eisenhower years were prosperous, placid, and very "American." Undercurrents of disaffection that hindsight has revealed didn't come to the fore until the troubled 1960s.

Much the same might be said of most Hollywood films of the 1950s in terms of placidity and Americanism—at least on the surface. The postwar years marked the beginning of a transition that would lead the American film industry from the hardened confines of a production-distribution-exhibition pattern that had lasted for over two decades into uncertainty and changing forms and functions. In film, what affects the industry affects the art; what happens in the United States influences the world.

A central factor accounting for and accompanying these changes was the decline in theater attendance from the booming war and postwar years (from 90 million weekly in 1948 to 51 million in 1952). The former "family audience" was now a minority audience, administered to mainly by Walt Disney Productions. Going to the movies, once the staple form of entertainment, became more of a special occasion somewhere between staying home to watch TV and attending live theater or a concert. With increased public affluence, motion pictures were now competing for leisure time with spectator sports, bowling, motorboating, hi-fi sets, and a whole range of new activities. Whereas in 1946, as *Variety* noted, almost $1.7 billion (or almost 20 percent of all U.S. expenditures for recreation) were paid in movie admissions; by 1962 that figure had plummeted to $930 million (or about 4.5 percent)—in spite of inflating ticket prices.

By 1952 the major studios had had to divest themselves of their theater holdings. After a decade of litigation, from 1938 to 1948, the Supreme Court finally ruled, in *U.S. v. Paramount Pictures et al.,* that the practice of "vertical control" was in restraint of trade and tended toward monopoly. The majors might continue to produce and distribute but not exhibit. In the mid-1940s about 400 features were produced annually—300 by the major studios, 100 by independents. Every week between 80 and 100 million persons had paid admission to see the movies in 18,719 "hard-top" theaters and 300 drive-ins. By 1960 the average weekly attendance—in 13,200 indoor and 4,600 outdoor theaters—had dropped to an estimated 46 million. Of the 136 features produced that year, only 70 came from the major studios, whereas 66 were from the independents. Those trends—fewer pictures, more of which were by independents; smaller audiences; and a decrease in the number of theaters, with the proportion of drive-in theaters increasing—would continue throughout the 1960s and into the 1970s.

Television

It was TV, of course, that occupied most of the leisure time of the public who formerly would have gone to the movies. The shifting relationship between motion pictures and broadcasting is one of the main chapters in the history of those two industries during the 1950s and 1960s. Television had begun on an experimental basis just before World War II, but wartime priorities and shortages had frozen its development until the postwar years. From five stations and a few hundred sets in 1946 it expanded rapidly to the first year of big-time television in 1948, when Milton Berle and Ed Sullivan were seen and heard in the large urban centers. Between 1948 and 1952 approximately 17 million TV sets were sold. In 1951 coaxial cable and microwave relay had connected the nation coast to coast. In that year major TV production began its move from New York to Hollywood. From the early 1950s the audience continued to expand. Today there are more television sets than persons in the country. The most popular television series (*ER,* for example) average between 25 and 30 million viewers a week. A special occasion (such as the last episode of *Seinfeld* in 1998) may attract more than 60 million; even greater numbers worldwide watch some big sporting events.

Until 1948 the motion picture industry's reaction to the TV threat was ostrichlike. At one studio it was reported to be forbidden even to use the word *television* in executive conversation. Then the stance shifted to passive resistance through deliberate withholding of the enormous resources of talent and reservoir of product. No actors, writers, or directors under contract were permitted to work for television. No feature films produced by the major studios were offered for airing. Films playing in theaters were not advertised on television. Revenues from the box office continued to decline, and complaints from stockholders about dwindling dividends steadily increased.

The critical problem was finding access to an audience. Since the production companies no longer owned the theaters, which anyway were being converted into supermarkets or razed to make way for parking lots, their loyalty to the theater owners and resolve to try to protect them from even greater television competition was weakened. When the pressures finally became too great, the studios followed the old industry saw about if you can't beat 'em, join 'em. They began by making available to TV the vast libraries of feature films that had accumulated during the past decades. The popularity of theatrical feature films with television audiences has, of course, been enormous. When *The Bridge on the River Kwai* was aired by ABC-TV on Sunday night prime time in 1966, the audience was estimated at 60 million. By the early 1970s not only had the backlog of old features been used up, but the supply of recent theatrical film releases was far below the television demand.

The ultimate response of Hollywood to television was to undertake production directly for the tube. It began in 1952 when Columbia Pictures formed the first of the television subsidiaries among the major studios—Screen Gems. This television film making started with the half-hour entertainment series, which became hour-long and, in some instances, even ninety minutes in length, resembling more and more the old "B" pictures that were no longer a profitable kind of production for the more choosy audiences who went out to the theaters. In 1957 Desilu, the company formed by Desi Arnaz and Lucille Ball out of the extraordinary success of their *I Love Lucy* series, shot more film than all the major studios together. By the mid-1960s Hollywood began to make feature films directly for TV rather than for initial theatrical showing.

The production for television exerted a gravitational pull toward the West Coast. Soon virtually all nighttime television entertainment was being produced in the Los Angeles area. Only news, documentary and public affairs, and some daytime game shows and soap operas continued to come out of New York. As television became established, people and product began to flow from it into film. Out of the so-called Golden Age of live TV drama in the late 1940s and early 1950s, theatrical feature films were created from the writings of Paddy Chayefsky, Rod Serling, and others. *Marty* (1955), *Twelve Angry Men* (1957), and *Requiem for a Heavyweight* (1962) had all appeared live on the tube. Direc-

Marty ★ United States,
1955, Delbert Mann; Ernest
Borgnine and Betsy Blair.

tors as well as writers came to features from television: John Frankenheimer, Sam Peckinpah, and Norman Jewison among them. Some of the new stars—Steve McQueen, James Garner, Clint Eastwood (male only, it seems) also got their start in television. Financial control, studio facilities, story material, production personnel, and performers have continued to move back and forth between film and television.

New Screen Processes

All three major technological additions to the silent black-and-white film—sound, color, and wide screen—were around from the very beginning. Their introduction was in every case dependent more on economic considerations than on technical feasibility. Whenever the industry is in trouble somebody will say, "There's nothing wrong with the movies that a few good pictures can't cure." But if producers knew how to make consistently profitable films, there wouldn't have been any trouble in the first place. Although popular success can't be guaranteed, technical novelty can be tried. Sound came in 1927 because of the competition radio then offered for the audiences of silent films, and because Warner Bros. was attempting corporate expansion. Technicolor was added to feature film production in 1935 in an attempt to remedy the continuing Depression slump. In 1952 the failing box office and television competition once again goaded the industry into introducing a number of "new screen processes." All were designed to offer sights and sounds that the competitive medium could not duplicate, and to give the screen a greater illusion of depth.

Stereoscopic, or 3-D, feature films first appeared in the fall of 1952. (In the 1930s there had been a series of M-G-M black-and-white 3-D shorts; polaroid lenses now permitted the addition of color.) With *Bwana Devil* it seemed to the audience that a lion was charging them (promotion promised "A lion in your lap") or a spear was being thrown over their heads.

At first, the 3-D films were extremely successful, but their attraction wore off within less than a year. It was said that audiences didn't like the special glasses required. By the time any substantial work was undertaken in 3-D (such as Alfred Hitchcock's *Dial M for Murder,* released in 1954), the audience had lost interest. 3-D came and went while the wide screen has lasted in one form or another ever since. It was the grandeur the wide screens added (in the late 1920s a wide-screen system called Magnascope had been referred to as the "grandeur screen") that caught public fancy. The first of the new wide-screen processes was the biggest and best of them in terms of spatial illusion. *This Is Cinerama* opened in New York City in September 1952. Developed by Fred Waller in 1939, it had been used in an earlier version by the Armed Forces during World War II for aircraft identification and mock gunnery practice. The screen, with a 2.85 to 1 ratio of width to height, was deeply curved and vast. A necessarily small audience sitting well forward had virtually everyone's whole field of vision filled by the image. Viewers felt they really were on that roller coaster or on that plane coming in over the Chicago skyline. Accompanying the visual format of great width and depth was a hi-fidelity, stereophonic, magnetic sound system. Its enormously increased range of frequencies brought sound reproduction much closer to life than the woefully inadequate optical recording in standard use.

Dial M for Murder   ★   United States, 1954, Alfred Hitchcock, in 3-D; Grace Kelly.

The development of Cinerama had been backed by people outside the Hollywood industry—Mike Todd, Louis de Rochemont, Lowell Thomas, and others—but the studio heads could scarcely be blind to its huge financial success. *This Is Cinerama* was soon numbered among the great moneymakers of all time, and the several features that followed it, playing in only a few specially equipped and converted "legitimate" theaters at live theater prices, consistently appeared high on *Variety*'s box-office tallies. But Cinerama's cumbersome technology and the small audiences that could be accommodated at each showing presented too severe a wrench to existing production and exhibition practices to be contemplated without alarm. Furthermore, the Cinerama films were essentially a group of travelogue shorts anthologized to feature length. The kinds of stories that might fill that monstrous screen seemed extremely limited. An appropriate size and shape for parades down Fifth Avenue, a train speeding across the Mojave Desert, or two boa constrictors copulating, as someone observed, it offered no clear advantage in dealing with individual human beings (who happen to stand upright), unless they were in quantities of thousands. Even more basically, the use of closeups and editing, essential to screen narrative technique as practiced, would be greatly reduced if not prohibited by what seemed acres of image. What was needed was a sort of poor man's Cinerama—one that spiced up but didn't depart too much from the existing standard.

Artist's representation of an audience watching *This Is Cinerama* ★ United States, 1952, Merian C. Cooper.

It was Spyros Skouras, head of Twentieth Century-Fox, who performed the trick. The rabbit he pulled out of the hat was called CinemaScope (and better not forget to capitalize the middle *S* if you were a Fox employee). It was based on a principle worked out in the 1920s by a French inventor, Henri Chrétien. Its wide screen was less wide than Cinerama's and curved only enough to accommodate focus. Though wider than standard (2.55 to 1 rather than 1.33 to 1), CinemaScope did not approximate peripheral vision. It was accompanied in its premiere by hi-fidelity four-track stereophonic sound.

Unlike the inauguration of the earlier 3-D, CinemaScope was launched with a feature that probably would have made money no matter what size and shape the screen. As it was, *The Robe,* which opened in September 1953, proved a tremendous success with its DeMille-like blend of spectacle and religiosity. It was followed by a series of expensive and well-made features, musicals and comedies especially, equally designed to show off the attractions of the new screen process—for example, *Gentlemen Prefer Blondes* (1953), *A Star Is Born* (1954), and *Seven Brides for Seven Brothers* (1954). Frequently featured trios of stars called attention to the expansiveness of the visual field, such as Marilyn Monroe, Lauren Bacall, and Betty Grable in *How to Marry a Millionaire* (1953) and Dorothy McGuire, Jean Peters, and Maggie McNamara in *Three Coins in the Fountain* (1954).

Fox was to wide screen what Warner had been to sound, and again the rest of the industry soon followed along. CinemaScope proved the almost ideal compromise between Cinerama and the conventional screen ratio. It required no major change in production technology or even technique, and it was simple and inexpensive to install in existing movie houses. Although it favored certain film types—historical spectacles, musicals, and westerns—and was awkward for others—intimate romances and social dramas—stories could be told in it, with fewer camera setups and less editing required. Some of the purists complained that the image it offered was like looking at the world through a postal slot, and Jean Cocteau is credited with remarking that he recognized progress when he saw it and henceforward would put paper in the typewriter sideways when he wrote his poems. But who cared about the purists?—the box office was registering public response in large figures. As with sound, directors learned to work with CinemaScope, many reluctantly at first. The new technology was incorporated into the medium, with resultant aesthetic shifts and even some gains—like all of the earlier technological additions. In *East of Eden* (1955), for example, director Elia Kazan and cinematographer Ted McCord made stunning and highly dramatic use of the new proportions for what was essentially an intimate story of family strife. Other wide-screen systems soon appeared. VistaVision, from Paramount, was a good alternative, providing a sharper image than CinemaScope. Todd A-0 was the first to use 70mm film, a gauge still employed for a few prestige productions. But the extremely wide screens didn't become the exclusive shape, as some feared they might when CinemaScope first appeared. Rather, they eventually became reserved for the extravaganza—the big musical (*My Fair Lady,* 1964, and *The Sound of Music,* 1965), the blockbusting war picture (*The Guns of Navarone,* 1961, and *The Longest Day,* 1962), and the historical spectacular (*Lawrence of Arabia,* 1962, and *Doctor Zhivago,* 1965). For more conventional pictures what is called the "standard wide screen"—1.85 to 1 its most common ratio—has replaced the former 1.33 to 1 "Academy ratio" that has remained standard for television sets.

Lawrence of Arabia   ★   United States, 1962, David Lean; Peter O'Toole, in Arab dress.

Fall of the Studios,
Rise of the Independents

Another result of the pressures and changes experienced by the industry in the early 1950s was a shakeup in production-distribution practices, which also affected the content and form of the films being made. Among the producing companies it was the former giants, now stripped of theaters, that were hit hardest by the dwindling and erratic earnings of their films. The enormous overhead in real estate, sound stages, expensive equipment, and high-salaried technical and creative personnel under long-term contracts could no longer be supported by the fewer, costlier films that current audience response dictated. Whereas M-G-M had once boasted as its greatest asset "More Stars Than There Are in Heaven," expensive nonworking actors, along with the writers and directors, had become a liability. All of the major studios except one were keeping their books in red ink.

That exception was United Artists (UA), which had never owned theaters and didn't even have a studio. Instead, it had acquired films from independent producers and distributed them to theaters owned by others. It would choose from among the projects presented to it, perhaps supervise the scripts, put up some money, and go to the bank for more. What it could guarantee to its producers was major distribution, for which it took a healthy cut. Its production overhead consisted mostly of offices, secretaries, and smart lawyers good at contracts and finance. Billy Wilder, one of United Artists' top producer-directors, observed ruefully, "We used to make pictures; now we make deals." A weak competitor in the old days, when the larger studios controlled exhibition, under the new conditions UA prospered and became the model others would imitate.

The rest of the studios freed themselves from employees under long-term contracts, except for skeleton technical crews. The actors, directors, and former staff producers went into production for themselves, or worked for other independents, with corporate profits and shares in the income from a picture replacing salaries. The studios rented out production space and facilities to the independents, financed their productions wholly or in part, and distributed the completed films. Rather than reading simply "Produced by," Paramount or Warner Bros., opening credits now read "A Judd Bernard-Irwin Winkler Production for Metro-Goldwyn-Mayer" or "A Horizon Picture, Released through Columbia Pictures Corporation," and the like.

The independent companies were by no means totally independent, however, and the kinds of films they produced departed very little from those that had preceded them. The domination once exercised by the heads of five studios (Metro-Goldwyn-Mayer, Paramount, Warner Bros., Twentieth Century-Fox, and RKO) was steadily being reduced. But the independents still had to play ball with the majors, whose remaining strongholds were their worldwide distribution organizations. This gave them power to exercise substantial control over the choice of subject matter and its presentation.

Another reason there was less change than might have been expected in the kinds of films being made with this new independence was that the smaller companies were subjected to exactly the same necessity for popular appeal as the large ones had been. In fact, in the case of the independents, the pressure was even greater. With only one picture produced at a time on borrowed money, rather than an annual production program of forty or fifty features financed out of studio reserves, each film had to be a success. Hits couldn't pay for flops. In some respects there seemed less room for experiment and risk than there had been under the old system. Many of the former studio personnel who formed their own companies stuck even closer to tested ingredients than the studios had done. Those who had cried for freedom from the repeated formulas of studio production and expressed the desire to strike out into bold new areas, to do something "really worthwhile," settled for the tried and true. To paraphrase G. B. Shaw, there's nothing as timid as several million dollars.

It is more than coincidental that in those years of the 1950s in which the studios were declining, directors were gaining a new status. When M-G-M, once biggest and proudest of the studios, virtually went out of the motion-picture business altogether in the 1970s, the film makers who would have worked for M-G-M still found their way to film making if they were smart enough and tough enough—constant prerequisites to creation in motion-picture art. If film artists spent a lot of their time making deals, as Wilder quipped, they were free from the power and overzealous supervision of production chiefs such as Irving Thalberg, and from conceptions of God, country, and motherhood, as revealed to Louis B. Mayer.

Internationalization

Along with all the other sweeping changes there even seemed some danger that Los Angeles might cease to be the film capital of the world, and fall into ruins like Carthage or ancient Rome. American films were in increasing competition with foreign ones—especially with those of Britain, Italy, and France—for audiences abroad and even in this country. Conational productions and multinational crews and casts became commonplace. And "American" films themselves were as likely to be shot anywhere in the world as within proximity of Hollywood Boulevard and Vine Street.

The first consideration to prompt this increased internationalization may have been in part an artistic one. Wide screens encouraged special emphasis on authentic and exotic locales. For conventional sorts of love stories that formerly would have been shot on sound stages and back lots, film makers now journeyed to Rome (*Three Coins in the Fountain,* 1954), Hong Kong (*Love Is a Many-Splendored Thing,* 1955), or Tokyo (*Sayonara,* 1957). Audiences of the 1950s began to get moving-picture postcards along with stars and stories. Some of the spectacles made for the wide screen were very much about the places and terrain where the stories took place—such as the Southeast Asian jungle for *The Bridge on the River Kwai* (1957) and the Middle Eastern desert for *Lawrence of Arabia* (1962).

The secondary considerations were exclusively financial. First, by shooting abroad, American producers could more easily assemble a cast drawn from a number of countries to better ensure warm reception of their films in various parts of the globe. Then, too, there was the advantage, for the Americans involved, of delayed payment of U.S. corporate and income taxes on work done outside the country. Also, it was thought to be, and in many cases actually was, cheaper to make films abroad. Generally costs were less in Mexico, Spain, and Italy, for example—especially for labor. (A counterargument was that the apparent saving was often canceled out in working with less-efficient crews who used unfamiliar methods and languages.) There was no doubt that the various schemes of subsidy offered by most foreign governments to encourage national production was a real incentive. Many essentially American films were disguised as British—for instance, their production set up in a way that met minimum requirements for assistance from Britain's

National Film Finance Corporation. In addition, where a quota system existed for proportionate release of foreign to domestic films, as in Britain and elsewhere, a film flying the local flag would be assured immediate exhibition there rather than having to wait among the films of other nations. In some cases—India, for example—American profits had become "frozen currency" and couldn't be taken out of the country. One way to make use of that money was to spend it on a production that could then be distributed worldwide and earn revenue elsewhere.

Distribution along with production became increasingly internationalized. American companies began to seek income from the distribution of foreign films in the United States as well as elsewhere. Also, as their own production expenses increased and the size of the domestic audience decreased, they attempted to earn back more and more of their costs from abroad. In former years the huge American market could return a profit on a film, and what was earned elsewhere was gravy. Now over 50 percent of the income from American films came from overseas. More than ever, Hollywood courted the world audience.

Finally, the motion-picture industry developed its own equivalent to the plants set up abroad and the multinational corporations that had become common practice among other industries. Not only was there a British M-G-M, as there was an English Ford, but the United States dominated and to some extent controlled foreign financing of production and international distribution. In terms of financial backing and distribution, Antonioni's *Blow-Up* (1966), made in England, was as much an American film as his *Zabriskie Point* (1970), made in the United States. American influence began to reach even into films that appeared to be totally French. Jean-Luc Godard's *A Married Woman* and *Band of Outsiders* (both 1964) were financed by Columbia Pictures. Four of François Truffaut's films were financed by United Artists. Although the European Economic Community tried to set up an alternative financing-distribution pattern to counter American domination, little came of the effort.

Loosened Controls on Content

In the United States, social controls placed on the content of motion pictures began to be eased in the 1950s. This encouraged, if not always a greater maturity, at least a new freedom and frankness in the presentation of sexual behavior, states of undress, and kinds of language. During those years, the United States Supreme Court rendered a series of decisions that curtailed the activities of state and local censoring bodies. The Motion Picture Association of America liberalized its code of self-regulation and then started to classify rather than regulate screen content. Organized pressure groups—religious, ethnic, and political—turned their attention away from what was showing in the theaters to what was appearing ever more widely on the tube. Producers eagerly, some desperately, took advantage of the new freedom to try to attract audiences away from television and to compete with the forthrightness of European films.

In 1952, in *The Miracle* case, the Supreme Court delivered what became a historic decision. The Rossellini short (which had been packaged with Pagnol's *Joffroy* and Renoir's *A Day in the Country* to be shown as *The Ways of Love*) had incensed Catholics in the New York City area, especially a Catholic veterans' organization. A modern parable of Christ's birth, *The Miracle* stars Anna Magnani as a feeble-minded peasant "Mary"; a bearded Federico Fellini appears as an itinerant "Joseph." After a round of contretemps,

The Miracle ★ Italy, 1948, Roberto Rossellini; Anna Magnani, center foregound.

including picketing and bomb threats, the New York State Board of Regents, the censoring agency, revoked the film's license on grounds that it was "sacrilegious." When the case eventually reached the Supreme Court, the Court seemed to reverse its own precedent. In 1915, in *Mutual Film Corporation* v. *Ohio,* it had been held that motion pictures were "business pure and simple . . . not to be regarded as part of the press of the country or as organs of public opinion," and hence not subject to the freedom from censorship guaranteed by the First Amendment to the Constitution. The 1952 Court did not rule on the constitutionality of film censorship as such, however. It simply stated that "sacrilege," particularly one faith's conception of it, was not sufficient grounds for the Board of Regents' action. Nonetheless, the decision suggested some sympathy toward affording the motion picture the same freedom from restraint prior to release as that enjoyed by the other media of communication and art. There followed a succession of cases in which the decisions seemed to support that interpretation of the Court's position.

With a later shift in Court membership toward the conservative, however, a 1973 decision regarding obscenity cases was rendered that many, not just those within the motion-picture industry, regarded with consternation. It altered and clarified the former criteria for determining what constituted obscenity. Specifically the Court mandated that the affront need be only to local—as opposed to national—community standards, and that local standards were employable in determining appeal to prurient interest. Additionally the Court withdrew the "utterly without redeeming social value" test and substituted for it a mere lack of "serious literary, artistic, political, or scientific value."

The way now seemed open for every interested local body to impose conflicting sets of requirements on every film released within conceivably thousands of areas of jurisdiction. That this was not an imaginary danger was made clear when, less than a month after the Supreme Court ruling, the Georgia Supreme Court confirmed a ban on *Carnal Knowledge* and the conviction of a theater owner for showing it. While the citizens of Albany, Georgia, were prevented from seeing Mike Nichols's serious dark comedy about sex, the exploitive and frankly pornographic *Deep Throat* was playing to packed houses in other communities across the land. (The U.S. Supreme Court subsequently reversed the Georgia decision on *Carnal Knowledge,* holding that no jury could legally find that film obscene, and indeed it looks tame today.)

During the same years the Motion Picture Association of America was making its own efforts, on the one hand to allow producers greater freedom of subject and treatment, and on the other to fend off attacks from those who protested that what had resulted was license rather than freedom. Since 1934 no important picture had been distributed without the seal of the MPAA's Production Code Administration. In the 1950s, when two "A" features of United Artists were denied a Code seal, UA released them anyway, without it. The MPAA, now that the theaters were no longer owned or controlled by the studios, was unable to prevent the films from playing to large audiences. The first, *The Moon Is Blue* (1953), was from a popular stage comedy and would appear today patently moral. It was in fact about Maggie McNamara's successfully resisting the charms of David Niven. But it did contain considerable talk about sex and the words *virgin* and *pregnant* were used. The Code office subsequently conceded that it had been unwise in refusing that film a seal. No such option existed for the second one, *The Man with the Golden Arm* (1955). Taken from the Nelson Algren novel, it dealt directly with narcotic addiction, a subject expressly forbidden by the Code.

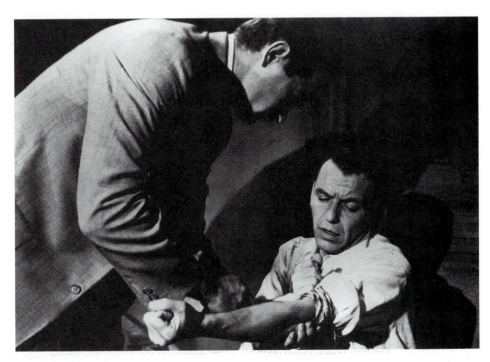

The Man with the Golden Arm ★ United States, 1955, Otto Preminger; Frank Sinatra, right.

Both films were produced and directed by Otto Preminger, who made much of the publicity and set himself up as a champion of free speech. In a show of self-righteous indignation United Artists withdrew from the MPAA; however, it rejoined after it had collected all its profits from the two offending films. This defiance of the Production Code Administration clearly threatened the whole system of self-regulation, and other production companies, especially the independents, were becoming restive. In 1956 the Code was revised, the main change being to permit the treatment of narcotics.

A decade later Jack Valenti succeeded Eric Johnston as president of the MPAA. Since pressures from producers for increased freedom from restraint had continued to mount, and an ever-increasing number of films were being released without the Code seal (distributors of foreign films rarely bothered to apply), one of Valenti's first acts was to further liberalize the Code. Among the concessions in the 1966 revisions were permitting the use of common profanity (*Gone With the Wind*'s famous final line, "Frankly, my dear, I don't give a damn," had required a special ruling in 1939), the treatment of abortion, and justifiable suicide. In general the Code language was softened, with phrases such as "good taste" and "dramatic necessity" replacing the strict prohibitions of the earlier Code.

Still, the onrush of new explicitness continued. Inasmuch as the trend seemed irreversible and the outcries provoked were largely on behalf of impressionable children, the MPAA decided that rather than attempt to control screen content, it would regulate audience attendance. The shocking language and sexual intensity of *Who's Afraid of Virginia Woolf?* (1966) were allowed when its advertising carried the statement "Suggested for Mature Audiences." In 1968 the MPAA adopted, not without protest from members of the industry who objected to potential earnings being limited in any way, a system of age classification like those already operating in many countries, such as the United Kingdom. The rating "G," for "general," meant suitable for all. "M" advised parents that the content was "mature" (subsequently this became "GP" and then "PG"—"parental guidance suggested"). "R" stood for "restricted": Those under age seventeen had to be accompanied by a parent or adult guardian. "X" indicated that only those age eighteen and older would be admitted.

By 1990 the X rating had come to imply the frankly pornographic; it drastically limited distribution, advertising, and hence box-office returns. To avoid the stigma of the X rating and acknowledge films with adult themes and serious intentions, a new classification was devised: NC-17 (no one under age seventeen admitted). *Henry and June,* about writers Anaïs Nin and Henry Miller in Paris of the 1930s, was first to receive it.

What had been the Production Code Administration became the Classification and Rating Administration. Enforcement was left to the theaters. Much dissatisfaction about classification was expressed. Producers complained when they felt their films had been given a too-restrictive rating. Theater owners resented the encroachment on their domains and the nuisance involved. Organized pressure groups, notably the National Catholic Office of Motion Pictures (which replaced the Legion of Decency), protested that the ratings were too laxly administered. All pointed to the inevitable inconsistencies in the labeling of particular films. Even so, in the face of the continuing threat of legal censorship, most of the industry accepted the MPAA classification system as the least of possible evils.

By the turn of the twenty-first century a new tempest had erupted as politicians called for further clarification and better enforcement of the ratings. Films now were required to carry descriptive language indicating why they had received the rating they had (for example, " 'R' for language and sexual content"). The big studios were further enjoined not to flaunt their disregard for the spirit of the Code by testing "R"-rated movies on teenage audiences. Although Hollywood paid lip service to the sentiment that prompted these reforms, little was actually altered. *Plus ça change, plus ça même chose* (i.e., "The more things change, the more they stay the same") appeared to be the film industry's response, as had been the case so often in the past.

Liberalism, Communism, and Anti-Communism: The House Un-American Activities Committee and Blacklisting

Although in some ways World War II was a cataclysmic event in the history of the United States, in other ways it proved to be only an interruption of some of the tensions of the 1930s, especially the political ones. In the decade before the war left-wing activities in the United States had achieved an unprecedented vigor and popularity. Whereas the forces of conservatism and reaction feared the "communist influence" at home and abroad, and attempted to check it through the power of capitalist business and government, they were ultimately ineffectual in halting a leftward swing. Some felt the New Deal itself represented a kind of totalitarian communism, with its powerful presidential leader and its sweeping program of social change. Even more unsettling, during the war the preeminent communist state, the Soviet Union, became a U.S. ally in the fight against fascism.

In the United States following the war, after a brief period of optimism about the recently established United Nations and attempts to ameliorate racial and ethnic discrimination and class and partisan differences, a new climate, or a return to an older climate, developed. By the late 1940s, the United States was locked into a fierce struggle with the U.S.S.R. and international communism, and had become prey to fears of communist subversion. Now the reactionaries, supported by great numbers of unthinking conservatives and some frightened liberals, led to a period of military belligerence and political repression that would climax in the early 1950s in the Korean War and in congressional investigating committees.

Films of the time reflected the prevailing shift in political sentiment. When the Soviet Union had been our ally during World War II, Hollywood had made some pro-Soviet films, most notably *Mission to Moscow* (1943), *The North Star* (1943), and *Song of Russia* (1944). By 1951 one of the increasing number of anti-communist films, *I Was a Communist for the FBI,* was nominated by the Academy of Motion Picture Arts and Sciences as best feature-length documentary. In 1952 another anti-communist film, *The Hoaxters* (more recognizably a documentary), received a nomination for the same award, and the anti-communist fiction feature *My Son John* was named by the National Board of Review among its ten best for the year. The rest of the films receiving major awards in 1952 were noticeably removed from contemporary domestic reality and its problems.

The appearance of the first anti-communist films after the war occurred following an investigation in 1947 by the House Un-American Activities Committee (HUAC) into alleged communist influence in Hollywood. Initially the industry united to oppose such an inquiry as unnecessary, punitive, and itself un-American in infringing civil liberties. In Hollywood a Committee for the First Amendment (which guarantees freedom of speech and opinion) was organized by film directors William Wyler and John Huston, and screenwriter Philip Dunne. A sizable delegation from the industry, headed by Eric Johnston, president of the Motion Picture Association of America, and including such celebrities as Lauren Bacall, Humphrey Bogart, Gene Kelly, Danny Kaye, and Jane Wyatt, appeared before HUAC in Washington to protest its activities.

They weren't called on immediately, however. Instead the committee called on a series of witnesses whose ties or sympathies with the Communist Party had been suggested by its earlier investigations. John Howard Lawson, screenwriter and leader in Hollywood guild and union organizing, was first to be heard. He angrily denounced the committee and refused to answer its questions. His prepared statement, which he was not allowed to read, began: "For a week this committee has conducted an illegal and indecent trial of American citizens, whom the committee has selected to be publicly pilloried and smeared." Lawson was followed by nine other "unfriendly" witnesses, who also refused to answer the committee's questions about their political beliefs and associations and invoked the First Amendment to the Constitution. The "Hollywood Ten," as they came to be known, comprised, in addition to Lawson, screenwriters Alvah Bessie, Lester Cole, Ring Lardner, Jr., Albert Maltz, Samuel Ornitz, and Dalton Trumbo; directors Herbert Biberman and Edward Dmytryk; and producer Adrian Scott. All were cited for contempt of Congress.

In the face of the unfavorable publicity occasioned by the truculent defiance of these ten witnesses and the allegations of communist infiltration made by "friendly" ones (including actors Adolphe Menjou, Robert Taylor, Robert Montgomery, George Murphy, Ronald Reagan, and Gary Cooper; producer-directors Sam Wood, Leo McCarey, and Walt Disney; and executives Jack Warner and Louis B. Mayer), the Committee for the First Amendment collapsed. The studio heads and principal independent producers hastily met at the Waldorf-Astoria Hotel in New York City. The resultant Waldorf statement deplored the action of the ten men who had refused to testify. Its key concession, a complete reversal from the producers' earlier opposition to the intentions and procedures of HUAC, read as follows: "We will not knowingly employ a Communist or a member of any party or group which advocates the overthrow of the Government of the United States by force or by any illegal or unconstitutional methods" (aims alleged to be those of the Communist Party U.S.A.).

The Hollywood Ten were sent to prison, and the industry moved into the era of blacklisting, in which people who were suspected of opinions and activities on the political left were denied employment. Failing to establish the presence of communist propaganda in the Hollywood film, HUAC sought to remove from the industry those who might have been able to support communism through their incomes and prestige. The studio heads were not concerned primarily with either possible communistic subversion or with violation of democratic principles. What rendered them compliant with the committee's wishes was the fear of boycott and picketing of theaters by indignant citizens. Such picketing did actually occur and numerous pressure groups joined HUAC in attacking the industry. The largest, most energetic, and most powerful of these was the American Legion, which insistently demanded that Hollywood "clean house."

In 1951 and following, in the Hollywood "mass hearings," more than two hundred motion-picture workers were named by HUAC as suspected communists or communist supporters. These congressional investigations into communism, in fact, became trials of the witnesses called. Those appearing before the committee who claimed protection under the Fifth Amendment to the Constitution (designed to protect witnesses from incriminating themselves) were automatically assumed to be guilty. A bizarre extralegal system of "clear-

ances" was set up by the industry and representatives of the pressure groups to "rehabilitate" those accused individuals who were willing to meet the requirements made of them.
Public confession and recantation, including the naming of former political associates, was
required from the admitted communists. Noncommunists with suspicious liberal tendencies had to repudiate their past political attitudes and behavior and promise to sin no more
in a letter to the studio executive employing them. Those named by HUAC or one of the
anti-communist organizations who were unwilling to take such steps could no longer find
employment in the Hollywood industry. Some screenwriters were able to sell their work
under assumed names, at greatly reduced rates; some directors worked under pseudonyms
on low-budget productions abroad. The blacklisted actors and actresses, whose presence on
the screen could not be concealed, had no recourse. Blacklisting continued even after
HUAC's final Hollywood hearing in 1954. The economic damage suffered by hundreds of
individuals and their families—with accompanying anger, fear, bitterness, and humiliation—
was matched by the corrosive effect on the morale of the industry as a whole.

A director whose work was deeply marked by his experiences with HUAC was **Elia
Kazan.** An almost mythic presence on the New York theater scene, he was famed primarily through his work with actors. But Kazan's career is also notable because of its connection with the communist scare. In 1952, he was called before the House Un-American
Activities Committee, confessed to his own Communist Party membership between 1934
and 1936, and named those he had known as Party members. He placed an ad in the *New
York Times,* justifying his change of political attitude and calling on others to join him in
confessing past error and denouncing communism and communists.

Elements of self-justification repeatedly cropped up in Kazan's subsequent films. *On
the Waterfront* (1954), the most powerful and empathic of these social-political statements,

On the Waterfront ★ United
States, 1954, Elia Kazan;
John Hamilton, Pat Henning,
and Marlon Brando.

is from a script by Budd Schulberg, who also had confessed past Party membership to the House of Un-American Activities Committee and named people he had known as communists. The film deals with the matter of informing to a government crime commission. Longshoreman Terry Malloy (Marlon Brando) comes to realize that in order to stand upright as a moral being he must expose the gangster forces controlling the waterfront labor unions and inform on his former associates. (Lee J. Cobb, who plays the union boss, and Leif Ericson, who plays one of the Waterfront Crime Commission investigators, were others involved in the production who had confessed and named names to HUAC.) The symbolism built around Terry's care and training of his flock of pigeons takes on a special significance when we remember that screenwriter John Howard Lawson, one of the "unfriendly witnesses," had charged that HUAC's "so-called 'evidence' " had come from a parade of "stool pigeons, neurotics, publicity-seeking clowns, Gestapo agents, paid informers and a few ignorant and frightened Hollywood artists."

Major Genres

The film industry's desire to overwhelm audiences with awesome visual spectacles in vivid color mounted in generous widescreen formats led movie makers to return with renewed energy to the most visually enticing formulas of earlier eras. Three genres that flourished most prominently during this decade—westerns, musicals, and Biblical epics—answered this need. Some of the greatest films of the decade grew out of these tried-and-true generic patterns. By contrast, a new genre, the juvenile delinquency film, looked to the future, defining a new audience of teenagers that Hollywood began to court during this decade and continued to woo ever more assiduously as the century progressed.

In an era when many people were moving into homes of their own on sizable plots of land in suburbias all over the nation, Hollywood produced a series of westerns that provided glorious vistas of the American landscape (frequently seen in sweeping wide-screen compositions), taking advantage of location shooting to show filmgoers unfamiliar views of their country's terrain. Many of the most enduring examples of the genre were produced during this decade, including films by directors Howard Hawks (*Red River,* 1948), Anthony Mann (*The Man from Laramie,* 1955), Budd Boetticher (*The Tall T,* 1957), and John Ford (*The Searchers,* 1956).

One of the most famous westerns ever made was *High Noon,* released in 1952. Produced by Stanley Kramer, directed by Fred Zinnemann, and photographed by Floyd Crosby, whose credits include most of the major documentaries of Pare Lorentz, it is tightly scripted along generic lines. In allegorical fashion it deals with the political paranoia called McCarthyism. Only the sheriff (Gary Cooper) will stand up against the vengeful outlaw and his gang as other members of the community think of reasons they cannot act. The sheriff finds his most sympathetic ally in a Mexican woman who owns most of the property in the town, but whose minority status prevents her from aiding him and ultimately forces her to leave the community altogether. Carl Foreman, the scriptwriter of *High Noon,* was one of the Hollywood professionals who, because of being blacklisted following his testimony before the House Un-American Activities Committee, exiled himself in England.

Another classic western, *Shane* (1953), was filmed mostly on location in Wyoming under the direction of George Stevens. Its setting is a lovely valley enclosed by snow-

High Noon ★ United States, 1952, Fred Zinnemann; Lon Chaney, Jr., and Gary Cooper.

capped mountains seen in expansive panoramic shots (VistaVision and Technicolor). A drab clapboard settlement squats along a muddy street in the middle of the valley. The farmers settling the valley look real enough and seem to have real problems—with the land and with the ranchers who don't want them on it. Into this community rides the mysterious title character (played by Alan Ladd in white buckskin) at the time the homesteaders need someone to face up to the cattle baron's hired gun, the black-garbed Wilson (Jack Palance). The simple story is seen through the eyes of a boy (Brandon de Wilde) who idolizes Shane. Shane almost becomes part of the community, almost acknowledges the attraction he and the wife (Jean Arthur) of the farmer (Van Heflin) feel for each other. But the gunfight with Wilson is what he has to do. After Wilson's death, Shane rides off into a mountain sunset. When asked where he's headed, he replies, "Someplace I've not been." When asked what it is he wants, he says, "Nothing."

   A less troubled view of the world is offered in the musicals made during the 1950s. Film scholar Richard Dyer has argued that these films present a utopian vision that sets forth a world filled with abundance and pleasure. The slender plot lines of such productions were designed to maximize the opportunities for major stars of the decade—such as Fred Astaire, Vera Ellen, Doris Day, and Gene Kelly—to display their considerable singing and dancing skills. The unabashedly romantic view of life offered in these delicious confections was set off by cinematography based on smooth tracks and crane shots that picked up the lyrical rhythms and cadences of music composed by some of the masters of the classical pop style, such as Cole Porter, Richard Rogers, and George Gershwin. The most accomplished examples of the form were produced at M-G-M by a tightly knit group of craftspeople under the supervision of producer Arthur Freed. The glossy M-G-M house style and the studio's generous production budgets created an atmosphere in which this team could function at top form.

An American in Paris was one of a number of memorable musicals the Freed unit turned out during these years. Released in 1951, it featured the work of seasoned talent in every department: music and lyrics of George and Ira Gershwin, choreography and dancing by Gene Kelly, with Leslie Caron as his partner in her first screen appearance. The film's director, Vincente Minnelli, is responsible for its expressive use of color and lighting. In the elaborate twenty-minute daydream ballet sequence, set to the Gershwin music of the title, the changing settings mimic the styles of various painters—Renoir, Rousseau, Toulouse-Lautrec, Dufy, Van Gogh, and Manet. Within those artistic worlds, the dancers interpret the feeling evoked by each painter with American energy and grace. It is a dazzling, breathtaking climax.

The following year the Freed unit produced another classic of the genre, *Singin' in the Rain,* this one codirected by Gene Kelly, its star, and Stanley Donen. A light-hearted spoof of the difficulties created in Hollywood by the coming of sound in the late 1920s, *Singin'* features memorable numbers such as "You Are My Lucky Star," "Make 'em Laugh," and, of course, the inimitable title tune. In addition, the film boasts a deliciously over-the-top performance by Jean Hagen as a spoiled movie star with a voice like chalk on

An American in Paris ★ United States, 1951, Vincente Minelli; Leslie Caron and Gene Kelly, foreground.

a blackboard. Its script, by Betty Comden and Adoph Green, is surely one of the cleverest ever to come out of the Hollywood dream factory.

The Band Wagon (1953) is to the musicals of Fred Astaire what *An American in Paris* and *Singin' in the Rain* are to those of Gene Kelly: top drawer. Yet another production of the Arthur Freed group at M-G-M, *The Band Wagon* couples Astaire with leggy dancer Cyd Charisse. It is about theater people, and though rampant egos are kidded, director Vincente Minnelli's view of them is gently affectionate. Astaire more or less plays himself as a former song-and-dance man of the Broadway stage who has gone to Hollywood and attained widespread popularity. In fact, the title, *The Band Wagon,* is that of a 1931 Broadway revue Astaire had starred in. The big number is "The Girl Hunt Ballet," in which Mickey Spillane and New York City private-eye toughness are burlesqued.

Scores of other musicals were released during the 1950s, including Howard Hawks's and Anita Loos's arch *Gentlemen Prefer Blondes* with Marilyn Monroe in 1953 and a series of Doris Day vehicles produced at Warner Bros. Like the westerns of the period, these were regarded at the time as highly professional but undistinguished undertakings aimed at pleasing the mass audience—not as Oscar material. However, time has proved kind to them. When the British film journal *Sight and Sound* conducted a poll of critics from around the world in 1992, a 1950s western, *The Searchers,* was named the tenth-best film of all time. And the 1950s musical, *Singin' in the Rain,* placed tenth on the American Film Institute's 1999 list of the greatest American movies ever. The other major cycle of film spectacles that flourished during the 1950s, Biblical epics, fared less well in the eyes of latter-day scholars. Although productions with Biblical themes—such as *Quo Vadis* (Mervyn LeRoy, 1951), *The Robe, The Ten Commandments* (Cecil B. DeMille, 1956), and *Ben-Hur* (William Wyler, 1959)—won a fair share of Academy Awards when they were released, they have subsequently lapsed into critical obscurity.

In search of new, more specialized audiences, Hollywood also developed a new movie formula during the 1950s, this one aimed at youth: the juvenile delinquency film. The label *juvenile delinquent* was coined during this era to refer to a rebellious young person. The increasingly widespread idea that adolescence should be viewed as a special stage of life that carried with it unique psychological challenges formed the background of this new interest in troubled youth. Hollywood's juvenile delinquent movies responded in kind by foregrounding tormented teenage heroes. Productions such as the 1955 *The Blackboard Jungle* also drew on the emerging musical style of rock music to appeal to youthful audiences.

The juvenile delinquent genre gained momentum from the excitement generated by a new crop of young male actors, including Marlon Brando and James Dean, who were dubbed "rebel heroes." Both Brando and Dean were trained in the performance style known as "the Method," which had originated in the Russian theater of Konstantin Stanislavsky. As interpreted in 1950s America, the Method emphasizes the fusion of performer and role through what is termed *affective memory.* Method actors are trained to relate their own experiences to those of the characters they play. To maximize this identification, improvisatory techniques are used. Method acting is particularly effective when employed in emotionally charged melodramas set in the present that call for the depiction of extreme anguish or rage—the kind of stories actors can readily relate to their own deepest frustrations and traumas. The juvenile delinquent films, which put adolescent passions and angst at center stage, were perfectly suited to showcase this approach to performance. Both

Brando and Dean developed some of the tics of the Method style along with its other techniques; they slouched, mumbled, and glowered through their parts in a provocative manner that made an almost visceral connection with teenage audiences.

The young Brando first defined the rebel hero type in the 1953 production *The Wild One,* in which he played a reckless, hostile leader of a motorcycle gang. When asked what he was rebelling against, Brando responded, "What've you got?" But it was James Dean who made the most lasting impression as a juvenile delinquent type. As a result of his early death, he was forevermore identified as a tragic symbol of troubled youth. Dean's 1955 release *Rebel Without a Cause,* directed by Nicholas Ray, marked the high point of the genre. As Jim Stark, the confused son of a dysfunctional suburban family, Dean created an arresting portrait of an alienated teenager. Although Dean's character in this film is depicted as unambiguously heterosexual, his sympathetic response to the homosexual advances of Sal Mineo's Plato (though, in keeping with the times, only obliquely hinted at) set a newly accepting tone for the representation of gay interactions on screen. Directed by Nicholas Ray in his customary overheated manner, the film's style was perfectly adapted to its melodramatic story about tortured youth. The look is marked by strong colors and odd camera angles. (In one scene, an inebriated Jim watches as his parents come down the stairs of his house upside down.) Wide-screen compositions alternate empty, alienating outdoor scenes with claustrophobic interiors.

Rebel was loosely based on a book written by clinical psychologist Robert M. Lindner, in which he described one of his cases. Though the staid *New York Times* described it as "a picture to make the hair stand on end," the film was a tremendous hit, especially with its target teenage audience. The red cotton windbreaker Dean wore in most of his scenes began a fad for such jackets in high schools all over the nation. Having thus discovered a lucrative new audience for whom filmgoing represented an opportunity to escape from parental control and to enjoy the company of peers, Hollywood never looked back. Youth movies, in endless variations, were here to stay.

Rebel Without a Cause ★ United States, 1955, Nicholas Ray; Ann Doran, James Dean, and Jim Backus.

American Directors of the 1950s

Among the most illustrious film makers of the postwar era were Vincente Minnelli, George Cukor, Billy Wilder, Douglas Sirk, and Alfred Hitchcock. Although all worked before and afterward, their work at this time fairly represents the qualities of American film most valued by those within the Hollywood industry, by the major critics, and by the domestic audience. The success of each was founded on his ability to remain safely within the conventional boundaries that defined industry practice at the time while creating bodies of work that were identifiably unique.

Hollywood's foremost director of musicals, **Vincente Minnelli,** arrived in Hollywood in 1940 after a substantial career as a stage designer and director. Following an apprenticeship at M-G-M, his first film direction was a version of the all-black Broadway musical *Cabin in the Sky* (1943). Minnelli proceeded to produce a series of distinctive musicals during the 1940s, including *Meet Me in St. Louis* (1944) and *The Pirate* (1948), but he directed noteworthy films in other genres as well, such as *The Clock* in 1945 (a romantic drama) and *Father of the Bride* in 1950 (a domestic comedy, remade in 1991 by Charles Shyer with Steve Martin in the Spencer Tracy role). During the 1950s Minnelli continued to alternate between musicals, such as *An American in Paris, The Band Wagon, Brigadoon* (1954), and *Gigi* (1960), and melodramas, such as *The Bad and the Beautiful* (1952), *Lust for Life* (1956), *Some Came Running* (1958), *Home from the Hill* (1960), and *Two Weeks in Another Town* (1962).

Much of Minnelli's best work brings art and life together, relying on reflexive strategies before the notion of film being about film had achieved currency. Some of his productions *(The Bad and the Beautiful* and *Two Weeks in Another Town)* are about the film-making process itself; others *(An American in Paris, The Band Wagon, Lust for Life,* and *Some Came Running)* feature artists, theater people, or writers. Minnelli's penchant for letting his audience in on the spirit of creation adds a playfulness to his musicals; in the serious dramas it provides an irony that amplifies and intensifies the strong emotionality.

Like Minnelli, **George Cukor** came to Hollywood after a successful stage career. He was the consummate professional, his direction stylish and impeccable. He began in theater in 1919 as stage manager and then director, and his films always had qualities traceable to theater. Invariably his productions were praised for their performances, especially those of women: Katharine Hepburn, Norma Shearer, Greta Garbo, Joan Crawford, Judy Holliday, Judy Garland, and Marilyn Monroe among them. Cukor frequently captured the interactions between various pairs of such charismatic stars in extended two-shots.

Cukor specialized in literary adaptations, sophisticated comedies, musicals, and period pictures. With *A Double Life* (1947), he began a collaboration with Garson Kanin and Ruth Gordon, the husband-wife screenwriting team, which lasted through six more of their original scripts. *Adam's Rib* (1949), starring Spencer Tracy and Katharine Hepburn, with Judy Holliday in a supporting role, was the first of a series of intelligent, witty, and urbane battle-of-the-sexes comedies. It was followed by *Born Yesterday* (1950), starring Judy Holliday. These performers—Tracy, Hepburn, and Holliday—continued working with Cukor in breezy vignettes of middle-class American life, much of them shot on the East Coast. With *A Star Is Born* (1954) Cukor was back to Hollywood full scale, and then some. This CinemaScope Technicolor extravaganza musical-melodrama was not only shot on the

A Star Is Born ⋆ United States, 1954, George Cukor; James Mason and Judy Garland.

sound stages and back lots of Hollywood but it was also about Hollywood. Although it was passed over at Academy Award time, Cukor eventually received his first and only Oscar for directing another musical, the lavish *My Fair Lady,* in 1964.

Billy Wilder, a film maker with a more sardonic turn of mind, began his Hollywood career as a scriptwriter during the 1930s, coauthoring a series of sophisticated comedies for directors such as Ernst Lubitsch (*Ninotchka,* 1939), Mitchell Leisen (*Midnight,* 1939), and Howard Hawks (*Ball of Fire,* 1941). Wilder, the consummate creator of well-made plots and witty dialogue, frequently claimed that he had turned to direction only "to protect my scripts." After a series of atmospheric *film noir* projects during the 1940s, including *Double Indemnity* (1945) and *Sunset Boulevard* (1950), he turned back to comedies during the 1950s. *Ace in the Hole,* released in 1950, was Wilder's first film after the breakup of his fruitful scriptwriting collaboration with Charles Brackett, which had begun in 1938. A darkly cynical satire on the exploitative nature of the modern media, it tells the tale of an ambitious reporter (played by Kirk Douglas) who puts a man's life at risk to get a scoop. The film's overall tone is conveyed in an offhand remark delivered by Jan Sterling, who plays the wife of the victimized man. "I never go to church," she confesses, "because kneeling bags my nylons."

Wilder next turned to another cynical tale, *Stalag 17* (1953). Based on a Broadway hit about American prisoners of war held by the Germans during World War II, it starred

William Holden. Although it was popular with audiences, some reviewers complained of the story's nihilism and tastelessness. Wilder followed *Stalag 17* with three frothier productions: *Sabrina* (1954), *The Seven Year Itch* (1955), and *Love in the Afternoon* (1957). All are very Lubitsch-like, a comparison Wilder readily acknowledged. The last was Wilder's first film with the screenwriter who would become his second long-lasting collaborator, I. A. L. Diamond. The next three comedies produced by the team—*Some Like It Hot* (1959), *The Apartment* (1960), and *One, Two, Three* (1961)—are very Wilder-Diamond-like. In them there is a fusion of the acidic *film noir* with the *joie de vivre* of the Lubitsch comedies.

Some Like It Hot, which some critics have called the funniest film ever made, combines elements of the gangster film, knockabout farce, fast-paced witty dialogue *à la* screwball comedy, and transvestism. (To escape mobster Spats Colombo, played by George Raft, stars Tony Curtis and Jack Lemmon become "girls" in an all-female band that includes Marilyn Monroe.) Confused identities and sexual mismatches escalate to incredible limits. The film's inimitable closing line is delivered by lustful millionaire Osgood Fielding III (Joe E. Brown). When his fiancée (Jack Lemmon in drag) confesses she's a man, he scarcely skips a beat before responding, "Nobody's perfect."

Another German emigré who achieved considerable Hollywood success during the 1950s is **Douglas Sirk,** whose most memorable work includes a number of highly profitable women's pictures produced by Ross Hunter for Universal, many starring Sirk's

The Apartment ★ United States, 1960, Billy Wilder; Jack Lemmon and Shirley MacLaine.

favorite leading man, Rock Hudson. The term *Sirkian irony* was later coined to describe his distinctive style, which never condescended to his tearjerker plots but overlaid them with a layer of self-consciousness and distance.

Sirk was a master at employing *mise-en-scène* to comment on character. Mirrors and glass surfaces abound in his films, repeatedly suggesting the complicated relationship between identity and role. An especially admired instance of this technique occurs in his 1956 production *All That Heaven Allows* when the film's main character (played by Jane Wyman) gazes at her likeness reflected in a television set her children have purchased for her and foresees herself as being trapped within its confines for the remainder of her days. The conclusion of the film finds her looking with similar disillusionment out of a picture window at a fawn grazing in the winter landscape outside: The glass separating her from this vision seems an impassible barrier between her "natural" desires and her position in an endlessly constricting culture.

Sirk's typically wide-angle compositions frequently juxtapose characters and their surroundings in revealing ways. In his 1957 *Written on the Wind,* for instance, Dorothy Malone, playing the spoiled daughter of a powerful oil baron, is shown at one point against a background of oil derricks, suggesting the devastation wreaked by her father's industrial prowess and, by implication, the devastation she herself seeks to impose on others through sexual manipulation. Sirk also employed costuming to comment on his characters and their world. In his last major production, *Imitation of Life,* released in 1959, Lana Turner's

Written on the Wind ★ United States, 1957, Douglas Sirk; Rock Hudson and Dorothy Malone.

gowns become ever more artificial and affected as she increasingly loses sight of what truly matters to her in life.

Yet another emigré, this one from England, **Alfred Hitchcock** hit the peak of his Hollywood career during the late 1940s and 1950s. "Cinema is not a slice of life," he once said, "It's a piece of cake." In this spirit, he produced a series of hugely entertaining thrillers that often explored the dark recesses of his audience's fascination with the cinematic image. His motto, "Always make the audience suffer as much as possible," was fulfilled with particular relish in tense mysteries such as *Notorious* (1946), *Strangers on a Train* (1951), *Rear Window* (1954), *The Man Who Knew Too Much* (1956), *Vertigo* (1957), and *Psycho* (1960). Such disturbing exercises in murder and espionage (the latter capitalizing on America's fearful Cold War mentality) were alternated with more purely enjoyable roller-coaster rides on similar topics, such as *To Catch a Thief, The Trouble with Harry* (both 1955) and *North by Northwest* (1959). Many of these productions were filmed in such colorful tourist locales as Monaco (*To Catch a Thief*), Marrakesh (*The Man Who Knew Too Much*), and Mount Rushmore (*North by Northwest*).

Hitchcock's distinctive visual style is based on the strict control of the audience's point of view, often isolating objects and people ominously in the frame (such as in the repeated shots of stuffed birds of prey in *Psycho*). Heavy editing, most famously in *Psycho*'s terrifying shower scene, created bravura set pieces filled with terror and suspense. The dizzying tracking shots that circle around embracing couples in *Notorious, Vertigo,* and *North by Northwest* evoke the sensation of sexual euphoria. In *Vertigo* Hitchcock also introduced an even more perceptually disorienting track in–zoom out technique that reproduces the unsettling emotional state referred to in the film's title. Supporting these displays of visual pyrotechnics in most of Hitchcock's productions of this era were tense, modernist-inflected scores by the great Hollywood composer Bernard Herrmann.

Hitchcock's films often feature coolly glamorous blonde heroines—for instance, Grace Kelly, Kim Novak, Eva Marie Saint, and Tippi Hedren—whose sexual allure becomes a trap for the male protagonists, typically played by familiar stars such as James Stewart and Cary Grant. The eroticism that hovers over most Hitchcock productions is countered by stern references to the punishing power of the police as well as by frequent allusions to his characters' own guilty consciences. The films also examine the perverse pleasures offered by the spectacle of cinema and the complicity of audiences who partake in this kind of pleasure. In a tacit acknowledgment of this motif, Hitchcock scholar William Rothman subtitled his book on the director, "The Murderous Gaze."

Hitchcock's films have been extraordinarily attractive to both pit and gallery. Huge audiences have gone to see each release because it carries his name. As much serious critical writing has been published about the Hitchcock films as about those of any other film maker. His films represent the fusion of the popular and the critically acclaimed. Like many of the most honored artists of other eras, such as Shakespeare and Dickens, Hitchcock, along with the other Hollywood directors of the postwar era discussed here, developed a style that managed to combine popular appeal with profundity.

The changes that followed in the wake of television's impact on the American motion picture were pervasive—technological, economic, and sociological. It took the industry time to absorb the changes and to adjust to the newly reduced and more specialized sorts of production, distribution, and exhibition that emerged. Changes in the actual content and form of American films during this period—except for those caused by the wide screen, stereophonic sound, and increased use of color—were not nearly so evident. As distinguished as was the work of the directors discussed in this chapter, and of other American film makers in the 1950s, it came out of firmly established tradition. Not until the middle and late 1960s did American films begin to take on some of the characteristics identified with trends of modern cinema that had begun germinating in Europe from the mid-1950s on. Moreover, the distinctive youth culture that emerged during the 1950s and was addressed in the juvenile delinquency films of that era was destined to develop into a far more radical force in the decade ahead.

Films of the Period

1946
The Best Years of Our Lives (William Wyler)
The Big Sleep (Howard Hawks)
It's a Wonderful Life (Frank Capra)
My Darling Clementine (John Ford)
Notorious (Alfred Hitchcock)

1947
A Double Life (George Cukor)
Fort Apache (John Ford)
The Lady from Shanghai (Orson Welles)
Monsieur Verdoux (Charlie Chaplin)
Red River (Howard Hawks)
Sleep, My Love (Douglas Sirk)
They Live by Night (Nicholas Ray)
The Treasure of the Sierra Madre (John Huston)

1949
Adam's Rib (George Cukor)
On the Town (Gene Kelly and Stanley Donen)
White Heat (Raoul Walsh)

1950
All About Eve (Joseph L. Mankiewicz)
The Asphalt Jungle (John Huston)
Born Yesterday (George Cukor)
Father of the Bride (George Cukor)
In a Lonely Place (Nicholas Ray)
Sunset Boulevard (Billy Wilder)

1951
Ace in the Hole (Billy Wilder)
An American in Paris (Vincente Minnelli)
A Place in the Sun (George Stevens)
Strangers on a Train (Alfred Hitchcock)
A Streetcar Named Desire (Elia Kazan)

1952
The African Queen (John Huston)
The Bad and the Beautiful (Vincente Minnelli)
The Greatest Show on Earth (Cecil B. DeMille)
High Noon (Fred Zinnemann)
Limelight (Charles Chaplin)
The Quiet Man (John Ford)
Singin' in the Rain (Gene Kelly and Stanley Donen)
Viva Zapata! (Elia Kazan)

1953
The Big Heat (Fritz Lang)
From Here to Eternity (Fred Zinnemann)
Gentlemen Prefer Blondes (Howard Hawks)
The Robe (Henry Koster)
Roman Holiday (William Wyler)
Shane (George Stevens)
This Is Cinerama (Merian C. Cooper)
The Wild One (Laslo Benedek)

1954
Dial M for Murder (Alfred Hitchcock)
On the Waterfront (Elia Kazan)
Rear Window (Alfred Hitchcock)
Sabrina (Billy Wilder)
A Star Is Born (George Cukor)

1955
The Blackboard Jungle (Richard Brooks)
East of Eden (Elia Kazan)
Kiss Me Deadly (Robert Aldrich)
The Man from Laramie (Anthony Mann)
The Man with the Golden Arm (Otto Preminger)
Marty (Delbert Mann)
The Night of the Hunter (Charles Laughton)

Rebel Without a Cause (Nicholas Ray)
Written on the Wind (Douglas Sirk)

1956
All That Heaven Allows (Douglas Sirk)
Around the World in Eighty Days (Michael
    Anderson)
The Man Who Knew Too Much (Alfred Hitchcock)
The Searchers (John Ford)
The Ten Commandments (Cecil B. DeMille)

1957
The Bridge on the River Kwai (David Lean)
Funny Face (Stanley Donen)
Paths of Glory (Stanley Kubrick)
Shadows (John Cassavetes)
The Sweet Smell of Success (Alexander Mackendrick)
The Tall T (Budd Boetticher)
Twelve Angry Men (Sidney Lumet)
Vertigo (Alfred Hitchcock)

1958
Anticipation of the Night (Stan Brakhage)
Gigi (Vincente Minnelli)
A Movie (Bruce Conner)
Touch of Evil (Orson Welles)

1959
Anatomy of a Murder (Otto Preminger)
Ben-Hur (William Wyler)
Imitation of Life (Douglas Sirk)
North by Northwest (Alfred Hitchcock)
Some Like It Hot (Billy Wilder)
Window Water Baby Moving (Stan Brakhage)

1960
The Apartment (Billy Wilder)
Home from the Hill (Vincente Minnelli)
Primary (Richard Leacock, Albert and David
    Maysles, Terence McCartney-Filgate)
Psycho (Alfred Hitchcock)

1961
The Birds (Alfred Hitchcock)
Breakfast at Tiffany's (Blake Edwards)
Lolita (Stanley Kubrick)

1962
The Cool World (Shirley Clarke)
Lawrence of Arabia (David Lean)
The Manchurian Candidate (John Frankenheimer)
The Man Who Shot Liberty Valance (John Ford)

Books on the Period

American Film Institute Staff. *The American Film Institute Catalog of Motion Pictures Produced in the United States: Feature Films, 1941–1950.* 3 vols. Berkeley: University of California Press, 1999.

Bernstein, Matthew, ed. *Controlling Hollywood: Censorship and Regulation in the Studio Era.* New Brunswick, NJ: Rutgers University Press, 2000.

Black, Gregory D. *The Catholic Crusade Against the Movies, 1940–1975.* New York: Cambridge University Press, 1998.

Brown, Gene. *Movie Time: A Chronology of Hollywood and the Movie Industry from Its Beginnings to the Present.* New York: Macmillan, 1995.

Couvares, Francis G., ed. *Movie Censorship and American Culture* ("Studies in the History of Film and Television"). Washington, DC: Smithsonian Institution Press, 1996.

Davis, Ronald L. *The Glamour Factory: Inside Hollywood's Big Studio System.* Dallas: Southern Methodist University Press, 1993.

Lyons, Charles. *The New Censors: Movies and the Culture Wars.* Philadelphia: Temple University Press, 1997.

Maltby, Richard, and Ian Craven. *Hollywood Cinema: An Introduction.* Malden, MA: Blackwell Publications, 1995.

Nowell-Smith, Geoffrey, and Stephen Ricci, eds. *Hollywood and Europe: Economics, Culture, National Identity, 1945–1995.* London: British Film Institute, 1998.

Schatz, Thomas. *Boom and Bust: Hollywood in the 1940s (Vol. 6, "History of the American Cinema").* New York: Charles Scribner's Sons, 1997.

Slide, Anthony. *The New Historical Dictionary of the American Film Industry.* Lanham, MD: Scarecrow Press, 1998.

Staiger, Janet, ed. *The Studio System.* New Brunswick, NJ: Rutgers University Press, 1994.

Whissen, Thomas. *Guide to American Cinema, 1930–1965.* Westport, CT: Greenwood Press, 1998.

16

American Reemergence

★ ★ ★ ★

1963–1974

On November 22, 1963, President John F. Kennedy was shot and killed in Dallas. Almost everyone who was an adult during that period remembers where he or she was when this event occurred. Not only was it a national tragedy, but it also heralded major changes for the country. The young president's White House had been held up as a modern Camelot; he was succeeded by his vice-president, Lyndon Johnson, a less popular figure who pursued an even less popular war in Vietnam. The mood in the United States shifted from the optimism of the 1950s toward a more self-critical stance, spearheaded initially by the development of the civil rights movement, with its sit-ins, marches, and riots; then by the rebellious spirit of a growing youth culture that called into question both the war in Vietnam and the bourgeois complacency into which the country had lapsed. The median age in the United States fell to below age twenty-five in 1964; an increasing number of these young people were clustered together on college campuses. For the rest of the decade and well into the 1970s, a youthful sensibility ruled. Then, in 1972, burglars broke into the Democratic offices in Washington's Watergate apartment complex; by 1974, then-President Richard Nixon, who had been implicated in the cover-up of this political skulduggery, resigned. The United States entered a new era of cynicism about its government officials, and the idealism that had fueled the reformist agendas of the previous decade was set aside.

For Hollywood, the 1960s and early 1970s were dismal years. Theater attendance dropped to half of what it had been ten years before. In 1963 only 121 features were released, an all-time low. Prestige productions such as *Cleopatra* (1963) and *Paint Your Wagon* (1969) bombed at the box office. In the studios, chaos reigned. Devastated and demoralized by the advent of television, the divestiture of their theaters, and the challenge of European art films, management was at a loss about where to turn. The old-time movie moguls who had ruled their empires with iron fists for so many years had died, retired, or been forced out. A series of sell-offs to large conglomerates made the studios part of much larger corporate entities, answerable to financial wizards who had little background in the movie business. In 1969 Warner Bros. was purchased by Kinney National Services, a company that owned parking lots and funeral homes. The once great and powerful Metro-Goldwyn-Mayer was sold to financier Kirk Kerkorian, who wanted the studio's logo to put on his Las Vegas hotel. M-G-M went out of business entirely for almost a decade, beginning in 1973. This corporate instability led to many inefficiencies, not the least of which was a revolving-door system for top executives. Each new regime was, quite naturally, inclined to ignore the films made under the auspices of the last group in its quest to make its own mark; thus, many worthy productions got dumped or shelved.

The new, green studio chiefs had less confidence and authority than the oldtimers did; popular stars who could promise an audience therefore gained more power, as did directors. As always, their interests were ably advanced by the Directors Guild of America, which negotiated ever-more directorial control over every aspect of the production process. In 1964 the Guild won the right for all its members to produce an initial director's cut on each of their films. But perhaps the biggest winners in the struggles following the breakup of the old-style studios were the agents, whose list of "bankable" clients and deal-making skills put them in the catbird seat in the new Balkanized climate of Hollywood. In fact, in 1962 a talent agency, MCA, gained control over one of the biggest studios: Universal.

Even though the Hollywood studios were floundering, film was far from dead. The youth movement had taken up movies in a serious way. Following the publication of Andrew Sarris's *auteurist* manifesto, *The American Cinema,* in 1963, a novel sort of creative vitality began to make itself felt, especially on college campuses—new kinds of films and new film makers. New genres emerged to capture the interests of a changed society. Among intellectuals, European art films by directors such as Ingmar Bergman, Federico Fellini, and Jean-Luc Godard became chic. In response, Hollywood began to hire younger, "hipper" directors whose movies had a European flavor. These new talents soon became known as the American New Wave. More radical kinds of films appeared as well—independent documentary and avant-garde productions that protested against prevailing conditions and affirmed the values of the youth culture.

Popular Genres

In response to the new mood of social unrest in the United States and the increasing visibility of groups with militant agendas, Hollywood scrambled to devise new genres that might appeal to these recently constituted specialized audiences. The juvenile deliquency films of the 1950s mutated into the youth films during the following decade; in the early 1970s a series of movies aimed at African American audiences, the so-called "blaxpoitation" cycle, were released.

Made for the youthful audiences who were now the principal patrons of the theaters, **youth films** were about young people and new lifestyles. All of them explored social, and some of them political, problems in one way or another. A few sounded strong notes of dissent. They also combined forms—documentary and experimental styles and subject matter along with those of conventional fiction—in ways that some of the recent films coming from abroad were doing (those of Godard, for example). The trend started off indirectly in 1967 with two of the most popular releases of that year: Arthur Penn's *Bonnie and Clyde* and Mike Nichols's *The Graduate. Bonnie and Clyde* was a sort of gangster film set in rural America of the 1930s, but encoded within it were themes of current youthful protest: the individual against the system; an unconventional and hedonistic lifestyle that put emphasis on "kicks"; and the implicit justification of violence directed against the impersonal institutions of society and against the conscientious, middle-aged, and humorless who served them. *The Graduate* more explicitly, if less boldly, expressed other manifestations of contemporary youthful tension and conflict.

It took Hollywood two years to contemplate those two films before producing more that incorporated some of the elements that seemed to have been responsible for their success. In 1969 the youth cycle proper began with *Easy Rider, Medium Cool, Zabriskie Point,* and *Alice's Restaurant. Easy Rider,* the seminal film, became an immediate favorite with the eighteen- to twenty-five-year-old audience. Directed by Dennis Hopper, who had learned about the potential of the youth genre when he was a supporting player in *Rebel Without a Cause* a decade before, *Easy Rider* starred Hopper and Peter Fonda, with support from a young Jack Nicholson. The episodic plot centered on two young men, Billy and Captain America, riding their motorcycles "in search of America," as pop-song lyrics of the time put it, and getting high on pot and LSD. Like Bonnie and Clyde, Billy and Captain America were quickly adopted as youth-cult heroes. *Easy Rider* spawned a profusion of features with related themes, some of them much more direct in their criticism of the dominant values of contemporary American society.

Two years later, in 1971, the **blaxploitation** genre was kicked off by the runaway success of Melvin Van Peebles's independent feature *Sweet Sweetback's Baadasssss Song.* Seeing a potentially lucrative and previously untapped market, Hollywood quickly jumped on the bandwagon with a series of action movies set in the urban ghetto featuring black heroes. Most of these played exclusively in inner-city theaters. The first of the cycle, *Shaft* (1971), directed by the award-winning African American photographer Gordon Parks, chronicled the adventures of a New York private eye played by Richard Roundtree. Shot on the gritty New York streets largely with telephoto lenses, *Shaft* depicts the in-your-face confusion of life in the big city with arresting *panache.* Its score, by Isaac Hayes, evoked a funky, with-it mood from the outset. Made for a paltry $1.2 million dollars, *Shaft* was an enormous hit and was quckly followed by two inferior sequels: *Shaft's Big Score* (Parks, 1972) and *Shaft in Africa* (John Guillerman, 1973). (The original *Shaft* was remade in 2000 with Samuel L. Jackson in the title role.) Other black action films appeared in short order, including *Superfly* in 1972 and *Foxy Brown,* starring Pam Grier, in 1973. Though all were popular, they proved controversial; groups like the NAACP protested their glorification of violence and criminality as well as their escapist mentality. A contemporary review in the *New York Times* by Clayton Riley voiced the concern. "Shaft Can Do Everything," the headline read. "I Can Do Nothing."

Around the same time, a series of more down-to-earth, sentimentalized, and comic productions aimed at black audiences were also released, including Parks's own *The Learning Tree* in 1969, Ossie Davis's *Black Girl* in 1972, John Berry's *Claudine* in 1974, Michael Schultz's *Cooley High* in 1975, and a series of films directed by black actor Sidney Poitier (*Buck and the Preacher,* 1972 and *Uptown Saturday Night,* 1974).

The Learning Tree ★ United States, 1969, Gordon Parks; Joel Fluellen, Kyle Johnson, and Mira Waters.

The American New Wave

During those years of national turmoil and dissidence, a number of young film makers working within the Hollywood system established careers, touching off a movement variously known as the American New Wave or the American Renaissance. The New Wave directors maintained a strong interest in critically examining aspects of American culture, including the violence so prevalent during the country's recent history. Some of these had established roots earlier; all continued their careers into the 1980s and most into the 1990s. The new interest in directorial styles manifested by the *auteur*-minded youth culture led Hollywood to give these new film makers unprecedented freedom—with the assurance that the movies they produced could be marketed as *auteurist* statements. Taking advantage of these new freedoms, the American New Wave directors developed stylistic signatures that were far more individualistic than the styles associated with the studio stalwarts of the 1950s. The European look cultivated by the New Wave group was characterized by loosely plotted storylines, ambiguous character motivations, low lighting levels, and jarring juxtapositions of tone (this last often achieved by the addition of already existing pop-music scores). These new Hollywood talents included Arthur Penn, Sam Peckinpah, Francis Ford Coppola, Robert Altman, Martin Scorsese, and John Cassavetes. Some of the group, such as Coppola and Scorsese, were trained in university film programs. Others—for example, Penn, Peckinpah, and Altman—got their start in television. Coppola and Scorsese also served apprenticeships under "B" movie entrepreneur Roger Corman.

Arthur Penn was the first of the New Wave directors to be widely recognized. Like others in the group, he was critical of prevailing mores. Every one of the films he directed explicitly examines a facet of American culture. The people who interest him most are the outcasts from this society—most typically, young ones. Some of his films, such as *Alice's Restaurant* (1969) and *Four Friends* (1981), explicity focus on youth cultures. Others enact stylish variations on traditional American genres: westerns (*The Left-Handed Gun,* 1958; *Little Big Man,* 1970; and *The Missouri Breaks,* 1976), gangster stories (*Mickey One,* 1965, and *Bonnie and Clyde,* 1967), and private-eye tales (*Night Moves,* 1975).

Although Penn's preoccupation with things American has remained a constant throughout his work, of all the American New Wave directors he had the strongest attraction to the kind of artistic modernism in film that had been emanating from Europe since the late 1950s. *Bonnie and Clyde* was originally conceived by its scriptwriters, David Newman and Robert Benton, for direction by Truffaut or Godard. *Mickey One* and *Night Moves* are the full-scale examples—what the trade would call art movies—experimental and philosophical within their genre trappings.

Almost all of Penn's productions take up violence as a major motif. *Mickey One* explores the fear and threat of violence omnipresent in American cities through the eyes of a paranoid and desperate nightclub comic pursued by the Mob. *The Chase* (1966) follows that same climate of violence into a small southern town and adds to it the general erosion of sexual morality. "I think that one of the functions of art is to purge or exorcise the crap that encrusts society," Penn once commented when asked about his repeated use of violence, "to blow out those undesirable capacities in all of us."

Penn's *Bonnie and Clyde,* surely among the most influential of American films, sets real-life bank robbers of the 1930s in the light of the myth they themselves had helped create. The film's star, Warren Beatty, who had earlier worked with Penn in *Mickey One,* acted as producer. As Bonnie, Faye Dunaway sported a stylish 1930s wardrobe that started a fad for such clothes. The film's bone-chilling violence was rendered even more shocking by its incongruous musical score, an upbeat banjo number, "Foggy Mountain Breakdown," by country-and-western composers Flatt and Scuggs. The narrative concluded with an innovative and stunning slow motion sequence, superbly edited by Dede Allen, featuring an ultra-violent, yet strangely romanticized, ambush in which the title characters are killed.

Like Penn, **Sam Peckinpah** came to features from television. He had been a writer-director on several TV western series and remained mostly loyal, even when working in a form that was not outwardly a western, to that most American of film genres. To the basic elements of the formula he added his attraction to the grandeur of nature, which he celebrated in resplendent location photography, and his absorption with violence. Among the most memorable of his many variations on the western formula are *Deadly Companions* (1961), *Ride the High Country* (1962), *Major Dundee* (1964), *The Ballad of Cable Hogue* (1970), *Pat Garrett and Billy the Kid* (1973), and *Bring Me the Head of Alfredo Garcia* (1974). He died in 1984 at the age of fifty-nine. Best remembered for his uncompromising vision of the lost values of heroic individualism represented by the closing of the American West, Peckinpah celebrated traditional, larger-than-life masculinity. His stories focused on loners and losers who have outmoded responses to cultural change.

Bonnie and Clyde ✶
United States, 1967, Arthur
Penn; Warren Beatty and
Faye Dunaway.

Often considered Peckinpah's greatest achievement and one of the greatest westerns ever made, *The Wild Bunch* (1969) brings violence to the fore—gross and gruesome, yet also poetic. Its opening sequence, in which a group of children torture a scorpion, has been widely lauded for the bitter, uncompromising statement it makes about the ingrained nature of human cruelty. At the same time, however, the film is deeply committed to the values of heroism and honor. For example, a famous exchange between two of the members of the story's eponymous outlaw gang, Pike (William Holden) and Dutch (Ernest Borgnine), focuses on the ethics of promises. Discussing a former gang member, Thornton (Robert Ryan), who has made a deal with the law-enforcement establishment to hunt them down, Pike defends Thornton's disloyalty by declaring, "He gave his word." Dutch responds passionately, "It's not whether you give your word; it's who you give your word to." The film's final episode, an extended slow-motion sequence in which the heroes are brutally massacred by a degenerate Mexican general and his forces, was shot in elegiac slow motion that took the technique of the similar closing scene in *Bonnie and Clyde* several steps further.

Like Penn and Peckinpah, **Robert Altman** came to film out of directing for television. *M*A*S*H* (1970), his first substantial success (which spawned an even more successful long-running TV show), rode the crest of the youth cycle and launched Altman's subsequent career. An outrageous satire of both the military and medical professions, it simultaneously desecrated our memories of *All Quiet on the Western Front* and *Young Doctor Kildare*.

Of all the American New Wave directors, Altman is the most prolific, averaging over a film a year. Many of his productions—including *M*A*S*H* (1970), *Brewster McCloud*

The Wild Bunch ★
United States, 1969, Sam
Peckinpah; Ben Johnson,
Warren Oates, William
Holden, and Ernest Borgnine.

(1971), *McCabe and Mrs. Miller* (1972), *The Long Goodbye* (1973), and *Nashville* (1976)—dissect the traditional American movie genres, in the course of which he pokes fun at, questions, and attacks the values and shibboleths that their conventions support. Another group of Altman's films, more mysterious and dreamlike, explore the interior lives of women (*That Cold Day in the Park,* 1969; *Images,* 1972; and *3 Women,* 1978). Each of his productions has a unique look, ranging from the foggy, desolate air that hangs over the town of Presbyterian Church in *McCabe and Mrs. Miller* to the postcard brassiness of *Nashville* to the quaintly cartoonish ambience of *Popeye* (1981). Altman's 1992 production, *The Player,* catapulted him into a new prominence near the end of the century, after a period of obscurity during which he was unable to find commercial backing for his projects. It was followed by a number of diverse productions, the most notable of which are *Short Cuts* in 1993, *Kansas City* in 1996, *The Gingerbread Man* in 1997, and *Dr. T. and the Women* in 2000.

Altman's accomplishment has been aided by a group of actors who appear regularly in his work during the 1970s: Shelley Duvall, Keith Carradine, Sissy Spacek, Geraldine Chaplin, and Elliott Gould among the stalwarts. Like Ingmar Bergman, he invariably obtains distinctive and compelling performances. But Altman, the playful postmodernist, is an artist of a different order from the somber Swedish director. "This is just like Bergman," comments Geraldine Chaplin's Opal upon arriving at a garden party in *Nashville.* "Of course, the people are all wrong for Bergman." Altman's predilection for in-jokes like this one and the easygoing satirical jabs he takes at his characters have led some commentators to denounce him as glib and condescending; critic Robin Wood's essay about the director is entitled "Smart-Ass and Cutie-Pie."

Altman's style is perhaps best described as fragmented. He has claimed that he is interested in "splitting areas of reality—in other words, dealing with emotional reponses rather than intellectual responses." He frequently employs wide-screen compositions in which many interactions happen simultaneously, all rendered in overlapping dialogue. "Found" musical scores, such as the Leonard Cohen songs that run through *McCabe and Mrs. Miller,* often have a contrapuntal relation to the film's narratives rather than simply underlining story points. Altman is also fond of pausing to zoom in or shift focus in order to emphasize objects in the environment that hold particular fascination—for example, the stained glass in *That Cold Day in the Park* and the pool murals in *3 Women.*

Improvisation adds to the sense of fragmentation in Altman's work. It is no accident that *Kansas City* is about jazz. To give free rein to his actors, he favors loose-jointed narratives that will accommodate frequent digressions, like the riff about a parrot Elliott Gould delivers in the 1974 *California Split.* In a spirit of open-endedness, Altman shot so much footage of actors' improvisations in *Nashville* that at one point he spoke of making two films of it: "Nashville Red" and "Nashville Blue."

A big, ambitious film, some regard *Nashville* as its director's crowning achievement; Altman himself has referred to it as his "metaphor for America." Its twenty-four characters are caught up in the music industry and in the presidential campaign of a populist demagogue. The movie's plot advances by intercut episodes from the lives of each of the characters, all of whom become involved in putting on a show for the political rally that forms the story's grand finalé. The subjects of parody and satire here are popular music and popular politics, the sorts of performance and manipulation involved in both, and the audiences to which both appeal.

Nashville ★ United States, 1975, Robert Altman; Ronnee Blakley and Henry Gibson.

Another director who has given us indelible portraits of America is **Francis Ford Cop-pola,** the first major American director to have graduated from a university film program (UCLA). Given that academic training, with its emphasis on personal expression, it is inter-esting that during the first part of his career he largely withheld or concealed his own per-sonality in his work, opting instead for a "professional" range of subjects and styles in productions such as *Dementia 13* (1963), a low-budget horror film; *You're a Big Boy Now* (1967), a charmingly light and unpretentious comedy; and *Finian's Rainbow* (1968), a semi-blockbuster musical. Beginning with *The Rain People* (1969), however, his work became more distinctive. Flawed in part, and oddly unresolved, *The Rain People* nonetheless gets at the stresses felt by a particular American woman, which cause her to leave her husband, though she is several months pregnant, to try to find herself in a cross-country journey by car.

With *The Godfather* (1972), adapted from a popular novel by Mario Puzo, Coppola's career took off in a rocketlike trajectory. What quickly became one of the great financial successes in the history of cinema is also a work of enduring value. Expert in every respect, the great appeal of the film clearly comes from the warm glow of people and times re-membered, when not only were men men and women women, but families were families, including especially the Mafia. The sentiments expressed were especially close to Coppola, who was himself from an Italian American background. The film portrayed the Mob as a more naked form of capitalist competition in which business rules and competition are literally cut-throat. "Basically, both the Mafia and America feel they are benevolent

The Godfather ★ United States, 1972, Francis Ford Coppola; Al Pacino and Marlon Brando.

organizations," the director once said. "And both the Mafia and America have their hands stained with blood from what it is necessary to do to protect their power and interests."

With deeply saturated, chiaroscuro images contributed by cinematography's "dark prince," Gordon Willis, and an unfogettable score by Fellini's favorite composer, Nino Rota, *The Godfather* brought a new level of European-style artistry to mainstream American cinema. To play the role of godfather Don Corleone, Marlon Brando stuffed his cheeks with cotton and adopted the raspy tones of an aging potentate who speaks softly but carries a very big stick. As the Don's youngest son, Michael, Al Pacino undergoes a major transformation in the course of the story, from an innocent and protected family favorite to the next Mob chieftain. The turning point occurs when Michael is forced to commit murder to save the family business. At this moment, the movie's sound editor, Walter Murch, added the screech of an L-train to the film's mix; the grating noise subtly signals the mental agony Michael's bland exterior conceals.

The Godfather, Part II and *The Godfather, Part III* expanded on the cinematic fresco outlined in the first movie. But Coppola's subsequent work encompassed other subjects as well. *The Conversation,* which won the Palme d'Or at the Cannes Film Festival in 1974, is an intimate portrait of a single individual, Harry Caul, played by Gene Hackman. An electronic eavesdropper who applies his expertise impartially and amorally, Harry gains his only satisfactions from his considerable skill and from vicariously experiencing fragments of other lives. The searing Vietnam War chronicle *Apocalypse Now* (1979) won Coppola yet another Palme d'Or at Cannes. In 2001 he took a recut version featuring fifty-four minutes of added scenes and entitled *Apocalypse Now Redux* back to the French festival. In the 1980s and 1990s Coppola went on to numerous other projects, including the musicals *One From the Heart* in 1982 and *The Cotton Club* in 1984, and the biopic *Tucker* in 1988. In 1992 he directed a lush, romantic horror story, *Bram Stoker's Dracula,* which manages to be both a faithful adaptation of the classic novel and a self-reflexive study of the nature of the modern world.

Coppola's style has been justly described as operatic. He often focuses on the complexities of obsessive, larger-than-life heroes such as Preston Tucker or *The Godfather's* Michael Corleone. At its worst, this approach leads to productions that feel bloated and overblown. "If he directs a little romance," critic Kenneth Tynan once remarked, "it has to be the biggest, most overdone little romance in history." On the other hand, Coppola has given us some of the most riveting set pieces in cinema, including the famous baptism scene that concludes *Godfather I,* in which a solemn organ piece plays over dynamic images of carnage taking place in numerous locations, and the helicopter attack in *Apocalypse Now,* which is accompanied by an actual operatic score, Wagner's "Ride of the Valkyrie."

In addition to his career as a director, Coppola played a key role in the reorganization of Hollywood during these uneasy years through his role as an entrepreneur. He founded Zoetrope studios in San Francisco in 1969 following his experience working on *The Rain People.* In typically 1960s fashion, he used the studio not only to make his own films but also to produce and distribute movies by European *auteurs* Wim Wenders (*Hammett,* 1982), Hans-Jurgen Syberberg (*Our Hitler,* 1979), Jean-Luc Godard (*Sauve qui peut [La vie],* 1980), Agnieska Holland (*The Secret Garden,* 1993), and Kenneth Branaugh (*Mary Shelley's Frankenstein,* 1994). He also arranged, in 1981, for the American release of French director Abel Gance's classic *Napoleon* as an event movie that played in

major cities with live musical accompaniment by his father, Carmine. Coppola also functioned as producer on American projects such as George Lucas's *American Graffiti* in
1973, Paul Schrader's *Mishima* in 1985, and Gregory Nava's *My Family/Mia Familia* in
1995. In part as a result of these grand undertakings, Coppola's finances have been subject
to more major roller-coaster rides than those of most Hollywood players. His desperate fi-
nanical straights forced him to sell Zoetrope in 1984. But he has never stayed down for
long. His universally acknowledged talent has always assured him of prestigious directing
assignments that return him, at least temporarily, to financial health.

Martin Scorsese, born in 1942, is the newest and youngest of the major mainstream
directors who emerged in the early 1970s; Coppola, born in 1939, is next. The careers of
these two Italian American film makers in some ways parallel one another. Both attended
university film departments (New York University in Scorsese's case). But Coppola has
ranged widely in terms of his subjects and forms, whereas Scorsese has stuck quite closely
to what he learned while growing up in New York's Little Italy. When Coppola tried his
hand at a musical, it was *Finian's Rainbow,* a bit of Irish whimsy replete with leprechaun
and a pot of gold at the rainbow's end; Scorsese's musical was *New York, New York* (1977),
about a self-absorbed tenor saxophone player obssessed with jazz.

After a few apprentice works, including *Who's That Knocking at My Door?* (1968)
and *Boxcar Bertha* (1972), Scorsese made *Mean Streets* (1973), a fuller, tougher, more assured treatment of the same sorts of characters, themes, and milieu that had appeared in
Who's That Knocking? In *Mean Streets* the protagonist (Harvey Keitel) attempts to recon-
cile his persistent sense of decency and concern for others with his ambition to succeed in
the Mafia-imbued life around him. His maddeningly irresponsible buddy is played by
Robert De Niro, who would subsequently become a fully participating collaborator in the
expression of Scorsese's mythos. Since *Mean Streets,* Scorsese has managed his career
with canny pragmatism, alternating the crime stories he is most famous for with chancier
experiments involving an array of genres and subjects. The most notable examples of the
former group include *Taxi Driver* (1976), *Goodfellas* (1990), and *Casino* (1995). Among
the latter endeavors are *Alice Doesn't Live Here Anymore* (1975), *The Age of Innocence*
(1993), and *Kundun* (1997).

Scorsese's visual style—edgy and kinetic—pegs him as a New Yorker. His crime
films have a dark and often gritty appearance. The jerky, hand-held camera work that characterized early efforts such as *Mean Streets* has given way in later productions to the
smoother rhythms made possible by the development of the more stable, shoulder-mounted
Steadicam (which was introduced in 1976). *Goodfella*'s long Steadicam shot of Ray Liotta
and Lorraine Bracco entering the Copacabana nightclub through a back door and winding
their way through the kitchen and back hallways before arriving at their front-row table is
often held up as a textbook example of the bravura effects the Steadicam has made possible. Scorsese's noncrime films have provided him with opportunities to experiment with
other styles and effects, such as the shimmering glow of the sea behind Michelle Pfeiffer's
silhouetted figure in *The Age of Innocence* and the lengthy montage of the Dalai Lama's
vision of his devasted nation that ends *Kundun.*

Although he has become famous for his depictions of the seamy side of life, Scorsese's first ambition was to be a priest, and his interest in religion is directly expressed in
films such as *The Last Temptation of Christ* (1988) and *Kundun* (which takes the Dalai
Lama as its subject). Even when his subjects are not overtly relgious, symbolism often adds

a spiritual dimension to Scorsese's stories, as when the image of a pool table takes on a sacramental character at a certain moment in *The Color of Money* (1986) or when Bach's "St. Matthew Passion" can be heard over a panorama of gambling tables in *Casino.* From this perspective, much of Scorsese's *oeuvre* can be viewed as an attempt to portray a fallen world filled with people desperately trying, by whatever perverse means, to find salvation.

Taxi Driver (1976) might be seen as an extreme variation on the failed saint figure who appears as protagonist in many of Scorsese's films. Here, the character, played by De Niro, is locked into near catatonia and becomes obsessed with cleansing the world's evil through a bath of blood. The isolation of the De Niro character is truly frightening and the homicidal violence unnerving. The film, which deals with attempted political assassination, was released immediately following a time when prominent U.S. leaders (Martin Luther King, John F. Kennedy, and Robert Kennedy) had been gunned down. *Taxi Driver* also featured Jodie Foster, the obsessive love object of the man who would wound Ronald Reagan.

Scorsese's *Raging Bull* (1980), which a poll of critics later ranked as the best film of the 1980s, has the New York City setting and Italian American context of many of the director's other works. What is different about this film is its tone. The life of fighter Jake La Motta, who rose to become middleweight champion and then descended into dissoluteness and a self-parodic nightclub act, is presented with what seems to be La Motta's own lack of understanding of his animal violence and self-indulgence. The film won Academy Awards for Robert De Niro, who gained fifty pounds to play La Motta, and Thelma Shoonmaker, Scorsese's long-standing editor. Also nominated for an Oscar was

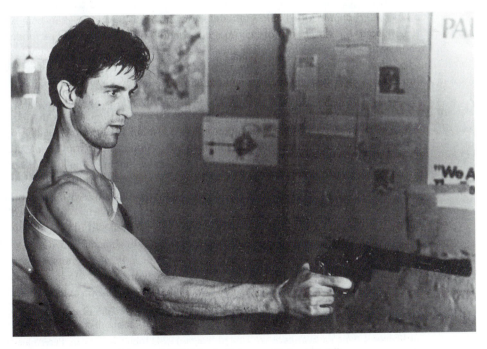

Taxi Driver ★ United States, 1976, Martin Scorsese; Robert De Niro.

cinematographer Michael Chapman, whose silvery black-and-white photography overlaid the film's brutal storyline with a patina of delicacy and elegance.

Of all the American New Wave directors, probably the most radical was **John Cassavetes.** Operating on the fringes of the Hollywood industry with a group of actor-collaborators, most notably his wife Gena Rowlands, Cassavetes created a series of films that he financed primarily through his work as an actor in mainstream productions such as *Rosemary's Baby* (1968). His own movies are built around performance, making extensive use of improvisation, loose storylines, and accommodating hand-held camera work. "I've been concerned from the beginning with the problems confronting real people rather than emphasizing dramatic structure or bending characters to the plot," he once said. Deeply committed to the Method acting technique, he created a series of highly charged melodramas about characters at turning points in their lives, foregrounding the kind of emotional venting for which the Method style is famous. His first effort, *Shadows* (1960), developed out of a Method acting workshop he was teaching. Among the most well-regarded films he made subsequently are *Faces* (1968); *Minnie and Moskowitz* (1971); *A Woman Under the Influence* (1974); *Gloria,* which won a Golden Lion at Venice in 1980; and *Love Streams,* which won at Berlin in 1986. Cassavetes died in 1989.

Though some commentators complained that his plots lack form, his technique is sloppy, and his scenes run far too long, Cassavetes stuck with his vision and produced a body of work that steadily gained ground with the critics. Fascinated by the intensity of people's inner lives, and the capacity of cinema to expose this intensity to view, he

A Woman Under the Influence ★ United States, 1974, John Cassavetes; Peter Falk and Gena Rowlands.

consistently focused on the problem of finding emotional stability and order in a world of self-indulgence and overprivilege.

Independent Voices

The counterculture mentality of the 1960s and early 1970s created a climate in which film makers whose ambitions went beyond creating entertainment for the masses were motivated to abandon Hollywood in favor of artisanal methods that could speak to larger social concerns or make more thoroughgoing individual statements. Many of those who had social or political agendas turned to documentary film making; others, wanting to express more personal or purely asthetic visions, looked to the traditions of the *avant garde*. Both groups were aided by the advent of cheaper 16 mm equipment as well as by avid audiences who congregated at museums, galleries, and college campuses, and responded enthusiastically to their efforts.

The documentary film movement that had begun in the 1920s with productions such as Robert Flaherty's *Nanook of the North* (1921) and had continued with New Deal–sponsored projects in the 1930s by directors such as Pare Lorentz was taken up by a group of left-leaning film makers in the 1960s who wanted to put the spotlight on social and political trends and events. Disdainful of the the heavy-handed educational tone and barely disguised ideological agendas of most television documentaries, they looked for fresher approaches to nonfiction movie making. Some—for instance, Emile de Antonio—made films that openly advocated political positions (*Year of the Pig,* 1969). Others developed a style of "direct cinema" in which the director(s) recorded contemporary events in a putatively neutral manner. This mandate was enabled by the development of relatively cheap portable cameras and lightweight sound-recording devices that could be taken to various locations so that events could be recorded as they occurred.

Prizing the principle of collective rather than individual authorship, the practitioners of direct cinema often worked in groups. The first major documentary to illustrate the method was *Primary,* an examination of John F. Kennedy's Wisconsin primary campaign for president. Released in 1960, it was produced by a team called Drew Associates. David and Albert Maysles, who customarily worked with Charlotte Zwerin, also practiced the direct cinema technique in documentaries such as *Salesman* (1968), a chronicle of the life of a Bible peddler, and *Grey Gardens* (1975), a look at two eccentric cousins of Jacqueline Kennedy Onassis. Shirley Clarke (*Portrait of Jason,* 1967) was another major figure in this movement. A popular series of "rock docs" used direct cinema methods to chronicle the massive gatherings of young people at the music festivals of the era, most notably *Monterey Pop* (D. A. Pennebaker, 1968) and *Woodstock* (Michael Wadleigh, 1970). *Gimme Shelter* (Albert and David Maysles), also released in 1970, marked something of an end point of the youth culture by inadvertently capturing an incident in which a member of the Hell's Angels motorcycle gang stabbed and killed a member of the audience at a Rolling Stones concert. The direct cinema style continued to be employed in later years, with major productions such as *Harlan County, USA* (Barbara Kopple, 1976), *Hoop Dreams* (Steve James and associates, 1994), and *The War Room* (D. A. Pennebaker and Chris Hegedus, 1998).

The most famous and prolific exponent of an approach that closely approximates the direct cinema mode was **Frederick Wiseman.** Wiseman's first film was an exposé of a

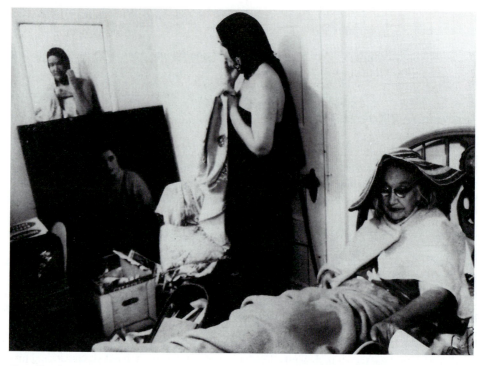

Grey Gardens ★ United States, 1975, Albert and David Maysles, Ellen Hovde, and Muffie Meyer; Little Edie and Big Edie Bouvier.

Woodstock ★ United States, 1970, Michael Wadleigh.

396

Harlan County, U.S.A. ✳
United States, 1976,
Barbara Kopple.

Massachusetts mental hospital, *Titticut Follies* (1967). Since then, he has continued to produce increasingly lengthy film examinations of an array of social institutions, including the educational system (*High School,* 1968), the police (*Law and Order,* 1969), and public housing (*Public Housing,* 1997). Wiseman has claimed that he tries to give his films the greatest possible sense of immediacy "so there is no separation between the audience watching the film and the events in the film."

At the same time the documentarians were examining political and social phenomena, another group of independent movie makers focused on personal emotions, developing lyrical forms rather than essayistic ones. Calling themselves "underground film makers" to emphasize their antiestablishment orientation, they were inspired in large part by the pioneering work of Maya Deren in the 1940s. Deren's cinematic poems, including *Meshes of the Afternoon* (1943) and *Ritual in Transfigured Time* (1946), had in turn been inspired by the European avant-garde movements of earlier eras. Following the pattern Deren and others had laid out, the underground film makers of the 1960s and 1970s worked either alone or in small, close-knit coteries, creating highly idiosyncratic, painterly works. The most prominent members of the group included Bruce Conner (*A Movie,* 1958), Jack Smith (*Flaming Creatures,* 1963), and Kenneth Anger (*Scorpio Rising,* 1964).

The father figure of 1960s underground film making was Jonas Mekas, whose magazine *Film Culture* and column in the *Village Voice* introduced and explained the work of these *cinéastes* to an ever-growing audience. Mekas also founded the Film-Makers Cooperative to distribute avant-garde and documentary works, and he cofounded the Anthology Film Archives to provide regular screenings and archive writings related to the movement's key figures. Mekas was himself a film maker, the creator of lengthy cinematic ruminations

Law and Order ★ United
States, 1969, Frederick
Wiseman.

on his life, family, and friends (*Diaries, Notes, and Sketches,* 1964–1969 and *Lost Lost Lost,* 1976).

Foremost among the practitioners of avant-garde movie making during this era was the prolific **Stan Brakhage,** who produced approximately 250 films between 1952 and 1995. Early in his career, Brakhage received the imprimateur of Mekas, who declared in his *Village Voice* column in 1961, "Brakhage is one of the four or five most authentic film artists working in cinema anywhere, and perhaps the most original filmmaker in America today." Working alone, often with low-tech, 8 mm stock, Brakhage turned out a series of movies, almost all without sound, to correspond to his belief in the expressivity of what he called "pure film." Many of his productions are autobiographical (*Dog Star Man,* 1961–1964); others are abstract (*Mothlight,* 1963). To express the nature of the cinematic medium itself in these works, Brakhage sometimes scratched the film or painted directly on it. Explaining his approach, he wrote in his 1963 book, *Metaphors of Vision,* "Imagine an eye unruled by man-made laws of perspective, an eye unprejudiced by compositional logic, an eye which does not respond to the name of everything but which must know each object encountered in life through an adventure of perception."

An almost polar opposite approach to movie making governed the work of the other major avant-garde film artist of the era, **Andy Warhol.** Warhol's cinematic technique could fairly be described as involving no technique at all. Having begun his career as a commercial artist, he had gone on to fame in the New York art world as one of the chief exponents of the Pop Art movement by making silkscreens of everyday objects such as soup

Meshes of the Afternoon ✫ United States, 1943, Maya Deren and Alexander Hammid; Maya Deren.

cans and movie-star portraits. He began his film making work with a series of productions that enshrined his belief in boredom. (He was fond of asserting, "I love to be bored.") The six-hour *Sleep* (1963) showed a man sleeping; *Empire* (1964) went even further, consisting of a single, eight-hour view of the Empire State Building. Warhol's next group of films made good on another of his beliefs—"Everyone should be famous for fifteen minutes"—by alotting somewhat more than fifteen minutes to showcase the antics of the denizens of his New York studio (called "The Factory"). These productions, including *Chelsea Girls* (1966) and *Lonesome Cowboys* (1968), were made in collaboration with Warhol's associate, Paul Morrissey. Iconoclastic in nature, they consisted of fragmentary narratives that pushed the limits of censorship with semipornographic representations of sexuality and displays of drug use. Warhol, who died in 1987, ultimately turned the directorial reigns over to Morrissey. Morrissey proceeded to make a number of more conventional films under the Warhol banner—including *Trash* (1970), *Andy Warhol's Frankenstein* (1974), and *Andy Warhol's Bad* (1975)—moving away from the ultra-passive filming technique favored by Warhol himself to introduce more traditional plots, camera work and continuity editing. Despite these innovations, however, Morrissey's commitment to shocking

Lonesome Cowboys ★ United States, 1968, Andy Warhol; Joe Dallesandro, on left.

audiences with explicit sexuality and bloody violence continued to tie his films to the Warholian aesthetic.

During the 1970s a new avant-garde movement came to the fore. Called *structuralist film making,* it highlighted the process of creating and viewing film in a highly abstract and self-reflexive manner. The name *structuralist* was suggested by critic P. Adams Sitney, a major interpreter of avant-garde cinema. "The film insists on its shape," he wrote, "and what content it has is minimal and subsidiary to its outline." The structuralist film movement's most famous exponent is Canadian artist Michael Snow, whose 1967 *Wavelength* consists of a forty-five-minute slow zoom in on a photograph of waves attached to the wall of a loft apartment. Other structuralist film makers of note include George Landow (*Remedial Reading Comprehension,* 1970), Ernie Gehr (*Serene Velocity,* 1970), and Hollis Frampton (*Zorns Lemma,* 1970).

By the early 1970s feminism had produced a new crop of independent movie makers who were committed to women's issues. Some, interested in unearthing facets of women's history and the conditions of women's lives, made documentaries such as *Janie's Janie* (Geri Ashur, New York Newsreel, 1971), *Union Maids* (Jim Klein and Julia Reichert, 1976), and *The Life and Times of Rosie the Riveter* (Connie Field, 1976). Others, taking to heart the feminist adage "the personal is political," made confessional films; this group included Carolee Schneemann (*Fuses,* 1964), Joyce Chopra (*Joyce at 34,* 1972), and Barbara Hammer (*Sap-*

The Life and Times of Rosie the Riveter ★ United States, 1980, Connie Field.

pho, 1978). Still others worked with mixed forms, including the Canadian Joyce Wieland (*Reason Over Passion,* 1969), Michelle Citron (*Daughter Rite,* 1978), Sue Friedrich (*The Ties That Bind,* 1984), and Trinh Minha (*Surname Viet, Given Name Nam,* 1989).

The most important avant-garde film maker to emerge from the feminist movement of the early 1970s was **Yvonne Rainer.** Like Deren before her, Rainer had started out as a dancer. Absorbing a range of influences, from the structuralism of Snow to the Brechtianism of Godard to the poststructuralism of contemporary film theory, she has produced a series of films that feature fragmented, self-reflexive narratives, printed texts, clips from films of the past, and documentary materials, all combined in collage-like structures. Feminist critic B. Ruby Rich has characterized the ultimate effect of these highly original and challenging works as "landmining emotional terrain." Rainer's first production, *Lives of Performers* (1971), grew out of the dance performance art in which she had previously been engaged, but she moved quickly beyond this beginning effort to create more abstract, theoretically informed works, most notably *Film About a Woman Who . . .* in 1974 and *The Man Who Envied Women* in 1985. In 1990, she made her most accessible film, *Privilege,* which focuses on a woman dealing with menopause.

By the mid-1970s the radical impulse that had powered the cinematic breakthroughs of Rainer and other film makers of the 1960s and early 1970s had run its course. Most of the

Privilege ★ United States, 1990, Yvonne Rainer.

directors who had launched their careers during this period continued to work on into the next decades, but the new film makers who appeared were of a different stripe. By this time, however, the United States had regained its place among the leading nations of film art.

Films of the Period

1963
The Birds (Alfred Hitchcock)
Flaming Creatures (Jack Smith)
Dr. Strangelove (Stanley Kubrick)

1964
Cheyenne Autumn (John Ford)
Dog Star Man (Stan Brakhage) (1962–1964)
Empire (Andy Warhol)
My Fair Lady (George Cukor)
Scorpio Rising (Kenneth Anger)

1965
The Sound of Music (Robert Wise)

1966
Chelsea Girls (Andy Warhol)
Don't Look Back (D. A. Pennebaker)

1967
Bonnie and Clyde (Arthur Penn)
The Graduate (Mike Nichols)
Guess Who's Coming for Dinner (Stanley Kramer)
Portrait of Jason (Shirley Clarke)
Titticut Follies (Frederick Wiseman)
Wavelength (Michael Snow)

1968
Faces (John Cassavetes)

High School (Frederick Wiseman)
Lonesome Cowboys (Andy Warhol)
Rosemary's Baby (Roman Polanski)
Salesman (Albert and David Maysles)
The Year of the Pig (Emile de Antonio)

1969
Butch Cassidy and the Sundance Kid
   (George Roy Hill)
Diaries, Notes, and Sketches (Jonas Mekas)
   (1964–1969)
Easy Rider (Dennis Hopper)
Law and Order (Frederick Wiseman)
The Learning Tree (Gordon Parks)
Medium Cool (Haskell Wexler)
Midnight Cowboy (John Schlesinger)
The Wild Bunch (Sam Peckinpah)

1970
Gimme Shelter (Albert and David Maysles
   and Charlotte Zwerin)
Little Big Man (Arthur Penn)
M*A*S*H (Robert Altman)
Trash (Andy Warhol and Paul Morrissey)
Woodstock (Michael Wadleigh)

1971
The French Connection (William Friedkin)
The Last Picture Show (Peter Bogdanovich)
McCabe and Mrs. Miller (Robert Altman)
Minnie and Moskowitz (John Cassavetes)
Shaft (Gordon Parks)
Sweet Sweetback's Baadasssss Song
   (Melvin Van Peebles)

1972
Cabaret (Bob Fosse)
The Godfather (Francis Ford Coppola)

1973
American Graffiti (George Lucas)
Badlands (Terence Malik)
The Exorcist (William Friedkin)
The Long Goodbye (Robert Altman)
Mean Streets (Martin Scorsese)

1974
Chinatown (Roman Polanski)
The Conversation (Francis Ford Coppola)
Film About a Woman Who . . . (Yvonne Rainer)
The Godfather II (Francis Ford Coppola)
A Woman Under the Influence (John Cassavetes)

Books on the Period

American Film Institute Staff. *The American Film Institute Catalog of Motion Pictures Produced in the United States: Feature Films, 1961–1970.* Berkeley: University of California Press, 1997.

Biskind, Peter. *Easy Riders, Raging Bulls: The Generation That Transformed Hollywood.* New York: Simon and Schuster, 1998.

Black, Gregory D. *The Catholic Crusade Against the Movies, 1940–1975.* New York: Cambridge University Press, 1998.

Brown, Gene. *Movie Time: A Chronology of Hollywood and the Movie Industry from Its Beginnings to the Present.* New York: Macmillan, 1995.

Curran, Daniel. *Guide to American Cinema, 1965–1995.* Westport, CT: Greenwood Press, 1998.

Lyons, Charles. *The New Censors: Movies and the Culture Wars.* Philadelphia: Temple University Press, 1997.

Maltby, Richard, and Ian Craven. *Hollywood Cinema: An Introduction.* Madden, MA: Blackwell Publications, 1995.

Man, Glen. *Radical Visions: American Film Renaissance, 1967–1976.* Westport, CT: Greenwood Press, 1994.

Muse, Eben J. *The Land of Nam: The Vietnam War in American Film.* Lanham, MD: Scarecrow Press, 1995.

Nowell-Smith, Geoffrey, and Stephen Ricci, eds. *Hollywood and Europe: Economics, Culture, National Identity, 1945–1995.* London: British Film Institute, 1998.

Slide, Anthony. *The New Historical Dictionary of the American Film Industry.* Lanham, MD: Scarecrow Press, 1998.

17

Recent National Movements

1959–

The last half of the twentieth century saw important cinema movements develop in countries beyond the orbit of Europe, the United States, and the major Asian nations. Postcolonial cultures in Latin America and Africa have nurtured distinctive movie-making traditions, as have the former commonwealth nations of Australia and Canada. Most recently, films from Middle Eastern countries, especial Iran, have appeared on the global stage. Early films from developing nations, which attracted international attention, generally expressed a strong sense of nationalism, frequently accompanied by anti-imperialism and sometimes a call to revolution. Film making in some of the Latin American countries, as well as in Africa, especially, conformed to these generalizations. Other places, such as Mexico and the British Commonwealth countries, have developed nationalist cinematic agendas in less politically stressed climates. The Middle East has its own political issues; in Iran, these are closely tied to questions of religious propriety, and its films reflect this concern.

Latin America

Although each Latin American country has given birth to its own, particularized cinematic culture, a common heritage, along with abundant opportunities for cross-fertilization, have led to a common set of principles and values. All of the Latin American film movements have built on a shared aesthetic in the other arts. The surrealist strain so prominent in Spanish painting and sculpture found its way into the New World as well. These nations, in turn, added their own brand of what has come to be called *magic realism* to the mix. Out of these ingredients Latin Americans have crafted a literary tradition that has proved to be a major wellspring for postmodernist narrative explorations—the writings of José Luis Borges, Carlos Fuentes, Gabriel García Márquez, and others. Filled with hallucinatory fantasies, labyrinthine mysteries, and unexpected shifts in character, style, and structure, these works have become the very definition of the postmodern aesthetic.

To this rich artistic heritage, most Latin American film makers have added strong political commitments, reacting against the military and fascist ruling elites and oppressive colonialist policies that have long governed the affairs of most of these countries. Unlike other third-world directors, such as Satyajit Ray of India, the Latin Americans made their films for local audiences, not international festivals. Although most of these movie makers come from upper-class backgrounds, their goal is to connect with the peasantry and the urban poor of their countries in order to raise social awareness and ultimately improve conditions. "By testifying, critically to [the reality of] misery, cinema refuses it," Argentinean director Fernando Birri, a leader of the movement, once wrote, "because it shows matters as they irrefutably are and not as we would like them to be."

Principles derived from the Italian neorealists were a major inspiration to many Latin American movie makers—particularly since several had been trained at Italy's documentary film school, the Centro Sperimentale, in Rome. Other Latin American directors attended the documentary school in Santa Fé, Argentina—La Escuela Documental de Santa Fé—set up in the 1950s by Birri, a graduate of Italy's Centro Sperimentale. To the neorealist principles of shooting on location, using nonprofessional actors, and focusing on lower-class lifestyles, accents, and dialects, the Latin Americans have added their own carnival-esque flavor, a style called *tropicalism,* consisting of surrealism, allegory, vivid color, flashy images, and powerful music. Their preferred subjects include contemporary social and political issues (for example, Bolivian Jorge Sanjinés's 1969 *Blood of the Condor,* which deals with the attempts by the American Peace Corps to sterilize Bolivian Indian women) as well as historical stories, especially those dealing with slavery (such as Brazilian Carlos Diegues's 1964 *Ganga Zumba* and Cuban Sergio Gilal's 1973 *The Other Francisco*). After many Latin American film makers were driven out of their countries by political crackdowns, exile films (Chilean Miguel Littín's 1975 *Letters from Marusia* and Argentinean Fernando Solanas's 1985 *Tango: the Exile of Gardel)* became another favored genre.

In 1954 a film festival was set up in Montevideo, Argentina, providing the region's directors with both a venue for showing their work and a forum for exchanging ideas. In 1958 the festival honored British documentary pioneer John Grierson. The occasion drew film makers from all over South America, including Birri, who screened his collectively produced documentary, *Throw Me a Dime,* and the Brazilian Nelson Pereira dos Santos, who showed his neorealist fiction film, *Rio, North Zone.* In 1967 another meeting of directors from an array of Latin American nations was held in Viña del Mar, Chile. Out of this came the label *Nuevo Cinema Latinamericano* to designate the new movement that was afoot.

Among Latin American cinematic traditions, **Cuba**'s has been preeminent. Movies have always been popular there. Moreover, with its socialist revolution achieved in 1959, Cuba was able to offer inspiration, encouragement, and actual assistance to the independent leftist film makers in the neighboring countries of South America. The Cubans had rebelled against foreign (i.e., American) domination as well as the Fulgencio Batista government. Following from this anti-American sentiment, the revolution's triumph brought

Blood of the Condor ★ Bolivia, 1969, Jorge Sanjinés.

sweeping changes in the Cuban motion-picture industry that sought to sever its relationship to Hollywood. Like Russia following its revolution in 1917, or the Eastern Republics
after 1945, Cuba established a government agency to organize and regulate all production,
distribution, and exhibition. Called *Instituto Cubano del Arte y Industria Cinematográfi-
cos (ICAIC),* it created first-rate production facilities, and invited Czechoslovakian film
makers in to train Cuban personnel.

    Consistent with Lenin's advice to the earlier Soviet film makers, the Cubans used
newsreels and documentaries to meet the needs of the people as seen by the new state. The
leading figure of this nonnarrative short-film output was Santiago Alvarez, who made documentaries such as *L.B.J.* (1968) and *79 Springtimes* (1969, about Vietnamese leader Ho
Chi Minh). The ironic and experimental forms of attack on the violence of the United
States in these films, and their lyrical portrayal of "the struggle of the underdeveloped and
small peoples for their human dignity," as Alvarez has put it, place him among the leading
innovators in art used for political persuasion.

    The best-known Cuban director is **Tomás Gutiérrez Alea,** whose *Memories of Un-
derdevelopment* (1968) was the first Cuban feature to achieve international recognition. Far
from serving any obvious agitprop function, it chronicles the spiritual displacement of a
bourgeois intellectual within postrevolutionary Cuban culture with a kind of cinematic sophistication and emotional detachment that place it within the mainstream of modern world
cinema. Alea's *Up to a Point* (1983) deals with the problems raised by a long tradition of
Latin American *machismo.* The title comes from one of the brief interviews with real work-

Memories of Underdevelopment ☀ Cuba, 1968, Tomás Gutièrrez Alea; Sergio Corrieri, on right.

ers interspersed throughout this fictional narrative. A young black male questioned about *machismo* laughingly replies, "Oh, they've managed to change my attitudes on that score: I've certainly changed up to a certain point. I'm probably 80% now. Maybe they can work on me and get me to, say, 87%. But they will never, never get me up to 100%, no way."

The topic of *machismo* has also been taken up in the many Cuban films that focus on issues facing women, including Humberto Solás's *Lucía* (1968) and Pastor Vega's *Portrait of Teresa* (1979). *One Way or Another* (1977), a fiction-documentary mix, is an especially memorable example of Cuban feminist discourse. Directed by Sara Gómez, who died before editing was completed, its plot concerns a young, idealistic social worker who, while trying to teach ghetto kids, falls in love with a local man struggling to break out of the neighborhood's deprived existence. Alea's own *Strawberry and Chocolate* in 1994 carries the gender issue into the realm of gay sexuality, which poses a further challenge to Latin *machismo*.

In **Brazil,** an upsurge of nationalism occurred at about the same time as the Cuban Revolution. In response, a cooperative formed by Glauber Rocha, Nelson Pereira dos Santos (*Barren Lives,* 1963), and Ruy Guerra *(The Guns,*1964) produced what they called *Cinema Nôvo.* Ironically, the group got their start through support from Embrafilme, a state funding agency set up in the 1960s by the reigning military government to promote Brazil abroad through films praising the existing regime. Needless to say the productions of the Cinema Nôvo directors were of quite a different order. But they got funding all the same. The abolition of Embrafilme in 1990 caused a major setback for the country's production activities, but in 1994 the institution of another system of government grants revitalized the industry once again.

The Cinema Nôvo group offered a more applicable model than did Cuba for other Latin American film makers on the left working independently within entrenched capitalist regimes. Dedicated to a principle of "miserabilism," which pledged them to focus on the poor and needy, these directors quickly moved away from the documentary-type approach of neorealism to develop a cinema in which dark political allegories were rendered in an exuberantly tropicalist style. Rocha was the Cinema Nôvo's leader and spokesman, labeling the movement's approach an "aesthetics of hunger." Another member of the group, Joaquin Pedro de Andrade, took this allusion to starvation to its logical conclusion in his 1969 production, *Macunaima,* a carnival-esque tale of cannibalism. "Cannibalism is an exemplary mode of consumerism adopted by underdeveloped peoples," he later commented by way of explanation.

Glauber Rocha's own films, including *Black God, White Devil* (1964) and *Antonio das Mortes* (1969), are set in the barren northeastern region of the country and explore the mythic folk roots of banditry and mystical religion that extreme poverty had bred. Strange and haunting in their combination of severe naturalism and stylized ritual, they portray a world of violence and madness. Following the release of *Antonio das Mortes,* Rocha left Brazil and worked abroad. He made films in Europe and Africa that attempted to deal with the problems of the third world—underdevelopment and neocolonialist exploitation—and to explore the possibilities for political action to bring about radical social change. In 1976 he returned to Brazil, but completed little of significance before his death in 1981.

Post-Cinema Nôvo production has become prolific. A line of leftist criticism has been maintained but added to it is a diversity of popular films. Pereira dos Santos contin-

Black God, White Devil ★ Brazil, 1964, Glauber Rocha.

Kiss of the Spider Woman
☆ Brazil, 1985, Hector
Babenco; Raul Julia and
William Hurt.

ued the political line in, for instance, *How Tasty Was My Little Frenchman* (1971), *Amulet of Orgum* (1974), *Tent of Miracles* (1977), and *Prison Memories* (1984); as did Carlos Diegues in *Xica* (1976) and *Bye Bye Brazil* (1980); and Argentine emigré Hector Babenco in *Pixote* (1981). For the most part, however, revolutionary Brazilian film makers have blended into the commercial film industry, which became more visible following the wide showing of Bruno Barreto's *Dona Flor and Her Two Husbands* in 1978. The international popularity of Brazilian cinema reached its peak in 1985 with Babenco's first English-language film, *Kiss of the Spider Woman,* a U.S.-Brazilian coproduction that centers on the relationship of two very different prison cell mates: a sensitive, imaginative, homosexual "queen" (William Hurt) and a tough-minded Marxist militant (Raul Julia). In 1999 Brazilian cinema again stepped into the international cinema spotlight with Walter Salles's *Central Station,* a socially progressive, if sentimentalized, tale about the relationship between a single woman and a destitute child; it garnered an Oscar nomination for its star Fernanda Montenegro.

In **Argentina** in the 1960s another group of political film makers set up an independent cooperative, in their case called *Grupo Cine Liberación (GCL).* Its manifesto, "Toward a Third Cinema," advocated film making that was "independent in production, militant in politics, and experimental in language." The group's program also called for collective film authorship and audience involvement in political discussion as part of the film experience. (The manifesto defines the first two cinemas as the Hollywood studio system and *auteur* films; films made according to Grupo Cine Liberación principles was the third.) The GCL's principal organizer was Fernando Solanas and its major work was his *The Hour of the Furnaces* (1968, codirected with Octavio Getino). This huge documentary (nearly four-and-a-half hours long) is in three separate parts: "Neo-Colonialism and Violence," "An Act for Liberation," and "Violence and Liberation." The first part presents a historical, geographical, economic, and social analysis of Argentina. The content of the second and third parts was developed out of points raised during audience discussion following the necessarily clandestine screenings of the first. Because of the time at which it appeared, its ambitious scope, its formal eclecticism, and the circumstances surrounding its production and distribution, *Hour of the Furnaces* has been regarded as the single-most influential documentary to have come out of the entire Cinema Latinamericano movement. With the resumption of military rule in Argentina in 1976, not only were the films of the GCL no longer smuggled abroad but they were not shown in Argentina itself, even clandestinely, because of the severe penalties attached to any activities critical of the government.

With the defeat of Argentina in the Falklands War of 1982, the military was weak enough to be opposed. Following the election of a civilian government in 1983, *The Official Story* was produced. The plot deals with the disappearance of roughly thirty thousand Argentinians—the *desaparecidos*—between 1976 and 1983. The first feature of Luis Puenzo, a director of television commercials, it won the 1985 Academy Award for Best Foreign Film. Solanas continued to produce works of value throughout the 1980s and 1990s, including *South* (1988), about a newly released prisoner wandering the night streets of Buenos Aires, reawakening memories and ghosts; and *The Voyage* (1991), a biting comedy-satire of a weak and ineffectual Argentina, representative of South America as a whole. Other Argentinean directors who came to the fore at the century's end have also adopted a tough line of political and social criticism, including Eliseo Subiola (*Man Facing Southeast,* 1986) and Maria Luisa Bemberg, who crafted a distinguished series of

The Hour of the Furnaces ★ Argentina, 1969, Fernando Solanas and Octavio Getino.

The Official Story ★ Argentina, 1983,
Luis Puenzo; Norma Aleandro.

Man Facing Southeast ★ Argentina, 1986, Eliseo Subiola; Hugo Soto.

searching feminist cinematic studies before her death in 1995, including *Camila* (1984), *Miss Mary* (1987), *I, the Worst of All* (1990), and *We Don't Want to Talk About It* (1993).

In **Chile** a group of political film makers developed in the 1960s in support of Salvador Allende's socialist movement. Their cooperative was called *Cinematographia Tercer Mundo.* Its best-known film is *The Jackal of Nahueltero* (1969), directed by **Miguel Littin,** a semidocumentary reconstruction of a mass murder committed by a peasant brutalized and driven mad by hopeless poverty. After Allende's election in 1970, Littin was appointed head of the newly nationalized Chile Films, which began producing a program of newsreels and documentaries following the Cuban pattern. (Of these, *The First Years,* 1971, made by Patricio Guzman, received the widest distribution; his later *Battle of Chile,* 1973, is even better known.) After the military coup of 1973, which deposed Allende, Littin left Chile and resumed work in Mexico. In Cuba, he finished *The Promised Land* (1971), another fictional account of an incident in Chilean history—in this case, the establishment and destruction of a socialist republic in the 1930s. Subsequently he lived in Spain and made films in exile. *Alsino and the Condor* (1982), a young boy's view of the Nicaraguan conflict between the Somoza government and the Sandanista rebels, may be his most widely seen film.

Chile's best known director, **Raúl Ruiz,** is more an international than national figure. Though he attended the Escuela Documental de Santa Fé in Argentina, he made only a few films in Latin America, including *Three Sad Tigers* (1968) and *The Penal Colony* (1971),

The Battle of Chile ★ Chile, 1973, Patricio Guzman.

City of Pirates ✶ France, 1983, Raúl Ruiz.

before being forced into exile by the Pinochet regime. Living in Paris since 1974, Ruiz began steady film making for France's National Audiovisual Institute in 1977. His amazingly prolific output, averaging six films a year, has been produced on minuscule budgets at incredible speed. And they are of all sorts: shorts and features, documentary and fiction, and mixtures of modes, most of them made originally for television. Whatever their form, they carry avant-garde inflections and a virtuosity that opens up new ways of storytelling, new kinds of imagery, and new interrogations of cinematic language. Even the titles suggest the fabulous and metaphysical aspects of his work: *Dog's Dialogue* (1977), *The Hypothesis of the Stolen Painting* (1978), *The Territory* (1981), *The Roof of the Whale* (1982), and *City of Pirates* (1983). You might think with *Treasure Island* (1991) you would be on familiar ground, but it turns out to be a wildly mythic and incoherent parody, stories within stories in the form of a child's game, connecting only occasionally with the Robert Louis Stevenson novel. In the late 1990s Ruiz showed signs of becoming more mainstream. He completed his most accessible film, *Three Lives and Only One Death,* a comedy starring Marcello Mastroianni, in 1996. At the dawn of the twenty-first century, he looked back to the past with a lavish adaptation of *Time Regained,* the last of Marcel Proust's famous trilogy about memory and desire.

As a country with a less turbulent political history throughout most of the twentieth century than most other Latin American nations, **Mexico** has not witnessed the genesis of the kind of radical film movement that came to the fore in other parts of the Hispanic New World. Its cinema has been most consistently notable for the broad distribution of its formulaic genre productions, called *churros,* throughout the region. Mexico has also produced numerous actors who later found success in Hollywood, including Dolores del Rio, Anthony Quinn, Ricardo Montalban, Katy Jurado, and Salma Hayek.

Mexico's own film culture, however, has produced works of enduring value as well as mass appeal. The 1940s and 1950s are thought of as a Golden Age, crowned by the films made by Spanish director Luis Buñuel from 1945 to 1960. During this period Mexico produced more than one hundred movies a year. Among the most highly esteemed of Buñuel's films made during this time are *Los Olvidados* (*The Lost Ones*), a searing exploration of the lives of young slum-dwellers in Mexico City; *A Mexican Bus Ride* (1951), an unusually gentle Buñuelian comedy featuring a warm description of Mexican peasant life; *Él* (1953), a study of sexual obsession; and *Nazarín* (1958), a dark satire of the Catholic Church. Many of these featured striking visuals executed by world-class Mexican cinematographer Gabriel Figueroa. Figueroa also worked extensively with Emilio Fernandez, another star director of the period, most notably on the classic cinematic ode to Mexico's Indian culture, *María Candelaria* (1945).

Following World War II a group of Mexico City–based directors began to create challenging, surrealist-tinted films; this group included Paul Leduc (*Reed: Insurgent Mexico,* 1973, and *Frida,*1986) and Arturo Ripstein (*The Castle of Purity,* 1973, and *The Beginning and the End,* 1993). In 1992 Mexican film achieved an unprecedented international visibility with the runaway success of Alfonzo Arau's erotic, magic realist fantasy, *Like Water for Chocolate,* adapted from a novel by his wife, Laura Esquivel. By the beginning of the twenty-first century, talk of a revival of Mexico's Golden Age was in the air in the wake

Maria Candelaria ★ Mexico, 1945, Emilio Fernandez; Pedro Armendáriz and Delores del Rio.

of critical and commerical hits such as the moving melodrama *Midaq Alley* (Jorge Fons, 1995), the daring political satire *Herod's Law* (Luis Estrada, 1999), and most of all, the riveting *Amores Perros* (Alejandro González Iñárritu, 2001), with its brutal images and complex, interwoven narrative.

The climax of South American political film making, reached at the end of the 1960s, receded into an unpromising denouement. In the 1970s many of the principal film makers were working in exile abroad, without benefit of the strengths they had derived from their native cultures and the national political goals that had infused their work with revolutionary energy. Those at home were forced to remain silent or work within the noncommitted commercial film industries. In the 1980s and 1990s Cuba continued steadily on a modest scale, attracting little attention abroad. Among the other Latin American nations, both Brazil and Argentina achieved sporadic successes without eschewing altogether earlier political commitments. Many films from Latin America that found international success at the end of the century were directed by women, including Venezuelan Fina Torres's 1985 *Oriane* and Helena Solberg's postmodern documentary about Brazilian star Carmen Miranda, *Bananas Is My Business* in 1995. Mexico's Jaime Humberto Hermosillo has brought a gay sensibility to bear on an array of issues in films such as *Appearances Deceive* (1977) and *Dona Herlinda and Her Two Sons* (1984), providing further evidence to support the contention that in Latin America, as elsewhere, the meaning of politics has expanded to include gender politics.

Africa

In Africa—except Algeria and other Arab countries of the North, where a certain amount of noteworthy production is evident—the development of national film industries has been limited. The region is among the poorest in the world; at the millennium, 42 percent of Africa's population was living on less than $1 per day. In such a climate of economic scarcity, it is hardly surprising that sub-Saharan cinema of the late 1950s and early 1960s was little more than the work of a few isolated creators. Although white South African Jaime Uys's 1980 hit comedy, *The Gods Must Be Crazy,* drew world attention to the African continent, it took longer for the films of black African movie makers to find audiences abroad. As in Latin America, African films, when they finally appeared, were socially and politically inspired, post- (and anti-) colonialist, part of what was then called "third-world Euphoria."

Most of the important black African film makers to emerge since the 1970s are from countries that had been colonies of France or Belgium, with French their common language. (More than 80 percent of African films are made in French.) In large part this situation stemmed from the hands-on colonialist policies of the French, who, unlike the less involved British, have been ready to supply money and know-how to aspiring film makers in Francophone countries. Many African directors have been trained in France or Moscow. Under such a paternalistic system, however, censorship, in all of its forms, has played a major role.

The process of making films in Africa has been characterized as *mégotage*—like making cigarettes from discarded butts, an allusion to the difficulty of finding usable film stock. The Africans have also encountered major barriers when attempting to break into an entrenched distribution system dominated by Americans, Europeans, and East Indians. In such a context, international cooperation has been essential; the Africans have achieved this goal through the *Fédération Pan-Africane des Cinéastes (FEPACI),* an entity that established film centers around the continent, which in turn set up production and distribution facilities. The FEPACI also instituted the region's first film festival in Ouagadougou. In the 1990s, funding for African films from France was cut back and production slowed. At the turn of the century, however, the European economic community stepped in, beginning a funding program to compensate for the loss. But because the procedure requires submission by local governments rather than by individual film makers, censorship remains a factor. In addition, obstacles to adequate distribution remain.

The film-making style that has emerged in the region has sometimes been described as *folkloric*. Many African films build on the tradition of the *griot,* or oral storyteller. Political criticism is frequently softened in these works by their beguiling look; bathed in the clear light of the tropics, they typically feature lambent pastel hues and sun-drenched settings that overlay their forceful political messages with a fairy tale-ish patina. Senegal assumed early leadership in the development of the favored approach, especially in the work of Ousmane Sembène.

Novelist as well as film maker, **Ousmane Sembène,** more than any other figure, has come to represent the values and style of black African cinema. With painful irony, his first film, *Black Girl* (1966), attacked the exploitation and racism to which blacks were subjected by the French colonists. In *Xala* (1974), using satire and bawdy humor, he shows how the leaders of the new black state mimic the ways of their former colonial masters to the continued detriment of the people. With *Ceddo* (1977), Sembène continues his attempts to develop a truly African film language, making use of the griot as the center of the nar-

Black Girl ☆ Senegal, 1966, Ousmane Sembène.

rative. His next feature after *Ceddo, Camp de Thiaroye* (1987), made with Thierno Faty Sow, deals with an event of World War II in which a group of West African infantrymen awaiting demobilization after active service in Europe were suspected of mutiny and fired on by the French. Sembène maintained his preeminence as the father of black African film throughout the 1990s with productions such as *Guelwaar* (1995), a droll comedy about a misplaced corpse, and *Faat Kine* in 2001.

Following Sembène were a group of younger film makers whose films have been inspired by the oral tradition of African narrative and deal with indigenous subjects close to the people. Angolan film maker Sarah Maldorer's visually ravishing 1972 *Sambizanga,* for example, focuses on the political awakening of its female protagonist. Med Hondo's *Sarraounia* (Mauritania, 1986) recounts the story of the successful resistance against the French in the 1890s. Led by the queen of the Aznas, the rebellion united pagan and Moslem Africans to defeat a powerful and well-armed invading force. (African film scholar Nwachu Frank Ukadike has called *Sarraounia* the most ambitious African production ever in terms of its inventiveness and professionalism.) Souleymane Cissé's *Yeelen (Brightness,* Mali, 1987), set in a remote desert area in the sixteenth century, is concerned with superstitions and the supernatural invoked in a conflict between son and father, and the impact of these forces on the people. Shot in mellow tones of beiges, tans, and chocolate browns, it is a work of arresting dignity and visual power. Idressa Ouedraogo's *Yaaba (The Grandmother,* Burkina Faso, 1989) takes place in a village near the film maker's home and performances are by the villagers and some of his relatives. It is built around an African tale of the oral tradition, as is *Yeelen.* Both films won the Jury Prize at Cannes. The 1990s brought other admirable examples of African folkloric cinema, most notably Malian director Cheik Oumer Sissoko's historical allegory *Guimba, the Tyrant* (1995), which the director has called "a fable about power—its atrocities and its absurdities."

Australia

In 1970 the Australian government established an experimental fund for neophyte film makers, a film and television school, and a national development corporation to provide starting money for film productions. Although a distribution network dominated by Hollywood continued to pose a formidable barrier, the Australian movie industry began to show signs of life. Before that time Australia had been known on the screen chiefly in a few films made by Britons and Americans. (During the entire decade of the 1960s, Australia itself produced only eight features.) Once Australians were able to make their own films, they tended to feature the history and topography of their subcontinent, with its vast, wild outback and pioneer heritage. Australia's indigenous people, the Aborigines, also figure in many of these films. In addition, after an initial period in which male values were celebrated, Australia has nurtured a vigorous tradition of women's cinema.

The first evidence of the newly revitalized Australian film industry came in the form of reliable genre pictures. The popular "Ocker" comedies featured a (male) protagonist presented as being "typically" Australian: naive, vulgar, not too bright, good hearted, and down to earth. An early version was *The Adventures of Barry McKenzie* (1972), the first feature directed by Bruce Beresford. The pinnacle of the Ocker comedies was *"Crocodile" Dundee* (1986), the biggest box-office hit ever in Australia. In addition, George Miller's privately financed "Mad

"Crocodile" Dundee ★ Australia, 1986, Peter Faiman; Paul Hogan.

Max" road warrior movies (1971, 1981, 1985) created a genre of their own and made an international star of Mel Gibson. Miller went on to establish yet another viable franchise in 1982 with *The Man From Snowy River,* which married an Australian outback setting to an American western plot and an American star (Kirk Douglas); it was followed by a sequel in 1988.

In 1975 an *auteur*-oriented art cinema emerged when Ken Hannam's *Sunday Too Far Away,* an engaging film about the lives of itinerant Australian sheep shearers, was shown at the Cannes Film Festival. It was followed the next year by **Peter Weir**'s *Picnic at Hanging Rock* (1975), the first Australian art film to achieve significant commercial success both in Australia and abroad. Weir's film was also the first of what would prove to be an enduring genre of Australian heritage productions set at the end of the nineteenth century when the country had declared nominal independence from Britain. A haunting story of a girls' boarding-school outing on which a number of the students disappear mysteriously, it evokes turn-of-the-century dress and manners and makes stunning use of its country's scenery.

Weir went on to become one of the leaders in the new Australian cinema with productions such as *The Last Wave* (1977), about a lawyer who becomes engulfed by the tribal mysteries of his aboriginal clients; *Gallipoli* (1981), a big-budget spectacular about Australians fighting under English command in Turkey during World War I; and *The Year of Living Dangerously* (1982), partly financed by M-G-M, about an Australian journalist in Indonesia in the mid-1960s, around the time of Sukarno's fall from power. At this point Weir moved on to Hollywood, directing a string of critically acclaimed, star-driven projects, including *Witness* (1985), *The Mosquito Coast* (1986) (both with Harrison Ford), *Dead*

Road Warrior ★ Australia, 1981, George Miller.

Picnic at Hanging Rock ★ Australia, 1975, Peter Weir.

Poets' Society (1989, Robin Williams), *Green Card* (1990, Gerard Depardieu and Andie MacDowell), and *The Truman Show* (1998, Jim Carrey).

Possessed of a mystical, poetic sensibility, Weir has a penchant for enigmatic, un-resolved narratives, most prominently on display in *Picnic at Hanging Rock, The Last Wave,* and *The Truman Show.* He is frequently drawn to stories about charismatic individuals such as the scientist in *The Mosquito Coast* and the teacher in *Dead Poets Society.* Weir's sensi-tivity to mood and nuance has enabled him to create scenes of tremendous erotic power, like Mel Gibson and Signorey Weaver's kiss in the rain in *The Year of Living Dangerously* and Harrison Ford's impromptu dance with Kelly McGillis in *Witness.* He has said that his ini-tial image for each of his films has been a musical one. Given this approach, it is not sur-prising that a number of his productions feature stunning set pieces in which music takes center stage: the long tracking shot over a group of heartbreaking photographs backed by one of Richard Strauss's four last songs in *The Year of Living Dangerously,* and the barn-raising scene in *Witness,* which is brought alive by the addition of Maurice Jarré's stately fugue.

Films by other Australian film makers have achieved considerable international suc-cess as well. *Newsfront* (1978), directed by Phillip Noyce, weaves actual newsreel footage into its fictional plot about Australian newsreel companies after World War II. Aboriginal culture is the subject of Fred Schepisi's *The Chant of Jimmie Blacksmith* (1978), about a young half-caste who turns to violence and revenge after being exploited by whites. Gillian

The Chant of Jimmie Blacksmith ★ Australia, 1978, Fred Shepisi; Tommy Lang and Freddy Reynolds.

Armstrong's *My Brilliant Career* (1979) chronicles the progress of a spirited young woman from a poor farming family who persists in her resolution to become a writer; it became a feminist rallying cry at the time of its release. *Breaker Morant* (1980), directed by Bruce Beresford, dramatizes the politically motivated court martial of Australian soldiers fighting under the English in the Boer War in South Africa. Joselyn Moorhouse also garnered accolades for her 1991 production of *Proof,* which took as its subject the unlikely character of a blind photographer.

Among a newer generation of film makers, **Jane Campion,** originally from New Zealand but based in Australia, is most prominent. Campion's recurring concerns center on women's issues, especially female sexuality, which she often examines using an unlikely blend of surrealistic fantasy and tacky realism. Her first widely distributed film was *Sweetie* (1989), a tragicomedy about a pair of bizarre and mismatched sisters. A controversial entry in the Cannes Film Festival, it was subsequently released to great acclaim. Campion followed up with *An Angel at My Table* (1989), an adaptation of the autobiography of New Zealand writer-poet Janet Frame, which originated as a television miniseries. Campion's most resounding success came with her next film, *The Piano,* in 1993, a French-Australian-New Zealand coproduction that shared the top prize at Cannes and won an Academy Award. Like *An Angel at My Table,* it features magnificent New Zealand landscapes. Its story concerns a nineteenth-century mail-order bride who refuses to speak and falls in love with her husband's neighbor, to whom she is giving piano lessons. This gothic tale was based on an original script by Campion herself, who claimed that it was inspired by Emily Brontë's *Wuthering Heights.* Campion's next film, *Portrait of a Lady* (1996), was financed and shot abroad; *Holy Smoke* (1999), brought her back to Australia for the filming, although the production's funding came from Hollywood.

Holy Smoke ✶ Australia, 1999, Jane Campion; Kate Winslet.

Oscar and Lucinda ☆ Australia, 1998, Gillian Armstrong; Ralph Fiennes, on wagon.

During the 1980s and 1990s most directors of the important Australian films of the 1970s followed the example of Weir and Campion and began making films abroad. By 1984 those with international reputations—Fred Schepisi, Phillip Noyce, Bruce Beresford, and Gillian Armstrong—were all working in the United States. Armstrong found success in Hollywood with films such as *Mrs. Soffel* (1984) and *Little Women* (1994). But, like Campion, she returned home to helm other projects, including *The Last Days of Chez Nous* (1990), *Oscar and Lucinda* (1998), and *Charlotte Gray* (2001). The protean Mel Gibson also succumbed to Hollywood. His roles included several in the American films of Australian directors.

Australian films are not noticeably to the left politically; their contemplation of their own culture and past is mainly nostalgic (with a few swipes at the former British Empire, to be sure). The problem for Australian films seems to be the familiar one of hanging on to "Australianness" and international success at the same time within a global industry dominated by the United States. Gillian Armstrong's 1998 heritage production, *Oscar and Lucinda,* is a good example of this dilemma. A period melodrama set at the turn of the twenieth century with a long concluding section centering on a journey into the Australian bush, it features a strong female leading role played by Aussie actor Cate Blanchett and an interest in Aboriginal culture; at the same time, however, this Australian core is somewhat compromised by the presence of a "bankable" British star, Ralph Fiennes, and a gentile Eurofilm ambiance.

Canada

If antipodal Australia has had a problem overcoming the domination of the U.S. film industry, Canada, just across the border, has been affected far more profoundly. The country's situation vis-á-vis its powerful neighbor was once described by its longtime Prime Minister Pierre Trudeau as "like sleeping next to an elephant." Talented Canadian actors and directors have repeatedly been lured across the border by the promise of money and fame, including Mary Pickford, Walter Pigeon, Norma Shearer, Donald Sutherland, Norman Jewison, Michael J. Fox, James Cameron, and Mike Meyers. In addition, Canada has long served as a favorite location for "runaway" Hollywood productions attempting to escape high union costs and take advantage of unspoiled scenery and favorable exchange rates. And, of course, Hollywood productions continue to flood Canadian screens.

Canada's quest to develop a strong national cinematic identity has also been hampered by its history—or lack of it. Unlike the United States, which has endured the Revolutionary War in the eighteenth century and the Civil War in the nineteenth century, Canada has known only peace since the European settlement. The nation's most contentious political issue has arisen in the present, as its large French-speaking population, concentrated mostly in Quebec, debates the wisdom of seceding from the rest of the country, a movement called the *révolution tranquille*.

Insofar as Canadian cinema can be said to have achieved a distinctive character, it is the National Film Board of Canada (NFB) that deserves the credit. Set up in 1939 under the direction of legendary British documentarian John Grierson, the NFB was shrewdly designed to establish a cinematic culture that would not attempt to compete with Hollywood but would establish an alternative tradition. The result was an unqualified success. By 1945

John Grierson, at the National Film Board of Canada, looking over a recently released poster that Art Director Harry Mayerovitch has just produced, January 1944.

the NFB was producing three hundred movies a year, the great majority of which were short documentaries and newsreels targeted for nontheatrical distribution rather than for the theaters. The board dealt with a variety of subjects, including intimate regional studies (for example, on the life of a Quebec priest), the building of the Alaska Highway, and the workings of credit unions. An animation unit was also set up; it supported, among others, Norman McLaren, who created a noteworthy series of classic animated films, winning an Oscar in 1952 for *Neighbors*. In 1962 a separate unit was established to sponsor the work of Québécois directors. The Francophone film makers focused their energies on producing documentaries that employed variants on the direct cinema approach, including Gilles Groulx's *Les Raquetteurs* in 1958 and Pierre Perrault's *Pour la suite du monde* in 1963.

To bring NFB productions to audiences around the nation, a comprehensive system of nontheatrical distribution and exhibition was developed, including rural circuits, national trade union circuits, and industrial circuits. Showings were also sponsored by women's clubs, libraries, YMCAs, and schools. As a result of these efforts, the annual audience for NFB productions during the 1940s was larger than the national population. *Audience response* was a key term, uniquely important in the growth of the movement.

The work of the NFB has shaped all subsequent developments in Canadian cinema, either directly or indirectly, both by training production personnel and by creating a model of non-Hollywood film-making practice. In later years the Canadian Council opened up another avenue of funding, providing support for an internationally honored group of avant-garde film makers, including Michael Snow and Joyce Wieland, whose work was discussed in Chapter 16, as well as Guy Maddin. Avant-garde and related nontheatrical traditions have also influenced many Canadian feature film directors, notably Patricia Rozema (*I've Heard the Mermaids Singing,* 1986) and Canada's most internationally celebrated movie makers, David Cronenberg and Atom Egoyan.

David Cronenberg's early avant-garde films, including *Stereo* (1969) and *Crimes of the Future* (1970), were funded by the Canadian Film Development Corporation, but he caught the wave of horror-film fever that hit during the 1970s to establish a career in commercial cinema. Today, many of his films are funded by Hollywood, although he maintains a home base in Toronto, where he also shoots most of his productions. Actor James Woods has observed that Cronenberg "works from his dreams." Obsessed with the interplay of technology and the human body, he has produced a highly idiosyncratic *oeuvre* consisting of a series of bizarre, ghoulish studies of physicality in the modern world, most notably *Videodrome* (1982), *Dead Ringers* (1986), and *The Fly* (1986). His most honored production, *Dead Ringers,* features a virtuoso performance by Jeremy Irons as a pair of twin gynecologists, one of whom is going insane. In the 1990s Cronenberg moved on to other, less horror-bound projects, including an adaptation of William S. Burroughs's novel, *Naked Lunch,* in 1992 and a version of David Henry Hwang's play, *M. Butterfly,* in 1993. He created an international scandal in 1996 with the release of *Crash,* starring Holly Hunter and James Spader. Based on a novel by science fiction writer J. G. Ballard, it tells a tale in which sexual desire, physical mutilation, and automobile crashes are combined in a phantasmagoric stew that borders on the pornographic. Cronenberg returned to the project of filming his dreams in 1999 with *eXistenZ,* a thriller about a video game designer that he wrote himself.

A less controversial figure is Armenian-born **Atom Egoyan,** who, like Cronenberg, began his career with an avant-garde orientation. Influenced by avant-gardist Michael Snow as well as by mainstream and art cinema directors such as Martin Scorsese and In-

Dead Ringers ⋆ Canada, 1986, David Cronenberg; Jeremy Irons.

gmar Bergman, Egoyan makes films that are noticeably self-reflexive. "In my films," he has said, "you're always encouraged to remember that you're watching a collection of designed images." His 1993 *Calendar* cunningly blends documentary and fiction in a tale about a photographer who embarks on a project to film a dozen Armenian churches for a calendar but gets sidetracked by his growing jealousy over his wife's attraction to their Armenian guide. In 1997 Egoyan won the grand prize at Cannes with a more conventional production, *The Sweet Hereafter,* about a lawyer working with a group of families in rural British Columbia whose children have been killed in a bus crash.

In the meantime, Québécois cinema has continued to thrive, spurred by the success of Claude Jutra's 1971 hit, *My Uncle Antoine,* about a young boy growing up in rural Quebec at the turn of the century. The most notable Québécois film maker to emerge since then has been Denis Arcand, who, like so many other Canadian directors, began his career at the National Film Board. Arcand has helmed such widely screened features as the Oscar-nominated *Decline and Fall of the American Empire* (1986), about the decadent sexual mores of modern middle-class culture, and *Jesus of Montreal* (1989), a tale about an actor who begins to live his on-stage role as the Messiah.

Given Canada's diverse cinematic traditions of documentary, avant-garde, and gothic genre pictures, as well as its two languages, how is it possible to discern a common thread? What does *My Uncle Antoine* have to do with *Crash?* In other words, is there any quality that can be said to constitute "Canadianness"? Director Atom Egoyan has described the Canadian experience as one shaped by its location at the edge of a vast northern wilderness. "You can't but be aware of the idea of space and what it means to live on the fringe of this unexplored territory and of possibility," he has said. "We're sort of overwhelmed by it." The idea that the Canadian character is defined by the country's proximity to the Arctic tundra is rendered with

The Sweet Hereafter ★ Canada, 1997, Atom Egoyan; Ian Holm and Sarah Polley.

emphatic self-consciousness in a 1980 film called *Why Shoot the Teacher?* directed by Silvio Narrizanno. In it, a young schoolteacher from the urban center of Toronto finds work in Bleke, Saskatchewan, educating the children of the local farm families. His classroom is a drafty schoolhouse in the middle of a vast, featureless tract of northern prairie. In such a setting, he finds that the concept of geographical difference means nothing to his students. Despairing of success, he comes to sympathize with a local woman whose husband has driven her to the point of madness with the complacent phrase, "Winter never killed anyone."

Iran

If Canada has had difficulties establishing a recognizable national cinematic identity, the same cannot be said for the most recent country to emerge as a potent international film presence: Iran. In its early days, the Iranian film industry consisted of documentaries commissioned by and shown to the upper classes. As popular cinema developed, India and Hollywood models were drawn upon. Iran, however, has always nurtured a cinema of directors rather than actors, which laid a groundwork for the international preeminence of its current *auteurs*.

　　An oil-rich society, Iran has long harbored a tradition of Islamic fundamentalism, which came to the fore following the revolution against the Shah in 1979. Since that time, the Iranians have followed a policy of international isolationism. A war with Iraq in the mid-1980s brought with it an economic slowdown, but this setback proved to be only temporary.

Immediately after the 1979 revolution, Islamic fundamentalists, who had long opposed cinema in principle, destroyed 180 of Iran's movie theaters, leaving a shortage of screens, which has remained a problem today. But the revolutionary regime soon realized the worth of a cinematic tradition that could satisfy the desires of a local population that had always loved movie going and could also introduce international audiences to the values it held dear. Government supports for the film industry were accordingly strengthened and expanded, and Iran began actively to pursue a policy of entering its productions into international festivals. The pace of production accelerated: In 1983, twenty-two films were released; by 1986, the number had reached fifty-seven. As Iranian film scholar Hamid Naficy has observed, Iran has rethought the place of film in its culture. "Cinema, rejected in the past as a frivolous *superstructure*," he has written, "has been adopted as part of the necessary *infrastructure* of Islamic culture."

Under the new regime, censorship, long a major factor in the cultural life of the country, became even tighter. Women could not be shown unveiled, even within their homes (although, in fact, few Iranian women actually wear veils when at home); moreover, men and women could not be shown touching one another on screen. Even the nature of glances between men and women were proscribed, as the rules called for an "averted look" instead of a direct gaze. Given such a context, it is hardly surprising that many of Iran's movie makers have focused on films about children, some of which were supported by the well-funded Institute for the Intellectual Development of Children and Young Adults (IIDCYA).

The so-called Iranian New Wave was initially inspired in part by the example of Italian neorealism. The movement was initiated in 1969 with the release of Mas'ud Kimia'i's *Qaisar* and Dariush Mehrju'i's *The Cow*. Both films celebrated Iranian lifestyles and mores. In addition, *The Cow*, with its focus on the day-to-day existence of the peasantry, was readily traceable to a neorealist aesthetic. Many subsequent Iranian films have continued to follow this socially progressive neorealist mode by depicting the daily lives of the downtrodden (for example, *Bashu, the Little Stranger* [Bahram Baiza'i, 1985] and *The Runner* [Amir Naderi, 1985]). As the New Wave developed, however, more films took formal experimentation and self-reflexivity as their touchstone. The movement culminated in the widespread international critical and popular acclaim that greeted the release of a film cast in this more formalistic mode: Jafar Pahahi's *The White Balloon*, released in 1996, a simple but formally innovative tale about a little girl trying to buy a goldfish.

The White Balloon was scripted and edited by **Abbas Kiarostami,** who is generally regarded as the country's première director. Employed for many years by the IIDCYA, he frequently puts children at the center of his stories. Although his films use neorealist techniques such as nonprofessional actors, location photography, and real-time narratives, the ultimate impression they convey is one of studied formalism. This latter concern is especially evident in the endings of his stories, which, in films such as *The White Balloon* and *A Taste of Cherry*, veer off course to take in the activities of the director and crew. Other films—for instance, *Close-Up* (1989) and *Through the Olive Trees* (1994)—are self-reflexive throughout. Many of Kiarostami's movies are about journeys, and he has a penchant for dwelling for inordinate amounts of time on shots of characters traversing long roads or pathways, a process that encourages viewers to read their journeys as allegories of life itself (for example, in *Where Is the Friend's Home?* [1987] and *The Taste of Cherry* [1997]). In a sense, one could think of Kiarostami's technique as metaphysical, an exercise in questioning the nature of the world we live in and even the act of viewing film itself.

"We are never able to reconstruct truth as it is in the reality of our daily lives, and we are always witnessing things from far away while we are trying to depict them as close as we can to reality," he has said. "So if we distance the audience from the film and even the film from itself, it helps to understand the subject matter better."

Mohsen Makhmalbaf is the other Iranian director who has become an internationally recognized *auteur.* A former Islamic activist, he was imprisoned for four years before the revolution; subsequently, he turned to film making. In contrast to Kiarostami's contemplative long takes, however, Makhmalbaf has fashioned a more mercurial style that favors quick cuts, often among differing views of the same action, a technique that Chicago critic Jonathan Rosenbaum has labeled "the Makhmalbaf twitch." Following honored neorealist principles, his films often feature the poor; *The Cyclist* (1987), for example, is about a penniless Afghani immigrant who undertakes a week-long bicycle marathon to make money for his sick wife; similarly, the first episode of the three-part *Peddler* (1987) concerns an impoverished family who try to give away one of their children. During the 1990s Makhmalbaf turned away from his earlier neorealist agenda to make movies in the less politicized, self-reflexive mode favored by Kiarostami. His *Once Upon a Time, Cinema* (1992) takes movie-making as its subject, while *Salaam Cinema* (1995) focuses on the process of auditioning for film roles. His award-winning 1996 production, *Gabbeh,* is cast in the form of a folktale. Deeply indebted to the films of Russian director Sergei Paradjanov, *Gabbeh* has been described as "a symphony of color," especially in relation to the garb of its female characters (who appear in the vivid costumes of nomadic tribespeople in contrast to the all-

Gabbeh ★ Iran, 1996, Mohsen Makhmalbaf.

black clothing prescribed for most other Iranian women). "Life is color," a character says at one point. Makhmalbaf is also the father of Samira Makhmalbaf, herself a director; her first feature, *The Apple,* released in 1998, drew international praise.

The critical praise garnered by the films of the Iranian New Wave speaks for the success of the government's investment in cinema. Certainly, part of the interest generated by these films lies in the novel sensibilities at work in them—they are radically unlike anything that has come before. Rather than following the more common path of creating a movie-making tradition that declares its singularity by straining accepted boundaries of decorum, the Iranians have worked within a much narrower set of restrictions than any that would be tolerated in the West; yet they have produced a magisterial cinematic canon that has commanded the admiration of critics and audiences worldwide.

In an increasingly globalized environment, non-American films made in almost any other country face formidable obstacles, especially films from poor nations in Africa and Latin America. The dominant U.S. industry has always faced the same problem, of course; it has solved it with sufficient success so that what comes from the United States is popular around the world. The growing prevalence of video, however, is creating new options for film makers from other parts of the globe. The greater accessibility of video cameras and editing facilities and the greater ease with which these new technologies can be utilized, along with the proliferation of television channels in all parts of the world, are providing new avenues for the production and distribution of moving images, enabling the development of more localized film cultures. In the words of African film maker Jean-Marie Teno, "The new digital video technologies can liberate us, allowing us to create our own work, accessible to our own populations."

Films of the Period

ARGENTINA

1958
Throw Us a Dime (Tire die) (Fernando Birri et al.)

1968
The Hour of the Furnaces (La Hora del los hornos) (Fernando Solanas and Octavio Getino)

1983
The Offical Story (La historia official) (Luis Puenzo)

1984
Camila (María Luisa Bemberg)
A Funny, Dirty Little War (No habrá más penas ni olvido) (Héctor Olivera)

1985
Tangos: The Exile of Gardel (Tangos: el exilio do Gardel) (Fernando Solanas)

1986
Man Facing Southeast (Hombre mirando al sudeste) (Elisio Subiela)
Miss Mary (Mariá Luisa Bemberg)

1988
The South (Sur) (Fernando Solanas)

1990
I, the World of All (Yo, la pior de todas) (Mariá Luisa Bemberg)

1991
The Voyage (Fernando Solanas)

1992
The Dark Side of the Heart (El Lado oscuro del corazón) (Elisio Subiela)

BRAZIL
1957
Rio, North Zone (Rio, zona norte) (Nelson Periera dos Santos)

1963
Barren Lives (Vidas Secas) (Nelson Periera dos Santos)

1964
Ganga Zumba (Carlos Diegues)

1964
Black God, White Devil (Deus e o diablo na terra do sol) (Glauber Rocha)

1969
Antônio das Mortes (Glauber Rocha)
Macunaima (Joachin Pedro de Andrade)

1971
How Tasty Was My Little Frenchman (Como era gostoso o meu frances) (Nelson Pereira dos Santos)

1976
Xica de Silva (Carlos Diegues)

1977
Hour of the Star (A hora da estrela) (Suzana Amaral)
Tent of Miracles (Tenda dos milagres) (Nelson Pereira dos Santos)

1978
Dona Flor and Her Two Husbands (Dona Flor e seus dois maridos) (Bruno Barreto)

1979
Bye, Bye Brazil (Bye bye Brasil) (Carlos Diegues)

1981
Lucia (Bruno Barreto)

1982
Pixote (Hector Babenco)

1984
Prison Memories (Memorias do carcere) (Nelson Pereira dos Santos)
Quilombo (Carlos Diegues)

1985
Kiss of the Spider Woman (Hector Babenco)

1998
Central Station (Central do Brasil) (Walter Salles)

CHILE
1968
Three Sad Tigers (Tres tristes tigres) (Raúl Ruiz)

1969
The Jackal of Nahueltero (Miguel Littin)

1974
Dialogue of Exiles (Dialog de exilados) (Raúl Ruiz)

1975
The Battle of Chile (La Batalla de Chile: La lucha de un pueblo sin armas) (Patrizio Guzman)

1982
Alsino and the Condor (Alsino y el cóndor) (Miguel Littin)

CUBA
1966
Death of a Bureaucrat (La muerte de ub burocrata) (Tomás Guitiérrez Alea)

1967
The Adventures of Juan Quin Quin (Las aventuras de Juan Quin Quin) (Julio García Espinoza)

1968
Lucía (Humberto Solás)
Memories of Underdevelopment (Memorias del subdesarrollo) (Alea)

1973
The Other Francisco (El otro Francisco) (Sergio Gilal)

1976
The Last Supper (La Última cena) (Tomás Guitiérrez Alea)

1977
One Way or Another (De cierta manera) (Sara Gomez)

1983
Up to a Point (Hasta cierto puoto) (Tomás Guitiérrez Alea)

1993
Strawberry and Chocolate (Fresa y chocolate) (Tomás Guitiérrez Alea)

MEXICO
1943
María Candelaria (Emilio Fernández)

1945
The Pearl (La Perla) (Emilio Fernández)

1948
Maclovia (Emilio Fernández)

1950
Los Olvidados (The Young and the Damned) (Luis Buñuel)

1951
A Mexican Bus Ride (Subida al cielo) (Luis Buñuel)

1953
Él (Luis Buñuel)

1955
The Criminal Life of Archibaldo de la Cruz (Essayo de un crimen) (Luis Buñuel)

1958
Nazarin (Luis Buñuel)

1973
The Castle of Purity (El Castillo de la pureza) (Arturo Ripstein)
Reed: Insurgent Mexico (Reed: Mexico insurgente) (Paul Leduc)

1984
Dona Herlinda and Her Two Sons (Doña Herlinda y su hijo) (Jaime Humberto Hermosilla)

1986
Frida (Paul Leduc)

1992
The Beginning and the End (Principio y fin) (Arturo Ripstein)
Like Water for Chocolate (Como ague para chocolate) (Alfonzo Arau)

1995
Midaq Alley (El callegon de los Milagros) (Jorge Fons)

1999
Herod's Law (La Ley de Herodes) (Luis Estrada)

2001
Amores Perros (Alejandzo Gonzáles Iñárritu)

AFRICA
1966
Black Girl (La Noire de . . .) (Senegal, Ousmane Sembène)

1972
Sambizanga (Angola, Sarah Maldorer)

1973
Touki Bouki (Senegal, Djibril Diop Mambéty)

1974
Xala (Senegal, Ousmane Sembène)

1976
Ajani Ogun (Nigeria, Ola Balogun)

1977
Ceddo (The People) (Senegal, Ousmane Sembène)

1980
The Gods Must Be Crazy (South Africa, Jaime Uys)

1982
The Gift of God (Wend Kuuni) (Burkina Faso, Gaston Kaboré)

1986
Garbage Boys (Nyamanton) (Mali, Cheik Oumar Sissoko)
Sarraounia (Mauritania, Med Hondo)

1987

Camp de Thiaroye (Senegal, Ousmane Sembène and Thierno Faty Sow)

Life Is Rosy (La Vie est belle) (Congo, Mweze Ngangura)

Yeelen (Brightness) (Mali, Soueuymane Cissé)

1988

Dancing in the Dust (Bal Poussière) (Ivory Coast, Henri Duparc)

Whom Death Refused (Montu Nega) (Guinea Bissou, Flora Gomez)

Harvest: 3,000 Years (Ethiopia, Haile Gerima)

Heritage . . . Africa (Ghana, Kwaw Ansah)

Zan Boko (Homeland) (Burkina Faso, Gaston Kaboré)

1989

Finzan (Mali, Cheik Oumar Sissoko)

Yaaba (The Grandmother) (Burkina Faso, Idressa Ouedraogo)

1990

Tilai (Burkina Faso, Idressa Ouedraogo)

1991

Sango Malo (Cameroon, Bassek Ba Kobhio)

1992

Guelwaar (Senegal, Ousmane Sembène)

Quartier Mozart (Cameroon, Jean-Pierre Bekolo)

1993

Sankofa (Ethiopia, Haile Gerima)

1994

Black Light (Mauritania, Med Hondo)

Le Cri du Cour (Burkina Faso, Idressa Ouedraogo)

1995

Guimba (The Tyrant) (Mali, Cheik Oumar Sissoko)

Waati (Mali, Souleymane Cissé)

1996

Aristotle's Plot (Le Complot d'Aristote) (Zimbabwe, Jean-Pierre Bekolo)

1998

Napumocento's Will (O Testamento do Senhor Napumocento) (Cape Verde, Francisco Manso, 1998)

Pièces d'identités (Congo, Mweze Ngangura)

1999

Genesis (La Genèse) (Mali, Cheik Oumar Sissoko)

La Petite Vendeuse de Soleil (The Little Girl Who Sold the Sun) (Senegal, Djibril Diop Mambéty)

2000

Battu (Mali, Cheik Oumar Sissoko)

AUSTRALIA

1975

Picnic at Hanging Rock (Peter Weir)

1977

The Last Wave (Peter Weir)

1978

The Chant of Jimmie Blacksmith (Fred Schepisi)

1979

Mad Max (George Miller)

My Brilliant Career (Gillian Armstrong)

1980

Breaker Morant (Bruce Beresford)

1981

Gallipoli (Peter Weir)

1982

The Man From Snowy River (George Miller)

The Year of Living Dangerously (Peter Weir)

1986

"Crocodile" Dundee (Peter Faiman)

1989

Sweetie (Jane Campion)

An Angel at My Table (Jane Campion)

1990

The Last Days of Chez Nous (Gillian Armstong)

1991
Proof (Joselyn Moorhouse)

1992
Strictly Ballroom (Baz Luhrmann)

1993
The Piano (Jane Campion)

2000
Chopper (Andre Domineck)

2001
Charlotte Gray (Gillian Armstrong)

CANADA
1971
My Uncle Antoine (Mon Oncle Antoine)
     (Claude Jutra)

1979
Scanners (David Cronenberg)

1982
Videodrome (David Cronenberg)

1986
Dead Ringers (David Cronenberg)
The Decline of the American Empire (Le Déclin de
     l'empire Americaine) (Denys Arcand)
I've Heard the Mermaids Singing (Patricia Rozema)

1988
Tales from the Gimli Hospital (Guy Maddin)

1989
Jesus of Montreal (Jesus de Montréal) (Denys
     Arcand)

1993
Calendar (Atom Egoyan)
Love and Human Remains (Amour et restes
     humains) (Denys Arcand)

1994
Exotica (Atom Egoyan)

1996
Crash (David Cronenberg)

1997
The Sweet Hereafter (Atom Egoyan)

1999
eXistenZ (David Cronenberg)
Felicia's Journey (Atom Egoyan)

2000
Stardom (Denys Arcand)

2001
Atanarjuat, the Fast Runner (Zacharius Kunuk)
Maelstrom (Denis Villeneuve)

IRAN
1969
The Cow (Gav) (Dariush Mehrju'i)
Qaisar (Mas'ud Kimia'i)

1985
Bashu, the Little Stranger (Bashu, gharibeh-ye
     kuchak) (Bahram Baiza'i)
The Runner (Davandeh) (Amir Naderi)

1987
The Peddler (Daskforoush) (Mohsen Makhmalbaf)
Where Is the Friend's Home? (Khane-ye Doush
     Kodjast?) (Abbas Kiarostami)

1989
The Cyclist (Bicycleran) (Mohsen Makhmalbaf)

1990
Close-Up (Nema-ye nazdik) (Abbas Kiarostami)

1992
Life and Nothing More (Zendegi va digar hich)
     (Abbas Kiarostami)

1994
Through the Olive Trees (Zire darakhatan zeyton)
     (Abbas Kiarostami)

1995
Gabbeh (Mohsen Makhmalbaf)
Salaam Cinema (Mohsen Makhmalbaf)

1996
The White Balloon (Badkonake sefid) (Jafar Panahi)

1998
The Apple (Sib) (Samirah Makhmalbaf)
The Silence (Sokhout) (Mohsen Makhmalbaf)
A Taste of Cherry (Ta'm e guilass) (Abbas Kiarostami)

1999
The Wind Will Carry Us (Bad ma ra khahad bord) (Abbas Kiarostami)

2000
The Circle (Dayereh) (Jafar Panahi)

2001
Sun Behind the Moon (Qandahar) (Mohsen Makhmalbaf)

Books on the Period

LATIN AMERICA

Barnard, Timothy, and Peter Rist, eds. *South American Cinema: A Critical Filmography, 1915–1994.* Hamden, CT: Garland, 1996.

Johnson, Randal, and Robert Stam, eds. *Brazilian Cinema,* expanded edition. New York: Columbia University Press, 1995.

Maciel, David R., and Joanne Hershfield, eds. *Mexico's Cinema: A Century of Film and Filmmakers.* Wilmington, DE: Scholarly Resources, 1999.

Martin, Michael T., ed. *New Latin American Cinema: Studies of National Cinemas* (Vol. II). Detroit: Wayne State University Press, 1997.

Martin, Michael T., ed. *New Latin American Cinema: Theories, Practices, and Transcontinental Articulations* (Vol. I). Detroit: Wayne State University Press, 1997.

Newman, Kathleen, ed. *Latin American Cinema.* Bloomington: Indiana University Press, 1994.

Noriega, Chon A., ed. *Visible Nations: Latin American Cinema and Video.* Minneapolis: University of Minnesota Press, 2000.

Noriega, Chon A., and Steven Ricci, eds. *The Mexican Cinema Project.* Austin TX: UCLA Film and Television Archive/University of Texas Press, 1995.

Paranaguá, Antonio, ed. *Mexican Cinema* (trans. Ana M. López). London: British Film Institute, 1996.

Pick, Zuzana M. *The New Latin American Cinema: A Continental Project.* Austin: University of Texas Press, 1993.

Ranucci, Karen, and Julie Feldman, eds. *A Guide to Latin American, Carribean and U.S. Latino Made Film and Video.* Lanham, MD: Scarecrow Press, 1997.

Sanchez-H., José. *The Art and Politics of Bolivian Cinema.* Lanham, MD: Scarecrow Press, 1999.

Stam, Robert. *Tropical Multiculturalism: A Comparative History of Race in Brazilian Cinema and Culture.* Durham, NC: Duke University Press, 1997.

Stevens, Donald F. *Based on a True Story: Latin American History at the Movies.* Wilmington DE: Scholarly Resources, 1997.

Xavier, Ismail. *Allegories of Underdevelopment: Aesthetics and Politics in Modern Brazilian Cinema.* Minneapolis: University of Minnnesota Press, 1997.

AFRICA

Armes, Roy. *Dictionary of North African Film Makers.* London: Editions ATM, 1996.

Givanni, June, ed. *Symbolic Narratives/African Cinema: Audiences, Theory and the Moving Image.* London: British Film Institute, 1999.

Pfaff, Françoise. *Twenty-Five Black African Film-Makers and Films.* Westport, CT: Greenwood Press, 1998.

Russell, Sharon A. *Guide to African Cinema.* Westport, CT: Greenwood Press, 1998.

Shiri, Keith, comp. *Directory of African Film-Makers and Films.* Westport, CT: Greenwood Press, 1993.

Ukadike, Nwachu Frank. *Black African Cinema.* Berkeley: University of California Press, 1993.

AUSTRALIA

Australian Feature Films on CD-ROM: One Hundred Years of Australian Film Production. London: British Film Institute, 1996.

McFarlane, Brian, Geoff Mayer, and Ina Bertrand, eds. *The Oxford Companion to Australian Film.* New York: Oxford Unviersity Press, 2000.

Murray, Scott, ed. *Australian Film: 1978–1994.* New York: Oxford University Press, 1995.

O'Regan, Tom. *Australian National Cinema.* New York: Routledge, 1996.

CANADA

Armatage, Kay, and Kak Armatage, eds. *Gendering the Nation: Canadian Women's Cinema.* Toronto: University of Toronto Press, 1999.

Magder, Ted. *Canada's Hollywood: The Canadian State and Feature Films.* Toronto: University of Toronto Press, 1993.

MIDDLE EAST

Kronish, Amy W. *World Cinema: Israel.* Cranbury, NJ: Fairleigh Dickinson University Press, 1996.

Shafik, Viola. *Arab Cinema: History and Cultural Identity.* New York: Columbia University Press, 1999.

18

Here and Now: United States

1975–

In the summer of 1975 *Jaws* was released, and a blockbuster mentality was born that continued to shape Hollywood's attitudes toward movie making today. Audiences have responded to the blockbuster strategy; by 1997 American movie admissions had reached 1.38 billion, the highest figure since 1959. But some thought that quality had suffered and costs were out of line. In a piece called "Memo to the Multinationals" penned by *Variety* editor and former studio executive Peter Bart in the autumn of 2000, Bart complained, "Since taking over the studios a decade or so ago, your corporate leviathans have not contributed a single new idea to the production and distribution of motion pictures. What you've really done is drive up costs. You've achieved this by (a) tilting production slates toward star-driven films geared to the overseas audience, and (b) giving above-the-line performers and film makers whatever they want in the way of money and controls." Fortunately, alternatives emerged to counter this trend in the form of independent films, many of these produced on a shoestring. Hollywood also tentatively began to court niche markets with pictures aimed at audiences of women and ethnic minorities.

The Economy and Technology

As for the present Hollywood **economy,** the major studios—Warner Bros., Universal, Columbia/TriStar, Paramount, Disney, M-G-M/UA, and Twentieth Century-Fox—have tended to follow the pattern of acquisitions and mergers prevalent in U.S. industry in general. For example, in 1981, United Artists, then owned by Transamerica, was sold to Metro-Goldwyn-Mayer, which had earlier been purchased by Las Vegas real-estate magnate Kirk Kerkorian. Columbia Pictures was obtained by the Coca-Cola Company in 1982. In 1985, an incursion of foreign capital began with News Corporation (part of the media empire of Australian Rupert Murdoch) purchasing Twentieth Century-Fox. The major thrust of subsequent foreign investment came from Japan, especially from the electronic industry giants. Sony Corporation acquired Columbia Pictures in 1989 for $3.4 billion and merged it with its sister company, TriStar, in 1998; after a few hard years, the studio bounced back in 1997 with box-office revenues totaling $1.3 billion. Matsushita Electric Industrial Company (which includes brand names such as Panasonic, JVC, and Technics) purchased Universal Studios in 1991. These Japanese firms not only had excess capital they wanted to invest but they could also see that being able to provide software (movies) for the hardware they manufactured (home videos) made good business sense. Not to be outdone, two American firms—Time, Inc. and Warner Bros.—merged in 1989 to become Time-Warner, the biggest media company in the world. It owns/controls newspaper and magazine publishing, a cable television network with more than six million subscribers, the Home Box Office (HBO) cable channel, the world's largest music company, and the old Warner Bros. studio. In 1996 it took over Turner Broadcasting Company, paying $7.3 billion for it.

This activity continued into the 1990s. In 1993 entertainment conglomerate Viacom took over Paramount. Then, the Canadian-based liquor company Seagrams purchased MCA/Universal in 1995, and in the following year a consortium led by studio chief Frank Mancuso backed by Kirk Kerkorian bought the troubled M-G-M/UA from the French bank Crédit Lyonnaise for $1.3 billion—the same Kirk Kerkorian who bought and sold the studio in the 1970s. By the end of the century film studios were also joining with television networks (Disney and ABC, Paramount and CBS). Movie companies also became integrated with the new electronic environments of computers when the Internet provider America Online acquired Time-Warner at the end of the decade.

One new major media conglomerate was formed during the 1990s as well. DreamWorks SKG, launched in 1994, was the brainchild of three Hollywood heavyweights: music mogul David Geffen; director Steven Spielberg; and production executive Jeffrey Katzenberg, who had earlier left Disney in a highly publicized falling out with his boss, Michael Eisner. After an uncertain start with some embarrassing failures in its attempts to conquer new media frontiers, the new company achieved its first big hit in the business the triumvirate knew best—movies—with Spielberg's *Saving Private Ryan* in 1998. By 2000 DreamWorks had climbed to second place among all the studios in overall box-office take, with a 12.8 percent share of the market, and had far outstripped all others in terms of revenues for each film released, with three out of their seven productions grossing over $100 million by mid-September (*Gladiator,* $185; *Chicken Run,* $104.9; *What Lies Beneath,* $148.5). Although they handled their distribution needs through Universal, at century's end, they had no merger plans. "We started DreamWorks because it allows us to do what we do in an atmosphere where we are in charge of it," Geffen was quoted as saying. "We're not frustrated by having to deal with other people and their agendas and their priorities and their tastes. We're dealing with our own."

Fewer and bigger tends to be the pattern for the motion pictures produced as well as for the studios themselves. A major studio that used to produce around fifty films a year now frequently produces no more than twelve or fifteen, or fewer, although it will also distribute independently produced pictures. What seems clear is that a few movies on which a lot of money is spent can return huge profits: The studios and the independents try hard to make one of those few. In 1996 *Variety* published a survey that showed that movies budgeted at more than $60 million were more likely to make a profit than others. All of Hollywood's ten top-grossing films of all time have been released since 1975. The extraordinary success of *Jaws* made it a model that has been followed in subsequent films aimed at setting new box-office records.

Increasingly, Hollywood relies on foreign revenues; by 1995 the foreign box-office take topped $5.1 billion—as much as in the United States. This situation means that stars whose faces are known around the world are in great demand and can command astronomical salaries. The increased use of television and other national (and international) forums for advertising means that the older pattern of stepped releases, which would play first in a few major cities then trickle down to second- and third-run houses in neighborhoods and small towns, is no longer viable. The new pattern calls for a blanket release accompanied by a media blitz designed to create a "must see" attitude on the part of potential viewers who want to be among the first to experience the latest hit. The business generated on a film's first weekend determines what happens next. By 1997, the average cost of this marketing strategy had risen to $22.2 million per film, an increase of 166 percent from what it had been a decade before. Not only is this process costly in itself but it also means that many more 35mm prints must be struck for simultaneous distribution nationwide— another added expense. The cost of marketing also includes, in most cases, one or more test screenings and sessions with focus groups at $15,000 each.

In 1996 the special-effects blockbuster *Independence Day* took in a record $104.3 million worldwide in its first week after a saturation publicity blitz, becoming the fastest-grossing film to date. In 2000 *Blair Witch 2: The Book of Shadows* carried this process one step further by staging a globally coordinated release pattern in which the movie opened on the same day at 3,600 theaters around the world. The tremendous distribution networks of the big studios, with hundreds of offices in cities everywhere selling their product, has enabled this global strategy. No matter that in past years, many films that went on to become big money-makers (such as *Dances with Wolves, Driving Miss Daisy,* and *Fatal Attraction*) built audiences slowly; studios are locked into the opening weekend syndrome. As one studio executive complained, "There's no breathing room for good pictures that may have had mediocre openings."

Along with marketing goes merchandising: *Wedding Singer* nightshirts, *Mulan* Happy Meals at McDonald's, *Goldeneye* matchbox Aston Martins, *Austin Powers* talking key chains, and so on. The *Star Wars* franchise alone is estimated to have taken in over $2 billion in tie-ins over the years. The synergy works the other way as well: Manufacturers pay to have their products featured in the movies themselves. Thus, Superman is thrown into a Marlboro cigarette truck in *Superman II* (1982), and Pepsi Cola in futuristic bottles is the drink of choice in *Back to the Future II* (1989). In 1997 Reebok sued TriStar, producers of *Jerry Maguire,* for cutting out a final scene in which Reeboks would appear after the athletic shoe company had provided the production with more than $1.5 million in merchandise, advertising, and promotional support in exchange.

Despite Hollywood's growing marketing sophistication, however, theater attendance in the United States is becoming flat—just under 1.5 billion moviegoers in 2000, down 1 percent from the year before. Nonetheless, the ever-greater competition among theaters for this gradually shrinking audience has fueled an unprecedented overbuilding of multiplexes and luxurious megaplexes today. The 27,805 screens that existed in 1985 had swollen to 37,185 in 1995. By 2000 New York's Times Square had 38 screens on a single block. Many exhibition chains were close to bankruptcy. Some began to show ads to increase revenue, thereby canceling out some of their perceived superiority to television.

In the face of declining business at U.S. theaters, so-called back-end revenue from television, cable, and video sales has come to play a major role in the studios' profit column. In 1999 Americans spent more than $17 billion on the purchase and rental of videos; *The Sixth Sense* video release alone took in more than $150 million. By the turn of the twenty-first century, the major studios were hauling in $8.8 billion annually from this market. In addition, competition from cable and the need for high-profile "event" programming during crucial "sweeps" weeks, when advertising rates are set, has made television an ever-more-eager customer for high-profile films: In 2000 the twenty-one biggest-grossing summer movie hits raked in $385 million from TV sales (about 16 percent of domestic box-office revenue, up from 13 percent in the mid-1990s). Foreign television sales are also soaring; *The Matrix,* for example, was sold to Japanese television for $8 million.

Because foreign audiences frequently do not understand English dialogue, special effects and action are the most reliable gimmicks to sell movies overseas. Thus, superspectacles and science-fiction stories have been dominant among box-office winners. *Star Wars* (1977) set the trend. Its record $185 million in income from domestic rentals surpassed even *Jaws. Star Wars* also set a trend for sequels—presold properties—with follow-ups such as *The Empire Strikes Back* (1980) and *Return of the Jedi* (1983), seemingly completing a trilogy, until the 1998 blockbuster *Star Wars: Episode I—The Phantom Menace* made it a tetralogy.

There have been, of course, extremely successful films that were neither science fiction nor spectacular: *One Flew Over the Cuckoo's Nest* (1975), *Saturday Night Fever* (1977), and *Driving Miss Daisy* (1990) were all serious films about serious subjects. In 1999 the aptly titled *Titanic,* featuring teen idol Leonardo di Caprio, cost an astronomical $200 million but took in over $1 billion at the box office worldwide. "So does this prove, once and for all, that size does matter?" asked its director, James Cameron.

The 1980 film *Heaven's Gate* was a much-publicized financial disaster that led to the sale of United Artists to M-G-M and shook the industry considerably. The lesson learned from this debacle was not that less money should be spent on a given film. Film budgets rose from an average of $8.5 million per picture in 1980 to $75.6 million in 1997. But instead of gambling on the vision of a particular auteur/director such as Michael Cimino, the large budgets were allocated to comparatively safe projects. Consistent big money-makers included (1) the "heavy metal" films of Sylvester Stallone (*Rambo II,* 1984) and Arnold Schwarzenegger (*The Terminator,* 1984); (2) gimmicky comedies (*Ghostbusters,* 1984; *Honey I Shrunk the Kids,* 1989; *Home Alone,* 1990; *The Nutty Professor,* 1996; and *There's Something About Mary,* 1998); (3) corporate genre action adventure pieces (*Die Hard,* 1988 and *Indiana Jones and the Last Crusade,* 1989); (4) animations (*The Lion King,* 1994 and *Toy Story,* 1995); and (5) comic book adaptations (*Batman,* 1989; *Dick Tracy,* 1990; and *Teenage Mutant Ninja Turtles,* 1990). *Batman,* playing in more than 2,200 North American theaters at its peak, moved into the top-ten-grossing films of all time in a matter of months. Warner Bros. spent $63 million to advertise it—$10 million more than it cost to make. Its sequels were released to similar fanfare.

The money being spent and returned (or not returned) is up, and the technology being employed has reached a correspondingly high level. Great advances have been made in special effects. George Lucas's Industrial Light and Magic Company—which was organized in 1975 and created the sophisticated special effects for many of the science-fiction and action-adventure films just mentioned—can make almost anything appear to exist or happen. *Jurassic Park* (1993), *Titanic* (1997), and *The Matrix* (1999) are recent, extraordinary examples. Computers have assisted available technology to create these amazing effects.

For live-action cinematography, Steadicam permits the camera to move with a steadiness that formerly would have required a large hydraulic boom or a dolly and tracks. It was first used in 1976 with striking effect in the opening scene of *Bound for Glory* to follow David Carradine from overhead into a crowd of hundreds in a migrant labor camp, then in *Rocky* to run alongside Sylvester Stallone up the steps of the Philadelphia Museum of Art. Since that time its use has become commonplace. Arifflex or Panavision cameras, Nagra tape recorders, and location dollies comprise the standard apparatus. In the new look of films, hand-held camera technique has come a long way, as has the equipment designed for it: Cameras are lighter and better balanced, and cinematographers have learned to operate them with increased skill.

Sound, as well, has evolved during these years. Director Robert Altman's experiments with overlapping dialogue led to the development of an 8-track sound system at the small studio he once owned, Lionsgate, which was based on using tiny radio microphones attached to the actors rather than using cumbersome booms. At the turn of the century, digital sound systems are part of many new theater set-ups, allowing an enhanced audiotrack that retains its crispness through countless screenings. Warren Beatty's 1990 *Dick Tracy* was the first feature released with digital sound; now, all major Hollywood productions have it. Under the leadership of virtuosi such as Walter Mirsch, sound editor for many of Francis Ford Coppola's films, mixing has become a fine art with sound effects, music, and dialogue brilliantly orchestrated to play off one another and add to the drama of the story.

During the 1980s the colorization process, employing computer technology, was used to transfer black-and-white film to videotape in approximate color. The motivation for it was admittedly financial—to make profits by re-presenting films from the vaults on television and video cassette. The commercial argument is that audiences raised on color tend to skip black-and-white films (and old TV series) as they flip channels. When the colorized *Miracle on 34th Street* (1947) was shown on network television in 1985 it received the highest audience rating of syndicated films for that year. Colorized cassettes of *Yankee Doodle Dandy, The Maltese Falcon, Topper,* and *It's a Wonderful Life* became available soon after. The colorized *Casablanca* premiered in 1988. Along with colorization went a process called *panning and scanning,* which had long been used to reformat movies to fit the requirements of television. The process involves selecting part of the image so that the width of a film frame would be adapted to the more square TV set and increasing the projection speed slightly so that the length would fit into a predetermined time slot. In addition to these distortions, TV film editors often cut whole scenes and narrative linkages in the interests of brevity. Thanks largely to the efforts of the Artists' Rights Foundation, an offshoot of the Directors Guild of America, films that have been subject to such processes now must be labeled "formatted to fit your TV screens." Also, an increasing number of directors now have clauses written into their contracts restricting the liberties TV can take with their productions. But now all filming is done with an eye to the "safe zone"—the frame within a frame that signals which parts of the image will appear in TV and video formats.

Scholars, critics, and film makers have been loud in their denunciation of the distortions that colorization and panning and scanning cause to the creative intentions of the artists who created the films. Director Fred Zinnemann called such tampering "a cultural crime of the first order." He was joined by others expressing outrage, including Woody Allen, Martin Scorsese, Warren Beatty, John Huston, Steven Spielberg, and Elia Kazan—along with the American Film Institute, the Directors Guild of America, the Writers Guild of America West, the American Society of Cinematographers, and the Society for Cinema Studies.

Along with the economic and technological developments within the film industry is the excitement and uncertainty of the new electronic means of producing and distributing the moving image accompanied by sound. Videotape, electronic cameras, and editing machines are steadily replacing the photochemical system of the traditional motion picture. Electronic transmission and playback possibilities already include—in addition to broadcast television—satellite, cable, video cassette, disc recorders, laser disc players, and even computers. In 1999 *Star Wars: Episode I—The Phantom Menace* was the first film to be shown digitally, its images bounced off a satellite in a few theaters. Widespread availability of feature films for home video began about 1981; by 1987 the home video industry's annual gross rentals exceeded rentals paid for films by the theaters. At the turn of the century, DVD players began to proliferate. High-definition television (HDTV), also introduced in 1981, is still being worked on and debated. Standard HDTV systems more than double the number of lines currently available on a video screen (525), giving sharpness and detail of image comparable at least to 16mm projection. With the use being made of fiber optics and the advances toward high-definition television, in a comparatively short while the motion picture as art form, replete with computer graphics no doubt, will be part of the visual-audio material filling the walls of our living rooms with crisp wide-screen images accompanied by stereophonic digital sound.

Motion pictures made with and for such new technologies, as well as audience expectations regarding them, will likely be quite different from what we have experienced to date. Another aesthetic jump—like that taken from silence to sound, from black and white to color, from almost square to very wide screen and stereophonic sound—is beginning.

Mike Figgis's 1999 production, *Time Code,* takes the emerging technology to a new level, using real-time video technology to present the audience with four simultaneous interrelated stories and asking us to choose among them. By adjusting the sound tracks, our attention is directed to one or another of the four screens at any given moment, but the choice about where to focus is ultimately ours. As computer technologies are increasingly with us, a computer aesthetic of interactivity is bound to become more prevalent and pronounced. *Time Code* may be only the first of many more attempts to create a new aesthetic experience by integrating the values of traditional art forms with those of games where the outcome is uncertain and the audience exercises a certain degree of control.

Emerging Genres

American movie genres that flourished at the end of the twentieth century reflected society's growing attachment to the international marketplace. Social issues and a new cine-

Time Code ★ United States, 1999, Mike Figgis.

matic love affair with technology were also major factors in the popularity of certain kinds of movies during the period. As the century drew to a close, a genre labeled *action* consistently dominated Hollywood's thinking. At a more serious level, the 1970s and 1980s saw a cycle of Vietnam War films. Science-fiction stories, a staple of genre movie making since the earliest days, also came into their own during this period, fueled by the effects made possible by the cornucopia of technological gadgets available. New technological options also led to a resurgence of animated movies intended for families.

Most conspicuously, the broad category of action movies has been at the core of the studios' strategies to win thrill-seeking audiences—especially those powered by "bankable" male stars such as Bruce Willis, Mel Gibson, and Harrison Ford. The formula is simple: a minimal narrative framework on which numerous gory chases and scenes of general mayhem can be hung, preferably launched by a showy set piece that sets the tone. The first of the hugely profitable *Lethal Weapon* series, directed by action pro Richard Donner in 1987, is typical. Starring the racially mixed team of Mel Gibson and Danny Glover (to cast the broadest possible net across the potential audience of racially diverse males), *Lethal Weapon* begins with an episode in which Gibson, in a heart-stopping suicidal gesture, jumps off the top of a building. The film's subsequent string of car chases, explosions, and gunplay is orchestrated in loosely connected episodes that proceed at a relentlessly accelerating pace designed to supply the maximum visceral jolt. During the 1980s, the grotesquely overmusculatured physiques of action stars Arnold Schwarzenegger and Sylvester Stallone hinted at a renewed anxiety about masculinity; mercifully, by the end of the decade concern over the effects of steroids and other body-enhancing drugs brought an end (or at least a diminution) to this disturbing phenomenon.

Action was combined with substantive social issues in another genre of this period: the **Vietnam War** film, most notoriously in Stallone's bloodfest, *Rambo: First Blood, Part Two,* in 1985 (directed by George Pan Cosmatos, but coscripted by the star). Although the Vietnam War had ended a decade before, the films about it were unaccountably delayed. Hollywood frequently waits until after the tensions have somehow been resolved before dealing with large-scale stress and cultural dislocation, or deals with them obliquely. The film industry is loathe to offend segments of its audience by adopting a position on disturbing issues; it is generally believed that the audience pays its admission to experience something other than the serious and worrisome actuality existing outside the theaters.

Even allowing for this tendency, the Vietnam War is unique in having been absent from the screens of the United States until long after the event; even more puzzling was the sudden appearance of a number of films dealing with the subject five years after the last U.S. troops had left Vietnam. The only earlier exceptions to the rule were John Wayne's overstated *Green Berets* (1968) and Ossie Davis's overlooked *Gordon's War* (1973).

In 1978 the cycle of films about the Vietnam War began in earnest, including productions such as *Go Tell the Spartans, Coming Home, Who'll Stop the Rain?* and *The Deer Hunter.* In 1979, it reached its climax with *Apocalypse Now.* Then, after a hiatus of eight years, a second wave of Vietnam films began with *Platoon,* continued in 1987 with *Gardens of Stone, The Hanoi Hilton, Full Metal Jacket,* and *Hamburger Hill,* followed in 1988 by *Good Morning, Vietnam,* and in 1989 by *Casualties of War* and *Born on the Fourth of July.* Of these, *Platoon* received the widest public response.

It was *The Deer Hunter* (Michael Cimino) that seemed to touch the national nerve most directly. It deals with three buddies from a Pennsylvania steel town who volunteer for Vietnam. They experience dreadful violence and torture, physical and psychological. One dies in Saigon, one loses his legs, and the other has become truncated emotionally. The use of Russian Roulette in prison camp and as a game for Saigon gambling created a furor; Cimino acknowledged that it probably didn't happen but insisted on his artist's prerogative to use it as a metaphor for the war. The ending of the film is ambiguous but exalting, even if it might be argued what exactly is being exalted. At a funeral breakfast the returned veterans begin to sing "God Bless America" as a dirge for their dead friend. As they continue the song becomes a hymn to the country and to the values it traditionally holds, for which they and others had fought and died. This scene provides a catharsis of sorts; it is a sad moment but also curiously ennobling. Life goes on, it seems to mean, and Americans can again become the Americans they want to be.

Apocalypse Now (Francis Ford Coppola)—in its effort to fuse the mystery and gloom of Joseph Conrad's *Heart of Darkness* with the known and awful actualities of the Vietnam War—was the first film to excoriate directly American involvement. A behemoth of a film, it was years and many millions of dollars in the making. Its production became something like a re-creation of the war it was portraying. Shot in the Philippines, it ran over schedule and over budget; most critics and probably most viewers found that it did not conclude satisfactorily. However, it is a chilling and convincing vision of a kind of madness rampant in the U.S. military command: homicidal, conspiratorial, and megalomaniacal. It offers surreal experience of jungle and battle; colors and sounds overwhelm the senses, and we may feel that this is the way it must have felt to the American soldiers, especially if their sensations were heightened by fear and perhaps drugs.

Many people felt that *Platoon* came closest to what the combat experience in Vietnam must have been like of any of the films dealing with the subject. It centers on the experience of a rookie and can be assumed to be autobiographical to a degree. Its writer-director, Oliver Stone, volunteered for the army in 1967 and spent fifteen months in Vietnam. The fragmented structure—a sequence of events rather than a coherent narrative—and the number of characters involved (the men of the platoon) add to this sense of actuality. It is a tough film to watch; the violence, the jungle, the heat, and the stench all seem palpable. But there are also mythic elements involved, as in *The Deer Hunter* and *Apocalypse Now*—in this case, two sergeants of contrasting temperaments: one a hardened killing machine and the other serene and Christ-like. Whatever it was about the combination of its elements—painfully convincing naturalistic detail and mythic confrontation between representatives of good and evil—its reception was extraordinary. Not a film you would expect to be popular or honored, it was a box-office success and won four Academy Awards, including Best Picture and Best Director.

The new potentials of special-effects technology led to a renaissance of the science-fiction film, which was now taken to a whole new level of creative excitement, beginning with *Star Wars* in 1977 and going on to other cult favorites, such as the *Star Trek* series (nine in the cycle as of 1998). The genre's new vitality also manifested itself in such classic productions as *Alien* (Ridley Scott, 1979), *Blade Runner* (Scott, 1981), *Brazil* (Terry Gilliam, 1985), *Total Recall* (Paul Verhoeven, 1990), *Terminator II: Judgment Day* (James Cameron, 1991), *Strange Days* (Kathryn Bigelow, 1995), *Twelve Monkeys* (Terry Gilliam, 1995), *Contact* (Robert Zemeckis, 1997), and *The Matrix* (Andy and Larry Wachowski, 1998). Many science-fiction films (such as *Blade Runner, Brazil,* and *Strange Days*) exploited computer-generated special effects to create utopias and distopias of the future. Others (beginning

Platoon ★ United States, 1986, Oliver Stone; Tom Berenger, Charlie Sheen, and Willem Dafoe.

with the George Lucas–Ron Howard fantasy, *Willow,* in 1988) made use of the new, computer-generated technique of *morphing,* by which one thing gradually changes its shape and turns into another, to explore issues around the nature of the body and its relation to technology.

Terminator II: Judgment Day gave rise to especially lively discussion and debate centering on its portrayal of a gutsy mother figure (Linda Hamilton) and its meditations on the nature of fatherhood and its relation to a system of patriarchy. Starring Arnold Schwarzenegger as a good cyborg and Edward Furlong as a bad one, the film features some of the most spectacular morphing effects filmed to date. Although it reportedly cost between $80 and $100 million to make, it generated a healthy profit, becoming the top-grossing production of 1991.

Robert Zemeckis's *Contact,* from a novel by Carl Sagan, was another standout production with a feminist slant. Featuring Jodie Foster as a maverick astronomer who succeeds in locating intelligent beings elsewhere in the universe, the story builds to the first interaction between human and alien life forms. Using spectacular special effects, the climactic sequence depicts Foster's trip through holes in space to make contact with the other-worldly beings she has found using a machine they have designed for her. The film aroused considerable controversy on its release because of its portrayal of the superiority of science over religion as a way of putting humanity onto a higher spiritual plane.

The Matrix, released in 1998 and directed by former comic book creators Larry and Andy Wachowski, took special effects to a whole new level by borrowing techniques from Hong Kong action movies to create a story that featured sensational fight sequences, with characters flying through the air to attack one another. Like so many of the best science-fiction offerings, it focused on the nature of identity, this time playing off the unreality of its fake environment to suggest that in the technology-driven world of the future, it will become less and less possible for human beings to retain a grip on what is actually "real" and what is only "virtual" reality. The Wachowskis sold their script to action-movie producer Joel Silver by drawing it up as a 600-page comic book. "The script was a synthesis of ideas that sort of came together at a moment when we were interested in a lot of things: making mythology relevant in a modern context, relating quantum physics to Zen Buddhism, investigating your own life," Andy Wachowski later commented. "We started thinking of this as a comic book."

The Matrix ★ United States, 1998, Larry and Andy Wachowski.

The other genre resuscitated by special-effects technology, animation, takes the idea of comic books more literally by creating wholly manufactured images. New technologies have made this process both cheaper and richer in possibilities. As in earlier days, Disney has been the leader in this realm, kicking off the boom with *The Little Mermaid* (1989), a coproduction with Warner Bros. and Steven Spielberg's Amblin Entertainment. Disney followed this success with more projects in the same vein, such as *Beauty and the Beast* (1991), *Aladdin* (1992), and *A Bug's Life* (1998). Unlike the daring experiments with the science-fiction genre, these films, created mostly with children in mind, have remained fairly traditional, featuring musical scores that frequently won Academy Awards. Criticism of racist subtexts in earlier offerings, such as *The Lion King* (1994), led to gestures toward multiculturalism in later Disney films—such as *Pocahontas* (1995) and *Mulan* (1998)—where animation style was used to capture the flavor of ethnic differences. In 1995 Disney introduced computer-generated animation in *Toy Story,* taking both the public and the critics by storm. Although the figures produced by this process have a somewhat plastic appearance, they also possess a satisfying aura of roundedness.

In the late 1990s Jeffrey Katzenberg, who had been responsible for the animation revival at Disney when he served as head of production there, set up an animation studio at his new studio, DreamWorks, offering traditionally undervalued animators better terms of employment, including profit sharing. DreamWorks' animated features, including *The Prince of Egypt* (1998), *Antz* (1998), and *Chicken Run* (2000), have aimed at a higher level of sophistication than the Disney movies, opening up the genre to new audiences in the process.

A director who began his career as a Disney animator and continues to use animation and special effects extensively to create fantastical worlds is **Tim Burton.** Burton wrote and produced *The Nightmare Before Christmas* (1993), which is pure animation; other films under his direction, such as *Pee-Wee's Big Adventure* (1985), *Batman* (1989),

Batman ★ United States, 1989, Tim Burton; Kim Basinger and Michael Keaton.

Mars Attacks! (1996), and *The Legend of Sleepy Hollow* (2000), blend animation and live action, creating weird worlds and strange characters. Critic Robin Wood has characterized Burton's highly idiosyncratic *oeuvre* as one focused on freaks—social outsiders who are often physically deformed (*Beetlejuice,* 1988, and *Edward Scissorhands,* 1990).

Burton's films often feature Johnny Depp, an innocent but slightly off-center presence that adds to the surreal effect of these movies. Most memorably, Depp starred in what is usually thought of as Burton's greatest achievement, *Ed Wood,* in 1994. A fable about a man who has been labeled "The World's Worst Director," *Ed Wood* was shot in black and white and features a strangely assorted group of Wood's collaborators, including Bill Murray as a would-be transsexual, Lisa Marie (Burton's wife) as television personality Vampira, and Martin Landau in an Oscar-winning performance as a drug-addled, dying Bela Lugosi. A scene near the end of the narrative has Wood unexpectedly meeting Orson Welles (Vincent D'Onofrio), who urges him to remain true to his vision. Unfortunately, Welles neglects to mention that it is important to have talent as well.

Another genre that has flourished during these years is **comedy,** especially in forms conceived by such talented film makers as Mel Brooks (*Blazing Saddles,* 1974, and *Dracula: Dead and Loving It,* 1995), Albert Brooks (*Real Life,* 1979; *Modern Romance,* 1981; and *Mother,* 1996), James L. Brooks (*Broadcast News,* 1987, and *As Good As It Gets,* 1997), Cameron Crowe (*Jerry Maguire,* 1996, and *Almost Famous,* 2000), and the Farrelly

The Nutty Professor ★ United States, 1996, Tom Shadyac; Eddie Murphy.

Brothers (*There's Something About Mary,* 1998). In this often performance-driven mode, brilliant actors have also created distinguished bodies of work: Lily Tomlin (*Nine to Five,* 1980; *All of Me,* 1984; and *Flirting with Disaster,* 1996), Eddie Murphy (*Beverly Hills Cop,* 1985; *The Nutty Professor,* 1996; and *Bowfinger,* 1998), Bette Midler (*Down and Out in Beverly Hills,* 1985, and *Outrageous Fortune,* 1987), Kevin Kline (*A Fish Called Wanda,* 1988, and *Soapdish,* 1991), Bill Murray (*Groundhog Day,* 1993, and *Rushmore,* 1998), and Steve Martin (*All of Me,* 1984, and *Bowfinger,* 1998).

One of the most respected makers of film comedies today is **Woody Allen.** In *Annie Hall* (1977), Allen hit full stride with his own special and highly personal brand of humor. Based in New York City, it draws on Jewishness and psychoanalysis, and offers in-jokes about show business and films. But most essential to it are the gentle, recognizable, and amusing revelations about certain (male intellectual) sexual insecurities and inadequacies. "Love is the answer," Allen once said. "But while you're waiting for the answer, sex raises some pretty good questions." *Manhattan* (1979), in black-and-white Panavision, is more of the same. Although the humor is darker, it maintains the same high level of exact observation presented in the perfect nuances of Allen's and Diane Keaton's performances. Another Allen film that has found particular favor with audiences and critics is *Hannah and Her Sisters* (1985), which recalls Ingmar Bergman's valedictory *Fanny and Alexander.*

Annie Hall ★ United States, 1977, Woody Allen; Diane Keaton and Allen.

Allen followed his first serious drama, *Interiors* (1978), with others of similarly sober aspirations: *September* (1987) and *Another Woman* (1988). Allen's ability to persist in this vein seems commendable, yet the legions of Woody Allen fans and the reviewers favor the romantic comedies set in contemporary Manhattan (*Annie Hall, Manhattan, Hannah and Her Sisters,* and *Husbands and Wives,* 1992). The intellectual critics, on the other hand, are drawn to the self-reflexive films about the film maker, film making, and the film being made (*Stardust Memories,* 1980; *Zelig,* 1983; *The Purple Rose of Cairo,* 1985; and *Mighty Aphrodite,* 1995).

During the 1990s Allen's tumultuous personal life hit the media. The scandal involved Mia Farrow, actor in his films and longtime intimate companion, a child custody suit, and allegations of child abuse. Throughout all this Allen's output continued, although his audience dwindled. "Most of the time, I don't have much fun," he has commented. "The rest of the time, I don't have any fun at all." Yet out of this gloomy view of life, Allen has created a body of work that has provided a great deal of fun for his audiences.

Studio Stalwarts

Within mainstream production a number of film makers have been able to maintain sufficient control over their films to make personal statements representing their own ways of seeing and feeling. A list of this sort would include Clint Eastwood, Steven Spielberg, Jonathan Demme, and Oliver Stone, arranged in the order in which they directed their first features.

Actor **Clint Eastwood,** initially known as a TV cowboy star, he made his name in the movies by starring in the "spaghetti westerns" of Italian director Sergio Leone (*The Good, the Bad, and the Ugly,* 1966) and then in the American-style westerns of Don Siegel (*Two Mules for Sister Sara,* 1969). His oeuvre as a director includes westerns (*The Outlaw Josey Wales,* 1976, and *Unforgiven,* 1992) as well as thrillers (his first directorial outing, *Play Misty for Me,* 1971, and *Absolute Power,* 1997), comedies (*Bronco Billy,* 1980), and a miscellaneous assortment of other genres, including what some would refer to as a woman's picture (*The Bridges of Madison County,* 1995). A self-effacing directorial presence, his movies are marked by a relaxed pace, punctuated where appropriate with rousing action sequences and a recurring interest in the nature of masculinity. Eastwood's master work is surely *Unforgiven* (1992), in which he plays the role of a wandering gunman. Dedicated to Sergio Leone and Don Siegel, *Unforgiven* focuses on the pervasiveness of violence in American life and offers meditations on the western as genre and on Eastwood's own dominant persona.

Jonathan Demme—like Coppola, Scorsese, and others—began direction with exploitation films for Roger Corman's New World Pictures (*Caged Heat,* 1974, about women in prison; *Crazy Mama,* 1975, about three women on a crime spree; and *Fighting Mad,* 1976, about rampaging rednecks). His directorial career has allowed him to range widely among genres and types, from his early offbeat comedies (*Citizens Band,* 1977, and *Melvin and Howard,* 1980) to period pictures (*Swing Shift,* 1983, and *Beloved,* 1998) to thrillers (*The Silence of the Lambs,* 1996) to documentaries (*Stop Making Sense,* 1984; *Swimming to Cambodia,* 1987; and *Cousin Bobby,* 1992). No matter what their genre, all display a mastery of filmic narrative. Tightly constructed, well made, and compelling, they seem to

Unforgiven ✦ United States, 1992, Clint Eastwood; Eastwood.

grow out of intense concentration and an ability to find the exact way in which particular subjects and themes can best be presented. Also, his films are characterized by a kind of hipness, or street smarts. He seems to have an intuitive sense of current cultural issues and styles and sees them with toughness of mind and compassionate humor. His characters are fresh, individual, and frequently eccentric, with especial sympathy and understanding given to the female roles.

Demme's most famous project, *The Silence of the Lambs,* is about an FBI trainee (Jodie Foster) assigned to the case of "Buffalo Bill," a serial killer who skins the bodies of his young female victims. A huge success, with countless awards for picture, performances, and direction, it is unquestionably brilliant suspense film making. It took other dimensions as well: as the subject of considerable discussion among feminists regarding the Foster character's functioning in the patriarchal hierarchy of the FBI and as a potential victim of deranged male sexuality. It also was seen, especially in the gay community, as homophobic in its portrayal of "Buffalo Bill" and his insane desire to assume a female identity.

The phenomenal success of *Jaws* (1975), a dark myth about a white shark preying on a seaside community, fixed the direction **Steven Spielberg**'s career would subsequently take. Its popularity was repeated with *Close Encounters of the Third Kind* (1977), about an average guy who comes in contact with creatures from another planet. He followed this success with the *Indiana Jones* series: *Raiders of the Lost Ark* (1981), *Indiana Jones and the Temple of Doom,* (1984), and *Indiana Jones and the Last Crusade* (1989)—rousing, globe-circling,

The Silence of the Lambs ★ United States, 1991, Jonathan Demme; Anthony Hopkins and Jodie Foster.

action-adventures full of derring-do. *E.T.—The Extraterrestrial* (1982), with its lovable space creature in the midst of suburbia, achieved some sort of pinnacle in public response. *Hook* (1991) is a reworking of J. M. Barrie's turn-of-the-century play, *Peter Pan,* in the Disney manner. *Jurassic Park* (1993) and its sequel, *The Lost World* (1997), are heavy on fear; the magic is black. Like *Jaws,* these are monster films—in this case, genetically engineered dinosaurs. The themes implicit in many of these films are of a child's fear of growing up and the possibility that an adult can return to a magical childhood state.

After *Indiana Jones and the Temple of Doom,* Spielberg began to attempt more serious, adult-oriented fare. *The Color Purple* (1985), from a Pulitzer Prize–winning book, recounts the growing up (the film spans some forty years) of a black girl in the South during hard times. The film's somewhat softened interpretation of the book created some controversy. *Empire of the Sun* (1987) is about a privileged English boy who had been living in Shanghai at the outbreak of the Second World War, was separated from his parents, spent four years in a Japanese prison camp, and then has to fend for himself at the war's end in Japanese-occupied China as the prison camps are evacuated. Both films received mixed reviews. The reaction seemed to depend on whether the feelings Spielberg was attempting to evoke could be accepted or whether his kind of film making was thought to be contrived and inflated beyond what the content at any given moment warranted. He finally succeeded in this more adult forum with *Schindler's List* in 1993, a portrait of a German industrialist who saved thousands of Jews from concentration camps. *Schindler's List* won numerous Academy Awards, including ones for Best Picture and Best Director. Spielberg followed

E.T.—The Extraterrestrial
✶ United States, 1982,
Steven Spielberg; Henry
Thomas and friend.

up by arranging for the film to be shown in schools and creating the Shoah Foundation to document the atrocities of the Holocaust. In 1998 he turned his directorial talents to another highly successful serious effort, the World War II blockbuster *Saving Private Ryan,* starring Tom Hanks; although the film was critically lauded, it was overlooked at Academy Award time.

The ultimate question about Spielberg, the most commercially successful director the world has yet seen, is: Can his entertainments, constructed with considerable skill and ever-increasing technological virtuosity, be taken seriously as something resembling works of art that somehow contain personal statements? Of course, the corollaries are: Does that really matter? What criteria are applied to Spielberg's most popular works?

Clearly he is onto mythic material that has a wide, even universal, appeal. In addition, his films grow out of the same sort of familiarity with movies that characterizes the "film generation," both the makers and the viewers. Spielberg seems quite content in thinking it proper—even necessary perhaps—to make his films within standard genres. Furthermore, he employs the familiar, the clichéd, with knowing and affectionate expertise; his films are full of quotes from other films. At their best, they are movie-movies, as a student film maker might say about them, and are no doubt valued in that way by their vast audiences.

A more idiosyncratic directorial presence is **Oliver Stone,** whose first successes came as a writer of such films as *Midnight Express* (Alan Parker, 1978), for which he won an Academy Award. A product of the New York University film school, he is a true child of the 1960s: radical and angry. After his great success with *Platoon* in 1986, he settled into a pattern of bombastic and often controversial revisionist histories, including *JFK* in 1991 (which attempted to expose a conspiracy surrounding the Kennedy assassination), and *Nixon* in 1995 (which provided a version of the Watergate scandal). He also returned to the issue of American foreign policy in a series of examinations of people around the world who have been affected by U.S. incursions into their countries in productions such as *Salvador* (1986, about a journalist in Central America who discovers he must take a stand in support of the local population) and *Heaven and Earth* (1993, about Vietnamese refugees). Perhaps Stone's most controversial production was *Natural Born Killers* in 1994, a gory rendering of the adventures of a pair of serial killers. In 1987 he directed what is perhaps his best-known film, *Wall Street,* a satire of American big business in which Michael Douglas speaks a line that has passed into the language: "Greed is good."

Stone's visceral style relies on hand-held camera work and heavy editing. *JFK* featured an innovative intermingling of fictional and documentary footage, including the famous Magruder video of Kennedy's assassination. A Stone movie grabs the viewer by the throat and won't let go. And while people may not approve of everything he espouses, his films never leave them bored.

Other Hollywood A-list directors of note include British emigré Ridley Scott (*Alien,* 1979, and *Gladiator,* 2000), Robert Zemeckis (*Who Framed Roger Rabbit?* 1988, and *Forrest Gump,* 1994), and Paul Schrader (*Blue Collar,* 1978; *American Gigolo,* 1979; and *Affliction,* 1998). A somewhat special case is Terrence Malick, who, though repeatedly supported by the big studios, has produced work of a consistently delicate and specialized nature. In over twenty years, he has directed only three features: *Badlands* (1973), one of the outlaw-couple-on-the-run subgenre; *Days of Heaven* (1979), about two loners who commit murder in 1930s Texas; and *The Thin Red Line* (1998), an adaptation of the James Jones novel about the conflict in the Pacific during World War II. All of Malick's films feature voice-over narration: by a woman in *Badlands,* a child in *Days of Heaven,* and several different soldiers in *The Thin Red Line.* All are also filled with magical photography (in the

Days of Heaven ★ United States, 1979, Terence Malick; Richard Gere and Brooke Adams.

case of *Days of Heaven* all outdoor footage was shot at twilight in order to provide a precise quality of light). In addition, the musical scores Malick uses are uniquely moving and unexpected, from the selection from Saint-Saens's *Carnival of the Animals* in *Days of Heaven* to the ethereal Hans Zimmer score in *The Thin Red Line*. In total, Malick's cinema is that of an independent sensibility working within a studio context.

Independent Voices

Happily, the mainstream industry's preoccupation with high-tech, high-finance blockbusters has not completely absorbed American cinema. In some ways, and inadvertently to be sure, it may allow more space for resolute independent film makers appealing to minority audiences. Funding for these independent productions may come from completely outside the industry: from Public Television's *American Playhouse* series, the National Endowment for the Arts, and occasionally German television. Mostly, the film makers raise their modest (sometimes minuscule) budgets any way they can: from friends and relatives, hucstering, and delayed payment for services.

Worthy independent films are often premiered and may find distributors at the Sundance Festival in Utah. Started as the United States Film Festival in 1981 and absorbed into Robert Redford's Sundance Institute in 1985, the festival has become a hot ticket for aspiring independent film makers and would-be moguls since Steven Soderbergh's *Sex, Lies, and Videotape* was picked up there by upstart independent distributor Miramax in 1989. After being produced on a budget of $1 million, it went on to win at Cannes and gross $70 million worldwide. Subsequently, every young film maker sees the Sundance Festival as an entrée to the big time, and an ever-growing number of industry heavyweights go there searching for the next Soderberg. Predictable complaints about overcommercialization and declining quality have continued to surface, but Sundance just keeps getting bigger.

First into the field, as scriptwriter as well as director of his films, was **David Lynch.** His *Eraserhead* (1978), which carries its horror in a dark view of the world and deliberately repugnant images, has gained a considerable cult following. In *The Elephant Man* (1980) Lynch put his intelligence to work on another man cruelly afflicted with physical deformity. In this case the treatment of the protagonist is remarkable for its sensitivity and delicacy. A quite adequate budget (his first film had been made for a pittance) permitted the re-creation of a convincing Victorian London. *Dune* (1984), a huge, long version of Frank Herbert's fantasy novel, proved a disaster, critically and commercially. *Blue Velvet* (1986), on the other hand, is Lynch's most resounding success to date. It carries his attraction to the mysterious and perverse (it is his original script) into a picture-postcard American small town. Its underside is discovered by two teenagers who become involved with the awfulness they discover.

Nothing Lynch has done since has fulfilled the promise of that film (or of *Eraserhead,* for that matter). He next conceived, and directed some episodes of, the network television series *Twin Peaks* (1990–1991). It offered the same exposure of moral corruption beneath the surface of a small town (in this instance in Oregon, but read American society generally). It also had some of the same mixture of genres (mystery-horror-soap opera) and levels of reality, adding a juggling of narrative time to delve into the past. It achieved a cult following and added to the materials Lynch would continue to explore. *Wild at Heart*

Blue Velvet ☆ United States, 1986, David Lynch; Kyle MacLachlan and Dennis Hopper.

(1990), which won the top award at Cannes, draws on both *Twin Peaks* and *Blue Velvet* but takes the form of a (formless, one might say) road movie. The couple in this rambling and wildly undisciplined saga, which includes violent and sexual excesses like those of *Blue Velvet,* are deeply into mad love.

Then, returning to the TV series as source, in fact dealing with events in the characters' lives that preceded those of the series, was *Twin Peaks: Fire Walk with Me* (1992). This film seems seriously out of control, however. Lynch indulges his obsessive perversity in an unremitting nightmare of horror, which lacks completely the quirky charm and playfulness interlaced with crime, evil, and the supernatural that characterized the series. Lynch's avant-garde talent with images and sounds and the intermittent seductiveness of his inverse view of humanity may keep him afloat.

Jim Jarmusch's *Stranger Than Paradise* (1984) plummeted him into the international spotlight. It won the Camera d'or at Cannes (for Best New Director) and was voted best film of the year by the National Society of Film Critics in the United States. It is an engaging road comedy in which an unprepossessing young man, his emigré Hungarian female cousin, and a dull-witted friend take off on an odyssey that extends from New York's Lower East Side to Cleveland to Florida. *Down by Law* (1986) has some of the same qualities. Jarmusch described it as the story of "a pimp, a disc jockey, and an Italian tourist stuck in a Louisiana prison." They break out and wander off into the swamplands until they reach Luigi's Tintop, an isolated eating-joint near the Texas border run by Nicoletta, niece of the late Luigi. She and the Italian tourist, Roberto (or "Bob, itsa the same thing"), fall immediately in love. He remains and the other two men wander down the road, then separate to pursue their solitary ways.

Stranger Than Paradise ★ United States, 1984, Jim Jarmusch; John Lurie, Eszter Balint, and Richard Edson.

These films share with the others Jarmusch's offbeat and quite personal sense of narrative structure and visual style, which have earned him considerable respect at home and abroad. All involve foreigners exploring American culture on the fringes of society—tourists in a sense. Critic James Naremore has suggested that Jarmusch's concerns can be described by the phrase *cognitive estrangement* (a term taken from science-fiction scholar Darko Suvin), which points to his preoccupation with juxtaposing disparate cultural types: Japanese teenagers looking for the legacy of Elvis Presley in Memphis (*Mystery Train,* 1989), an Eastern dude thrust into the world of tribal beliefs and customs (*Dead Man,* 1995), and an African American who takes on the role of a samurai warrior (*Ghost Dog,* 1999). These encounters are presented in unusual narrative patterns: three interwoven stories in *Mystery Train* and a series of unrelated episodes in *Night on Earth* (1992). Jarmusch's camera style is also related to cognitive estrangement, for he likes to contemplate elements of the landscape after his characters have left the frame; in *Mystery Train,* for example, as the Japanese tourists pass through a run-down part of Memphis, the camera lets them walk on ahead as it lingers to gaze at the unprepossessing cityscape.

Brothers **Joel** and **Ethan Coen** also had their first big hit, *Blood Simple,* in 1984. Like Jarmusch, Joel is from New York University—the undergraduate film program in his case. He directed, Ethan produced, and they wrote the script together. It is a very clever, slick, highly stylized suspense-thriller in the manner of Hitchcock, or even more that of Brian De Palma. Action-horror is the Coens' label for it, and, to be sure, it has considerable shock value. Set in Texas, the beginning of its intricate plotting occurs when a cuckholded husband hires an unsavory character to kill his wife and her boyfriend. Deception and double-cross, a body thought to be dead buried alive and rekilled with a shovel, and the like occupy the remainder. *Raising Arizona* (1987) is a wacky farce about an ex-con husband and police officer wife. When they discover they cannot have a child they kidnap one of the newborn Arizona quintuplets, sons of Nathan Arizona, an unfinished-furniture tycoon.

The Coens brought their unique brand of black humor and over-the-top style to numerous other productions during the 1990s, most notably *Miller's Crossing* (1990, another gangster story), *Barton Fink* (1991, loosely based on the Hollywood experiences of Broadway playwright Clifford Odets), *The Hudsucker Proxy* (1994, a satire on the culture of big business), *Fargo* (1996, about a crime spree in Minnesota), and *O Brother, Where Art Thou* (2000, about members of a chain gang in the 1930s). Of these the most honored was *Fargo,* which won Oscars for the Coens' screenplay and for its star, Frances McDormand. As a local police chief, McDormand, along with the rest of the cast, managed perfectly tuned Minnesotan accents that added considerably to the movie's charm. In addition, Roger Deakins's cinematography, which featured endless snow-covered tracts, was dazzling.

David Mamet is also an astute and knowledgeable craftsman, but his craft so far has been more closely related to theater than to movies or novels. He was an established playwright (*American Buffalo, Sexual Perversity in Chicago,* and *Glengarry Glen Ross*) before he became a screenwriter (*The Verdict,* 1981; *The Untouchables,* 1987; and *Wag the Dog,* 1997). He became a writer-director of his own film, *House of Games,* in 1987, and went on to write and direct a series of tense thrillers and deadpan comedies, including *Things Change* (1988), *Homicide* (1991), and *The Spanish Prisoner* (1998). In 1999 he surprised

Barton Fink ★ United States, 1991, Joel Coen; John Goodman and John Turturro.

House of Games ★ United States, 1987, David Mamet; Joe Mantegna and Lindsay Crouse.

the critics by adapting and filming a play set in Victorian England, *The Winslow Boy,* but he returned to form in 2001 with *Heist.*

As one might expect, Mamet's strength is in his scriptwriting ability. His thrillers are intricately plotted and his dialogue is unmistakable, relying on laconic phrases, repetition, and a heavy use of profanity to create a kind of superrealist effect. In the Hitchcockian tradition, his visual style favors carefully composed point-of-view shots and a high degree of editing.

Another director who first achieved fame as a writer is **John Sayles.** Working from a reformist agenda, Sayles has written and directed a series of films about social issues, such as lesbian lifestyles (*Lianna,* 1982), labor unrest among West Virginia miners (*Matewan,* 1987), corruption in big-time sports (*Eight Men Out,* 1988), interracial friendship (*Passion Fish,* 1992), and small-town life (*Lone Star,* 1996, and *Alaska,* 1998). Always beautifully observed, Sayles's films avoid generic forms and conspicuous stylistic flourishes, focusing instead on characterization. "If storytelling has a positive function," he has said, "it's to put us in touch with other people's lives, to help us connect or draw strength or knowledge from people we'll never meet, to help us see beyond our own experience."

The hottest directorial talent to emerge in the 1990s was **Quentin Tarantino.** A former video store clerk and self-taught movie buff, Tarantino borrowed his slam-bang technique from Hong Kong action movies. His first production, *Reservoir Dogs* (1992), brought him instant fame with its ultra-violence, hyperkinetic style and offbeat conversations. His next effort, *Pulp Fiction* (1994), won the top prize at Cannes and an Oscar for Tarantino's screenplay. He followed up with *Jackie Brown* in 1997.

Eight Men Out ★ United States, 1988, John Sayles; Michael Rooker.

Pulp Fiction ★ United States, 1994, Quentin Tarantino; Uma Thurman and John Travolta.

Tarantino's major strength is as a scriptwriter, a talent that reached its zenith in the intricately plotted *Pulp Fiction,* where three different stories are followed as they gradually intertwine. He also has a pronounced flair for dialogue, such as in *Pulp Fiction* when John Travolta explains to fellow hood Samuel L. Jackson what a hamburger is called at McDonald's restaurants in Paris. Tarantino also excels in finding has-been or "B"-movie performers and revitalizing their careers, as he did for Travolta in *Pulp Fiction* and Pam Grier in *Jackie Brown.* His settings are most often sleazy, run-down parts of Los Angeles, the haunts of most of his characters, most of whom are low-level criminals.

Following the lead of other important film makers such as Francis Ford Coppola and Martin Scorsese, Tarantino has arranged American distribution deals for a number of foreign films; the most successful of these efforts was his sponsorship of *Chungking Express* (1994) by postmodernist Hong Kong director Wong Kar-Wei. By century's end, movie buff Tarantino was trying to drum up support for another of his discoveries, William Witney, the director of numerous Roy Rogers programmers during the 1950s. "His camera movements, when they happen, are so cool," he explained.

Other independent film makers who have achieved a certain degree of success in the last years of the twentieth century include Abel Ferera (*The Bad Lieutenant,* 1992, and *The Addiction,* 1995), Kevin Smith (*Clerks,* 1994; *Chasing Amy,* 1997; and *Dogma,* 1999), Todd Solanz (*Welcome to the Dollhouse,* 1995, and *Happiness,* 1998), and Hal Hartley (*Henry Fool,* 1997). Earlier independent presences such as Steven Soderberg (*Sex, Lies and Videotape,* 1988), Billy Bob Thornton (*Sling Blade,* 1996), David O. Russell (*Flirting with Disaster,* 1996), and Neil LaBute (*In the Company of Men,* 1997, and *Your Friends and Neighbors,* 1998) have moved into the mainstream with productions such as *Three Kings* (Russell, 1999), *All the Pretty Horses* (Thornton, 2000), *Out of Sight* (Soderberg, 1998), and *Nurse Betty* (LaBute, 2000).

Despite the growing activity in the independent sector of the industry, the audience for these films is not getting larger. From 1990 to 2000 theater revenues dropped by 31 percent to $185 million. Nonetheless, the big studios have shown an increasing proclivity for attaching themselves to small, specialized production houses, with Disney gobbling up Miramax, and other majors starting their own in-house independent production entities (Paramount Classics, Fox Searchlight, Sony Pictures Classics, etc.). The trend may be a response to the success of these smaller films at Academy Award time: In 1999 big studio pictures were cut out of the major awards entirely by independent productions such as *Shakespeare in Love.*

A few micro-distributors—for instance, New Yorker and First Look—are still out there, willing to release films that eke out only $1 million following a platform release schedule designed to build on good reviews and word of mouth. But for the studios, the opening week tells all; they roll the dice and wait for a big winner to emerge. "It's the studio mentality," says Sony Classics copresident Tom Bernard. "Buy ten and have the tenth one pay for the other losses."

Multicultural Agendas

At a certain point Hollywood executives figured out that their audience was made up of more than just white males like themselves. They had earlier learned this lesson with the so-called woman's film of the 1930s, 1940s, and 1950s and then forgot it during the 1960s. For a brief period in the 1970s, blaxploitation films targeted African American audiences. But it was during the 1980s and 1990s that attempts to understand that female, gay, and minority audiences might be interested in seeing something other than Sylvester Stallone shoot-em-ups really got underway. Of course, one way to attract these audiences has been to give jobs to female, gay, and minority film makers and performers. Gradually, this turnaround has been happening, with many of these new talents increasingly demonstrating cross-over appeal as well.

Sexism has long been notorious in Hollywood, from the storied casting couch to the demonstrable absence of **women** in key administrative and creative positions. In the 1980s some change began to occur in this situation, or at least a few more exceptions. For example, in an unprecedented appointment, Sherry Lansing became president in charge of film production at Twentieth Century-Fox in 1980. Other women soon followed her into top leadership positions (Dawn Steel at Columbia in 1987 and, during the 1990s, Lucy Fisher at Fox and Stacey Snider at Universal).

Among directors, Amy Heckerling had a solid hit with *Fast Times at Ridgemont High* in 1982, about teenage growing pains in southern California, one of the best of the genre and a big boost in the career of imminent star Sean Penn. Subsequently she directed *Look Who's Talking* (1989) and *Clueless* (1995).

Susan Seidelman's first feature, following graduate film school at New York University, was *Smithereens* (1982). It is an honest, tough-minded, painfully believable film about

Desperately Seeking Susan ★ United States, 1985, Susan Seidelman; Rosanna Arquette.

a near-psychotic young female hustler on the fringe of the punk-rock scene. *Desperately Seeking Susan* (1985) is about a bored New Jersey housewife (Rosanna Arquette) who pursues a bizarre woman being sought through a personal ad (Madonna). It was a smash hit.

Martha Coolidge seemed to be typed as a director of teenage flicks, of which her first, *Valley Girl* (1983), was the most interesting and successful. A departure with her fifth film, *Bare Essentials* (1991), made for television, was a generally agreed disaster. And then there was *Ramblin' Rose* (1991). In spite of its title (the role was played by Laura Dern, nominated for an Oscar as Best Actress; Diane Ladd, who played Mother, was nominated for Best Actress in a Supporting Role), it is really a coming-of-age story recalled by a man who returns home to visit his father in 1971. He remembers Rose, who came to work at their house during the Depression, and the various incidents and involvements growing out of her rampant if innocent sexuality (including the beginnings of his own sexuality, stimulated by her presence). A warm and nostalgic comedy of character and manners, its direction is coherent and controlled.

Other American-born female directors came to the fore in the 1990s, including Kathryn Bigelow (*Blue Steel,* 1989, and *Strange Days,* 1995), Allison Anders (*Gas Food*

Blue Steel ★ United States, 1990, Kathryn Bigelow; Jamie Lee Curtis.

Lodging, 1992, and *Grace of My Heart,* 1996), and Mary Harron (*I Shot Andy Warhol,* 1996, and *American Psycho,* 2000). These tended to be edgier talents, not always limited to making films about other women. Bigelow, for example, has established herself as an action director and Harron as a wry social satirist. During the 1980s and 1990s important female stars, such as Barbra Streisand and Jodie Foster, also established themselves as directors: Streisand with *Yentl* in 1983 and *The Mirror Has Two Faces* in 1996 and Foster with *Little Man Tate* in 1991 and *Home for the Holidays* in 1995.

If it is easier for women to become directors than it was at the beginning of this last period, it is still by no means easy. Female directors complain that they do not have access to the "boys' club"—that is, the predominantly male group of executives who have the power to "greenlight" projects. Moreover, they fall prey to male stereotyping that women cannot direct action pictures, cannot direct commercial movies, cannot control crews, and so on. Male prejudices within the industry are still a formidable barrier, it seems.

The so-called woman's film was also revived during these years, renamed "chick flicks" or "mom movies." Many of these were notable commercial and critical hits. Some focused on mother-daughter bonds (*Terms of Endearment,* James L. Brooks, 1983; *Steel Magnolias,* Herbert Ross, 1989; *Postcards from the Edge,* Mike Nichols, 1990; and *One True Thing,* Carl Franklin, 1998) or the bonds between sisters or women friends (*The Turning Point,* Herbert Ross, 1977, and *Beaches,* Garry Marshall, 1988). Others featured the trials and rewards of romance (*When Harry Met Sally,* Rob Reiner, 1988; *Pretty Woman,*

Thelma and Louise ★ United States, 1991, Ridley Scott; Susan Sarandon and Geena Davis.

Garry Marshall, 1990; and *Sleepless in Seattle,* Nora Ephron, 1993) and the power and jus-
tifications of female rage (*The Accused,* Jonathan Kaplan, 1988; *Thelma and Louise,* Ridley Scott, 1991; and *The First Wives Club,* Hugh Wilson, 1996).

Shirley MacLaine has established herself as one of the reigning divas of the genre
with a series of remarkable performances in films such as *Terms of Endearment, Steel Mag-
nolias,* and *Postcards from the Edge.* In both *Terms of Endearment* and *Postcards from the
Edge* MacLaine plays a vain, spoiled woman, but she appears without makeup in certain
scenes to show how deeply affected her characters are by what is happening to them. In
Steel Magnolias she portrays a woman who is unconcerned with her appearance, and
MacLaine's own appearance reflects this quality of character. She won a well-deserved
Academy Award for her role in *Terms of Endearment.*

Gender politics were taken to another level in the **gay** and **lesbian** cinema of the
1980s and 1990s. Gay-coded characters had always played a part in Hollywood productions, from the mannish behavior of the maiden aunt in Griffith's *Way Down East* (1919)
to the fussy *shtick* Edward Everett Horton perfected in the Astaire-Rogers musicals of
the 1930s to the demonized gay men featured in *film noir.* (To be sure, these characters'
sexual orientation was rarely explicitly stated, but many audience members could read
them easily enough.) In 1982 the first major mainstream film built around a gay issue
(in this instance, AIDS) appeared: *Philadelphia* (Jonathan Demme), although it was notably subtle in presenting gay lifestyles. There have also been a number of mainstream
films about cross-dressing and gender confusion over the years, from *Sylvia Scarlett*
(George Cukor, 1935) to *Some Like It Hot* (Billy Wilder, 1959) to *Victor/Victoria* (Blake
Edwards, 1982).

At the end of the 1980s a movement known as New Queer Cinema took root,
first among foreign film makers and then in America, following a trajectory feminist critic
Ruby Rich has described as a "short, sweet climb from radical impulse to niche market."
The godfather of the movement was British director Derek Jarman, whose 1986 *Caravaggio,* with its unabashed representation of gay sexuality, became a model others followed. From Isaac Julien, who is also British, came *Looking for Langston* (1988), a poetic
and evocative study of Langston Hughes, black poet and homosexual of the Harlem
renaissance of the 1930s. Julian's *Young Soul Rebels* (1991) focuses on the friendship of
two young men in London in 1977—one black and gay, the other half-black/ half-white and
heterosexual—who run a pirate radio station that plays black import records. In African
American director Marlon T. Riggs's expressionistic documentary *Tongues Untied* (1989),
a disparate group of unidentified black gay men relate their personal experiences. Jennie
Livingston's *Paris Is Burning* (1990), a more straightforward as well as an amusing and
skillful documentary, is about black drag costume balls in Harlem. These films suggest the
predominance of male homosexuality within the New Queer Cinema movement. Films
about male couples and coupling assumed the lead.

Gus Van Sant's *My Own Private Idaho* (1991) was the breakthrough feature. It concerns a young narcoleptic male hustler and his passion for an upper-class rich kid who is
part of the scene on the streets of Seattle but really just slumming. The film received wide
distribution (for such subject matter) and subsequently became available on video. Van
Sant's previous *Male Noche* (1987) also deals with homosexual obsessive desire but received only limited distribution. Other New Queer Cinema features that focus on male

My Own Private Idaho ★ United States, 1991, Gus Van Sant; River Phoenix and William Reichart.

homosexual lifestyles include *Poison* (Todd Haynes, 1990), *Swoon* (1991, Tom Kalin), *The Hours and Times* (1991, Christopher Munch), and *The Living End* (1992, Gregg Araki).

Lesbian films and film makers came to the fore in the mid- to late-1990s, with productions such as *R.S.V.P.* (Laurie Lynd, 1991), *Jollies* (1992) and *It Wasn't Love* (both Sadie Benning, 1992), *Go Fish* (Rose Troche, 1994), *Watermelon Woman* (Cheryl Dunye, 1997), and *High Art* (Lisa Cholodenko, 1998). *High Art,* about a lesbian photographer, is especially memorable for the way it captured the ambience of the New York art scene with its unique brand of gloomy chic.

By century's end gay themes and characters were integrated into mainstream film with productions such as *Gods and Monsters* (Bill Condon, 1998), *Being John Malkovich* (Spike Jonze, 1999), *The Talented Mr. Ripley* (Anthony Minghella, 1999), and especially *Boys Don't Cry* (Kimberly Pierce, 1999). Perhaps more significantly, gay-identified stars— for example, Anne Heche and Rupert Everett—began to be seen as viable romantic leads. Also, heterosexual stars began to appear as gay characters, including Cher, Sharon Stone, Tom Hanks, Antonio Banderas, Ally Sheedy, Cameron Diaz, and Hilary Swank. However, it is notable that when Swank accepted her Oscar for *Boys Don't Cry* she wore a very feminine ball gown and efusively thanked her husband in her acceptance speech.

Swank's Oscar for *Boys Don't Cry* represented a breakthrough for queer cinema, for director Kimberly Pierce had made a film that was quite a radical statement. Employing many of the techniques of avant-garde film making, it tells the tale of Teena Brandon, a young woman who lives as a man, and the emotional and physical costs of her decision. Based on a true story, the film is unsparing in its depiction of the bigotry Brandon's

Boys Don't Cry ★ United
States, 1999, Kimberly
Pierce; Hilary Swank.

behavior gives rise to in the midwestern town in which she lives. The images are dark, reflecting the mood of the story.

Another group that came a long way in relation to American cinema during the last part of the twentieth century are **black** film makers. The new visibility of African American films began with a radical group of black directors who came together at the UCLA film school in the 1970s and later came to be known as the L.A. Underground. The most famous members of the group are Charles Burnett (*Killer of Sheep,* 1977, and *To Sleep with Anger,* 1990), Ethiopan-born Haile Gerima (*Bush Mama,* 1974), Billy Woodbury (*Bless Their Little Hearts,* 1984), and Julie Dash (*Daughters of the Dust,* 1991). Mentored by UCLA faculty, such as Teshome Gabriel and British documentarian Basil Wright, the group formed a third-world film club that sponsored screening and discussions with leading third-world film makers, especially those from Latin America, during the late 1970s.

Probably the most important film made by a member of this group is *To Sleep with Anger.* Starring Danny Glover as a mysterious devil-figure that contaminates the affairs of a prosperous black family in Los Angeles, it explores the uneasy dynamics that relate blacks both to the American milieu they are part of and to a very different African heritage. The story is enhanced by the addition of an evocative gospel and blues musical score.

The breakthrough of black film making into the mainstream was *She's Gotta Have It* (1986), directed by Spike Lee, another New York University alumnus, who has become a sort of bellwether for black film making. He writes, directs, edits, and acts in his films and has built up a company of black collaborators, including his father as composer and his sister as writer and performer. *She's Gotta Have It* is not so much about blacks in this culture as about the relationships of Nola Darling with her three lovers and friends. She is a single, sexually emancipated commercial artist living in Harlem. The life she makes for herself includes the relationships available to her, but she maintains an attractiveness and a dignity that are her own. *School Daze* (1988), although it too is a comedy, is about class and color among black Americans. It takes place at Mission, a fictitious, predominantly black college in the South. The student body is divided into two factions: those who are lighter skinned and aspire to be like upper-middle-class whites and those who are darker, poorer, first-generation college students—the black interclass.

With *Do the Right Thing* (1989) Lee created a highly controversial, markedly successful direct attack on the problems of black-white (and Asian) relations in the urban ghetto, in this instance the Bedford Stuyvesant section of Brooklyn. It revolves around a pizzeria owned by an Italian (played by Danny Aiello) and his efforts to do business and live amicably in an indigent neighborhood of repressed and angry African Americans. His own anger eventually leads to murder, which triggers a race riot started by one of his employees (played by Lee) that includes the burning down of his pizza parlor. The film ends on a note of temporary reconciliation, which leaves the essential problems of racial discord unresolved, with contradictory quotes on the sound track from Martin Luther King, Jr., urging nonviolent protest, and Malcolm X, approving violence that is self-defense. This was

Do the Right Thing ★ United States, 1989, Spike Lee; Lee and Danny Aiello.

the most talked about film of the year, with critics and viewers alike taking sides. Lee continued his steady output during the late 1990s with productions such as *Clockers* (1995), *Get on the Bus* (1996), and *He Got Game* (1997). In 2000 he created a considerable stir with *Bamboozled,* a satire about television. The story concerns a new TV sitcom in which black actors appear in blackface.

The financial success of *She's Gotta Have It* (it grossed $8 million against a budget of $175,000) and *Do the Right Thing* ($28 million against $6.5 million) enabled Lee to continue making roughly a film a year (*Mo' Better Blues,* 1990; *Jungle Fever,* 1991; and *Malcolm X,* 1992) and led to a veritable explosion of black films in 1990–1991. Some nineteen features were released, first features for most of their directors, including *House Party* (Reginald and Warrington Hudlin, 1990), dealing with black hip-hop culture and rap music; *New Jack City* (Mario Van Peebles, 1991), a gangster ghetto melodrama of crack cocaine drug dealers and rebel cops; and *Straight Out of Brooklyn* (Matty Rich, 1991), a film much rougher in technique and narrative structure, the most bleak and hopeless of the black wave.

Boyz N the Hood (1991, John Singleton) was the most widely seen and discussed of the black films, apart from Spike Lee's productions. It is about four young black male high school students with different aims, ambitions, and family situations trying to survive amidst Los Angeles gangs and bigotry. Singleton went on to helm such other memorable films as *Higher Learning* (1995) and *Rosewood* (1997). Other black directors who emerged during the 1990s include Bill Duke (*A Rage in Harlem,* 1991, and *Deep Cover,* 1992), Carl Franklin (*One False Move,* 1991, and *Devil in a Blue Dress,* 1995), Allen and Albert Hughes (*Menace II Society,* 1993), and Boaz Yakin (*Fresh,* 1994). Later in the decade,

Boyz N the Hood ✶ United States, 1991, John Singleton.

black-helmed films aimed at African American women also began to appear, including *Waiting to Exhale* (Forrest Whitaker, 1995), *Set It Off* (Gary Gray 1996), and *Eve's Bayou* (Kasi Lemmons, 1997).

One of the most heartening developments that occurred during the 1990s was the work of major black performers who had achieved cross-over status to enable the production of ambitiously conceived black-made films. Danny Glover's willingness to back *To Sleep with Anger* was crucial in getting financing for it. *Eve's Bayou* was made possible by the support of star Samuel L. Jackson, who plays a meaty role as a beloved, but philandering, husband and father in 1950s Louisiana. The financing for both *Set It Off* and *Get on the Bus* was wholly supplied by blacks, including Will Smith and Danny Glover. And former basketball star Magic Johnson dedicated himself to building theaters in black neighborhoods to serve a previously neglected audience. (Blacks comprise only 12 percent of the population, but they purchase 25 percent of all movie tickets.)

By the turn of the century, however, there was still much to be achieved. In an article published in the *New York Times* in 1999, Spike Lee wrote, "There is no high-ranking African American who can greenlight a picture." Lee went on to observe that at least part of what stands in the way of the production of a broad array of black films is the audience. "Black people complain about black films," he wrote, "but nobody shows up to support a different type of film. Where was the black audience for *Daughters of the Dust, Rosewood, Eve's Bayou,* and *Beloved?* Where? Packing theaters to see *Set It Off* and *Booty Call.*"

If black film makers are still struggling to gain parity in Hollywood, **Latino** film makers have had an even harder time. A breakthrough of sorts occurred in 1987 with the success of Luis Valdez's *La Bamba,* which chronicled the life of Latino pop star Richie Valens, and "Cheech" Marin's *Born in East L.A.,* a clever comedy about a non-Spanish-speaking Chicano who finds himself trapped south of the border. These were followed by Raymond Menendez's *Stand and Deliver* (1989), about a Latino math teacher in an inner-city high school, and *The Milagro Beanfield War,* about Latino tenant farmers in the southwest. (Although directed by Anglo Robert Redford, it was Latino produced.) The next spate of Latino-themed films came in 1992 with Robert Rodriguez's *El Mariachi,* a rough, stylish action movie set in Mexico and reportedly made for a mere $7,000, and Edward James Olmos's *American Me,* a darkly disturbing tale of prison life as experienced by Latino inmates. In 1993 Anglo director Allison Anders directed *Mi Vida Loca (My Crazy Life)* about Hispanic teenaged girls in Los Angeles. Two interesting family dramas emerged from the movement in 1995: Gregory Nava's *My Family/Mia Familia,* which chronicled the tribulations of a close-knit Chicano family in Los Angeles, and Mira Nair's *The Perez Family,* which spurred controversy because many of the Cuban American roles were played by non-Latinos.

A moving force in the development of this tradition has been actor Edward James Olmos, who has been a loyal supporter of such films from his appearance in Robert Young's *The Ballad of Gregorio Cortez* in 1983. A beautifully poetic rendering of an actual court case in Texas at the end of the nineteenth century, this film raises difficult questions about the relation of language to culture. Olmos also starred in *Zoot Suit* (1981), *Stand and Deliver* (1988), and *My Family* (1995), as well as in his own directorial effort, *American Me* (1992).

Mi Vida Loca (*My Crazy
Life*) ⋆ United States,
1993, Allison Anders.

Possibilities now exist for feminist, gay, and minority-made films to be made inexpensively on video and Super-8mm and for bypassing conventional theatrical, nontheatrical, and television distribution to be sold and rented directly on videotape or disc or on the Web to persons interested in them. These developments mean that such works can be created and enjoyed much as literature and the other arts, which have long allowed for the innovative and specialized, and even the unpopular and outrageous.

Multinationalism

A profound change of recent years is the increasing internationalization of the industry, which internationalizes the art—for better or worse. It is no longer possible to draw distinctions among films of different nations with assurance; film money, film makers, and film production move across national boundaries. Some of the most important films of recent years are multinational mixes, not only of finance, crew, and cast but also of subjects, themes, and styles—"Euro-puddings," "transatlantic" productions, or US-Asian "fusion" cinema.

Among the most conspicuous examples of this trend is *The Last Emperor* (1987). A British-Italian-Hong Kong coproduction, its source was the autobiography of Pu Yi, *From Emperor to Citizen,* published in China in 1964. The screenplay was by Mark Peploe (English) and Bernardo Bertolucci (Italian). It had to be approved by the Chinese authorities

The Last Emperor ⋆ Italy-United Kingdom-China, 1987, Bernardo Bertolucci.

before production could proceed. The budget of $25 million was raised by British inde-
pendent producer Jeremy Thomas from five British and European banks. Principal crew
members were Italian: director Bertolucci; set designer Ferdinando Scarfiotta, and cinematographer Vittorio Storaro. The musical score was composed by a Japanese, Ryuichi
Sakamoto; an American, David Byrne; and a Chinese, Cong Su. The cast comprised a substantial number of Chinese Americans from California, plus Chinese nationals as well as
Irish Peter O'Toole. The leading role was played by Hong Kong–born John Lone. Shooting was divided between sixteen weeks in China and five weeks of interiors in the studio
in Rome. The film was distributed by Shoiku-Fugi, a Japanese entertainment conglomerate. Commenting on the production's subsequent success, its producer said that "it was presold virtually everywhere in the world."

The metaphor pursued throughout this book of a country stepping into the international spotlight with a particularly innovative national contribution to the evolution of film
art now has to be modified. Instead of more or less separable national developments, there
are now films from any country reaching audiences in any other—if not always easily,
certainly more readily than ever before.

As the old industry and old audiences give way to the new, individual artists are at
last beginning to receive the recognition in film they have always had in the other arts.
However, the motion picture remains an awesomely difficult medium in which to create.
The very characteristics that distinguish it from the older arts often impede the artist: the
massive and complex technology, the demands of high finance, and the necessity for a
huge and diverse audience. But, as the film made for theaters has yielded its place as mass

entertainer to television and now the Internet, and as the rigid production-distribution-exhibition systems have been shaken and cracked in many places, art of a new seriousness and difficulty, greater originality and individuality, has begun to appear. As Abbas Kiarostami once declared, "The best form of cinema is one which poses questions for the audience."

The flexible and subtle eloquence of modern film has been built on those periods of great national creativity surveyed in this history. The capacity of the medium for handling widely varied personal expression has been added to, bit by bit. Along with the ever-growing richness of the new, it is a further boon that we are able to go back and review the history of film through the work of film archives and museums, film history courses, retrospective series, and now, video cassettes and DVDs. In art there is rarely progress, only change. The works of Griffith, Murnau, Eisenstein, Ozu, and Buñuel are no less valuable now than when they were created. Each generation of viewers can find something new in them, sometimes more than was seen by the original audiences. Kurosawa, Bergman, Ray, Antonioni, Wajda, Zhang, Campion, and Sembène have replaced no one. Knowing as much as we can of the sum total of cinema helps us better appreciate the work of every film maker and each individual work. That is the use of the history of film.

Films of the Period

1975
Alice Doesn't Live Here Anymore (Martin Scorsese)
Grey Gardens (Albert and David Maysles)
Jaws (Steven Spielberg)
Nashville (Robert Altman)
One Flew Over the Cuckoo's Nest (Miloš Forman)

1976
All the President's Men (Alan J. Pakula)
Carrie (Brian De Palma)
Harlan County, USA (Barbara Kopple)
Heaven's Gate (Michael Cimino)
The Life and Times of Rosie the Riveter
   (Connie Field)
The Outlaw Josey Wales (Clint Eastwood)
Network (Sidney Lumet)
Rocky (John G. Avildsen)
Taxi Driver (Martin Scorsese)

1977
Annie Hall (Woody Allen)
Killer of Sheep (Charles Burnett)
New York, New York (Martin Scorsese)
Saturday Night Fever (John Badham)
Star Wars (George Lucas)
3 Women (Robert Altman)

1978
Days of Heaven (Terrence Malik)
The Deer Hunter (Michael Cimino)

1979
Alien (Ridley Scott)
American Gigolo (Paul Schrader)
Apocalypse Now (Francis Ford Coppola)
Manhattan (Woody Allen)
The Return of the Secaucus Seven
   (John Sayles)

1980
Bronco Billy (Clint Eastwood)
Dressed to Kill (Brian De Palma)
Gloria (John Cassavetes)
Heaven's Gate (Michael Cimino)
Love Streams (John Cassavetes)
Raging Bull (Martin Scorsese)

1981
Blade Runner (Ridley Scott)
Body Heat (Lawrence Kasden)
Raiders of the Lost Ark (Steven Spielberg)
Reds (Warren Beatty)

1982

The Ballad of Gregorio Cortez (Robert M.
    Young)
Chan Is Missing (Wayne Wang)
E.T.—The Extra Terrestrial (Steven Spielberg)
Fast Times at Ridgemont High (Amy Heckerling)
Lianna (John Sayles)
Tootsie (Sydney J. Pollack)
Victor/Victoria (Blake Edwards)

1983

The King of Comedy (Martin Scorsese)
The Right Stuff (Philip Kaufman)
Terms of Endearment (James L. Brooks)
Zelig (Woody Allen)

1984

Amadeus (Miloš Forman)
Blood Simple (Joel Coen)
Choose Me (Alan Rudolph)
The Cotton Club (Francis Ford Coppola)
El Norte (Gregory Nava)
Once Upon a Time in America (Sergio Leone)
Pretty Woman (Garry Marshall)
Stranger Than Paradise (Jim Jarmusch)
Surname Viet, Given Name Nam (Trinh Min-ha)
This Is Spinal Tap (Rob Reiner)

1985

Brazil (Terry Gilliam)
The Color Purple (Steven Spielberg)
Desperately Seeking Susan (Susan Seidelman)
Out of Africa (Sydney J. Pollack)
Prizzi's Honor (John Huston)
Witness (Peter Weir)

1986

Blue Velvet (David Lynch)
Down By Law (Jim Jarmusch)
The Fly (David Cronenberg)
Hannah and Her Sisters (Woody Allen)
Platoon (Oliver Stone)
A Room with a View (James Ivory)
She's Gotta Have It (Spike Lee)
Something Wild (Jonathan Demme)

1987

Broadcast News (James L. Brooks)
The Dead (John Huston)

House of Games (David Mamet)
The Last Emperor (Bernardo Bertolucci)
Radio Days (Woody Allen)
Raising Arizona (Joel Coen)
The Unbearable Lightness of Being
    (Philip Kaufman)
The Untouchables (Brian De Palma)
Wall Street (Oliver Stone)

1988

Bird (Clint Eastwood)
Tucker: The Man and His Dream (Francis
    Ford Coppola)
Who Framed Roger Rabbit? (Robert Zemeckis
    and Richard Williams)

1989

Batman (Tim Burton)
Do the Right Thing (Spike Lee)
Drugstore Cowboy (Gus Van Sant)
Eight Men Out (John Sayles)
The Little Mermaid (John Musker and Ron
    Clements)
Mystery Train (Jim Jarmusch)
Roger and Me (Michael Moore)
sex, lies, and videotape (Stephen
    Soderbergh)
The Thin Blue Line (Errol Morris)
When Harry Met Sally (Rob Reiner)

1990

Dances with Wolves (Kevin Costner)
Edward Scissorhands (Tim Burton)
Godfather III (Francis Ford Coppola)
Goodfellas (Martin Scorsese)
The Grifters (Stephen Frears)
Home Alone (John Hughes)
Miller's Crossing (Joel Coen)
Privilege (Yvonne Rainer)
The Sheltering Sky (Bernardo Bertolucci)
To Sleep with Anger (Charles Burnett)
Tongues Untied (Marlon Riggs)
White Hunter, Black Heart (Clint Eastwood)
Wild at Heart (David Lynch)

1991

Barton Fink (Joel Coen)
Beauty and the Beast (Gary Trousdale and
    Kirk Wise)

Boz N the Hood (John Singleton)
Daughters of the Dust (Julie Dash)
JFK (Oliver Stone)
My Own Private Idaho (Gus Van Sant)
One False Move (Carl Franklin)
Paris Is Burning (Jennie Livingston)
Rambling Rose (Martha Coolidge)
Resevoir Dogs (Quentin Tarantino)
The Silence of the Lambs (John Demme)
Terminator 2: Judgment Day (James Cameron)
Thelma and Louise (Ridley Scott)

1992

Aladdin (John Musker)
American Me (Edward James Olmos)
The Bad Lieutenant (Abel Ferera)
Bram Stoker's Dracula (Francis Ford Coppola)
Deep Cover (Bill Duke)
Gas Food Lodging (Allison Anders)
Howard's End (James Ivory)
My Own Private Idaho (Gus Van Sant)
The Player (Robert Altman)
Reservoir Dogs (Quentin Tarantino)
Unforgiven (Clint Eastwood)

1993

Jurassic Park (Steven Spielberg)
Philadelphia (Jonathan Demme)
Schindler's List (Steven Spielberg)
Short Cuts (Robert Altman)

1994

Clerks (Kevin Smith)
Ed Wood (Tim Burton)
Forrest Gump (Robert Zemekis)
Hoop Dreams (Steve James)
The Lion King (Roger Allers and Rob Minkoff)
Pulp Fiction (Quentin Tarantino)

1995

Babe (Chris Noonan)
Clueless (Amy Heckerling)
Crumb (Terry Zwigoff)
Devil in a Blue Dress (Carl Franklin)
From the Journals of Jean Seberg (Mark Rappaport)
Leaving Las Vegas (Mike Figgis)

A Little Princess (Alfonzo Cuaron)
My Family/Mia Familia (Gregory Nava)
Sense and Sensibility (Ang Lee)
Toy Story (John Lassiter)
The Usual Suspects (Brian Singer)
Waiting to Exhale (Forest Whitaker)

1996

Dead Man (Jim Jarmusch)
Fargo (Joel Coen)
The First Wives Club (Hugh Wilson)
I Shot Andy Warhol (Mary Harron)
Independence Day (Roland Emmerich)
Jerry Maguire (Cameron Crowe)
Lone Star (John Sayles)
Natural Born Killers (Oliver Stone)
The Nutty Professor (Tom Shadyac)
William Shakespeare's Romeo and Juliet (Baz Luhrmann)

1997

Boogie Nights (Paul Thomas Anderson)
Chasing Amy (Kevin Smith)
Henry Fool (Hal Hartley)
In the Company of Men (Neal LaBute)
L.A. Confidential (Curtis Hanson)
Titanic (James Cameron)

1998

Affliction (Paul Shrader)
Gods and Monsters (Bill Condon)
High Art (Lisa Cholodenko)
Out of Sight (Stephen Soderbergh)
The Prince of Egypt (Brenda Chapman)
Saving Private Ryan (Steven Spielberg)
A Simple Plan (Billy Bob Thornton)
The Thin Red Line (Terrence Malick)

1999

The Blair Witch Project (Daiel Myrick and Edwardo Sánchez)
Boys Don't Cry (Kimberly Pierce)
Dogma (Kevin Smith)
Ghost Dog (Jim Jarmusch)
Magnolia (Paul Thomas Anderson)
The Matrix (Andy and Larry Wachowski)
The Sixth Sense (M. Night Shamalyan)
Three Kings (David O. Russell)
Toy Story II (John Lassiter)

2000

Almost Famous (Cameron Crowe)
American Psycho (Mary Harron)
Being John Malkovich (Spike Jonze)
Cast Away (Robert Zemeckis)
Nurse Betty (Neal LaBute)
O Brother, Where Art Thou? (Coen)
Traffic (Steven Soderbergh).

2001

AI: Artificial Intelligence (Steven Spielberg)
Lord of the Rings: The Fellowship of the Ring
   (Peter Jackson)
The Man Who Wasn't There (Joel Cohen)
Moulin Rouge (Baz Luhrman)
Mulholland Drive (David Lynch)
Ocean's Eleven (Stephen Soderbergh)
Shrek (Andrew Adamson and Vicky Jensen)
The Gangs of New York (Martin Scorsese)

Books on the Period

Brown, Gene. *Movie Time: A Chronology of Hollywood and the Movie Industry from Its Beginnings to the Present.* New York: Macmillan, 1995.

Curran, Daniel. *Guide to American Cinema, 1965–1995.* Westport, CT: Greenwood Press, 1998.

Dale, Martin. *The Movie Game: The Film Business in Britain, Europe and America.* Herndon, VA: Cassell Academic, 1997.

Devine, Jeremy. *Vietnam at 24 Frames a Second.* Austin: University of Texas Press, 1999.

Ferncase, Richard K. *Outsider Features: American Independent Films of the 1980s.* Westport, CT: Greenwood Press, 1996.

Hillier, Jim. *The New Hollywood.* New York: Continuum, 1994.

Hillier, Jim, ed. *American Independent Cinema: A Sight and Sound Reader.* London: British Film Institute, 1999.

Levy, Emanuel. *Cinema of Outsiders: The Rise of American Independent Film.* New York: New York University Press, 1999.

Lewis, Jon, ed. *The New American Cinema.* Durham, NC: Duke University Press, 1998.

Lyons, Charles. *The New Censors: Movies and the Culture Wars.* Philadelphia: Temple University Press, 1997.

Lyons, Donald. *Independent Visions: A Critical Introduction to Recent Independent American Film.* New York: Routledge, 1996.

Maltby, Richard, and Ian Craven. *Hollywood Cinema: An Introduction.* Malden, MA: Blackwell Publications, 1995.

Moran, Albert, ed. *Film Policy: International, National and Regional Perspectives.* New York: Routledge, 1996.

Muse, Eben J. *The Land of Nam: The Vietnam War in American Film.* Lanham, MD: Scarecrow Press, 1995.

Neale, Stephen, and Murray Smith, eds. *Contemporary Hollywood Cinema.* New York: Routledge, 1998.

Nowell-Smith, Geoffrey, and Stephen Ricci, eds. *Hollywood and Europe: Economics, Culture, National Identity, 1945–1995.* London: British Film Institute, 1998.

Palmer, William J. *The Films of the Eighties: A Social History.* Carbondale, IL: Southern Illinois University Press, 1995.

Prindle, David F. *Risky Business: The Political Economy of Hollywood.* Boulder, CO: Westview Press, 1993.

Puttnam, David. *Movies and Money: The Undeclared War Between Europe and America.* New York: Random House, 1998.

Rines, Jesse Algernon. *Black Film/White Money.* New Brunswick, NJ: Rutgers University Press, 1996.

Slide, Anthony. *The New Historical Dictionary of the American Film Industry.* Lanham, MD: Scarecrow Press, 1998.

Vaz, Mark Cotta, and Patricia Rose Duignan. *Industrial Light and Magic: Into the Digital Realm.* New York: Ballantine Books, 1996.

Vineberg, Steve. *No Surprises, Please: Movies in the Reagan Decade.* New York: Schirmer Books, 1993.

Wasko, Janet. *Hollywood in the Information Age: Beyond the Silver Screen.* Austin: University of Texas Press, 1995.

Wollen, Tana, and Philip Hayward, eds. *Future Visions: New Technologies of the Screen.* London: British Film Institute, 1993.

Index

Á nous la liberté, 118
Abbas, Ahmad, 333, 335
Abbott and Costello Meet . . .
[series], 142
Absolute Power, 448
Abyss, The, 65, 254
academic films, 193–194
Academy Awards, 183, 184,
186, 193, 214, 260, 288,
290, 294, 295, 350, 367,
373, 376, 393–394, 409,
410, 421, 424, 425, 443,
445, 446, 450, 451, 456,
457, 459, 461, 463
Accatone! 170, 182, 184
Accident, 211–212
Accused, The, 463
Ace in the Hole, 376
Ackroyd, Dan, 98
action/adventure films,
100–101, 315, 384, 438,
441
Actor's Revenge, An, 323
Adam's Rib, 93, 375
adaptations (of literature/
drama), 148–149, 157,
194, 246, 315, 356,
404–405
Addiction, The, 459
Adoption, 293
Adventurer, The, 43
*Adventures of Baron
Munchausen, The,* 213
*Adventures of Barry McKenzie,
The,* 417
Adventures of Dollie, The, 15
*Adventurous Automobile Trip,
An,* 38
Affairs of Anatol, The, 93
Affliction, 452
African films, 414, 415–417,
429
African American films,
464–468
African Queen, The, 193–194
After the Truth, 269
Age d'or, L', 116, 270
Age of Innocence, The, 392
Agee, James, 97
Agnus Dei, 291
Aguirre, the Wrath of God, 267
Aiello, Danny, 466
Aimée and Jaguar, 269
Air Force, 152
Ajantrik, 337
Akerman, Chantal, 236,
238–239
Aladdin, 445
Alaska, 457
Alea, Tomás Gutièrrez,
406–407
Alexander Nevsky, 83
Ali: Fear Eats the Soul, 265
Alice, 296
*Alice Doesn't Live Here
Anymore,* 392
Alice in the Cities, 268
Alice's Restaurant, 384, 386

Alien, 443, 452
All About My Mother, 274
All of Me, 447
All Quiet on the Western Front,
110, 387
All That Heaven Allows, 265,
378
All That Jazz, 137
All the Pretty Horses, 459
Allen, Dede, 386
Allen, Robert C., 105
Allen, Vera, 371
Allen, Woody, 98, 440,
447–448
Almodóvar, Pedro, 271,
273–274, 275
Almost Famous, 446
Alone on the Pacific, 323
Alphaville, 232
Alsino and the Condor, 412
Altman, Robert, 385–386,
387–389, 439
Alton, John, 62
Alvarez, Santiago, 406
Amadeus, 297
Amarcord, 174, 183
Amelio, Gianni, 184, 188, 189
American Buffalo, 456
American films. **See** United
States
American Friend, The, 268
American Gigolo, 452
American Graffiti, 392
American in Paris, An, 372, 375
American Me, 468
American Playhouse [series],
453
American Psycho, 461–462
Amidei, Sergio, 162
Amor brujo, El, 272
Amores Perros, 414–415
Amour á mort, L', 237, 238
Amour en fuite, L', 234
Amour fou, L', 234
Amulet of Orgum, 408–409
And God Created Woman, 226
And the Ship Sails On, 177
Anders, Allison, 461–462
Anderson, Lindsay, 200,
201–202, 204
Anderson, Michael, 193
Andersson, Bibi, 257
Andrei Rublev, 304
Andy Warhol's Bad, 399
Andy Warhol's Frankenstein,
399
Anemic Cinema, 115
Angel, 207
Angel at My Table, An, 421
Angeli, Otello, 183–184
Anger, Kenneth, 397
Animal Crackers, 142
animated films, 20, 149–150,
296, 298, 438, 441,
445–446
Ankur, 338
Anne Boleyn, 96
Annie Hall, 447, 448

Another Woman, 448
Antoine Doinel [series], 227,
234
Antonio, Emile de, 395
Antonio das Mortes, 408
Antonioni, Michelangelo, 162,
169, 170, 171, 172,
177–179, 180, 184, 189,
363
Antz, 445
Aparajito, 335, 336
Apartment, The, 377
Apocalypse Now, 391, 442, 443
Appearances Deceive, 415
Apple, The, 429
Apple Game, The, 297
Arabian Nights, The, 182
Araki, Gregg, 463–464
Arau, Alfonzo, 414
Arbuckle, Roscoe "Fatty," 131
Arcand, Denis, 425
Arcelli, Kim, 184
Archers, The, 194, 205
Argent, L', 225
Argentina (films made in),
409–412, 415
Arif, K., 333
Arletty, 120, 121
Armstrong, Gillian, 420–421,
422
Arquette, Rosanna, 461
Arroseur arrosé, L', 5–6
Arsenal, 75
Artaud, Antonin, 265
Arthur, Jean, 133, 371
*Artists at the Top of the Big Top:
Disoriented,* 263
Aryan, The, 96
Arzner, Dorothy, 147
As Good As It Gets, 446
Ascent, The, 302
Ashes and Diamonds, 284, 285
Ashik Kerib, 304
Ashur, Geri, 400
Asia (films made in), 332. **See
also** China; India; Japan;
Soviet Union
Askoldov, Alexander, 302
Asphalt Jungle, The, 154
Asquith, Anthony, 70
Assassinat du Duc de Guide, L',
104
*Assassination of the Duc de
Guise, The,* 21
Assayas, Olivier, 247
Astaire, Fred, 139–140, 371
Astor, Mary, 154
Astruc, Alexandre, 220, 225,
226
Atalanta, L', 118, 119
Au revoir, les enfants, 239, 241
August, Bille, 259, 260–261
Austin Powers, 437
Australia (films made in), 404,
417–422
Autumn Afternoon, An, 321
Autumn Tale, An, 236
Aviator's Wife, The, 235–236

Avventura, L', 169, 170, 171,
177, 178–179, 184
Awara, 333–334
Awful Truth, The, 144
¡Ay! Carmela, 272
Ayres, Agnes, 145
Aznavour, Charles, 229, 230

Babenco, Hector, 409
Bacall, Lauren, 359, 368
Back to God's Country, 101
Back to the Future [series], 437
Backstairs, 54
Bad and the Beautiful, The, 375
Bad Lieutenant, The, 459
Bad Timing, 208
Badlands, 452
Baiza'i, Bahram, 427
Baker's Wife, The, 120
Balance, La, 246
Balcon, Michael, 196
Ball, Lucille, 147, 356
Ball of Fire, 142, 376
Ballad of a Soldier, 72
Ballad of Cable Hogue, The, 386
Ballad of Gregorio Cortez, The,
468
Ballad of Narayama, 325
Ballet mécanique, 115
Bamba, La, 468
Bamboozled, 467
Bananas Is My Business, 415
Band of Outsiders, 231, 232,
363
Band Wagon, The, 140, 375
Banderas, Antonio, 464
Bandit Queen, The, 339
Bandits of Orgosolo, The, 170
Bara, Theda, 47
Baranovskaya, Vera, 84
Bardot, Brigitte, 226, 241
Bare Essentials, 461
Baree, Son of Kazan, 101
Barkleys of Broadway, The, 140
Barney Oldfield's Race for Life,
42
Barnouw, Erik, 333
Barrault, Jean-Louis, 121
Barren Lives, 407
Barreto, Bruno, 409
Barrier, 286, 296
Barry Lyndon, 213
Barrymore, John, 105
Barrymore, Lionel, 109
Barstow, Stan, 200
Bart, Peter, 435
Barton Fink, 456
Bashu, the Little Stranger, 427
Bataan, 152
Batman, 438, 445–446
Battle, The, 33
Battle of Chile, The, 412
Battle of the River Plate, The,
193
Battleship Potemkin, 81–82, 83,
86, 155
Bazin, André, 120
BBC-TV, 196, 206, 212, 215

Beaches, 462
Beatles, The, 214, 248
Beatty, Warren, 386, 439, 440
Beau Serge, Le, 226
Beauty and the Beast, 150, 445
Beauty and the Bolshevik, The,
  72
Becker, Jacques, 220, 226
Becky Sharp, 148
Bed and Board, 234
Bed and Sofa, 72
Beetlejuice, 446
Before the Rain, 307
Before the Revolution, 184
Beginning of the End, The, 414
Beinex, Jean-Jacques, 247
Being John Malkovich, 464
Belasco, David, 92
Belle de jour, 270
Belle Époque, La, 274–275
Belle Équipe, La, 120
Belle Noiseuse, La, 234–235
Bellocchio, Marco, 184, 186,
  188, 189
Belmondo, Jean-Paul, 227, 230,
  232
Beloved, 448, 468
Bemberg, Maria Luisa,
  410–411
Ben-Hur, 91, 102, 103, 373
Benegal, Shyam, 335, 337, 338
Benigni, Roberto, 184, 189
Bennett, Joan, 153
Benning, Sadie, 464
Benton, Robert, 386
Beresford, Bruce, 417, 420, 422
Bergman, Ingmar, 171, 226,
  255, 256, 257–260, 261,
  269, 274, 275, 304, 305,
  388, 424–425, 447
Bergman, Ingrid, 151
Berkeley, Busby, 109, 138–139
*Berlin: Symphony of a Great
  City,* 54, 55
Berlin Alexanderplatz [series],
  51, 266
Berlin Film Festival, 186, 293,
  302, 341, 343, 394
Berliner, Alain, 246
Bernard, Tom, 459
Bernhardt, Sarah, 21
Berry, John, 384
Berry, Jules, 122
Bertolucci, Bernardo, 184–186,
  188, 189, 469, 470
Besieged, 186
Bessie, Alvah, 368
Besson, Luc, 247
Best Intentions, 259
Best Years of Our Lives, The,
  148, 149
Better Tomorrow, A, 345
Beverly Hills Cop, 447
Beware of a Holy Whore, 265
Beyond Rangoon, 206
Beyond the Clouds, 177
Bhumika, 338
Bhuvan Shome, 337
Biberman, Herbert, 368
Biblical epics, 370, 373
Biches, Les, 234, 235
Bicycle Thief, The, 165,
  167–168, 169, 175, 335
Bidone, Il, 174
Big City, The, 337
Big Parade, The, 100, 101, 343
Big Sleep, The, 152

Bigelow, Kathryn, 443,
  461–462
Billy Liar, 202
Birdcage, The, 246, 350
Birinski, Leo, 66
Birri, Fernando, 405
Birth of a Nation, The, 15, 18,
  20, 27–36, 83, 88, 91, 103,
  155
Birth of a Race, 103
Bitter Moon, 286
Bitter Rice, 164
*Bitter Tears of Petra von Kant,
  The,* 265
Bitzer, G. W. "Billy," 19, 37–38
Björk, 260
Black Cat, White Cat, 301
black films, 464–468
Black Girl, 384, 416
Black God, White Devil, 408
Black Narcissus, 205
Black Orpheus, 226
Black Peter, 294
Black Pirate, The, 101
Black Rain, 325, 326
Black River, 323
Blackboard Jungle, The, 373
Blade Runner, 211, 443
*Blair Witch 2: The Book of
  Shadows,* 437
Blanchett, Cate, 422
blaxploitation, 383, 383, 460.
  See also black films
Blazing Saddles, 446
Bless Their Little Hearts, 465
Blethyn, Brenda, 198
Blind Husbands, 95
Blithe Spirit, 194
Blonde Venus, 145
Blood of a Poet, The, 115
Blood of the Condor, 405, 406
Blood Simple, 455–456
Blood Wedding, 272
Blot, The, 99
Blow-Up, 171, 363
Blue Angel, The, 67
Blue Collar, 452
Blue Light, The, 68
Blue Sky, 211
Blue Steel, 461–462
Blue Velvet, 453, 454
Boat People, 346
Bob le flambeur, 226, 227
Boccacio 70, 176
Bodrov, Sergei, 306, 307
Body and Soul, 103
Body Heat, 154
Body Snatcher, The, 142
Boetticher, Budd, 370
Bogart, Humphrey, 151, 154,
  227, 368
Bogdanovich, Peter, 225
Boheme, La, 210
Bonheur, Le, 238
Bonnie and Clyde, 384, 386,
  387
Boorman, John, 205, 206
Booty Call, 468
Border, The, 211
Border Street, 282
Borgnine, Ernest, 387
Born in East L.A., 468
Born on the Fourth of July, 442
Born Yesterday, 375
Borowszyk, Walerian, 286
Bossak, Jerzy, 282
Boucher, Le, 234

Boudu Saved from Drowning,
  122
Bound for Glory, 439
Bow, Clara, 147
Bowfinger, 447
Bowie, David, 208
Boxcar Bertha, 392
Boy, 325
Boyfriends and Girlfriends, 236
Boyle, Danny, 203, 216
Boys Don't Cry, 464–464
Boyz N the Hood, 467
Bracco, Lorraine, 392
Brach, Gerard, 286
Brackett, Charles, 144, 376
Braine, John, 200
Brains Repaired, 20
Brakhage, Stan, 239, 398
Bram Stoker's Dracula, 391
Branaugh, Kenneth, 194, 391
Brandauer, Klaus-Maria, 292
Brando, Marlon, 370, 373–374,
  391
Brazil, 214, 443
Brazil (films made in),
  407–409, 415
Bread and Chocolate, 188
Breaker Morant, 421
Breakfast at Sunrise, 99
Breaking the Waves, 260
Breathless, 227–228, 229, 230,
  231, 232, 243
Brecht, Bertolt, 51, 52, 79, 156,
  231, 241, 242, 265
Breen, Joseph I., 131
Breillat, Catherine, 244
Bresson, Robert, 220, 222,
  224–225, 226, 248, 255,
  269
Brewster McCloud, 387–388
Bride Wore Black, The, 233
Bridge on the River Kwai, The,
  194, 356, 362
*Bridges of Madison County,
  The,* 448
Brief Encounter, 194
Briel, Joseph Carl, 28, 35
Brigadoon, 375
Brighter Summer Day, A,
  349–350
*Bring Me the Head of Alfredo
  Garcia,* 386
Bringing Up Baby, 134, 142,
  144, 145
British films. **See** Great Britain
British Sounds, 233
Brittania Hospital, 202
Broadcast News, 446
Broadway Melody, 138
Broken Blossoms, 27, 62
Bronco Billy, 448
Brooks, Albert, 446
Brooks, James L., 446, 462
Brooks, Mel, 98, 446
Brotherhood of the Wolf, 245
Brown, Clarence, 145
Brown, Joe E., 377
Brückner, Jutta, 264
Brusati, Franco, 188
Buck and the Preacher, 384
Buckland, Wilfred, 93
Bug's Life, A, 445
Bugajski, Ryszard, 286
Bunny, John, 47
Buñuel, Luis, 116, 255,
  269–271, 274, 414
Burgess, Anthony, 213

Burmese Harp, The, 322, 323
Burnett, Charles, 465
Burnt by the Sun, 305
Burton, Tim, 445–446
Bush Mama, 465
Bushman, Francis X., 47
Butterfly, 274–275
Buttoners, 297
Bye Bye Brazil, 409
Byrne, David, 470

Cabaret, 51
Cabbage Fairy, 15
Cabin in the Sky, 375
Cabinet of Dr. Caligari, The,
  52, 54–55, 56, 57, 63, 66
Cabiria, 22–23
Café au lait, 246
Cage, Nicholas, 269
Cage au folles, La, 246
Caged Heat, 448
Cahiers du Cinéma, 220, 221,
  225, 226, 231, 241–242,
  243–244
Caine, Michael, 194
Calendar, 425
California Split, 389
Calm Before the Storm, The,
  288
Cameron, James, 423, 438, 443
Camila, 410–412
Camille, 145
Cammell, Donald, 207
Camouflage, 286
Camp de Thiaroye, 417
Campion, Jane, 421, 422
Camus, Marcel, 226
Canada (films made in), 404,
  422–426
Cannes Film Festival, 184,
  198–199, 226, 248, 260,
  263, 268, 270, 288, 300,
  301, 325, 332, 341, 345,
  346, 347, 350, 391, 417,
  418, 421, 425, 453, 454,
  457
Cantata, 291
Canterbury Tales, The, 182
Canudo, Ricciotto, 115, 116
Capra, Frank, 127, 132,
  134–136, 142, 335
Captain Blood, 148
Caravaggio, 207, 463
Carax, Leos, 247
Carla's Song, 203, 204
Carmen, 182, 272
Carnal Knowledge, 365
Carné, Marcel, 120–121,
  152
Carnet de bal, 120
Carol, Martine, 223
Caron, Leslie, 372
Carpenter, John, 142
Carradine, David, 439
Carradine, Keith, 388
Carrey, Jim, 418–420
Carson, L. M. "Kit," 268
cartoons. **See** animated films
Casablanca, 151, 439
Casino, 392–393
Cassavetes, John, 347,
  385–386, 394–395
Castle of Purity, The, 414
Casualties of War, 442
Cat People, 142
Cattaneo, Peter, 216
Cavalcanti, Alberto, 196

Cavani, Liliana, 187
Cayrol, Jean, 237
Ceddo, 416–417
Celebration, The, 260, 261
Celine and Julie Go Boating,
    234, 236
censorship, 131–132, 281, 282,
    284, 363–370, 427
Center Stage, 346
Central Station, 409
Ceremony, The, 325–326
César, 118
Chabrol, Claude, 225, 226, 231,
    234
Chan, Jackie, 344–345
Chandler, Raymond, 152
Chang, 101
*Chant of Jimmie Blacksmith,
    The,* 420
Chaos, 186
Chapayev, 280
Chaplin, Charles, 27, 38–39,
    42–45, 47, 88, 97–98, 113,
    334, 335
Chaplin, Geraldine, 388
Chapman, Michael, 393–394
Chapter in Her Life, A, 99
*Charge of the Light Brigade,
    The,* 211
Chariots of Fire, 214, 215
Charisse, Cyd, 373
Charlotte Gray, 422
Charulata, 336–337
Chase, The, 386
Chasing Amy, 459
Chatman, Seymour, 178
Cheat, The, 92–93
Chelsea Girls, 399
Chen Kaige, 342–343
Cher, 464
Chess Players, The, 337
Cheung, Maggie, 247, 346
Chevalier, Maurice, 138
Cheyenne Autumn, 137
Chicken Run, 436, 445
Chien andalou, Un, 116, 270
Chienne, La, 122
Children Are Watching Us, The,
    166
Children of Paradise, 121
Children of the Earth, 335
Chile (films made in), 412–413
Chimes at Midnight, 157
China (films made in),
    340–351. **See also** Hong
    Kong; People's Republic
    of China; Taiwan
  actors in, 343–344, 346, 347
  American influence on, 340
  British influence on, 340
  distribution/exhibition of,
    344–345
  genres of, 344–345
  globalization and, 350–351
  social/political events
    and, 340–341, 344,
    347–348
China Is Near, 186
Chinatown, 154, 286
Chinoise, La, 242
Chopra, Joyce, 400
Choudbury, Sarita, 339
Chow, Rey. **See** Rey Chow
Chow Yun-Fat, 345–346
Chrétien, Henri, 359
Christ Stopped at Eboli, 182

Christiansen, Benjamin, 254
Christie, Julie, 208, 212
Christopher Strong, 147
Chronicle of a Death Foretold,
    182
Chronicle of a Summer, 246
*Chronicle of Anna Magdalena
    Bach,* 265
*Chronicle of the Gray House,
    The,* 63
Chungking Express, 248,
    346–347, 459
Churchill, Berton, 136
Churning, The, 338
Chuvelyov, Ivan, 84
Chytilová, Věra, 294, 297
Cider House Rules, The, 260
Cimino, Michael, 438, 442
Cinderella, 8
Cinema Nôvo, 407–409
Cinema Paradiso, 183, 189
cinéma pur, 115–117, 120
cinéma vérité, 73, 232, 246,
    294–295
CinemaScope, 359–360,
    375–376
Cinémathèque Française, 125,
    220–221, 241
Cinerama, 114, 358, 359–360
Circumstance, The, 181
Cissé, Souleymane, 417
Citizen Kane, 155–156, 157
Citizens Band, 448
Citron, Michelle, 401
City of Angels, 269
City of Pirates, 413
City of Sadness, 348
City of Women, 174
Clair, René, 116, 118
Clansman, The, 28
Clarke, Arthur, 213
Clarke, Shirley, 395
Clarke, T. E. B., 196
Class Relations, 265
Claudine, 384
Clayton, Jack, 200–201
Cleo from 5 to 7, 238, 239
Cleopatra, 163, 382
Clerks, 459
Clock, The, 375
Clockers, 467
Clockwork Orange, A, 213
Cloquet, Ghislain, 248
*Close Encounters of the Third
    Kind,* 449
Close-Up, 427
Closely Watched Trains, 295,
    297
Closet, The, 245
closeups, 16–17, 84
Clowns, The, 174
Clueless, 460
Cobb, Lee J., 370
Coca-Cola Kid, The, 300
Cocoanuts, The, 110
Cocteau, Jean, 115, 116, 220,
    360
Coen, Joel and Ethan, 455–456
Cohen, Leonard, 389
Cohl, Emile, 20, 38
Cohn, Henry, 88
Cohn, Jack, 88
Colbert, Claudette, 142
Cold Comfort Farm, 211
Cold Days, 296
Cold Heaven, 208
Cole, Lester, 368

Colonel Redl, 292
Color of Money, The, 392–393
Color of Pomegranates, The,
    303, 304
Color Purple, The, 450
colorization, 439, 440
Columbia/TriStar, 435, 436
Columbia Pictures, 88, 129,
    215, 356, 363, 436, 460
Come and See, 302
Comedies and Proverbs
    [series], 235, 236
comedy/comedies, 27, 38–44,
    85, 93, 96, 97–98,
    142–144, 188–189, 194,
    196–199, 212, 246, 344,
    359, 417–418, 438,
    446–447
Comfort and Joy, 198
comic book adaptations, 438,
    444
Coming Home, 442
Commissar, The, 302
Company of Wolves, 207
Condon, Bill, 464
Conformist, The, 184
Confrontation, The, 291
Conner, Bruce, 397
Connery, Sean, 194
Conquest of the Pole, 8
Contact, 443, 444
Contempt, 232
Contract, The, 286–287
Conversation, The, 391
Conversation Piece, 172
Conviction, The, 186
Cook, the Thief, His Wife, and
    Her Lover, The, 209
Cooley High, 384
Coolidge, Martha, 461
Cooper, Gary, 134, 135, 142,
    368, 370
Coppola, Francis Ford, 114,
    187–188, 287, 385–386,
    390–392, 439, 442, 448,
    459
Corman, Roger, 142, 386, 448
Cornelius, Henry, 196
Cotton Club, The, 391
Couer en Hivre, Un, 245
Courant, Kurt, 66–67
Courtenay, Tom, 200
Cousin Angelica, 272
Cousin Bobby, 448
Covered Wagon, The, 42, 97
Cow, The, 427
Craig's Wife, 147
Cranes Are Flying, 72
Crash, 424, 425
Craven, Wes, 142
Crawford, Joan, 145–146, 147,
    375
Crazy Mama, 448
Crichton, Charles, 196,
    215–216
Cries and Whispers, 258
Crime of Monsieur Lange, The,
    122
Crimes of the Future, 424
Crisis, 257
Cristaldi, Franco, 183
"Crocodile" Dundee, 417
Cromwell, John, 109
Cronenberg, David, 424
Crosby, Floyd, 370
*Crouching Tiger, Hidden
    Dragon,* 350

Crowd, The, 107
Crowe, Cameron, 446
Crucified Lovers, 318–319
Cruel Sea, The, 193
Cruise, Tom, 207
Cruze, James, 97
Crying Game, The, 207
Cuba (films made in), 405–407,
    415
Cukor, George, 109, 145,
    375–376, 463
Cummings, Irving, 110
Cure, The, 43
Curse of Frankenstein, The, 205
Curtis, Tony, 377
Curtiz, Michael, 146, 147
Cushing, Peter, 205
cut/cutting, 18, 71
Cutter's Way, 297
Cybulski, Zbigniew, 284–285
Cyclist, The, 428
Cyrano de Bergerac, 246
Czechoslovakia (films made
    in), 281, 293–298, 306

D'Onofrio, Vincent, 446
Dagover, Lil, 65
Daisies, 294
Dali, Salvador, 116, 270
Dam Busters, The, 193
Damned, The, 172
Dance, Girl, Dance, 147
Dance with a Stranger, 215
Dancer in the Dark, 260
Dances with Wolves, 437
Dangerous Liaisons, 204
Danny Boy, 207
Dante's Inferno, 22
Dardenne, Jean-Pierre and Luc,
    248
Daring Youth, 99
Darling, 248
Dash, Julie, 465
Daughter Rite, 401
Daughters of the Dust, 465, 468
David Copperfield, 148
Davies, Terrence, 203
Davis, Bette, 145–146
Davis, Ossie, 384, 442
Dawn Patrol, The, 133
Day, Doris, 371, 373
Day for Night, 231
Day in the Country, A, 363
Day of Wrath, 255
Daybreak, 120, 121
Days and Nights in the Forest,
    336–337
Days of Heaven, 452
de Andrade, Joaquin Pedro, 408
de Forest, Lee, 105
DeMille, Cecil B., 23, 52,
    91–94, 96, 101–103, 373
De Niro, Robert, 185, 187–188,
    392, 393
De Palma, Brian, 142
de Putti, Lya, 66
de Rochemont, Louis, 358
de Santis, Giuseppe, 177
de Seta, Vittorio, 170
de Sica, Vittorio, 166–167, 169,
    170, 172, 189, 227, 316,
    335
de Wilde, Brandon, 371
Dead End, 148
Dead Man, 455
Dead Poets' Society, 418–420
Dead Ringers, 424

Deadly Companions, 386
Deakins, Roger, 456
Dean, James, 285, 373–374
Dear Diary, 189
Death and the Maiden, 286
Death by Hanging, 248, 325
Death in Venice, 172
Death of a Salesman, 263
Decalogue [series], 288
Decameron, The, 182
Deception, 96
Decline and Fall of the American Empire, 425
Deep Cover, 467
Deep Throat, 365
Deer Hunter, The, 442, 443
del Rio, Dolores, 414
Delaney, Shelagh, 200
Deliverance, 206
Delluc, Louis, 113, 116, 125
Dementia 13, 390
Demme, Jonathan, 448–449, 463
Deneuve, Catherine, 234
Denis, Claire, 248
Denmark (films made in), 254–255, 260
Depardieu, Gérard, 185, 234, 418–420
Depp, Johnny, 446
Deren, Maya, 397, 401
Dern, Laura, 461
Déry, Tibor, 291
Desilu, 356
Despechin, Arnaud, 247
Desperately Seeking Susan, 460, 461
Destiny, 53
Détective, 243
Devi, 336
Devil in a Blue Dress, 467
Devil Is a Woman, The, 132
Devil Probably, The, 225
Devine, Andy, 136
di Caprio, Leonardo, 260, 438
Diagonal Symphony, 54
Dial M for Murder, 357, 358
Diamond, I. A. L., 377
Diamonds of the Night, 294, 295
Diaries, Notes, and Sketches, 398
Diary for My Children, 293
Diary for My Loves, 293
Diary for My Mother and Father, 293
Diary of a Chambermaid, 270
Diary of a Country Priest, 224–225
Diary of a Shinjuku Thief, 325
Diaz, Cameron, 464
Dick Tracy, 438, 439
Dickson, W. K. L., 105
Die Hard, 438
Dieguez, Carlos, 405, 409
Dietrich, Marlene, 128, 132, 145
Dimensions of Dialogue, 296
Directors Guild of America, 132, 383, 439–440
Dirty Dancing, 137
Disasters of War, The, 271
Discreet Charm of the Bourgeoisie, The, 270–271
Dishonored, 132
Disney, Walt, 149–150, 368. **See also** Walt Disney Studio/Productions

dissolve, 18
Distant Thunder, 337
Distant Voices, Still Lives, 203
Diva, 247
Divorce, Italian Style, 183, 188
Dixon, Thomas, 28, 30
Dmytryk, Edward, 152, 368
Do the Right Thing, 466–467
Do You Remember Daisy Bell? 300
Doctor Zhivago, 360
documentaries, 5, 9–10, 101, 116–117, 127, 165–166, 194–196, 206, 232, 238, 245–246, 263, 282–283, 302–303, 323, 367, 370, 383–384, 395–397, 404–406, 409–410, 423–424
Dodsworth, 148
Dog Star Man, 398
Dog's Dialogue, 413
Dogma, 459
Doillon, Jacques, 245
Dolce Vita, La, 170, 171, 175–176, 177
domestic melodramas, 145–146
Dommartin, Solveig, 268–269
Don Juan, 105, 106
Don't Change Your Husband, 93
Don't Look Now, 208
Dona Flor and Her Two Husbands, 409
Dona Herlinda and Her Two Sons, 415
Donen, Stanley, 140, 221, 248, 372
Donner, Richard, 441
Double Indemnity, 152, 376
Double Life, A, 375
Double Life of Véronique, The, 289
Double Suicide, 327, 328
Douglas, Kirk, 376, 418
Douglas, Michael, 452
Dovzhenko, Alexander, 75–76, 78, 79, 83, 178, 231, 303, 305
Down and Out in Beverly Hills, 447
Dr. Korczak, 286
Dr. Strangelove, or: How I Learned to Stop Worrying and Love the Bomb, 213
Dr. T and the Women, 388
Dracula, 67, 141, 194, 205, 391
Dracula: Dead and Loving It, 446
Draughtsman's Contract, The, 209, 215
Dream of a Rarebit Fiend, 14
Dream of Light, 273
Dreamlife of Angels, The, 248
Dreams, 318
Dreyer, Carl-Theodor, 254–255
Drive, She Said, 238
Driving Miss Daisy, 437, 438
Drunken Master, 345
Duchamp, Marcel, 115, 243
Duel in the Sun, 274
Duellists, The, 215
Dukakis, Olympia, 261
Duke, Bill, 467
Dulac, Germaine, 113, 116
Dumont, Bruno, 248
Dunaway, Faye, 286, 386
Dune, 453

Dunne, Irene, 142
Dunne, Philip, 367–368
Dunye, Cheryl, 464
Dupont, E. A., 59, 66
Duras, Marguerite, 226–227, 236, 237, 238
Duryea, Dan, 153
Dutt, Guru, 335
Duvall, Shelley, 388
Dyer, Richard, 371

Ealing Studios, 196, 198, 206, 216
Early Summer, 321
Earrings of Madame de . . . , The, 223
Earth, 75–76, 77, 303, 339
East of Eden, 350
Eastern Europe (films made in), 280–281, 306–307. **See also** Czechoslovakia; Hungary; Poland; Yugoslavia
Eastwood, Clint, 448
Easy Rider, 384
Easy Street, 43
Eat, Drink, Man, Woman, 350
Eclipse, The, 171, 177
Ed Wood, 446
Eddy, Nelson, 138
editing (of films), 85, 92–93
Edison, Thomas Alva, 2, 3, 4, 5–6, 10, 105
Edison Company, 2, 38, 45, 47
Educating Rita, 214
Edward Scissorhands, 446
Edwards, Blake, 463
Eel, The, 325
Eggeling, Viking, 54
Egoyan, Atom, 424–425
Eight Men Out, 457, 458
8½, 171, 174, 176, 280
Eisenstein, Sergei, 37, 74, 75, 76, 78, 79–83, 85, 86, 172, 178, 179, 231, 232, 305
Eisner, Lotte, 58
Eisner, Michael, 436
Él, 414
Elephant Man, The, 453
Elizabeth, 215, 339
Elsaesser, Thomas, 262
Elvira Madigan, 260
Emigrants, The, 260
Emperor and the Assassin, The, 343
Emperor's Nightingale, The, 296
Empire, 399
Empire of Passion, 326
Empire of the Sun, 450
End of St. Petersburg, The, 78, 84
End of the Affair, The, 207
English, Fred Karno, 43
English Patient, The, 145, 193, 215–216
Enigma, 215
Enjo, 322, 323
Enoch Arden, 18, 20
Enter the Dragon, 345
Entr'acte, 116
Entre nous, 244
Ephron, Nora, 462–463
Epstein, Jean, 113, 270
Eraserhead, 453
Erice, Victor, 271, 272–273
Ericson, Leif, 370
Eroica, 283

Esquivel, Laura, 414
Estrada, Luis, 414–415
E.T.—The Extra-Terrestrial, 450
Eureka, 208
Europa, Europa, 287, 288
Europe (films made in). **See** Eastern Europe; Western Europe
Europe 51, 173
Eustache, Jean, 247
Eve's Bayou, 467–468
Even Dwarfs Started Small, 267
Everett, Rupert, 464
Every Day Except Christmas, 200
Every Man for Himself, 242
Everything for Sale, 285
Eviction, The, 98
Evita, 211
Ex-Convict, The, 98
Excalibur, 206
Execution of Mary Queen of Scots, The, 101
eXistenZ, 424
Exterminating Angel, The, 270, 271
Eyes Wide Shut, 213

Faat Kine, 417
Fábri, Zoltán, 291
Face-Off, 345
Faces, 394
fade out/fade in, 18
Fahrenheit 451, 207
Fairbanks, Douglas, 44, 47, 88, 101, 141
Falcons, The, 291
Fall of Babylon, The, 36
Fall of the House of Usher, The, 142
Fall of Troy, The, 22
Fallen Angel, 152
Fallen Angels, 347
Fallen Idol, 194
False Movement, 268
Family Game, 327–328
Family Life, 203, 286
Fanny, 118
Fanny and Alexander, 258–259, 447
Fantômas, 20
Far from the Madding Crowd, 207
Faraway, So Close, 269
Färberböck, Max, 269
Farewell, 302
Farewell My Concubine, 343
Fargo, 456
Farrelly Brothers, 446–447
Farrow, Mia, 448
Fassbinder, Rainer Werner, 51, 262, 265–266
Fast Times at Ridgemont High, 460
Fata Morgana, 267
Fatal Attraction, 211, 437
Father of the Bride, 375
Faustus Faustus Faustus [series], 292
Fawlty Towers, 216
Fear and Desire, 213
Federico Fellini's Interview, 177
Feeding the Baby, 2
Feininger, Lyonel, 52
Fellini, Federico, 161, 163, 166, 169–170, 171, 172,

173–177, 178, 180, 183, 189, 234, 280, 285, 363, 391
Fellini Satyricon, 173–174
Fellini's Casanova, 173–174
Fellini's Roma, 174
feminism, 400–401, 469. **See also** women's films
Femme de nulle part, La, 113
Femme douce, Un, 225
Femme infidèle, La, 234
Femme Nikita, La, 247
Ferera, Abel, 459
Ferreri, Marco, 187
Feuillade, Louis, 20, 247
Fiancés, The, 170, 180–181
Field, Connie, 400
Fields, W. C., 142
Fiennes, Ralph, 292, 422
Fièvre, 113
Figgis, Mike, 211, 440
Fighting Mad, 448
Figuroa, Gabriel, 414
Film about a Woman Who . . . , A, 401
film noir, 67, 152–154
films d'art, 21, 22, 71, 113
Finian's Rainbow, 390, 392
Finney, Albert, 200
Fiorile, 187
Fire! 14, 339
Firemen's Ball, The, 294, 295, 296
Fires on the Plain, 323
Fires Were Started, 195
First Name: Carmen, 243
First Wives Club, The, 463
First Years, The, 412
Fish Called Wanda, A, 215–216, 447
Fisher, Lucy, 460
Fisher, Terrence, 204–205
Fists in the Pocket, 186
Fitzcarraldo, 267
Five Boys from Barska Street, 282
Flaherty, Robert, 195, 197, 232, 335, 395
Flaming Creatures, 397
Flaming Youth, 99
Flashdance, 137, 211
Flesh and the Devil, 145
Flirting with Disaster, 447, 459
Flowers of Shanghai, 348–349
Fly, The, 424
Flying Down to Rio, 140
Folie du Docteur Tube, La, 113–114
Fonda, Henry, 137
Fonda, Peter, 384
Fons, Jorge, 414–415
Fool's Paradise, 93
Foolish Wives, 42, 94, 95
For Better or Worse, 93
For Ladies Only, 99
Forbidden Fruit, 93
Forbidden Paradise, 96
Ford, Aleksander, 282
Ford, Harrison, 418–420, 441
Ford, John, 97, 132, 136–137, 221, 315, 335, 370
foreign films. **See specific countries**
Foreman, Carl, 370
Forman, Miloš, 294, 295 297
formula pictures, 46–47
Forrest Gump, 452
Forsyth, Bill, 194, 198

42nd Street, 138, 139, 140
Fosse, Bob, 231
Foster, Jodie, 393, 444, 449, 462
Four Feathers, The, 340
Four Friends, 386
400 Blows, The, 227, 228, 233
Four Nights of a Dreamer, 225
Four Weddings and a Funeral, 215–216
Fox, Michael J., 423
Fox, William, 67, 88, 106, 109
Fox Film Corporation, 88, 90, 106, 460
Foxy Brown, 384
Frampton, Hollis, 400
France (films made in), 112–126, 220–252
    actors in, 120
    American influence on, 221, 225, 244
    auter movement, 220–222
    directors of, 231–241
    documentaries, 245–246
    film length and, 20–21, 26
    genres of, 246
    Golden Age of, 117–125
    government support of, 225–226
    impressionism, 113–114
    Left Bank movement, 236–241
    New Wave movement, 220, 222, 225–236, 243–244, 248
    pure cinema, 115–117, 120
    social/political events and, 119, 221, 225, 241–242, 243–244, 247–248
    sound in, 116, 117
    techniques used in, 228–231
Franju, Georges, 125, 226
Frankenheimer, John, 356–357
Frankenstein, 67, 141–142, 194, 391, 399
Franklin, Carl, 462, 467
Fraser, Ronald, 200
Frears, Stephen, 203, 204
Fred Ott's Sneeze, 38
Frederick, Pauline, 47
Freed, Arthur, 140, 372–373
French Lieutenant's Woman, The, 210–211
Frend, Charles, 193, 196
Fresh, 467
Freshman, The, 98
Freund, Karl, 62, 66–67
Freyermuth, Ortwin, 269
Frida, 414
Friedrich, Sue, 40
Full Body Massage, 208
Full Metal Jacket, 442
Full Monty, The, 216
Full Moon in Paris, 235–236
Fuller, Samuel, 221
Fun in a Chinese Laundry, 3, 38
Funeral, The, 328, 329
Furie, Sidney J., 194
Fuses, 400–401

Gaál, István, 291
Gabbeh, 428–429
Gabin, Jean, 120, 121
Gable, Clark, 128
Gabriel, Teshome, 465
Gai Savoir, Le, 242
Gallipoli, 418
Game of Cards, A, 5–6

Gance, Abel, 113–114, 220, 391–392
Gandhi, 214
Ganga Zumba, 405
gangster films, 140–141, 221, 231, 324, 344, 386
Gans, Christopher, 245
Ganz, Bruno, 268–269
Garbo, Greta, 59, 65, 144–145, 254, 375
Gardens of Stone, 442
Garland, Judy, 375
Garner, James, 357
Garnett, Tay, 109
Gas Food Lodging, 461–462
Gas Masks, 80
Gate of Hell, 313, 314
Gatwik, Ritwik, 335
Gaucho Nobility, 20
gay and lesbian films, 463–465, 469
Gedeon, Sasa, 297
Geffen, David, 436
Gehr, Ernie, 400
General, The, 98, 206
General della Rover, 170
General Line, The, 83
Generation, A, 284
Genesis, 337
Genevieve, 196
Gentlemen Prefer Blondes, 359, 373
Gere, Richard, 318
Gerima, Haile, 465
Gerlach, Arthur von, 63
Germi, Pietro, 162, 173, 183, 188
Germany (films made in), 51–69, 261–269
    actors in, 64–65, 265
    documentaries, 263
    emigration and, 66–68, 96
    New German Cinema, 261–269
    origins of, 51–52
    post–World War II era of, 254, 261–269
    social/political events and, 51–52, 60, 66
    Soviet influence on, 70–71
    techniques used in, 61–65
Germany, Pale Mother, 264, 269
Germany in Autumn, 263
Gershwin, George, 371, 372
Gershwin, Ira, 372
Gertrud, 255
Get on the Bus, 467, 468
Getino, Octavio, 409
Ghost Dog, 455
Ghostbusters, 438
Gibson, Hoot, 97
Gibson, Mel, 418, 420, 422, 441
Gielgud, John, 209
Gigi, 375
Gilal, Sergio, 405
Gilda, 152
Gilliam, Terry, 194, 211, 214, 443
Gilou, Thomas, 244–245
Gimme Shelter, 395
Ginger & Fred, 177
Gingerbread Man, The, 388
Girl, The, 293
Gish, Lillian, 27, 33, 35, 65, 256
Gladiator, 211, 436, 452

Glengarry Glen Ross, 456
globalization, 350–351, 362–363, 429, 440–441, 469–471
Gloria, 347, 394
Glover, Danny, 441, 465, 468
Go Fish, 464
Go Tell the Spartans, 442
Go-Between, The, 211–212
Goalie's Anxiety at the Penalty Kick, The, 268
Godard, Jean-Luc, 16, 225, 227–228, 229, 231–233, 234, 237, 242–244, 285, 299, 325, 337, 363, 384, 386, 391
Goddess, The, 336
Godfather, The [series], 140, 187–188, 348, 390–391
Gods and Monsters, 464
Gods Must Be Crazy, The, 415
Godzilla, 324
Gold Diggers [series], 139
Gold Rush, The, 98
Goldwyn, Samuel, 88, 99
Golem, The, 55, 56, 63, 141
Golovnya, Anatoli, 74
Gombrowicz, Witold, 282
Gomery, Douglas, 105
Gómez, Sara, 407
Gone With the Wind, 27, 366
Gong Li, 343–344
González, Alejandro, 414–415
Gonzàlez, Felipe, 274
Good Marriage, A, 235–236
Good Men, Good Women, 348
Good Morning, Vietnam, 442
Good, the Bad, and the Ugly, The, 187, 448
Goodbye, South, Goodbye, 348
GoodFellas, 140, 392
Goon Show, The, 212
Gordon, Ruth, 375
Gordon's War, 442
Goretta, Claude, 200
Gorin, Jean-Pierre, 242
Gospel According to St. Matthew, The, 182, 183
gothic fantasy films, 194, 204–210. **See also** horror films
Gould, Elliott, 388, 389
Grable, Betty, 359
Grace of My Heart, 461–462
Graduate, The, 384
Grand Illusion, The, 122–123, 124
Grande Bouffe, La, 187
Grandmother, The, 417
Grant, Cary, 133, 142, 144, 379
Grass, 101
Gray, Gary, 467–468
Great Britain (films made in), 193–219
    actors in, 194, 197, 200, 204
    American influence on, 193, 210–214, 215, 362–363
    distribution/exhibition of, 193, 215–216
    Free Cinema, 200–204
    genres of, 193–199, 204–210
    ratings of, 366
    social/political events and, 199–200, 203, 215–216
Great Expectations, 194
Great Train Robbery, The, 12–14, 17, 49, 61, 96, 120
Greed, 94, 95

Green Berets, 442
Green Card, 418–420
Greenaway, Peter, 205, 207, 209
Greene, Graham, 194
Gregory's Girl, 198, 214
Grey Car, The, 20
Grey Gardens, 395, 396
Grido, Il, 177
Grier, Pam, 384, 459
Grierson, John, 194–196, 405, 423
Griffith, David Wark (D. W.), 15–20, 23, 27–38, 39, 40, 42, 44, 46, 61, 62, 64, 65, 71, 76, 78, 86, 88, 91, 101–103, 113, 231, 463
Griffith, Richard, 135
Grifters, The, 204
Grim Reaper, The, 184
Grotowski, Jerzy, 282
Groulx, Gilles, 424
Groundhog Day, 447
Gruault, Jean, 238
Grune, Karl, 58
Guelwaar, 417
Guerra, Ruy, 407
Guerre est finie, La, 237
Guillerman, John, 384
Guimba, the Tyrant, 417
Guinness, Alec, 197
Gun Fighter, The, 96
Guns, The, 407
Guns of Navarone, The, 360
Guy, Alice, 15
Guzman, Patricio, 412

Hackman, Gene, 391
Hagen, Jean, 372–373
Hail, Mary, 243
Hail the Conquering Hero, 144
Haine, La, 248
Hair, 297
Hallelujah! 110
Hallström, Lasse, 260
Hamburger Hill, 442
Hamilton, Linda, 444
Hamlet, 194
Hammer, Barbara, 400–401
Hammett, 391
Hammett, Dashell, 154
Handmaid's Tale, The, 263
Hands Over the City, 170, 181
Hanks, Tom, 451, 464
Hannah and Her Sisters, 447, 448
Hannam, Ken, 418
Hanoi Hilton, The, 442
Hanson, Einar, 59
Happiness, 459
Happy Together, 347
Harakiri, 324
Hard-Boiled, 345
Hard Day's Night, A, 212, 248
Hardy, Edith, 92
Hardy, Oliver, 42, 98
Harlan County, USA, 395, 397
Harlow, Jean, 142
Harmetz, Aljean, 151
Harris, Richard, 200
Harron, Mary, 461–462
Hart, William S., 46, 96
Hartley, Hal, 459
Has, Wojcieck, 286
Hathaway, Henry, 152
Haunted Castle, The, 8
Hawks, Howard, 132, 133–134, 136, 142, 152, 221, 370, 373, 376

Hawks and the Sparrows, The, 182
Hayakawa, Sessue, 92
Hayek, Salma, 413–414
Haynes, Todd, 463–464
Hays, Will, 105, 131
He Got Game, 467
Hearts of Glass, 267
Heaven and Earth, 452
Heaven's Gate, 438
Heche, Anne, 464
Hecht, Ben, 144
Heckerling, Amy, 460
Hedren, Tippi, 379
Heflin, Van, 371
Hegedus, Chris, 395
Heimat [series], 269
Heist, 457
Help! 212, 248
Henreid, Paul, 146
Henry and June, 366
Henry Fool, 459
Henry IV, 157
Henry V, 194
Hepburn, Katharine, 128, 142, 144, 147, 375
Hepworth, Cecil, 14–15
Herbier, Marcel L', 113
heritage films, 246, 260
Hermann, Bernard, 379
Hermann, Irm, 265
Hermosillo, Jaime Humberto, 415
Herod's Law, 414–415
Herzog, Werner, 262, 265, 266–267, 269
High and Dry, 196
High and Low, 315
High Art, 464
High Fidelity, 204
High Hopes, 198
High Noon, 370, 371
Higher Learning, 467
Hiroshima, mon amour, 226–227, 237, 238
His Girl Friday, 142
His Trust, 20
Histoire(s) du cinéma, 243
History Lessons, 265
Hitchcock, Alfred, 194, 208, 221, 233, 234, 357, 375, 379
Hoaxters, The, 367
Hoffman, Dustin, 263
Holden, William, 376–377, 387
Holland, Agnieska, 286, 287, 391
Holliday, Judy, 375
Holloway, Stanley, 197
Hollywood Revue of 1929, The, 137–138
Holy Smoke, 421
Holy Week, 286
Home Alone, 438
Home and the World, The, 336–337
Home for the Holidays, 462
Home from the Hill, 375
Homicide, 456
Honda, Ishiro, 324
Hondo, Med, 417
Honey I Shrunk the Kids, 438
Hong Kong (films made in), 340, 341, 344–347
Hook, 450
Hoop Dreams, 395
Hope and Glory, 206
Hopper, Dennis, 384

Horne, Denis, 200
horror films, 67, 141–142, 194, 221, 286, 424
Horse Thief, The, 342
Hou Hsiao-hsien, 348–349
Hour of the Furnaces, The, 409–410
Hours and Times, The, 463–464
House of Games, 456
House of Youth, The, 99
House Party, 467
House Un-American Activities Committee (HUAC), 367–370
How Tasty Was My Little Frenchman, 408–409
How to Marry a Millionaire, 359
Howard, Ron, 443–444
Hsiao-hsien, Hou. **See** Hou Hsiao-hsien
Hu, King. **See** King Hu
Hudlin, Reginald and Warrington, 467
Hudson, Hugh, 214
Hudson, Rock, 377–378
Hudsucker Proxy, The, 456
Hue and Cry, 196, 197
Hughes, Allen and Albert, 467
Hui, Ann, 346
Huillet, Danièle, 264–265
Human Beast, The, 124
Human Condition, The [trilogy], 323
Humanité, L', 248
Hungarian Rhapsody, 291
Hungary (films made in), 281, 290–293, 306
Hunt, The, 272
Hunter, Holly, 424
Hunter, Ross, 377–378
Hurry, Hurry, 272
Hurt, William, 409
Husárik, Zoltán, 291
Husbands and Wives, 448
Husbands for Rent, 99
Huston, John, 152, 153–154, 193, 335, 367–368, 440
Hypothesis of the Stolen Painting, 413

I Am Curious, 299
I Can't Sleep, 248
I Even Met Happy Gypsies, 299, 301
I Live in Fear, 332
I Shot Andy Warhol, 461–462
I, the Worst of All, 410–412
I Vitelloni, 173
I Walked with a Zombie, 142
I Was a Communist for the F.B.I., 367
Ice Storm, 35
Ichikawa, Kon, 322–323
Ideal Husband, An, 215
Identification Marks: None, 286
Identification of a Woman, 177
Idiots, The, 260, 315
If . . . , 118, 202
Ikiru, 313, 315, 316–317
Illumination, 286
Images, 388
Imamura, Shohei, 324–325
Imitation of Life, 378–379
Immigrant, The, 43
Impossible Voyage, An, 8
In Search of Famine, 337
In the Company of Men, 459

In the Mood for Love, 347
In the Name of the Father, 184, 186
In the Name of the Law, 173
In the Realm of the Senses, 325, 326, 327
Inagaki, Hiroshi, 314
Ince, Thomas H., 27, 46, 48, 91, 96, 113
Independence Day, 437
India (films made in), 332–340
actors in, 333
genres of, 333
New Indian Cinema, 337–340
social/political events and, 333, 334–335, 337
television and, 337
India Song, 238
Indiana Jones [series], 438, 449–450
Indochine, 246
Industrial Britain, 195
Ingeborg Holm, 255
Innocence Unprotected, 299
Insect Woman, The, 326
Insignificance, 215
Interiors, 448
internationalization, 350–351, 362–363, 429, 440–441, 469–471
Interview with the Vampire, 207
Intimate Lighting, 295
Intolerance, 20, 27, 28, 34–38, 44, 76, 78, 83, 101, 254
Invention for Destruction, An, 296
Invisible Man, The, 142
Ipcress File, The, 194
Iran (films made in), 404, 426–429
irises, 18
Irma Vep, 247
Iron Horse, The, 97
Is It Easy to Be Young? 302–303
It Happened One Night, 142
It Wasn't Love, 464
It's a Wonderful Life, 135–136, 439
Italy (films made in), 161–192
actors in, 165, 167
directors of, 166–168, 170–182
film length and, 22–23, 26
genres of, 188–189
neorealism, 163–179
neo-neorealism, 180–182
social/political events and, 161–163, 168–169, 172, 182–183
techniques used in, 165–166
Itami, Juzo, 328
Ivan the Terrible, 83
Ivan's Childhood, 304
Ivory, James, 194
Iwerks, Ub, 149–150

Jackie Brown, 457, 459
Jackal of Nahueltoro, The, 412
Jackson, Samuel L., 384, 459, 468
Jagger, Mick, 207
Jailor of Panama, The, 206
Jakubowska, Wanda, 282
Jalousie, 171
James, Steven, 395
James Bond [series], 194

Jamòn, Jamòn, 274–275
Jancsó, Miklós, 291–292
Janie's Janie, 400
Jannings, Emil, 59, 65, 66
Janowitz, Hans, 54
Jao, Steven, 345
Japan (films made in), 312–331
 directors of, 315–325
 distribution/exhibition of, 329
 documentaries, 323
 genres of, 312–313, 315, 324
 New Wave, 324–325
 origins of, 312
 social/political events and, 312–313
 studio system and, 312, 327
 techniques used in, 313–315, 319–321
 television and, 327
Jarman, Derek, 207, 463
Jarmusch, Jim, 454–455
Jaws, 435, 437, 438, 449
Jazz Singer, The, 106, 107, 137
Je t'aime, je t'aime, 237
Jeanne Dielman, 23 Quai de Commerce, 1080 Bruxelles, 239, 240
Jeanson, Henri, 120
Jennings, Humphrey, 196
Jerry Maguire, 437, 446
Jerusalem, 260–261
Jessel, George, 106
Jesus of Montreal, 425
Jetée, La, 238
Jewison, Norman, 356–357, 423
JFK, 451, 452
Jin, Xie. See Xie Jin
Joffe, Roland, 215
Joffroy, 363
Johnny Guitar, 274
Johnson, Julia Migenes, 182
Johnson, Magic, 468
Johnston, Eric, 366, 368
Joli mai, Le, 238, 240
Jollies, 464
Jones, Buck, 97
Jonze, Spike, 464
Jordan, Neil, 205, 207
Josephson, Erland, 304
Jour de fête, 222
Jour se lève, Le, 120, 121
Journey to Primeval Times, A, 296
Jouvet, Louis, 120
Joyce, James, 231
Joyce at 34, 400–401
Joyless Street, The, 58, 59, 65
Ju Dou, 343
Judex, 20
Judith of Bethulia, 20, 27, 28
Jules and Jim, 229, 233, 234
Julia, Raul, 409
Julien, Isaac, 207, 463
Juliet of the Spirits, 171
Jungle Fever, 467
Jurado, Katy, 413–414
Jurassic Park, 439, 450
Just Before Nightfall, 234
Jutra, Claude, 425
juvenile delinquency films, 370, 373–374, 383

Kadár, Ján, 294, 297
Kagemusha, 317, 318
Kaige, Chen. See Chen Kaige
Kaiser, Georg, 52

Kalin, Tom, 463–464
Kama Sutra, 339
Kaminski, Janusz, 290
Kanal, 284
Kanchanjungha, 336–337
Kandinsky, Vasily, 52
Kanin, Garson, 375
Kaplan, Jonathan, 463
Kapoor, Prithviraj, 333
Kapoor, Raj, 333–334
Kapur, Shakhar, 215, 339–340
Karina, Anna, 231, 232
Karmitz, Martin, 289
Kassovitz, Matthew, 246, 248
Katzelmacher, 265
Katzenberg, Jeffrey, 436, 445
Kaul, Mani, 337
Kawalerowicz, Jerzy, 286
Kaye, Danny, 98, 368
Kazan, Elia, 360, 369–370, 440
Keaton, Buster, 42, 97–98
Keitel, Harvey, 292, 392
Kelly, Gene, 140, 221, 368, 371, 372, 373
Kelly, Grace, 379
Kerkorian, Kirk, 383, 435–436
Kes, 203
Kessel, Adam, 42–43
Key Largo, 154
key light, 62
Keystone comedies, 38–39, 42, 43
Khan, Mehboob, 333, 335
Kiarostami, Abbas, 427–428
Kid, The, 98
Kieślowski, Krzysztof, 288–289
Killer, The, 345–346
Killer of Sheep, 465
Killer's Kiss, 213
Killers, The, 152
Killing, The, 213
Killing Fields, The, 215
Kimia'i, Mas'ud, 427
Kind Hearts and Coronets, 197
Kind of Loving, A, 200
Kinder, Marsha, 274
Kinetoscope, 2, 3, 38
King, Stephen, 213
King and Country, 211–212
King Hu, 345
King Lear, 243, 315, 318
King of Kings, The, 93–94, 103
King of the Children, 343
Kingdom, The, 260
Kings of the Road, 268
Kino-Pravda [series], 73, 74, 246
Kinugasa, Teinosuke, 313
Kiss Me Deadly, 152
Kiss of Death, 152
Kiss of the Spider Woman, 409
Klee, Paul, 52
Klein, Jim, 400
Klimov, Elem, 301–302
Kline, Kevin, 350, 447
Klos, Elmar, 294
Kluge, Alexander, 262, 263
Knife in the Water, 286
Knight, Shirley, 212
Kobayashi, Masaki, 322, 323–324
Kolya, 297
Kombrig Ivanov, 72
Kovács, András, 291
Kozintsev, Grigori, 74

Kracauer, Siegfried, 4, 58, 60, 66, 67, 70
Kragh-Jacobsen, Soren, 260
Kramer, Stanley, 370
Krauss, Werner, 65
Kriemhild's Revenge, 53
Krishnaswamy, S., 333
Kristin Lavanstdatter, 260
Kubrick, Stanley, 194, 211, 213–214, 304
Kuleshov, Lev, 74, 76, 77, 78, 83–84
Kundun, 392
Kureishi, Hanif, 204
Kurosawa, Akira, 313, 314, 315–318, 319, 320, 322, 332
Kurys, Diane, 244
Kusturica, Emir, 300–301
Kwan, Stanley, 346
Kyo, Machiko, 313, 314

La Cava, Gregory, 142–144
L.A. Confidential, 154
La Fête espanole, 113
Laborit, Henri, 237
LaBute, Neil, 459
Ladd, Alan, 371
Ladd, Diane, 461
Lady Eve, The, 144
Lady from Shanghai, The, 157
Lady Vanishes, The, 194
Lady Windermere's Fan, 96
Ladybird, Ladybird, 203
Ladykillers, The, 196, 197
Laemmle, Carl, 88
Lamerica, 184, 188
Lancaster, Burt, 172
Lancelot of the Lake, 225
Land and Freedom, 203
Land Without Bread, 270
Landau, Martin, 446
Landow, George, 400
Landscape after Battle, 285
Lang, Fritz, 53, 54, 63, 64, 66, 67, 152, 153, 221, 232, 234
Lang, Jack, 244, 246
Langdon, Harry, 42, 97–98
Langlois, Henri, 125, 241
Lansing, Sherry, 460
Lanzman, Claude, 245
Lardner, Ring, Jr., 368
Last Command, The, 107
Last Days of Chez Nous, The, 422
Last Days of Pompeii, The, 22
Last Emperor, The, 185–186, 469–470
Last Laugh, The, 55, 61, 62, 63, 65, 67
Last Metro, The, 234
Last of the Mohicans, The, 97
Last Stage, The, 285
Last Tango in Paris, 184, 185
Last Temptation of Christ, The, 243, 392
Last Tycoon, The, 91
Last Wave, The, 418, 420
Last Year at Marienbad, 229, 230, 237, 296
Late Autumn, 321, 322
Late Spring, 321
Latin America (films made in), 404–415, 429. See also Argentina; Brazil; Chile; Cuba; Mexico
 artistic basis of, 404–405
 documentaries, 409–410

 government support of, 406, 407
 Italian influence on, 405
 social/political events and, 405
Latino films, 468
Lattuada, Alberto, 173
Laura, 152
Laurel, Stan, 42, 98
Lavender Hill Mob, The, 196, 197, 216
Law and Order, 397, 398
Lawrence of Arabia, 360, 362
Lawson, John Howard, 368, 370
L.B.J., 406
Lean, David, 194
Learning Tree, The, 384
Léaud, Jean-Pierre, 227, 234, 247
Leaves from Satan's Book, 254, 255
Leaving Las Vegas, 211
Leconte, Patrice, 246
Leduc, Paul, 414
Lee, Ang, 350–351
Lee, Bruce, 344–345
Lee, Christopher, 205
Lee, Spike, 465–467, 468
Leenhardt, Roger, 220, 225
Left-Handed Gun, The, 386
Legend of Sleepy Hollow, The, 445–446
Legend of the Holy Drinker, The, 181
Legend of the Mountain, 345
Legend of the Suram Fortress, The, 304
Legends of Rita, 263
Léger, Fernand, 115
Legion of the Condemned, The, 100
Lehar, Franz, 137
Leigh, Mike, 194, 198–199
Leisen, Mitchell, 152
Lemmon, Jack, 377
Lemmons, Kasi, 467–468
length (of films), 20–23
Leni, Paul, 54, 66
Lenin, V. I., 71, 72
Leone, Sergio, 187–188, 448
Leopard, The, 172, 174
Leopard's Spots, The, 28
LeRoy, Mervyn, 141, 373
lesbian films, 463–465, 469
Lester, Richard, 194, 207, 211, 212, 213, 248
Letter, The, 149
Letter from an Unknown Woman, 223
Letter from Siberia, 238
Letters from Marusia, 405
Lethal Weapon [series], 441
Levring, Kristian, 260
Lewis, Jerry, 98
Lewton, Val, 142
Li, Gon. See Gong Li
Lianna, 457
Liehm, Mira, 184
Lies My Father Told Me, 297
Life and Times of Rosie the Riveter, The, 400–401
Life Is Beautiful, 184, 189, 275
Life Is Sweet, 198
Life of an American Fireman, 10–12, 74
Life of O'Haru, The, 318
Life on a String, 343
Lifeboat, 152

lighting (of films), 19, 62–63, 92, 93
Lightning Over Water, 268
Lights of New York, The, 107, 108
Like Water for Chocolate, 414
Lilac Time, 100
Lili Marleen, 266
Lin, Brigitte, 347
Linder, Max, 38
Ling-yu, Ryan, 346
Lion King, The, 438, 445
Lion's Love, 238
Lionsgate, 439
Liotta, Ray, 392
Lisztomania, 215
Littin, Miguel, 405, 412
Little Big Man, 386
Little Buddha, 186
Little Caesar, 140, 141
Little Foxes, The, 149
Little Man Tate, 462
Little Mermaid, The, 445
Little Vera, 303
Little Women, 422
Littlewood, Joan, 200
Lives of a Bengal Lancer, 148
Lives of Performers, 401
Living End, The, 463–464
Livingston, Jennie, 463
Lloyd, Harold, 42, 97–98
Loach, Ken, 194, 203–204
Local Hero, 198
location shooting, 86, 110, 362
Lock, Stock, and Two Smoking Barrels, 216
Loew, Marcus, 88
Lola Montèz, 223–224
Lolita, 97, 213
Lombard, Carole, 142
Lone, John, 470
Lone Eagle, The, 100
Lone Star, 457
Loneliness of the Long-Distance Runner, The, 201, 202
Lonesome Cowboys, 399, 400
Long Goodbye, The, 387–388
Long Live the Lady! 181
long shot, 16
Longest Day, The, 360
Look Back in Anger, 200, 201
Look Who's Talking, 460
Looking for Langston, 463
Loos, Anita, 373
Lorentz, Pare, 127, 370, 395
Losey, Joseph, 194, 211–212, 213
Lost Honor of Katharina Blum, The, 263
Lost Lost Lost, 398
Lost Ones, The, 414
Lost World, The, 450
Love, 291
Love Affair, or The Case of the Missing Switchboard Operator, 299
Love and Anarchy, 187
Love at Twenty, 234
Love in the Afternoon, 377
Love Is a Many-Splendored Thing, 362
Love Me Tonight, 138
Love on the Run, 234
Love Parade, The, 138
Love Streams, 394
Love, the Magician, 272
Lovers, The, 226

Lovers of the Arctic Circle, 274–275
Lovers on the Bridge, 247
Loves of a Blonde, 294
low-key lighting, 19, 62
Lower Depths, The, 315
Lozano, María, 275
Lubitsch, Ernst, 52, 53, 66, 95–96, 138, 142, 376
Lucas, George, 392, 439, 443–444
Lucía, 407
Ludendorff, Erich, 60
Ludwig, 172
Lugosi, Bela, 205, 446
Luis Borges, Jorges, 208
Luis Cuerda, José, 274–275
Lumière, Louis and Auguste, 2, 3, 5–6, 7, 105
Luna, La, 185
Lunacharsky, A. V., 71
Lunda, Bigas, 274–275
Lust for Life, 375
Lynch, David, 453–454
Lynd, Laurie, 464
Lyne, Adrian, 211

M, 67, 153
M. Butterfly, 424
Ma vie en rose, 246, 247
Macbeth, 157, 315
MacDonald, Jeannette, 138
MacDowell, Andie, 418–420
machismo, 406–407
Mackendrick, Alexander, 196, 197
Mackenzie, Compton, 197
MacLaine, Shirley, 463
MacPhail, Angus, 197
Macunaima, 408
Mad Max [series], 417–418
Mad Whirl, The, 99
Madadayo, 318
Madame Bovary, 122
Madame du Barry, 52, 53, 96
Madden, John, 216
Maddin, Guy, 424
Made in USA, 242
Madonna, 461
Maggie, The, 196
Magician, The, 258
Magnani, Anna, 161, 163, 363
Magnificent Ambersons, The, 391
Magnificent Seven, The, 315
Mahanagar, 337
Mahler, 215
Major Barbara, 256
Major Dundee, 386
Makavejev, Dušan, 299–300
Makhmalbaf, Mohsen, 428–429
Makhmalbaf, Samira, 429
Makk, Károly, 291
Malcolm X, 467
Maldorer, Sarah, 417
Male and Female, 93
Male Noche, 463
Malick, Terrence, 452–453
Malle, Louis, 226, 236, 239–240, 263
Malone, Dorothy, 378
Maltese Falcon, The, 152, 154, 439
Maltz, Albert, 368
Mamet, David, 456–457
Mamoulian, Rouben, 109, 138, 145
Man Escaped, A, 225, 226

Man Facing Southeast, 410–411
Man from Laramie, The, 370
Man from Snowy River, The, 418
Man in the Moon, The, 297
Man in the White Suit, The, 196, 197
Man Is Not a Bird, 299
Man of Aran, 197
Man of Iron, 285–286
Man of Marble, 285, 286
Man on the Track, 283
Man Who Envied Women, The, 401
Man Who Fell to Earth, The, 208
Man Who Knew Too Much, The, 379
Man with the Golden Arm, The, 365–366
Mancuso, Frank, 436
Manhattan, 447, 448
Mankiewicz, Herman J., 155–156
Mankiewicz, Joseph, 163
Mann, Anthony, 221, 370
Mansfield Park, 215
Manslaughter, 93
Manthan, 338
María Candelaria, 414
Mariachi, El, 468
Marianne and Julianne, 264
Marie, Lisa, 446
Marin, "Cheech," 468
Marius, 118
Mark of Zorro, The, 101
Marker, Chris, 214, 226, 236, 238, 242, 243–244
Marquise of O . . . , The, 235
Marriage Circle, The, 96
Marriage of Maria Braun, The, 265–266
Married Woman, A, 363
Mars Attacks! 445–446
Marseillaise, La, 124
Marsh, Mae, 37, 65
Marshall, Gary, 462–463
martial arts films, 344–345
Martin, Steve, 375, 447
Marty, 356
Marx Brothers, 142
Mary Shelley's Frankenstein, 391
M*A*S*H*, 387–388
Masina, Giulietta, 170, 174
masking, 18
Masque of the Red Death, The, 142
Mastroianni, Marcello, 175–176, 177, 413
Matewan, 457
Matrix, The, 438, 439, 443, 444
Mattei Affair, The, 181–182
Maura, Carmen, 273
Mauvaises rencontres, Les, 226
Mayer, Carl, 54, 58, 65, 163
Mayer, Louis B., 362, 368
Maynard, Ken, 97
Maysles, Albert, 395
Maysles, David, 395
Mazetti, Lorenzo, 200
McBride, Joseph, 134
McCabe and Mrs. Miller, 387–388, 389
McCarey, Leo, 109, 144, 368
McCord, Ted, 360
McCoy, Tim, 97

McDormand, Frances, 456
McGillis, Kelly, 420
McGuire, Dorothy, 359
McLaren, Norman, 150, 424
McNamara, Maggie, 359, 365
McQueen, Steve, 357
Mean Streets, 392
Mechanics of the Brain, 71
Medea, 182
Medem, Julio, 274–275
Medium Cool, 384
medium shot, 16
Meet John Doe, 135
Meet Me in St. Louis, 140, 375
Mehrju, Dariush, 427
Mehta, Deepa, 339
Mekas, Jonas, 397, 398
Méliès, Georges, 6–9, 10, 16, 18, 20, 21, 38, 40, 118
Mélo, 237
Melville, Jean-Pierre, 226, 227, 231, 263
Melvin and Howard, 448
Memories of Underdevelopment, 406–407
Memory of Justice, The, 245
Men Who Tread on the Tiger's Tail, The, 314
Menace II Society, 467
Menendez, Raymond, 468
Menjou, Adolphe, 368
Menzel, Jiří, 295, 297
Mephisto, 292
Mercer, David, 238
Merchant, Ismael, 194, 333
Merchant of the Four Seasons, The, 265
Merry Widow, The, 94, 137, 138
Merry Wives of Windsor, The, 157
Merry-Go-Round, 58, 291
Meshes of the Afternoon, 397, 399
Mészáros, Márta, 292, 293
Method actors/acting, 197, 212, 373–374, 394
Metro-Goldwyn-Mayer (M-G-M), 46, 67, 88, 90, 91, 107, 128–129, 138, 140, 150, 216, 361, 362, 371–372, 373, 375, 382, 418, 435–436, 438
Metropolis, 53, 64, 153
Mexican Bus Ride, A, 414
Mexico (films made in), 404, 413–415
Meyerhold, Vsevolod, 79
Meyers, Mike, 423
Mia Familia, 392, 468
Micheaux, Oscar, 103
Michi, Maria, 161
Mickey One, 248, 386
Midaq Alley, 414–415
Middle East (films made in), 404. **See also** Iran
Midler, Bette, 447
Midnight, 376
Midnight Cowboy, 211
Midnight Express, 215, 451
Midsummer Night's Dream, A, 148
Miéville, Anne-Marie, 242
Mifune, 260
Mifune, Toshiro, 313, 317
Mighty Aphrodite, 448
Mikhalkov, Milcho, 307
Mikhalkov, Nikita, 305–306

Milagro Beanfield War, The, 468

Mildred Pierce, 146, 147

Milestone, Lewis, 110

Mill on the Po, 173

Miller, George, 417–418

Miller's Crossing, 456

Million, Le, 118

Minbo; or, the Gentle Art of Japanese Exploitation, 328, 329

Mineo, Sal, 374

Minghella, Anthony, 216, 464

Minha, Trinh, 401

Minnelli, Vincente, 140, 221, 372, 373, 375

Minnie and Moskowitz, 394

Mira, Briggitta, 265

Miracle, The, 243, 363–364

Miracle in Milan, 164

Miracle of Morgan's Creek, The, 144

Miracle on 34th Street, 439

Miramax, 184, 215, 453, 459

Mirror, The, 304

Mirsch, Walter, 439

mise-en-scène, 184, 186, 203, 248, 287, 307, 344, 378

Mishima, 392

Miss Mary, 410–412

Miss Nobody, 286

Mission, The, 215

Mission to Moscow, 367

Mississippi Burning, 211

Mississippi Marsala, 339

Missouri Breaks, The, 386

Mister Shome, 337

Mitchell, Thomas, 136

Mitry, Jean, 125

Mix, Tom, 97

Miyamoto, Nobuko, 328

Mizoguchi, Kenji, 313, 314, 315, 318–320, 322

Mo' Better Blues, 467

Moana, 101

Moby Dick, 193–194

Modern Romance, 446

Molinero, Eduoard, 246

Momma Don't Allow, 200

Mon Oncle, 222

Mon Oncle d'Amérique, 237, 238, 242–243

Mona Lisa, 207

Monika, 257

Monroe, Marilyn, 359, 373, 375

Monsieur Hire, 246

monster films, 324

montage, 80, 83–87

Montalban, Ricardo, 413–414

Montenegro, 300

Montenegro, Fernanda, 409

Monterey Pop, 395

Montgomery, Robert, 368

Monty Python [series], 214

Moon Is Blue, The, 365–366

Moon Is Down, The, 152

Moorhouse, Joselyn, 421

Moreau, Jeanne, 230

Moretti, Nanni, 189

Morgan, Michèle, 120, 121

Morin, Edgar, 246

Morita, Yoshimitsu, 327–328

Morocco, 132, 145

Morricone, Ennio, 187–188

Morrissey, Paul, 399–400

Moses and Aaron, 265

Mosquito Coast, The, 418–420

Motel Chronicles, 268

Mother, 37, 78, 84, 446

Mother and Son, 306

Mother and the Law, The, 33–34, 36

Mother and the Whore, The, 247

Mother India, 333

Mother Joan of the Angels, 286

Mothlight, 398

Motion Picture Association of America (MPAA), 105, 129, 363, 365, 366, 368

Motion Picture Producers and Distributors of America (MPPDA), 105, 129, 130, 131

Motion Picture Production Code, 131–132, 365–367

Moulin Rouge, 193–194

Movie, A, 397

moving camera, 61–62, 71

Mozhukhin, Ivan, 84

Mr. Deeds Goes to Town, 127, 134

Mr. Hulot's Holiday, 222

Mr. Klein, 95

Mr. Smith Goes to Washington, 127, 134, 135

Mrs. Miniver, 148

Mrs. Soffel, 422

Mughal-e-Azam, 333

Mulan, 437, 445

Müller, Robby, 267

Mulvey, Laura, 210

Munch, Christopher, 463–464

Munk, Andrzej, 283

Murder, My Sweet, 152, 153

Muriel, 237

Murnau, F. W., 55, 58, 66, 67, 178, 268

Murphy, Eddie, 447

Murphy, George, 368

Murray, Bill, 98, 446, 447

music (in films), 42, 104, 319–320, 333, 371, 379, 384, 389

Music Room, The, 337

musicals, 137–140, 221, 359, 360, 370, 371–373

Mutiny on the Bounty, 148

Mutual Film Corporation v. Ohio, 364

My American Grandson, 346

My Beautiful Laundrette, 204, 205, 215

My Brilliant Career, 420–421

My Darling Clementine, 137

My Fair Lady, 360, 376

My Family/Mia Familia, 392, 468

My Favorite Season, 245

My Life as a Dog, 260

My Life to Live, 229, 231–232, 233

My Little Chickadee, 143

My Man Godfrey, 144

My Night at Maud's, 235, 237

My Own Private Idaho, 463, 464

My Sex Life (Or, How to Get Into an Argument), 247

My Son John, 367

My Uncle Antoine, 425

My Way Home, 291

Mystéres du Château de Dés, Les, 116

Mystery of Kaspar Hauser, The, 267

Mystery Train, 455

Nabokov, Vladimir, 213

Naderi, Amir, 427

Naficy, Hamid, 427

Nagata, Masaichi, 313

Nair, Mira, 339

Naked, 198–199

Naked City, The, 185

Naked Lunch, 424

Naked Night, The, 257

Nanny, The, 184, 186

Nanook of the North, 101, 335, 395

Napoléon, 114, 391–392

Naremore, James, 455

Narrizanno, Silvio, 426

Naruse, Mikio, 318

Nashville, 387–388, 389

Natural Born Killers, 452

Naughty Marietta, 138

Nava, Gregory, 392, 468

Navigator, The, 98

Nazarín, 414

Negri, Pola, 52, 65, 67

Nehru, Jawaharlal, 333, 334–335

Neighbors, 424

Němec, Jan, 294, 296, 299

New Babylon, 104

New Faces, 138

New Jack City, 467

New Land, The, 260

New Year's Eve, 65

New York, New York, 392

New York Hat, The, 19

Newell, Mike, 215–216

Newman, David, 386

Newsfront, 420

Next Best Thing, The, 211

Nibelungen, Die, 53, 64

Niblo, Fred, 103

Nice Time, 200

Nichols, Dudley, 136, 144

Nichols, Mike, 246, 365, 384, 462

Nicholson, Jack, 286, 384

nickelodeons, 48–49

Nielsen, Asta, 59, 65, 254

Night and Fog, 237

Night at the Opera, A, 143

Night in Tunisia, A, 207

Night Moves, 386

Night Porter, The, 187

Night Sun, 186–187

Night of the Shooting Stars, The, 186, 187

Night on Earth, 455

Nightmare before Christmas, The, 445–446

Nights of Cabiria, The, 174, 175

Nimoy, Leonard, 246

Nine to Five, 447

1900, 184

Ninotchka, 376

Ninth Gate, The, 286

Niven, David, 365

Nixon, 451

No End, 288

No Greater Love, 323

Normand, Mabel, 47

North by Northwest, 379

North Star, The, 367

Nosferatu, 55, 57, 67, 141

Nostalgia, 304

Not One Less, 344

Not Reconciled, 265

Notari, Elvira, 166

Nothing Sacred, 144

Notorious, 379

Notte, La, 171, 177

Nouvelle Vague, 243

Novak, Kim, 379

Noyce, Phillip, 420, 422

Numéro deux, 242

Nurse Betty, 459

Nutty Professor, The, 438, 447

Nykvist, Sven, 257, 304

O Brother, Where Are Thou, 456

O Dreamland, 200

O Lucky Man! 202

O'Hara, Maureen, 147, 148

O'Toole, Peter, 470

October, 83

Odd Obsession, 323

Oedipus Rex, 182

Official Story, The, 410, 411

Ogre, The, 263

Old and New, 74, 83, 172

Old Arizona, 110

Old Czech Legends, 296

Old Wives for New, 93

Oliver Twist, 194

Olivier, Laurence, 194

Olivier Olivier, 287

Olmi, Ermanno, 170, 180–181, 294, 295

Olmos, Edward James, 468

Olvidados, Los, 270, 414

On the Town, 140

On the Waterfront, 369–370

Once Upon a Time, Cinema, 428

Once Upon a Time in America, 187–188

Once Upon a Time in the West, 187

One A.M., 43

One and a Two, A, 350

One and Eight, 342

One False Move, 467

One Fine Day, 181

One Flew Over the Cuckoo's Nest, 297, 438

One from the Heart, 391

One Glance, and Love Breaks Out, 264

One Sings, the Other Doesn't, 23

One True Thing, 462

One Way or Another, 407

One, Two, Three, 377

Only Angels Have Wings, 133, 134

Open City, 161–162, 163, 165, 166, 169, 173

Ophüls, Marcel, 222, 245

Ophüls, Max, 220, 222–223, 225, 226

Ordet, 255

Oriane, 415

Orlando, 210

Ornitz, Samuel, 368

Orphans of the Storm, 28, 103

Osaka Elegy, 318

Osborne, John, 200

Oscar and Lucinda, 422

Oscars. **See** Academy Awards

Oshima, Nagisa, 248, 324–326

Ossessione, 166, 172

Ostrovsky, Alexander, 79–80

Other Francisco, The, 405

Ottinger, Ulrcke, 264
Our Daily Bread, 337
Our Dancing Daughters, 99
Our Hitler, 391
Out of Sight, 459
Out of the Past, 152
Out One: Spectre, 234
Outcry, 164
Outlaw and His Wife, The, 255–256
Outlaw Josey Wales, The, 448
Outrage, The, 315
Outrageous Fortune, 447
overbuying, 130
Ozu, Yasujiro, 315, 320–322, 337

Pabst, G. W., 58, 67–68, 71
Pacino, Al, 391
Padre Padrone, 186
Pagliero, Marcello, 161
Pagnol, Marcel, 118, 363
Pahahi, Jafar, 427
Paint Your Wagon, 382
Paisan, 166, 167, 173
Palance, Jack, 371
Palcy, Euzhan, 244
Pale Flower, 326–327
Palm Beach Story, The, 144
Palmetto, 263
Palminteri, Chaz, 339
Pan Tadusz, 286
Panavision camera, 439, 447
panning and scanning, 439–440
Paradjanov, Sergei, 303–304
Parain, Brice, 233
Paramount Pictures/Studio, 67, 88, 89, 90, 95, 108, 138, 360, 361, 435, 436
Paris Is Burning, 463
Paris nous appartient, 234
Paris, Texas, 268
Parker, Alan, 211, 215, 451
Parks, Gordon, 384
Part-Time Work of a Domestic Slave, The, 263
Pasolini, Pier Paolo, 170, 182
Passenger, The, 171–172, 179, 282
Passer, Ivan, 295, 297
Passion, 52, 53, 96, 243
Passion Fish, 457
Passion of Anna, The, 258
Passion of Joan of Arc, The, 255
Passport to Pimlico, 196, 197
Pat Garrett and Billy the Kid, 386
Pather Panchali, 332–333, 335–336
Pathetic Fallacy, 337
Paths of Glory, 213
Paul, R. W., 7, 14
Pauline at the Beach, 235–236
Pavese, Cesare, 171
Pavlovic, Živajin, 299
Pawnshop, The, 43
Peckinpah, Sam, 356–357, 385–387
Peddler, 428
Pee-Wee's Big Adventure, 445–446
peep shows, 1, 2
Peeping Tom, 194, 205–206
Peking Opera Blues, 345
Pelle the Conqueror, 260
Penal Colony, The, 412–413

Penn, Arthur, 248, 384, 385–386
Penn, Sean, 460
Pennebaker, D. A., 395
People v. John Doe, The, 99
People v. Larry Flynt, The, 297
People's Republic of China (films made in), 340, 341–344
Pépé le Moko, 120
Perceval, 235
Pereira dos Santos, Nelson, 405, 407, 408–409
Perez Family, The, 339
Performance, 207, 208
Perils of Pauline, The, 20
Perrault, Pierre, 424
Persona, 258
Peters, Jean, 359
Petit Soldat, Le, 232
Petrovic, Aleksander, 299, 301
Petulia, 207, 212, 248
Pfeiffer, Michelle, 392
Phalke, D. G., 333
Phantom Carriage, The, 256
Phantom Chariot, The, 256, 259
Phantom Lady, 152, 153
Phantom of Liberty, The, 271
Philadelphia, 463
Pialat, Maurice, 245
Piano, The, 421
Pick, Lupu, 58
Pickford, Mary, 44, 47, 88, 423
Pickpocket, 225
Picnic at Hanging Rock, 418–420
Pierce, Kimberly, 464–465
Pierrot le fou, 229, 232
Piesiewicz, Kryzysztof, 288, 289
Pigeon, Walter, 423
Pigpen, 182
Pillow Book, The, 209
Pinter, Harold, 211
Pirandello, Luigi, 18
Pirate, The, 375
Pitt, Brad, 207
Pixote, 409
Platoon, 442, 443, 451
Play Misty for Me, 448
Player, The, 388
Playtime, 222
Plow That Broke the Plains, The, 127
Pocahontas, 445
Poe, Edgar Allan, 113, 142, 233
Pointe courte, La, 226
Poison, 463–464
Poitier, Sidney, 384
Poland (films made in), 281, 282–290, 306
  American influence on, 289–290
  censorship of, 281, 282, 284
  directors of, 282, 283–289
  documentaries, 282–283
  French influence on, 282
  social/political events and, 282, 285–287, 290
Polanski, Roman, 286
Pommer, Erich, 66
Ponette, 245
Popeye, 388
Pornographers: An Introduction to Anthropology, The, 325
pornography, 324, 325, 344, 365, 424

Port of Shadows, 120, 121
Porter, Edwin S., 10–15, 17, 18, 20, 39, 40, 61, 71, 74
Portrait of a Lady, 421
Portrait of Jason, 395
Portrait of Teresa, 407
Postcards from the Edge, 462, 463
Postino, Il, 188
Posto, Il, 170, 180, 294
Potter, Sally, 205, 207, 210
Pour la suite du monde, 424
Powell, Michael, 193, 194, 205–206
Preminger, Otto, 152, 221, 232, 366
President, The, 254
Pressburger, Emeric, 193, 194, 205–206
Pretty Woman, 462–463
Prévert, Jacques, 120–121, 152
Primary, 395
Prince of Egypt, The, 150, 445
Princess Mononoke, The, 150
Princess Yang Kwei Fei, 318, 319
Prison Memories, 408–409
Prisoner of Shark Island, 136
Prisoner of the Mountains, 306, 307
Privilege, 401
problem pictures, 98–100
Production Code Administration, 131, 132, 365–367
Profession of Arms, The, 181
Professor Hannibal, 291
Promesse, La, 248
Promise, The, 264
Promised Land, 286
Promised Land, The, 412
Proof, 421
Prospero's Books, 209
Providence, 237, 238
Psycho, 379
Public Enemy, 140
Public Housing, 397
Pudovkin, V. I., 37, 71, 74, 75, 76–79, 83–86, 231, 305
Puenzo, Luis, 410
Pulp Fiction, 457–459
Pumpkin Race, 38
Punishment Island, 327
Puppetmaster, The, 348
Purple Rose of Cairo, The, 448
Puttnam, David, 215, 292

Qaisar, 427
Queen Christina, 145
Queen Elizabeth, 21–22
Queen Kelly, 95
Quinn, Anthony, 413–414
Quo Vadis, 22, 23, 373

racism, 28, 30–31, 103, 137
Radford, Michael, 189
Raft, George, 377
Rage in Harlem, A, 467
Raging Bull, 393–394
Ragtime, 297
Rahn, Bruno, 58
Raimu, 120
Rain People, The, 390, 391
Rainer, Yvonne, 401
Raining in the Mountains, 345
Raining Stones, 203
Rains, Claude, 146

Raise the Red Lantern, 343
Raising Arizona, 456
Raja Harishchandra, 333
Ramachandran, M. G., 338–339
Ramblin' Rose, 461
Rambo [series], 438, 442
Ran, 315, 317–318
rapid cutting, 17
Rappeneau, Jean-Paul, *246*
Rapper, Irving, 146
Raquetteurs, Les, 424
Rashomon, 313, 314, 315
Rasputin, 302
Rathnam, Mani, 339
Rasputin, 302
Ray, Man, 115, 116, 221
Ray, Nicholas, 268, 374
Ray, Satyajit, 332–333, 335–337, 340, 405
Real Life, 446
Rear Window, 379
Reason over Passion, 401
Rebel Without a Cause, 374
Red and the White, The, 291–292
Red Beard, 317
Red Desert, The, 177
Red Psalm, 291
Red River, 370
Red Shoes, The, 194, 205
Red Sorghum, 343
Redford, Robert, 453, 468
Redupers, or the All-Around Reduced Personality, 264
Reed, Carol, 194
Reed: Insurgent Mexico, 414
Reeves, Keanu, 186
Reichert, Julia, 400
Reimann, Walter, 54
Reiner, Rob, 462–463
Reinhardt, Max, 52, 57–58, 62, 96, 148
Reisz, Karel, 200, 210–211
Reitz, Edgar, 269
Religieuse, La, 234
Remains of the Day, The, 194
Rembrandt lighting, 93
Remedial Reading Comprehension, 400
Renoir, Jean, 122–125, 220, 258, 335, 363
Report on the Party and the Guests, 296, 298
Repulsion, 286
Requiem for a Heavyweight, 356
Rescued by Rover, 14–15
Rescued from an Eagle's Nest, 15
Reservoir Dogs, 457
Resnais, Alain, 226–227, 229, 230, 235, 236–238, 242–243, 263, 296
Return of Martin Guerre, The, 246
Return of the Idiot, 297
Rex, "King of the Wild Horses," 101
Rey Chow, 343
Rhapsody in August, 318
Rhythmus 21, 54
Rich, Matty, 467
Rich, Ruby, 463
Richard III, 194
Richardson, Tony, 194, 200, 201, 211, 248
Richie, Donald, 314, 317, 321

Richter, Hans, 54
Richter, Roland Suso, 269
Riddance, 293
Ride the High Country, 386
Riefenstahl, Leni, 68
Riggs, Marlon T., 463
Rin-Tin-Tin, 101
Ring with a Crowned Eagle, The, 286
Rink, The, 43
Rio, North Zone, 405
Rip Van Winkle, 3
Ripstein, Arturo, 414
Rise and Fall of Free Speech in America, The, 34
Rise to Power of Louise XIV, The, 184
Riskin, Robert, 134, 135, 144
Ritchie, Guy, 217
Ritt, Martin, 315
Ritual in Transfigured Time, 397
River, The, 127, 335
Rivette, Jacques, 225, 230, 234–235
RKO (Radio Keith-Orpheum), 108–109, 128–129, 361
Road to Eternity, 323
Road Warrior, 419
Robbe-Grillet, Alain, 171, 236, 237
Robbery of the Mail Coach, 14
Robe, The, 359, 373
Roberts, Rachel, 200
Robin Hood, 101, 102
Robinson, Edward G., 141, 153
Robson, E. W. and M. M., 66
Rocco and His Brothers, 170, 172, 173
Rocha, Glauber, 407, 408
"rock docs," 140, 395
Rocky, 439
Rodriguez, Robert, 468
Roeg, Nicholas, 207–208
Rogers, Ginger, 139–140
Rogers, Richard, 371
Rohmer, Eric, 225, 231, 235, 236
Röhrig, Walter, 54
Roja, 339
Role, The, 338
Romance, 244
Romantic Englishwoman, The, 211–212
Rome, Eleven O'Clock, 164
Romeo and Juliet, 106
Romero, George, 142
Ronde, La, 223
Roof, The, 170
Roof of the Whale, The, 413
Room, Abram, 72
Room at the Top, 200, 202
Room with a View, A, 194
Rosa Luxemburg, 264
Rosemary's Baby, 286, 394
Rosetta, 248
Rosewood, 467, 468
Rosi, Francesco, 170, 181–182, 183
Roskomkino, 305
Ross, Herbert, 462
Rossellini, Roberto, 161–162, 163, 166, 167, 169, 170, 172, 173, 184, 189, 243, 363
Rota, Nino, 170, 391
Rotha, Paul, 196

Rothman, William, 379
Rotunno, Giuseppe, 172–173, 187–188
Rouch, Jean, 73, 245–246
Roue, La, 114
Rouge, 346
Round-Up, The, 291
Roundtree, Richard, 384
Rowlands, Gena, 347, 394
Roy, Bimal, 333
Rozema, Patricia, 424
R.S.V.P., 464
Ruins, The, 337
Ruiz, Raúl, 412–413
Rules of the Game, The, 122, 124
Run for Your Money, A, 196
Run, Lola, Run, 269
Runner, The, 427
Running, Jumping, and Standing-Still Film, The, 212
Rushmore, 447
Russell, David O., 459
Russell, Ken, 215
Russell, Rosalind, 142, 147
Russell, Theresa, 208
Russia (films made in). **See** Soviet Union
Ruttmann, Walther, 54
Ryan, Meg, 269
Ryan, Robert, 387

Sabrina, 377
Sacrifice, The, 304, 305
Sadoul, Georges, 125
Safety Last, 98
Saint, Eva Marie, 379
St. Michael Had a Rooster, 186
Sakamoto, Ryuicihi, 470
Salaam Bombay! 339
Salaam Cinema, 339
Salesman, 395
Salles, Walter, 409
Salò—The 120 Days of Sodom, 182
Salvador, 452
Salvatore Giuliano, 170, 181, 183
Sambizanga, 417
Sammy and Rosie Get Laid, 204
Samson and Delilah, 208
Sander, Helke, 264
Sanders-Brahms, Helma, 264, 269
Sandra, 172, 183
Sanjinés, Jorge, 405
Sanjura, 315
Sans Soleil, 238
Sant Tukaram, 333
Sappho, 401
Saragossa Manuscript, 286
Sarraounia, 417
Sarris, Andrew, 221, 222, 383
Satantango,* 293
Satie, Eric, 116
Saturday Night, 93
Saturday Night and Sunday Morning, 200, 201
Saturday Night Fever, 137, 140, 438
Saura, Carlos, 271, 272
Sautet, Claude, 245
Sauve qui peut (la vie), 242, 243, 391
Saving Private Ryan, 436, 450
Sawdust and Tinsel, 257

Sayles, John, 457
Sayonara, 362
Scandalous Adventures of Buraikan, The, 327
Scandinavia (films made in), 254–261. **See also** Denmark; Sweden
Scar of Shame, 103
Scarface, 140
Scarfiotti, Ferdinando, 184, 470
Scarlet Empress, The, 132, 133
Scarlet Letter, The, 256
Scarlet Street, 152, 153
Scenes from a Marriage, 258
Schepisi, Fred, 420, 422
Schindler's List, 290, 450–451
Schlesinger, John, 200, 202, 207, 211, 248
Schlöndorff, Volker, 262, 263
Schneeman, Carolee, 400–401
Schnitzler, Arthur, 213
School Daze, 466
Schrader, Paul, 225, 392, 452
Schulberg, Budd, 369–370
Schultz, Michael, 384
Schwarzenegger, Arnold, 438, 441–442, 444
Schygulla, Hanna, 265, 266
science-fiction films, 324, 438, 441, 443–444
Scorpio Rising, 397
Scorsese, Martin, 243, 385–386, 392–394, 424–425, 440, 448
Scott, Adrian, 368
Scott, George C., 212
Scott, Ridley, 211, 215, 443, 452, 463
Searchers, The, 137, 370, 373
Seashell and the Clergyman, The, 116
Seastrom, Victor, 256. **See also** Sjöström, Victor
Seberg, Jean, 232
Seclusion Near a Forest, 297
Secret, The, 346
Secret Garden, The, 287, 391
Secrets and Lies, 198
Secrets of a Soul, 71
Secrets of Women, 257
Seduction of Mimi, The, 187
See You at Mao, 233
Seedling, The, 338
Seidelman, Susan, 460–461
Selznick, David, 129
Sembène, Ousmane, 416–417
Sen, Mrinal, 335, 337
Sennett, Mack, 27, 38–39, 40, 41–43, 46, 65, 97
Sense and Sensibility, 350
Senso, 172
September, 448
sequence, 17
Serene Velocity, 400
Serreau, Coline, 246
Servant, The, 211
set design, 63–64
Set It Off, 467–468
Seven Beauties, 187
Seven Brides for Seven Brothers, 359
Seven Samurai, 313, 314, 315–316, 317
Seven Year Itch, The, 377
Seventh Seal, The, 257–258, 259, 304
79 Springtimes, 406

Sex, Lies, and Videotape, 453, 459
Sexual Perversity in Chicago, 456
Seyrig, Delphine, 239
Shadow Warrior, The, 317
Shadows, 394
Shadows of Our Forgotten Ancestors, 303
Shaft [series], 384
Shahini, Kumar, 337
Shakespeare in Love, 193, 216, 275, 459
Shame, 304
Shane, 370–371
Shanghai Express, 132
Shanghai Triad, 343
Shantaram, V., 333
Shattered, 54, 65
She's Gotta Have It, 465–466, 467
Shearer, Norma, 375, 423
Sheedy, Ally, 464
Sheik, The, 145
Sheltering Sky, The, 186
Shepard, Sam, 268
Sheptiko, Larisa, 302
Shimura, Takashi, 315
Shine, 275
Shining, The, 213
Shinoda, Masahiro, 324–325, 326–327
Shipman, Nell, 101
Shoah, 245
Shoeshine, 165, 166–167, 227
Shoot the Piano Player, 229, 230, 233, 234
Shop on Main Street, The, 294
Short Cuts, 388
Short Film about Killing, A, 288–289
Short Film about Love, A, 288
Shoulder Arms, 43
Shriek of Araby, The, 42
Shyer, Charles, 375
Siegel, Don, 448
Siegfried, 53, 54
Sign, Slobodan, 301
Signora di tutti, La, 223
Silberling, Brad, 269
Silence, The, 257, 258
Silence and Cry, 291
Silence of the Lambs, The, 448, 449, 450
Silent Touch, The, 287
Sillitoe, Alan, 200
Silver, Joel, 444
Sim, Alistair, 197
Simon, Michel, 120
Sinbad, 291
Singin' in the Rain, 107, 140, 372–373
Singleton, John, 467
Siodmak, Robert, 152
Sirk, Douglas, 221, 265, 375, 377–379
Sissoko, Cheik Oumer, 417
Sisters, or the Balance of Happiness, 263–264
Sisters of the Gion, 318
Sitney, P. Adams, 400
Six Moral Tales [series], 235
Sixth Sense, The, 438
Sjöberg, Alf, 257
Sjöman, Vilgot, 299
Sjöström, Victor, 255–257, 259, 261

Skelton, Red, 98
Skolimowski, Jerzy, 286, 296, 299
Skouras, Spyros, 359
Sleep, 399
Sleepless in Seattle, 462–463
Sling Blade, 459
Smalley, Phillips, 99
Smiles of a Summer Night, 257, 258
Smiling Madame Beudet, The, 113, 114
Smith, George Albert, 14
Smith, Jack, 397
Smith, Kevin, 459
Smith, Will, 468
Smithereens, 460–461
Snapper, The, 204
Snider, Stacey, 460
Snow, Michael, 239, 400, 424–425
Soapdish, 447
Soderbergh, Steven, 453, 459
Sokurov, Alexander, 306
Solanas, Fernando, 405, 409
Solanz, Todd, 459
Solaris, 304
Solás, Humberto, 407
Solberg, Helena, 415
Soldier's Prayer, A, 323
Some Came Running, 375
Some Like It Hot, 377, 463
Something to Think About, 93
Song of Ceylon, The, 195
Song of Russia, 367
Song of the Exile, 346
Sorrow and the Pity, The, 245
Soufrière, La, 267
sound (in films), 104–110, 116, 117, 157
Sound of Music, The, 360
Sous les toits de Paris, 118
South, 410
South, The, 273
Southern, Terry, 213
Southerner, The, 335
Soviet Union (films made in), 70–87, 301–306
    directors of, 231
    distribution/exhibition of, 36–37
    documentaries, 302–303
    emigration and, 71
    government support of, 70–71, 86, 305–306
    origins of, 70–74
    social/political events and, 70–74, 86, 280–281, 301–302, 305–306
    techniques used in, 71, 83–87
Sow, Faty, 417
Spaak, Charles, 120, 122
Spacek, Sissy, 388
Spader, James, 424
Spain (films made in), 254, 269–276
Spanish Prisoner, The, 456
Sparkuhl, Theodore, 66–67
Spartacus, 213
spectacle films, 101–103, 438
Spider's Stratagem, The, 184
Spielberg, Steven, 290, 436, 440, 445, 448, 449–451
Spiral Staircase, The, 152
Spirit of St. Louis, The, 272–273

Spooky Bunch, The, 346
Squaw Man, The, 92
Stagecoach, 136, 137
Stalag 17, 376–377
Stalker, 304
Stallone, Sylvester, 438, 439, 441–442, 460
Stand and Deliver, 468
Stanislavsky, Konstantin, 79, 373
Stanwyck, Barbara, 142, 145–146
Star Is Born, A, 359, 375–376
Star Trek [series], 443
Star Wars [series], 20, 437, 438, 440, 443
Stardust Memories, 448
Starfish, The, 115
Starski, Allan, 290
Stavisky, 237
Steadicam, 392, 439
Stealing Beauty, 186
Steamboat 'Round the Bend, 136
Steamboat Willie, 149
Steaming, 211–212
Steel, Dawn, 460
Steel Magnolias, 462, 463
Stella Dallas, 146
Stereo, 424
Sterling, Ford, 43
Sterling, Jan, 376
Stern, Seymour, 28
Sternberg, Josef von, 67, 132–133, 136, 140, 145
Stevens, George, 370
Stewart, James, 128, 134, 137, 142, 379
Stiller, Mauritz, 256–257
Stolen Children, 188
Stolen Kisses, 234
Stone, Oliver, 443, 448, 451–452
Stone, Sharon, 464
Stop Making Sense, 448
Storaro, Vittorio, 184, 470
Storey, David, 200, 202
Storm Over Asia, 78
Story of G.I. Joe, The, 152
Story of Gösta Berling, The, 256–257
Story of Qiu Ju, The, 343, 344
Story of Sin, 286
Story of the Last Chrysanthemum, The, 319
Strada, La, 170, 171, 173, 174
Straight Out of Brooklyn, 467
Strange Days, 443, 461–462
Stranger, The, 172, 228–229
Stranger Than Paradise, 454, 455
Strangers on a Train, 379
Straub, Jean-Marie, 264–265
Strawberry and Chocolate, 407
Street, The, 58
street films, 58–59, 61, 62, 67
Street of Shame, 318
Streisand, Barbra, 462
Strike, 74, 78, 80–82
Stroheim, Erich von, 91, 94–95, 123, 137
Strong Man, The, 98
studio system, 128–130, 157, 312, 327, 361–362
Sturges, John, 315
Sturges, Preston, 144
Sturm group, 52

Subiola, Eliseo, 410–411
Sugar Cane Alley, 244
Summer, 235–236
Summer Interlude, 257
Summer Snow, 346
Summertime, 194
Sunday Bloody Sunday, 211
Sunday in the Country, A, 245
Sunday Too Far Away, 418
Sunrise, 67, 268
Sunset Boulevard, 376
Sunshine, 292
Superfly, 384
superimposition, 18
Supermarket Woman, 328–329
Surname Viet, Given Name Nam, 401
Sutherland, Donald, 208, 423
Švankmajer, Jan, 296
Sverák, Jan, 297
Swaim, Bob, 246
Swank, Hilary, 464
Swann in Love, 263
Sweden (films made in), 254, 256–260
Sweet Dreams, 210–211
Sweet Hereafter, The, 425, 426
Sweet Movie, 299, 300
Sweet Sweetback's Baadasssss Song, 384
Sweetie, 421
Swimming to Cambodia, 448
Swing Shift, 448
Swing Time, 139
Swoon, 463–464
Syberberg, Hans-Jurgen, 391
Sydow, Max von, 257, 269, 287
Sylvia Scarlett, 463
Sympathy for the Devil, 232
Szabó, István, 291, 292

Taipei Story, 349
Taiwan (films made in), 340, 347–351
Taking Sides, 292
Tale of the Springtime, A, 236
Talented Mr. Ripley, The, 464
Tales of Hoffman, 205
Tales of the Four Seasons [series], 236
Tall T, The, 370
Tampopo, 328
Tango, 272, 405
Tanner, Alain, 200
Tarantino, Quentin, 346–347, 457–459
Tarkovsky, Andrei, 304–305
Tarr, Béla, 293
Tarzan of the Apes, 100
Taste of Cherry, A, 427
Tati, Jacques, 220, 222, 225
Taxi Driver, 392, 393–394
Taxing Woman, A, 328
Taxing Woman Returns, A, 328
Taylor, Robert, 368
Taylor, William Desmond, 131
Téchiné, André, 245
Technicolor, 148, 341–342, 343, 357, 371, 375–376
technological developments, 439–440
Teenage Mutant Ninja Turtles, 438

television, 253, 262, 327, 337, 355–357, 379–380, 382
Tempest, The, 209
Ten Commandments, The, 93, 103, 373, 438
Ten Days That Shook the World, 83
Teno, Jean-Marie, 429
Tent of Miracles, 408–409
Teorema, 182
Terje Vigen, 255
Terminator [series], 438, 443, 444
Terms of Endearment, 462, 463
Terra Trema, La, 165, 172, 182
Territory, The, 413
Terrorizer, The, 349
Thackery, William, 213
Thalberg, Irving, 91, 128, 313, 362
That Cold Day in the Park, 388, 389
That Sinking Feeling, 198
theaters, 48–49, 88–91, 105, 108, 128–129, 355, 361, 437–438, 468
Thelma and Louise, 211, 462, 463
There's Something about Mary, 438, 447
Thewis, David, 198–199
Thief of Bagdad, The, 101
Thin Red Line, The, 452–453
Things Change, 456
Third Man, The, 194
Thirty Seconds Over Toyko, 152
36 Fillette, 244
Thirty-Nine Steps, The, 194
This Is Cinerama, 357, 358, 359
This Sporting Life, 200, 201–202
Thomas, Jeremy, 470
Thomas, Lowell, 358
Thompson, Emma, 350
Thornton, Billy Bob, 459
Three Brothers, 182
Three Coins in the Fountain, 359, 362
Three Colors [trilogy], 289
3-D films, 357, 359
Three Foolish Weeks, 42
Three Kings, 459
Three Lives and Only One Death, 413
Three Men and a Baby, 246
Three Men and a Cradle, 246
Three Musketeers, The, 101
Three Sad Tigers, 412–412
Three Sisters, 263–264
Three Strange Loves, 257
3 Women, 388, 389
Threepenny Opera, The, 51, 68
Thriller, 210
thrillers, 194, 246, 379. **See also** horror films
Throne of Blood, 315
Through a Glass Darkly, 257
Through the Olive Trees, 427
Throw Me a Dime, 405
Thulin, Ingrid, 257
Ticket of No Return, 264
Ties That Bind, The, 401
Tight Little Island, 196, 197, 198
Tillie's Punctured Romance, 43, 44
Time Code, 440, 441
Time of the Gypsies, A, 301

Time Regained, 413
Tin Drum, The, 263
Tisse, Eduard, 74
Titanic, 27, 145, 438, 439
Titfield Thunderbolt, The, 196
Titticut Follies, 395–397
To Catch a Thief, 379
To Live, 343
To Live in Peace, 164
To Sleep with Anger, 465, 468
Todd, Mike, 358
Toeplitz, Jerzy, 282
Together, 200
Tokyo Olympiad, 323
Tokyo Story, 322
Toland, Gregg, 156
Toller, Ernst, 52
Tom Jones, 248
Tomei, Marisa, 339
Tomlin, Lily, 447
Tongues Untied, 463
Toni, 122
Topper, 439
Topsy Turvy, 199
Torment, 257
Tornatore, Giuseppi, 183, 189
Torres, Fina, 415
Total Recall, 443
Touch of Evil, 157
Touch of Zen, A, 345
Tourneur, Jacques, 152
Tourneur, Maurice, 97
Tout va bien, 231, 242
Toy Story, 150, 438, 445
Track 29, 208
Tracy, Spencer, 375
Traffic, 222
Tragedy of a Ridiculous Man,
     185
Tragedy of a Street, 58
Tragic Hunt, 164, 165, 177
Trainspotting, 203, 216
Tramp, The, 43, 333
Tramp, Tramp, Tramp, 98
*Transformation of the World
     into Music, The,* 267
Trash, 399
Trauberg, Leonid, 74
Travolta, John, 459
Treasure of Arne, The, 256–257
Tree of Wooden Clogs, The, 181
Tretyakov, Sergei, 80
Trevor, Claire, 136
Trial, The, 157
Trial Marriage, 99
Trial of Joan of Arc, The, 225
Trier, Lars von, 260
Trikal, 338
Trip to the Moon, A, 8–9, 13
Triumph of the Will, 68
Trnka, Jiří, 296
Troche, Rose, 464
Troell, Jan, 260
Troisi, Massimo, 189
Trotta, Margarethe von, 262,
     263–264
Trouble in Paradise, 132, 142
Trouble with Harry, The, 379
Trouper of Troup K, The, 103
True Heart Susie, 27
True Story of Ah Q, The, 341
Trueba, Fernando, 274–275
Truffaut, François, 205, 207,
     220, 221, 222, 225, 227,
     229, 230, 231, 233–234,
     236, 237, 238, 285, 363,
     386

Truman Show, The, 418–420
Trumbo, Dalton, 368
Tucker, 391
Tumbleweeds, 97
Turner, Lana, 378–379
Turning Point, The, 462
Turpin, Ben, 42
Tushingham, Rita, 200
Twelve Angry Men, 356
Twelve Monkeys, 214, 443
Twentieth Century, 134, 142
Twentieth Century-Fox, 108,
     109, 128–129, 359, 361,
     435, 436, 460
25 Fireman's Street, 291
Twin Peaks [series], 453, 454
Two Acres of Land, 333
Two Cents Worth of Hope, 164
Two for the Road, 248
Two Mules for Sister Sara, 448
Two Stage Sisters, 340, 341
2001: A Space Odyssey, 213,
     304
Two Weeks in Another Town,
     375
Two Women, 170
Tykwer, Tom, 269
Tynan, Kenneth, 391
typage, 86

Ufa (Universum Film A. G.),
     60, 64, 66, 67, 117, 263
Ugetsu, 313, 314, 319–320
Ukadike, Nwachu Frank, 417
Ullman, Liv, 257, 260
Ulmer, Edgar, 221
Umberto D., 164, 165, 169,
     315
Uncle Tom's Cabin, 12, 14
Uncovered Wagon, The, 42
Under the Sun of Satan, 245
Underground, 301
Underworld, 140
Unforgiven, 448, 449
Union Maids, 400
United Artists (UA), 44, 88,
     129, 361, 363, 365, 366,
     435–436, 438
United States (films made in),
     26–50, 88–111, 127–160,
     354–381, 382–403,
     435–474
     actors in, 47, 357, 359, 368,
        371, 375, 379, 388,
        414–415, 447, 464
     attendance at, 354–355, 382,
        435, 437–438, 459
     censorship of, 131–132,
        363–370
     cost of, 362–363, 436–437,
        438
     directors of, 356–357,
        375–379, 385–395,
        448–453
     distribution/exhibition of, 46,
        48–49, 88–91, 129–130,
        354–355, 361, 363, 382,
        437, 459
     documentaries, 127, 367,
        370, 383–384, 395–397
     earnings of, 436–438, 439,
        467
     genres of, 38–44, 85, 97–103,
        137–150, 152–154,
        370–374, 383–384, 438,
        440–448
     German influence on, 66–68

     independent producers of,
        45–46, 88–91, 361–362,
        453–459
     internationalization and,
        362–363, 440–441,
        469–471
     merchandising of, 437
     multicultural issues in,
        459–469
     New Wave, 385–395
     origins of, 26–27, 49
     production centers for,
        45–46, 108
     promotion of, 47–48, 437
     ratings of, 131, 366–367
     social/political events and,
        127–128, 150–152,
        354–355, 367–370, 382
     studio mergers, 435–436, 459
     studio system, 128–130, 157,
        361–362
     techniques used in, 46–47,
        92–94, 109–110, 128,
        357–360
     technological developments
        and, 439–440
     television and, 355–357,
        379–380, 382, 438
     video releases of, 438, 440
Universal Studios/Pictures, 67,
     88, 90, 128–129, 377–378,
     383, 435, 436, 460
Untouchables, The, 456
Up to a Point, 406, 407
Uptown Saturday Night, 384
Ustinov, Peter, 223
Uys, Jaime, 415

Vadim, Roger, 226
Vagabonde, 238
Valdez, Luis, 468
Valenti, Jack, 366
Valentino, Rudolph, 42,
     144–145
Valley Girl, 461
Valmont, 297
Vampires, Les, 20, 21, 247
Vampyr, 255
Van Peebles, Mario, 384, 467
Van Sant, Gus, 463
Vanishing Lady, The, 8
Varda, Agnes, 226, 236, 238
Variety [film], 59, 60, 61, 62,
     63, 66–67
Variety [journal], 276, 354–355,
     358, 435, 437
Variety Lights, 173, 174
Veber, Francis, 245
Vega, Pastor, 407
Veidt, Conrad, 65, 67
Vengeance Is Mine, 325
Venice Film Festival, 170, 172,
     183, 238, 239, 243, 300,
     313, 318, 341, 348, 394
Verdict, The, 456
Verhoeven, Paul, 443
Veronica Voss, 266
vertical control, 128–130, 355
Vertigo, 208, 379
Vertov, Dziga, 72–74
Very Private Affair, A, 239–241
Victor/Victoria, 463
video releases, 438, 440
Videodrome, 424
Vidor, Charles, 152
Vidor, King, 100, 110, 146
Vie est un roman, La, 237, 238

Vietnam War, 238, 241, 382,
     391, 441, 442
Vigne, Daniel, 246
Vigo, Jean, 118
Vinterberg, Thomas, 260
Viridiana, 270, 271
Visconti, Luchino, 163, 166,
     170, 171, 172–173, 178,
     180, 182, 183, 189
Vitelloni, I, 173, 175
Voyage, The, 410
Voyage to Italy, 169
Voyager, The, 263

Wachowski, Andy and Larry,
     443, 444
Wadleigh, Michael, 395
Wag the Dog, 456
Waiting to Exhale, 367–368
Wajda, Andrzej, 284–285, 286,
     287
Wake Island, 152
Walkabout, 208
Walker, Joseph, 134
Walkover, 286
Wall Street, 452
Waller, Fred, 357
Wallis, Hal, 128
Walsh, Raoul, 100, 110, 221
Walt Disney Studio/
     Productions, 129, 150,
     354, 435, 436, 445,
     459
Walthall, Henry B., 33
Wanger, Walter, 129
war films, 100, 193, 206, 221,
     281, 360. **See also** Vietnam
     War
War Game, The, 196
War Room, The, 395
Warhol, Andy, 398–400
Warm, Hermann, 54
Warner, Jack, 88, 368
Warner Bros., 88, 105–106,
     107, 108, 128–129, 138,
     141, 150, 287, 357, 361,
     373, 383, 435, 436, 438,
     445
Warnier, Régis, 246
Washington, Denzel, 339
Washington Square, 287
Watermelon Woman, 464
Watkins, Peter, 196
Watt, Harry, 196
Wave, The, 337
Wavelength, 400
Way Down East, 463
Way We Laughed, The, 188
Wayne, John, 136, 137, 442
Ways of Love, The, 363
We Are the Lambeth Boys, 200
We Don't Want to Talk about It,
     410–412
Weaver, Sigourney, 350, 420
Weber, Lois, 99
Wedding Banquet, The, 350
Wedding March, The, 94
Wedding Singer, 437
Weekend, 242
Wegener, Paul, 55
Weill, Kurt, 51
Weinstein, Bob, 184
Weinstein, Harvey, 184
Weir, Peter, 418–420, 422
Welcome to the Dollhouse, 459
Welles, Orson, 155–157, 221,
     446

Wellman, William, 144, 221
Wenders, Wim, 262, 265, 267–269, 391
Wertmüller, Lina, 187
Wesker, Arnold, 200
West, Mae, 142
Western Europe (films made in), 253–254, 275–276, 363. **See also** Denmark; France; Germany; Great Britain; Italy; Sweden
westerns, 42, 46, 97, 136–137, 187, 221, 315, 360, 370–371, 373, 386, 448
Westfront, 68
Wetherby, 215
What Lies Beneath? 436
What Price Glory? 100
What's Eating Gilbert Grape? 260
When Father Was Away on Business, 300–301
When Harry Met Sally, 462–463
When I Was Dead and White, 299
Where Are My Children, 99
Where Is the Friend's Home? 427
Where the Heart Is, 206
Whiskey Galore, 196, 197
Whitaker, Forrest, 367–368
White Balloon, The, 427
White Heat, 140
White Nights, 172
White Sheik, 173, 174, 177
Who Framed Roger Rabbit? 150, 452
Who'll Stop the Rain? 210–212, 442
Who's Afraid of Virgina Woolf? 366
Who's Singing Over There? 301
Who's That Knocking at My Door? 392
Why Change Your Wife? 93
Why Shoot the Teacher? 426
Why We Fight [series], 135–136

Widerberg, Bo, 260
Wieland, Joyce, 401, 424
Wiene, Robert, 54
Wild at Heart, 453–454
Wild Bunch, The, 387, 388
Wild One, The, 374
Wild Party, The, 147
Wild Reeds, 245
Wild Strawberries, 256, 257, 258, 259
Wilder, Billy, 144, 152, 335, 361, 362, 375, 376–377, 463
Wilder, Hagar, 144
Williams, Richard, 150
Williams, Robin, 418–420
Williamson, James A., 14
Willis, Bruce, 441
Willis, Gordon, 391
Willow, 443–444
Wilson, Dooley, 151
Wilson, Hugh, 463
Wind, The, 107, 256
Wine of Youth, 99
Wings, 100
Wings of Desire, 268–269
Winslet, Kate, 350
Winslow Boy, The, 457
Winter Light, 257
Winter Wind, 291
Wise, Robert, 221
Wise Man, The, 79–80
Wiseman, Frederick, 395–397
Witchcraft through the Ages, 254
Witches, The, 208
With Beauty and Sorrow, 327
Within Our Gates, 103, 104
Without Anesthetic, 286
Without Pity, 164, 173
Witkiewicz, Stanisław Ignacy, 282
Witness, 418
Witney, William, 459
Wollen, Peter, 133–134
Woman in the Window, The, 152, 153, 154
Woman Is a Woman, A, 231, 232, 243

Woman Under the Influence, A, 394
Women of the Night, 318
Women on the Verge of a Nervous Breakdown, 273, 274
women's films, 144–148, 263–264, 318, 326–327, 343, 377–378, 388, 400–401, 407, 448, 459–463
Wong, Faye, 347
Wong Kar-Wei, 248, 346–347, 459
Woo, John, 345–346
Woo-ping Yuen, 345
Wood, Robin, 388, 446
Wood, Sam, 378
Woodbury, Billy, 465
Woods, James, 424
Woodstock, 140, 395, 396
Workers Leaving the Factory, 7
World of Apu, The, 335, 336
WR: Mysteries of the Organism, 299, 300
Wright, Basil, 195, 196, 465
Wringing Good Joke, A, 38
Written on the Wind, 378
Wuthering Heights, 149, 421
Wyatt, Jane, 368
Wyler, William, 148–149, 221, 335, 367–368, 373
Wyman, Jane, 378

Xala, 416
Xica, 409
Xie Jin, 340

Yaaba, 417
Yakin, Boaz, 467
Yang, Edward, 349–350
Yankee Doodle Dandy, 439
Year of Living Dangerously, The, 418, 420
Year of the Pig, 395
Year of the Quiet Sun, 287
Yellow Earth, 342
Yentl, 462
Yesterday Girl, 263

Yi yi, 350
Yimou, Zhang. **See** Zhang Yimou
Yoda, Yoshikata, 318
Yojimbo, 315
You Shouldn't Worry, 244–245
You're a Big Boy Now, 390
Young, Loretta, 52
Young, Robert, 468
Young Doctor Kildare, 387
Young Mr. Lincoln, 136
Young Soul Rebels, 207, 463
Young Törless, 263
Your Friends and Neighbors, 459
youth films, 383–384
Yugoslavia (films made in), 281, 298–301, 306
Yun-Fat, Chow. **See** Chow Yun-Fat
Yutkevitch, Sergei, 74

Zabriskie Point, 171, 363, 384
Zanuck, Darryl F., 28
Zanussi, Krzysztof, 286–287
Zardoz, 206
Zavattini, Cesare, 163–164, 166–167, 169, 227, 316, 335
Zazie dans le Métro, 239–240
Zecca, Ferdinand, 38
Zelenka, Petr, 297
Zelig, 448
Zeman, Karel, 296
Zemeckis, Robert, 150, 443, 444, 452
Zero for Conduct, 118, 119
Zhang Yimou, 342, 343–344
Ziegfeld, Florenz, 138
Ziegfeld Follies, 138
Zinnemann, Fred, 370, 440
Zonka, Eric, 248
Zoot Suit, 468
Zorns Lemma, 400
Zukor, Adolph, 22, 88, 89
Zvenigora, 75
Zwerin, Charlotte, 395